Irish
Classics

Irish Classics

Declan Kiberd

Harvard University Press
Cambridge, Massachusetts
2001

In memory of Fred Kiberd, 1911–1995

First United Kingdom publication by
Granta Books 2000

Printed in the United States of America

Library of Congress Cataloging-in-Publication Data

Kiberd, Declan.
Irish classics / Declan Kiberd.
p. cm.
Includes bibliographical references and index.
ISBN 0-674-00505-8 (alk. paper)
1. English literature—Irish authors—History and criticism.
2. Irish literature—History and criticism.
3. Ireland—In literature I. Title

PR8714.K54 2001
820.9'9417—dc21
00-054073

Contents

Acknowledgements

The author and publishers thank the following: the Society of Authors and the Bernard Shaw estate for permission to quote from *Arms and the Man*; A.P. Watt Ltd and Michael Yeats for permission to quote from *Collected Poems* and *Autobiographies*: Colin Smythe Ltd, Gerrards Cross for permission to quote from Augusta Gregory's *Cuchulain of Muirthemne*; Extracts for *Ulysses* reproduced with the permission of the estate of James Joyce, © copyright Estate of James Joyce; Pegeen O'Sullivan and the estate of Liam O'Flaherty for permission to quote from *The Informer* and *Shame the Devil*; Faber and Faber, Macnaughton Lord representation and the Estate of Eileen O'Casey for permission to quote from Sean O'Casey's *Juno and the Paycock*; Stephen P. Maher, executor and trustee of the late Evelyn O'Nolan for permission to quote from Flann O'Brien's *At-Swim-Two-Birds*; David Higham Associates Ltd, Virago Books and the Estate of Kate O'Brien for permission to quote from *The Ante-Room*; the Educational Company of Ireland and the Estates of Tomás Ó Criomhthain and Peig Sayers for permission to quote from *An tOileánach* and *Peig*; Máire Ní Chíobháin Ó Súilleabháin and the Estate of Muiris Ó Súilleabháin for permission to quote from *Fiche Blian ag Fás*; David Higham Associates and the Estate of Louis MacNeice for permission to quote from the writings of Louis MacNeice; John Colder Publications and the Sammuel Beckett Estate for permission to quote from the Beckett Trilogy – *Molloy, Malone Dies* and *The Unnamable* – © copyright Samuel Beckett 1959, 1970 and © copyright the Samuel Beckett Estate 1993, and to Faber and Faber publishers and the Samuel Beckett estate 1993 for permission to quote from *Waiting for Godot, Endgame* and *All That Fall*; the Trustees of the Estate of the late Katherine Kavanagh for permission to quote from the writings of Patrick Kavanagh; to Sáirséal Ó Marcaigh Teoranta and the Estate of Seán Ó Ríordáin for permission to quote from *Eireaball Spideoige, Brosna* and *Línte Liombó*, and for permission to make translations; to Sáirséal Ó Marcaigh Teoranta and to Caoimhín Ó Marcaigh for permission to quote from and translate passages of *Cré na Cille*.

Introduction

Mark Twain once defined the classic as a book which nobody wants to read but everyone wishes to have read. That may be another way of saying that 'classics' are what once gave pleasure to our ancestors, while 'literature' is what lifts the heart of a reader today. The notion that texts have their season was proposed by Scott Fitzgerald when he said that 'an artist writes for the youth of today, the critics of tomorrow and the schoolmasters of ever after'. Somehow, the literary classic has become more and more associated with the educational process. The compulsory study of set texts has become one of the defining experiences of childhood and adolescence. Some adults who make young people read *Gulliver's Travels* or *Cúirt an Mheán-Oíche* may be unaware of the undeniably subversive potentials of those texts. Others may be passing on to youth what they see as another worthy but tedious chore. 'As for reading, our children can do that for us' would seem to be the motto of the past century. Many of those texts that now feature on course lists were once deemed injurious to public morality and especially inappropriate for the young: that very group which is now most encouraged to read them.

My conviction in writing this study has been quite different from that of Mark Twain. For me a classic is like a great poem, 'news that stays news'. It is in fact the sort of book that everybody enjoys reading and nobody wants to come to an end. It owes its reputation, undoubtedly, to its initial impact on its own generation, without which few books ever survive: but after that it displays a capacity to remain forever young and fresh, offering challenges to every succeeding generation which must learn anew how to be its contemporary. It reads each passing age at least as intensely as it is read by it.

There are two ways of approaching a classic and both have great value. The first is to interpret it historically, in terms of the ideas and events of its own age. One of the most useful services a scholar can perform is to re-create the conditions and materials out of which a work of art first came. This always increases our sense of the wonder of human creation, even if it can never fully account for the miraculous process by which ordinary matter was transmuted into pure art: and it also induces in readers a proper awareness of the limitations within which all authors must work. There should always be, even in the most exacting criticism, a compassionate reference of human achievements to actual human abilities: and that empathy may be the right spirit with which to greet a classic. As Alexander Pope wrote:

> *A perfect judge will read each work of wit*
> *With the same spirit that its author writ.*

One of my objectives has been to convey some sense of how the texts treated here were interpreted in their own time. Our understanding of the role played by two very different works, such as *The Rivals* and *Caoineadh Airt Uí Laoghaire*, in the ebb and flow of Anglo-Irish relations can be greatly enhanced by such knowledge, making much that might otherwise baffle seem pointed and exciting.

That said and done, the greatest pleasure offers itself to those modern readers who know how to make the classics thoroughly their own. A great saga, such as the tale of Cuchulain, will reveal disparate meanings to different ages. If the monks of early Christianity had a right to interpret it by their own lights, so had those who came after them, from the Anglo-Irish lords and ladies, through the rebels of Easter 1916, down to today's Ulster Defence Association (which, not unreasonably, celebrates the hero as a protector of the province). That is the sacred right of every future reader of these texts too. One of the elements that keeps a book a classic is its usefulness and resonance in the here-and-now. The critic is simply a person who may find yet newer meanings and values in a text, meanings and values which might well surprise the original author and will surely dismay and even outrage previous readers. For it is a feature of classics to be open to an almost endless play of meanings.

Every selection of a canon of classic writings has an arbitrary, personal quality about it, revealing not just the tastes of the selector but also the tolerances and limitations. Hence my somewhat qualified title, *Irish Classics* rather than *The Irish Classics* or even *The Classic Irish Writers*. I have tried to pay homage in what follows to two languages, which have often been considered inimical in their histories and workings: and I have suggested that their fortunes were utterly connected over more than five centuries, for all the antagonism between them. My materials are drawn from oral as well as written lore, from popular as well as high culture.

To my mind there are three sorts of Irish classic. The first is a work of art in which human energies are shaped to produce words and images of awesome beauty and internal rigour – some poems of the Gaelic bards and of Yeats, some plays of Synge and Beckett, and of course Joyce's *Ulysses* fall easily into this category. The second is a narrative which generates a myth so powerful as to obscure the individual writer and to unleash an almost superhuman force – the Cuchulain story, the lament for Art Ó Laoghaire and, indeed, *Dracula* all have that mesmeric power. The third is a text that has had, by virtue of its eloquence and insight, a palpable influence upon the course of human action or the prosecution of public policy – the *Drapier's Letters* of Swift, the speeches of Edmund Burke or the autobiography of Wolfe Tone might be mentioned in such a context. Each of the works chosen for separate treatment in this volume earns its place under at least one of these headings; many might stake a claim under two; and some rare but brilliant instances may deserve mention under all three.

The word 'classic' once denoted the revered texts of ancient Greece and Rome, but the curricular study of those literatures has for over a century been challenged by courses in modern languages. The yoking together of the words 'modern' and 'classic' no longer seems a trite paradox, although attempts to enlist living authors as recruits to the pantheon may be overenthusiastic. I have limited myself here to the treatment of dead artists whose reputation seems secure, for, as Dr Johnson said, about those subjects on which the public thinks long, it commonly thinks aright. A study of the contemporary movement in Irish writing, say from 1950 to the present, is a project for another volume. It would not be surprising if it were to reveal many continuities with the forces and themes to be found here.

Ireland has always felt itself in some need of the 'classical' tradition. The poetry of the *filí*, composed between 1200 and 1600, was classical in the sense that it adhered to very strict rules, was written by and for an elite, and had as its main purpose the desire to voice a shared communal philosophy with unparalleled verve and wit. Even after the collapse of the bardic system in the early 1600s, those ideals survived, and for a very long time. Greek and Latin were often taught in hedge schools, and the already threatened Irish language was also felt to be part of that continuum. For this reason, the defence of classicism became, in the peculiar conditions created by the English plantation and colonization, also the radical, rebel option. This helped to create that strange blend of the conservative and the revolutionary which is such a feature of the great texts in both languages, linking writers as outwardly disparate as Swift and Ó Bruadair, Yeats and Flann O'Brien. It also meant that the gap between high and popular culture was greatly reduced in Ireland long before this could happen in most other parts of Europe.

Once the old system of patronage had been replaced by the conditions of an open market, Irish culture provided a case of modernity *avant la lettre*. Those who wished to defend ancient values under the new conditions had to evolve new, experimental forms in which to protect those priceless things; and those who welcomed modernization often felt obliged to cloak their new ideas in the forms of tradition, the better to secure a hearing in a land filled with nostalgia. These were the two major ways of coping with the onset of modernity, while seeking to hold onto what was useful from the past. The Irish writer became in consequence a type of the Tory Anarchist, at once a defender of old values and a fomentor of rebellion: and this personality structure may be found as often in such Anglo-Irish figures as Swift and Edgeworth as in Irish-language authors like Merriman and Eibhlín Dhubh Ní Chonaill. Even the politics of the independent state seemed to feed off such ambivalences, as those in government soon learned to speak in the tones of an outraged opposition, and those in opposition bore themselves like rightful dukes exiled to some Forest of Arden.

The collapse of the bardic system after 1600 did not signify the defeat of classical ideals in Irish writing. The attack on those ideals had come, after all, not from within but from without: it was not – as it would be in other parts of Europe – the revolt of an 'unhealthy' romanticism against a 'healthy-minded' neoclassical style. Long before the emergence of the romantic movement, Irish classicism had already won for itself the weird glamour of the beleaguered rebel: and the resistance literature produced even in the nineteenth century by William Carleton and Standish J. O'Grady insisted on maintaining its own access to the Greek and Latin world. That continued to spectacular effect in the use made of Homer by authors like Yeats and Joyce. The classical conception of literature as definitive of social ideals was never lost through all the centuries of occupation: if anything, that view was strengthened, as literature became the one remaining social institution through which an underground consciousness might reveal itself. When the great modernists like Eliot and Pound emerged in the early decades of the twentieth century, they found in the example left by Swift, Joyce and others a ready template of the revolutionary use of tradition, of how the classics might be invoked as part of the hypermodernity embraced by the new experimentalists.

There were many other features of Irish writing that offered case studies of how the classical and the modern might be creatively reconciled. Because there were two powerful cultures in constant contention in Ireland after 1600, neither was able to achieve absolute hegemony. One consequence was that no single tradition could ever become official: the only persistent tradition in Irish culture was the largely successful attempt to subvert all claims to make any tradition official. In conditions of ongoing cultural confrontation, most of the great works of literature produced on either side took on something of the character of anthropology. They raised questions not so much *within* their own culture as *of* the very notion of culture itself. They were aware, almost from the outset, that cultures can be construed from without as well as within. The liquidation of seemingly sacrosanct values and ideas, especially those of the recent past, became a *sine qua non* of Irish modernity; the phenomenon was to be found also in the willingness of writers to repudiate or rewrite their own earlier works. With the constant attack on the recent past went a corresponding celebration of the art of the ancient world. Ireland in these guises was no provincial backwater, however, but in the eyes of authors from Swift to Joyce, from Céitinn to Ó Cadhain, a test-case of the modern world. One of their recurrent tactics was the suggestion that theirs was an age of crisis, in which all the old values stood in danger of imminent death. Granted the gift of perpetual old age, the culture found in it the sources of a vitality that has lasted to this very day.

All translations, except where otherwise indicated, are by the present author.

I owe thanks to many who have assisted me over the years in which this study took shape. The President of University College Dublin, Dr Art Cosgrove, made me an award that freed me from teaching duties in the session 1998–9, when much of the writing was done. I am grateful also to Derek Hand who took my place in the classroom with superb ability.

I have been much inspired by the teaching and conversation of

John McGahern during his period as writer-in-residence in my department. Without those conversations and the illumination they brought, this book would have had a very different shape. The writings of Edward Said and Brian Friel have remained a priceless touchstone, as I moved from postcolonial studies into a more anthropological kind of investigation. In that changing context, the work of the New Voices in Irish Criticism collective has been a constant challenge: I want to acknowledge P.J. Mathews, Noreen Doody, Edna Longley, Aaron Kelly, John Kenny and many others.

My own recent students Jarlath Killeen, Diana Pérez Garcia, Seokmoo Choi, Li Yuanhong, Conor McCarthy, Nancy Watson, Heather Laird and Neil Murphy have all added a lot to the thinking behind this volume. So also have Ron Callan, Sarah Fulford, Beth Wightman, Catherine Wynne, Desmond O'Rawe, John Alderson, David Cotter, Taura Napier, Gearóid O'Flaherty, and Frankie Sewell. I am very much indebted as always to Éamon Ó Tuathail and Sean G. Ronan for hospitality and guidance in the field of international cultural relations; and to Frank McGuinness, Alan Sinfield, Helen Vendler and Fred Jameson for shrewd counsel. My mother Eithne Kiberd, my brother Damien Kiberd and my sister Marguerite Lynch have all been generous not just with encouragement but with ideas, as have my friends Adrian and Rosaleen Moynes, Caroline Walsh and James Ryan, Carol Coulter and Harry Vince Coulter, Richard Murphy and Brendan Kennelly, Marie and Seamus Heaney, Lyn Innes and Paddy Lyons, Bob and Angela Welch, Nicky and Eleanor Grene, Glenn Hooper and Oonagh Walsh, Terence Brown, Roy Foster, Susan Sailer, Tony Roche and Katy Hayes, Brian and Trish Donnelly, and Catriona Clutterbuck. I would also like to thank Maureen Murphy, Bernard O'Donoghue, Munira Mutran, Peter Kuch, Bob and Becky Tracy, Norma McDermott and Sinéad MacAodha, Richard and Catherine Rose, Richard and Anne Kearney, Judy Friel and Aedeen Howard for help and inspiration. My ideas have been sharpened by many conversations and exchanges with Dillon Johnston and Guinn Batten, Rosangela Barone, Shaun Richards, Robert Ballagh, Rand and Beth Brandes, Seán Ó Mórdha and David Dickson, and Gabriel and Brenda Fitzmaurice.

Philip O'Leary and Seamus Deane have been flawless guides through much unfamiliar terrain; and Elizabeth Butler Cullingford has been a wonderful ally and kindly supporter. Some of the ideas and chapters were first tried on audiences at seminars at University College Dublin, Trinity College Dublin, Yale University, the University of West Virginia, Cambridge University, the British Association of Irish Studies, the Abbey Theatre, the Joyce International

Foundation, the University of Rome, the University of São Paolo, the Foreign Languages Institute of Beijing, the Frankfurt Book Fair, and at many Irish summer schools. I want to thank all my hosts.

For assistance with specific details in particular chapters I wish to express heartfelt gratitude to: Michael Smith, Rory Rapple, Gearóid Ó Crualaoich, Alan Titley, Tom Dunne, Alasdair Macrae, Andrew Carpenter, Anne Fogarty, Michael Moses, John Devitt, Jeff Holdridge, Wanda Balzano, Luke Gibbons, Brendan Barrington, Clíona Ó Gallchóir, Owen Dudley Edwards, Christopher Murray, J.C.C. Mays, Janet Clare, Lucy McDiarmid, Tony Coughlan, Desmond Fennell and Paul Gillespie. I should also acknowledge Lindsay Waters, Pat Sheeran, Nina Witoszek, Michael D. Higgins, Lance Pettit, John Brannigan and Moyra Haslett.

A study which traverses so many centuries and such varied terrain leaves an author especially reliant on the help of friends – and wary of over-identifying any of them with a text which, even after such assistance, must be open to many criticisms. I wish, however, to thank Marc Caball for his generously detailed critique of my chapters on the decline of the *filí*. Angela Bourke has been for over a decade my main source of inspiration on the subject of eighteenth-century Gaelic poetry. Our student Sarah McKibben wrote a powerful thesis on attitudes of writers to the 'death' of the Irish language. Both of these scholars have greatly enriched my thinking. Likewise, Joe McMinn, Tom Bartlett and Jeff Holdridge have read the chapters on Swift, Tone and Burke with great kindness and many creative suggestions. All of these good people will see from what follows just how often I attended to their advice: and they should not be held accountable for the fact that sometimes I didn't.

Owen Dudley Edwards read the entire manuscript. His comments were always shrewd, often hilarious, and saved me from many errors. He is the Sherlock Holmes of Irish studies and, like countless others, I am massively indebted to him. His learning is exceeded only by his generosity. I wish to make a special acknowledgment of three texts: Breandán Ó Buachalla's seminal essay "Canóin na Creille"; Fiona Macintosh's luminous monograph *Dying Acts;* and Nina Witozsek and Pat Sheeran's wonderfully contentious *Talking to the Dead: A Study of Irish Funerary Traditions.*

My intellectual debt to Neil Belton grows with every passing year. I am fortunate once again to have him publish a book which I might never have contemplated without the knowledge that he was available with shrewd criticism and warm support. The scrupulous and scholarly copy-editing of Pat Harper was absolutely invaluable and the work was much improved by her care. I have many reasons to be grateful to Angela Rose of Granta for wise advice and cheerful help.

To my mother Eithne I owe a love of Irish literature in both of our languages: it was she who introduced me to most of the writers treated here and who taught me that books are the signals that we send into the future. *Ise a chothaigh ionam dílseacht don dúchas.* My wife Beth and my children Lucy, Amy and Rory have offered endless kindness and love (tempered with shrewd and sensible warnings). My dead teachers and friends Máirtín Ó Cadhain, Dick Ellmann, Vivian Mercier and Éilís Dillon have been more present and helpful than ever; and the most urgent, cajoling and tenderly quizzical presence of all has been my dead father, a consummate Tory Anarchist even in the manner of his dignified departure. To his memory *Irish Classics* is dedicated with respect and with love.

DECLAN KIBERD
Clontarf, Dublin
January 2000

1

Gaelic Ireland: Apocalypse Now?

On September 4th, 1607, a big boat set sail from Lough Swilly bearing ninety-nine passengers. Among them were earls whose families had dominated the north-western part of Ireland for centuries; priests and clerical students bound for Louvain; a Spanish sailor who had been stranded in the time of the Armada and had married and settled in Ireland; and a bardic historian named Tadhg Ó Cianáin, who kept a vivid record of their progress. Foremost among the company was Hugh O'Neill, earl of Tyrone, who had in the previous decade sought to unite the disputatious leaders of Gaelic Ireland against the expansionist policies of English monarchs. He had led his troops to a tremendous victory at the Battle of the Yellow Ford in 1598, the only serious military defeat sustained by English forces on Irish soil: but that had been followed by the wholesale slaughter of the Irish at Kinsale in 1601.

After that, the power of the Gaelic princes was curbed and they seemed a spent force. Their departure in 1607 was so hurried that some men's wives and other men's children were left behind in the confusion. O'Neill's son was seized by the English and raised as a Protestant; the wife of Rory O'Donnell, a prince of Tyrconnell, stayed on and later married a Dublin nobleman named Sir Nicholas Barnwell; and Ó Cianáin's wife and children were left as virtual hostages, soon to be stripped of cattle and lands which were his inheritance as a man of learning. All in all, it was a messy departure: some relations refused to leave with the earls, while others who wanted to go with their loved ones got news of the flight only when the boat had sailed.

Tadhg Ó Cianáin's account captures something of that disorder, but later versions smooth such untidiness over. In the canon of Irish nationalist history, the Flight of the Earls was the moment when Gaelic Ireland finally collapsed, that conjuncture which saw an entire people robbed of those natural leaders who might have given shape to their aspirations. For it was the northern princes who had done most not only to resist English armies but to promote the culture of Gaelic poets and historians. In their apparent ruin, one of the *filí* (poets), Eoghan Ruadh Mac an Bhaird, was able to read his own and that of his country:

> Anocht is uaigneach Éire,
> do-bheir fógra a fírfréimhe
> gruaidhe a fear 'sa fionnbhan flioch,
> treabh is iongnadh go huaignioch . . .
>
> Gan rádha rithlearg molta,
> gan sgaoileadh sgeól gcodalta;
> gan úidh a fhaicsin leabhair,
> gan chlaisdin nglúin gheinealaigh.[1]

Tonight Ireland is lonely: the outlawing of her people has left tears on the cheeks of her men and fair women. It is amazing that such a people should be lonely . . . Without the recital of praise poems, without storytelling before bed, without passion for the study of books, without listening to the announcement of genealogies.

Those earls had abandoned the land of Ireland, so often imagined as a bereft and betrayed woman. Mac an Bhaird predicted doom for the Gael – Troy and Babylon provided precedents, but hardly Israel, for now the Gaelic people had no Moses to lead them from captivity. Other poets lamented Ireland as a tragic woman caught in a bad relationship with a tyrannical foreigner and tried to call forth a new leader in place of O'Neill.[2]

Nobody was quite able to account for the flight, which seemed out of character for a strong, uncompromising warrior such as O'Neill. A year later, he would send an apologia to the authorities in London, outlining his reasons – the measures against the Catholic religion; the seizure of lands to provide wealth for the bishops of the Anglican Reformation; the appointment of sheriffs in areas once controlled by

his men; and so on. This may have been window-dressing. Earlier in
1607, O'Neill had heard that King James wanted him jailed in the
Tower of London. Having been condemned in his absence, perhaps
he resolved to be punished in his absence too. As soon as the earls
had fled, the authorities circulated a rumour that they had been plotting to seize Dublin Castle. In the eyes of officialdom, they were
traitors and so their lands might lawfully be seized.

The image of their boat taking to the waters entered Irish iconog-
raphy as an emblem of desolation: 'with these / our very souls pass
overseas'. Subsequent accounts develop the emotion evoked in Mac
an Bhaird's poem: 'it is said that, as the ship that carried them away
set sail down Lough Swilly, a great cry of lament and farewell went
up from their followers left upon the shore'.[3] With that sentence the
Celtic scholar Robin Flower brings his study of Gaelic literature
towards its conclusion in a chapter entitled 'The End of a Tradition'.
But what is a terminal point for some may be a launching pad for
others. The radical novelist Peadar O'Donnell laughed out loud on
reading Flower's lines: for, according to the folk memory of his
people, the peasantry of Donegal and Derry stood on the shores of
Lough Swilly and cheered as the boat moved away.[4]

What fell with Hugh O'Neill was not a Gaelic civilization so much
as an aristocratic order: and the departure of the earls merely signalized prior changes in the social structure. One of the complaints
O'Neill made to the London authorities in his 1608 apologia concerned the severe reduction in his taxes following the freeing of the
serfs three years earlier – for not only were serfs freed from bondage,
but now they might seek redress in courts of law against the Gaelic
chieftains. The new central administration in Dublin was interfering
far too much in the affairs of local overlords. Perhaps O'Neill and his
followers hoped to secure military help from the Catholic armies of
Europe under the direction of the Pope in Rome: that at least was the
justification for the Flight put about by their admirers. But they were
hopelessly out of date in their thinking: the Pope had no intention of
breaking the peace between Spain and England, and he even counselled O'Neill against coming to Rome at all.[5]

In the event, the noble Catholic families whom they encountered
on their progress across Europe paid due respect to the travellers.
Many offered hospitality and a chance to view masterpieces of painting in Louvain or the frescoes of Giotto in Assisi – before quickly
moving them on. Most of the refugees would die overseas, caught in
a time-warp of nostalgia for a Gaelic order that now existed solely in
the writings of Ó Cianáin. His ancient duty was to record the doings
of his lord, which he faithfully did until his own death in 1614; but

the language of his chronicle, though sometimes beautiful, was a symptom of the underlying problem of his lord. Ó Cianáin had 'a liking for archaic forms which must have passed from the spoken language at least five centuries before';[6] so, in describing a squall at sea, he could not resist an old run such as 'd'éirigh an fharraige ina tonnta tubhorba tinneasnacha tréantuinsiúla dóibh'[7] (the sea rose in rude, painful, strong-leaping waves against them). He never contented himself with one verb when three might cover the case equally well: 'ghabh siad ag aithrí agus ag urnaí agus ag idirghuí Naomh Muire Ógh i bhfrithchéadfá na híomhá'[8] (they began to repent and pray and intercede with the Virgin Mary in the sensory shape of that image). There were moments in his narrative when, confronted with the baroque foppery of a French ambassador at the Papal Court, Ó Cianáin seemed dimly to register a version of his own anachronism:

> . . . ach cheana ba neamhchónaitheach dá lámh ag síorbhaint an hata sin de, ag tabhairt umhlaíochta agus cúirtéise do lucht a fheicseana agus a fhorbháiltithe.[9]

> . . . but still his hand was never resting, eternally doffing his hat, offering humility and courtesy to his listeners and welcomers.

In the end, however, his eye saw only what it wanted to see, a Europe filled with gallant courtiers and noble kinsmen. For Tadhg Ó Cianáin was, even by the admission of an English pardon which had been granted to him in 1602, a 'gentleman'.[10]

The bardic order, which was now collapsing, had always been unapologetically aristocratic, with certain families serving as hereditary poets to the Gaelic leaders. They stood second only to the chieftain in the pecking order and might even wield power over him: for it was their duty not only to praise a wise and generous ruler (saying that the land, always female, was beautiful under his lordship) but also to denounce a bad leader (even to the extent of raising boils or blisters on his shamed face). Bardic training was long and arduous, as befitted a mandarin class. Up to twelve years were served in mastering a complex system of quatrains under the guidance of an *ollamh* (professor). The poet's self-image was accordingly high and all were jealous in guarding their rights. They flourished between 1200 and the early 1600s. One of the finest, Muireadhach Albannach Ó Dálaigh, was once so incensed by a churlish tax demand from a steward of the O'Donnells that 'he seized a sharp axe and instantly cut him down'.[11] O'Donnell was outraged and the poet had to flee into the territory of Richard de Burgo, an Anglo-Norman lord whose court was by 1213 already so Gaelicized as to be addressed 'a dhream ghaoidhealta ghallda' (o people both Gaelic and foreign) and which the poet assumed to share in the *sprezzatura* of the natural aristocrat:

> *Beag ar bhfala risin bhfear,*
> *bachlach do bheith dom cháineadh,*
> *mé do mharbhadh an mhoghadh –*
> *a Dhé, an adhbhar anfholadh?*[12]

Little our dispute with the man, that a churl was denouncing me to the effect that I'd killed a serf – o God, is that a basis for bloodletting?

Moghadh was the classical Irish word for 'serf': one of the low food producers who would finally be given their freedom under the English dispensation. After that date, these people were able to save money by dint of hard work and even to buy land, unlike the remnants of the old Gaelic aristocracy, most of whom felt themselves to be above common toil. Previously, the serfs had been expected to provide free field labour for the Gaelic nobles, who offered protection and sustenance in return: now, they were to be paid for all work done.

Not all members of the old bardic caste quit the country. A very few, such as Eochaidh Ó hEódhusa, were pardoned by the new rulers and granted landholdings; and some of the new leaders were cunning enough to offer limited patronage to the remaining *filí*, perhaps fearing that they might otherwise encourage rebellion.[13] Most of the poets who stayed on were virtual outcasts, keen to mock the beneficiaries of the new money-order, which emerged at its fullest point of development after the Plantation of Ulster in 1610. Clearly, the planters were a minority group in most areas and so 'the tillers of soil necessarily remained the same':[14] but, with pastorage rapidly giving way to tillage, there was good money to be earned and life became easier. The former serfs were soon outbidding the fallen noblemen or bards for rented or even for purchased tracts of land.

Some time between 1607 and 1620, one of the ruined artists wrote an attack on the *arrivistes* in *Pairlement Chloinne Tomáis* (The Parliament of Clan Thomas), a work which mocks their lineage and boorish manners. Lacking the noble genealogies of the older patrons, the Clan Thomas are described as descendants of Beelzebub on the paternal side. They were recalcitrant even to Saint Patrick, who failed to teach them Christian doctrine. As a punishment, the saint put them under a sort of curse so that their music would be screeching and their food the feet of beasts. They were also condemned to eternal labour 'do chothú an uasail' (to nurture the nobility). As a sign of their doltishness, they left no good turn unpunished:

> . . . an tí do-dhéanadh math agus mórchosnamh dhóibh, go mbadh é budh lugha orra – agus an tí do bhuailfeadh agas do cháinfeadh iad, go mbadh é budh annsa leo d'fhearuibh an bheatha.[15]

> . . . whoever offered them kindness or great protection was thought least by them – and whoever attacked or denounced them was closest to them above all men in the world.

A second version of *Pairlement Chloinne Tomáis* was written after Cromwell's campaign. Its author was a master of the classical language (including its poetic quatrains) and was filled with distaste for the emerging tenant farmers who imitated English customs, food and clothes. Accordingly, he offered a savage ventriloquism of their barbarous, halting language, as they portentously arrogated to themselves a parliament. This was the political institution which had brought misery to Ireland, and the lower orders are considered tainted by association with it. The Clan Thomas is accused of these qualities: sloth, slovenliness and timidity. However, its members are in turn permitted to make a somewhat similar set of allegations against the parasites of the Gaelic nobility, 'sladuighthe satha . . . do bhíodh ag caitheamh lóin ar na fíorbheachuigh i. na lábánuigh'[16] (drones who were accustomed to eat at the expense of the worker bees, i.e. the poor). It may well be that the author was, by the time of writing, equally dismissive of a weak-kneed Gaelic nobility which should have fought harder for its code and supported poets but instead (in his view) simply rolled over in submission. Its remnants are called 'na huaisle meata' (the cowardly nobles) in the text.

If parody is the act of a trapped mind which cannot create anew but has just enough energy to mock what has gone before, then the *Pairlement Chloinne Tomáis* is indeed a parody. This might explain the frequent notes of coarseness in a tale that at times seems to savour the very boorishness it affects to regret. It is one thing for its high-minded author to jeer at the broken English of the new pretenders: 'what the bigg greate órdhlach for the what so penny?' (how much per inch?).[17] There the same mockery of the 'brogue' associated with renditions of the stage Irishman in London theatres is enacted by a fastidious Gaelic artist working in a Gaelic framework: and the cream of the jest is that the serfs are abject in their admiration of such dubious fluency, assuring the speaker 'dhubhshloigis rogha an Bhéarla' (you have swallowed the choicest English whole).[18] It is quite another thing, however, for the author to blend the noble metres in which a bard bade farewell to a dying tanist with a low-budget account of riff-raff who snore and fart:

> Slán do Bhrian Ó Bhriolláin tshuairc,
>   fear crónáin i gcluais a mhic,
> Slán do Mhuirghuill is do Mhéidhbh,
>   nár leig braidhm is nár ith min.[19]

Farewell to affable Brian Ó Briolláin, a man to snore in the ear of his son; farewell to Muirghull and Maeve, who never let a fart nor ate coarse meal.

That is a quatrain worthy of Flann O'Brien (and in *At Swim-Two-Birds* he would bring off such fusions of high art and low comedy), but the combination humiliates the ancient form even more than the modern target.

The energies unleashed in *Pairlement Chloinne Tomáis*, though ostensibly gathered in defence of tradition and against modernity, are deployed in a manner that comes perilously close to nihilism. (This would be true, some decades later, of Jonathan Swift's *The Battle of the Books*.) Everything is set into contest with everything else: and *everything* is finally levelled in a desperate mimicry of modern democracy. It is as if the author sees all around him a world in which each restraint of civilization has been lost. Where once the codes of rich and poor, though different, generated systems of self-control, now the fusion of systems leads one to cancel the other out, with the consequence that people fall into the chasm of barbarisms that opens between them. If there is one group which provides the major target for all this mockery, it is the one that is neither noble nor base, 'na meathaigh uaisle', those weak nobles who did not flee with the earls but who cannot labour:

> Beag an mhaith na meathacháin
>   mheathas a leith na huaisle,
> Ní thiubhruinn mo leathshrubhán
>   orra riamh nó an uair si.[20]

Little good are the weak-kneed – half the nobility are weak. I
would not give half my barleycake for them, now or ever.

These are accused of idleness: and the serfs assert their right to adopt
surnames and lands left by the vanished princes.

A representative of the ruined Gaelic elite, Séamas an Seabhac
(James the Hawk) is allowed to state their case: but, just like the freed
serfs, he is permitted only to condemn himself out of his own mouth:

> . . . nach fuil a fhios agaibh gurab ó ifrionn táinig bhur sinnsior,
> gurab do chloinn dílis Dé sinne? . . . Thugamuir sean-bhróga
> agus sean-stocaidhe dhibh, agas sean-éadach do chuiremaois
> dár gcorpaibh fein . . . agas go gtugamuir coimhéad bó agas
> caorach agus capuill dibh . . . agas an tan do-cunnarcamuer
> sibh ag teacht ar bhur n-aghaidh, gur léigeamuir seisear nó ochtar
> ar aonbhaile amháin dibh ag cur agas ag treabhadh ar chíos
> agas do léigeamuir bhur gclann len ar gcloinn chum sgoile . . .
> Annsin budh miann leis gach aonduine aguibh dochtúir dlighe
> nó duine eaglaise do dhéanamh dá mhac . . . An tráth do léigea-
> muir bhur srian féin libh, chuaigh sibh i bhfiántas orainn, mar
> as gnáth libh bheith míchoinghíollach ionar n-aghaidh.[21]

> Don't you know that it was from hell your people came and
> that we are the faithful family of God? . . . We gave old shoes
> and stockings to you, and old clothes from our own bodies . . .
> and we gave you work tending cows, sheep and horses . . . and
> when we saw you progress, we allowed six or eight of you to
> plough land on rental and permitted your families schooling
> with ours . . . and now every one of you wants to make his son
> into a lawyer or priest . . . When we gave you your head, you
> went wild on us, for you were forever treacherous.

If the work really were a satire on the lower orders alone, that passage would have to be read literally. However, it is clearly intended as
a moral exposure of the pusillanimity of the upper class.

Some have taken the *Pairlement Chloinne Tomáis* for a risky
attack on the new order by an overdog turned underdog, yet its purchase seems wider. It is hardly a conventional satire at all, for at its
end there is no code left intact by which all others might have been
found wanting. The English satirists of the period hoped to make
their readers into more civilized persons, whereas here the mocker
despairs of any human improvement. In fact, he reserves some of his
bitterest invective for those who seek advancement. In order that

satire should work effectively, there must be some human norm against which all infractions can be measured. Here, on the contrary, even the implied stability of the bardic quatrain is fractured when the old form is employed in an absurd praise-poem to Cromwell, appended to later versions. The great puritan radical is called a king:

> *Treise leat a Chromuil.*
> *A rígh chroinic na sgulóg,*
> *As red linn fuaireamar suaimhneas,*
> *Mil, uachtar agus onóir.*[22]

> More power to you, Cromwell,
> O king in the chronicles of the lowly.
> From you we derived comfort,
> Honey, cream and honour.

The second version circulated very widely winning many readers for its author. Like other parodists, he may have written for his own relief and amusement, discharging the bile of a marginalized man and jeering at all who cared to notice that they were under attack. The pervasive coarseness and slang ensured that the *arrivistes* got the message in a work whose subject is a straightforward question: who is to inherit Ireland? The answer is given in a scene where all chivalric rituals are inverted by a people who prefer an English to an Irish overlord, and who would wrestle a lady into bed rather than engage in the protocols of *amour courtois* poetry. When one of the daughters of a remaining prince is ready for marriage, a man of Clan Thomas offers his hand, but her father is advised by his poets that noble and base blood should never be mingled. He disregards the advice and speaks the very death-sentence of the *filí*:

> *Ná grádhaigh an taos uasal*
> *is ná tabhair dualgas don éigse;*
> *ná héist le foghar orgán*
> *'s ná creid comhrádh cléire.*[23]

> Do not love the nobility and do not discharge obligations to the poets: do not listen to the sound of the organ and don't believe the talk of clerics.

The poets would not have been poets if they hadn't lamented the collapse of their patronage: and it was in their interest to equate

that with the defeat of Ireland itself. For centuries, a favourite theme
of poets had been the suggestion that their lord deserved 'the sovereignty of Ireland': now, for many of the *filí*, this was no longer a
conceit but an urgent summons to dynasts to defend a threatened
way of life.[24] However, in older days, the poets often had little compunction about praising any chief, native or foreign, who paid for the
text: their ultimate loyalty was to their artistic profession and they
would transfer their allegiance from one lord to another, if rewards
seemed likely to be greater with the new man. What had begun to
trouble them after 1541 was the system of 'Surrender and Regrant',
whereby the English legal code now being introduced had no clear
role for *them*. As primogeniture took the place of Gaelic custom, the
notion of the poets as interpreters of rightful sovereignty became
redundant. No longer could the *file* record the beneficence or otherwise of a man's rule; no longer would he offer the rod at the
investiture of the *tánaiste* named by a sept to succeed a dead lord, for
now primogeniture was the iron rule.[25] No wonder that after the
decree of 1541 (which had to be read in Irish by the earl of Desmond
at the Dublin Parliament), the more alert among the poets sensed the
long-term implications of such anglicization.

One of them had in fact named and shamed the defaulting
chieftains:

> *Fúbún fúibh, a shluagh Gaoidheal,*
> *ní mhaireann aoinneach agaibh;*
> *Goill ag comhroinn bhur gcríche;*
> *re sluagh síthe bhur samhail.*
>
> *Fúbún fán ngunna ngallghlas,*
> *fúbún fán slabhra mbuidhe,*
> *fúbún fán gcúirt gan Bhéarla,*
> *fúbún séana Mheic Mhuire.*[26]

Shame on you, Gaelic ones, not one of you lives; foreigners are
dividing your lands and you are like the fairies [i.e. under-
ground].
Shame on the green-tinted foreign gun; shame on the golden
chain. Shame on the court without a poetic language. Shame on
those who deny the Son of Mary.

The poets, because of their possible mobility from lord to lord, had
some sense of the scale of the new opposition. This was no incursion by a rival grandee into a local ruler's lands, but a systematic

revolution. Most of the lords in the later 1500s had little sense of the invaders as representatives of a modern nation: for them the Tudor forces were just a foreign element, another in the seemingly endless sequence of contestants from the dawn of time who fought for control of land.

Over time, however, it became obvious that the process of anglicization would go deep indeed. The sons of those lords who had accepted Surrender and Regrant in 1541 had been sent to England to learn English and English ways. The earl of Desmond's own boy became a playmate of Prince Edward. Sir William Parsons outlined the official thinking behind these policies:

> We must change their course of government, apparel, manner of holding land, language and way of life. It will otherwise be impossible to set up in them obedience to the laws and to the English Empire.

The Elizabethan poet Edmund Spenser agreed:

> It hath ever been the use of conquerors to despise the language of the conquered, and to force him by all means to learn his ... the speech being Irish, the heart must needs be Irish.[27]

Just how important the English administrators considered the *filí* is not easily estimated, for the evidence which survives is contradictory. For example, George Carew, the President of Munster in the 1600s, is said by some to have collected Gaelic manuscripts for their safe keeping and preservation, and by others to have cut up the old vellum to make covers for English-language grammar books.[28] The document-driven English may have considered that some bardic poems amounted to validations of a sept's traditional claim to land. Sir John Perrott was accused of imprisoning and hanging poets – but also of asking one to write a praise-poem for his monarch. 'Treise leat a Chromuil' may have been a parody, as well as an extension, of that mode.

The English, in their attempt to streamline Irish administration, wished to unite all in the community of their own language. Sir John Davies, the main organizer of the Ulster Plantation, expressed the hope that 'the next generation will in tongue and heart and every way also become English'.[29] Obviously, the *filí* were an impediment to that policy. They had a vested interest in the defence of a Gaelic system which paid well for their expertise. Once the shadow of English fell upon them after 1541, many began to use loan words

from that language ('bríste', 'clóca', cóta', 'scarfa') not only to disparage new fashions in clothing but also to register nervousness
about this extraneous new element in the population. As a privileged
caste, they had always known that they would stand or fall with the
system and that it would stand or fall with them. The 'honour' of a
lord had always been articulated by a poet: and it was through the
poet's memorable lines that rulers might leave 'names upon the harp'.
That sense of the future shape of things, which the *filí* were expected
to imagine, was in part a residue of their ancient prophetic function
as seers. Fame and repute, those most precious possessions of a
grandee, were impossible without a *file*.

Under stress of the anglicization thrust of the Elizabethans, the
poets naturally continued to praise those who supported the Gaelic
way of life. Edmund Spenser had some of the bardic poems translated. Although he praised their pretty flowers, he added, '. . . it is
great pity to see so good an ornament abused to the gracing of
wickedness and vice'.[30] Thomas Smyth, a Dublin apothecary,
accused the *filí* of inciting rebels, 'and further they do cause them
that would be true to be rebellious thieves, extortioners, murderers,
raveners, yea and worse if it were possible'.[31] In all of these statements, one thing comes through very clearly: the English already
had a notion of 'common weal', of national self-interest, whereas the
strongly communal identity of the Irish was still not fully national.[32]
Yet many of the *filí* helped to hasten its development. Some, like
Tadhg Dall Ó hUiginn, envisaged a fusion of Anglo-Norman and
Gaelic stock under the common name of 'Éireannaigh' (Irish people)
as opponents of Tudor expansionism; this note was struck increasingly by poets during the period of militancy in the 1590s.[33] They
well understood that their own positions would disappear if the
English won.

The streamlined, unitary organization of English forces convinced
Irish intellectuals of the need for a similar degree of cohesion on
their own side: and the native-versus-foreigner theme of ancient
poems was soon reactivated. A national consciousness would soon
develop further among the Irish, as one consequence of enforced
exile. In Rome or Louvain or Salamanca, Irish men of learning would
soon discover ways of seeing Ireland clearly and seeing it whole. Yet
not even the poets, who had been paid handsomely to foretell the
future, managed to anticipate the depths of their degradation, when
finally it came.

2

Bardic Poetry:
The Loss of Aura

Deprived of their patrons, those *filí* who stayed in Ireland found themselves at the mercy of new market forces. It was probably inevitable that they would end up hitting out impartially at all sides in this new order. For four centuries they had shown nothing but contempt for the common people: and they had developed a mandarin language which was comprehensible only to the elite. That language, priding itself on its archaic qualities, over the centuries had grown resistant to further development or change. The virtuosity of the poets was, for the most part, of that kind which leaves an artist invulnerable to criticism and yet incapable of evolution.[1] Now the *filí* found that, if they wished to survive, they would have to employ the language of a more vulgar market.

Mathghamhain Ó hIfearnáin advised his own son not to practise poetry and then sarcastically committed his own productions to the humiliation of popular suffrage:

> *Ceist! cia do cheinneóchadh dán?*
> *a chiall is ceirteolas suadh:*
> *an ngéabhadh, nó an áil le haon,*
> *dán saor do-bhéaradh go buan?*
>
> *Gé dán sin go snadhmadh bhfis,*
> *gach margadh ó chrois go crois*
> *do shiobhail mé an Mhumhain leis –*
> *ní breis é a-nuraidh ná anois.*

Ceard mar so ní sochar dhún,
  gé dochar a dul fá lár:
uaisle dul re déiniomh cíor –
  ga bríogh d'éinfhior dul re dán?[2]

A question! who will buy a poem, whose content is the proper knowledge of scholars? Will anyone accept or does anyone want a fine poem that will last forever?

Although this is a well-made poem, every fair from cross-roads to crossroads have I walked through Munster with it – and no sale last year or this year.

A trade like this is no good to us, even though it may be sad to see it die. It would be better to manufacture combs. What good to anyone to practise poetry?

There were many such begging letters, disguised as satiric lyrics, in this period of change before and after 1600. As old retainers of lords who no longer needed their ratification in order to rule, most poets suffered greatly. Their position was rather like holders of contemporary academic doctorates who cannot find a market for their expertise and are compelled to take menial employment: or like Beckettian tramps who once had learning but now face a deteriorating situation. In fact, what the *filí* were undergoing, somewhat sooner than their colleagues in other parts of Europe, was what would much later be called the loss of aura, in the decline from aristocratic patronage to commercial conditions. There had, of course, been a simulacrum of the market in the ability of poets to move from one lord to another, but selling combs to coxcombs was the real thing.

Like the *flâneur* of later centuries in the capitals of Europe, Ó hIfearnáin was seeking the right moment at which to bring together a buyer and a commodity. His predicament would be experienced all over again, two centuries later, by the French decadent poet Charles Baudelaire in 'Au Lecteur':

Pour avoir des souliers, elle a vendue son âme;
Mais le bon Dieu rirait si, près de cette infâme,
Je trenchais du tartufe et, singeais le hauteur,
Moi qui vends ma pensée et qui veux être auteur.[3]

In order to have shoes, she has sold her soul; but the good Lord would laugh if, beside that infamy, I were to play hypocrite and to affect hauteur – I who have sold my thoughts and wish to be an author.

Walter Benjamin has observed that, in his identification with the abandoned prostitute, Baudelaire 'knew what the true situation of the man of letters was: he goes to the marketplace as a *flâneur*, supposedly to take a look at it, but in reality to find a buyer'.[4] The Gaelic poets merely fell well before their sell-by date and the patronage system with them.

Thereafter, their role was that of the dandy, the courtier without a court: and it took a heroic constitution to live at that level of exposure, 'a Hercules without work'. As dandies, the *filí* tried to appear impressive and undeterred amidst the deteriorations, but it was a hard act to sustain. Those who had once lamented dead grandees were now keening the death of an entire cultural system, while remaining desperate for *any* patrons who might present themselves, Gaelic or foreign. It was, in rudimentary terms, patronage rather than Ireland that was often being lamented, though the two could never be fully distinct in many poetic minds.

A somewhat similar poem was composed in 1603 by Eochaidh Ó hEódhusa, who now found himself in the position of 'a poet laureate seeking engagements at a music hall'.[5] Denied his learned audience, he was forced downmarket to write in a more popular idiom. The *filí* had long made a virtue of obscurity in their *bélra na bhfile*, a mandarin jargon clear only to the initiated, who had always equated profundity with complication. Now they were forced to accept the adage that unless a person is a genius, it is best to be comprehensible. Ó hEódhusa's problem *was* that he was a genius: some of the lines of his most inspired compromise with the new conditions remain obscure to the most intrepid scholars:

> *Ionmholta malairt bhisigh:*
> *tarraidh sinde 'san amsa*
> *iomlaoid go suarach sona,*
> *do-chuaidh a sochar dhamhsa.*

> *Do thréig sind sreatha caola*
> *foirceadal bhfaobhrach ffrithir*
> *ar shórt gnáthach grés róbhog*
> *is mó as a moltar sinde.*

> *Le dorchacht na ngrés snoighthe*
> *do bhinnse ag tuilliodh gráine:*
> *fa hí ughachta mhóráin*
> *nár dhíol róghráidh ár ndáinne.*[6]

A change for the better is to be praised: in this time there has

come to pass a poor but happy transformation, which brings
profit to me.

I have abandoned the refined series, the sharp, fluent compositions, for a more commonplace and facile art, which brings
me greater praise.

With the darkness of well-wrought verses I once incurred
unpopularity: many gave as their opinion that my poetry was
unworthy of acclaim.

Nevertheless, this new fashion won for the poet an entirely new
audience, to whose demands he submitted, but with a glint of mocking condescension:

> Is iomdha tré dhán bhfallsa
>   lán dom annsacht a mbliadhna:
> do thuillfinn tuilleadh cheana
>   muna bheith eagla an iarla.[7]

Many because of my false poetry were full of acclaim for me
this year. I could earn even more plaudits, but for my fear of the
earl.

But not even the remaining lords can prevent the emergence of new
forms:

> Beag nach brisiodh mo chroidhe
>   gach dán roimhe dá gcumainn:
> is mór an tadhbhor sláinte
>   an nós so táinig chugainn.
>
> Dá lochtaighe triath Bearnais
>   énrand dá ndealbhthar linde
> budh iomdha ag cor 'na aghaidh –
>   ionmholta malairt bhisigh.[8]

Every poem I used to compose almost broke my heart: a great
source of good health is this new mode which has come to us.

If the chief of Barnesmore find fault in any verse made by
me, there will be many to dispute that – a change for the better
is to be praised.

A paradox lies coiled in those two final stanzas: for even though they
express a fastidious contempt for the mass mind, they are already

embracing it. The opening phrase of the poem becomes by the time of its repetition at the close almost fully drained of the attendant irony. This growing discrepancy between buoyant form and depressive content becomes a characteristic of many lyrics written in the period of *suathadh* or transformation.

It may be found also in Fear Flatha Ó Gnímh's poem addressed to Art Magennis, the inheriting son of a noble family in County Down, who claimed descent from the ancient kings of Ireland:

> *Mairg do-chuaidh re ceird ndúthchais:*
> *rug ar Bhanbha mbarrurthais*
> *nach dualghas athar is fhearr*
> *i n-achadh fhuarghlas Éireann.*
>
> *Ní sníthe snátha an fheasa,*
> *ní leanta craobh choibhneasa,*
> *gréas duan ní déanta d'fhighe,*
> *luach dréachta ní dlighfidhe.*[9]

Woe to him who pursued a family calling: it has happened in fresh, soft Ireland that duty no longer passes from father to son, in the cold green land of Ireland.

The threads of learning are not to be woven; the genealogies not followed; the patterns of a poem are not to be woven; it is not lawful to compose.

The lines that proclaim the banning of all poetry are deeply, richly poetic, in a way which will become familiar, three centuries later, in the writings of Samuel Beckett, which also seek to express the impossibility of all expression. Ó Gnímh is, in this lyric, discovering just how sumptuous destitution can be. Yet the more life he infuses into his quatrains, the more dead he proclaims the tradition, paradoxes fully explored by Sarah McKibben:

> *Mairg d'ollamh dá nárbh aithnidh*
> *ceard nábudh cúis iomaithbhir,*
> *d'uaim chláraidh, do dheilbh dhabhcha,*
> *sul tárraidh feidhm foghlamtha.*
>
> *Ní fhuighthe ar uaim ná rithlearg*
> *umhla ó fhearaibh ísilcheard:*
> *mon-uar gan aoibh na moghadh*
> *gan chaoir shuadh ar shaothrughadh.*[10]

Woe to the bardic poet who knows no trade that would keep
him free from insults. He might be a carpenter or a vat-maker,
before he attained the practice of learning. For the alliterating
rhapsody no recognition can be won from those low tradesmen. Alas, that not even the comfort of serfs is available for the
work of the scholar.

In fact, Ó Gnímh had hit upon a new theme: failure, loss and death.
Back in 1260, Giolla Brighde Mac Con Midhe had foretasted the end
of the tradition in a famous quatrain:

> Da mbáidhthí an dán, a dhaoine,
> gan seanchas, gan seanlaoidhe,
> go bráth, acht athair gach fhir,
> rachaidh cách gan a chluinsin.[11]

If poetry were destroyed, o people, and there were no old
stories or songs, nobody would know anything ever again
about generations before their own.

Ó Gnímh went one better than that and wrote the tradition out. His
verse derived muscular strength and sinewy force from the prospect
of its own demise.

It was as if the capacity to survey an entire tradition from its
beginning to its end had led to the onset of a new power and a new
authority:

> Ós aca tar fhéin mBanbha
>   tarla tús na healadhna –
> síol Róigh na sliomaitreabh sean –
>   tiomáintear dhóibh a deireadh.[12]

Since among the people of Ireland the origins of art were
found – the seed of Róigh, of ancient, beautiful houses – its end
is entrusted to them too.

Yet strangely, having announced the demise of the code in mid-
lyric, Ó Gnímh went on to praise Art Magennis as the new hope of
Gaeldom. Perhaps that final surge of anticipation was formulaic
and merely courteous (it would become so by the eighteenth century): but the reader is left wondering whether the death of 'Gaelic
glory' at the centre of the poem may not be something of a conceit.
The *suathadh*, even if it disempowered many poets, also gave rise to

many powerful poems: far more than were written by the *filí* in the days of their prosperity.

If the poets faced popular modes with some reluctance, that was hardly surprising. 'How much do they give in the pawnshop for a lyre?' would be Baudelaire's cryptic description of the modern plight of poets expelled from the fair courts of life. Henceforth, the lyric poet with an aura would be seen as antiquated. All poets, being fastidious souls, would still fear the crowd, but at a yet deeper level many would now yearn to speak for the entire community.

In a late prose work called 'A Lost Halo', Baudelaire offered an image of the modern poet deprived of an aura:

> Some while back I was rushing through the streets, and among the early-morning disorder, in which death threatens from all sides at once, I must have jerked myself, because the halo fell from my head onto the dirty asphalt pavement. I lacked the courage to pick it up and decided that it was less humiliating to lose my insignia than to have my bones broken. I told myself also that every cloud has a silver lining. Now I am able to travel incognito, do bad things, and engage in common behaviour like ordinary mortals. So here I am just like you.
> 'But you should report your lost halo to the lost property office.'
> I wouldn't dream of it. I prefer it here. You're the only one who has recognised me. Anyway, dignity fatigues me: and I like to think that some bad poet will retrieve the halo and won't be slow to adorn himself with it. There is nothing I like more than making a person happy – especially if the happy man is someone I can mock. Imagine X wearing it, or Y. Won't that be hilarious?[13]

That is the voice of Ó hIfearnáin, Ó Gnímh and, even, of the authors of the *Pairlement Chloinne Tomáis*, marvelling at the pretentious *arrivistes* who adopt the old, noble names. But the tone of light mockery possible to Ó hIfearnáin in 1603 could not survive for much longer, as the depth of the crisis became clearer.

For the Gaelic poets, as later for Baudelaire, the crowd was that which beckoned and repelled. In the figure of the prostitute, above all, Baudelaire found a metaphor for his own thoughts on 'the possibility of a mythical communication with the crowd'.[14] Prostitution offered a means of survival in a market where even persons were as interchangeable as physical objects: and well the *filí* knew it. In some of their greatest lyrics from the ninth century to the seventeenth, the poet had imagined himself caught between rival patrons, sharing the

plight of a woman who passed from one partner to another. Forced
out onto the streets for the practice of what they called *sráidéigse*
(street art), the poets were all too well aware of one possible meaning of their equation of Ireland with an abandoned woman. The
cultural anxiety that lay behind a lyric by Ó hEódhusa or Ó Gnímh
was the terror that they would never again assert a courtly identity
which broke free of the types of the mass market. As a *fear* that was
most ironic, given that the old bardic system, with its strict metrical
rules, scarcely encouraged any great individuality.

'The loss of aura concerns the poet first of all,' wrote Walter
Benjamin. 'He is forced to exhibit his own person in the marketplace,' whereas the exhibition of aura from now on 'becomes an
affair of fifth-rank poets'[15] (such as those mocked in the *Pairlement
Chloinne Tomáis* for taking up the old nobility's surnames). So it was
for the ruined *filí*: they must have been among the first poets in the
world to seek an originality that was market-oriented. Yet, even in
that perilous task, as they became dedicated followers of fashion,
they felt obliged to keep on insisting that the new things they did
made positively no contribution to progress. It would be unfair to
call them hidebound conservatives, for many displayed a flexibility,
in meeting the new challenges, that freed them from some very suffocating conventions. Even their 'adherence to tradition may in itself
have been a strategic response to the chaotic socio-political factors',[16]
as well as an attempt to protect a communal code that seemed on the
point of disintegration. Being dandies, whose tradition seemed to
flower late, they were without any great belief in their own immediate future. Their urge to consume a new experience was but another
expression of their longing for death: hence that strange mingling of
vitality and morbidity in Ó Gnímh's poem. Yet they went to that
death unillusioned, with no fully developed political programme by
way of response to the English, other than a reliance on old notions
of territorial sovereignty under the name of *Éireannaigh*. They tried
to sell their wares to the crowd and at the same time they voiced
patrician contempt for that crowd. They were the earliest poetic dis-
coverers of the modern world, a world of de-creation: and their
stanzas grew fat on denial (*gan seo, gan siúd*), as they listed the
good things gone. They were among the first to learn that price for
which the sensations of modernity may be had: 'the disintegration of
the aura in the experience of shock'.[17] But they paid that price and
looked up into a sky without stars.

One person's end is another's beginning. Reports of the death of
Gaelic Ireland after the Flight of the Earls were much exaggerated.

These reports were first syndicated by ruined poets, who immodestly equated their own dynasts with Ireland itself: a common conceit was that, with the passing of this or that lord, the country itself died. It was an ancient cliché, of course, but after 1607 one or two of the *filí* may have genuinely believed that it now carried some force. Over subsequent centuries it would carry all the conviction of a narrative conclusion. Gaelic Ireland always seemed to be dying – if not at the funeral of a lord, then on the deathbed of a poet, if not in the loss of native speakers to death or emigration, then in the sheer impoverishment of the words in the spoken language. The very tradition seemed to draw sustenance from the prospect of its own death. Like monks who slept in their coffins as *memento mori*, the Irish seemed to grow vital at the prospect of an imminent death. It was as if the corpse of a dead person might achieve in death that which had so often eluded it in life: success and popular acclaim. 'There's something respectable about a clean and tidied corpse,'[18] observed an old woman at a Connemara wake: the dead in Ireland clearly had a secure place in the privileged classes.

The moments of animation in the culture, from the days of Eochaidh Ó hEódhusa to those of James Joyce, have all been created in the face of possible extinction. The Fenians of the 1860s found Ireland like a corpse on the dissecting table and proceeded to administer the kiss that brought it back to life. Their very symbol was the phoenix, that mythical bird which arose from its own ashes. Likewise, the young Joyce feared at the start of the twentieth century that the abandoned woman was about to die: 'If she is truly capable of reviving, let her awake, or let her cover up her head and lie down decently in the grave forever.'[19] There is an amusing note of irritation there at her many revivals, faints and rallies: but nine years after Joyce wrote those lines in 1907, the same fear that the nation might be about to disappear in the trenches of World War One led Patrick Pearse and James Connolly to lead an uprising against British rule. Ireland was forever dying and getting born again. Even in the decades after independence, books continued to appear under titles such as *The Vanishing Irish* or *Is Ireland Dying?* or *Can Ireland Survive?* All of which seemed an illustration of Samuel Beckett's bleak aphorism that it is the search for the means to put an end to things which enables discourse to continue.[20] The deeper the Irish crisis went, the more words it seemed to elicit.

Gaelic Ireland was never afraid of death but, like Woody Allen, it 'just didn't want to be there when it happened'.[21] Of it might be said what that great comedian observed of his own literary productions: 'I don't want to achieve immortality through my work . . . I just want to achieve it through not dying.'[22] Discretion in such a context might be the better part of valour. The soldiers who had followed Hugh O'Neill into battle quickly learned how to sham death in order to survive the enemy onslaught. The lesson wasn't lost on the poets. They learned fast how to play dead for the greater protection of life. Yet later commentators took their protestations of ruin literally: anything that came after was a footnote to the main narrative. There were plenty of Gaelic scholars to lend support to that reading: for academics prefer to study dead things rather than moving objects. They prefer autopsies to engagements.

Literature, of course, does not work like that. In fact, each account of the collapse of one civilization invariably ends up becoming the master narrative of another. So it was in Ireland. Far from dying, Irish-language literature underwent a revival after 1607, invigorated not just by the personal and social crisis of the remaining poets, but also by the new literary conditions which forced them – almost two hundred years before Wordsworth's Preface to the *Lyrical Ballads* – to speak to the masses rather than the classes. The result was a vibrant literature which, at its best, was based on a creative fusion of the diction of the bardic tradition with the robust idiom of the streets. Bereft of their former patrons, many Irish-language intellectuals joined the forces of the Counter-Reformation as Catholic priests. The *filí* had remained rather reticent on religious themes (perhaps sensing that their near-druidic powers were regarded with suspicion by the clergy), but the developments after 1600 forced them to propose 'an essentially Christian analysis of Gaelic misfortune' and to enter 'the mainstream of European political debate'.[23] Some poets-turned-priests translated major works of Continental theology into Irish: and the need to make these texts comprehensible to ordinary people had a tonic effect on their art.

Flaithrí Ó Maolchonaire, for example, made a rather free version of *El Desseoso* from the Spanish. The demands of fidelity to his source acted as a powerful restraint on the native tendency of learned men to archaism; indeed, the effect of his source material may also be traced in the high incidence of loan-words (*devóision*, *rebherens*, *blaisféim*). The title means 'Yearner' and the text is a treatise on how to attain perfection in the religious life. In effect, *Desiderius* became a sort of anticipatory Gaelic version of *The Pilgrim's Progress*, written as an allegory with the Yearner on a road that leads him to encounters with stylized characters such as 'Fear-of-God' or 'Unconcern-for-Anything'. The brilliance of its best chapters – for instance, the second – arises from its exploitation of the verbal clash between the learned and the conversational registers, just as their delicacy lies in the refusal to overwork such contrasts. Ó Maolchonaire says at the outset that he wrote 'chum leasa na ndaoine simplidhe'[24] (for the benefit of simple people). *Desiderius* may be taken as representative of a large body of religious texts printed and published in Irish as a counterblast to the Protestant bibles and prayer books being printed in Irish by the English authorities.

Ó Maolchonaire was described in one contemporary account as 'per Anglos proscriptus' and so were many other men of Gaelic and Catholic learning. Irish students at Louvain were described as traitors, and spies reported of one Jesuit, James Archer, that 'he did swear against His Majesty's jurisdiction in Louvain and he swore to read no English book'.[25] The most famous of all the priestly authors was Seathrún Céitinn who, with the use of a good library, compiled his *Foras Feasa ar Éirinn* (The Basis for Knowledge of Ireland), a collection of great stories from the country's history. Céitinn clearly believed that Gaelic Ireland was in danger of eclipse under the new system. He wrote his book, he says in the Introduction,

> . . . de bhrí gur mheasas nár b'oircheas chomh-onóraí na hÉireann do chrích agus chomh-uaisle gach fóirne dar áitigh í, do dhul i mbáthadh gan lua ná iomrá do bheith orthu.[26]

> . . . because I thought it was not fitting that a country like Ireland for reputation, and people as honourable as those who lived there, should go into oblivion without any word or mention to be made of them.

The rather apologetic tone of that last sentence grew more and more widespread in the writing of the 1600s. Obviously, artists like Céitinn believed that they were now in a position to survey a whole phase of civilization, from rise to fall. Indeed, the very structure of their narrative seemed to mimic that of the *dán díreach*, the bardic poem whose end was its beginning, whose last line often repeated its first. To write with such a sense of an ending was to give a total, finalized shape to a narrative. It may well be, however, that the preponderance of Catholic priests and Catholic intellectuals in the literature of the period added to its millennial edge. The old pagan world of the Celts had been one without beginning or end: an eternal now. In the Bible, on the other hand, 'the world is made out of nothing', and Christians must correspondingly invest all their belief in the prospect of a meaningful end to all stories.[27] The havoc wrought by the English must have looked to many Catholic priests like a rehearsal of apocalypse. Indeed, some of those who brought the havoc may themselves have thought of it in that way: the poet Spenser, for instance, saw 'mutabilitie' as the mark of all created things which must come to a final term.[28] In his mind, the deaths and humiliations endured by rebels and priests may have been a fitting Last Judgement, or at least an intimation of it. To that extent, he and Céitinn may not have wholly differed in their interpretation of the meaning of events. Both men, after all, were courtiers by right who had lost access to their courts and were left to contemplate a more religious set of meanings.

With men like Céitinn, the sense of a modern crisis enters Irish-language writing. Over previous centuries, bardic modes had been stabilized to the point of stasis, as once-live form turned into dead formula. Now, however, culture was under dire stress, and for the next four centuries writers of Irish would know only turbulence and change, forever declaring themselves to be at the end of an era. Like all predictors of apocalypse, many said that the end would come very soon. When the promised cataclysm never quite opened out, they went cheerfully back to work on a revised schedule, predicting a new termination. Their religion had, after all, advised them to be ever watchful for the appointed end. As the seventeenth century progressed, Gaelic poets abandoned all hope of earthly amelioration and put their trust in God, who must (they thought) have devised these punishments as part of some wider, more merciful, long-term plan.

Yet the moment of apocalypse never did come; and the culture did not die. Instead, the terrors of apocalypse were absorbed by narrative.[29] As in *King Lear*, death was terribly delayed, while grim prognosticians said, 'the worst is not / So long as we can say "this is the worst"'.[30] Writers began to discover a certain bleak pleasure in stating that worst superbly well, for the sheer awfulness of experience might be mitigated by the intellectual control their words could exercise over it. Even destitution could be turned into a tragic tale. In due course, some of the priestly authors came to view their apocalyptic statements as a sin of pride, a bid to hurry on eternity rather than live in God's slowly evolving time.[31]

3

Saving Civilization:
Céitinn and Ó Bruadair

Men like Seathrún Céitinn, as they gathered Gaelic lore into comprehensive narratives, might be compared with Erich Auerbach, who three centuries later would collect the master texts of another civilization, this time of Europe itself, which seemed about to expire under the Nazis. Of course, neither civilization did go under – each, in the event, was augmented by a brilliant new contribution. If it is the mark of the modern imagination always to feel itself 'at the end of an era',[1] that may well be a device for spurring the mind on to ever greater achievements. For the crisis is never wholly inherent in a culture so much as in the false leadership offered by an exhausted class. So it was in Ireland at the start of the seventeenth century, the first of a seemingly endless sequence of ages of transition in modern Irish culture. After that, authors attempted to make sense of their relation to their own past. The continuing fortunes and misfortunes of the Irish language were to prove that in tragedy the end as expected never comes: there would be an ending of some kind, but the death that was announced at the beginning would not be the one enacted.

This has not always been understood, and it has been least understood by some of the English-language writers of modern Ireland. Frank O'Connor once described Irish literature in the seventeenth century as dying in its sleep.[2] Patrick Kavanagh wrote a surly little lyric about Mícheál Ó Cléirigh, accusing this leader of the Four Masters of succumbing in his annals of Ireland to a cult of the past:

It would never be morning, always evening,
Golden sunset, golden age –
When Shakespeare, Marlowe and Jonson were writing
The future of England, page by page,
A nettle-wild grave was Ireland's stage.

It would never be spring, always autumn,
After a harvest always lost,
When Drake was winning seas for England
We sailed in puddles of the past,
Chasing the ghost of Brendan's mast . . .

Culture is always something that was,
Something pedants can measure,
Skull of bard, thigh of chief,
Depth of dried-up river.
Shall we be thus forever?
Shall we be thus forever?[3]

Kavanagh had taken the laments of bards too literally, failing to notice the strange energy of the language in which they were made. So did many others. O'Connor, for instance, found that the 'Elizabethans adopt courtly love with all the enthusiasm that young people in the twenties showed over free love': but, he darkly added, 'it may be significant that one of the finest Irish-language poems of the period is about a man so old and physically exhausted that he can no longer have sexual relations with the woman he loves'.[4]

This poem has sometimes been attributed to Céitinn and is written in one of the bardic metres, *leathrannaíocht mhór* (major half-versification):

A bhean lán de stuaim
  coingibh uaim do lámh;
ní fear gníomha sinn,
  cé taoi tinn dár ngrádh.

Féach ar liath dem fholt,
  féach mo chorp gan lúth,
féach ar thraoch dem fhuil –
  créad re bhfuil do thnúth?

Ná saoil mé go saobh,
  arís ná claon do cheann;
bíodh ár ngrádh gan ghníomh
  go bráth, a shíodh sheang.

Druid do bhéal om bhéal –
   doiligh an scéal do chor –
ná bíom cneas re cneas;
   tig ón teas an tol.

Do chúl craobhach cas,
   do rosc glas mar dhrúcht,
do chíoch chruinngheal bhláith,
   tharraingeas mian súl.

Gach gníomh acht gníomh cuirp
   is luighe id chuilt shuain
do-ghéan féin tred ghrádh,
   a bhean lan de stuaim.

A fhinnebhean tséimh shéaghanta shárchaoin tsuairc
na muirearfholt réidh raonfholtach fá a ndíol gcuach,
is iongnadh an ghné thaomannach fhasaíos uait;
gé doiligh an scéal, tréig mé agus táig dhíom suas.

Do-bheirimse fém bhréithir dá mbáití an slua
san tuile do léig Venus 'na táclaí anuas,
a bhurraiceach-bhé mhéarlag na mbánchíoch gcruaidh,
gur tusa mar aon céidbhean do fágfaí im chuan.[5]

O woman full of wantonness, keep your hand from me; I am not a loving man, even if you are sick for love.

Look at how my hair has greyed; look at my stiff body; consider how tired is my blood – what is it that you long for?

Do not think me soft; do not toss your head again; let our love be without action for ever, slender fairy.

Take your mouth from my mouth – distressing is the story of your plight – let us not go skin against skin, for desire grows from heat.

Your branching curly hair, your eye green as dew, your bright, blossoming, pointed breast would attract the heart's desire.

Every act but that of the body or lying in your quilt of sleep I would do for love of you, woman full of desire.

O gentle, accomplished, refined and excellent fair lady of the flowing hair with heavy locks and ringlets, your fitful appearance amazes me. However hard it be, leave me and give me up.

I give my word that if the crowd were drowned in the flood let down by Venus's curls, o full-figured lady of delicate fingers and firm white breast, you are the first woman who would be left in my company.

The looser, accented *amhrán* (song) metre of the closing two stanzas exists in tension with the older, syllabic quatrains of the *dán díreach* (strict poem): and the lyric itself issues from a tension in the mind of the author between pagan energy and Christian denial. All great poetry arises from a clash between freedom and system, between the idiom of conversation and the idiom of the academy: and here the author is enacting a quarrel not with others but within himself. The female figure addressed may well be a type of the Muse, in whose service the poet would have lived but for the social changes that left him a priest, enjoined to other duties. If so, this was a poem that would be much rewritten in later times – by Art Mac Cumhaigh in *Úirchill an Chreagáin*, by W.B. Yeats in 'He Wishes His Beloved Were Dead', and by Beckett in 'I Would Like My Love to Die'.

In the *rannaíocht mhór* (major versification, based on lines of five syllables ending always on a single syllable), the speaker attempts to dismiss the woman, but then in the *amhrán* he seems to relent. Throughout the poem the very lines in which he disclaims her body serve only to heighten his throbbing awareness of her loveliness. Of the eight lines in the *amhrán*, the last alone implies his abstinence, but what is that against seven lines filled with flowing adjectives which fasten obsessively on every detail of a body he thinks he is renouncing? So, even within the *amhrán*, the conflict persists. The entire lyric is an inversion of the *amour courtois* convention of the *dánta grá* (love poetry), whereby a young lover pines for an unattainable lady: and Céitinn's use of that tradition was masterly, for he invoked it the better to reject it. This hardly indicates a loss of vitality of the kind diagnosed by Frank O'Connor, for often the surest way of safeguarding a tradition is to attack it. The writer here has simply looked behind the *amour courtois* convention to a human truth that few others would dare to face: and he has attacked the convention with a reminder of the other kinds of relationship it may have ignored. The reverse of formulaic, his work is at once a magnificent parody of the *dánta grá* and a passionately personal utterance.

The lines of the *rannaíocht* throb with a sinuous energy, and the vowels seek to seduce even as the words voice a ban. The poem is a paradigm of much that was to follow in Irish literature of both languages: the form and style are buoyant, experimental, energetic, even as the content grows ever bleaker and more depressive. Perhaps it was a subliminal sense of its transgressive rhythms that led some rather puritanical scholars of the Irish Revival to deny that these lines could ever have been composed by a priest. Eugene O'Curry flatly denied the possibility and was supported in this by Fr Peter O'Leary who said: 'this rebuke of lawless desire, framed in the subtle *deach-nadh beag*, could not be Keating's'. Patrick Pearse, who would himself write a somewhat similar inversion of a *dán grá* tradition in 'Fornocht do Chonac Thú', was a great admirer of Céitinn and accused the puritans of foolishly assuming that a priest could not be a poet.[6]

   The lines have Céitinn's fluency, and the flickering ironies are certainly within the tradition of *dánta grá*, which were never guilty of taking themselves overseriously. As an inheritor of bardic tradition, someone like Céitinn would be as likely to compose a love poem as a religious lyric or encomium. What marks this exercise off is the pressure of a real passion which can be felt alongside the light ironies in the very rhythm of the lines. The word 'gníomha' in the opening stanza, for example, was often used in the old Irish medieval texts as a technical term for coitus: so here the writer uses it somewhat loftily, dignifying the act of love with no more specific mention. The word 'folt' was often employed sensuously to describe a beautiful woman's thick, curling tresses, but here it is applied to the speaker's grey head, in a stanza that goes on to list the images of an exhausted Oisín, returned from Tír na nÓg after three hundred years, to find the days of wine and roses are over. That the woman should feel the courtly yearning (*tnúth*) for such a wasted body is ironic indeed: a deft collocation of two very different poetic discourses, those of *dánta grá* and *Fiannaíocht* (Fenian balladry). So far, it appears that all the desire is on her side and that the poet feels none: but in the third stanza the phrase 'ár ngrádh' admits that the love is mutual. Thereafter, it becomes less clear whether the poem is really an attempt to spurn her or a devious means of further inflaming her frustrated desire. To forbid the woman to incline her head is virtually to invite a repetition of the act: and the word 'arís' is beautifully ambiguous in this context, since it may mean that he has to repeat a request already made, or that she may yet provoke him again. Likewise, the very physical possibilities of their proximity ('bíodh ár ngrádh gan gníomh') are somewhat deflected by the immediate suggestion that she is incorporeal, a sprite. 'Seang' was a staple term of love poems (sometimes used as a noun in its own right rather than an adjective, to denote the body), so the very grammar of the language seems to enact the poet's tussle with himself, as body and spirit are locked in combat ('a shíodh sheang').

   The speaker doesn't deny his love for the woman – so why does he spurn her? Is 'spurn' the right verb? 'Druid do bhéal óm bhéal' implies that a kiss has already occurred and that the injunction of the first three stanzas has been happily disregarded. In the next line 'cor' can mean either 'trick' (as if the woman had taken advantage in planting the kiss) or 'plight, shift of fortune' (as if he were taking pity on her situation, which has left her the lover of a physically exhausted man). If the second meaning is the more likely, it would add a note of compassion to his forbidding of bodily contact, in the course of which 'heat' will only generate 'will' or 'assent' (*tol*). But consent is gaining the upper hand, for the next stanza is no more than a delighted inventory of her beautiful hair, eye and breast, and as such a violation of the speaker's own interdiction. In the final stanza of the *leathrannaíocht*, he tries to solve the conflict by consenting to all action but that of the body: and then proceeds to closure by the old bardic device of repeating the opening line. By this stage, however, the word 'stuaim' has acquired several new layers of meaning.

The poetry and prose of Céitinn were to prove popular among the common people in the centuries after his death, despite his rather aristocratic mien (he was a descendant of the Old English Anglo-Norman families who became 'more Irish than the Irish themselves'). In part this was because of the manifest patriotism which animated his writings. Trained in Bordeaux, he learned by distance to see Ireland as a whole and to call for unity in the face of the English onslaught. His mastery of the *amhrán* form helped to ensure its growing popularity, especially in a lyric such as 'Óm Sceol ar Árdmhagh fáil':

> *Óm sceol ar ardmhagh Fáil ní chodlaim oíche*
> *is do bhreóidh go bráth mé dála a pobail dílis;*
> *gé rófhada atáid 'na bhfál re broscar bíobha,*
> *fá dheoidh gur fhás a lan den chogal trithi.*[7]

Since I heard news of high-plateaued Ireland I don't sleep at night; and the tales of her dear people sickened me forever. Even though they have held out a long time against a hostile rabble, in the end a lot of cockle grew through amongst them.

The word 'dílis' is beautifully ambiguous here – does it mean faithful or beloved? If the first meaning seems dominant, it must carry a heavy freight of irony, for Céitinn had a low opinion of the Irish forces of resistance, as is clear from the rest of the stanza: it is among the Irish themselves that traitors have emerged. Again and again he laments that Gael and Norman could not be united against the invader, at one point in the poem calling Ireland 'práis' (faithless), a word that bounces by way of clarification off the earlier 'dílis' (faithful).

The poets in the 1610s and 1620s divided down the middle on this question. Most, like Céitinn, called for national unity and castigated the contributors to *Iomarbhá na bhFilí* (The Contention of the Bards), in which various writers asserted the claims of this or that region and its rivers to pre-eminence. For the majority, the participants in the *Iomarbhá na bhFilí* were guilty of an ethical failure to pull together against a common enemy. Hugh O'Neill had achieved a sort of unity, but after his departure there was only further dissension. The results were described in Céitinn's poem:

> *Deor níor fágach i gclár do bhrollaigh mhínghil*
> *nár dheólsad ál gach cránach coigríche.*

A drop wasn't left in your bright gentle breast, that was not slurped down by the farrow of every foreign sow.

The image, though ferocious, has been universally praised for its uncompromising accuracy. It would be taken up by the young James Joyce from J.C. MacErlean's edition of 1900 and further developed on the lips of Stephen Daedalus, who inverts it bitterly: 'Ireland is the old sow that eats her farrow.'[8] Céitinn had no compunction about contrasting the harsh consonants that described the English invader (cránach coigríche) with the sweet vowels of Irish place names (ár náitibh eochar-aoibhne); and his use of compound words would be imitated by Yeats, even as his programmatic opposition of English consonance and Irish assonance would be redeployed by Heaney.

Céitinn's technical virtuosity has long been admired. At the end of the poem he says that if God will not aid the Irish

> *ní mór narbh fhearr gan chairde a bhfoscain-díolaim*
> *'s a seoladh slán i bhfán tar tonnaibh Clíona.*

then it is better of necessity that those without relief should be winnowed and gleaned and sent safe far away across the wave of Clíona.

This reads like yet another prophecy of dissolution and might be accused of overemotionalism: but the verb 'foscain-díolaim' represents a canny development of the opening image of the cockles which have grown through the good crop. Céitinn had the confidence to extend a metaphor over an entire poem. Even if his prophecy is dire, the metre in which it has been written has been justly described as militant by a critic who found 'in its thunderous accents an advantage over the sternly restrained manner of poems on the same theme in syllabic metres. Here we have the means of a popular rhetorical poetry – inevitably this form prevailed'.[9]

Among Céitinn's poetic contemporaries were Pádraigín Haicéad and Piaras Feiritéar: all three came from Old English or Norman families, and in their work was canvassed the possibility of a middle style, above grossness and below preciousness, where propriety might reside. Some of them also wrote well in English: a number of Piaras Feiritéar's love poems were addressed to English ladies, as if he were still hoping to build the 'middle nation' epitomized by one of his forerunner love poets, Gearóid Iarla, the earl of Desmond. The work produced by this trio is of major quality: so much so that it is no exaggeration to speak of their period (1600–50) as the first of many 'revivals' in modern Irish writing. Like other revivals to follow, it had certain qualities of the swan-song: perhaps this was why Anglo-Irish artists at the start of the twentieth century (especially Synge and Yeats) identified so much with it, for in the collapse and regrouping of one aristocratic order they must have found an anticipatory illumination of their own experience.

But the mere Irish of the twentieth century, the O'Connors and the Kavanaghs, when they came to consider this literature, often found themselves underwhelmed. O'Connor could never bring himself to admire the new accented (rather than syllabic) verse of the *amhrán*: 'Every peasant poet was hammering it out with hobnailed boots like an ignorant audience listening to a Mozart minuet. It is no wonder it offended O'Hussey's delicate ear: it often offends mine.'[10] Doubtless, the repetitive structures of the *amhrán* could prove wearisome to the ear, but at its best the form was powerful. Nor is it true to say that the old mandarin codes were entirely smothered by popular discourse. The philosophical content of early seventeenth-century literature remained so high that, three centuries later, when Patrick Pearse attempted to reactivate an intellectual tradition in Irish, it was to the example set in this period that he turned:

> . . . a living literature cannot (and if it could), should not be built up on the folktale . . . Why set up as a standard of today a standard at which Seathrún Céitinn and Aodh Ó Dálaigh would have laughed? . . . Irish literature, if it is to live and grow,

must get into contact on the one hand with its own past and on the other with the mind of contemporary Europe . . .[11]

Part of the attraction of Céitinn and others for the Revival generation was their European sensibility, their easy commerce with French, German and Italian literatures, and their knowledge of Latin. Douglas Hyde did more than anyone to nurture that interest, when in his *Literary History of Ireland* he saluted the brilliant success of a group that broke all bardic rules and 'suddenly burst forth in all the freedom of the elements'. No begrudger, he stretched credibility, praising it as 'the most sensuous attempt to convey music in words ever made by man'.[12] Nor was he alone. Cainneach Ó Maonaigh, writing half a century later, agreed, arguing that no other literary period in Ireland could match it for variety of themes or energy of forms.[13]

The measures taken against Catholics by Oliver Cromwell's armies after 1649 and by the Williamite forces after 1690 left the Irish language in a far less happy state. It ceased to be the language of power and became instead that of the victim and the underdog. Removed not only from the world of politics and law but from government and high commerce, it was bound to suffer a decline in prestige.

The poetic chronicler of that collapse was Dáibhí Ó Bruadair (1625–98). Like Feiritéar, he was by all accounts an accomplished poet in English, but, even though more of his Gaelic poems survive than are attributed to any other poet in the language, that other aspect of his work is lost to us. His English was not fluent (he called it 'Béarla pléascach', explosive English). His Irish was by contrast both rich and strange, so much so that some remains incomprehensible (perhaps a sign of that baroque splendour so common in the art of the seventeenth century). He himself was not above boasting about his aristocratic indecipherability, but he also accused the exponents of popular metres of lacking any great substance. He penned a parody of the *amhrán* that would have raised Frank O'Connor's heart: each individual line makes sense but the aggregated lines of the poem as a whole say precisely nothing. Perhaps Ó Bruadair sensed within the tradition the tendency to lapse into mere formula. Some commentators believe that he had a hand in later versions of *Pairlement Chloinne Tomáis*. That would certainly accord with poems which denounce with impartial fury both the new planters and the spineless Irish who have submitted to them.

Ó Bruadair's attitude remained candidly aristocratic, even though he ended his days as a labourer in the fields. His writings can read like covert responses to the English authors of his age: for instance, he appears to have read John Milton's works and to have mocked the names of puritan planters, much as Milton had jeered at the names of Gaelic nobility in his writing. Ó Bruadair composed a number of long poems that ranged obsessively over the political history of Ireland in the seventeenth century, as if seeking that moment of weakness which might account for all the suffering: but he never really found a convincing explanation. In his final days, he lived in fear that his hearth-rug might be seized by bailiffs. By then he saw himself as a broken old man, like Oisín living on in old age after the heroes of the Fianna:

> Cé síleas dá saoirse bheith seascair sódhúil
> Im stíobhaird ag saoi acu nó im ghearra-phrobhost,
> Ós críoch di mo strócadh go sean-bhrógaibh,
> Finis dom scríbhinn ar fhearaibh Fódla.[14]

Although I'd hoped to be settled, happy and free, as a steward to a learned man or as a vice-provost, since my end sees my reduction to old shoes, a finish to my writing about the people of Ireland.

Ó Bruadair loaded every line with rich content, proving that the *amhrán* form need not necessarily preclude complex syntax or phrasing. If some lines grew cryptic, that was probably for want of the discipline imposed by a ready audience. On occasions, he seemed to confuse criticism with denunciation, judgement with disparagement, for he lived at odds with his age, becoming for that very reason its truest chronicler.

The poem by which he is best remembered, 'Mairg nach fuil 'na dhubhthuata', is itself riven into two forms, that of *ae freislighe* (a mode of awesome complexity, with seven syllables per line and each final word being of three syllables) and the four-line looser *amhrán* at the close:

> Mairg nach fuil 'na dhubhthuata,
>   gé holc duine 'na thuata,
> i ndóigh go mbeinn magcuarda
>   idir na daoinibh duarca.

> Mairg nach fuil 'na thrudaire
>   eadraibhse, a dhaoine maithe,
> ós iad is fearr chugaibhse,
>   a dhream gan iúl gan aithne.

Dá bhfaghainn fear mo mhalarta,
    ris do reacfainn an suairceas;
do-bhéarainn luach fallainge
    idir é 'gus an duairceas.

Ós mó cion fear deaghchulaith
    ná a chion de chionn beith tréitheach,
truagh ar chaitheas le healadhain
    gan e a-niog ina éadach.

Ós suairc labhartha is bearta gach buairghiúiste
gan uaim gan aiste 'na theangain ná suanúchas,
mo thrua ar chréanas le ceannaraic cruaphrionta
ó bhuaic mo bheatha nár chaitheas le tuatúlacht.[15]

Woe to those who are not boors,
    however bad it is to be a boor,
better for me to be in the company
    of the sullen men.

Woe to whoever isn't deaf
    among you, noble people,
for such are welcomed better by you,
    a people without knowledge or breeding.

If I could find a bargainer
    to whom to sell my pleasing wit;
for the price of a cloak
    I would come between him and sadness.

Since there is more respect for a fop
    than all the respect given to an accomplished artist,
it's a pity that all that I spent on learning
    I should not have now in the form of clothing.

Since the saying and deeds of every boor are pleasing – one without skill, personality or creativity of language – pity all energy wasted on the challenge of learning, and pity that from youth I didn't study boorishness.

The mode is that of so many Gaelic works: *caoineadh ar chéim sios na nuasal* (a lament for fallen nobility): but what makes this a great lyric is the fact that it doesn't just assert its judgements but it enacts them in the very movement of the verse. The disparity between the austere elegance of the *ae freislighe* and the looser refrain illustrates the poet's thesis: the coincidence of both forms in a single poem was by then conventional. The author, however, pierces remorselessly through the convention to the uncomfortable truth it reveals – that something good has gone. A *file* by inheritance, Ó Bruadair was no longer able to use the bardic metres with literal commitment and so he filled the form with bitter, corrosive ironies. The use of the *amhrán* at the close is equally parodic. Like Jonathan Swift, his near contemporary, he could not really bring the old and new learning into a fruitful fusion and so he contented himself with exacerbating the manifest conflicts between them.

In the manner of preceding *filí*, the poet laments that he isn't a churl, 'however bad it is to be a boor' – that second line ironizes the first in a way that will also be characteristic of Aogán Ó Rathaille. The tone struck is of haughty, glacial disdain. In the second stanza, however, this composure is lost, as the speaker deliberately insults his listeners. This is intriguing, for it may be assumed that the boors themselves would not fully understand a syllabic poem. Is Ó Bruadair, from the depths of despair, making his complaint to a people who cannot even guess that they are being insulted? Is he, in short, talking to himself, relieving a purely personal pain in his outburst? If so, perhaps the *amhrán* at the close will offer some hint to the uncultured of what he has just been saying.

Words are the weapons of the disarmed. *Ae freislighe* was one of those metres in which a poet spoke to noble patrons. Despite the fact that those nobles and their descendants have made many compromises in the intervening period, they can still be spoken to, if only by way of condemnation. After the arrival of the Earl of Ormond as Lord Lieutenant in the 1660s, many of the Gaelic nobility had taken to English ways. Ó Bruadair was targeting these, much as the author of the *Pairlement Chloinne Tomáis* attacked weak-minded nobles: and there must have been still some among their number who understood the syllabic poetry. This might explain the phrase 'a dhaoine maithe' (good people), an ironic usage of the old courteous address and a deliberate dissonance with 'tuata'. Now it may function as a put-down of the former serfs.

Ó Bruadair goes on to employ an extended metaphor of clothing, just the sort that would be used by Swift a few decades later. The dead lords would have paid the cost of a cloak for a cheerful poem, but now there is more respect for English clothing than for Gaelic art. The new overlords are foppish philistines, without literary sensibility. Swift and Goldsmith would pen equally furious denunciations of foreign frippery and imported fashions in their critique of luxury, though the emphasis in their case would be on French as Ó Bruadair's was on English modes.

There is about Ó Bruadair's performance an element of the broken dandy, not only in his baroque discourse but also in his ever-frustrated desire for finer apparel. He was a sort of Gaelic anticipation of Baudelaire, a downstart who found himself among ordinary people for whom he could never summon much respect. Of this declension Baudelaire would later write:

> ... lost in the villainous world, among fools, I am like a worn-out man whose eye, looking back far into the years, sees nothing but disillusion and bitterness, and before him nothing but a storm which heralds nothing new, neither wisdom nor sadness.[16]

Ó Bruadair called this state 'longbhriseadh' or shipwreck.

He was a man whose private life had been swamped by terrible public events. For all his assumed snobbery, he felt along the lines of his own sensibility the suffering of a people. The fall of a once-great family was for him no disinterested exercise in modernization on the part of English rulers: rather it was a consequence of the persecution, both religious and political, of an entire race. To read some latter-day commentators on the social transformation of seventeenth-century Ireland, one might be forgiven for seeing that transformation as a high-minded rationalization of the administrative structures; but that was hardly the case. True, an old Gaelic aristocracy was destroyed. What replaced it, however, was not a genuinely radical alternative but a pseudo-aristocracy, far less cultured than what it displaced. Many of its members were not just philistine but militantly so. Ó Bruadair's own indictment of them would be repeated a century later by Oliver Goldsmith, who accused them of spending more in a single year on horses than in two centuries on learning and books.[17] Most of the new planters were puritans by religious conviction and turned out to be opposed not just to *filí* but to all forms of art. Their scruples about mimesis would find their way, in time, into the artistic productions of their more independent-minded descendants. The displaced poets like Ó Bruadair could not help noticing how little culture was brought by the new order to the recently enfranchised serfs. Not for these 'liberated' ones the rich hybridity of a Piaras Feiritéar – instead a zone of emptiness opened between two contesting cultures, a chasm into which they like Clan Thomas fell.

Revivalist readings of this literature at the start of the twentieth century could never be wholly innocent. Some Celtic scholars like Fr Patrick Dinneen overstated the esteem of ordinary people for the old Gaelic grandees: and many Anglo-Irish scholars have subsequently overstressed the modernizing benefits of the new dispensation. Nationally minded scholars overpraised the *filí* as early patriots, defenders of an all-Ireland concept:[18] however, the poets were not only culpably haughty and archaic on occasion, but sometimes astonishingly slow to register the wider political implications of the cultural conflict. Whether the English had imposed themselves or not, the days of the *filí* might have been numbered. The very fact that noblemen had begun to write poems, and soon after them clergymen, signalled the end of a purely professional caste.[19] Under pressure of this change, some poets after 1600 began to speak for more than themselves, their art or their lord. Most continued to lament not so much a lost community as a seigneurial life of cattle raids, warrior feuds, high culture and immense wealth. The propagandists of England presented their world as a viable modern alternative, but it was never fully convincing. It was simply a bourgeois formation masquerading as an aristocracy and (as Gaelic poets often sourly noted) not very assured in that role. The next great Gaelic *file* would call these new men 'upstarts': but by the time Aogán Ó Rathaille put pen to paper they were in near-total control.

4

Dying Acts:
Ó Rathaille and Others

Every sentence is a death sentence, in the sense that every statement is no sooner begun than it is already starting to die on an
exhalation of breath. No writer has understood this better than
Samuel Beckett for whom the much-reported death of Irish was no
more than a foretaste of the fate awaiting all language. The conversation between Mr and Mrs Rooney in *All That Fall* might almost be
a literal translation of an exchange between the Gaelic bards as they
moved to dissolution:

> MR ROONEY: Never pause . . . safe to heaven . . . Do you know,
> Maddy, sometimes one would think you were struggling with a
> dead language.
> MRS ROONEY: Yes indeed, Dan, I know full well what you mean. I
> often have that feeling, it is unspeakably excruciating.
> MR ROONEY: I confess I have it sometimes myself, when I happen to
> overhear what I am saying.
> MRS ROONEY: Well, you know, it will be dead in time, just like our
> own poor dear Gaelic, there is that to be said.[1]

A post-mortem on any language conducted in that language is, of
course, a deeply paradoxical enterprise, portending a possible
rebirth. As Jacques Derrida wryly observed 'one should never pass
over the question of the tongue in which the question of the tongue is
raised'.[2] Beckett in his youth was hugely suspicious of the antiquarian

devotees of Gaelic Ireland's death cult. In his literary criticism he mocked their attempts to reactivate old metrical forms, yet he seems also to have been deeply sceptical of the success with which the 'revivalists' had proclaimed the death of the culture, the better to present themselves as its rescuers. Not only that, but the ease with which Anglo-Ireland had allowed itself to be convinced of the alleged *rigor mortis* evoked his amused contempt. In his first full collection of stories, some graduates of Trinity College Dublin return from the funeral of a young friend:

> 'Now in Gaelic', said Hairy on the way home, 'they could not say that.'
> 'What could they not say?' said the parson. He would not rest until he knew.
> 'O Death where is thy sting?' replied Hairy. 'They have no words for these big ideas.'[3]

In his later, more anorexic writings, Beckett would develop a voice very close to that of the Gaelic bards: his protagonist would lie on his back in the dark, summoning voices, working on a set exercise. Invariably, he would offer to do something rather strange: both to die and in the very act of dying narrate an account of his own passing. *Malone Dies* is the classic text.

There were precedents for this also in the practice of the *filí*. Even in their heyday they had written of the death of a gifted poet as somehow marking the very demise of poetry itself. As early as 1391, Tadhg Dall Ó hUiginn had written of the death of his older brother and teacher Fearghal Ruadh:

> *Gan mharthain do mhac Áine,*
> *rug don éigse a hamháille:*
> *mar théid clár a taoibh thunna,*
> *do sgaoil fál na foghluma.*[4]

The death of Ann's son took from artists their joy; just as a plank breaks from the side of a cask, the protecting wall of poetry has toppled.

That, despite the pressure of a personal loss behind the lovely lines, was a conceit: but three centuries later it had become, like so many other metaphors of cultural despair, more literal. As Eochaidh Ó hEódhusa lay dying of his last illness, a fellow poet opened his lament:

Fogus orchra don éigsi:
gá ttás cur ré coiméidsi?
do bhean sí céill do chabhair;
ní réidh í ó orchradhaibh.[5]

Decay is near to poetry. How can she be saved? She has given up hope. She isn't safe from eclipse.

Just a few years later, another *file* lamented the closing of the last bardic schools in lines of spare urgency, bespeaking a rain of real tears:

Aonar dhamhsa eadar dhaoinibh,
atú anocht go neamhfhaoiligh:
am aonarán a ccionn cháigh,
's ionn gan aobharán d'fhagháil.

Ní thuig mé an lucht so ag labhra
gá dtá ar tteanga mháthardha:
ar naos aithnigh ní léir linn,
mh 'aithghin féin ó nach faicim.

Dursan an taobh dhá dtáinig
a mhoille thrá thionáilid;
fatha sgaoilidh na scoile
Gaodhil Macha ag moghsoine.[6]

Lonely am I among people, tonight I am without joy. I'm lonely above all others, without food for thought. I don't understand those who speak our mother language: I don't recognize our people, since I see none like me. Woe to the place where they were slow to meet together. The cause of the school's break-up is that the Gaels are in bondage.

These accents would in time inform the *caoineadh* or lament, which was soon adopted as *the* representative poetic form of a Gaelic Ireland in terminal collapse. One result of the isolation of the scattered poets who remained was that many were compelled, for want of mourners, to lament themselves. Thus was born the cult of last words, the poem voiced by a poet as he lay dying, *an file ar leaba a bháis*. Some of these were prayers of repentance after a riotous, self-indulgent life. Others were last-minute requests that the speaker be taken for burial back to his ancestral homeland. A few really powerful exercises conflated both traditions. The Ulster writer Séamas

Dall Mac Cuarta produced a famous specimen: it began

> *Is fada mé a mo luí i Lúbhadh*
> *i mo scraiste brúite, mo mhíle crá;*
> *Dúisígí is cruinnígí na seabhaic lúfar'*
> *is iompraígí an túrmhac go cuail na gcnámh.*

I am long lying in County Louth, a broken man with a thousand troubles. Rise up and gather the young warriors and carry this son to the place of bones.

And it ended:

> *Cha ndearna mé aithreachas riamh mar ba chóir dom,*
> *ach ag déanamh ceolta ar feadh mo shaoil,*
> *ach anois ó tá mé tréithlag breoite,*
> *a Dhia, déan trócaire ar Shéamas chaoch.*[7]

I never repented as I should have, but spent my life making songs: but now that I am weak with sickness, o God have mercy on blind James.

Generations of Irish schoolchildren, set to the formal study of these poems, have pestered teachers with the predictable question: if the poet really were about to breathe his last, how did he manage to gather his energy for so forceful an utterance? For the convention to work properly, the reader must be convinced that the very culture is expiring with its latest performer, but the deathbed scenario was endlessly repeatable. Far from indicating the weakness of a culture, it drew sustenance from its continuing strength.[8]

The 'last words' convention was a vestige of the old bardic arrogance. It was as if each poet who composed one saw himself as history's cutting edge, the only true custodian of the tradition. The conceit (in the literal sense, this time) was awesome, for the claim was that the poets alone could survey a whole civilization in every aspect from beginning to end. Moreover, they affected to write the account of their own death even as they underwent it, so that teller and tale would finally be one. They would somehow do what no writers in human history had been able to do, for the pen had always dropped from enfeebled hands even as they made the attempt. And this superhuman feat would mark the death of a culture, so to speak, while really being its transfiguration, its assumption onto a new, even higher plane. The artist, out of his solitude and desperation, would give to his own life a sense of final shape that previous writers like Ó Gnímh could only confer upon the lives of others. The attempt has persisted ever since in Irish culture, in the diaries of hunger strikers and the poems of condemned rebels on the eve of execution: those critics who have interpreted *Malone Dies* as a radically new narrative without precedent may have ignored these earlier examples.

The regret for cultural decline voiced in Gaelic poems created in many readers a sense of the staunch conservatism of their authors, but the predicament out of which the works were written was wholly modern. The marginalization of all poetry would become a pervasive modern theme – of Baudelaire, Eliot and Pound no less than of Ó Bruadair, Yeats and Mahon. By the end of the seventeenth century the hereditary *filí* had been broken down and compelled to work as schoolteachers, farm labourers and journeymen. Political turbulence had simply speeded up these developments. One consequence was that the writers who emerged from this mauling found themselves cast in the role of *radical* traditionalists. Even as the poets lost standing as full-time professionals, the range of functions open to them widened. Addressing a popular audience, they could proclaim themselves at once rebels against England and conservators of Gaeldom. Hence the dissonance felt in most subsequent Irish writing between form and content, the sense that each severely strains the resources of the other. At times that is the strain felt when ideas of tradition are defended in experimental new forms: or it can involve a somewhat ironic use of an ancient mode to contain new ideas, new themes.

Every other poet now saw himself as a representative example of the tragedy of an enforced modernity: and each of these read the collapse of a whole civilization into a set of personal discomforts and humiliations. This might seem a monumental vanity until one recalls that it is a major technique of major modern poets, from the Pope of *The Dunciad* to the Eliot of *The Waste Land*, from the Wordsworth of *The Prelude* to the Pound of *Hugh Selwyn Mauberley*. Behind it lies another modern idea: that man is not just the measure of all things, but also the measurer. What was enacted in Gaelic poetry was another 'dying act', a recognition that death is not so much a termination as another career move. Like the details of an examined life, it had to be staged. It was after all a part assigned to every person and the poets prided themselves on playing the part well. They would teach their followers how to turn even death into a play, of which each person was author, actor and sole producer. And so, like the Mabel Beardsley celebrated in a Yeats poem, they would die game.

*

The 'last' great poet of eighteenth-century Ireland was Aogán Ó Rathaille. If Turlough Carolan was mourned as the last of the harpers at his funeral in 1738, Ó Rathaille had already been dubbed the last of the bards at his death ten years earlier. He may even have believed this publicity himself, for he wrote as if his own life and career were a final test case for Gaelic Ireland. His deathbed poem is the most famous of all for its racial pride, bitter wit, and panoptic view of an entire tradition from pagan days to recent deteriorations. The metre quivers with righteous indignation, and yet the speaker is sophisticated enough to mock his own seriousness as hopelessly redundant:

> Cabhair ní ghairfead go gcuirtear mé i gcruinn – chomhrainn:
> dar an leabhar dá ngoirinn níor ghairide an ní domsa –
> ár gcodhnach uile, glac-chumasach Shíol Eoghain,
> is tollta a chuisle, is d'imigh a bhrí ar feochadh.[9]

I shall not call for help until I am put in the coffin: by the book, if I did, it would bring help no nearer. For the ruler of us all, our strong-handed son of Eoghan, has found his pulse weakened and his strength gone.

The usual scenario involved a call by the poet for younger disciples about his bedside as a prelude to an act of Christian repentance, as in Mac Cuarta's lyric. Ó Rathaille's art of impoverishment refuses such obvious gestures: he simply announces that there is no point in this observance, because the breath of life is gone. The words in which this is said throb with the very life they deny: the refusal is really a covert affirmation, the denial a way of asserting the haughty pride of past poets who would seek favours from nobody. The hauteur of line one is undercut by the bitter pragmatism of line two, and what might have seemed a pose of self-sufficiency is revealed to be an enforced predicament. The initial word 'cabhair' may be taken to mean not charitable help but the ancient patronage due to a *file*.

Ó Rathaille's rightful patrons, the MacCarthys, have been stripped of their lands: and so he unleashes the roar of a wounded animal, with the word 'glam' marking the nearness of death. The landlord now dominant in the lands of the MacCarthys would not even offer 'fabhar' (the favour of alms), not to mention 'cabhair' (help) to his closest relation; the use of 'fabhar' is accentuated at the start of the final line of stanza five in order to compound the poet's insult to the new order.

In the third stanza, Ó Rathaille lists the rivers of Ireland as they weep for lost leaders and in the fourth he evokes a waterfall. In the fifth he mingles falling teardrops with the weeping river Blackwater, in a daring equation of his own ruined body with the wasted landscape. The contrast from stanza to stanza is between land and water, the former plundered as only the rivers run free to lament the new conditions. If the opening stanza had voiced a reluctance to perform traditional duties, those that followed have in fact honestly discharged them. That entitles the poet to conclude with a stanza which voices a more purely personal statement:

> *Stadfadsa feasta, is gar dom éag gan mhoill*
> *ó treascradh dreagain Leamhain, Léin is Laoi.*
> *Rachad a haithle searc na laoch don chill –*
> *na flatha faoi raibh mo shean roimh éag do Chríost.*

I will stop henceforth, for death comes close to me without delay, since the lords of the rivers Leamhan, Léin and Laoi have been overcome. I shall go after the beloved warriors into the graveyard, those princes whom my ancestors served before the death of Christ.

Here also an earlier image is revised: if tracts of land were seized by planters, at least this poet will have the 'cabhair' of his own plot of earth. There is a sublime indifference to all ideas of repentance in this closure. The poet mentions Christ, but solely as the marker of the limits of a pre-Christian dispensation, according to which a warrior asked only to be buried with his lord.

Commentators have linked this stoical, even pagan, obsession with burial in the proper cemetery to the ending of J.M. Synge's *Riders to the Sea*, where also there is no talk of Christian consolation in an afterlife.[10] There is an element of *Blutsbrüderschaft* about the ending: if the poem begins with a denial of secular assistance, it ends with another sort of negation, a denial of any facile spiritual comfort. Synge on Aran had felt that the people were fundamentally pagan with a thin overlay of Christian doctrine[11] – and so it was for Ó Rathaille. Anglo-Irish writers at the start of the twentieth century found in his closing lines intimations of their own fate. W.B. Yeats quoted them in 'The Curse of Cromwell', a poem which equated the philistine planters who refused patronage to Gaelic poets and the new-rich Catholic rulers of the Irish Free State:

> *You ask what I have found, and far and wide I go:*
> *Nothing but Cromwell's house and Cromwell's murderous crew,*

The lovers and the dancers are beaten into the clay,
And the tall men and the swordsmen and the horsemen, where
*   are they?*
And there is an old beggar, wandering in his pride –
His fathers served their fathers before Christ was crucified.
                           O what of that, O what of that,
                                   What is there left to say?[12]

The psychologist Carl Gustav Jung once remarked that it was the sign of fully mature persons that they could imagine their own deaths. Yeats himself said that a fully lived life was completed rather than negated by death: 'we begin to live', he said, 'when we have conceived life as a tragedy'.[13] The Gaelic poets saw themselves as recorders of tragedy, and in this they were rather like the obituarists who, working for today's newspapers, must imagine a death and its effects well before the actual event comes to pass. Harder still would it be for them to imagine the full implications of the death of a cultural order, yet there is evidence that such an imagination existed not just in the Gaelic Ireland of the eighteenth century but in Anglo-Ireland too.

'Cabhair ní Ghairfead' is routinely described as emitting the same *saeva indignatio* as the work of Jonathan Swift; but in truth the more interesting analogy is with the poem in which the Dean of St Patrick's Cathedral anticipates the effect of his own demise, 'Verses on the Death of Dr Swift'. There also the writer contemplates the defeat of his body as a metaphor for a decayed civilization: and there too the wit which permits a negation of that negation results in a sort of intellectual triumph too harrowing to be ultimately acceptable. Swift 'turned to poetry towards the end of his career in order to present a "public image" for posterity':[14] for once he began to contemplate his testament, all he could feel was a terrifying sense of the speed with which life could be emptied of all significance:

The Dean is dead (and what is Trumps?)

The bitter truth is that each writer is 'no more . . . missed / Than if he never did exist', and the author who has broken all other reputations consents finally to break his own.

Like his Gaelic counterparts, Swift was capable of lashing out against the inadequacies and weaknesses of the very Irish whose cause he espoused:

He gave the little Wealth he had
To build a House for Fools and Mad:

And shew'd by one satyric Touch
No nation wanted it so much . . .[15]

Although these lines may be more sportive than Ó Rathaille's, their ultimate import is even more annihilating: for the Gaelic artist, at least, the death of the poet will be kept from the poems. The literature in which both men passionately believed was being displaced; and so they wrote their death-poems in the certain knowledge that they would be 'the first to which the future would turn' for an account of their authors.[16] Like Ó Rathaille, of whom we have no certain picture or likeness, Swift realized that after his death he would be no more than the name to which a tissue of quotations was appended.

But who was Ó Rathaille? Details are sketchy. He was born near Killarney, twenty years before the defeat of Jacobite forces by King William at the Boyne in 1690. This defeat shattered the hopes of his patron, Sir Nicholas Brown. When Brown lost his remaining lands in 1700, Ó Rathaille and his young family were left without financial support: a poem written by him in 1705 marvels that he is now so reduced that he must eat periwinkles from the sea cliffs. By way of compensation, he developed a rhetoric of satire and irony. He watched the local planters felling the woods and selling them off at sixpence a tree. Some of those planters were given land on estates run by men with Gaelic names such as Ó Gríofa and Ó Cróinín: sometimes it was Protestant families with names like Warner or Herbert who supported Gaelic culture in the area, a proof that even at that stage Catholic did not necessarily equal Gaelic.[17]

In early poems Ó Rathaille saluted Sir Nicholas Brown as 'árdrí' (high king), but he soon learned that this man could never return to Ireland, and so he placed his hopes in the son, Valentine. His return would be as important as that of the defeated James, promised in dozens of *aisling* (vision) poems by virtually every practising poet. In the event, when the young man did come Ó Rathaille was bitterly disappointed, for Sir Valentine had no training in Irish (being rather a student of French literature) and no understanding of the ancient duties towards a *file*. When Ó Rathaille paid a formal call on his mansion to seek the return of his lands, he was kept waiting in the vestibule for a great length of time and then received only a resounding refusal. To Sir Valentine, here was no aristocrat seeking restitution but a beggar seeking alms. However, Ó Rathaille, like Swift, was able to ventriloquize the philistine thinking of his enemy and so he took revenge in the bitterest of animal images. He described the returned lord as a foreign raven who had evicted the local birds and gone against the very order of nature:

> D'aistrigh fia an fialchruth do chleachtadh sí ar dtúis
> ó neadaigh an fiach iasachta i ndaingeanchoill Rúis,
> seachnaid iaisc griantsruth is caise caoin ciúin
> fá deara dhom triall riamh ort, a Vailintín Brún.[18]

The deer has changed the very form to which it is accustomed, since the foreign raven has nested in the deep woods of Ross. Fish avoid the sunlit streams and the silent, gentle brooks, which is why I am looking for you, Valentine Brown.

The lyric works by virtue of its mingled tones of outrage and sarcasm, of hot anger and cold irony, and by virtue of its old bardic mode of address to a chieftain now manifestly incapable of understanding a single word of it. There are accordingly two registers in the vocabulary: one vicious and deliberately insulting (diabhal iasachta) and the other stately and restrained (fearann Choinn): and they enact the conflict in the writer's mind between his noble self-image and his low social standing. If all art is trapped energy held down at will, then this captures that throb of outrage with which Ó Rathaille delivers his damning verdict on yet another lord who has spurned high art.

After such an experience in the year 1721, the poet would have been in an excellent position to provide Dr Samuel Johnson with an advance warning of the collapse of the system of literary patronage in the new money economy. Had they ever met, he might have been enabled to save the lexicographer his frustrating visit to Lord Chesterfield. He would certainly have endorsed the doctor's haughty ironies:

Seven years, my Lord, have now passed since I waited in your outward rooms, or was repulsed from your door; during which time I have been pushing on my work through difficulties of which it is useless to complain, and have brought it at last to the verge of completion without one act of assistance, one word of encouragement, or one smile of favour. Such treatment I had not expected, for I never had a patron before.[19]

Thomas Carlyle saw this passage as the decisive blow against a corrupt system of supercilious patronage, and so it was. Ó Rathaille could not afford to take so sanguine a view. Henceforth the English author had access to printing presses and could afford to strike bargains with publishers and booksellers, but for the Gaelic writer a lukewarm patron would have been preferable to none at all. Ó Rathaille's situation would, however, be repeated two centuries later in the genteel tramps of W.B. Yeats, J.M. Synge and Samuel Beckett, whose derelicts wear the dregs of old learning.

For Ó Rathaille had known real affluence in his youth, as well as patronage from the Browns and MacCarthys. Only after they were extirpated did he learn that there would be no further support for Gaelic poetry. A Jacobite himself, Ó Rathaille was forced to flee to Corca Dhuibhne, where he was given a small plot of land. There he wrote poems that rejected the pathetic fallacy: rather than see nature as a source of comfort, he read in the sea storms a version of the tempest in his mind. He declared war on the very waves that other poets hoped might bear ships of succour from Catholic Europe:

> *Cabhair dá dtíodh arís ar Éirinn bhán*
> *Do ghlam nach binn do dhingfinn féin id bhráid.*[20]

If help ever came again to fair Ireland, your tuneless roar I would shove back down your throat.

He learned early how to balance the voice of tradition against the needs of an individual talent. Unchastened by the old syllabic rules, he was free to realize the soundscape of the Irish language.

The poets of Munster met together, when circumstances permitted, at a local court of poetry, which served as a Gaelic equivalent to the gentlemen's club in London. Whilst most of the Augustans met in coffee houses, the Irishmen gathered in a local tavern: but the functions of both institutions were remarkably similar. The poets came to the court in order to read their poems aloud to one another for criticism and correction, to exchange manuscripts and to defend their literary inheritance. Although they were no longer fully professional authors, they tried to maintain the standards of men who saw themselves as vocational bards, lacking only the patronage of vanished princes. They enjoyed one another's peculiarities, as well as the pleasure of coming to terms with the intricacies of a colleague's mind.

Just as the denizens of the Dublin or London coffee houses chose to admire or abuse each other in the form of a verse epistle, so the Gaelic authors adapted that form known as *barántas* or warrant. The Court of Poetry was ruled over by a Judge or High Sheriff who was responsible for issuing such warrants. The whole convention was a parody of the processes of the despised English law, since the

High Sheriff gave each poem the semblance of a legal document, by signing his name on the manuscript along with the date and county of issue. It was also, however, a variant of the 'familiar epistle' of Augustan England. The High Sheriff ruled over his court with all the magisterial efficiency of Mr Spectator in London, and his style had a similar formality, acceptable to men who looked up to a self-declared leader in all discussions. Richard Steele derived the idea of Mr Spectator's club from the numerous classical dialogues then fashionable, in which each interlocutor was intended to represent a point of view.[21] The same idea underlies the *barántas*, which was often but the first salvo of a developing controversy, eliciting replies from other poets.

Since the Middle Ages, it had been a custom of European nobles to send mocking, enigmatic letters to one another.[22] The verse epistle and warrant were versions of this. The eighteenth century was the golden age of letter-writing, doubtless due to the improved mail and transport facilities. On those occasions when the Corkmen could not met at their court in Macroom, they sent warrants and epistles to one another by the mails. They loved to make play with the mechanics of the form, just as Swift in the *Journal to Stella* delighted in references to her distance from Dublin, the need to fill a certain amount of paper, and so on. The portentous alliterative prose introductions to the trivia that often filled the warrants have a similarly self-referential quality. Even when the poets were free to meet together at the court, they sometimes preferred to send a message in writing, the better to enjoy the niceties of the genre. Ó Rathaille might have enjoyed Horace Walpole's remark that he often refrained from visiting a neighbour, so that a good letter should not be spoiled by tiresome first-hand exchanges.[23]

There is a strong element of stage management in the warrants, no less than in the Augustan epistles, a tongue-in-cheek solemnity visited upon such relatively insignificant details as the loss of a pair of spectacles, the failure to return a borrowed book, or – as in this effort by Ó Rathaille – an alleged theft of a cockerel. The poem tells how a pious Christian priest named Aonghas (the pagan name raising a question as to whether all priests can be pious and Christian), having purchased a prize cock at Dingle fair, entrusted it to one Séamas Ó Síobharáin (a name that sounds as if it comes straight out of *Pairlement Chloinne Tomáis*) for transport to his rectory. It never arrived and the priest made a jocular complaint to the sheriff, John Blennerhasset, who is imagined by Ó Rathaille responding with the following decree:

Whereas *Aonghas fáithchliste –*
    sagart cráifeach críostaitheach –
do theacht inniu i'm láthairse
    le gearán cáis is fírinne:

Gur cheannaigh coileach ard-shleachta
    dá chearcaibh sráide is tí-bhaile,
ba bhreátha scread is bláfaire,
    is baic le scáil gach líondatha;

Thug sé caogad mínscilling
    ar an éan do b'aoibhinn cúlbhrice,
gur sciob síobhra draíochta é
    ó aonach chinn na dúiche seo.

Ba ghá dá shamhail, d'áirithe,
    coileach screadaithe is dúisithe
do bheith dá fhaire ar shámhchodladh
    in am gach easpairt urnaithe.

M'órdú dibh, an tábhar sin,
    a bháillí stáit mo chúirte-se,
déinig cuardú ardshlite,
    is sin le díograis dúthrachta;

Ná fagaig lios ná sí-chnocán,
    ina gcluinfidh sibh glór ná gliogarnáil,
gan dul i ndiaidh an tsíchonáin,
    do rinne an gníomh le plundaráil.

Wheresoever *cuainseachán*
    ina bhfaighidh sibh an tórpachan,
tugaig chugamsa é ar ruainseachán,
    go gcrochad é mar dhreoileacán.

For your so doing, *d'oibligeáid,*
    ag seo uaim dibh bhur n-údarás,
mar scríobhas mo lámh le cleiteachán
    an la seo d'aois an Uachtaráin . . .[24]

Whereas philosophic Aonghas, a pious Christian priest, came before me today with a truthful case to plead: that he had bought a high-pedigreed cock better than town or manor hens, possessed of a fine screech and beauty and a neck bright with many colours. He gave fifty shillings for the bird with a pleasant comb, until a fairy sprite snatched it from the chief market of this townland. He needed, in particular, a crowing cock to waken him from his comfortable sleep at the time of vespers and devotions. My order to you, on account of that, state bailiffs of my court, search all the highways with zeal and rigour. Do not leave a *lios* or fairy rath in which you might hear a crow or cackling out of your search, but go after the urchin who did this deed of plunder. Wheresoever hiding place in which you find this crab, bring him to me on a thin rope, so that I can hang him like an oaf. For so doing, as is due, here is my authority, written in my hand with a quill, in this day of our president's reign . . .

The poem is written in *casbhairdne*, a complex metre once reserved for such noble subjects as the death of a chief. The mock-heroic strategy is obvious as the poet plays off a stately form against a trivial topic: the technique of deliberate deflation is that employed by Alexander Pope in *The Rape of the Lock*:

> *Here thou, great Anna! whom three realms obey,*
> *Dost sometimes counsel take – and sometimes tea.*[25]

A mischievous irony flickers through Ó Rathaille's lyric, where haughty terms (ard-shleachta) once applied to proud aristocrats are now attached to stolen farmyard fowl.

The controlled exaggeration of the performance is delightfully sustained through compound words (fáithchliste, líondatha) and assertions that are frankly incredible – in those days fifty shillings would cover the cost of a prize cow rather than a cock. This irony of accumulating detail is the very device employed in *The Rape of the Lock*: the domestication of the epic. Pope in his poem lists the details that inflate a lovers' tiff to heroic proportions, while his actual idiom works simultaneously to diminish it all by programmatic contrasts, as when a lady passes to her beau nothing more lethal than a pair of scissors:

> *Just then, Clarissa drew with tempting Grace*
> *A two-edged weapon from her shining Case:*
> *So Ladies in Romance, assist their Knight,*
> *Present the Spear, and arm him for the Fight.*[26]

That same disparity between tone and topic may be found throughout the prose of Joseph Addison, in the mocking contrast between elaborate clauses and homely objects. The delicacy, as in Ó Rathaille, lies in the equipoise of overstatement and covert irony, for the speaker does not finally commit himself either way.

A similar ambivalence may be found in the warrant, which oscillates between self-mockery and self-righteousness. Seán Ó Tuama has shown how the metre grows looser and less stately as the poet rushes headlong to his conclusion, skilfully suggesting the excitement of the chase. Slang terms and anglicized borrowings ('plundaráil') take over from the elegant diction of the opening, as if to hint at a self-deflation by the poet.[27] Each grandiose term is pushed just beyond its compass until, towards the end, the writer tips the wink to the reader, inviting a comparison of the two styles. The warrant works, correspondingly, in two ways. On the surface, it is placed in the mouth of Blennerhasset, a practising sheriff, and so the threat to hang the culprit may be real enough. Daniel Corkery inclined to this belief and accounted for the popularity of the warrants with the explanation that they were an unironic imitation of the only remaining ceremonial institution with which the people came into contact. 'With the law and its forms,' he suggested, 'they then began to associate all ideas of ceremony, judgements and authority.'[28]

That may well be too obvious a reading. It takes no account of the deliberate exaggeration with which Ó Rathaille propels his subtext. That text mocks rather than apes the self-importance of the legal profession, which administered the hated new laws. It is very likely, however, that he also intended some sly deflation of the self-image of the bardic order, whose leading members had once combined the functions of *file* with that of *breitheamh* (judge). With his highfalutin talk of courts and warrants, the ventriloquist poet is scarcely convincing as a sheriff. In fact, he slips in and out of the persona, much as Swift in his writings may oscillate between a chosen role and an opportunist self. Ó Rathaille is clearly *imagining* himself as an ancient poet/judge, so that the threat to hang the miscreant is more rhetorical than real. It is a threat to enact the customary bardic revenge, that is, to write a satire on the culprit. In the deepest sense of all, however, this grandiloquence cannot conceal the poet's marginality and powerlessness, by contrast with his bardic ancestors. This explains the undercurrent of self-mockery, emphasized by the lapse from metrical intricacy into loose slang. It is as if the very idiom of the stanzas were enacting in its free fall that decline of cultural tradition which was Ó Rathaille's obsessive theme.

The tonal range and technical virtuosity mastered by Ó Rathaille were awesome, fully earning him his standing as a major artist. His willingness to read the fate of a nation into his own tragedy appealed greatly to Gaelic revivalists at the start of the twentieth century. The aristocratic fetishism displayed in many poems had its attractions: it allowed a lower-middle class to assert a new social self-respect (as, in truth, did the mandarin poetry of the professional *filí*). But such a response begged certain questions. The sheer versatility of Ó Rathaille's verse would hardly have been possible in a badly maimed or debilitated culture. His achievement is of an order that suggests that not only did he tap the still-vital energies of the Irish language but that that language realized its genius in a spectacular fashion through him. The expressive achievement of forerunners in the seventeenth century was available to him and he did not fail to exploit it to the full. It also seems likely that, in Munster at least, the literary public for poetry in Irish may have grown rather than shrunk after the collapse of the bardic order.[29]

Ó Rathaille's is only the most striking voice to come down to us from the eighteenth century, but there were many more, so many as to provoke the envy of many writers of our own time, including the poet, Thomas Kinsella. He finds there 'a world suddenly full of life and voices' and locates its appeal in the shared intensity of a thousand-year-old tradition, 'which is precisely what is missing from Irish literature, in English or Irish, in the nineteenth century and today'.[30] Among those who wrote powerfully after Ó Rathaille were Eoghan Rua Ó Súilleabháin and Piaras Mac Gearailt.

5

Endings and Beginnings: Mac Cuarta and After

The Munster Poets were celebrated by Daniel Corkery in *The Hidden Ireland* (1925) and this reflected the high standing enjoyed by that region's dialect among teachers and learners of the Irish Revival: but the evidence of cultural activity from Gaelic Ulster is almost as extensive. After the Flight of the Earls the centre of gravity in poetic activity shifted from the north-west to the south-east of the province: and the work of Séamas Dall Mac Cuarta (1647–1732) was the basis for a tradition that blossomed also in the poetry of Peadar Ó Doirnín and Art Mac Cumhaigh in the first half of the eighteenth century. There had been no strong poetic tradition in this rather anglicized area of south-east Ulster and north Leinster before Mac Cuarta. Perhaps it was the fact that this was border country which caused English forces to attack Gaelic culture in the area and prompted a defiantly creative response from the community. After all, theirs was the landscape of the *Táin*, of *Oidhe Chlainne Uisnigh*, of Emain Macha and St Patrick's Armagh. The border out-post of Glassdrummond Castle became for Mac Cuarta the symbol of Gaelic pride and when it was demolished in 1700, he lamented the collapse of an old world.

Later poets like Ó Doirnín and Mac Cumhaigh were involved on the fringes of rebel movements against the English and both had friends who were hanged as traitors by crown forces. The political changes in the period did not affect all the Gaelic nobility. A few saved themselves by tactical conversions to Protestantism or by making treaties with the English. In the towns many Catholics took

advantage of the improved transport systems and circumvented the
Penal Laws by profitable engagement in trade. These quickly abandoned their allegiance to Gaelic culture. That commitment was
maintained by some, but by no means all, of the hedge schoolmasters
who had a hard life, often facing summary eviction by a Protestant
minister before they had time to collect their fees. (That happened
repeatedly to Ó Doirnín.) Those who sent their children to hedge
schools were not the poor, but ambitious farmers and middlemen.
Some of the poet-schoolmasters would hardly have shared the pragmatic outlook of their customers.

The poets symbolized the victory of the English by the cutting
down of the woods. What they failed to understand was that, revolution or not, the woods were being felled all over Europe, since
charcoal was needed for smelting purposes. A patriarchal society was
giving way to modern capitalism: and one economic historian has
seen in poets like Ó Bruadair and Mac Cuarta 'the last articulate
protest at the passing of medieval society'.[1] It is foolish to look to
such poets for an account of the poor, for no account of them survived. The Gaelic poets tended to migrate to the remoter regions,
where old ways lived on: hence the move of Mac Cuarta's family from
Tyrone into the south-east of Ulster. That tendency – along with the
new willingness among ordinary people to attempt verse – may well
be a further explanation for the revival of poetry in the region.

Mac Cuarta was born in Omeath, County Louth and, according
to local lore, he caught a fever which left him blind but was compensated with the gift of words. His mindset was formed before the
defeat of James at the Boyne and so he believed that patronage was
due to a poet, even as he lived a reality which was very different.
Located on the cusp between tradition and modernity, he perfected
the form known as *trí rainn agus amhrán* (three stanzas and a song).
The *amhrán* verses attached to syllabic poems had not always been
composed by the same author who had written the main text: but the
sheer continuity of style suggests that Mac Cuarta treated the new
form as an artistic unit. In his work the *amhrán* offers a real development rather than mere repetition of prior themes. Because of its
brevity, the new form was well suited to occasional poetry on the
joys and sorrows of everyday life.

His best-known lyric is 'Tithe Chorr an Chait':

> *Uaigneach sin tithe Chorr an Chait,*
> *Is uaigneach a bhfir is a mná;*
> *is dá bhfaighdís ór is fíon,*
> *cha dtig aon díobh i gceann cháich.*

I gceann cháich cha dtig siad,
ar ar cruthaíodh thiar is thoir;
ar ar cruthaíodh ó neamh go lár –
ionann sin is béasa an bhroic.

Béasa an bhroic bheith ag tochailt faoi
i ndorchadas oíche is lae;
ar ar cruthaíodh ó neamh go lár,
i gceann cháich cha dtig sé.

Ní hionúin leis an ríbhroc aoibhneas, aiteas, ná spórt;
ní hionúin leo saoi, draoi, ná cumadóir ceoil,
ni hionúin leo Séamas caoch ná cuidiú Néill óig –
is fanadh gach aon mar a mbíd ag tochailt an phóir.[2]

Lonely are the houses of Corr an Chait, and lonely are their men and women. Even if they were given gold and wine, they would not one of them greet people.

They would not greet people for all the created world, east and west; for the created world from heaven to earth – that is like the habit of the badger.

The badger's habit is to dig beneath himself into the darkness, night and day; for the created world from heaven to earth, he would not greet people.

The chief badger doesn't like joy, pleasure or sport. The badgers don't like learned men or druids, or music-makers. They don't like blind Seamus, nor the company of young Niall, so let each one stay where he is wont, digging in soil.

This is a satire on skinflints who refuse traditional hospitality to an arriving poet and instead lock themselves away in their houses. It identifies that meanness with a locality, Corrakit. A somewhat similar sort of satire emerged in English in this period also, and for identical reasons. 'The growth of public credit and financial institutions of government caused a realignment of moneyed as against landed interests,' observes Pat Rogers; 'satire is normally engaged in detecting infractions of a norm: and one common theme is the picture built up of the "new men", the invaders of established society, the pretenders to taste, the *nouveau riche*, the pushing outsiders'.[3] The Protestant ethic now taking hold brought the spirit of capitalism with it, to the detriment of the poets, who suffered because of their ambiguous class position. Many took revenge by describing the newly rich in images of avaricious animality. Swift in *A Tale of a Tub* compared the *arriviste* to the spider who spins wholly from himself and scorns any obligation to other beings. Mac Cuarta compared the Corrakit people to burrowing, indifferent badgers.

His poem inverts the old *dinnsheanchas* code, by which a poet praised the lore of a particular place. Now, like the *filí* whose work was spurned, he must take revenge. It is not just the meanness to a guest that appals him, but the insult to a bearer of a noble tradition. The form makes the point for him, because the syllabic metres are as refined in manner as the old aristocratic code:

internal rhyme: fíon/díobh   faoi/oíche   lár/cháich
final rhyme: mná/cháich   toir/broic   lae/sé

Unlike many bardic poems, the stanzas here are well integrated into a coherent sequence, with the last line of one being recast as the first of the next, for the purpose of refining (not repeating) an idea. The suggestion is of a speaker too outraged to let go of the sentence, someone unable to purge his sorrow in a definitive declarative statement. Just when he thinks that he has done with it, the wave of sadness breaks again with each opening line. The playwright Synge would employ a similar device:

> BARTLEY: It's hard set we'll be from this day with no one in it but one man to work.
> MAURYA: It's hard set we'll be surely, the day you're drowned with the rest.[4]

or

> BARTLEY: . . . the fair will be a good fair for horses, I heard them saying below.
> MAURYA: It's a hard thing they'll be saying below if the boat is washed up and no man in it to make the coffin.[5]

The stanzas are integrated in other ways too: line three of the second and third is pure repetition, and the final line of the syllabic form has been uttered twice already. Out of twelve lines in the *dán díreach* only six are truly new, in this technique of deliberate self-limitation. The poet grows as miserly in his use of words as the people of Corrakit are with the goods of the world. The entire lyric works off a series of contrasts between miserliness and prodigality, spatial openness and limitation, as in the second stanza, where the beauty and scope of nature seem boundless:

ar ar cruthaíodh thiar is thoir
ar ar cruthaíodh ó neamh go lár

Against such a backdrop of openness, the cramped hunkering-down of the people seems a sin against poetry but also against nature itself. The widening scope of the second stanza contrasts utterly with the delimitation of space and light in the third, where there is no new thought and no new line. The objects of the satire are evoked as underground folk, already half-dead because devoid of any creativity or capacity for celebration. Hence the similitude of the badger. The blind poet, who lives perforce in darkness, cannot credit that these people would choose such a condition.

The repetitions in the *dán díreach* are subtle, covert, inflected: but in the *amhrán* they are obvious (Ní hionúin . . . ní hionúin . . . ní hionúin . . .). This seems like rhetoric, but it is rhetoric used to a poetic point, by way of illustrating that decay that has coarsened manners and simplified verse. Though the *amhrán*, built around hard consonants rather than soft words, seems loose, its lines are filled with telling ambiguities. 'Ríbhroc' may denote either the king of badgers or it may deploy the reinforcing word 'rí' to indicate the badger as the ultimate in rapacity. As a spurned poet Mac Cuarta defiantly asserts that he will none the less return to his time-honoured duty ('Ag tochailt an phóir') of excavating the lineage of noble families, even as the badger-humans dig themselves deeper into the earth ('pór' can mean earth or race). Two apparently opposed meanings may in fact be linked: for death awaits all parties. Whatever form of digging is done, it may be no more than a rehearsal for the diggers of the ancestral grave.

Mac Cuarta, though technically gifted, was like many artists in that he wrote one basic poem over and over again in varied ways. His other great lyric, 'Fáilte don Éan', appears to tackle a very different subject, yet the same theme underlies it: a welcome that should have been extended is somehow aborted. The poet recalls how the local community migrated to the woods, as in every April in search of the cuckoo, leaving the blind poet behind to write lines whose vowel music celebrates the bird's very notes:

Fáilte don éan is binne ar chraoibh,
labhras ar chaoin na dtor le gréin;
domhsa is fada tuirse an tsaoil,
nach bhfaiceann í le tíocht an fhéir.

Gach neach dá bhfaiceann cruth na n-éan,
amharc Éireann, deas is tuaidh,

bláth na dtulach ar gach taoibh –
is dóibh is aoibhinn a bheith dá lua.

Cluinim, gé nach bhfaicim a gné,
seinm an éin darb ainm cuach;
amharc uirthi a mbarraibh géag,
mo thuirse ghéar nach mise fuair.

Mo thuirse nach bhfuaireas bua ar m'amharc a fháil,
go bhfaicfinn ar uaigneas uaisle an duilliúir ag fás;
cuid de mo ghruaim nach gluaisim ag cruinniú le cách,
le seinm na gcuach ar bhruach na coilleadh go sámh.[6]

Welcome to the sweetest bird on the branches, who speaks
from the bushes' foliage to the sun. To me the weariness of the
world is long, that I don't see her with the ripening of the grass.

Everyone who sees the form of birds, the sight of Ireland
south and north, the flower of the hills on every side, loves to
be able to talk of that.

I hear, although I can't see anything, the playing of the bird
that is called cuckoo. To see her in the topmost branches – it is
sharp sadness that I have not the means.

My sadness that I did not get the virtue of my own sight, to
see in solitude the nobility of the foliage ripening; part of my
gloom is that I can't congregate with all people when the
cuckoo sings luxuriously on the forest's edge.

The metre is a strict version of *rannaíocht mhór* with internal rhyme
between *craoibh* and *caoin*, as well as final rhyme between *craoibh*
and *saoil*. The poet manages to re-create the rhythms of everyday
speech within the metrical strictness: and again in the *amhrán*, where
the *a/uu* vowels of sorrow gradually win out over the *e/i* sounds of
joy as loneliness overwhelms the promised greeting.

The welcome is suffused with bitter irony from the outset. If the
poet is able to re-create the cuckoo's music, that is only because
blindness has compelled him to a more heightened sense of hearing.
This poem, like the earlier one, works off familiar contrasts between
assertion and denial, welcome and keening, light and darkness, sky
and land. The seekers of the cuckoo must look up to the tops of the
trees, but the blind man can better sense the coming of summer in the
new lushness of grass beneath his feet. Again, the contrast between
unlimited space and the confined world of the sightless is accentuated: and it is (again) the second line of the second stanza that evokes
the scope of the natural world for those with the spirit to relish it.

In that second stanza the flowers on the branches are likened to the cuckoo's song from the same bushes in stanza one: the sensory world is a continuum in which fragrant smells, beautiful sights and sweet sounds merge. But for Mac Cuarta that continuum is broken: he can hear but not see the song of the bird 'that is called cuckoo': and the literal-mindedness of that phrasing reminds us that for him the cuckoo is but a name used by those people who have gone to the woods. The phrase sounds deliberately childish, as if used by a learner slowly feeling his way into a strange world, one who cannot be completely certain in the absence of visual confirmation that a cuckoo is indeed what he hears. The uncertainty of the speaker is contrasted in the third stanza with the emphatic nouns with which the central lines begin, 'seinm', 'amharc'; that emphasis necessitates a reversal of the usual syntax, as if to suggest the slightly skewed experience of a world which is a blind man's. More conventionally, he might have written 'mo thuirse nach bhfuair mise amharc . . .', but here the emphasis is placed on the opening ('amharc') and closing ('fuair') words, just as in the previous stanza a technique of retardation is used to throw the key verb ('lua') into relief at the end. This delay rouses the reader's faculties, an appropriate effect in a poem about the meaning and use of the senses.

Some might feel that the writer indulges in self-pity. In fact a poised equilibrium is maintained between positive and negative throughout. The opening welcome is brave in coming from a blind man (all the braver when one recalls that the cuckoo's sound was dreaded by the *filí* who knew it marked the break-up of their school for summer). The poet – rather like Keats and the nightingale or Shelley and the skylark – senses that he may be able to assimilate the birdsong to his own music. Since the cuckoo is heard more often than seen, it provides a working metaphor for one whose poems are heard even as his personality goes unrecognized in the community. That would explain Mac Cuarta's solitude at the close, for he also lives on the edge of things – there is an absolute contrast between the rich scope of the world in stanza two and the drastic limitations of the first-person world evoked in stanza three. The healthy members of the community have gone to the woods to greet the cuckoo: but the large-scale irony is that they have abandoned an even more tuneful singing-bird at home. There could hardly be a more poignant, or more subtle, lament for the collapse of the poetic tradition: for what is lamented is not so much any inherent weakness in the poetry as a weakness in its intended audience. The poet isn't even playing (as Raftery would in the next century) for empty pockets: he is playing solely for his own relief and he knows it.

Unlike Munster poets, who tried to speak for a community, the Ulster writers were individualistic, independent-minded, and even cynical. They took the decay of Gaelic poetry for granted. Mac Cumhaigh, even further removed from bardic days than Mac Cuarta had been, compared himself to a drop of water awaiting the Flood. Like Ó Doirnín, Ó Bruadair and even Ó Súilleabháin, he had a good knowledge of English, a language that was widespread by the mid-eighteenth century. Reports by visitors repeatedly describe an essentially bilingual community. In the 1730s Arthur Young found that one-third of the citizens of Dublin were Irish-speaking; three decades later John Bush found that even in the countryside 'very few of the lowest class are met with that cannot speak English'.[7]

Not surprisingly, texts that recognized the bilingual nature of the society were popular. In Dublin Seán Ó Neachtain produced *Stair Éamuinn Uí Chléire* (The Story of Eamon O'Clery, 1710), a parody of the old romantic tales, with mockeries of literal-minded English translations from the Irish: 'Nine God to you' for 'hello' (i.e. go mbean naoi Dia dhuit).[8] The author, caught between a desire to mock the old heroes in a hilarious parody and the wish to supply a more complex, modern psychological motivation, opted for a mock-heroic strategy. A similar exercise in picaresque anti-heroism was *Mac na Míchomhairle* (The Ghost of the Ill-starred Son), composed in the later seventeenth century by Brian Dubh Ó Raghallaigh. Here the hero, fancying his chances with a noble lady, is told that he must defend her father in battle. He breaks into a cold sweat and, dispensing with all courtly preliminaries, tries to trundle her straight into bed.[9] This is a far cry from those warriors who refused no battle and defended maidenly honour: and so in his essay 'The End of a Tradition' R.A. Breatnach found in such parodies 'a noteworthy phenomenon which suggests decline in cultural standards'.[10] Thus Celtic scholarship sought to roll back the eighteenth century. Those developments could with more justice be described as a positive evolution, in keeping with the 'comic epic poem in prose' being perfected by Henry Fielding in England. There was little enough difference between the Gaelic anti-heroes and such picaresque rascals as Tom Jones and Joseph Andrews.

What prevented the refinement of such tales into the forms of the early novel was simple enough: the lack of a proper system of printing presses for secular texts in Irish.[11] Only such religious works as the sermons of James Gallagher were printed, and these proved hugely popular, passing through twenty-five editions between 1735 and 1911. Composed on the shores of Lough Erne while their author lay in hiding from English forces, they offered a spiritual analysis in artful but clear language, and a pungency that verged on epigram:

> *Cia aige a bhfuil gach én ní réir a thola?*
> *Ní thusa é, nó mise é, nó duine ar bith air a' talamh.*[12]

> *Who has every single thing according to his desire?*
> *It is not you, or I, or anybody on the earth.*

The art of such sermonizing was close to that of the periodical essay, then being refined by men like Joseph Addison and Richard Steele. The manuscripts left by Addison show that he wrote out his essays in a print-like hand, so that he might test them aloud on a select audience in a coffee house. The published essays were read aloud in every coffee house in London and discussed afterwards by the company, much as a congregation might debate a sermon on leaving church. In Scotland many Sunday congregations did not disperse until they had heard and dissected the latest *Spectator*. This practice of reading prose aloud induced in the essayists an awareness of the need for a clear, sequential style, and words that were memorable.[13] Topics covered by Addison parallel almost exactly those treated in Gallagher's sermons. They were often pragmatic: the dignity of hard work; the need to curb vandalism; the ways of domestic hygiene; the means of securing good employment for children; and so on. The object in both cases was the refinement of life and manners among the emerging middle class.

Ireland in the eighteenth century may have been a land of two languages, but the evidence suggests that bilingualism rather than biculturalism was the order of the day. If Ó Súilleabháin could write the ballad 'Rodney's Glory' celebrating an English naval victory, Ó Doirnín could praise the ways of 'The Independent Man' in another English-language song. The immense demand for macaronic ballads suggests a cheerfully bilingual community, whose members admired and enjoyed fluency in both languages. Far from indicating a loss of purity in Gaelic tradition, the very fact that the framing language in most of these ballads is Irish indicates a culture still confident of its ability to hold its own.[14]

Why, then, the widespread determination among many Celtic scholars to read these signs as the end of a tradition? To ask that is to enquire why Irish has been pronounced dead or dying in almost every decade since 1607. One answer might be that the imminent death of Irish was proclaimed by its lovers in order to shock an apparently indifferent populace into an awareness of the long-term implications of its own decline.[15] The apparatus of state grew in importance through the eighteenth century and its affairs were now conducted solely in English: even those groups like the Whiteboys or United Irishmen who mounted effective critiques from the Irish side found it effective to use the planters' language. But there were other factors at work too.

Jonathan Swift once observed that 'it is impossible that anything so natural, so necessary and so universal as death, should ever have been designed by providence as an evil to mankind'.[16] People have often welcomed death as a clarification, something that ends the intolerable ambiguity of being caught between the living and the dead, that zone of uncertainty in which so many painful questions may be raised. To live always on the verge of death is bad enough; to live on the brink of apocalypse is exhausting, especially when the dead-by date has to be eternally revised and postponed. One way to annul those pains is to hurry death on. Over time, and for many different reasons, it may have come to suit both the Irish and the English to proclaim Irish dead.

As long as the language was endangered, that situation was a standing rebuke to the lack of will among Irish persons to protect and save it. Once it was safely dead, the English could be blamed for killing it off and the Irish could adopt a role that would make them notorious, as champion whingers of the western world. The English, for their part, could happily shoulder this burden, since it confirmed the superior durability of their own culture: but they were then free to suggest that, though losing their own tongue, the Irish had been compensated by the injection of toxins of energy from the dying syntax and, as a result, now enjoyed an unrivalled eloquence in English. Many Irish people were ready to buy into such analyses, congratulating themselves on their eloquence in English, even while they remained dumb in Irish.[17]

Much of the theorizing about language was based on arrant self-deception. Irish was neither dead nor dying, but it suited most people to pretend that it was. It suited revivalist intellectuals, for it gratified their vanity with the suggestion that they alone had the power to breathe it back to life, to make it young again (an interpretation much enhanced by the cult of youth and of Tír na nÓg in Celtic literature, a theme to be taken up by Wilde and Yeats). It suited Celtic scholars who believed that their studies and translations of a dead but beautiful culture could make its energies current again among a new generation of readers: they needed it to be lost, if ever it was to be recovered. An Irish that was alive but threatened remained a potent rebuke to such established powers, if only because it induced guilt feelings on all sides: but an Irish dead could be simply waked and buried, a process well documented by Sarah McKibben.[18]

As soon as Irish-language authors understood that the shock value of announcing its death had become counterproductive, they abandoned that claim. Henceforth, it would be left to scholars, often writing in English, to fret about the apparent decline in the vocabulary and syntax of the language. As recently as 1969 one lamented that 'the ordinary Gaeltacht dweller of today does not speak Irish with the same fluency, the same precision and the same vigour as did his grandparents'.[19] It became a habit to compare the dense vocabulary of Tomás Ó Criomhthain with that of later Blasket authors such as Peig Sayers or Muiris Ó Súilleabháin: but such lamentations could also be heard regularly in French, German and every other language. It is one of the functions of a living language to be constantly accused of lacking the richness it once had: the snows of yesteryear were always a matter of words. No book written in the Gaeltacht (the Irish-speaking area) ever voiced any great lament for a decline in the vitality of the language. As Sarah McKibben has brilliantly observed: 'while it is possible to find Irish dying in any language, English is the language in which it is usually buried'. She adds a stinging comment: 'it is also, alas, too often the language in which Irish is revived'.[20]

The Irish have always derived a sense of their own vitality from the very prospect of death. In this culture, there has usually been a better than even chance of a life after death – indeed, that option is often considered superior to any offered by this world. ('Is there a life before death?' was one of the more striking graffiti on Belfast walls during the recent war.) The tale of the corpse that sits up and begins to speak is of ancient vintage, but it has been repeated in every generation, at wakes and weddings, in the plays of Boucicault, Synge, Beckett and Behan. A culture that can frame life's most extreme challenges can hardly be said to be dead, for the very capacity to describe a terrible situation with accuracy is an answer to hopelessness. In the hidden powers of that descriptive faculty lurk the codes of a solution: and in Irish the rejected codes continued to live vibrantly in the laments for their passing.

For centuries the national literature has been written not just to be heard but to be overheard. Political poets of Gaeldom in the seventeenth century, like the *aisling* poets of the eighteenth, though faced with a calamity, never lost the sense of its underlying meaning. They saw in communal suffering a just retribution for sin, the English being no more than the stick wielded by the almighty. The poems were often addressed, explicitly or implicitly, to an overwatching, overhearing God, who would (it was assumed) see everything right in the end. Indeed, the proud capacity of the people to endure even more than the English could ever inflict became a new sort of existential challenge to the vibrancy of a threatened culture. From such an experience emerged the Beckettian idea that one would have to learn to suffer and to 'be there' even more patiently than before, if one was to weary the torturers. And if God would not hear the righteous voices raised in Irish, then later – especially after the Great Famine of the nineteenth century – those voices raised in English were further amplified in the hope that the better sort of Saxon liberal would, on hearing the cry, know what to do.

W.B. Yeats often said that only a life that can come to terms with death is a life worth living. James Joyce was obsessed (according to his brother) with the steady course of the past through the present: and he liked to say that 'death is the highest form of life'.[21] He caused his greatest fictional creation, Leopold Bloom, to remark that 'the Irishman's house is his coffin'[22] and to speculate about the possibility of setting up telephone links to the coffins in Glasnevin Cemetery, on the off-chance that some people buried there might yet be alive. The notion that the dead may continue to speak links documents as different as Patrick Pearse's speech at the grave of O'Donovan Rossa (often quoted at election time by gleeful personators of deceased voters: 'The fools, the fools, the fools, they have left us our Fenian dead'),[23] Máirtín Ó Cadhain's great experimental prose masterpiece *Cré na Cille* (1949), or the final section of the trilogy by Samuel Beckett. Democracy demands that the dead cast votes and voice opinion as well as the living.

This is because in Ireland the past is never a dead letter: it isn't even over. Like the corpse that snaps upward and forward, it retains a radical potential to disrupt the complacent world of the present. Bram Stoker was not the first or last author to sense the power of the Undead. In such a culture, the past can form a constellation with the present, flashing forth as a challenge: and then the *status quo ante* turns out to be the radical option. The effect of the Penal Laws against Catholics after 1691 was that a conservative, even aristocratic longing on the lips of poets acquired a radical, even populist purchase, because of the extensive repression: and ever since the Irish have produced a strangely traditionalist radicalism, which looked back in order to look forward. One consequence was that old-fashioned ideas were often framed in experimental new forms (a feature linking, say, the *trí rainn agus amhrán* as perfected by Mac Cuarta with the Yeats who defended tradition in the experimental narrative of *A Vision*). Another consequence is that revolutionary ideas were sometimes encased in very traditional forms (an element that connects the author of *Pairlement Chloinne Tomáis* with the Joyce who framed his *Ulysses* with the structuring device of Homer's

Odyssey). Throughout the Irish-language poetry of the eighteenth century, artists who were living in reduced circumstances spoke in the accents of the declining aristocracy: and at the same time they showed themselves more and more willing to celebrate the culture of the masses.[24] In effect, they became linkmen for those former aristocrats who wished to take on the protective coloration of the emerging bourgeoisie, even as they also provided a bridge in the cultural continuum which permitted new money to ape the values of the older elites. That ambiguous class position which caused such humiliation to an Ó Rathaille became, in time, the basis for new cultural possibilities.

Even if the English had never imposed a new order, the bardic schools would have been compelled to take stock of a new world. The vitality in any literature springs from an ever-varying tension between the rhythms of current speech and the formal generic schemes, and there is a similarly healthy tension between the language of an age and the language of its poetry. Sometimes, the two come close together; but if they remain too close for too long, the result is an unimaginative limitation on the themes and emotions with which writing can deal, for poetry is rightly expected to cope with experiences more intense than just the quotidian. On the other hand, if the divergence between the language of literature and the idiom of an age goes too far or lasts too long, the danger is that poetry will develop a factitious dialect divorced from the springs of life. That was what happened to the bardic schools, but the writing that followed hard on their collapse was animated by the pressure of a felt experience. Long before the Romantic poets of England insisted on using the language of men speaking to men, the poets of Gaelic Ireland had made that breakthrough. If the Romantics would in time reject the gaudy and inane diction of predecessors, the Irish writers voiced identical reservations about the standards of the bardic poets.

Yet the extreme buoyancy of their forms could never quite conceal the sadness of their contents, a disjunction which was to become a global characteristic of postcolonial writing. The wake, with its vibrant celebration of the passage through death, became a paradigm not just of the Irish language but of Irish culture more generally; and the rituals associated with it may explain the pervasive cult of death. Even after life had left the body, it was assumed to hover in its vicinity: the dead person was not imagined as 'crossing over' from the living world right away. The question put by the Tramp concerning the corpse laid out at the start of Synge's *The Shadow of the Glen* is pertinent here: 'Is it departed he is? . . . It's a queer look is on him for a man that's dead.'[25] In fact old Dan is very much alive and a testament to the inability of his young wife to determine the moment of death with any exactitude. This may well have been Synge's own metaphor for a Gaelic tradition which would have to die many times before a certificate could be issued.

The devices and symbolic visions foreshadowing death in Gaelic folklore are well known, and the words actually spoken by the dying are ritually invested with great significance. But the real fear which haunts the carriers of Irish culture is the one with which Synge and Joyce deal: that of being waked and even buried alive. One way of meeting this anxiety is to have a telephone installed in your coffin; another is to be both a witness of and participant in your own death, to report what you undergo, as in Greek tragedy.[26] Acts of mourning of others are, of course, ways of rehearsing for the death that some day will be one's own. This may explain the stubborn persistence of the wake as a crucial ritual in Irish society: and that persistence may in turn raise questions about the health of other 'modern' civilizations which are organized around a 'denial of death'.[27]

Not all of the modern Irish would see things in this way. Some will contend that the argument concerning Irish is no longer about survival or revival but rather about who owns the corpse. The poet Patrick Kavanagh was one of these:

> At wakes nothing serious is ever discussed. Nobody is ever angry or destructive. At a wake everyone speaks in a hypocritical whisper: 'God be good to him, he was a decent man.'
> 'Raised a good family,' says another.
> . . . A wake is what is in progress in this country, a wake at which there is lashings of eating and drinking . . . We came to the wake that has been going on uproariously for at least thirty years and at the moment we are trying to get the family to remove the corpse – the corpse of 1916, the Gaelic language, the inferiority complex – so that the house may be free for the son to take a wife. Will they take our advice or will the wake proceed to explosion point?[28]

Kavanagh offered 'a few uncultured peasant facts'. The Gaelic language was no longer the native language: 'it is dead yet food is being brought to the graveyard'.[29] However much the creature had been loved when alive, it was time to accept that it could never be revived either as a spoken or as a written language. What was being enacted was a propping-up of the corpse with pillows. This motif – of the postponed burial[30] – is pervasive through modern writing: Old

Mahon in Synge's *Playboy of the Western World*, like the Undead in *Dracula*, or the Irish language itself, just will not be buried.

There is something rather pagan about the idea of dead people being fed, propitiated and even kept unburied in the manner described by Kavanagh: and there is a fiercely pagan quality to many of the games played at wakes, a fact that led to their denunciation by the Catholic clergy in both the nineteenth and twentieth centuries. Yet Kavanagh chose not to indict the tradition on those grounds, instead pressing home the argument that neither Carleton nor Liam O'Flaherty could have done any good as writers in Irish. 'If the subject or the language is dead or dying,' he contends, 'it will come to pieces in the writer's hands.'[31] This was hardly true of Ó Rathaille or Mac Cuarta, much less of O'Flaherty himself, who was about to publish some of the most brilliant short stories in the language when Kavanagh published his essay. But Kavanagh was never a great expert on Gaelic culture: he had got the seventeenth-century revival hopelessly wrong and was as likely to misread the modern equivalent. Eventually, he conceded that his sarcastic poem 'Memory of Brother Michael' was 'good poetry but bad history'.[32]

What is remarkable, however, is just how much of that Gaelic poetry he despised lived on in Kavanagh's own art: in his compulsive desire to praise the good and slam the bad; in rivalry with poetic competitors from his own townland; in his willingness to 'rhyme up' an enemy; and in his view of the public role of the poet. Believing that the artist is a lightning conductor for misfortune, he came (inevitably perhaps) to celebrate his own local *file* of the eighteenth century, Art Mac Cumhaigh. 'Art McCooey' was published in *The Bell* of April 1941 and there the poet appears as a version of Kavanagh himself.

The lyric is ostensibly a record of the small talk and minor rituals of rural life. It is based on a local tradition that Mac Cumhaigh, while employed by a farmer to cart dung to outliers on his land, became so distracted by composing a poem that he drove the same load back and forth four or five times, until his employer broke into his reverie with a roar of complaint.[33]

> *We played with the frilly edges of reality*
> *While we puffed on cigarettes;*
> *And sometimes Owney Martin's splitting yell*
> *Would knife the dreamer that the land begets.*[34]

The lines move from death back to life. In the labourer's delivery of dung to farmers, there is an image of the artist handling a seemingly dead, even deathly, tradition; but the excrement nurtures the earth back to life and allows for a celebration of rural ritual in this text written for townies:

> *Wash out the cart with a bucket of water and a wangel*
> *Of wheaten straw. Jupiter looks down.*
> *Unlearnedly and unreasonably poetry is shaped*
> *Awkwardly but alive in the unmeasured womb.*

Mac Cumhaigh is described by Kavanagh as one who, though not a great poet, became authentic by absorbing the little fields and lanes, and was thereby enabled to grow into his locality as naturally as a child nestling in the womb.[35] In his art, if not in his cultural polemics, Kavanagh saw just how clearly the dung dropped by Gaelic tradition signposted a path back to life.

The very brilliance of the English-language literature of Ireland may be a direct consequence of the reported loss of Irish, a massive attempt at psychological compensation. That brilliance is connected in large part with its exploration of the question of identity, a theme that pressed all the more strongly in the vacuum left after hundreds of thousands stopped speaking Irish in the mid-nineteenth century. If nationalism was one force that filled the ensuing vacuum, Anglo-Irish literature was another. But just how empty was that emptiness? In 1840 Irish was still vibrant enough for the Protestant authorities at Trinity College Dublin to appoint a professor in the subject, whose main function was to prepare clergymen to preach in the native language. In the census taken eleven years later, many denied a knowledge of the language – this denial, even among fluent speakers, would persist until the Gaelic League began to restore some pride in the 1890s. Whether its campaigns – still active in the government-funded television and radio stations – were largely symbolic or practically effective is something the present generation (like all its predecessors) may yet decide. For Irish is not dead, but still very much alive. If it disappears, it will be because Irish people themselves decide to have done with it, and for no other reason.

6

Jonathan Swift:
a Colonial Outsider?

Jonathan Swift was nothing if not conflicted. Born in the parish of St Werburgh's, Dublin in 1667, he liked to pretend that he was really an Englishman, stolen from his country of origin as an infant and brought over in a bandbox.[1] The truth was only a little more mundane. His father died before he was born and the family went back to England, but a nursemaid who loved the child brought him with her to Whitehaven, when he was just a year old. Even in his cradle he was marked out for spiritual hyphenation: and in the years of his greatest power and influence in England, he was invariably treated as an Irishman.

At Kilkenny School he mixed with boys from all corners of Ireland, yet he felt himself a loner, on the edge of life. Much of the poignancy and all of the comedy in his subsequent writing arises from his sense of the fish-out-of-water state. In Ireland he might feel like a stranger in a strange land, but he found things no different in England. He was arguably one of the very first postcolonial writers, in the sense of one who feels cast out by the mother country and yet imperfectly assimilated by the new one. In Swift's case, of course, it would have been hard to say which that mother country was: he might have said England in his younger days, but in the end it hardly mattered, for he had no place like a home in which to hang his hat. Hence, perhaps, his love of travelling and travellers. This may also account for the early diminishment of his sense of reality, for the

homeless, houseless youth found himself accustomed at an early age
to the experience of disappointment:

> I never wake without finding life a more insignificant thing
> than it was the day before ... but my greatest misery is recol-
> lecting the scene of twenty years past, and then all on a sudden
> dropping into the present. I remember when I was a little boy,
> I felt a great fish at the end of my line which I drew up almost
> on the ground, but it dropt in, and the disappointment vexeth
> me to this very day, and I believe it was the type of all my
> future disappointments.[2]

He was one of the first in a long line of Anglo-Irish writers who
would find their lives a preparation for something that never happened. No mere frustration in the progress of a career can account
for such ontological insecurity, but the sense of being estranged from
one's natural element just might explain things. Swift in that anecdote invites us to identify with his loss of the great fish (a rise to
ecclesiastical power in England). However, his real identification is
with the struggling animal itself, briefly out of the water before it
falls injured back into the zones of the unconscious, where it is hap-
piest of all. And that unconscious zone may well have been Ireland.
As always, when he seems to tell one story, however simple, Swift is
really narrating another.

He was sent by a kindly uncle at a remarkably early age to Trinity
College Dublin but he was not grateful for the favour: 'he gave me
the education of a dog'. At the time the college's reputation was very
high. Swift did not excel at his studies, developing a distrust of professors, experts and theorists that would stay with him for life. One
Trinity man reciprocated, finding him 'remarkable for nothing but
making a good fire'.[3] The Church of Ireland was Swift's chosen
career. His fellow-clergymen never questioned his devotion to their
institution, but often wondered whether he was in his beliefs any
kind of Christian at all. His early book A Tale of a Tub shocked
many with its apparent blasphemies and formal audacity. The
English queen, having read it, felt unable to recommend the author
for anything. Many thought Swift an arrant nihilist: yet his despon-
dency was utterly connected to his religious experience rather than
being based on any kind of alternative, secular analysis. As a young
clergyman in Kilroot, County Antrim, he had seen Anglican churches
despoiled, bishoprics reserved for mediocre Englishmen, and tithes
reduced as the economy failed and the numbers of Dissenters grew.
His sermons there were, he said, 'for a church without a company or

a roof'.[4] Out of this humiliating initiation, he developed a sense of solidarity with lower clergy as against bishops and a rooted distrust of autocratic English careerists. Ireland might be displaying its fatal propensity to turn even the more humane Englishmen into tyrants, but already it was converting Swift into a radical critic of power elites.

Back in England where he worked for Sir William Temple, Swift rapidly proved his abilities as a propagandist, helping to take the country out of an expensive Continental war: but he was ill rewarded. In fact he felt infantilized by all the fawning on royals, lords and ministers necessary to a career: so much so that he would later warn his friend Bolingbroke against assuming a cold severity such as that with which schoolboys might be treated. He was astute enough to notice the low regard in which English people held visitors from the neighbouring kingdom: 'The Irish brogue is no sooner discovered, than it makes the deliverer in the last degree ridiculous and despised; and from such a mouth an Englishman expects nothing but bulls, blunders and follies.'[5] He warned Irish gentlemen to avoid speaking Irish, the fatal source of that brogue; but he couldn't help criticizing the Anglo-Irish landlords for their absenteeism, 'thinking themselves too good to live in the country which gave them birth and rather choosing to pass their days among those who heartily despise them'.[6] Swift would reverse that trajectory, passing over to a despised Ireland where he would in time be acclaimed as a popular patriotic hero. In England, for all his gifts, his central experience had been one of frustration. Even before the reversal of all his ambitions, he could sense his fate. Almost two centuries before Oscar Wilde, he knew what it meant when people called him by his forename. 'They call me nothing but Jonathan, and I said, I believe they would leave me a Jonathan as they found me.'[7] As they duly did. Among the giants of London he was a mere spectator, a nobody; among the pygmies of Ireland, he might cut a figure yet. His very predicament in England seemed to prove that he must really be an Irishman: or, as he said to Francis Grant, 'I am a Teague, or an Irishman, or what people please.'[8] Yet the man who penned that line had bolted for England with the best of them at the outbreak of war in Ireland in 1689.

What exactly were the politics of Swift? The very slippage in the terms of his self-description just quoted suggests that he hardly knew himself. History would reveal that he was at once a frustrated loyalist and a precursor nationalist. He railed against the inefficiency and incompleteness of the anglicization process in Ireland and, having despaired of it, he seems in later years to have sought impatriation among the Irish. An early work of 1707 (cannily withheld from publication at a time when he still hoped for English success) was an allegorical account of the wrongs endured by Ireland: 'The Story of an Injured Lady Written by Herself'.[9] This *anti-aisling* plays with the personification of Ireland as victimized woman so prevalent from the days of the *filí* to Ó Rathaille: but this woman is loyal in a way that no *spéirbhean* (skywoman) ever was – she rejects the Pretender and France. She has been abused by her intended partner (that England which refuses a Union such as Scotland is to enjoy) and has instead seen her estate reduced by stewards. In Swift's eyes these middlemen lived off parasitical rents while producing nothing themselves. The Lady wants nothing more than a proper marriage, of the kind that had been envisaged by William Molyneux in 1698 when he urged that Ireland be treated as an equal rather than depending kingdom under the crown. (His pamphlet was burned by the common hang-man.)[10]

By 1707 such a request was tantamount to treason, and so Swift borrowed a device of Gaelic tradition to humanize the political relation between England and Ireland and to 'appeal to political decency' in the face of a broken contract.[11] Even as the contractual imagery testified to his Protestant biblical training, the woman-image identified the author with an old Irish tradition. The very gesture that seeks assimilation seems written in a language which repudiates that possibility. To imagine Ireland as female was in effect to take sides.

The tract ends with a friend counselling the Lady. If her resolutions fail, he promises to think of something that will be more effectual – a veiled threat that the loyalty of the Anglo-Irish might snap, leaving them at one with the mere Irish. Some Gaelic poets had imagined the wronged woman as also 'fallen' – the harlot figure again – and so it is here. Swift emulates such poets in suggesting that the lady somehow deserves the fate against which none the less he protests. That ambivalence would mark all his later judgements of the Irish people, making him in George Orwell's memorable phrase a Tory Anarchist, at once conservative moralist and cheeky rebel. He returned to live among the Irish as Dean of St Patrick's Cathedral, a post which he thought beneath him but which he held with such distinction as to leave him the most famous Dubliner of the century.

At the core of Swift's case against English policy in Ireland was an allegation of inefficiency. Through most of his life the Penal Laws against Catholics were on the statute-book, maintaining a system of apartheid between the one-fifth Anglican minority and the rest of the population. Catholics could not become lawyers, purchase land, bear swords or firearms, own a horse worth more than five pounds, employ more than two apprentices. Catholic schools and seminaries were banned, and in 1719 the Irish Privy Council recommended the castration of all unregistered priests, a black joke against clerical celibacy. The House of Commons reduced the enactment to branding all priests with the letter *P*.[12] The Lord Chancellor opined that the law supposed no such person to exist as a Roman Catholic. Yet four-fifths of the population, despite this judicial fantasy, continued to eat, breathe and go about business.

The laws were indeed ferocious. The violence of their language may at times have been rhetorical in a land that lacked a fully compliant police force or, for that matter, a comprehensive system of prisons. The enactments were despicable, but have been read by some commentators as exercises in a radical irony which Swift would soon parody.[13] That irony arose from the discrepancy between the official version of reality and the actual state in which people lived. That affected both sides. Gaelic poets sang about Cathleen Ní Houlihan when they really meant to celebrate Ireland; or they decried the felling of the woods when what they truly lamented was the fall of a native aristocracy, whose rebel sons still found shelter in what forests remained; or they implored women to shelter gallants from the storm, the gallants being rebels and the storm English fire-power. On the ascendancy side, laws were equally ambivalent. Catholics were compelled to work on their own church holidays, but justices and constables who refused to implement that law were to be jailed. In the words of Andrew Carpenter, the very law which outlaws the Catholics seems to concede the impossibility of its own application: 'The law acknowledges that it is merely one way of looking at life and seems to accept that the other perspective is *de facto* to remain in existence.'[14] One penal statute maintained that maidens who married Roman Catholics ('to the great dishonour of almighty God') were to be considered dead (though the usual number continued to breathe). The enactments were on occasion a rather shrill attempt to substitute moral authority for physical power: and the harshness of some laws may have been a sign of their inoperability. Yet the world of the demented 'projector', which would be mocked so harshly by Swift, was latent in these measures of manic, racist wish-fulfilment.

Swift never denounced the code as penal and will never be forgiven by some writers for that failure, but he wrote with real eloquence castigating its social effects. Although the well-being of his own church was tied to that of ascendancy landlords, he denounced each one for avarice and oppression, and for acting the part of 'a tyrant in the neighbourhood over slaves and beggars, whom he calleth his tenants'.[15] Given that Swift believed popery to be a system of superstitions and that he profited from land rents in rural Ireland after appointment as dean, this may have been as far as he felt he could go. He supported charter schools for Catholic children, but only if they trained them to be servants to Protestant gentlemen: any educating of them above their station was wicked.[16] Yet, since the whole colonial system tried to justify itself as an improvement of agricultural holdings and land use, Swift's indictment of neglectful or absentee landlords carried a subversive, long-term implication. 'By unmeasurable screwing and racking their tenants all over the kingdom,' he charged, 'they have already reduced the miserable people to a worse condition than the peasants in France.'[17] Properly managed, the land could easily support four times its current population.[18]

The problem was pastoralism: the replacement of tillage by grazing and the usurpation of men by mere animals. Although economic theorists still held that the wealth of a nation lay in its people, that rule seemed to have no application in Ireland. People, Protestant as well as Catholic, were leaving in droves. Much of Swift's later writing derives its charge from his strong feeling on this point: the prioritizing of animals over humans, the suggestion that man's only chance in life is to compete on level terms with beasts. The Archbishop of Dublin bore Swift out in a letter written in 1718: 'One half of the people in Ireland eat neither bread nor flesh for one half of the year, nor wear shoes nor stockings; your hogs in England and Essex calves lie and have better than they.'[19] Grazing was less expensive for landlords than tillage, but it was (said Swift) 'an absurdity that a *wild Irishman* would be ashamed of'.[20] Restrictions by England on the wool and cattle trade (wool was sent for processing to English manufacturers) further reduced profits, inducing Swift's rage against pastoralism: 'Ajax was mad when he mistook a flock of sheep for his enemies: but we shall never be sober until we have the same way of thinking.'[21] The poet who liked to reveal the carcass beneath a cosmetic female beauty was anxious to replace idealized images of Augustan landscape with a truer account.[22] English painters could afford to indulge sentiment, but Irish writers had to be realists from economic necessity. In this process Swift substituted good journalism for poetry, raising discursive prose to an artistic form. 'I never yet saw in Ireland a spot of earth two feet wide, that had not in it something to displease.'[23] The Injured Lady was all too like the land: overploughed by heedless tenants without respect for her future and then set aside as hopeless.

Many of Swift's anxieties – about economy, agriculture, sexuality, art itself – found a focus in the female body, which was a sort of mannequin symbolizing the real state of a national culture. Clothing

in the eighteenth century was a subject of energetic debate and the
new power of a social group manifested itself in props (snuffboxes,
watches, cases, lorgnettes, wigs).[24] To be aware of one's appearance
was not seen as self-regarding, provided that one dressed to one's station. Swift, however, was enraged by the propensity of many
Irishwomen to disdain products from their own country and to buy
costly imports. His views were shaped by the plight of unemployed
weavers near his house in the Liberties of Dublin: on a notorious
occasion one of these men spat on ladies in foreign clothes. Swift
advised the Irish House of Commons 'to exclude all silks, velvets,
calicoes, and the whole lexicon of female fripperies' and declared
opponents of the measure 'an enemy to the nation'.[25] Eventually, he
would urge men as well as women 'never to appear with one single
shred that comes from England' – an anticipation by over one hundred and fifty years of Douglas Hyde's call to Gaelic enthusiasts for
a programme of self-help initiated by the wearing of homespuns.[26]

The new money economy had brought with it a pursuit of luxury
which distressed traditionalists. The rural landscape, like the cities,
was being 'improved' for the delectation of those with money to pay
for new pleasures. In a similar fashion, the bodies of women bore
increasing evidence of the wealth of families. Swift's attacks on frippery have often been dismissed as examples of pure misogyny or of
ways of defending himself against the guilty attraction he felt
towards the female body. They might better be read as critiques of
corrupt consumerism. He believed after all in intellectual equality
between men and women: and he objected (as did many Gaelic
poets) to the fetishizing of the woman's body by puritan merchants.
His desire was for what was honest, candid and unadorned: things in
their natural shape were good and became corrupt only with refinement. Those wives who used foreign drugs, costumes and cosmetics
'spend the revenue of a moderate family to adorn a nauseous
unwholesome living carcass'.[27] His poems often dismantle the fetish
created for the pleasure of males less intrepid than he:

> Four storeys climbing to her bow'r;
> Then, seated on a three-legg'd chair,
> Takes off her artificial hair.[28]

Such strictures were not peculiar to Swift. Bishop Berkeley asked
in *The Querist* whether 'an Irish lady, set out with French silks and
Flanders lace, may not be said to consume more beef than a hundred
of our labouring peasants'.[29] The venom with which Swift wrote of
such pampered belles was very detailed:

Now listen while he next produces,
The various combs for various uses,
Filled up with dirt so closely fixed,
No brush could force a way betwixt . . .

or

A glass that can to sight disclose
The smallest worm in Celia's nose,
And faithfully direct her nail
To squeeze it out from head to tail . . .[30]

This connects with the nausea felt by Lemuel Gulliver at the magnification of the female breasts among the giants: but it also anticipates the Gaelic satire by Art Mac Cumhaigh against the flashy women of a family grown rich on distilling. Here are lines from 'Bodaigh na hEorna' (The Churls of the Barley):

Níl aon chailleach bhuí chrón a lásaibh ag stró
   Dá gcruinneoidh dornán saibhris,
Nach mbeadh síoda 'gus sról agus sciorta ar a tóin,
   Agus putóg nó dhó ina héadan.

Is tócúil an tseoid níon bodaigh sa ród
   Is cha ghlacann sí cóiriú Gaelach,
Mur mbeadh hata uirthi ar dóigh, is crios air den ór,
   Is cleite ag treabhadh na gaoithe.

Na sneadh 'na ndornaibh casta 'na cóip,
   A putóg 's ag dortadh dréise,
Is amach ona srón teacht theas na Féil' Eoin
   Go bhfaicfí an míol mór 's é ag aoibheall.[31]

There is no tanned hag struggling in her laces who, if she gathers a fistful of money, doesn't start wearing silk and satin and a skirt on her bum, and a ringlet or two down her forehead.

The churl's daughter is a proud jewel on the road and she refuses to wear Gaelic styles, but prefers a hat of fashion and a golden chain and a feather ploughing the wind.

The nits come out in fistfuls from her and her ringlets drip with grease. Out from her nose on the feast of St John, the great monster snot comes gadding.

Swift had a lot in common with Gaelic poets. Like them, he felt himself to be writing out of a tradition in danger of imminent collapse, and he used animal images to render the predators of the new money order. In such a predicament, options were limited and it was difficult to articulate even those values that were in eclipse, and so Swift, like his Gaelic counterparts, often chose to offer mocking impersonations of the hated enemy. This is why their works take bad new writing as a literal pre-text, accused of driving out the good: the bitter invective of an Ó Bruadair or of *Pairlement Chloinne Tomáis* would have resonated with the Dean. The battle of the books between ancients and moderns was being fought in both languages and not just between them. Swift's famous contrast between the bee, who turned available forms into sweetness and light, and the spider, who selfishly refused any obligation to tradition or environment, was rehearsed in many Gaelic lyrics. Uilliam Óg Mac an Bhaird had, as early as the 1570s, compared the Irish to noble bees whose honey has been stolen by thieves.[32]

Equally, the satire written in both Irish and English was directed at pushy *arrivistes*, pretenders to learning and taste, who might now enjoy power but could none the less be cursed according to the tradition of the *aoir* (satire), which left physical marks on the victim. Swift's octosyllabic couplets against two Dublin politicians perfectly invoke the remedy:

> *Both are apt to be unruly,*
> *Lash them daily, lash them duly;*
> *Though 'tis hopeless to reclaim them,*
> *Scorpion rods perhaps may tame them.*[33]

The Dean shared with Gaelic scholars a fear that language itself was in decline. Like them he resorted frequently to the use of word-lists and inventories, even within poems, as a half-conscious attempt to save idioms from eclipse. Both sides called for the 'fixing' of their languages by dictionaries – yet Swift rather touchingly failed to realize that his own writings would be of far more value in preserving the energies of his language. Here, at least, the Gaelic writers were one step ahead of him.[34]

Swift clearly knew some Irish, for his 'Dialogue in Hybernian Style' is a witty exemplification of the many loan-words rapidly entering English usage in the period. His version of 'Pléaráca na Ruarcach' (O'Rourke's Feast), while it may be based on a prose crib, captures the sound-music of the lyrics (for instance, 'glug, glug i na mbróg' becomes 'splish, splash in their pumps').[35] His verse contestations with his friend Thomas Sheridan are very much in the

tradition of *Iomarbhá na bhFilí*: and his visits to Sheridan's rather
decrepit home in Quilca, County Cavan – the roof leaked and the fire
smoked – were marked by real *bonhomie* with local characters.
Sheridan later recorded such visits in verse:

> *So far forgetting his old station,*
> *He seems to like their conversation.*
> *Conforming to the tatter'd rabble,*
> *He learns their Irish tongue to gabble.*[36]

While sojourning there, Swift was amused by the discrepancy in size
between the massive labourers on Sheridan's farm and the dwarf-like
workers on the lands of the nearby Brooke family. Whether or not he
heard those field labourers sing the great Gaelic lament for fallen
forests 'Cill Cais' (later to be published by Charlotte Brooke in
Reliques of Irish Poetry),[37] he would certainly have been told how
deeply the cutting down of the woods violated the rural community's
sense of propriety. Like Edmund Burke in later years, whenever he
needed a metaphor for the state or its economy, he often described it
in terms of a slow-maturing tree lopped before its due time. It was
yet another image shared with the Gaelic poets: whilst Ó Rathaille
observed the 'upstart' planters huckstering the woods 'at sixpence a
tree',[38] Swift would defend the Irish economy against Wood's brass
money by saying that 'now that the branches are all cut off, Woods
stands ready with his axe at the root.'[39]

Folk tradition claims to record one meeting between the two great
Irish satirists of the age. It may well be fabrication, but even as such
would tell us what ordinary people wished to believe. Hearing that the
Dean was in Kerry, Ó Rathaille disguised himself as a herdsman; as
Swift passed, he began to talk to one cow in Greek, to another in
Latin, to the next in Irish, and so on. 'The herds here speak seven
languages,' marvelled the Dean, aghast: 'what must their scholars be
like?' Unwilling to find out, he scurried back to the capital.[40] The ease
with which tales about 'the Dane' entered Gaelic lore suggests that
Swift's increasing identification with the Irish was understood and
welcomed. Though appalled by their submission to so many disasters
brought on by English policy, he often wrote about the ordinary
people with a tenderness that never informed his comments on landlords. Pouring scorn on racist theories that the Irish were inherently
lazy, unproductive, even cannibalistic, he suggested that the real
man-eaters came from outside. The defects of the people were not
innate, 'arising only from the poverty and slavery they suffer from their
inhuman neighbours'.[41] For hinting at the reasons for his accusations,

Swift found that the printers of a pamphlet like his *A Short View of the State of Ireland* could be prosecuted and jailed, so he needed to be careful. In letters he was more candid, remarking thus to John Gay:

> Here I will define Ireland a region of good eating and drinking, of tolerable company, where a man from England may sojourn some years with pleasure, make a fortune, and then return home, with the spoils he has got by doing us all the mischief he can, and by that make a merit at court.'[42]

Swift never wanted to be Dean and felt himself a sort of 'exile' in the land of his birth. Yet he soon found that this was a plight shared with dispossessed Gaelic aristocrats, evicted cottiers and even those Anglo-Irish professional men who lost out to the English interest. An England under the Whig oligarchy established in 1714 could hardly be called 'home'. Swift experienced the telltale distress of the colonial expatriate at the failure of the mother country to remain as it was. At the same time, he felt an interloper among the mere Irish, along with a real affinity with their Gaelic culture now in apparent decline. This aloofness from both cultures, this homelessness of mind, accounts for the coldly anthropological strain in Swift, his willingness to ask questions *of* a culture and not just *within* it.[43] Such questions include: what kind of a creature is mankind? It was as if his experience enabled the writer to take a stance beyond culture, perhaps even above it. His foremost biographer believes that this was his way of responding to Ireland's littleness: 'To dignify Irish politics, one had to see them not as directing a nation but as testing mankind.'[44] It may be that he had little choice, for he could sense from the start that no culture in Ireland had truly official status. There was unofficial – and unofficialer. Other Anglo-Irish artists from Goldsmith to Yeats would find themselves grappling with similar themes; and later Anglo-Irish political leaders like Parnell would find that it was a condition of their headship of the nation that they should never be allowed to feel fully at home in it.

For the Anglo-Irish, impatriation could never be total. 'I am only a favourite of my old friends the rabble', Swift wrote in a letter, 'and I return their love, because I know none else who deserve it.'[45] Most of his friendships were in fact with persons of middle rank, affording him a good opportunity to sense the cohesiveness of the emerging Irish polity. In time he came to enjoy the experience of being 'rather a freeman among slaves than a slave among freemen' (as he said to Gay).[46] But his sympathies, though extensive, were never unconditional. That is clear from his proposal to issue the beggars of Dublin with badges for the purposes of identification and regulation.

While his Anglo-Irish coreligionists were building country houses with the look of eternity about them, Swift wrote like one who knew that their tenure was utterly provisional. Colonial decorum could never mask the sheer anxiety of a power that was already deeply divided against itself. The resulting personality, 'as anxious as it is assertive',[47] was no sooner able to declare its mastery than it found it eroded – an apt account of the narrative strategies that would link *Gulliver's Travels* and *A Modest Proposal*. The world of Gulliver, like the Ireland of Swift, is a place where the observer all of a sudden becomes the observed, while 'the look of surveillance returns as the displacing gaze of the disciplined'[48] (as in the story of the encounter with Ó Rathaille). In such a place, it makes little sense to speak of official culture – all are in contention. Even as the planter writes back to the homeland, he may feel himself going native, gabbling the local tongue, lapsing into brogue. If he is alert to danger, he may wonder whether he may be falling into the chasm between two cultures, a perilous zone in which all restraints could be lost.

For the plain fact was that Swift was not English. He could only ever hope to be *anglicized*, a flawed mimesis of the real thing. Such a figure was born to be a parodist of the available forms, initially in a serious attempt at their imitation:

> *If you have London still by heart,*
> *We'll make a small one here by Art.*
> *The difference is not much between*
> *St James's Park and Stephen's Green.*[49]

Later, this would turn into a corrosive mockery of all attempts at 'mastery':

> *Instead of Bolingbroke and Anna*
> *Shane Tunnelly and Brian Granna.*[50]

Sheridan (who wrote that couplet) encouraged Swift to create an alternative set of criteria by which all masters would seem weak, presumptuous and foolish. That is why Swift's use of forms – travelogues, *contes*, philosophical treatises, economic tracts – was always somewhat mocking. He pulverized each to the point where it was almost unrecognizable, often doing so by an intergeneric conflation of one with another. His mimicry emerges, therefore, 'as the representation of a difference that is itself a process of disavowal' by one colonial of the code he is supposed to represent.[51] Swift was much too sharp an observer not to have noticed how the ordinary

Irish themselves were learning the same sort of trick: both city and country were awash with macaronic songs and poems that often disrupted the settled authority of both languages. He was a keen student of fetishes and knew well how they could mimic an authority in the very act of deauthorizing it. What else was afoot in those poems of his which dismantled the cosmetic femininity of the period? But the same unmasking might be done to the colonial authority itself, whose culture was 'potentially and strategically an insurgent counter-appeal'.[52] It is just such an appeal that lies behind the *Drapier's Letters*.

In 1724 an English tradesman named Wood, by bribing a lady of title, won the right to produce coins for Ireland to the value of £100,800, over one-quarter of the currency supply. The Irish were not consulted. The patent allowed Wood a vast, unreasonable profit, even as the low value of his brass halfpence posed a serious threat to the nation's gold and silver supply. The executive in Dublin was deeply opposed to the measure and set out to break the patent, but it was Swift who wrote the words of opposition which seared themselves into popular memory. Even more important, his pamphlets forged an unprecedented alliance between the administration and the common people, which would have long-term effects more lasting than any he had dreamed of. Not only would his face grace many a shop-sign and his birthday be marked by the ringing of bells across Dublin, but in later years the arguments he used would be appropriated by Irish and American patriots, helping to undermine the very institutions of English power.

Swift believed that the Irish should strike their own coin. Four years earlier, just before the official celebrations of the sixtieth birthday of King George, he had printed a sentence urging his fellow citizens to 'burn everything that comes from England except their people and their coals'.[53] Now he adopted the mask of a Dublin draper in order to play upon the fear and anger of the city's tradesmen. Such a figure was cannily chosen. As one of the middle rank, he could appeal to other shopkeepers but also to those higher on the social scale than himself. Moreover, as a man paid to see his customers as they really were before donning those clothes that marked one class off from another, he was able to appeal to a common humanity.[54] Being neither rich nor poor, the Drapier could afford to be civic-minded and argue for the social good.

The Drapier's early pamphlets are in the candid style of one who favours plain clothes and unfussy learning; but with each success Swift grew more intrepid, deliberately complicating his approach, even to the point of condescending to his Drapier persona. It was as if he really wanted his readers to savour the delicious danger of a major ecclesiastic donning a rebel mask. Caught between a self and a role, Swift enjoyed the ambiguity, and especially those moments when his mask slipped just a little to reveal the laughing face beneath. That mask freed him to be far more resourceful, playful and creative than he had ever been when he wrote under his own name. His appeal was to a very Protestant notion of contract: Ireland no more depended on England than England did on Ireland, for both were sovereign kingdoms subject not to the parliament of London but to the crown. This view, taken also in the poems of Ó Rathaille and Ó Bruadair, had been articulated most memorably by William Molyneux: 'we are in a miserable condition indeed, if we may not be allow'd to complain, when we think we are hurt'.[55] Now, Swift suggests, even a man on the rack may be refused the liberty of roaring as loudly as he thinks fit. Through the decades, Swift's physical sufferings would seem to be assimilated to those of the ordinary people; and he was not slow to exploit the image of a martyr, denied even the right to give voice to his torment. What amused him in the midst of pain, however, was the fact that lawful protest might carry a whiff of treason. Here was another case of the Tory Anarchist, 'an extraordinary example of the application of irony to mass action'.[56]

Although he was writing in the role of a trader, Swift dealt with Wood in the same tone with which Gaelic poets condescended to the 'upstart' planters. He pointed to the anomaly of an English regime that set one insignificant hardware man above the dignity of a sovereign nation. He wondered how a great kingdom could be brought to the edge of destruction not by a tyrant prince, 'for we never had one more generous', but by an 'insignificant mechanic'.[57] In the early pamphlets, Swift addressed his coreligionists as victims of a broken contract: his repeated references to 'brass' touched on a word associated with the hated Stuart dynasty. With each pamphlet, however, he grew more bold and more extensive in his address, until by the fourth he was appealing beyond the Protestant interest to 'the whole people of Ireland'.

Here he suggests that the English prime minister Walpole would need 50,000 operatives to force the coin down Irish throats; he mischievously attributes to Walpole the charge that the Irish now seek 'to shake off their dependence upon the crown of England'.[58] He, on the contrary, protests himself to be a rebel loyalist, appealing to the monarch for protection from the political elite. 'Am I a freeman in England, and do I become a slave in six hours, by crossing the channel?' This claim made little sense in terms of existing English law, but it did invoke *tradition*, a force which, for Swift as for Gaelic poets, was more telling. On that ancient basis he would make a thoroughly modern proposition: that 'all government without the consent of the governed is the very definition of slavery'.[59]

Here, in clear language, was the insurgent counter-appeal. A man of Swift's intelligence must have grasped the obvious application of his precept to the disenfranchised four-fifths majority in Ireland. No wonder that, over a century later, the English conservative Walter Bagehot could call the *Drapier's Letters* absurd: 'a clever appeal to ridiculous prejudices'.[60] Swift's language must have frightened even those Anglo-Irish administrators who opposed the patent, for the limited authority they had did not derive from the common people and would crumble as soon as those people were united. A jury in Dublin, convened to try the printer, refused to present; a second panel sat only to return a verdict against the fraud perpetrated by the English government. They had been warned by Swift that Wood was no more than a well-rewarded stooge: the real power lay with the prime minister Walpole. A large sum of money was offered for information leading to the discovery of the Drapier's real identity, but no Dublin workman could be found to betray Swift. It was his finest hour, as the patent fell.

Wood was quietly paid off with £24,000 in compensation, but Swift had turned a set of disparate Irish groupings into a people capable of purposeful action. He may not have intended so much at the outset: events, however, acquired a momentum of their own. His expressions of nationality were largely instinctual: only later would they achieve conceptualization. It was as if he had assumed the existence of a patriotic entity named 'Ireland' in order to prove a constitutional and economic one. Having willed it into being, he could not walk away from it. The Drapier would pass into history: the nation was waiting to be born. Three years later, he tried honestly to explain the problems of Ireland to Walpole, but it was 'a dose to the dead'.[61] Whether he meant to imply that Ireland or Walpole was dead is still not fully clear. When, at the end of the century, Theobald Wolfe Tone gave a classic definition to the modern Irish nation, he attributed its evolution to sentiment evoked among the 'middling ranks' by writers like Swift.[62] In the nineteenth century, the Dean would be praised as the founder of Anglo-Irish literature, 'the first Anglo-Irish writer who felt that he was an Irishman'.[63] Later still he would be celebrated as a wily subversive who pleased the Young Ireland movement by the skill with which he used Anglo-Irish ballads, turning them like captured weapons against the English interest.[64]

7

Home and Away:
Gulliver's Travels

Like many another classic, *Gulliver's Travels* has been filed by nervous adults under the heading of Children's Literature. In this way the authorities have managed to recognize its entertainment value and, at the same time, to deflect its satiric ferocity. It is, all the same, a strange fate for a book whose author was accused of having 'blasphemed a nature a little lower than that of the angels and assumed by far higher than they'.[1]

Swift was fearful of the future and uninterested in children. The young were hardly on his mind as an intended audience, though he made it clear that his book was for 'the vulgar more than the learned'.[2] Yet they have always been far less frightened than adults when confronted with its scenes. Those to whom the world seems very big can enjoy the joke of looking down on Lilliputians or in pondering the fate of a grown man trapped in a child's body. Those who play in dirt may relish the nervousness of Gulliver about Yahoos or the idea of animals taking control of a society.[3] Such inversions make children laugh as they see a middle-aged ship's captain reduced to the condition of an infant, in need of care, tuition and protection. Yet coded into the story is an insuperable truth known to children, if not always admitted by adults: that size matters. The little people are vain, the large ones dignified, and the child eavesdrops on the book knowing that its intended adult reader is expected to identify with the bigger people in every chapter.

An Irish reader may feel like a similar sort of eavesdropper on a tale that sometimes reads like a document in Swift's private quarrel with those English who spurned him. He must have felt a thrill as he deposited with the London printer a text which contained the King of Brobdingnag's verdict on England: 'I cannot but conclude the bulk of your natives to be the most pernicious race of little odious vermin that nature ever suffered to crawl upon the surface of the earth.'[4]

The *Travels* were written by a man who had just won a great victory for Ireland and was relaxing into the role of Hibernian patriot. The early drafts were completed at Quilca in the company of Thomas Sheridan, a great lover of jokes and squibs. Sheridan liked to chide Swift for his earlier career as an honorary Englishman:

> *He seems to gain by his distress,*
> *His friends are more, his honours less.*[5]

It would not be surprising if such a critique of power elites were one of the book's major themes.

Sheridan's son certainly thought so: 'As to the upper class of mankind, he looked upon them as incorrigible, and therefore had scarce any intercourse with them.'[6] More than one critic has urged us to read *Gulliver's Travels* as yet another of the Irish Tracts, a further anatomy of human perversity.[7] Once again, the Irish offer Swift a version of the dilemma of all humans, whose cruelty to one another, though awful, is as nothing compared with the cruelty of *being human*. Their sufferings seem deserved, because provoked by their own weakness, yet unfair, in so far as the uncontrolled punishment always exceeds the crime. Beyond these anthropological analyses, however, it may also be possible to read *Gulliver's Travels* as a study in avoidable suffering brought on by projectors and professors, with Ireland cast in the role of a spectacular victim of *theory*.

Most travel books of Swift's age used a distant society to expose the limitations of a home country. Many were also narratives of discovery. Although Gulliver sets out with a rather condescending English view of foreigners, he does not seek to discover anything or bring home major booty, preferring to learn the customs of faraway peoples who, for all their strangeness, seem rather like those at home. The comparison between 'home' and 'away' exposes the foreignness of both places. If the object of the English in Ireland was, as Friedrich Engels later wrote, to turn the natives into strangers in their own land,[8] then Swift knew that experience sooner than most. So, *Gulliver's Travels* reads at times as if England had been placed, palimpsest-like, atop of Ireland and the ensuing landscape had been traversed by a slightly paranoid lunatic. After each trip Gulliver is expelled, like his author, for some imagined flaw, rather than being punished for one or other of his real failings.

Gulliver is only at home when travelling or crossing from one zone to another. So also for Swift: Anglo-Irishmen existed fully only on the hyphen between two secure codes. Swift explained to Alexander Pope that the magic lands discovered by Gulliver came to the eye of the mind as he moved from London to Dublin: 'What a quick change I made in seven days from London to the Deanery, through many nations and languages unknown to the civilised world. And I have often reflected in how few hours . . . a man may come upon a people as unknown to him as the Antipodes.'[9] Swift's travels through Ireland, as he worked on the book, help to explain why *Gulliver's Travels* is an exercise in comparative literature, of a kind so often produced by exiles who find themselves estranged from all official codes. The very stories of big people and little people *may* have been suggested by a classic Gaelic tale *Imtheachta Tuaithe Luchra* (The Events of the People of Luchra), in which the king of the leprechauns behaves much like the vain emperor of Lilliput during a visit by Ulstermen, who admire the beautiful, unblemished skin of the natives.[10] However, when the leprechaun-poet Eisirt goes to Ulster, he experiences a life like Gulliver's in Brobdingnag, almost drowning in a container of ale, as did Gulliver in a bowl of cream. The ever-shifting double perspectives allowed by such a tale could be applied also to Anglo-Irish relations, undermining the composure of the English side. *Gulliver's Travels* was an early instance of the empire 'writing back', engaging in reverse anthropology, sitting in judgement on an England that liked to sit in judgement on others.

Gulliver's arrival in Lilliput in Book One might be taken as a version of Swift's in Ireland. (A recent advertisement at the Irish terminal of Heathrow Airport had the English rugby captain urge passers-by to 'Come on over and meet the little people'). There Gulliver is a huge success, marvelled at as almost godlike by the folk. But, equally, the analogy could be with the reception of an Irishman in England, for as the Drapier observed, 'upon the arrival of an Irishman to a county town, I have known crowds coming about him, and wondering to see him look so much better than themselves'.[11] That double-exposure effect will work all through the first two books. Sometimes the 'Irish' Gulliver, as he permits the little people to walk all over him, will convey the sense of a massive destructive power held in check (as if Swift were marvelling at the acquiescence of the Irish majority to the planter elites). At other times, the 'English' Gulliver will himself become the object of a native ethnography, as the Lilliputians try to translate his consultations of his watch ('the god that he worships')[12] into religious meaning. They survey him even as he surveys them: but he implicitly asks us to believe that he knows more of them than they can of him. The naïveté of the Lilliputians lends credence to that view, especially when their pompous ruler describes himself as 'the delight and terror of the universe',[13] a universe no more than twelve miles in extent. The arbitrary nature of all cultural signs is emphasized by Swift's account of wars fought solely on the basis of whether an egg was to be broken at the big or little end: and the deceiving, self-interested nature of official histories is exposed by the fact that all books by Big-Endians have been outlawed in Lilliput.

With his immense strength, Gulliver immobilizes the Blefuscu fleet, prompting the emperor of Lilliput to fantasies of reducing Blefuscu to a province under his own appointed viceroy: but Gulliver refuses on grounds that 'I would never be an instrument of bringing a free and brave people into slavery.'[14] Nothing chastened, the emperor compels some prisoners from Blefuscu to explain themselves in the Lilliputian tongue, an imposition of which Gulliver cannot approve, since he himself is always open to learning the language of a new interlocutor. Yet many of the customs of Lilliput seem to be analogous to practices encountered in rural Ireland; the burying of the dead heads downward in a vertical position (as at Knockarea), the notion that an unjust accusation (or *mallacht*) will rebound on its author, and so on.[15] The people's incredulity at a legal system based on the deterrent power of penalties echoes that of a Gaelic order that preferred to emphasize reward for those who virtuously upheld tradition. Their nurseries for children who are removed from parents recall the fosterage systems under the Brehon Laws. Yet they reject elite hierarchies, believing that notions of truth and justice should be 'in every man's power'.[16] Certain contradictions emerge, however: their honour system, by which Gulliver is named a Nardac, leads a man who was previously 'a stranger to courts' to start pulling rank on others.[17]

Lilliput is, in fact, hopelessly confused in its politics – and in its view of Gulliver. Deciding that his vast consumption of food and goods puts too great a strain on Lilliput's budget, their treasurer seeks his death. The emperor commutes that sentence to the gouging out of his eyes – much as the Privy Council of England commuted the castration of Catholic priests to mere branding of their faces. The metaphor is extended when a friendly secretary tells Gulliver that the real intention is to starve him by degrees, which was effectively what Swift accused the English of doing to Anglo-Ireland. The harsher the emperor's punishments, the more lavish the encomia to his mercy. Swift had not to look far for inspirational analogies: Ireland had been repeatedly told that, as she benefited from the prosecution by England of Continental wars, she must repay that debt by accepting restrictions on trade.[18] Small wonder that, following his courtesy visit to Blefuscu, Gulliver resolves never more to place confidence in princes or ministers.

Although the double-exposure effect is deliberate, the landscape of Lilliput seems more like that of Ireland than that of England. Gulliver feels himself a prisoner there, yet he can warm to its beauty. He has to crouch on entering cabins much as Swift and all visiting gentlemen did in rural Ireland. He strikes fear into the hearts of the rulers of the place, who exploit his talents as far as they can for their purposes; yet in the end he shrewdly refuses to use his immense power either to destroy the emperor or to subjugate the people.

In Book Two, however, Gulliver puts his trust in a prince and offers to teach the king of Brobdingnag how to develop gunpowder and master the world. Such inconsistencies are Swift's earliest hints that the character may be a victim of his satire, as well as its vehicle. Most of Swift's fictions end up by subverting the very orthodoxies they had seemed to embrace, like the travelogues that placed home and host countries in an implied critique of one another. As the book unfolds, it will become harder and harder to know just how much of what Gulliver says is to be taken seriously, and harder still to discover just how much of what survives all mockery may safely be attributed to Swift. Book Two, for instance, offers itself as a history, even as it concedes that all histories are lies compiled by prostitute hacks.

In that book Gulliver, once an opponent of slavery, now prates of the conquests of England. It is as if he begins each new book with his mind a *tabula rasa*, registering little or nothing of his prior experience. So he becomes by Book Four an illustration of the maxim that no colonizer ever believes in colonialism, for his own practice is always dignified by some other name: 'but this description, I confess, doth by no means affect the British nation, who may be an example to the whole world for their wisdom, care and justice in planting colonies'.[19] Here, once again, Swift seems fascinated, as in the *Drapier's Letters*, by those who take on the role of anti-colonial colonialist: 'the coloniser who accepts' (in the words of Albert Memmi), becomes harder and harder to distinguish from 'the coloniser who refuses'.[20] There is something almost hysterical about Gulliver's desperate defence of the British nation: if he were a slightly more complex thinker, the sentence might be taken as sarcasm on his part, but it is safer to attribute that to Swift. Lacking inner depths,

Gulliver is, like most travellers, engrossed in mere surfaces which he finds exhausting enough. He is put to the pin of his collar to adjust to each new situation and, as such, he is a modern type, a personality with a shifting context rather than a character of fixed principle.

That diminished inner life has led some to deny him the status of a novelistic character and to treat him more as a satirical device – but in each particular scene a reader will suspend such disbelief and find him real enough. And the predicaments in which Gulliver finds himself do give rise to much subtle analysis. In Brobdingnag, which may be taken as a picture of what England would have been like had the Tories continued to rule, Gulliver is fêted and treated as a great entertainment. The Irishman who hated being patted on the head as a 'Jonathan' in England was able to infuse some conviction into Gulliver's revolt against such theatricalization: 'I was a favourite of a great king and queen, and the delight of the whole country, but it was upon such a foot as ill became the dignity of human kind.'[21] Yet Swift has seen enough of the 'sly civility' of the natives in Ireland to register the ways in which the surveyed one can suddenly turn surveyor. So, with Gulliver, we watch in fascinated horror as the queen crunches the bones of a skylark between her teeth. Yet to the Brobdingnagians themselves Gulliver appears less than fastidious, boasting of the English scheme of things ('the mistress of arts and arms, the scourge of France')[22] in a style that would come more appropriately from the emperor of Lilliput.

The king of Brobdingnag stands, in truth, a lot closer to Swift's philosophy than does Gulliver. Under his rule the nation engages in no quarrels with nature, being self-sufficient but untainted by the debilitating luxuries and excessive profits that are the effect of foreign trade. The king's caustic commentary on mankind is offered while he is stroking Gulliver – a version of Swift's method which caused him to lash the vice but spare the name. Gulliver, as literalist, learns little in either Lilliput or Brobdingnag: one might expect that the two extremes were established so that a truly Augustan *via media* could be recommended, but Gulliver comes to no such conclusion. Like Swift he can find no norm and is reduced to the *via negativa* of defining mankind in terms of what it is *not*. For most of Book One he could not think himself superior to the vain Lilliputians; and for all of Book Two he cannot concede that he might be inferior to the Brobdingnagians. What might seem at first blush like a stubborn democracy of spirit turns out in the end to be an invincible slowness on the uptake.[23] So when he returns to England, he fails to notice that its people are much the same as himself and insists on calling them pigmies. He is still in a Brobdingnag of the mind.

Nevertheless, Brobdingnag as a device allows Swift to pursue his comparative ethnography. Here the aesthetic dimension is explored by a Gulliver who is nauseated by the monstrous breasts and open pores of the women. English skins, he surmises, appear fair only because not seen through a magnifying-glass. Distance lends enchantment – to the body as much as to England. In Lilliput Gulliver had revealed 'great holes in my skin'[24] to the little people who stood close to him: in the *Imtheachta Tuaithe Luchra* the leprechauns had objected to the ugly skins and smelly breaths of the Ulstermen. As an artist Swift knew that he could see more of humanity than most people considered decent – and that such an intrepid observer would seldom be thanked for looking so closely at things. Yet it is Gulliver rather than the Brobdingnagians who feels diminished by all the comparisons, as when the queen holds him on her hand and they both stand before her looking-glass.

One subject on which Gulliver remains a wise guide is the pretension and uselessness of much learning. As the professors of Brobdingnag pontificate on the diminutive creature before them, theorizing that it might be an embryo or a field animal, he is amused at their retreat into pompous Latin. Swift's memories of Trinity still rankled, and so he has the king dismiss the professoriat. That wise man constructs a critique of human grandeur

> . . . which could be mimicked by such diminutive insects as I: and yet, said he, I dare engage, these creatures have their titles and distinctions of honour, they contrive little nests and burrows, that they call houses and cities . . .[25]

The king is something of an anarchist (like his Lilliputian counterpart) and pronounces himself appalled to learn of the existence of a standing, specialist army among a free people in peacetime England. He denies that government is a refined art to be practised only by experts: whoever can make two ears of corn grow where only one grew before is better than any politician. Being anarchists, the Brobdingnagians have no specialist conception of art or mathematics other than 'what is useful in life'.[26] Likewise in language, they avoid all pedantry, keeping laws terse and comprehensible . . . as opposed to England where they are so convoluted that a caste of lawyers devote all their energies to confounding, perverting and eluding them.

The Flying Island of Laputa is featured in Book Three. It is there that the relationship between England and Ireland is most obviously treated. The Laputans rule over the distressed people of Balnibarbi, who live in rags. Even its landlords who wish to improve things are compelled by Laputan policy to submit to the general demoralization. 'I never knew a soil so unhappily cultivated,' writes Gulliver in a paraphrase of Swift's letters to Pope on the state of Ireland, 'houses so ill contrived and ruinous, or a people whose countenances and habit expressed so much misery and want'.[27] The nobles of Balnibarbi, like absentee landlords, spend much time at court to the neglect of their demesnes. The citizens are constantly on the verge of rebellion, with the consequence that the Laputans are often tempted to lower their island down over the Balnibarbans, crushing them forever. However, they cannot do that lest the adamantine bottom of Laputa be destroyed. This may signal a reluctance to imperil the English monarchy and constitution by an outright military repression of the 'other kingdom'.[28] By a similar analogy, the rebellion sparked in the capital city of Lindalino, when its citizens use magnetic towers to disrupt the path of the Flying Island, seems a version of the Wood's halfpence affair, an example of subjects invoking the authority of monarchy against crown policy itself. Swift understood the relentless reciprocity that bound colonizer to colonized. If Ireland really was a depending kingdom, that dependency might be seen as mutual, for England was nothing without her holdings, and so an effect of Ireland as much as an influence on it. Indeed, the initiative might be said to lie with Balnibarbi, a place controlled by that which it alone controls. The very failure of the English system to transplant itself to Ireland raised, as Seamus Deane has written, radical questions as to the limits of that system itself, with the consequence that Ireland might suddenly emerge as the reader and interpreter of English failure.[29] Swift insists that Laputa cannot survive without Balnibarbi: 'this island cannot move beyond the extent of the dominions below, nor can it rise above the height of four miles'.[30]

Even more radical is the implication that Balnibarbi has been martyred not to political hatred but to demented, misplaced theory. The Laputans are shown to be addicted to intrigue and also to abstraction. Out of touch with reality, their ruling elites feel free to weave crazy administrative fantasies. Balnibarbi is sufficiently distant for them to feel no need to check the theories against human experience: hence its ruinous condition. Yet that authority is weakened by that very remoteness which makes its prescriptions seem possible – for it takes the Laputans eight months to respond to the revolt of Lindalino (much as it took as long for London to come to terms with Dublin over the halfpence). The Flying Island, with its centralized authority in control of the latest scientific methods, finds itself all but helpless when confronted with an intelligently organized rebellion.

The implication was so blatant that this section of Book Three was dropped from all editions published in Swift's lifetime, and for some years after. Yet its inclusion is crucial to the overall unity and meaning of *Gulliver's Travels*, which is a study of the abuse of intellectual and political power.[31] The citizens of Lindalino shut their gates and force the Laputans to give them their demands: the very memory of the Wood affair was subversive, even in the disguise of fiction. Worse still, however, was the linked account of an agricultural landscape, such as Balnibarbi's, when it becomes the playground for deranged projectors of economic theory and for the academy of Lagado (Swift's code-name for Trinity College Dublin). 'The only inconvenience is that none of these projects are yet brought to perfection; and in the meantime, the whole country lies miserably waste, the houses in ruins, and the people without food or cloaths.'[32]

In Swift's view, projectors used a ridiculous jargon which ordinary people couldn't follow in order to hide the poverty of their ideas. The Laputans are absent-minded professors who need blows to the body to bring them back to reality. When they design a suit of clothes, they use quadrants and compasses to bring forth a misshapen article after days of labour. Their cult of expertise has led to a chasm between intellectuals and workmen, with the result that instructions given in too refined a language lead to perpetual mistakes. At Lagado the mad projectors believe that they can extract sunbeams from cucumbers and that they can replace words with things carried around by speakers of a new, universal language. The elaboration of these fantastic programmes can provide a playground for paranoia, as in the kingdom of Tribnia, when its rulers decide to accuse someone of concocting a plot: the suspect's letters are seized and freely decoded, so that any symbol can mean anything else in a sort of surreal nightmare: 'For instance, they can discover a close-stool to signify a privy-council; a flock of geese, a senate; a lame dog, an invader . . .' Similarly, they can deduce political meanings from mere letters of the alphabet: 'Thus N. shall signify a plot; B. a regiment of horse; C. a fleet at sea . . .' This is not just an attack on overinterpretation but a reminder of a time, soon after his arrival in Dublin, when Swift's own post was seized on suspicion that he might be a Jacobite plotter exchanging cryptograms with Francis Atterbury.[33]

Gulliver is a great scourge of professors, having seen the effects of their handiwork. When the governor of Glubbdubdrib calls up the ancient authors, Homer and Aristotle emerge as 'perfect strangers' to their learned commentators. Equally, the noble families thus summoned turn out to have suspect lineages, including fiddlers and barbers in their pedigrees. This mockery of unjustified reputation and unearned wealth is sourced, perhaps, in Swift's own awareness that the Protestant ascendancy in Ireland was nothing more than a random assembly of middle-class careerists, whose influence had been won by dubious means. Far from indicating a civilization on the rise, it signified a world on the wane.

Decay assails Gulliver's eyes everywhere he goes. Compared with the ancients, the moderns prompt him to 'observe how much the race of human kind was degenerated among us, within these hundred years past',[34] due to the debilitating effects on the human body of the pox. That nausea had already been felt by him in Brobdingnag, where the sight of beggars crowding around his carriage 'gave me the most horrible spectacle that ever an European eye beheld'[35] – a leit-motif in Irish writing from Burke to George Moore. Swift's resolute dismissal of the benevolists and optimists of eighteenth-century Ireland was notorious in its day. However, the appalling famines that racked Ireland seemed to bear him out in the century following his death.[36] The few English visitors who came over to Ireland began to understand his meaning.

The projectors of Swift's day – men like Sir William Petty – were meliorists, but for the Dean they simply epitomized an abuse of intellectual powers. 'Professors in most arts and sciences are', he said, 'generally the worst qualified to explain their meanings to those who are not of their tribe.'[37] For him textuality was almost always a form of self-importance, as with the pedantic laws of the Lilliputians: the only possible value of writing was as a guide to right action. Whenever he spoke for the value of concrete experience against the more abstracted forms of knowledge, he included professors in the indictment, for the fate of a country that had become an open-air experimental laboratory in the hands of projectors was argument enough: 'There is not an acre of land in Ireland turned to half its advantage, yet it is better improved than the people; and all these evils are effects of English tyranny, so your sons and grandchildren will find to their sorrow.'[38] No grass grows in Balnibarbi, which is a living refutation of the wise Brobdingnagian monarch's maxim about ears of corn and politicians.

Book Three nears its close with an account of life among the Struldbrugs. Each of these wears a red spot on the forehead, like the *ball seirce* (spot of love) described by Gaelic storytellers, as a sign that they should never die. This section is in the mode of the old *Fiannaíocht* story of how Oisín returned from Tír na nÓg (the Land of Youth) and, setting foot again in Ireland, found himself aged three hundred years in a country that had long since been left by his former comrades, all of them dead. The only thing worse than dying, suggests Gulliver, would be to live forever. The older Struldbrugs lose their social esteem after the age of eighty, and such is the pace of change that they live on as speakers of a dead language. Swift was thinking of elderly Irish-speakers met in the vicinity of Quilca when he has Gulliver describe some Struldbrugs: 'they acquired an additional ghastliness in proportion to the number of their years, which is not to be described'.[39] Eating and drinking without relish or appetite, they are indeed a version of *Oisín i ndiaidh na Féinne* (Oisín after the Fianna). They are also an example of another persistent Irish paradigm for, estranged by their distinctive language from others of their kind, they 'lie under the disadvantage of living like foreigners in their own country'.[40] Gulliver sees them as a potentially valuable object lesson for English people, who might be induced to take warning against the fear of death. The Irish needed no such lessons: for them death was a way of life.

T.S. Eliot described Book Four, the voyage to Houyhnhnmland, as 'one of the greatest triumphs that the human soul has ever achieved'.[41] Here Swift adopts a sort of God's-eye view of the human world, pressing further his thesis on degeneration. Each of Gulliver's voyages suggests that he can learn nothing from an experience of homelessness which must be endlessly repeated, yet there is a suggestion from book to book of the growing depravity of those whom he encounters. At first, he is cast away by chance; next he is abandoned by colleagues; then he is put upon by pirates; and now, as if to enforce the lesson, he is marooned by mutineers. He loves to compare one experience with another, in the conviction that whatever of his original beliefs may survive these challenges will offer a bedrock of sense. What survives by the end of Book Four will be little and strange enough.

Arriving among the Houyhnhnms, whose name means 'perfection of nature' and who appear to be rational horses, he assumes that they must be magical shape-changers – a type common in Gaelic sagas. The Irish-language poets of the period would characterize the turning upside-down of their world in the image of horses who now dictated terms to humans – in the lines of Peadar Ó Doirnín:

> *Ach ó chuaidh an saol fó seach is gur éirigh*
> *An teach ar chléith an mharcaigh fá dheoidh, mar chím . . .*[42]

But since life was overturned and the steed mounted on the rider's breast, as I can discern . . .

What Gulliver encounters is no magic: rather a breed of beings who are incapable of lying and who are so perfectly attuned to the natural world that they 'have not the least idea of books or literature'.[43] The only shadow darkening their world is the foul race of Yahoos, filthy-smelling creatures who pelt Gulliver with excrement.

His main problem is that he appears to be one of them, decently draped (it may be), less hirsute, but in essence akin. That poses a challenge for the Houyhnhnms, much like that posed for the English in Ireland, who felt threatened by the 'white chimpanzees' among the peasantry staring back at them, and who wondered why the Irish were not more like the Africans or Asians. In a letter to the Archbishop of Dublin as he travelled the countryside, Swift wondered 'whether those animals which came in my way with two legs and human faces, clad and erect, be of the same species with what I have seen very like to them in England, as to the outward shape, but differing in their notions'.[44] The Houyhnhnm master 'could hardly believe me to be a right Yahoo, because my body had a different covering from others of my kind'. Yet Gulliver concludes that he must be one, differing only in whiteness, smoothness 'and my affectation of walking continually on my two hinder feet'.[45]

The Houyhnhnms are of course something less than perfect, though Gulliver is only intermittently able to see this. He senses that they, like the projectors, have carried rationalism to a point where it becomes self-defeating: 'I thought it might consist with reason to be less rigorous.'[46] Such manic rationalists will end up being faced by those elements of life that lie beyond reason, and they will be predictably bestial when unleashed. The sleep of reason will bring forth monsters: for if Yahoos had never existed, the Houyhnhnms would have been brought into the world to invent them. Claims to pure reason made little sense amid the disorder of eighteenth-century Ireland: hence that defiant use of animal imagery by its writers.

A major flaw of the Houyhnhnms is their inability to live at peace with Gulliver's liminality: they must assign him to either the Yahoo race or their own. He has a similar problem. They want him to be a higher Yahoo type, while he craves recognition as a Houyhnhnm (attempting to speak like them, presumably avoiding Yahoo brogue); neither he nor they appear to be able to live with ambivalence. The result is a cultural crisis in which he will finally be cast in every conceivable part except his own. But why should he feel obliged to make such a dreary and predictable set of choices? Swift knew only too well that one of the effects of the colonial experiment was to create the illusion that such binary choices were inevitable. Gulliver is a human but he tries to make himself a horse (the animal worshipped by so many Anglo-Irish). Colonialism is revealed to be as daft as that – it teaches the natives how to neigh.

For his abject deference to these horses, Gulliver becomes a butt of Swift's satire. The superiority of horses is assumed rather than proven, a matter more of style than of earned respect. Swift finished this volume after his tour of the south of Ireland. In Book Three (written later still) he would insist that the great families achieved their spoils by theft; and as he witnessed wealth and poverty in close proximity across Munster, he concluded that the Anglo-Irish ascendancy would have seemed mediocre in any other setting. The too-easy submission of the natives to these overlords would later drive the Modest Proposer to despair. It was, however, the coldness of the new master-class that struck him even more forcefully, perhaps because he sensed something of it in himself.[47] The fourth voyage permitted him to express and explore both aspects of the Irish predicament, as well as his own mingled feelings about it. Gulliver's horror at finding in the abominable Yahoos a perfect human figure is all too close to the Swiftian bone. So is his recoil from the overtures of one of their females.

However tangled Swift's response, he wrote of the Yahoos with great honesty. The Yahoos, like Dr Johnson's Irish, never speak well of one another and can learn nothing. Gulliver cannot, therefore, be a Yahoo for, despite his slowness, he learns a lot and that knowledge forms the basis of many cultural comparisons. The Houyhnhnms have concocted a history to legitimate their lordship, according to which the Yahoos are not really aborigines, being traced back rather to the appearance of two brutes produced on a mountainside by the effect of the sun's rays on slime. This sounds suspiciously like Edmund Spenser's insistence that the 'salvage' Irish were nomads and cannibals, without any real title to the land. Earlier books of the *Travels* have already exposed the fact that most official histories are self-flattering fictions: all that will remain for Swift, having thus undermined those of Spenser and Clarendon, is to erode what little authority may survive in his own. That act of undermining will be connected in Swift's mind with his own social and political self-positioning.

The very existence of the Yahoos as such poses immense questions for the Houyhnhnms, whose politics are now so consensual that they have but one remaining debate: whether or not to exterminate the brutes. If they do that, of course, they may abolish the very grounds of their own being, for without the colonized the colonizer is a nobody, a nothing. The Yahoos are both intolerable and indispensable, a little like the Catholic Irish under the Penal Laws. On the surface level, the replacement of aristocratic Gaelic chieftains by middle-class careerists was about as logical as putting horses in charge of humans. At a deeper level, Swift may have sensed that real Gaelic aristocrats featured nowhere in his landscape, since they were fled before his own family arrived: but he would have known enough of the history of that family and of many others to wonder whether the ancestors of the Anglo-Irish were not Yahoos.[48] The thesis had been already advanced by Gaelic authors. Swift's own class position was ambiguous. In England he had hated the coldness assumed by a real aristocrat like Bolingbroke; in Ireland he was distressed by a similar coldness assumed by the Anglo-Irish to the sufferings of the natives. He was not a nobleman himself and so was perfectly willing to question an Anglo-Irish nobility that was not really 'noble' at all.

There is accordingly a double irony in the solemn account of English policy that Gulliver gives to the master Houyhnhnm:

It is a very justifiable cause of a war to invade a country after the people have been wasted by famine, destroyed by pestilence, or embroiled by factions among themselves. It is justifiable to enter into war against our nearest ally, when one of his towns lies convenient for us, or a territory of land that would render our dominions round and complete. If a prince sends forces into a nation, he may lawfully put half of them to death, and make slaves of the rest, in order to civilise and reduce them from their barbarous way of living.[49]

So much for the anti-colonialist Gulliver of Book One, who found such logic refutable on the lips of the emperor of Lilliput.

The Houyhnhnms are anarchists, seemingly so attuned to their environment that they have nothing left to struggle for – no art, no passion, no party politics. George Orwell astutely noted in them a strange blend of the radical and the reactionary, 'despising authority, while disbelieving in liberty'.[50] They have no use for a state, but neither do they care for debate. In that limited sense, they represent one aspect of Swift – the part of him that feared social discord and the irruption of his own subconscious. They are creatures of the daylit world. Their value in this narrative is tactical rather than intrinsic: they exist as a rationalist utopia to expose some flaws of the real world. They remind Swift of all that man is not, or not quite yet. Their utopia, like all utopias, verges at moments perilously close to a dystopia. The critique of professions, whether soldier (a Yahoo hired to kill inoffensive members of his own species) or lawyer (profiteers who represent nothing but their own interests), offered in dialogue with the master Houyhnhnm is impeccable anarchist philosophy, a refinement of much that has gone before in the *Travels*. However, Gulliver parts company with the Houyhnhnms on the difficult issue of social class. Throughout his voyages, he has generally mocked the pretension of any social group to superiority over another (which explains his openness to new languages and customs). England is by Book Four so defamiliarized that its tongue can be called barbarous, even as Gulliver writes in it. However, his anarchist consensus with his master is abruptly broken when Gulliver complains that 'the bulk of our people were forced to live miserably, by labouring every day for small wages to make a few live plentifully'.[50] His interlocutor cannot share his outrage, for the Houyhnhnms have a colour-coded system of social hierarchies.

Given that the whole book is an assault on elitism, the insistence of the Houyhnhnm on special comforts for the leaders of society is a tell-tale flaw. Gulliver inveighs against young noblemen who are 'bred from their childhood in idleness and luxury'.[51] It is, of course, at such noblemen that the book is directed, as the Publisher informs the Reader in the prefatory material – for their amendment if not approbation. Like all believers in hierachy, the Houyhnhnm masters are invincibly complacent, finding fault with Gulliver's body which had seemed perfectly serviceable up to this point. That he should become infatuated with upholders of such an imperfect system is Swift's hint to the reader that Gulliver will end the tale as a target of his satire. True, he does revert to his anti-imperial philosophy in his closing warning against any attempt to colonize Lilliput, Brobdingnag or the Flying Island: and his description of the cynical use of religion to justify plunder might nowadays be called Shavian:

> Here commences a new dominion acquired with a title by *divine right*. Ships are sent with the first opportunity; the natives driven out or destroyed, their princes tortured to discover their gold; a free licence given to all acts of inhumanity and lust, the earth reeking with the blood of its inhabitants: and this execrable crew of butchers employed in so pious an expedition, is a *modern colony* sent to convert and civilise an idolatrous and barbarous people.[52]

However, having produced a perfect account of what England did in the previous century in Ireland, he then embarks on the famous paragraph that begins 'But this description, I confess, doth by no means affect the British nation', before listing those very elements (devout pastors, selfless administrators, virtuous governors) which justify the claim for English superiority first made in Book Two.[53] Gulliver is frankly addled, a cautionary example of the sort of intellectual exhaustion that may overcome any too-travelled protagonist. He shares in the civilized recoil from cannibalism, yet uses Yahoo skin to make a canoe. So this man who genuinely opposed all calibrations of class now glows with pleasure at the very thought of being addressed by a Houyhnhnm and so distinguished from the rest of his species; and when he returns to his family, he can scarcely tolerate the company of those dreadful Yahoos, his wife and children. The enemy of colonialism has become a perfect *colon*, the scourge of social class an inveterate snob. He dreams that someday the horses will come and civilize his own people, the English. Swift wrote these closing passages of the book in an adjoining country to which those horses had already come: and there is little reason at the end to treat them as the perfection of nature. After all, they expel their greatest admirer.

The master Houyhnhnm is appalled to hear of the barbarisms perpetrated by the leaders of England. His diagnosis, however, rebounds on his own breed: for he wonders whether the corruption of the rational faculty in such beings might not be 'worse than brutality itself'[54] Gulliver is equally guilty, of course: in fleeing terrified from the female Yahoo, he denies part of his own humanity. Book Four, like most of what precedes it, is a warning about what is likely to happen to those benevolists and rationalists who try to account for human virtue without reference to original sin.[55] Expecting too much of their fellow beings, they are likely to lapse into misanthropy when schemes fail.

In that regard, *Gulliver's Travels* might be read as a prophecy of the French Revolution and of the terror that followed. Swift could see so deeply into his own time that the shape of the future became discernible: and he could do that because the same irrational attempt to impose a rational theory had been tried in Ireland. The attempt by Gulliver to make himself over as a Houyhnhnm is doomed. To separate reason from emotion in that schematic way was in effect to discredit both: each was bound in its isolation to be cultivated to an unhealthy extreme. The more Gulliver seeks to deny emotion, the more it erupts: that is why Book Four is 'the most passionate denunciation ever penned'[56] His mistake is to make an absolute of one extreme point in the kaleidoscope of ever-changing norms encountered on his voyages, 'reason alone'; as a result, his predilection for mildness and moderation is couched in a language that is ferocious and even violent.

Swift was aware of the need for moderation in all things, even in moderation. The speaker in *A Tale of a Tub* had admitted that the rationalist was often the one who fell at the first fence: 'even I myself, the author of these momentous truths, am a person whose imaginations are hard-mouthed and exceedingly disposed to run away with his reason, which I have observed from long experience to be a very light rider, and easily shook off'.[57] Though not the gravest of divines, Swift was a believer in Christian orthodoxy as something badly needed to repair man's fallen nature. *Gulliver's Travels* is not a dramatization of Christianity but of the need for it in a fluctuating world. In Swift's view religion might express, even if it could never explain, the human mystery. That is why Eliot spoke so highly of Book Four as Swift's greatest work, for it assumes the failure of a secular theory to produce human happiness. Coming from a bleak perspective, Swift believed that, although religion could not be vindicated in theory, its value in practice lay in its ability to keep madness at bay. Even the attempt to establish a notional human norm, uninformed by a sense of God, was likely to end in the rational madness of the Houyhnhnms. The question may then be raised: did Swift believe in belief? The answer is unknowable, for to give it would have been to degrade Christianity to the level of just another theory.

That Swift doesn't want us to endorse Gulliver's misanthropy at the end is clear enough: the protagonist's behaviour to the seamen who save him is understandable but inexcusable. Even when he abuses and rebuffs them, they humbly act in the knowledge that they are responsible for him, thereby saving his life. The text in the reader's hand has often put other texts into question and is now somewhat undercut by the discovery that its author, if no longer mad, is certainly a grumpy old man. If this subverts some of the more superficial satire offered by Gulliver, that is so that an even more radical kind of mockery can now do its work. The consequence is that the reader is asked to supply some sort of mental qualification to the more extreme judgements made by Gulliver all through. In other words, the subversion of textual authority actually works to a moderating effect. Here again is an example of Swift's formal innovation producing rather traditionalist results. *Gulliver's Travels* pleads to be not just read, but reread. Its ironies and doublings work to make an increasingly vigilant reader supply a countervailing or opposing thought.

The deepest irony is this: that Gulliver has tried to transcend the code of his birth only to discover that it and it alone is the instrument by which anything else can be known at all. What is profoundest in life is reached when the dreamer or theorist or traveller is reaching honestly back towards reality: for as Swift had written in *The Examiner*:

> . . . a man may speculatively prefer the constitution of another country, or an utopia of his own, before that of the nation where he is born and lives: yet from considering the dangers of innovation, the corruptions of mankind, and the frequent impossibility of reducing ideas to practice, he may join heartily in preserving the present order of things, and be a true friend to the government already settled.[58]

The two impulses were at work in *Gulliver's Travels*: the anarchist employment of other codes with which to criticize one's own, and then the final, weary acceptance of the established order. But the implication of that sentence just quoted, as of the narrative thrust of *Gulliver's Travels*, is that it was of dubious value to disrupt the Irish order for the sake of a new-fangled theory. Swift's Gulliver knew one big thing which would be discovered again two centuries later by another ethnographer, Claude Lévi-Strauss: that our own society is the only one we can reform without destroying.[59]

Gulliver's Travels never stabilizes itself into the form of a single, identifiable genre: instead it troublingly mingles genres, being part *conte*, part treatise, part travelogue. It is hardly a novel, for the protagonist becomes more and more decentred as the tale proceeds, a man on the periphery of things, so tentative at the end that he seems to retain the views of the last person talked to. As an act of radical parody, the book isn't limited by its targets, however, and provides the intergeneric shape of many later classics of Irish modernism: from Edgeworth to Joyce, from Carleton to Flann O'Brien. In its nihilism about the secular world, it would also be profoundly influential, most of all in its use of one style to annul another and in its final undercutting of its own narrative. Swift's followers would all adopt his sardonic address, treating a joke as a serious matter and a serious matter as a joke. Most would be driven by the extremity of the Irish situation to employ the technique of the Tory Anarchist: using radical experimental methods to project surprisingly traditionalist views.

Never again, however, would a major artist offer quite such an extreme dichotomy between the surface composure of his utterance and the violent rages that tore at the subtext beneath. To find an analogy for that, one would have to turn back to the Gaelic poetry of Ó Rathaille and Ó Bruadair, artists who faced identical technical problems. The classical ideals they had inherited from the *filí* could no longer be embodied or even described in contemporary social terms: they could only be inferred by a savage irony of indirection as existing in a purely imaginary world. Their ultimate ploy in their greatest poems was to employ satire and then to discredit the norms that gave it meaning but patently could not sustain the values off which it fed. They were, quite bluntly, enraged with the ancients for not surviving in better shape, even more than they were contemptuous of the moderns who replaced them – exponents of militant vulgarity, shallowness, dullness. And their method was very like Swift's.

Edward Said has saluted Swift as the first major writer to register the fact that modern literature is simply the displacement of older writing and that a modern author writes, therefore, *during* the loss of a tradition.[60] It is this element which gives such poignancy to the closing pages of *Gulliver's Travels*; the resigned awareness that 'writers of travels, like dictionary-makers, are sunk into oblivion by the weight and bulk of those who come after, and therefore lie uppermost'[61] (a beautifully used verb). They will 'jostle me out of vogue, and stand in my place'. This sense of his own death as an author is what links Swift to Ó Rathaille and the Gaelic poets, a conviction that their words are dying even as they are given birth, that literature itself is but a brief postponement of mortality. Writing, unless it achieves its immediate goals of mending the world, lives on only as a sort of excrement, buried under more.

In Ireland, Swift soon discovered that he was on the wrong side. He himself wrote that 'the great men sent hither from the other side were by no means upon the same foot with his majesty's other subjects in Ireland. They had no common ligament to bind them to us.'[62] The real defenders of tradition, classical learning and ancient morality seemed to be the natives and their artists. Their common guru, Seathrún Céitinn, had compiled his great books to prevent those values from going into oblivion and had also offered 'written imitations of the enemy',[63] imagined as a dung-beetle rolling in mud. Céitinn's rebuttal of Spenser's calumnies informs Gulliver's strictures on false histories and may well have been summarized for Swift by his friend Anthony Raymond, who began work on its translation. What Swift had in common with those Gaelic writers was 'an extraordinarily proleptic sense of himself as a problem for the future',[64] a sense that at the very least they were all bearers of an emotion of loss that would have to be more fully processed by later generations. They were the question to which only the future could be an answer. They could express what their descendants might conceptualize. They understood literature as an attempt to imagine a death.

Ireland was a problem for all writers caught up in it. Its situation converted upholders of Gaelic tradition into protesting rebels; and it turned many among the modernizing colonial intelligentsia into violent traditionalists. A political commitment did not travel easily from one island to the other. Edmund Burke was not the first (or last) to find that the outer Whig did not wholly conceal the inner Jacobite. Swift used masks and narrators in order to conceal his more subversive ideas: and so did the Gaelic poets. Sometimes the man and masks fitted so snugly as to be indistinguishable: and then there was trouble. The ferocity with which Swift spoke from behind the mask of projector, blasphemer or bawd suggested to some that he had lost his critical distance: yet, in truth, he was just illustrating with energetic bitterness how much easier it was to be a modern than an ancient. *Mairg ná fuil ina dhubhthuata* ('Woe to those who are not boors'). He, however, had the luxury (if such it was) of being able to remove the mask and satirize the utterances to which he had just committed such energy: the Gaelic poets could not. Yet he and they endured the daily humiliation of giving their allegiance to a cultural order whose values, they knew, could never be fulfilled.[65]

One effect of the social changes was that upholders of tradition acquired the *cachet* of dissidents, so that apparently monstrous ideas could be put in the mouths of seemingly reasonable speakers and, as a corollary, deeply wise observations could be made to issue from the lips of extremists. This is what links Swift forward to Goldsmith and Burke, for each writes in the tones of a well-bred eighteenth-century gentleman but employs those decorous modes to raise ultimate and shocking questions about what kind of creature man really is. In their hands the modes of Augustan writing are used to write anthropology; this produces a central tradition of Irish Modernism structured around a recognizable personality type – the aristocratic radical, the protesting nostalgist, the dynamic traditionalist, in short the Tory Anarchist. These disjunctions are less a sign of hypocrisy than of the tactics necessary for a cultural worker in a transitional society. Swift would serve, in such terms, as both the founder and the subverter of Anglo-Irish literary tradition.[66]

His biographer, Irwin Ehrenpreis, has noted the paradoxical workings of such a traditionalism. The Dean is described as brave in conscience but timid by instinct, with the result that his most daring ideas were often published discreetly in some distant place. His traditional piety screened, and was screened by, an unconventional personality; and his deceptively simple language was used to convey astoundingly complex thought. Ireland, says Ehrenpreis, stung him into such lucidity, tempering English restraint with

Hibernian exuberance, Anglo-scepticism with Gaelic fantasy.[67] Without it, there would have been no Drapier, no Gulliver, no Modest Proposer. Swift's signed writings can seem official and predictable, while his pseudonymous productions remain open and performative: yet there is a continuity, for the use of masks permits him to explore extremes without succumbing to extremism, to be balanced without being boring. He wrote better when he didn't try to express himself directly: long before Wilde and Yeats, he illustrated the truism that man is least himself when he talks with his own face but, given a mask, is likely to blurt out the truth.

Swift insisted that English visitors see the latent Ireland of suffering and want, as well as the manifest land of hospitality and grace. He feared the unconscious but couldn't help peering into it: he adopted the style of a gentleman to make some very ungentlemanly points. The more his tone presupposed assent, the greater the likelihood that his content would provoke dissent. In the end it was the vitality with which he stated his negations that linked him back to Ó Rathaille and forward to Beckett. Unlike these, however, he turned to God to save the appearances. Nor was his religion just a matter of keeping up appearances, for he hoped that its observance would produce a better reality in time, as men sought to live up to its precepts. He used the surreal juxtapositions of modern ethnography to shock gentle readers and ultimately to enforce a Christian ethic: but he was subtle enough to leave it to be inferred rather than stated. An ancient bee trapped in a flashy spider's web had little choice.

8

Nostalgia as Protest: Goldsmith's 'Deserted Village'

Of all the Irish-born writers of the eighteenth century, Oliver Goldsmith in his life and work most anticipates future developments of the tradition. His youthful travels among the Continental peasantry would be repeated by Synge, even as his abortive career as medical student would be emulated by Joyce. The inner split in his personality between private genius and public humiliation seems to prefigure not just the Marlow of *She Stoops to Conquer* but also the Gar of Brian Friel's *Philadelphia, Here I Come*. Goldsmith's decking of an ungainly body in costly clothes looks forward to Wilde, as does his conviction that man was born for pleasure rather than toil. His most famous poem, 'The Deserted Village', is a protest against the flight from the land and a plea for frugal comfort, such as would animate the speeches of Éamon de Valera and the poetry of W.B. Yeats. Even his uncertain romance with his native country prefigures that of Shaw and of tens of thousands of others.

For all that, commentators have found it difficult to locate him in any identifiably Irish tradition. Seamus Deane has said that Goldsmith viewed Ireland 'almost with the eyes of a foreigner' and that he treated it 'as a slightly exotic variation on the English norm'. His nostalgia was deep but rose-tinted, so that (Deane alleges) 'his is not the Ireland of the penal laws and occasional famines, agrarian disturbances and judicial murders' but a remembered idyll. Compared with such figures as Swift, Burke or Sheridan, he was 'the least affected by national sentiment'.[1] W.B. Yeats was even more caustic, finding it hard to believe that Goldsmith had come out of Ireland at all.[2] Yet 'The Deserted Village' is filled with images of famine, eviction and forced migration, alongside passages of nostalgia for things past (the more dubiously quotable bits which tend to be anthologized in children's school books). And the class tensions of a transitional society lie not far below the surface of *She Stoops to Conquer*. Goldsmith liked to consider himself a citizen of the world, but he was more effortlessly national than many who painted their Irishness on from the outside. Wearing the mask of honorary Englishman, as Beckett would later wear that of Frenchman, he was free to tell the underlying truth about a deeper self.

He was born in 1728 at Pallas, a village in County Longford, but his clergyman father was soon moved to a better living at Lissoy, in County Westmeath. Surrounded by the dispossessed Catholic poor, this kind man found scope for a charitable nature and taught his children to be (in the phrase of one daughter) 'machines of pity'.[3] Oliver, the third of five children, was his mother's favourite. His free hours were spent roaming the fields, and his schooldays were sweetened by a teacher named Thomas Byrne, a retired soldier who told stories of Red Hugh O'Donnell and who recited Virgil's *Eclogues* to the boys. Later, Goldsmith would learn French from a Catholic priest. Interchurch relations, despite the Penal Laws, were good in the area: and the Goldsmiths were of mingled background anyway, for though they were now minor gentry, their ancestors had included a Spanish Catholic priest.

Oliver, though clever, early won a reputation for idleness, buffoonery and practical jokes. At Trinity College Dublin, he was a sizar, which meant that he had to wait on wealthier students at the evening meal, in return for which his board was free. He was also prevented from wearing the magnificent gowns sported by better-off classmates.[4] These wounds rankled and he later wrote: 'it implies a contradiction for men to be at once learning the liberal arts, and at the same time treated as slaves, at once studying freedom and practising servitude'.[5] His subsequent love of fine clothes may have been an attempt not just to distract from his odd face (the chin too short, the mouth massive, the forehead bulging) but also to live down those humiliations. He disliked the lofty pose struck by some Trinity teachers, notably the mathematician Theaker Wilder who broke up more than one of his raucous parties. 'Mathematics seems a science to which the meanest intellects are equal' was his aphoristic revenge.[6]

He often gave what little he had to poor people of Dublin. A classmate one morning found him asleep half-buried in a college mattress, having given his blankets and greatcoat away to a starving woman and her children. Among the poor of London he would often give his own pot of coal to a freezing family. However, some English commentators, from the snobbish Sir Joshua Reynolds to the Marxist Terry Eagleton, have suggested that all this was a disguised form of vanity, rooted in the desire to be admired.

Reynolds said that Goldsmith moved simple people by asking them to treat him as an equal:[7] such a request struck him as sheer vanity, but perhaps Reynolds himself felt demeaned by the thought that rude folk were close to a man who was his particular friend. (The poet William Blake would marvel at the foolishness of Goldsmith in associating with the mandarin Sir Joshua.) Eagleton also sees Goldsmith's charity as an attempt to bolster a tenuous self-hood: his Goldsmith exists only in the good will of English friends, returning otherwise to 'a kind of solitary non-being'.[8] All very convincing, were it not for the fact that Goldsmith's kindnesses were mostly done in secret for poor people, whose opinion could count for nothing in that world. The old Gaelic tradition of *flaithiúlacht*, which he honoured, becomes in the analyses of English critics nothing more than a token of exchange in the making of a reputation.

At Trinity College Dublin, Goldsmith was never wholly comfortable among the gilded youth. He ran away more than once, and when his father died in 1747 he pawned his books and got caught up in a riot. An older brother, Henry, already a clergyman, secured Oliver's return to the college following expulsion, and he eventually got his degree; but even after that, he remained feckless. He wore flaming scarlet breeches when presenting himself for possible ordination to the Bishop of Elphin: perhaps it was a way of telling the world that he wasn't really interested.[9] Deciding to emigrate, he got as far as Cork, where he bought a ticket to America but managed to miss the boat. His relations with his mother were complicated, for he had never bothered to take a formal leave of her. She began to despair of him, until a helpful uncle offered him £50 if he would use it to study law at London's Inner Temple. He got as far as Dublin before losing it all at cards. Eventually, the family prevailed on him to become a medical student at Edinburgh.

Although he seems not to have taken a degree, the experience in Edinburgh was decisive. Already the thinkers of the Scottish Enlightenment were emphasizing the value of feeling over analysis: and from them Goldsmith learned the value of a natural style in speech and writing, free of false refinement yet purged of any vulgarity. His own style of writing would be amenable, easy, user-friendly, drawing attention not to itself but to its object. The lover of ostentatious clothes was never guilty of showy prose. But in

Edinburgh the obsession with clothes only deepened. Goldsmith
affected a scarlet coat, long wig and gold-tipped cane and sword,
prompting bystanders to jibe at 'the fly with the long pin stuck
through it'.[10]

Thus accoutred, he was invited to soirées at the Duke of
Hamilton's, where he was soon a figure of fun more than of elegance.
'They like me more as a jester than as a companion,' he reported
sadly in a letter home. 'I shew'd my talent and acquir'd the name of
the facetious Irishman.'[11] In another letter to his friend Robert
Brizanton, he hinted at some near-irreparable breach with his
mother: '. . . give my service to my mother if you see her for as you
express it in Ireland I have a sneaking kindness for her still.'[12] The
note of distancing qualifies the rather ironical attempt at *tendresse*.
The knockabout treatment of the mother figure Mrs Hardcastle at
the end of *She Stoops to Conquer* may have its source in the desire
for revenge by a buffoon son, who is in the play but the half-son of
the house. Perhaps Goldsmith sensed that his pattern of learned helplessness derived from his mother's early cosseting. In the play Tony
Lumpkin intuits something almost erotic in his mother's drive
towards him: and the device of a mother who hides from her son the
knowledge that he has come of age suggests that he is being held in
a posture of dependency against his real interests. Goldsmith may
have feared a mother-love that was suffocating, denying him his
youthful autonomy.

The family romance in Ireland often enables initial growth, but
then prevents any further development within that structure.
Goldsmith's abortive attempts to leave, via Cork or Dublin, may be
seen as deliberately botched rehearsals for a final departure, as if he
were aware that exile would exact a high price. He obviously found
it hard to break with his mother in any sociable way and harder still,
having broken, ever to return. Yet the guilt of that breach was massive and may explain why so many of his subsequent acts of kindness
were to abandoned mothers (as if he were atoning for a wrong done).
The family unit remains the norm to which he appeals in much of his
writing, from *The Vicar of Wakefield* to 'The Deserted Village': and
that writing may be a reporting back to his own clan, in the style of
those early letters from Edinburgh. This is often overt, as in the dedication of 'The Traveller' to his older brother Henry, enjoying
domestic bliss in his vicarage family, unlike the 'Remote, unfriended,
melancholy, slow' Oliver: the poet envies the 'spot' which he might
have had himself.[13] More often, however, it is implicit, as if
Goldsmith's work is a 'writing back', an exercise in comparative cultural study by a travelling theorist, who began that labour in his

account of the Duke of Hamilton's drawing room. His central point of reference would always be the Irish midlands, even when he wrote from a London whose citizens generally took it for the epicentre of the civilized world. Flumstead Hill might be handsome, but 'I had rather be placed on the little mount before Lishoy gate, and take in, to me, the most pleasing horizon in nature.'[14]

He had 'left behind in Ireland everything that I think worth possessing, friends that I love and a society that pleased while it instructed'.[15] In an essay he tried to imagine 'the enthusiasm with which I again revisit the happy island where I drew my first breath, and received the early pleasures and institutions of life'.[16] Yet he never did return, even when wealthy enough to afford a trip to his blind mother; when she finally died, he unsettled his more pious London acquaintances by wearing only half-mourning and insisting that he had lost only a distant relation.[17] He could control his feelings about his mother only by icing them over.

Yet the family remained for him the ideal unit by which to measure the state of society, being itself a haven in a heartless world. Goldsmith's exile was more from the family than from any idea of 'Ireland' (for him that term was but a code word for family life). Over a century later, G.K. Chesterton would remark on the intensity of family life among Irish people, who could give their consent to no larger institution, whether the colonial state or the established church.[18] Goldsmith understood early the *subversive* quality of the family, whose members within the secrecy of the home's four walls might enter into a conspiracy against the codes of a new commercial order. The more remote and secretive such people might be, the more subversive, finding in the family a unit of resistance. That may be the poignant meaning of that moment when the Vicar of Wakefield leaves his boots outside the hall door, as an offering which may be enough to keep robbers at bay and outside. Although such familial loyalty will prove stronger by far than the loyalty of external enemies to their codes, it will never, alas, be quite enough, because the hearth can never be fully sealed off from the forces of the outer world. Exiled from the intimacies of family life, Goldsmith felt himself an outsider looking longingly in. So he idolized the family, much as de Valera would in the twentieth century and for similar reasons: his early uncertainties about his mother led him to idealize as an absolute moral value the parental world he had 'lost'.

Having gone, Goldsmith discovered that nobody really emigrates: people simply bring their native landscape and personal baggage with them wherever they go. After wandering on the Continent and

ushering at a London school, Goldsmith settled to the life of a professional writer. Yet he felt a foreigner in England: so much so that he
adopted the pose of a Chinese visitor in describing its effects on an
Anglo-Irish temperament. The Anglo-Irish, being a spiritually
hyphenated people, felt forever estranged from whatever surroundings they found themselves in: and so their writings often tilted
towards the anthropological, as if adopting that point from which to
view man as if he were a non-human witness of himself. Once out,
the only way to heal such estrangement was to exacerbate it: and so
Goldsmith in London accentuated rather than concealed his Irish
accent. 'An ugly and a poor man is society only for himself,' he
bleakly quipped, 'and such society the world lets me enjoy in great
abundance.'[19] He was one of the earliest intellectuals to come in
from the colonial periphery in search of a cultural centre, there to
make the painful discovery that the 'enigma of arrival' was that there
would be no discovery at all.

London was just another place, bigger, noisier, smellier than the
rest. 'I have passed my days away among a number of cool designing
beings and have contracted all their suspicious manner in my own
behaviour.'[20] But there was no point now in trying to return to the
source: the penalty of being a citizen of the world was that it left a
man with no home to go to. 'I should actually be as unfit for the society of my friends at home as I detest that which I am obliged to
partake of here.' His lament – that his family members were doomed
to love every place but that in which they resided – is now more
familiar in an age of postcolonial writing than it was in 1759. In
Edinburgh he had found his *maladie du pays* unaccountable; in
London he began to realize that a return home was unthinkable for
the expatriate intellectual. To Henry he wrote with plaintive jocu-
larity that London offered a writer a viable living, but 'I know you
have in Ireland a very indifferent idea of the man who writes for
bread'.[21]

The trouble with London was that his friends there tended to
laugh at him. He learned that he would be forever 'on', and disarmed
would-be mockers by learning to laugh first and foremost at himself.
In the process, he became a superb actor and mimic. By a radical
irony, he who had refined the role of bright buffoon set out for him
by his mother and family fled that particular form of inauthenticity
by taking to the life of the stage that was literary London. Thus, the
lad who had narrowly escaped holy orders became a lay preacher
and an essayist, making the transition from play-acting to self. For
even as he humiliated himself by playing some assumed part in Dr
Johnson's circle, the sense that he was being false at least reassured

him of the continuing existence of a deeper self that he was being false to. James Boswell fed Dr Johnson the predictable line on this:

> BOSWELL: For my part, I like well to hear honest Goldsmith talk away carelessly.
> JOHNSON: Why yes sir, but he should not like to hear himself.[22]

Almost alone among his English contemporaries, Sir Joshua Reynolds noted the sophistication of Goldsmith's mockery (misread by many as mere clownishness). In Ireland, if you tell people that you're a fool, they will know you are really a clever fellow: but in literal-minded England the danger is that they may take you at your word. It was only after Goldsmith had died that Dr Johnson could bring himself to call him a great man: and even a century later Thackeray was still patronizing him with the judgement that 'your love for him is half pity'.[23] Nobody took with full seriousness a man who had spent £8.2s.6d. on a pair of blue silk trousers.

Perhaps that was all to the good, for Goldsmith's own opinion of English literary culture was less than flattering. The new primacy of the bookseller over the old system of patronage he bewailed with a ferocity that would have done justice to a Gaelic poet: it would be impossible to imagine a combination more prejudicial to taste than mercenary bookseller and jobbing drudge, 'addressing the Muse as the Russian addresses his mistress, by falling asleep in her lap'.[24] If the repressed unconscious of English society had been visible in an Ireland of famines, beggars and irresponsible gaiety, the official face it presented in London was hardly conducive to feats of literary insight. 'Among well-bred fools we may despise much but have little to laugh at; nature seems to present us with an universal blank of silk, ribbands, smiles and whispers: absurdity is the poet's game, breeding is the nice concealment of absurdities.'[25] England, for all its talk of liberty, was the sort of place where being known as Irish was enough (he contended) to keep a man unemployed.

Ireland, now that he was safely out of it, was – or should have been – a zone of pleasure, excitement and fun. Its people were by nature innocent of the cash nexus which reduced men to wage-slaves and rent-payers: their true destiny was to be as free-spirited as the nomads and shepherds of a happy pastoral. Unfortunately, the English had short-sightedly decided to treat these people as expropriable subjects rather than as free citizens, with the result that the old pleasure-seeking life had been destroyed. It was not now replaced by one of wealth and efficiency. Goldsmith inveighed against 'the manifest error, in politics, of a government which endeavours to enrich one part of its dominions by impoverishing another, and of choosing to have but one flourishing kingdom when it might be possessed of two'.[26] There is every reason to believe that it was a resentment such as this which gave its emotional tone to 'The Deserted Village'.

By 1759 England's economy was beginning to boom, following some military successes in the Seven Years War, but Goldsmith did not share in the general exaltation. He had studied Virgil's *Eclogues* too closely not to sense what was coming: those who would grow rich by the trade of war would do so only at the expense of vulnerable rural communities. Even if the First Eclogue had not enforced the lesson, the state of affairs in Ireland would have. The wars of the seventeenth century had seen a new money economy replace the old land system: and the new bourgeois elites refused to recognize the old *geasa* which had so frequently bound Gaelic princes and peasants in a code of mutual obligation. In remoter places, traces of that old regime remained, but in *The Vicar of Wakefield* Goldsmith could evoke the security of that medieval world only in terms of a comparison with an encroaching modernity:

> As they had almost all the conveniences of life within themselves, they seldom visited towns or cities in search of superfluity. Remote from the polite, they still retained the primaeval simplicity of manners; and frugal by habit, they scarce knew that temperance was a virtue. They wrought with cheerfulness on days of labour; but observed festivals as intervals of idleness and pleasure.[27]

The paragraph can, significantly, define past virtues only in terms of what they are not (superfluous, urban, polite).

In England there was now an obsession with calibrations of social class: but in the Ireland of Goldsmith's youth the lines of demarcation were still rather fuzzy. In a letter purporting to be written by an English gentleman of 1759, Goldsmith described 'The Manners and Customs of the Native Irish'. The essay has a set-piece quality, which derives as much from Gaelic as from English tradition. The gentleman finds a young 'goddess of beauty' lodged 'meanly' in a hovel: an image from the *aisling*, as is the account of her alertness 'though nothing seemed more wretched than her situation'.[28] Father and son of her family invite the guest to lodge, since the nearby inn is overflowing. The visitor misreads the overture and confuses things by offering half a crown for his keep to the father. 'This he refused with the utmost indignation, telling me at the same time that he scorned to keep an inn, and was resolved never to be such a disgrace to his family.'[29] The daughter then refuses the visitor a requested kiss, which more 'fast' English girls would (we are assured) think nothing of bestowing.

At the centre of 'The Deserted Village' is a protest against the commodification of the rural landscape and of the human relations enacted within it. British readers, while admiring the poetry as poetry, have fretted about its sociology and have accused Goldsmith of exaggerating the effect of enclosures, clearances and even famine-induced emigration. If the village of 'sweet Auburn' is imagined as English, such reservations carry weight, for many improving land-lords increased the productivity and happiness of their tenants: but Goldsmith's diagnosis was all too fitting in Ireland. He implied that entire English villages such as Nureham Courtenay, Oxfordshire, were victims of the same fate. However, the analysis is more persua-sive if one thinks of the setting as Lissoy (its inhabitants certainly did, renaming their village Auburn).

'What is strangest in the poem', wrote Raymond Williams, 'is its combination of protest and nostalgia, and the way these emotions are related, consciously and unconsciously, to the practice of poetry.'[30] In Ireland, where poets held open utopian potentials which formed constellations with blessed moments from a happier past, there would have been nothing 'strange' about that at all. In England the liberals were futurologists, intent on liquidating past relations; in Ireland, as we have seen, to be nostalgic was to be a radical dissident. There the traditionalist was the true rebel. T.S. Eliot was closer to the truth when he praised Goldsmith's technical gift for keeping 'the old and new in such just proportion'. His praise of the form and style of the poem might also be read as an inadvertent statement of one of its central themes: 'to be original with the minimum of alteration is sometimes more distinguished than to be original with the *maxi-mum* of alteration'.[31]

The couplets of 'The Deserted Village' are traditional, urbane and normative, but they exist in a state of some tension with the heart-rending events reported. The Augustan structure implies a sort of sunny, condescendingly invoked norm whose very composure seems out of proportion to the revealed situation. Though invoked deadpan at the outset, its use by the end comes to seem auto-satirical, even par-odic. The form which at the start suffices to 'place' a local character like the village schoolmaster in the report of a more sophisticated world

While words of learned length, and thundering sound,
Amazed the gazing rustics ranged around,

> *And still they gazed, and still their wonder grew,*
> *That one small head could carry all he knew.*[32]

is shown later to have appealed implicitly to a 'superior' code which is
not in any sense superior at all. The couplets which begin by placing the
rustics end with accounts of their displacement: and the antithetical
structure becomes the medium for a violently indignant analysis, which
becomes ever more protective of the very persons who seemed at first
in danger of being tokenized. That same technique would be applied,
three years later, in Goldsmith's most famous play, where a country
bumpkin moves from being a comic butt to a source of moral meaning.

English readers have sensed that something more is going on in
'The Deserted Village' than seems to be the case. Macaulay, for
instance, explained this by saying that the happy landscape was
English, the decayed one Irish, and that they 'belong to two different
countries, and to two different stages in the progress of society'.[33]
However, the opening lines invoke a sunny pastoral, the 'seats of my
youth', a phrase that had only one meaning for a man who took care
never to lose his Irish accent. Moreover, most of the crucial early
phrases are within Irish, even Gaelic, poetic traditions. There is the
ritual hope for *bás in Éirinn*:

> *I still had hopes, my long vexations past,*
> *Here to return – and die at home at last.*[34]

Ireland is personified as an old woman driven back to the forces of
nature:

> *She, wretched matron, forced, in age, for bread,*
> *To strip the brook with mantling crosses spread . . .*[35]

The returned spendthrift might be taken as a version of Goldsmith
himself, for he was eternally in debt and in the grip of bailiffs: against
that image of precarious living the solid preacher has been identified
by Goldsmith's sister, Catherine, as their father.[36] The exactness of
the household detail is irrefutable:

> *The white-washed wall, the nicely sanded floor,*
> *The varnished clock that clicked behind the door;*
> *The chest contrived a double debt to pay,*
> *A bed at night, a chest of drawers by day . . .*
> *While broken tea-cups, wisely kept for shew,*
> *Ranged o'er the chimney, glistened in a row.*[37]

Contra Macaulay, the happy section seems Irish enough: but, contra Deane, so also do the unhappy images of hunger amid plenty:

> *No surly porter stands in guilty state*
> *To spurn imploring famine from the gate . . .*[38]

or again

> *While scourged by famine from the sinking land,*
> *The mournful peasant leads his humble band;*
> *And while he sinks without one arm to save,*
> *The country blooms – a garden, and a grave.*[39]

The heroic couplet is well fitted to deliver a truly dialectical image, which captures the awful disparities of the new regime:

> *The robe that wraps his limbs in silken sloth,*
> *Has robbed the neighbouring fields of half their*
> *growth . . .*[40]

One critic has pointed to the brilliance of the unexpected, hissing sibilant 'sloth' rather than the more predictable 'cloth' in the first line:[41] but what is truly uncanny is the use of those balanced Augustan periods to describe the *méirdreach* of Gaelic poetry: the woman, once beautiful, who must now clothe herself in frippery and baubles in order to sell her country to the highest bidder:

> *But when those charms are past, for charms are frail,*
> *When time advances, and when lovers fail,*
> *She then shines forth solicitous to bless,*
> *In all the glaring impotence of dress . . .*[42]

That is an image out of the world that produced 'Bodaigh na hEorna': but it will recur in the poignant desire of the ageing Mrs Hardcastle in *She Stoops to Conquer* to sport her niece's jewels.

One could in fact reverse Macaulay's reading, for when the speaker moves his evicted, exiled peasantry into a fallen, urban setting, there to witness a profusion in which they cannot share, the backdrop seems remarkably close to Goldsmith's London. Here the dialectical contrasts, between fine clothes and their exhausted wearers, are more vivid than ever:

Here, while the courtier glitters in brocade,
There the pale artist plies the sickly trade;
Here, while the proud their long drawn pomps display,
There the black gibbet looms beside the way . . .[43]

Although the scene may well be London, Ireland is still a presence in
these lines, for in 1768 seven Irish coal-heavers had been hanged following their agitation for better wages. This was the period in which
Goldsmith had done something he rarely ever did: refuse a writing
commission. The radical followers of Wilkes had been massacred in
St George's Fields, and the writer amazed many friends by spurning
an invitation to write propaganda for the government led by
North.[44]

The closing sections describe the emigration of cottiers to North
America at a time when it was the Irish rather than English peasantry
that was travelling there in numbers:

Ah no! To distant climes, a dreary scene,
When half the convex world intrudes between . . .[45]

The irony was that in due time many villages founded in that new
world would be named 'Auburn', as if in fulfilment of the hopes
recorded in the poem:

And took a long farewell, and wished in vain
For seats like these beyond the western main.[46]

In such a way would the 'foreign' be rendered 'native'. A great persistent theme in Goldsmith is the pretence that one place may really
be another: an Irish village may be an English village, a home an inn,
an inn a home, and so on. In the lines quoted, Goldsmith raises the
possibility that colonial settlements overseas may be less offensive
than defensive, arising from a desire that was thwarted at home:
and that desire leads the settler to turn the colony into a replica not
of what the old country is but of what it was.

Goldsmith was, however, a genuinely dialectical thinker and so he
wishes to show how *home* is itself an effect of what happens *away*.
Even as a peripheral setting like Lissoy is ruined by the commercial
values of the metropolis, so the metropolis itself is distorted and corrupted by the colonial mission.[47] Virgil's *Eclogues* had shown how
soldiers returning from overseas in triumph would be given lands
seized from vulnerable farmers: and even as Goldsmith formulated
his prophecy of imperial self-destruction, the young Edward Gibbon

was imagining his *Decline and Fall of the Roman Empire*. Irish intellectuals in London, such as Burke and Sheridan, were well schooled
from their experience of the two countries to sense that something
had to give, but Goldsmith phrased the theme most graphically:

> *Till sapped their strength and every part unsound,*
> *Down, down they sink, and spread a ruin round.*[48]

Moving from Lissoy to London, Goldsmith could see earlier than
most the link between clearances in Ireland and corruption in the
imperial metropolis. The 'junto of robbers', as Burke contemptu-
ously called the planters of Ireland, were now jostling through the
drawing rooms of London, 'buying their way into the English aristocracy',[49] and the earlier clearances in Ireland that had so enriched
certain landlords were inspiring a later generation of landowners in
England to adopt more rapacious policies towards their own tenantry. Moreover, newly rich adventurers were returning from India in
search of estates without manorial duties. A new kind of agriculture
was being developed. Food was no longer produced to feed the tenantry but for export to distant cities, where it would generate for the
landlord plenty of much-needed cash. Laws of private property now
superseded ancient customs of reciprocal obligation, and the new
relationships at home began to mimic those of colonial societies
abroad:

> *The wealth of climes, where savage nations roam,*
> *Pillaged from slaves, to purchase slaves at home.*[50]

The cult of luxury had created an elite geared to consumption
rather than production, and the pursuit of foreign trade had led to an
'aristocratical' style of government. Where once communal festivals
had illuminated entire societies, now the solitary sports of fishing and
shooting grouse had taken their place, enjoyed only by a privileged
few. The lament made centuries earlier by a Gaelic poet

> *Gan gáire fá ghníomhradh leinbh,*
> *cosc ar cheol, glas ar Ghaoidhilg . . .*[51]

without laughter about the behaviour of a child, music banned
and Irish outlawed . . .

is now repeated by a poet who knows that 'rural mirth and manners
are no more', as even 'sweet poetry' is silenced on the margins. Now,

instead of sweeter modes, the muse must learn the harsher notes of
social protest:

> *Aid slighted truth, with thy persuasive strain*
> *Teach erring man to spurn the rage of gain.*[52]

What follows is a denial of any justification of empire as a means
of saving heathens or spreading sweetness and light: the real motive
is revealed as avarice brought on by unequal trade. Dr Johnson wrote
the last four lines for Goldsmith in a fitting prophecy of the ruin to
come:

> *That trade's proud empire hastes to swift decay,*
> *As ocean sweeps the laboured mole away,*
> *While self-dependent power can time defy,*
> *As rocks resist the billows and the sky.*[53]

Whether the two friends knew it or not, this prophecy of imperial
decline, made even before the heyday of empire in the nineteenth century, was itself an ancient theme of Gaelic poets:

> *Time has triumphed, the wind has scattered all,*
> *Alexander, Caesar, empires, cities are lost,*
> *Tara and Troy flourished a while and fell*
> *And even England itself, maybe, will bite the dust.*[54]

The radical effect of 'The Deserted Village' can be attributed to its
author's deep emotional engagement in its themes and to his sense of
a still-shared language in which his appeal to a cultural heritage
could be made. The details of Lissoy life are sharp but never
overindividualized, because what is lamented is a whole way of life
which was the antithesis of selfishness. What is invoked is a sense of
popular desolation, which would be felt as keenly in England as in
Ireland. The lost world of festivals and feasts had its victims also, of
course, but communal vision and energies could have been tapped in
the transition to an even more caring society. Instead, they were
simply suppressed. Yet even radical critics have found in Goldsmith's
protest a rather eccentric attempt by one slightly unhinged poet to
stand in the way of 'progress'. In fact, what Goldsmith regrets most
of all is the *lack* of any improvement around Lissoy village, the fact
that its houses and lands are reverting to nature and to the 'hundred
years of solitude' that are bound to follow, as only the lapwing and
bittern, those birds who love solitude, frequent the local land.

Some commentators suggest that Goldsmith overinvested in his images, re-creating a merely personal loss of Lissoy as the defeat of an entire rural class. Raymond Williams insists that in England, after the changes, there was an increased use of land rather than a desert landscape, and that 'the assertion of nature against industry and of poetry against trade' was a consequence of 'a dubious isolation of humanity and community into the idea of culture'.[55] However, even in England that was only intermittently so. Within sixty miles of London, Goldsmith could point to landlords who levelled entire villages to make way for a personal pleasure ground. The worst thing about this process was that the judges who signed for the eviction of families were all political appointees:

> *Each wanton judge new penal statutes draw,*
> *Laws grind the poor and rich men grind the law.*

'All my views and enquiries have led me to believe those miseries real, which I here attempt to display,'[56] said Goldsmith in his dedication to Reynolds. He humbly emphasized the word 'attempt', for he feared that poetry was itself a casualty of the new order and might not be up to the task of capturing its barbarity. However, the barbarous process took hold fast in Ireland, that crucible of modernity: near Lissoy itself a community of cottiers was broken up by General Robert Napier for 'intended improvements of what was now to become the wide domain of a rich man'.[57] Events so near to Goldsmith's family home exerted the pressure of a real experience:

> *The man of wealth and pride*
> *Takes up a space that many have supplied.*[58]

To protest against such devastation in couplets is scarcely to fall into the trap of insisting that 'to be a poet is to be a pastoral poet', as Williams alleges.[59] In fact Goldsmith insists that what is needed is a new kind of poetry to match the unprecedented crisis, one combining nostalgia and protest.

The models were already well honed, of course, in Irish: but there is no reason to think of their sponsors as propagandists for a paternalistic aristocracy opposed to social progress. Like many Gaelic poets of his day, Goldsmith was appalled by the rupture of traditional values and natural rhythms by a predatory class which knew the price of everything. His lament for an organic social order would inspire later writers on the left and on the right, from William Blake to William Faulkner. Within Ireland, his profound pity for those violently shunted into smoky cities became a powerful example to leaders of the national renaissance at the start of the twentieth century. There is a clear lineal descent from lines like

> *Ill fares the land, to hastening ills a prey,*
> *Where wealth accumulates, and men decay . . .*
> *But a bold peasantry, their country's pride,*
> *When once destroyed can never be supplied.*[60]

to a speech given by W.B. Yeats at Trinity College in 1900:

> I think that the best ideal for our people, an ideal very generally accepted among us, is that Ireland is going to become a country where, if there will be very few rich, there will be nobody poor. Wherever men have tried to imagine a perfect life, they have imagined a place where men plough and sow and reap, not a place where there are great wheels and great chimneys vomiting smoke . . .[61]

to the much-cited, little-read speech of Éamon de Valera on St Patrick's Day 1943:

> The Ireland we have dreamed of would be the home of a people who valued material wealth only as a basis of right living, of a people who were satisfied with frugal comfort and devoted their leisure to the things of the spirit, whose villages would be joyous with the romping of sturdy children, the contests of athletic youths, the laughter of maidens; whose firesides would be forums of old age.[62]

De Valera's debt to Goldsmith may be a direct one, for the idylls of the village schoolmaster and preacher ('passing rich with forty pounds a year') were staples of the school primers which he read. The political leader knew a good deal about the disruptive effects of forced migration upon the fabric of rural life. The graphic conciseness in Goldsmith's account of broken families must have scored itself into the memory of successive generations, for whom he became the most quoted and beloved of poets:

> *The good old sire, the first prepared to go*
> *To new-found worlds, and wept for others' woe . . .*[63]

The natural rhythms and honest emotion of the passage owe much to the fact that it was rehearsed in the prose of 'The Revolution in Low Life'. Goldsmith had the ability to present a sophisticated analysis in the language of ordinary people who trusted his words as fully as he had trusted their experience:

> The modest matron followed her husband in tears, and often looked back at the little mansion where she had passed her life in innocence, and to which she was never more to return; while the beautiful daughter parted forever from her lover, who had now become too poor to maintain her as his wife. All the connections of kindred were now irreparably broken . . .[64]

If there is one passage that chronicles this process with even greater emotional force than Goldsmith, it must be the famous paragraph by Karl Marx and Friedrich Engels that describes how commercial pressures have destroyed a culture that had lasted for centuries:

> Uninterrupted disturbance of all social conditions, everlasting uncertainty and agitation, distinguish the bourgeois epoch from all earlier ones. All fixed, fast-frozen relations, with their train of ancient and venerable prejudices and opinions, are swept away; all new-formed ones become antiquated before they can ossify. All that is solid melts into the air, all that is holy is profaned, and man is at last compelled to face with sober senses his real condition of life and his relations with his kind.[65]

9

Radical Pastoral: Goldsmith's *She Stoops to Conquer*

What happens when a home ceases to be a haven and becomes a business, invaded by forces of the outside world? Are its members then compelled to face their real relations with their kind? The plot of *She Stoops to Conquer* (1773) revolves around such questions, which had been raised for Goldsmith by a hilarious mistake made in his early youth. On a journey from Lissoy to Edgeworthstown, the thirteen-year-old wished to put up for the night at 'the best house in the town of Ardagh'. A local trickster, taking the word 'house' literally, sent the naïve boy to the largest residence, which he naturally mistook for the local inn. Calling for an ostler to tend his tired horse, he pulled off his boots at the blazing parlour fire and said 'I believe a bottle of wine could not be bad this cold night.' The owner, Sir George Fetherstone, went along with the young man's act, pretending to be a docile innkeeper. Magnanimously, the young lord, growing in confidence, invited him, his wife and family to share his wine. Next morning, after a sound sleep in the best guest-room, he called for hot cake and his bill, before being told the facts.[1]

That incident is a telling inversion of a story told a century earlier by Seathrún Céitinn in *Trí Bhiorghaoithe an Bháis* (The Three Shafts of Death). This concerned a young Irish innocent abroad in England for the first time. Unaware of the world of money, he proceeded gingerly, for he had been warned that the people he would meet might seem more formal and less hospitable than his own. Entering an attractive-looking house, he was at once overwhelmed by the generosity of the host, who set the finest of food and drink before him. He ate until he was full and was dozing off to sleep when he heard what seemed like someone's name being called out insistently: 'Mac Raicín, Mac Raicín'. Thinking he was being paged, he pleasantly explained that he was not the Mac Raicín being sought. It was only when the host began to shake him violently that he learned that he was in an inn, whose proprietor was saying 'Make reckoning! Make reckoning!'[2] The story was, of course, told in reverse in Goldsmith's account of an English gentleman visiting a hovel in the west of Ireland: there the visitor offered half a crown for sheer hospitality, whereas the Irishman in England mistook for hospitality what was in fact a commercial service.

In Goldsmith's play the young buffoon Tony Lumpkin tricks two visiting gentlemen, Marlow and Hastings, into the belief that the home of his stepfather, Mr Hardcastle, is really the local inn. Marlow has come to pay court to Lumpkin's half-sister Kate Hardcastle and to offer respects to her father, a friend of his father. Both of the older men hope for a marriage between their children. Lumpkin, kept in ignorance by a doting mother of the fact that he is already of age, is in open rebellion against his constricting life. This helps to explain why he turns his house into an inn for the visitors, even as he converts a pub called the Three Jolly Pigeons (where he is worshipped as a father figure) into his true spiritual home. All the characters, however, seem bifurcated, with personalities constructed along similarly contradictory lines. Marlow stammers shyly in the presence of gentlewomen, yet behaves with seigneurial confidence in the company of a barmaid.

Long before the audience is confronted with Marlow's split personality, it is faced with the dual nature of his 'intended'. Kate Hardcastle wears her 'superfluous silk' in the mornings to the chagrin of her old-fashioned father, who denounces luxury: 'the indigent world could be clothed out of the trimmings of the vain'.[3] In the evenings she dons a plain housewife's dress to please the old man. Although she is far more adept than Marlow at negotiating this division of her world, the fact that they are both divided suggests that, like two antithetical Augustan couplets, they are bound to be conjoined before the end. At this early stage, however, Marlow's reticence ('so formal, so like a thing of business', as she moans)[4] implants in Kate the fear that the new commercial ethic is invading the courtship as fast as the follies of London are penetrating the provinces by stagecoach.

Tony Lumpkin has meanwhile been introduced as a robust boy, whose doting mother is sure that he is ailing and consumptive. He seems the typical Anglo-Irish squireen: feckless, good-natured, improvident, yet he is also a force of nature and a lord of misrule. In his squireen role, he is a mordant comment by the playwright on the philistinism of those Anglo-Irish families who felt that fifteen hundred pounds a year was all a man needed to cut a figure in the world. Goldsmith, of course, had himself complained of this class that they spent more in a single year on horses than in two centuries on books;[5] Louis MacNeice would much later elaborate by suggesting that the big houses contained no culture worth speaking of, 'nothing but an insidious bonhomie, an obsolete bravado and a way with horses'.[6] Such houses would be brought down less by rebels outside the walls than by internal decay, a combination of fast women and slow horses: and the sexist equation of the two resounds through the play, as when Tony's friends in the pub praise his father, the late Squire Lumpkin, who 'kept the best horses, dogs and girls in the whole county'.[7] Even Kate Hardcastle, when Marlow clasps at her in a later scene, will joke that he seems to want 'to know one's age as they do horses, by mark of mouth'.[8]

Goldsmith's attitude to Lumpkin is more complex than this might suggest, for he uses Lumpkin to disarm those contemporary critics who were accusing him of introducing low, vulgar characters to the drama. These devotees of genteel and sentimental comedy (which he dubbed a tradesman's tragedy) were fearful that Goldsmith might coarsen public taste, so he responded by placing their reservations in the mouths of Tony Lumpkin's associates, who praise Tony thus: 'he never gives us nothing that's *low*', 'o damn any thing that's *low*, I cannot bear it'.[9] This dread of vulgarity is itself deeply vulgar, especially when a gentleman is in a 'concatenation' because of it. A London audience might have seen Tony Lumpkin as an Irish buffoon and Marlow as a type of English gentleman, assuming perhaps that if 'The Deserted Village' could conflate Irish and English elements to tragic effect, this play might do likewise for comical scenes of knockabout farce.

Yet the initial impression is eventually dispelled: the genteel narrative becomes the subplot, while Tony's low machinations come to dominate a play that turns all the old priorities of English drama inside out. The public and private zones are hopelessly confused, as are rich and poor, the smart and the silly, and so on. Goldsmith had incurred the wrath of the actor–manager Garrick by suggesting that the contemporary stage was run by blockheads, but here he makes a blockhead the hero of the action.[10] Kate Hardcastle's ploy of descending to the role of barmaid in order to spy on her prospective husband is but a version of Goldsmith's own technique, for he also stooped to conquer. The work was a huge success: just five days after the opening performance, its printed version had sold out.[11] It did so because, like Merriman's poem of the same decade, it appealed to nature as the real arbiter of human lives – 'both accuser and healer'.[12] As Dr Johnson said, it answered the great end of comedy by making its audience merry.

Marlow's mistake, like that of young Goldsmith in Ardagh, could only have been made in a transitional society where there was real fluidity of movement between the social classes. The decline of some hereditary houses in the new money-economy compelled some gentlemen to open their homes as upmarket inns; equally, the growth of the liquor industries allowed many families to make fortunes in the tavern trade. An inn, like a modern-day airport, was a place where distinctions between public and private grew unclear: and it is precisely such ambiguities that Tony Lumpkin feeds off in setting up his little joke. He tells Marlow and Hastings, 'the landlord is rich, and going to leave off business; as he wants to be thought a Gentleman, saving your presence, he, he, he'.[13] Lumpkin has his own agenda, somewhat insurrectionary, for he has already told his pals to quit the inn because the visiting gentlemen may not be good enough company for them.

The irony that underwrote 'The Deserted Village' heightens the comedy here: the fact that snobberies are a result of the emergence of a middle class, which might have been expected to soften the difference between high and low. At Hardcastle's house, near the start of Act Two, the servants have to be coached in the new London ways of waiting on table. In the old days, when the master drank, they drank with him; when Hardcastle laughed, they laughed too. Relations were somehow more equal, but must now be set aside in a separation of realms for the sake of fashionable appearance. However, even as he trains his servants, Hardcastle's belief in the new system breaks down against the shared hilarity of recalling the story of Old Grouse in the gunroom. 'Well, honest Diggory', he chortles, 'you may laugh at that.'[14] What the joke was we are never told. If there are only two kinds of joke – those that were once funny and those that were never funny – it must have been of the former type. The vanishing of a class system is the utopian moment that was briefly glimpsed at old Hardcastle's table; but those rich potentials are now lost, as family retainers are taught to act the part of servants for onlookers, and every participant in this performance will be overdetermined. That disappearance of class distinction in a mode of relaxed, informal courtesy is the 'old' style for which Hardcastle pines – but for Goldsmith it carries also the seeds of a better future, to which humanity may awaken after 'the mistakes of a night'.

Shyness is Marlow's major problem: he would prefer to lose his way than undergo the horror of seeking directions from total strangers. He also suffers 'the Englishman's malady': he lacks assurance with women of his own class, relaxing only in the presence of those to whom he feels superior. Goldsmith was himself a shy, stumbling fellow and the malady he describes may have afflicted the Irishman in London. Even in Dr Johnson's club he was an outsider pretending to be an insider, so he knew something of Marlow's syndrome. 'No man', said Sir Joshua Reynolds, 'ever wrote so much from his feelings as Dr Goldsmith.'[15] He re-created features of his own shyness not only in Marlow but also in Tony Lumpkin (who shuns polite society when he can) and in Kate Hardcastle (who, after all, spends most of the play in disguise).

Each of these characters experiences a very modern dilemma. They desire a clear role, yet fear being trapped in it completely. Kate solves the problem most effectively with her skilful changes of costume: but even she, like each of the others, feels her self to be more real than the part assigned to her by events. In the Three Jolly Pigeons Tony knows his part and can play it well, for it is one of his own devising. The Pigeons is the 'other stage', the real inn, of which his home is but a virtual version in which he, the half-son, is never really sure what he should do. Inside and outside the family at one and the same time, he has no clear sense of identity, and no awareness of the limits to admissable behaviour which might have been set by his long-dead father. When they aren't acting, each of these young people experiences a consciousness that is often humiliating, for it is then that the gap between a role and self looms widest. Hence those strange moments when two characters must sort things out together out of the audience's earshot in the recessed part of the stage.

Marlow is all antitheses: warm friend and cool lover. He needs to woo by proxy. Yet, far beyond the divisions of social class, his problem is a version of Tony Lumpkin's. Seeming opposites, they are secret doubles, for each needs to be indulged like a capricious child. They appear to defer to social norms, while secretly revolting against them. If Marlow is overbred, Lumpkin is underbred. Both are examples of that loss of balance between feeling and expression that is a mark of the new class system. It is this system that has destroyed the 'unity of culture' known once between Hardcastle and his retainers. If one man knows how to feel but not how to express, the other seems willing to articulate emotions that he has yet to know with any fullness.

The sexual instinct, like the impulse to laughter, is capable of posing challenges to the class system. Tony Lumpkin's presence as stepson in Hardcastle's house is proof enough of that. Likewise, Marlow can show feeling to underlings but has blocked it out at the level of polite society. These splits in personality may easily be interpreted as rooted in Goldsmith's own contradictory experience of London codes: that element in him which craved acceptance endorsed the codes, but his unconquerable part (much the stronger one) mocked them to perdition. The Irish fish-out-of-water-in-England shrewdly noticed a similar distress in the newer types of English once they left their own social groupings. Yet Marlow clearly needed to leave his own family, for within it – like Goldsmith – he felt himself caught in a restricted role of others' devising.

To Hardcastle-the-innkeeper he behaves with a curt dismissiveness that borders on rudeness ('this fellow forgets that he's an innkeeper, before he has learned to be a gentleman');[16] but Hardcastle-as-anxious-father rejects as 'modern modesty'[17] what is really 'old-fashioned impudence'.[18] If the retainers of Hardcastle's household had enjoyed a cheerful egalitarianism, repeatedly crossing class lines in the remote intimacies of big-house life and conversing easily with their 'betters', the new modes introduced by the London gentlemen seem much more snobbish. They reduce a servant from a comrade to an underling, a visitor from an honoured guest to a paying customer, and a landlord from a *paterfamilias* to a tradesman. In the guise of a democratic levelling the new money order is creating – just as Gaelic poets predicted – endless calibrations of snobbish sentiment.

The indifference of Hardcastle's rural circle to the clothes they wear may be seen as one sign of the older freedoms. It is also a mark of such people's confidence in the singular self. Marlow, on the other hand, frets about the disorder of his fashionable dress as he awaits his interview with Kate Hardcastle, only to be rebuked by her friend Constance Neville: 'the disorder of your dress will show the ardour of your impatience'.[19] His concern is an indication of nervousness rather than self-assertion: with each change of costume he hopes to feel himself a different person and to know a self in the very act of performing one. The danger is, as Constance hints, that he may get lost in one of these roles and fail to distinguish acting from reality – another weakness he shares with Tony Lumpkin. In a period of social transition, men are no longer sure how to act on every occasion, and this uncertainty affects Marlow as surely as it distresses Tony Lumpkin. Kate Hardcastle, on the contrary, flawlessly distinguishes playing and reality, being such a mistress of herself that she can act any role with conviction, knowing it to be only that.

Marlow's dressing to code, like Goldsmith's adoption of the costume of the medic, is one way of pinning down a role in the midst of these fluctuations. By the year 1757 Jean-Jacques Rousseau had noted how the conventions of urban life compelled men to behave like actors in order to be sociable with one another: many dressed accordingly to a station, even if the profession they dressed to was no longer necessarily their own:

> Whether people were in fact what they wore was less important than their desire to wear something recognisable in order to be someone in the street. At home, one's clothes suited one's body and its needs; on the street, one stepped into clothes whose purpose was to make it possible for other people to act as if they knew who you were.[20]

The more exalted a person was, the more free to play with appearance: Marlow, by concealing the traces of nature with costly clothes, is seeking to reduce his own vulnerability in the eyes of others.

'I have kept very little company,' he explains to Constance Neville. 'I have been but an observer upon life, Madam, while others were enjoying it.' He speaks, therefore, in the most correct clichés of refined sentiment to Kate Hardcastle and can hardly bring himself to look her in the eye. Yet, she muses, 'the fellow, but for his unaccountable bashfulness, is pretty well too. He has good sense, but then so buried in his fears, that it fatigues one more than ignorance. If I could teach him a little confidence.'[21] This reversal of the more usual gender role, whereby a man took it upon himself to explain the ways of the world to a sensitive woman, is delicious. (It may even carry an element of wish-fulfilment on Goldsmith's part.) It is based on a shared shyness; but Kate solves her uncertainties by throwing herself into a series of roles (barmaid, poor relation etcetera), from the safety of which she can study the true nature of her proposed husband, while Marlow opts in her presence for sheer passivity. His shyness allows him to stand back and observe from a position of relative anonymity, and this may ultimately leave him freer to act.[22] Yet it leaves him also in a double bind: shrinking from Kate Hardcastle's notice, yet wearing fine clothes to stand out (much as his ostentatious reticence may be a sublimated plea for special treatment).[23]

Marlow epitomizes a new crisis in manhood: a desire to be at once singular and representative. Dependent upon others for a sense of identity, he fears that others have the capacity to destroy it, either by exposing flaws in his underlying self or by spurning to know him at all. His shyness is but the sign of an extreme preoccupation with self and a fear of hostile judgements. Like other retiring types, he manages to be often intolerant of others (Hardcastle, Lumpkin, Kate), while at the same time being less self-confident than any of them.[24] A corollary is his fear that he and they may be forever acting a self not really their own. Among simple women, he plays the rake; among genteel ones, a shrinking violet.

The polarity in Marlow of aristocratic seducer and timid bourgeois may illustrate one of the problems of the New Man who finds the limits of the old behavioural codes no longer clearly demarcated. The predatory *hauteur* of a militarist aristocracy may be no longer serviceable in an age that calls for a more malleable kind of male: and in such confusing circumstances the shrewdest ploy may be to wait for the woman to make all the first moves. After all, Marlow senses that he can be both passive and successful with Kate, his seeming pliability an intrinsic part of his attractiveness in her eyes. Of course, in the end it doesn't really matter whether he is chaste, for although his friend Hastings suggests that it could be a consideration, Kate herself seems scarcely to bother. Marlow is not finally a commodity on the sex market, even if she enjoys the momentary pleasure of pretending that he is, appraising his looks far more obviously than he appraises hers. Although he is the observed and she the observer, he retains the ultimate power to say yes or no.

Kate, however, is determined to do the deciding. If Marlow is the sullen fellow she met, she won't have him, while her father vows that if Marlow is the crude churl whom he encountered, he will give no consent either. Each seems to want a Marlow available only to the other. Can they reconcile such contradictory desires? When Kate appeared before Marlow as a bargirl, he hauled her about like a milkmaid before her outraged father's eyes. Yet her disguise afforded her a precious opportunity, as she tells her friend: 'But my chief aim is to take my gentleman off guard, and like an invincible champion of romance examine the giant's force before I offer to combat.'[25] Through her disguise as a humble girl, she manages to see Marlow as he really is, off guard and among friends. Equally, there are recurrent hints that he may have sensed subliminally that Kate truly is one of the Hardcastles. At a telling moment he observes how the way of the barmaid 'drives out the absurdities of all the rest of the family'.[26]

Kate is a kind of throwback to Shakespeare's Rosalind, whose male disguise allowed her to see her lover as he was among his own comrades. There are also important differences, however. In *As You Like It* Rosalind-as-Ganymede is valued as a person (and not just for her gender as a woman), and so the marriage at the comedy's end is a true bonding, in the sense of a transcendence of gender roles. In *She*

Stoops to Conquer what is transcended is the division of social class, which allows Marlow to plight his troth to someone he believes no more than a poor relation of the Hardcastles: yet the victory may seem a little hollow, since such class divisions had been overcome already, in the prior informality of exchanges between master and servants in the Hardcastle home. It was the need to accept a brief incursion from the outside world, for the sake of an approved marriage, that curtailed and disrupted those happy civilities.

Marlow himself is on the high road to a new relation between master and servants, encouraging his men to drink even though he abstains. He tells the outraged Hardcastle (whom he still thinks a money-making innkeeper): 'I ordered them not to spare the cellar.' Yet he persists in taking the view that a barmaid, like a drink, can be paid for. 'I don't intend to rob her,' he assures Hastings, the sentimental lover; 'there's nothing in this house I shan't pay for'.[27] With such free-wheeling attitudes he converts the stately home of his friend's father into an alternative version of the Three Jolly Pigeons. By mistaking a domestic for a public setting, he permits the anthropologist in Goldsmith to examine the working fictions on which the society is based, and to show that at the core of the commercial ethic there may be something deeply insulting to traditional codes.

Goldsmith is, however, just as caustic about the deceptions made possible under the old aristocratic system. Marlow's servant, fired by drink, insists that he is as good as any gentleman: and the interchangeability of classes is proved very soon in a variety of ways. The sliding-scale between innkeeper and gentleman is mocked by the newly arrived Sir Charles Marlow in Act Five, who laughingly tells his old friend that his son mistook him not for a common but for an uncommon innkeeper. When Tony Lumpkin brings his mother (as she thinks) forty miles from home, in fact the pair are in their own darkened estate, where she mistakes her own husband for a highwayman. And Marlow, now aware of the error, softens the class divide by falling in love with Kate even though he believes her to be a poor relation of Hardcastle. 'By heaven, she weeps', is his response; 'this is the first mark of tenderness I ever had from a modest woman'.[28] That is a further jibe by Goldsmith at the vogue for genteel lovers in sentimental comedy, but its *reductio ad absurdum* is the Hastings–Constance Neville relationship, which is only allowed to come to the fore at the close.

Lumpkin's mother supposes him to be 'in love' with Constance and he hams the role dreadfully: 'I'd sooner leave my horse in a pound, than leave you when you smile upon one so.'[29] However, she foolishly divulges her letter of elopement to Mrs Hardcastle, imperilling the plan she hatched with Hastings. Unable to tell 'the difference between jest and earnest',[30] the blockhead seems carefree and promises to set all to rights. It is in the final act that Goldsmith subjects the plot of genteel lovers to the systematic humiliation of Tony Lumpkin's farce. Their fortunes depend on his skill in deceiving his mother into the belief that he has taken Constance and herself forty miles hence. The scene is, of course, utterly implausible and raised jeers on the opening night. The theatre manager George Colman tried to reassure a nervous Goldsmith: 'Psha! don't be fearful of *squibs*, when we have been sitting almost these two hours upon a barrel of gunpowder.'[31] It was a shrewd observation, for the whole play is constructed on the understanding that settings are made more in the mind than in the concrete: if a home could be an inn, an inn might serve as a home. Goldsmith knew as well as Tony Lumpkin that those who travel bring all their mental landscapes with them.

Constance Neville is surprisingly unwilling to seize the opportunity provided by Tony's ruse for a first elopement: instead she tells Hastings, 'I am unable to face any new danger. Two or three years' patience will at last crown us with happiness.'[32] They must wait until Tony is officially of age to state his own desire in the matter. This rather bourgeois notion of delayed gratification has also been a recurring theme: after all, Tony Lumpkin is being forced by a deceitful mother to wait for a long-past coming-of-age; and Kate Hardcastle fears that she may be 'engaged to wait' at the end. Yet one of the implications of the plot is that, if you suspend the desire for instant gratification and immerse yourself in the rules of a game, you will gain control of the situation and ultimately your heart's desire. Kate Hardcastle, a woman who can both show feeling and control it, triumphs. She does so because of her conviction that she can play better than anyone in a world whose conditions, like its environments, are plastic.

At the close Marlow defends such plasticity in a speech to Kate that softens and even effaces all divisions between the codes of low farce and genteel sentiment: 'What at first seem'd rustic plainness, now appears refin'd simplicity. What seem'd forward assurance, now strikes me as the result of a courageous innocence, and constant virtue.'[33] Old Hardcastle is not amused, accusing the young man of saying and unsaying things at pleasure, offering one story to him and another to his daughter; but the irony is that Marlow is being convicted of a double standard just moments after he has resolved that the woman, though poor, is fully worthy to join his family. Moreover, it is he who must now face the embarrassment of discovering that the poor relation is really the splendid Kate. He is led to the back of the stage speechless, but at last possessed of his identity, to sort things out with her.

In theatrical terms it is a complex moment. Just like the Old Grouse joke that was never told, here the painful clarifications between the pair have to be guessed at by an audience which again witnesses a character who, even when 'acting', is experiencing a heightened form of consciousness. Mrs Hardcastle may complain that 'this is all but the whining end of a modern novel',[34] but a novelist might not be sufficiently subtle to permit Marlow's embarrassment to be merely inferred. Yet the comedy ends on a note of real farce, with Tony Lumpkin now happily aware that he is of age, free to ensure that the jewels which once adorned his ageing mother's neck can now pass to their rightful owner, Constance Neville. Better still, he is also enabled to deliver her over to her sentimental lover by an act of anti-marriage: 'I, Anthony Lumpkin Esquire, of BLANK place, refuse you, Constantia Neville, spinster, of no place at all, for my true and lawful wife.'[35]

If *She Stoops to Conquer* were only a farce, it would hardly allow for the pressure of complex emotion felt by most of the principal characters. Though Goldsmith cannily advertised his play as an attack on sentimental comedy, it was more subtle than that: one in which sentiment and farce existed in a productive tension. The true centre of the play is neither Constance nor Tony but Kate, and with her Goldsmith returned to the Shakespearean and Restoration tradition of the witty, resourceful heroine. Not only that, but he used her mastery of disguise to compose a play impossible to Shakespeare, one that anatomized the hidden injuries of social class. Overt commentary on politics had been banned from the stage with the new Licensing Act of 1737, but with this drama of astute implication Goldsmith wrote a deeply political play. *Déclassé* as well as *déraciné*, he had lived on the edge of the London slums and been asked for alms by near neighbours. His self-image might have been that of the lower Anglo-Irish gentry, but in London even at his most successful he was a jobbing middle-class writer. Treated as a licensed clown by the Johnson circle, even while penning the most elegant prose of his age, he knew the angst of negotiating between a role and a self. His style drew its natural force from an appeal to shared values but it was in a sense just another mask. In a period of rapid social change it was no longer always clear how a person should speak, write, act. All around him he could witness the disintegration of old certainties in the growing theatricalization of city life. Like Goethe, he could forgive the faults of men in actors but not the faults of actors in men. That was why he observed of Garrick:

> *On the stage he was natural, simple, affecting;*
> *'Twas only that, when he was off, he was acting.*[36]

Something similar was said of Goldsmith by the victim of that couplet, who remarked that he 'wrote like an angel and talked like poor Poll'. In the act of writing alone did Goldsmith find a zone of freedom, where he could play off his confidence against his own timidity, his urbanity against his social anger, his resourcefulness against his conventionalism.

There, in the republic of letters, he saw the future. Even his Irish contemporary Sheridan, for all his republican philosophy, never wrote a play so radical as *She Stoops to Conquer*. If in *The School for Scandal* the voices of feeling win out over the peripheral wits, in Goldsmith's work the exponents of high sentiment are thoroughly conscripted by the forces of natural honesty. In *The Rivals* a gentleman would pose as a member of the lower class in order to catch a woman unawares, but his object (and Sheridan's) was to expose gender sentiment rather than class tension. In *She Stoops to Conquer* the question of class is centralized by Kate Hardcastle's twin disguises, while the very fact that she can convince with her performances indicates a real fluidity in the class system, even as the middle class emerges into prominence.

The new protagonists, Goldsmith intuited, would be the Tony Lumpkins (men free of filial pieties) and Kate Hardcastles (women of wit and despatch). It is they who propel the twin strands of the plot from start to end. Some of today's commentators suggest that Kate might in fact be a perfect male fantasy-figure: the genteel woman who can also play the part of barmaid, vamp and wit.[37] It could be argued even more strongly, however, that she also represents a *female* fantasy: one in which women learn to exploit the ambiguities of society, as did the king in Jacobean England, posing as an underling in order to learn what was really going on and what his subjects thought of him. By a similar logic, Kate gets to know others in order to find out what they think of her.

She Stoops to Conquer swept the boards. Even the usually jealous James Boswell was heard to say with pride that one of his daughters was born under a happy star on its triumphant opening night.[38] But Goldsmith had little time left to savour the victory. Within a year he was grievously ill with kidney trouble. He took medical advice but insisted on prescribing Dr James's Powders for himself. They only made him worse. On learning of his death Edmund Burke burst into tears and Samuel Johnson finally asserted his greatness. Everyone seemed suddenly to be taking him more seriously. One of the doctors who had attended at his bedside published a tract warning of the dangers of Dr James's Powders, and their producers were so dismayed that they issued counter-statements. Already the legend of the 'gentle master' was taking shape. In the next two centuries, he would become one of the most beloved of all writers in Ireland and in England.

At Goldsmith's deathbed, Dr Turton, who had worried about the dying man's irregular pulse, asked him: 'Is your mind at ease?' 'No, it is not,' came the simple reply. Goldsmith was far too radical an analyst to quit the world of 1774 in any kind of peace.

10

Sheridan and Subversion

An actor who was capable of great sincerity, a philanderer with a puritanical streak, an exponent of aristocratic *sprezzatura* who preached the virtues of middle-class radicalism, Richard Brinsley Sheridan was a complicated man. His own circle of friends in London thought that, as a speech-writing intimate of the Prince Regent, he would some day become Prime Minister; others, especially his critics, confidently predicted that he would fetch up in the Tower of London as a traitor. He is remembered today as one of the great political orators of the eighteenth century and as the author of two of the foremost comedies in English literature. His plays, *The Rivals* and *The School for Scandal*, have always been popular with playgoers, yet are sometimes dismissed by intellectuals as sentimental comedies of no great originality. His political speeches are now little known to the general public, but their prophetic analyses of the forces at work in British and Irish society are much quoted by intellectuals.

He was first and last an Irishman. His father, Thomas Sheridan, was a voice coach and playwright, whose own father had been a schoolteacher in Dublin and Cavan, as well as an intimate of Jonathan Swift. His mother, Frances, was also a dramatist, a career that represented her open defiance of a father who thought it improper that his daughter should even learn to read.[1] Richard Brinsley Sheridan, born in 1751 as the second child, seemed at first an aimless, drifting fellow, and so his disdainful father packed him off to a public schooling at Harrow. There he was laughed at for his Irish brogue and for being a mere actor's son among heirs of the English aristocracy. Deprived of parental tenderness, he became chronically insecure and developed a tendency to burst into tears whenever left in the dark. Perhaps the capacity of his plays to arouse intense feeling only to deflate it had its origin in this early pattern of experience, for Sheridan learned young that to survive the world you must always ensure against excessive sentiment. His family had gone from Dublin to escape pressing debts and his mother died in France. Even in the midst of his woe, however, the young boy was learning that the roles of actor and gentleman might not be as opposed as his schoolmates seemed to think. In order to maintain respectability, he asked his uncle in London for the black clothes of mourning. Already, the Irishman was learning how to impersonate the sort of Englishman his teachers felt he ought to be.

At the outset he threatened to put what genius he had into his life rather than art. Like Oscar Wilde a century later, he existed in an allegorical relation to his age. After the miseries at Harrow, he met a ravishing singer named Eliza Linley. She had many suitors. One old man gave her money, despite her lack of interest in him; a younger candidate named Mathews pressed his claim so hard that she escaped in the company of Sheridan to France, where she took refuge in a convent.[2] Sheridan's father had by this time set up an academy of oratory in Bath and become a partner with Eliza's father, the musician Thomas Linley. Richard's conduct with Eliza was impeccable: he may have gone with her in some concern for her well-being or in hopes of excitement. Such superficial feelings soon gave way to passionate love, however. The couple married in secret in a Catholic church and returned to England, where Sheridan felt obliged to fight two duels with his rival Mathews. He entered the first, it seems, to defend his own honour and the second to afford his opponent the opportunity of defending his. His older brother Charles, long a favourite of their father, voiced admiration: 'You risked everything where you had nothing to gain, to give your antagonist the thing he wished, a chance for recovering his reputation.'[3]

The vulnerability of young women in an age of libertines troubled the youthful Sheridan, who proposed that the monarch should set up a special college for the daughters of clergymen and army officers.[4] There they could study all the arts in safety: history, languages, astronomy, literature, music, drawing, embroidery and dance. Eventually, he theorized, such colleges could be thrown open to all interested young women, who would thereby be prepared for companionate marriages as the intellectual equals of their husbands.

Those radical ideas drew something from Swift's writings and, further back, from Thomas More: but they also fit well with theories enunciated in the eighteenth century by Irish-language writers from Dónal Ó Colmáin to Brian Merriman.

In those days the standing of playhouses was akin to that of today's strip clubs, and even the more respectable career of singer was seen as too commercial to be truly dignified. Sheridan was without a fortune of his own, yet he insisted that his status as a gentleman would be compromised if his wife were to sing for money or if her sister were to act in the commercial theatre ('in a profession which I think so ill of').[5] Somewhat perversely, he told Eliza's father that his own lack of 'birth, fortune or connections' would raise her even higher in the estimation of an adoring world, 'far above what any man of fifty times my advantages would have raised her to'. In theory she was not to earn money because she was now the wife of a gentleman; in practice he was implying that the depth of her love could be attested only by marriage to a poor man. In this way he evolved a philosophy of aristocratic radicalism, which managed to be at once deeply traditionalist and potentially modern: for the poor man, of course, might win great wealth by sheer merit in the more democratic world now emerging. Sheridan saw himself as a rising comet of the new order: 'and as God very often pleases to let down great folks from the elevated stations which they might claim as their birthright, there can be no reason for us to suppose that he does not mean that others should ascend'.[6]

But how to rise? Ironically, he was driven back to the very institution about which he had such divided feelings: the commercial theatre. This was a place no longer frequented solely by aristocrats; members of the middle class and even lowly servants came, some of them to study ways of impersonating (and maybe some day supplanting) their betters. The writer John Dryden had already noted the 'mixed' form of comedy being developed in the early eighteenth century: its compound of wit, humour and intrigue appealed to very different sections of the audience – the wit to the rakes and sparks of the pit, the sentimental humour to the ladies of the boxes, and the complications of plot to the servants in the gallery.[7] The world of the theatre might seem vulgar and amoral to fastidious souls, but it was open to all social classes, like the British constitution in which (said an admiring Sheridan) 'no sullen line of demarcation separates and cuts off the several orders from each other'.[8] Here the lowly could imitate the exalted in what amounted to rehearsals for a more modern world.

Sheridan's career as dramatist was a short one and a merry one.

Because theatre was seen as trivial, the playwrights of the Restoration had wished the public to suppose that their works were dashed off in early youth: and Sheridan's comedies really were. They earned a small fortune, which he spent as quickly as he acquired it: yet, despite their huge popularity, he refused to publish them. At a period when print seemed a powerful new technology adopted by the emerging middle classes, this reluctance aligned him once again with the older aristocratic code. One of his characters, Sir Benjamin Backbite, provides a kind of rationale for this attitude in conversation with a fellow gossip, Lady Sneerwell: 'To say truth, ma'am, 'tis very vulgar to print. And as my little productions are mostly satires and lampoons on particular people, I find they circulate more by giving copies in confidence to the friends of the parties.'[9] Yet Sheridan's ambivalence is also in evidence here, for the upper class has no better use for its leisure than the endless circulation of slander.

The plot of Sheridan's first play *The Rivals* (1775) revolves to a great degree around questions of reading and of the new sentimental literature of the middle class. It also draws on its author's formative experiences, for it includes a father/son altercation, a possible elopement of a poor man and his genteel lover, and two threatened duels. Sir Anthony Absolute wishes his son to unite his inheritance with that of the beautiful heiress Lydia Languish. She, however, has fallen in love with a poor ensign named Beverley and, as a keen reader of the sentimental novels of the period, she wishes to prove that love by giving up her fortune for a risky life with him. Her aunt Mrs Malaprop stands guardian of her virtue, which is assailed also (as Eliza's was) by an elderly, importunate suitor – in this case the Anglo-Irish buck Sir Lucius O'Trigger, who is keen to fight a duel with anybody who crosses his path.

Summarized in that way, the plot seems hackneyed, yet for Sheridan its situations had all the force of autobiography. He was able to inflect them with the pressure of experience. Even the debate into which his mother had been drawn on the merits and demerits of reading helped to propel his action. Confronted by Lydia Languish's refusal to submit to an arranged marriage, Sir Anthony Absolute laments that 'this comes of her reading'.[10] If he had a thousand daughters, he tells Mrs Malaprop, he would sooner teach them the black arts than the alphabet, for 'a circulating library in a town is as an ever-green tree of diabolical knowledge'.[11] Sheridan as a radical might have been expected to support female literacy, but on this too he had conflicting thoughts. He had after all been born in a land most of whose inhabitants still believed in the power of oral tradition and in the notion of literature as recorded speech.

He was, moreover, the son of a voice coach who asserted the superiority of the spoken over the printed word. All writing was a writing *down*, a pale imitation of the human voice in all its glory: a fact well recognized by the authors of the Bible who had always imagined God as a voice speaking. The whole human body was used to underwrite the appeal of the spoken word, heightening the attendant emotion in an appeal to more than just the sense of sight. The act of writing was artificial, deliberated, even knowing, but the speech of people welled unbidden from the subconscious. It was not only more dramatic but more sincere. Those were strong arguments in favour of theatre as a warmly social institution which privileged the speaking voice, but they also augmented the case against the silent, solitary consumption of modern novels. In the play Sheridan has a good deal of fun at the expense of Lydia's undiscriminating reading. It might also be said that, by introducing into plays many features that had ensured the success of Henry Fielding's novels of domestic sentiment, he himself was seeking to forestall the spread of private reading. A playwright who could cannibalize the major attractions of the novel might in time help to reverse the popularity of that still-new form.

In the Ireland from which Sheridan came, a novel was read not just for its storyline, but also as a manual of etiquette among a middle class that equated modernization with anglicization. From such novels a wholly new type of society might eventually be inferred. Sir Lucius O'Trigger may be responding to this very process at work in Mrs Malaprop, when he marvels at a woman who is 'quite the queen of the dictionary – for the devil a word dare refuse coming at her call'.[12] The malapropisms may be a painful if comic reminder of those Irish people who learned their English directly from books, rather than from free conversation with other persons fluent in the language. The result was that many spoke it almost as a learned language and, since orthography was a notoriously unreliable guide, with inevitable mispronunciation. Sheridan's grandfather had been a schoolmaster and must have encountered many travelling teachers who used ostentatious 'jawbreakers' to advertise their eloquence and learning in the new tongue. 'Words of learned length and rumbling sound' were a mechanism of compensation for more than Goldsmith's village schoolmaster.[13] Frances Sheridan had used malapropisms *avant la lettre* in *A Journey to Bath*: and before her there had been precedents in the Dogberry and Mistress Quickly of Shakespeare.

Although the device can seem mechanical if overused, at its best it is side-splittingly funny. Here is Mrs Malaprop on travel:

Nobody can be embellished that has not been abroad, you know. Oh if you were to hear him describe contiguous countries, as I have done, it would astonish you. He is a perfect map of geography.[14]

So potent did this tradition become in Irish writing that three-quarters of a century later it was still vibrant in the stories of William Carleton. His Mat Kavanagh emerges from a drugged sleep:

I'm all in a state of conflagration and my head – by the sowl of Newton, the inventor of fluxions, but my head is a complete illucidation of the centrifugle motion.[15]

Seventy-five years after that, it was still an audible tradition in the struggle of Sean O'Casey's character Fluther Good with words such as 'derogathory'. By then another audience, many of whose members had recently learned to read, could find matter for comedy in the spectacle of a workman whose linguistic reach exceeds his educational grasp: but across the centuries the same implicit appeal is made to the audience to find some poignancy in a character's losing struggle with writerly modes. Fluther Good becomes, after all, an inadvertent hero of O'Casey's play and Mrs Malaprop is not laughed off the stage but admired and defended by Sir Anthony Absolute at the end.

Sheridan, thinking of his own mother's struggle to read, was well aware of all that poignancy. Although he couldn't fail to extract comedy from the malapropisms, he was also alert to the fact that they represented one woman's attempt to inhabit a more spacious intellectual world than that allowed to most females of the age. A believer in the democracy of intellect, he understood that books offered the one way forward for many people (men as well as women) who felt their social constrictions all too keenly. Mrs Malaprop is not finally mocked, for if some of her shots are near-misses, a surprisingly high proportion are deliciously unintentional hits. Early on she urges Sir Anthony Absolute to speak well of Lydia Languish to his son: 'I hope you will represent her to the Captain as an object not altogether illegible.'[16] Or later, when she meets Captain Absolute, she speaks a degree of truth in confiding that 'few gentlemen nowadays know how to value the ineffectual qualities in a woman'.[17] The truth in art is a statement whose opposite may also be true: and Mrs Malaprop seems to half-anticipate this Wildean doctrine. Captain Absolute agrees, of course: young women of blossom lack knowledge, he regrets, whereas older ones gain respect for knowledge only after losing that blossom. He pretends that Mrs Malaprop has both virtues, while secretly believing that they may be reconciled in Lydia.

Writing some decades after the play's entry to the canon, Elizabeth Inchbold feared in 1808 that the character of Mrs Malaprop might suggest to future generations that 'the advance of female knowledge in Great Britain was far more tardy than in any other European nation'.[18] But Sheridan's play is an implicit plea for the proper education of women: his condemnation is of reading misapplied by persons without adequate tutelage – Lydia's booklist combines the trashy and the sublime in an undiscriminating heap. Sheridan well understood the value of reading in the education of a person, despite Shelley's belief that the library scene in *The School for Scandal* was an attack on the literary tradition as such. His real quarrel was with those foolish enough to confuse literature and life. The mockery of Mrs Malaprop is aimed at a woman who has allowed everyday conversation to be contaminated by writerly phrasing. The laughter at Lydia is directed at a debutante who insists that love affairs should be conducted in freezing gardens under a 'conscious moon' of a sort essential in romantic books.

Sheridan was sufficiently bourgeois to share some of the puritan distrust of actors and impersonators – hence the endless asides with which he has his dissemblers, both good and bad, puncture their own performances. Yet he was also anxious to adjust the earlier aristocratic values of Restoration comedy to those of the new sentimental modes of the middle class. The 'laughing comedies' were giving way (in the words of Goldsmith) to those gentler dramas that exhibited the virtues of a private life and 'the distresses rather than the faults of kind'.[19] In such a new landscape, even comic butts have their moments of wisdom: and the astounding rightness of many of Mrs Malaprop's mistakes suggests a more modern, latent, subconscious element at work. Sheridan's father had praised the spoken word as issuing from a man's innermost depths in statements of unrehearsed honesty. Through all of his son's plays there runs an obsession with distinguishing truth from appearance, the latent from the manifest content of a moment or a situation. So the wrong-looking suitor (Ensign Beverley) may turn out be the right one (Captain Absolute), or the misfired phrase may score a bull's eye. Sheridan himself delighted in puncturing social disguises, once dressing as a policeman for the pleasure of arresting a lady of title at an illegal gamblers' den in Brighton Pavilion. The fact that Ireland had functioned for well over two centuries as a zone of dark unconsciousness to England's daylit world may explain his glee at pulling away the social covers.

Born Irish but functioning as an English intellectual, Sheridan may have felt in some confusion as to his role. When Captain Absolute is asked (by his father, of all people) 'Who the devil are you?' the reply suggests some self-doubt: 'I am not quite clear myself; but I'll endeavour to recollect.'[20] The character of Sir Lucius O'Trigger emphasizes still more directly a possible Irish subtheme, for as he moves across the world of the English aristocracy, he enacts a version of Sheridan's own struggle to be recognized as at once an Irishman and a gentleman. By 1775 the stereotypical view of the native Irish as wild, impulsive drunkards had been extended to include the Anglo-Irish aristocracy as well. Exactly thirty years earlier in *The Brave Irishman*, Thomas Sheridan had immortalized a laughable, upper-class Protestant, Captain O'Blunder, whose massive frame caused English people to gape, before his exclamation: 'Well, you scoundrels, you sons of whores, did you never see an Irish shentleman before?'[21] The republican dream – to unite Catholic, Protestant and Dissenter under the common name of Irishmen – was being implemented on the London stage, but in a debased fashion: no distinction was any longer made between the mere Irish and the gentry, for all were 'wild Irish' now.

Sir Lucius O'Trigger is a credible portrait of the sort of Anglo-Irish landlord who, having frittered away his inheritance, came over to England during the eighteenth century in search of a wealthy wife. His high spirits verge on neurosis and he converts every scene of his progress into melodrama, as if he is trying to convince himself that he still has the capacity to feel. The sheer excess of gesture hints at an inner doubt. The 'mansion-house and dirty wares' have slipped through his fingers, alas, but he can still find comfort in the knowledge that 'our honour, and the family pictures, are fresh as ever'.[22] Sheridan had learned enough from his two duels to realize that 'honour' may be no more than the last luxury item hoarded by a discredited upper class. Sir Lucius may fulminate 'What the devil signifies *right*, when your *honour* is concerned?'[23] but it appears that, like many another buck, he fights to uphold the tradition of the fight rather than being able to articulate what exactly he is fighting for: 'Pray sir, be easy: the quarrel is a very pretty quarrel as it stands; we should only spoil it by trying to explain it.'[24] Sir Lucius, being a gentleman, assumes that, old and penniless though he be, a pretty face such as Lydia's is his by right; Captain Absolute, now certain that he has lost Lydia with the revelation that he tricked her into the belief that he was the poor ensign, is reckless enough in mood to accept the idiotic challenge. Asked by his father for some explanation, he simply shouts, 'Sir, I serve his majesty' – Sheridan's sure diagnosis, as a committed republican, of the link between two out-worn codes.

The dramatist's real feelings about the duels he had so recently fought may be deduced from an exchange in which a county squire Bob Acres is educated to a more modern attitude by his servant David:

ACRES: David, no gentleman will ever risk the loss of his honour.
DAVID: I say then, it would be but civil in honour never to risk the loss of the gentleman.[25]

This anticipates O'Casey's jibe that instead of gunmen dying for the people, the people are dying for the gunmen. Sheridan was material-ist enough to revise his notions of honour: for he has David suggest that the grave 'is just the place where I could make a shift to do with-out it'.[26] In that sane view of things, the best way of honouring dead ancestors is to keep as long as possible out of their company.

The transitional nature of Sheridan's society may be inferred from the fact that the servants not only speak the soundest sense in the play but also propel the main turns in the plot. No longer passive spectators of aristocratic foibles, they have minds and agendas of their own. Lydia's chamberwoman Lucy adopts a mask of silliness beneath which she goes to work. She extracts payments from the impecunious 'Ensign Beverley' for bearing messages, even as she fools Sir Lucius into the belief that his correspondence is with the ravishing Lydia rather than the ageing Malaprop: 'for, though not over-rich, I found that he had too much pride and delicacy to sacri-fice the feelings of a gentleman to the necessities of his fortune'.[27] Sir Lucius is one of the earliest in a long line of aristocrats who find that the titled property which gives them prestige also prevents them from keeping it up. So, in a rich anticipation of the plot of *Castle Rackrent*, he defeats his own agenda by his naïveté, arrogance and sheer pretension.

The actor who played Sir Lucius in the original production was by most accounts drunk, and his exaggerated gestures so incensed the audience that the play had to be withdrawn for eleven nights so that cuts and revisions could be made. By 1775 the London-Irish had clearly begun to wield some power as a lobby, and they were under-standably sensitive to misrepresentations in plays composed by Irish authors, who might be seen to ratify false stereotypes. These, after all, were those of whom Dr Johnson jibed that the Irish, being a fair people, never spoke well of one another. The controversy that erupted around *The Rivals* might seem to have borne him out, for there was little enough in the text (whatever about the acting) to justify the audience's tetchiness.

In the Preface he attached to the revised version, Sheridan insisted that he had no intention of offending 'the country supposed to be reflected on'.[28] The word 'supposed' is crucial: Sir Lucius was not intended to represent a people, merely the degenerate members of the Anglo-Irish aristocracy. The protesting London press had, nevertheless, read the part as one with more general implication: it was 'an ungenerous attack upon a nation' according to the *Morning Post* and 'so far from giving the manners of our brave and worthy neighbours that it scarce equals the picture of a respectable Hottentot', according to the *Morning Chronicle*.[29] By 30 January the *Chronicle* was offering forgiveness and absolution but still missing the point: the new Sir Lucius was, it opined, 'no longer designed as an insult on our neighbours on the other side of St George's Channel'. Sheridan, for his part, continued to suspect that the whole attack had been orchestrated, a case of malice aforethought rather than honest criticism.[30]

Certainly, the Anglo-Irish had grown ever more touchy about their image in the eyes of the world. If in an earlier part of the century Goldsmith had mocked their philistinism, by 1789 the Cavan noblewoman Charlotte Brooke published her *Reliques of Irish Poetry* with the intention of clearing the name of her class and defending it against the charge of lacking any enlightened interest in Gaelic culture. Sensing the growing mood of patriotism, Sheridan shrewdly turned the misinterpretation of his play to his own devices, much as a wrestler might use the very force of an attack against the opponent himself:

> If the condemnation of the comedy . . . could have added one spark to the decaying flame of national attachment to the country supposed to be reflected on, I should have been happy in its fate; and might with truth have boasted, that it had done more real service in its failure, than the successful morality of a thousand stage-novels will ever effect.[31]

This managed to suggest that *he* was really a frustrated patriot, appalled by the apparent collapse of national sentiment in Ireland.

If Sir Lucius is one of the decaying Anglo-Irish gentry whom the Sheridans had left in their native land, Captain Absolute seems to represent the sort of youth whom Sheridan felt himself to have been in England – calculating but good-natured, pushy but charming. Less cynical than the protagonists of Restoration comedy, he practises his deceptions not to further his progress as a rake but to win the woman he loves. The plot might accordingly be accused of a certain tameness. In effect Sir Anthony is attempting to compel his son to marry the very woman whom he has been secretly courting under the disguise of Ensign Beverley. Captain Absolute's problem is clear: he must play at being a poverty-stricken, modern, sentimental lover, while knowing himself to be really a conventionally moneyed aristocratic buck: 'I am by no means certain that she would take me with the impediments of our friend's consent, a regular humdrum wedding, and the reversion of a good fortune on my side; no, no, I must prepare her gradually for the discovery . . .'[32]

It is the new cult of sentiment that compels 'Ensign Beverley' to shiver in a freezing January garden as he plots elopement with Lydia, She takes a suspicious pleasure in these shared sufferings and in the prospect of more to come: 'How persuasive are his words! How charming poverty will be with him!' Lydia is already on the high road to romantic catastrophe:

Ah my soul! what a life will we then have? Love shall be our idol and support . . . proud of calamity, we will enjoy the wreck of wealth; while the surrounding gloom of adversity shall make the flame of our pure love show doubly bright.[33]

This is one of the earliest parodies of left-wing pastoral and of assumed poverty in modern writing. Out of her own mouth, Lydia convicts herself of pseudo-radicalism, of playing at dissent from a position of remarkable comfort.

Of course, Sheridan is wily enough to sense that he too could be accused of similar bad faith. His mockery of Lydia's novels loses its edge when presented in a play that is itself quite novelistic; and though he may drench the lines in an atmosphere of Restoration wit and depravity, that is only an atmosphere. His plot, deep down, is not only sentimental but downright conservative. In the final marriage between two wealthy aristocrats the old social system will be upheld. It is as if the illicit pleasures of Restoration subterfuge can be harnessed to the needs of a now-romantic upper class. Pretending to be a bold deceiver while actually being a straight lover, Captain Absolute can laugh at the ambiguity of his situation: 'My father wants to force me to marry the very girl I am plotting to run away with.'[34] He stands happily enough on the cusp between two worlds, a new sort of likeable rogue who pretends to be bad while secretly being good all along. He is one of the first in a line of youths who commit some understandable indiscretion so that their admirers can have the greater pleasure of forgiving them. Sir Anthony Absolute is rather relieved to discover that the son, who had seemed cravenly willing to enter the forced match, is not such a dullard after all. Lydia is slower to come round, accusing the Captain of playing the radical lover whom she alone managed to be: 'What, you have been *treating* me like a *child* – humouring my romance.'[35] Her thrilling scenario – a ladder of ropes, four horses and a Scottish parson – now recedes as she is 'made into a mere Smithfield bargain'.[36]

There is real sentiment as well as high ridiculousness in this scene, because throughout the play Lydia has been trying to believe in the reality of her own feelings, to make them more than mere conventions. That is an aspiration she shares with as unlikely a counterpart as Sir Lucius: both attempt to register emotion in a world where real feeling has been buried very deep. The remembered image of the Ensign kneeling to her prompts her to blurt to her friend: 'Ah, Julia! that was something like being in love.'[37] Yet perhaps Lydia herself was only playing a part too. Her life is so conditioned by wealth that even her gestures of revolt turn out to be rank self-indulgences: 'while I fondly imagined we were deceiving my relations, and flattered myself that I should outwit and incense them all . . .'[38] The unmasking of parental hypocrisy may have been higher on her agenda than a real relationship with a young man. Her servant Lucy is more adept at working within the constraints of her station in life, partly because she is better reconciled to it. She is, therefore, more able to manipulate it for her own ends under a mask of silliness, much as Sheridan himself employed the shell of Restoration comedy to contain his drama of feeling.

Likewise Fag, servant to Captain Absolute, sometimes needs to coach his master in his assumed roles, anticipating the Jeeves-like tradition by which the servant will from time to time deftly extricate his master from shared scrapes: 'I beg pardon, sir, but should Sir Anthony call, you will do me the favour to remember that we are *recruiting*, if you please.'[39] It is, none the less, a sign of health that the Captain needs such reminding, a proof that he has not been fully taken over by his role. Lydia has been overwhelmed by hers. Her supreme disillusion is her discovery that she has been liberating an already free man. In the words of one commentator: 'she is not the radical critic of her culture that she imagines herself to be; she is rather the mildly self-deluded comic heroine'.[40] The Captain is a truer radical, in the sense of one who solves the problem of reconciling tradition and innovation by the invention of a double persona. If he absconds with her, she loses two-thirds of her money; if he admits his real identity too soon, he loses her. The plot centres on his need to educate her out of her literary postures, much as the male protagonists of Jane

Austen novels some twenty-five years later would educate her heroines.

This conveys some sense of Sheridan's innovation. Yet his pose was that of an artistic traditionalist, reworking the modes of earlier comedy and the domestic manners of the Fielding-type novel. He posed as a cultural conservative, while being genuinely in sympathy with the emerging new structures of feeling and of form. There are moments in *The Rivals* when each of the main characters might, with a slight twist of fate, have plunged suddenly into a tragic world of suffering and loss: but the romantic agony is kept at bay by a modicum of sense.

Some critics have accused Sheridan of being a little like Lydia and the Captain, of playing the rebel while secretly being an arch-traditionalist. In their reading, he is in bad faith – a playwright who attacks the sentimentalism of Lydia only to fall back on it at the end. Needing money, the dramatist is accused of pandering to his immediate audience: 'a greater or more serious dramatist might have succeeded in reanimating the traditions rather than simply and haphazardly borrowing from them'.[41] His immense and continuing popularity has evoked much suspicion among intellectuals with a principled aversion to general public taste. Yet the public is more quickly bored by repetition than are most intellectuals. Sheridan must have been on to something more than that.

His success can be traced to his mingling not just of the laughing comedy and the sentimental comedy but of the modes of drama and novel. The new sentimental comedy was a hybrid in which tears were shed but nobody got badly hurt: by disrupting genres, moreover, the playwright could make comedy weep and tragedy laugh. Sheridan infused old forms with real feeling, reconciling the theatricality of the well-made plot with the pressure of actual emotion. Lydia Languish may be at times as ridiculous as her name, but she is also natural on many occasions, and by no means always predictable or 'legible'. In a world that offers only assigned scripts to heiresses, she seeks to write her own, even fabricating a letter to herself about the Ensign's reported infidelity. Her attempt to create a role for Beverley suggests a desire to smite rather than be smitten: and the freezing conditions she imposes may hint at a covert revenge for all the power wielded by men. This oscillating psychology is the equivalent of the intermittent bursts of misogyny on the part of such otherwise courtly fellows as Anthony Absolute and Faulkland – the former threatens his son with an heiress possessed of skin like a mummy and the beard of a Jew, while the latter vows to punish himself with some ancient virago if he loses his darling Julia. Beneath the bland social surface one detects a battle of the sexes, which could break out at any moment if instincts are not held in some sort of check. If the political problem of the eighteenth century was the avoidance of another Civil War, its social correlative was a desire to end the war between men and women, to rationalize the sexual instinct with social needs, as Merriman tried to do in *Cúirt an Mheán-Oíche*. Far from being a trivial concern, this was a test of the very feasibility of civilization itself.

Restoration comedy had been established in the age of the microscope on the sense of a perpetual discrepancy between outer form and inner essence. Its heroes and heroines were those who negotiated that discrepancy with panache; its fools and fops simply got these things confused. Much of its mockery had been against exponents of 'enthusiasm', which led them to take the world or themselves too seriously. Yet there had been in many plays a growing impatience with made marriages and a rival claim on behalf of the emotions and the needs of the human body. That is one reason why both lovers are endowed with fortunes in *The Rivals*: to show that they love one another for themselves and not their gold. It is her money (the very thing she wants to give up) that leaves Lydia free to choose with all the social independence of a man – or of a free citizen. There is a demonstrable link between the ideas of Sheridan and Merriman: both address the problem of women's autonomy in a system that reduces each to a Smithfield bargain or else a leftover like Mrs Malaprop, in whose head the whole system has built a demeaning replica of itself.

Had Sheridan simply mirrored his age, his art would soon have been forgotten, but because he existed in an allegorical relation to his times he was able to float free of them. His transcendence of the limits of his age was made possible, like Merriman's, by a dynamic traditionalism. He used the cynical shell of Restoration comedy to insure against his own sentimentality: and yet he saw beyond that sentiment to the romanticism of the next age. The character of Faulkland represented a new kind of protagonist, a male neurotic riven by doubt and self-cancelling instincts. His misplaced suspicions of the ever-faithful Julia contrast utterly with Malaprop's misplaced confidence in the never-reliable Lucius O'Trigger. Compared with him, a good-bad son like Captain Absolute seems the very picture of rude health – yet Sheridan acutely senses that this new self-divided protagonist might prove endlessly fascinating in the role of male coquette forever teasing some unfortunate woman. Julia gamely explains her love: 'his humility makes him undervalue those qualities in him, which would entitle him to it; and not feeling why he should be loved to the degree he wishes, he suspects that he is not loved enough'.[42] Toying with his own scruples, Faulkland can seldom feel worthy of his beloved. Immobilized by the very intensity of his feeling, he will in time become a subject better suited to a lyric poem or *Bildungsroman*, but in a play where even sentiment is open to suspicion, his sexual ardour is tolerated rather than celebrated. The rules of Restoration comedy, after all, had insisted that naked passion was risible as well as disruptive: and *The Rivals* is in the end 'a nice derangement of epitaphs' on earlier English comedy, 'one of those jaunty epitaphs that delight in rehearsing and summarising the main features and signal achievements of that which has passed from the world'.[43]

Yet in Sheridan's hands, as in Gaelic tradition, old forms can be filled once again with the breath of life. His next major play, *The School for Scandal* (1777), has also been written off by some carpers as a botched splicing of Restoration comedy and the novel of manners. Undeniably, there are one or two scenes where the joins show. Sheridan nervously explored his own doubts about such splicing in Sir Benjamin Backbite's savage commentary on a Mrs Evergreen at the play's outset:

> . . . 'tis not that she paints so ill – but when she has finished her face, she joins it on so badly to her neck that she looks like a mended statue, in which the connoisseur sees at once that the head's modern, though the trunk's antique.[44]

With his interest in the apparent and the real, Sheridan was far too conscious a stylist not to be aware of the implications of such a conceit for his own theatrical practice. There were many who said that he had done the theatrical equivalent in *The Rivals*, and the *Morning Chronicle* made the same claim in relation to *The School for Scandal*:

> Several of the situations approach so very nearly to those in other plays that nothing but the great skill of Mr Sheridan, in giving an originality of dialogue to the characters, could have saved them from being direct imitations of other works.

That is far too harsh. Every artist borrows but the test of a great artist is, as T.S. Eliot said, how he or she uses the borrowings. Sheridan's use of surface parallels and ironical contrasts with Restoration drama might be more fully understood in terms of Eliot's manipulation of ancient myth. To superficial eyes and ears, Eliot's use of myth in *The Waste Land* might have seemed a weak mimicry of James Joyce's handling of *The Odyssey* in *Ulysses*, but future users of myth, Eliot insisted, 'will not be imitators, any more than the scientist who uses the discoveries of an Einstein, in pursuing his own, independent, further investigations'.[46]

For Sheridan the prior forms of comedy had all the revelatory power of myth. They are effectively pronounced dead by the young heroine Maria at the start of the play, when she repudiates the scandal-mongers, telling Lady Sneerwell: 'For my part, I confess, madam, wit loses its respect with me when I see it in company with malice.'[47] Yet the superannuated forms of raillery and wit come back to a kind of life, despite that denunciation. They remain, however, on the periphery of the action, managing only to draw the more impressionable female characters into their field of force: Maria and Lady Teazle may find in them the lure and glamour of the forbidden in a world where the roles available to women are paltry indeed. The play, by opening with the scandal-school, seems to promise one kind of work, while proceeding to deliver quite another, as it moves with astonishing speed from witty cynicism to naked sentiment. Most of the characters of the school remain undeveloped, two-dimensional.

Sheridan was invoking dangers here. His play, though it veers away from the school, runs dangerously close to its central tenet, which is that sentiment is merely the reverse side of the coin of wit. The last line of the opening scene admits as much in Lady Sneerwell's advice to Joseph Surface: 'In the meantime I'll go and plot mischief – and you shall study sentiment.'[48] Joseph is a bad-good man, who affects virtue while harbouring rakish designs on Maria. Lady Sneerwell justly remarks: 'I know him to be artful, selfish and malicious – in short, a sentimental knave.'[49] He decides to recruit the young Lady Teazle (already frustrated by her recent marriage to the elderly Sir Peter) as an ally and lover. Meanwhile, Joseph's brother Charles, as good-bad man, cheerfully accepts the world's valuation of him as a spendthrift wastrel, while secretly remaining loyal to his true love, Maria, who returns his love. Sir Peter Teazle complains that this defection by Maria (who is his ward) appears to match that of his frustrated wife: she 'is determined to turn rebel too, and absolutely refuses the man whom I long resolved on for her husband – meaning, I suppose, to bestow herself on his profligate brother'.[50]

The uncle of the Surface brothers, Sir Oliver, returns with riches from India, giving both men grounds for hope: but he is equal to their wiles. He disguises himself as a Mr Stanley, a poor relation whom Joseph unfeelingly turns away, and then as Mr Premium, a

moneylender, to whom Charles sells off the family pictures (something not even Sir Lucius O'Trigger would part with). 'Sure, you
wouldn't sell your forefathers, would you?' asks an anxious 'Mr
Premium', only to discover that his nephew is one who would happily give up art for an enhanced quality of life. 'To be sure, 'tis very
affecting,' Charles muses, 'but rot 'em, you see they never move a
muscle, so why should I?'[51] If books were summoned to be thrown
aside in the earlier play, much the same happens to paintings in this
one. There is, however, just one portrait that Charles insists on
retaining: that of the young Sir Oliver, for whose generosity he feels
an unfeigned gratitude. In this he reveals – for all his dubious dealings with moneylenders and servants – an essential goodness of heart.
Such a good-bad man proves as irresistible as Captain Absolute had
been to his father. Once again the apparent intolerance of meddle-
some older folk masks a tender concern for the young. 'For my part,'
says Sir Oliver, 'I hate to see prudence clinging to the green suckers
of youth; 'tis like ivy round a sapling and spoils the growth of the
tree.'[52] Neither he nor his brother was a very prudent youth and so
he can forgive Charles's high spirits.

Charles appears for the first time at a rather late stage in the third
act. By then, he is less a person than a whole climate of opinion, created largely on the basis of gossip and rumour. He is never shown in
a romantic scene with Maria, so the audience (like the characters)
must guess at his honesty of purpose. Sir Peter Teazle is sure that he
is paying illicit court to Lady Teazle: in fact, this is being done by
Joseph, much to the chagrin of Lady Sneerwell, who urges him to be
constant to one roguery at a time.

In many ways, Joseph Surface is an inchoate character, very hard
to pin down. He is not even coherent in his villainies, maintaining a
pointless mask of rectitude among the cynical wits. He acts as a sort
of shadow side to the more sunny Charles, a foil to set off the inadvertent decency and instinctive virtue of the other man. With his
rascally asides, he seems less a person than the embodiment of the
social force of hypocrisy. Like all shadows and doubles, he must disappear from the daylight world of the stage when his brother finally
sorts his own life out. At that moment of exposure by Sir Oliver, the
two men share something as intimate as their lines of mutual recognition. Having shared his love of plotting, not to mention his witty
one-liners, the audience does not wish him to be entirely undone. His
punishment will be a very modern one – to have to know his self and
also to know that it has been revealed to the world. The unmasker
will be unmasked.

By the time he wrote *The School for Scandal*, Sheridan was the manager of the Drury Lane Theatre. In the period preceding his play, he staged three plays by Congreve and one by Vanbrugh, reminding his audience of the rules he was about to redesign. Joseph Surface's penchant for plotting and gossip is wholly within the tradition, but it predisposes the audience in favour of the man of feeling and instinct. The young Lady Teazle's restlessness in marriage to an old husband is also within the mode, but her assignation with Joseph in her husband's library tilts her life in the darker direction of domestic tragedy. Joseph, within the tradition, suggests that her goodness will be too great to be credible: unless she sins soon in her own defence, questions will be asked and tongues will wag. When her husband arrives to confide his doubts to Joseph, she hides behind a screen. Despite his honest admission that the difference in age makes it unlikely that she could love him, he resolves to treat her generously: and she, who was intended to hear nothing of this, hears all. Next Charles arrives and Sir Peter must hide behind another screen. He is less willing to believe that 'a little French milliner' stands behind the other screen and throws it down. The dénouement is remarkable; for Lady Teazle explodes Joseph's attempt to explain her presence away and she asserts her own shame, as well as her undying love for her husband. This is an utter reversal of the modes of Restoration comedy, for it declares the priority of the heart over the head, marriage over libertinism, the domestic over the sexual.

All this is not yet fully clear, however, for the shadow of tragedy still threatens. Sir Peter fears that he will be a laughing-stock if he accepts the renewed vows of his wife. Lady Teazle, who has only flirted with Joseph, complains, 'I'll not be suspected without cause, I promise you,' but her husband's initial instinct is to make 'an example of myself for the benefit of all old bachelors'.[53] The gossips, meanwhile, have put it about that he was injured in a duel with Charles. Sheridan, once again, having read the more preposterous rumours circulated about his own duels, had a well-developed contempt for the slanderers. When Sir Peter re-emerges at the close, Sir Oliver mocks the man's blithe refusal to play the part assigned him by the gossip machine: 'Why man, what do you out of bed with a small sword through your body, and a bullet lodged in your thorax?' The energy of such gossip had been defended by Joseph as a sign of creativity, but Maria was never convinced: 'Then is their conduct still more contemptible, for, in my opinion, nothing could excuse the intemperance of their tongues but a natural and ungovernable bitterness of mind.'[54] Sir Peter is disinclined to forgive his wavering partner, lest he be a joke among the scandal-mongers, but his servant Rowley teaches him a domestic virtue: to be happy in spite of wagging tongues. He seems on the verge of propounding some Addisonian moral, but Sir Peter cries halt: 'If you have any regard for me, never let me hear you utter anything like a sentiment: I have had enough of them to serve me the rest of my life.'[55] Instead of being voiced in words, the sentiment should be embodied at once at the level of action: and so at the close Sir Peter can confront the slanderers whom he feared with his own slander on them: 'Fiends! Vipers! Furies!'[56]

The slanderers are wholly repudiated and that repudiation has been long in the preparation. They are minor characters with grudges to bear from past hurts; and all their attempts to make new recruits fail. Their slow but steady relegation dramatizes onstage the gradual death of Restoration culture, with its satiric and aristocratic codes. The play may end with a dismissal of *sententiae*, but it implements a sentimental morality, made tolerable by bouts of wit and flashes of real danger. That danger never distresses for long and the wit is always more genial than cutting. This has led some critics to accuse Sheridan of being a crowd-pleaser. A century later, for example, George Bernard Shaw complained that a man who acted like Lady Teazle in outing a putative lover would rightly be called a bounder and hypocrite: 'I cannot for the life of me see why it is less dishonourable for a woman to kiss and tell than for a man.'[57] Of course, Shaw wanted an Ibsenite problem play, not a sentimental comedy.

Sheridan did supply his own innovations. If the manifest form of *The School for Scandal* was satiric comedy, the latent content was that of the new romanticism. When the man of feeling, Charles, knocked down the screen in Act Four, the roar of the audience was so loud that a passing boy ran away in terror, thinking that the theatre was about to collapse.[58] In fact, what collapsed was the code of the older comedy. The scene cried out for interpretation. Within the proscenium arch, as Katharine Worth has observed, the screen that shielded Lady Teazle was a frame-within-a-frame, the still centre of an ever-changing picture, as first her husband and then Charles Surface made their visits. Onto its surface might be mapped the growing anxieties of the previous century. On the side walls of the stage in the original production were painted representations of a theatrical audience, as if to emphasize not just the false play-acting of all parties but also the stage as 'a place where actors and audience come close in confrontation'.[59]

One effect of that confrontation was the collapse of a fashion system. Henceforth the offence of the villain would not be against manners but against domestic virtue; and the scandals of such villains would be printed (rather than spoken) in the newspaper, the chosen medium of the new bourgeoisie. In a Restoration play like *The Country Wife* Lady Teazle would have been laughed to scorn as a stumbling rustic. In *The School for Scandal*, once the screen falls, she becomes the centre of all moral meanings. Even the new kind of villain, for all his malicious intent, gets to do remarkably little damage: neither Lady Teazle nor Maria have a glove laid on them. The practised performances of Lady Sneerwell, Joseph and their circle help to drench the play in an aura of cynicism, even as the inner movements of the plot remain proof against their stratagems. Sheridan rewrote the drama for an audience now composed of all social classes: and to do that he had to blend contrary forces in his art. The screen scene would have been far less explosive for that first-night audience if Drury Lane had been filled with sparkish aristocrats, but the presence of merchants and even servants ensured that the old cynicism could not survive. Behind the fallen screen opened a space which might have been filled with prolonged suffering and a decline into domestic tragedy. By appealing to feeling within the wider context of dramatic artifice, Sheridan fused the truly dramatic with the utterly quotidian.

Not everyone has felt caught up in such moments, and some audiences hanker after something deeper. Louis Kronenberger has contended that the playwright was too dependent on worldly success to become a convincing delineator of worldliness, and that, for the sake of popularity, he remained a willing prisoner of the rudimentary tastes of his audience. The characters are not deep, he suggests, and what they discover at the end is not the wisdom of the ages but the nature of one another.[60] But that may be enough to be going on with. As in all drama, the lines written for an actor and the stage directions are no more than hints at how the role might be played: much more can be implied by a movement of the eye or a catch in the voice.

Some great writers, from Shakespeare to Eliot, have invented little. What gives their work its power is its ability to create new alignments of thought and feeling from a language and a genre which to lesser imaginations seemed incapable of renewal. It was William Hazlitt, another visionary radical, who captured best the nature of Sheridan's genius. Anticipating Eliot's comment on the manipulation of myth, Hazlitt wrote with beautiful tact that 'he could imitate with the spirit of an inventor'. Yet Sheridan has often been called a fretful plagiarist. Far from soothing audiences with images of concord, his plays touched off immense insecurities, as people heard familiar phrases used in utterly new ways and saw stock situations run counter to all expectation. Hazlitt, a man who well understood the subversive potential of any dynamic engagement with tradition, precisely described Sheridan's process: 'He wrote in imitation of Congreve, Vanbrugh or Wycherley, as those persons would have written in imitation of themselves, had they lived at the same time with him.'[61]

That method would be practised by many later Irish writers, who quickly learned how to present new ideas in old packages. In a land where tradition was glorified to precisely the extent that it came under attack, that was often a wise option. An immediate contemporary of Sheridan, the Gaelic poet Merriman, gift-wrapped a modern philosophy of sexuality in the forms of *aisling* lyricism. Over a century later, thinkers like Patrick Pearse and James Connolly would secure a hearing for their new-fangled theories in an identical way. Pearse assured his followers that the Montessori method of education which he favoured would be nothing more than a return to Gaelic methods of fosterage; and Connolly contended that his desired socialism would remould the old Gaelic property system, in which a chieftain held the land in the name of all the people, except for the fact that in future the role of chieftain would be discharged by a caring state. Sean O'Casey, another socialist, would encase his ideas in the forms of a music-hall variety show. His debt to Sheridan was arguably the greatest of all: his use of the pseudo-couple for comic purposes, his obsession with misused words, his mingling of tears and smiles, his conviction of the essential goodness of persons and his melodramatic reversal-and-recognition scenes all owe a huge debt to his predecessor.

The price of promoting new ideas is often the need to clothe them in familiar garments in order to make them seem cosily unremarkable. One consequent danger is that covert innovators may go under-celebrated, if not unrecognized. Even Sheridan's greatest admirers have argued that 'instead of proposing alternative modes of understanding or feeling, he operated entirely within those that were given to him, but seized control of them and made them serve his own purposes'.[62] He did a lot more than that implies, yet he gave to his writings the *look* of a tame traditionalism. Earlier in the eighteenth century, a much more conservative thinker, Swift, had performed a reverse feat, equally paradoxical, for he expressed his defence of past culture in styles that were audaciously new. In that way he hoped to defeat the moderns on their own ground, encasing his ancient ideas in a set of experimental forms that gave them some chance of survival in a fast-changing world. That strain in Irish writing would prove even more potent, issuing in the dynamic archaism of a Yeats or a Synge. Yet the sponsors of the two traditions had something in common: a belief that all truly vibrant cultures are Janus-faced, capable of looking backward and forward at the same time. In their different ways, they refused to see past and future as zones of opposition, celebrating instead the exponents of paradox who undid such oppositions – aristocratic radicals, liberal Tories, libertine moralists, and so on. In doing so much, they remembered the future and anticipated the past, along the very lines proposed by Mrs Malaprop: 'We will not anticipate the past – our retrospection will be all to the future.'[63]

Sheridan's life as a dramatist soon gave way to his interest in politics. He became one of the greatest orators of his time, and with Edmund Burke supported the impeachment of Warren Hastings and the East India Company. At Hastings's trial in 1788, Sheridan spoke for four days before collapsing into Burke's arms. It was a consummate performance, which many titled people paid fifty pounds to witness (some duchesses lost their shoes in the scramble for seats). But it was also a sincere expression of outrage against a set of colonial thugs who had bled India and set children there against parents. The Vizier in India extorted treasure from his mother to bankroll the East India operatives, while all the time Hastings worked 'to harden the son's heart, to choke the struggling nature in his bosom'.[64] In Sheridan's view, the bond between parent and child was stronger than that between lovers: and, as Burke had done in his strictures against the Penal Laws in Ireland, he evoked its violation in a charged language: 'The morality, the instinct, the sacrament of nature' that was filial love had been outraged by the colonial buccaneers.[65] He was even more scathing of Hastings than of the Vizier, and his portrait of an almost gratuitous love of malice recalls that of Joseph Surface: 'if there is anything worse than a wilful persecutor of his mother – it is to see a deliberate, reasoning instigator and abettor to the deed: this it is that shrieks, disgusts and appals the mind much more than the other . . .'[66]

Sheridan fretted much about his own children, perhaps because he had felt abandoned himself when young. The early deaths of Eliza and their daughter Mary devastated him. He was never astute in handling cash, yet his lifestyle called for endless injections of money. His affairs with society ladies were a further drain on his pocket. The consequences were dire. A friend at the Opera House said that he could not doff his hat to Sheridan without it costing fifty pounds: if he stopped to speak, he was touched for a hundred.

As a theatre manager, Sheridan was ineffectual. Even as a playwright, he sent his scripts in late: the fourth act of *The School for Scandal* was written in a single day with the under-prompter taking each sheet away on completion so that the cast might commit the lines to memory. In 1794 Drury Lane, which Sheridan had built in a drive for bigger audiences and productions, burned down. He left his seat in the House of Commons and watched the blaze from a coffee house: 'a man may surely be allowed to take a glass of wine by his own fireside', he quipped.[67] That refusal to take his own concerns too seriously was seized on by political opponents. Sheridan's conservative enemy William Pitt liked to dismiss him as an Irish purveyor of fancy, epigram and histrionic speeches, accusing him of an overtheatrical mode of address.[68]

Ireland remained a great concern, for Sheridan was an anti-imperialist. If Burke castigated the East India Company as an abuse of empire, Sheridan saw it as abuse by empire. Unlike Burke, he had no patrons among the aristocracy and so felt free to attack the behaviour of absentee Irish landlords and the restrictions placed by Pitt upon Irish trade. He was a keen supporter of the republican movement in the 1790s and defended its right to use force. Accordingly, the *Sun* of London accused him of supporting 'traitors'. Opposing the decision to send militias to Ireland to quell the 1798 rising, he insisted that it was the war of a nation against a government. 'To keep Ireland against the will of the people is a vain expectation,' he said. He denounced the Act of Union and averred, 'we shall love each other, if we be left to ourselves. It is the union of minds which ought to bind these nations together.'[69]

In a play called *Pizarro* put on in 1798, Sheridan described the behaviour of the Spanish in Peru with the kind of emotion that arose from his feelings about Ireland. Some of his best friends among the rebel leaders were now dead, others in jail. A matter of months before the passing of the Act of Union, he had a character named Rolla object to the European colonialists in words of wide implication:

> They offer us their protection. Yes, such protection as a vulture gives to lambs – covering and devouring them. They call on us to barter all of good we have inherited and proved, for the desperate chance of something better which they promise – Be our plain answer this: The throne we honour is the *people's choice* – the laws we reverence are our brave fathers' legacy – the faith we follow teaches us to live in bonds of charity with all mankind, and die with hope of bliss beyond the grave. Tell your invaders this, and tell them, too, we seek no change; and least of all, such change as they would bring us.[70]

In the play another character, Alonzo, says: 'I have not warred against my native land, but against those who have usurped its power.' If justice is denied, he adds, he has no country. *Pizarro* was a success, yet everyone knew that its author might be branded a traitor. He never did fetch up in the Tower, but he was jailed for debt. Even in his later years, he was still planning that the heir-apparent to the British throne should go to Ireland as President of a new council: in 1803 he suggested that he himself should accompany him as a member of the council to oversee Catholic Emancipation. His last message to the House of Commons was: 'Be just to Ireland, as you value your own honour – be just to Ireland as you value your own peace.'[71] He died in poverty.

Sheridan's weakness was a desire to have things both ways – and that was also his strength. He consorted with French and Irish rebels against the crown, yet aspired to be loved by the English people (and he often was). He tried by sheer force of personality to reconcile republican notions of citizenship and universal rights with the finer residues of English culture. English radicals like Hazlitt blessed his memory and recalled with fondness their enjoyment of *The School for Scandal*, which had come to the stage at that moment of optimism between the American and French revolutions, when human nature seemed about to be born again. It wasn't to be. Sheridan made the mistake of believing that he could effect a real breakthrough in politics and art by using forms bequeathed to him by a society whose pageants and plays proved its members to be deeply attached to tradition. It was the traditionalist Burke rather than the radical Sheridan who would wield tangible influence in the end, not least on the question of how best to understand Ireland. Yet Sheridan, a likeable optimist, remained convinced that English society contained the seeds of its own renovation. As he lay dying in July 1816, he may have wondered whether his art and his thought might not have been better served had he conducted his search for innovation in his own country.

11

Eibhlín Dhubh Ní Chonaill: The Lament for Art Ó Laoghaire

If you intend to marry, warned Chekhov, prepare to be lonely. So it was for Eibhlín Dhubh Ní Chonaill. Raised at Derrynane, County Kerry, in one of the last Gaelic mansions, she grew up against a background of real affluence, amidst retinues of servants. Her people were at once heirs to 'the full Irish cultural tradition, aristocratic as well as popular' and confident participants in the English-language life of the merchant and administrative classes of late-eighteenth-century Ireland.[1] Her mother was a poet and a proud, independent spirit; the furniture in her home was of the finest mahogany and her dresses were made of silk. Eibhlín married and was widowed while still very young. Then in 1767, while in her late twenties, she fell in love with a 21-year-old captain, Art Ó Laoghaire, who had served in the Hungarian Hussars.

Her family was devastated and utterly opposed to the runaway match, made in the same year. Ó Laoghaire already had a reputation for headstrong, flamboyant behaviour: he wore a sword openly in public defiance of the Penal Code, and a favourite hobby of his was to stand on a rolling barrel in the main street of Macroom, in his native County Cork, causing the townsfolk to scatter in his path. By contrast, the O'Connells, living in a remote part of Kerry, did all they could to avoid brushes with the hated English authorities. Eibhlín's father could not forgive her folly in marrying Ó Laoghaire, a young buck who seemed bound to come to a bad end. Her mother simply refused to speak to her after the elopement.

Their worries were well grounded. The Munster gentry was taking a dim view of uppity Catholics: in 1766 a priest named Nicholas Sheehy had been hanged on trumped-up charges, to the outrage of Edmund Burke, who had been to school in the area some years earlier. Wealthier Catholics considered that under the Penal Laws discretion might be the better part of valour, but Burke did not agree. He said they 'should be assertive, and that their own timidity had contributed to their plight'.[2] Burke masterminded the defence of a case brought against forty well-to-do Catholics in 1766–7. This may have emboldened young bloods like Ó Laoghaire to thumb their noses at the gentry. He was, after all, young, inexperienced and imbued since his Continental tour of duty with the certainty that Catholics had a right to wield traditional power. Various rumours circulated about him: that he was a rake who took advantage of poor local women; that he rode a mare worth well over five pounds in breach of the Penal Laws; that he was in open contest with a former sheriff named Abraham Morris for the favours of a lady.

As God made Ó Laoghaire and Morris, so he matched them, for one was as headstrong as the other. In July 1771, a Muskerry Constitutional Society was founded to seek complaints from 'injured poor persons of the barony'.[3] Ó Laoghaire went to see the magistrate Morris, perhaps to protect some of his own retinue from charges of rakish behaviour. Morris, keen to cut his rival down to size, invoked the Penal Code and offered five pounds for his beautiful brown mare. Ó Laoghaire refused. As he left, he was followed by Morris and one of Morris's servants: the servant shot at him and Ó Laoghaire seized the gun, before making his escape. This was another, even graver, breach of the code. In October 1771 Morris offered a reward for the arrest of Ó Laoghaire, who responded to the allegations in the newspaper that carried them. At that stage, the dispute was more personal than legal in character: the gentry of Cork seemed disinclined to pursue a legal case, and no evidence was adduced by the common people.

Eibhlín had by now borne Art two children, but his life was hardly one of domestic ease. He was living just an inch inside the law, in constant fear of summary arrest. Perhaps the uncertainty finally wore him down. At all events, he resolved to seek his old enemy out. Some versions narrate that the two men agreed to a duel and that Morris, never one of nature's gentlemen, brought a troop of soldiers as a reserve to help him finish his enemy off. A more widespread tradition has it that Art visited his wife, now pregnant a third time, on 4 May 1773 before setting out to ambush and kill Morris. Ó Laoghaire's planned itinerary was revealed to Morris by a local informer named

Cooney. However, Art seemed to have escaped Morris's men and was resting in a field near Carraig an Ime, when 'a one-eyed soldier shot him clean off his beloved brown mare'.[4] The mare galloped the seven miles back to Ó Laoghaire's home, where his wife was awakened by the horse's hooves, ran out the gate and jumped into the saddle. She did not rest until she found her fair-haired husband already dead but still covered in warm blood. She cupped some of that blood in her hands and drank it, before launching into the *caoineadh* that has been described by Peter Levi as 'the greatest poem written in these islands in the whole eighteenth century'.[5]

Some say that it shouldn't be called a poem at all, since it is possibly the work of many different women artists, all exponents of a largely anonymous oral tradition of lamentation. It is undeniable that professional keening women, usually old and poor, were hired by mourning families at funerals to praise the dead, vindicate their reputation and castigate their enemies. More than one commentator believes that the various laments made for Ó Laoghaire out of the charged political atmosphere in the Cork of the 1770s were simply attached to the name of his widow. Why she alone among the women who mourned murdered husbands should have been recognized as authoress of all the lines has never been fully explained: one theory holds that her aristocratic background was shrewdly invoked by the lamenters in the knowledge that it could ensure the survival of their verses. This doesn't explain, however, why the speech acts of poor, old women would be attributed to a wealthy young aristocrat. The problem posed for scholars by the name Eibhlín Dhubh Ní Chonaill is like that raised by an even more famous name, Homer. Was the named person a genuine author, in the sense of one who stitched together the new and prefabricated parts of a brilliant narrative poem; or was he or she just an assembly-line worker to whose name the products of an entire community were appended?[6]

Literate cultures place a premium on individuality and go in dread of clichés: but almost one-third of the *Caoineadh Airt Uí Laoghaire* is based on the time-honoured conventions of an essentially oral civilization.[7] Those conventions have long been known: that keening was a woman's prerogative; that the lament for a nobleman described the rich food and material comforts offered generously in his home; that someone had a premonitory vision of that home destroyed; that many nobles attended the funeral, and that regrets were sent by those who could not. The dead person was addressed, urged to rise and live again. Though (perhaps because) they were delivered extempore, the laments borrowed heavily from this pool of common sources and from one another. The lament spoken by the heroic Deirdre for her lover Naisi in the fifteenth-century manuscripts included her act of drinking the dead warrior's blood. Laments in keeping with this general formula were found from the Hebrides to Kerry in the later seventeenth century: 'the handful of fine keens which arose at this time testifies to the existence of a developed, and therefore immensely long, sub-literary stream of tradition'.[8]

Nobody can know for sure whether or not Eibhlín Dhubh truly was the author of all the lines that have come down to us. Her *caoineadh* is much longer than most and may have been added to over time, not only by herself but by others, with the full sanction offered by oral tradition. Yet the lament has about it a quality of passionate utterance that bears the stamp of a personal suffering: its enduring fascination, for illiterate as well as literate audiences, lies less in the aristocratic glamour of the speaker than in the compelling rhythm and tone of her voice. Visitors to Ireland who happened to hear such laments often spoke of the 'uncontrollable cry of the widow'.[9] What is striking about this lament is its strange fusion of deep feeling and utter technical control, of powerful utterance dramatically disciplined. This may indeed have been a major part of its appeal in nineteenth-century Ireland, a country caught between two languages and one that often seemed to seethe with *inarticulate* rage.

All great artistic works trap human energy in its defining moments, but they live on by virtue of their style even more than their content. What this keen offered was a style of endurance among a people who were defeated but not destroyed. Eibhlín Dhubh had come from a family that continued to live as if the earls had never fled, and so did Art Ó Laoghaire, but the strain was beginning to show, for their lands were no longer their own, but rented. Younger noblemen like Art had little choice but to take out commissions in foreign armies. These were proud people, in whom the manners of the old aristocracy remained intact even after the matter had gone, but they lived their lives on the verge of breaking point – a truth hinted in Art's warning, often repeated, that he might not return on this occasion. To keep this awesome threat under some kind of control, they had to cultivate a style; and this was itself a rehearsal for that moment, possibly not far off, when style would be all that remained for them. They were, in a sense, the last of the Gaelic dandies.

It is possible that Eibhlín Dhubh, inheriting her mother's gift for poetry, set down the template, on which others based their own additional stanzas. Such a collaboration would be wholly within the convention. But the current insistence on such an anonymous shaping seems as debatable, in its way, as the nineteenth-century portrayal of Eibhlín Dhubh as sole author in the approved mode of Wild Irish Girl. If the story of a handsome rebel cut down by official criminality and mourned by a beautiful widow had an appeal in the heyday of romantic nationalism, with the result that the real Eibhlín was 'obscured by time',[10] that was itself an uncanny repetition of the much earlier process that saw the lamenting Deirdre transformed from 'a wild woman' into 'the Lydia Languish of a later age'.[11] There is, however, an equal danger that the urgent personal rhythms of Eibhlín Dhubh will be lost to us a second time by virtue of a current determination to read the work as incorrigibly plural, completely collaborative.

So little is known about Eibhlín or Art that the text has become a happy hunting-ground for all kinds of theorists and controversialists. Good work has been done by historians to fill in some gaps. However, the critics of Gaelic literature have been strangely reluctant to make a formal analysis of the inner workings of the text. Some prize it for the light shed on the wider social crisis; others point to its linguistic richness and deployment of keening metres. The rooted unwillingness to make a sustained analysis of the text as text has prevented any embarrassingly first-hand confrontations. Indeed, many revivalist critics have positively warned against such interpretative criticism:[12] and the current uncertainty as to the nature of its authorship is a further explanation of the widespread shyness.

The need now is less to endow the author with a clear identity than to recover a sense of the lament as work-in-progress, a becoming. Why should Eibhlín Dhubh have to be given a believable personality when she already possesses something more telling, an urgent voice? Technique in this case is far more pressing a consideration than character, and sometimes altogether detachable from human agency. The refusal of the speaker to advertise self is really a sign of strength, and her openness to tradition a mark of self-confidence. The power of such a performance hardly needs to be transformed into a set of Ideas. Like the hero of an old tale, the keener must be at once exceptional and representative. This doesn't mean that she transcends the communal tradition with an intensely personal utterance; rather, it suggests that she understands the enabling links between the two. Far from being a backward or medieval attitude, this is profoundly modern: for it is based on the understanding, implicit in works as different as *Moby-Dick* or *The Waste Land*, that styles and formulations precede us to those experiences we think most personal.[13]

This is not to deny individuality to the speaker of the *caoineadh*, for only those who have personalities know what it is to want to transcend them in moments of deep feeling expressed through ritual. *The Waste Land* of T.S. Eliot is of course such an instance: in its case, also, perhaps one in every three lines is a quotation or a received convention. Although others (notably Ezra Pound) played a part in its construction, it bears none the less the stamp of a single mind and a singular sensibility. So with the *Caoineadh Airt Uí Laoghaire*. The same motifs and iterative images are developed in it from section to section; the metrical template, once laid down, is adhered to faithfully; and although other personae are introduced as speakers (Eibhlín's jealous sister-in-law, Art's father), behind all their construction is the suggestion of a single mind at work. If all the characters in a play by Oscar Wilde talk like the author, here all inflect their statements in the rhythms of Eibhlín Dhubh.

The very fact that the lyric has been carefully attributed to her in all its passages through oral and manuscript tradition suggests that she was the primary author. The lines were created, after all, in the 1770s and among a family that had a strong sense of its own property rights. If Ó Laoghaire had been discredited on the local rumour machine as a wife-beater and skinflint, it's very likely that his widow composed the lines to protect his reputation and, with it, her own. In Ireland the standing of a widow depended greatly on that of her dead husband. And if the rumours against Art had some basis, that simply added to the stoic poignancy of her lament, that of a true lover who could honestly register her man's flaws yet still end up loving him.[14] The Ó Conaill family, always ambivalent about Ó Laoghaire,[15] had no similar ambivalence about the *caoineadh*, in which they took pride for some decades after Eibhlín's death. In 1834 Daniel O'Connell's son Maurice wrote to a researcher: 'my father desires me mention that one of the finest Irish keens is that of his aunt, the widow of Arthur O'Leary'.[16] Forty years earlier, in Kerry during the 1790s, the visiting Coquebert de Montbret found the same attitude: 'the song of Mme O'Leary on the death of her husband is praised above all others'.[17] There, just a few years after the events narrated, she was unproblematically taken to be the author. It might even be said that people were at pains to preserve the attribution, because they realized that the self-sacrificing widow had attempted to save his reputation by immortalizing it, even as she herself submitted her words to the anonymity of a poor people's tradition.

Eibhlín Dhubh Ní Chonaill would certainly have understood modern notions of literate authorship, as well as the communal oral mode. The family in which she grew up was bilingual, using Irish among themselves and with servants, and English with the outside world. She would have been at ease with the Irish-language poetic tradition: and the fact that the *Caoineadh Airt Uí Laoghaire* is the only work to be linked with her doesn't impugn the attribution – such passionate utterance is reserved for one lover and for one only. It lived on the lips of the people into the second half of the nineteenth century. By then the political backdrop of the piece would have been a dim memory. Most members of Eibhlín's family affected to know nothing of a lament that was seen after the 1850s as part of a semi-barbarous oral culture, best transcended by the newly literate, newly empowered class of prosperous farmers.[18] It lived on because of the beauty of its language, the rigour of its spare imagery, and because it celebrated a fulfilled love.

The lyric begins with an epiphany: Art Ó Laoghaire is sighted at a market-house in 1767, and that singular image is enough for Eibhlín. She must have him, even if that means elopement 'i bhfad ó bhaile' (far from home).[19] His own desires don't enter into consideration, for this is a masterful woman in the Gaelic tradition of Deirdre and Medbh. In that extreme independence of mind lurks also her greatest vulnerability: if Englishwomen of the time felt surrounded by precipices, how much truer was that of Eibhlín, estranged from her own people, distrusted by her in-laws, her third child yet unborn as she stands over the body of her dead husband? She who gave up much for love must now assert what has been gained. The listing of the comforts provided by him might seem self-regarding, but it has at once a traditional and a personal value: it exhibits his princely generosity while offering a sound defence against the distrust of both families.

Already, the technique is manifest: a rapid telescoping of images, with a drastic suppression, for the sake of speed and passion, of all banal links in the expository chain. Hence the almost cinematic 'cut' from first sighting to magnificent house-warming on the wedding night. Speed is crucial to the rapid shorthand of successive images, the headlong rhythms of elopement feeding into the urgent mourning. That first image of transgression is now linked with a second: Art's wearing of costly clothes and a bright sword as he rode the majestic mare in defiance of the Penal Code. The proud horseman will become a leitmotif through the lament, an image of Gaelic nobility which the English seek to erase, by taking the mare away, but also a sign of the rider's manliness and sexual power. Another leitmotif is introduced in the third stanza: the bowing of terrified Englishmen to the proud rider will be repeated by the selfsame verb 'umhlú go talamh' (genuflect to the ground) later used to recount the curtseys of the buyers' wives in Cork city, who know a potent man when they see one. Sex and power are fused in the speaker's imagination whenever Art is evoked astride his horse.

That the horse has returned riderless from the scene of his murder is a fair image of a Gaelic Ireland left leaderless, with only a pregnant young woman to take up the challenge. Though riderless, the mare also gives a sign that the order of nature at least knows the fitness of things, for the horse that could never be put up for sale recognizes who to summon in the moment of crisis. Here follows a third act of transgression: Eibhlín jumps across threshold (táirseach) and gate (geata) onto the horse. Already she is breaking out of the purely domestic role evoked and embraced so happily at the start. There is a further transgression here, in that she is adopting a traditionally male role as she puts herself astride his steed.

This is true in more ways than one. Many of the greatest classical women's laments for dead warriors were in all likelihood composed by *fili* mourning a chieftain. Créidhe, for example, bemoaned 'an laech ro laiged liom' (the warrior who used to lie with me), just as here Eibhlín praises Art 'gur bhreá an leath leaba tú' (You were the fine bedmate).[20] Such a bardic lament for a fallen chief was often erroneously treated as a love poem by being given a false, saga setting.[21] Aware of that aristocratic tradition, Eibhlín Dhubh may have taken a perverse pride in the thought that instead of a male poet assuming a female voice, the old roles were being reversed as she lamented the fallen prince. In Jungian terms, she was already incarnating within herself elements of the lost male, much as the women of the 1920s assumed the masculine styles of short hair and flat chests, as if to impersonate the missing soldiers who would never return from the wars. Part of the wisdom of her lyric is its recognition that, in a relationship such as hers with Art, death was always imminent. To conceive of life as tragedy was, for her, to form a conception of his possible death. In order to prepare for that, she must be already whole in herself, so that when the moment of parting came, she would be able to rely on the masculine as well as feminine resources within.[22] That must be why the word 'cara' (comrade) is used, rather than 'grá' (love) in this part of the poem.

Eibhlín incarnates more than her dead husband's masculinity: she also embodies all elements of the lost Gaelic tradition. Again the telescoping of images in fast-forward mode brings her to the sight of the dead body:

> *Go bhfuaireas romham tú marbh*
> *Cois toirín ísil aitinn,*

Gan Pápa gan easpag,
Gan cléireach, gan sagart
Do léifeadh ort an tsailm,
Ach seanbhean chríonna chaite
Do leath ort binn dá fallaing –
Do chuid fola leat 'na sraithibh;
Is níor fhanas le hí ghlanadh
Ach í ól suas lem basaibh.[23]

Until I found you dead before me, beside a low furze, without pope or bishop, cleric or priest who would read a psalm for you, but one withered, spent old woman who spread her cloak over you – while your blood came in spurts. I did not stop to clean it, but drank it up from my hands.

The onrush of rhythm as she gallops to the scene slows to a more stately measure in the presence of death after 'aitinn'. She, a noble, must now do what the women of Carraig an Ime should have done by tradition: speak his lament over the body. That is why her lyric is exceptional: it overrides all boundaries of class and gender to capture a sense of loss so deep that many of the dispossessed were scarcely aware of the tradition they had lost. Only one old woman could be found to show faith with the better days by spreading the cloak.

Blood-drinking may be a metaphor for the sexual act, for the mingling of bodily fluid certainly suggests an utter identification with Art. In a lyric that shows the ways in which one person's identity can be replaced or usurped by another's, it is a telling image. However shocking, it has the sanction of tradition, being done by Deirdre in the legend. Spenser had marvelled at how the Irish drank not their enemies' but friends' blood 'saying that the earth was not worthy to drink it'.[24]

Ó Laoghaire dies in wild country, whose people are ignorant of the ancient rites to which a dead chief might be entitled. He becomes in life and then in death a symbol of the older Gaelic society, naïvely convinced of his invulnerability and then awfully abandoned. Eibhlín urges him to rise up and come home, where she would like to do what he so magnificently did: welcome a visitor from a strange, unfamiliar world. The image of his deathbed by the furze bush dissolves into that of their bridal bed, as she assumes the role of welcomer discharged once by him. The patterning of *a* vowels is sumptuous:

Go gcóireod duitse leaba
Faoi bhairlíní geala,

Faoi chuilteanna breátha breaca,
A bhainfidh asat allas
In ionad an fhuachta a ghlacais.[25]

Until I make your bed with bright sheets and fine, spotted quilts, which would make you hot with sweat instead of this coldness which you have taken on.

This is the moment when, in the tradition surrounding the poem, Art's sister interjects, seeking to usurp the mourning intensity of the wife. Her claim that many fine women would have brought a dowry in marrying Art introduces a false note, sounded again in her jibe that Eibhlín slept at her own husband's wake. Not even the love of a dead man seems safe from recrimination in a Gaelic Ireland now fatally divided against itself. Sensing that the recently deceased live in some proximity to those who survive, Eibhlín responds as if in fear that Art might actually hear such allegations. Her sleep was that of an exhausted mother who sought to soothe her bereaved children with a lullaby: in seeking to defend her own passion, she may also be attempting to convince herself of his. The strangeness of the moment is deep: for the sister has taken over Eibhlín's very metre, rhythm, something as intimate as her very inhalations of breath. Such a takeover was routinely conducted by a second or third keener at a wake, but rarely to dispute the honest feeling of the chief mourner. It has its part, however, in a lyric that deals with the supplanting of one code by another. If Eibhlín has drunk Ó Laoghaire's blood by now, perhaps it isn't quite so shocking that a sister of the man should drink her literary forms. The effect (unintended by the sister) is to ratify Eibhlín as main mourner, who has laid down the template to which all must conform.

Ó Laoghaire's father speaks in the same metres, voicing a curse on his son's enemies. Since a widow's curse was all-powerful, the audience may sense that he is coaching Eibhlín in this necessary new role. He also urges Art to leap onto his steed and drink wine at the end of his gallop to Macroom: the effect is eerie, for this is what Eibhlín has in fact done, in mounting the mare and drinking the blood. It is as if she alone can do what the father would want. His lament

Is gan aon fhear in Éirinn
A ghreadfadh na piléir leat[26]

And not a single man in Ireland who would fire a bullet for you . . .

will be answered not by a man but by Eibhlín. If necessary, she will enact vengeance herself, the red blood triumphing over the black:

> *Go dtiocfad ar ais arís*
> *Go bodach na fola duibhe*
> *A bhain díom féin mo mhaoin.*[27]

Until I come back again to the black-blooded churl, who took from me my treasure . . .

As yet, she isn't ready for such brutality, as she seeks for a tender identification with her dead love. In imagination she becomes a warrior, taking the bullet in his stead, so that Art might retreat again to the mountains, those repositories of Gaelic culture, like the rapparees of old. On this occasion, the reworking by Art's sister of earlier lines seems but a sad, dim plagiarism, as if her incapacity to achieve creative utterance is the mark of her inability to suffer at all. She is already deathly herself, turning Eibhlín's live form into dead formula. Her barren repetitions develop nothing, serving only as a foil to the authentic emotion.

Through all this time Eibhlín has been talking to the dead man as if he were living: and so she revolts against dressing him in his funeral clothes. Now, at last, she begins to curse Morris, for it is burial morning and she is already losing the immediacy of that sustained address to Art. So in stanza nineteen, for the first time, she moves from the vocative *tú* at the start to the third person ('dá chaint', to his talk) at the close. Again the image is uncanny, for it combines premonition and return, two powerful currents in the keen. Art is recalled at the moment of his departure when, with a flash of anticipation, he returned through the gate to coach her in her imminent role. There is a tragic chord sounded here: for the gate he reopens is the one we have already seen her cross to journey to his dead body. That tragic foreknowledge now adds to the painful sweetness of the moment, for he kisses her on the hands ('barra baise', tip of the palms), as if somehow he already *knows* that they will soon be cupping his blood. His return is like that of a somnambulist, yet *he* tells *her* to rise, as if she is the true sleepwalker, the half-dead one, and he the warrior leaving home, perhaps never to return. Here Art speaks for the only time in the poem and the first thing he says is her name. The gorgeous arrangement of *ai* sounds perfectly interweaves their discourse into a stanza that suggests just how married they are in the depths of the imagination:

Mo chara thú is mo thaitneamh!
Nuair ghabhais amach an geata
D'fhillis ar ais go tapaidh,
Do phogaís do dhís leanbh,
Do phogaís mise ar bharra baise.
Duraís, 'A Eibhlín, éirigh id sheasamh
Agus cuir do ghnó chun taisce
Go luaimneach is go tapaidh.
Táimse ag fagáil an bhaile,
Is ní móide go deo go gcasfainn.'
Níor dheineas dá chaint ach magadh,
Mar bhíodh á rá liom go minic cheana.[28]

My comrade and my delight, when you went out the gate you came back fast and kissed your two infants. You kissed me on the tips of my palms and said 'Eileen, stand up and put an end to your work fast and soon, for I am leaving home and may not be returning.' I made nothing of his talk but mocked it, for he had often said such things to me.

In a wonderful triple-take, she fastens upon a phrase that he first used and she later repeated ('Éirigh suas', rise or stand up): but in the poem she uses it first, and only later do we realize with dismay that those were his last words to her. She orders him to don his fine clothes, mount the mare and parade through the countryside. As he travels, he is to observe how the very streams and trees pay homage to the proper ruler: here also she arrogates to herself the right of the male *file* to make that judgement. However, the stanza moves on this occasion to a closure that is annulled and withdrawn, for she doubts whether the people will perform a similar homage:

Má tá a mbéasa féin acu . . .

If they have their own manners . . .

and so she adds the fatal afterthought that records the breaking of all tradition:

's is baolach liomsa ná fuil anois . . .[29]

And I fear that they do not now . . .

The alterations of rhythm can be very subtle within the tight structure of the *caoineadh* and the use of bathos in many stanzas, such as this one, is deliberate. The technique of retardation before Eibhlín's bleak postscript to the stanza here is masterly. Her bathetic insight at the close renders the leftover absurdity of a world from which Art is gone.

Still, she bravely repeats the order 'Éirigh suas' (Rise up). Perhaps she is summoning his ghost, the pale rider on the brown horse, to frighten the complacent living; but she has recognized already that only nature (and no mere mortal) can know true nobility. She lists her own family tree with real pride. The implication, however, is that all this is secondary to her love for the dead man, who is 'go singil' (single) with her now as in the days of their first love. She tortures herself with the thought that the mill-women of Carraig an Ime (as black as the blood of Morris) who first saw the body could not lament him properly. Then, as a sort of counter-melody to her own, she names his genealogy, augmenting it by reference to the forces of nature (the beautiful crops signalling that he is the rightful ruler) and to his power as a horseman to outrun the hunt and hounds. She had considered him immortal when she bought his uniform (so much more fitting than this shroud). The fact that she is still speaking to him suggests, of course, that he will be forever immortal to her, and (if she keens him rightly) to all who can hear her lament.

It is now the sister's turn to apologize in tones of defensive self-justification. Her relations from Cork, who could have mourned him, are absent from the wake, being either sick or dead of the pox: there can be no shame, she asserts, in such an absence. In fact, many were wary of identifying with Ó Laoghaire, but the impression the sister conveys is of a general malaise gripping the land. Hence, perhaps, her strange *aisling* in which she saw their family home being destroyed, and with that the silencing of its birds and hounds, as if the loss of the house signified the end of discourse itself. Now the word 'traochadh' used earlier by Eibhlín of the 'exhausted' hunt is employed by the sister: and where once the hounds had merely stopped for rest, now they too are entirely dumb.

Art's attractiveness to many women is a theme rather cuttingly taken up by the sister in a brilliantly physical image:

> *Is mó ainnir mhodhúil mhúinte*
> *Bhíodh ag féachaint sa chúl ort . . .*[30]

It's many a comely, well-bred maiden looked at your behind . . .

The taunt is unworthy and Eibhlín Dhubh's reply has a grave dignity. Developing the image rather than deflecting it, she suggests that, yes, even in hostile settings such as the Cork butter mart, the merchants' wives bowed in deference to his charisma as lover, athlete, father. If his manliness is celebrated all through, Eibhlín speaks more than once as if he were so secure in it that he could explore his own 'womanly' side as well. A man who is strong enough to bring his *anima* into such conscious recognition will never be an unconscious slave to it. Rather than place a woman on a distant pedestal, he will know her as a comrade and feel free to explore all his own contrasexual aspects. In this, Art was utterly unlike the planters, who struck macho poses but distrusted the *anima* (the feminine element in men), which they repressed back into the unconscious and demonized accordingly (much as they banished the womanly man of Gaelic Ireland to the forests). Eibhlín Dhubh is therefore celebrating a relationship of real freedom with a good companion, a relationship sensed by those women in the anglicized towns (but seldom possible to them). She was beyond the conventions which bound such commodity-wives and could sense their frustration in their fascination with her man.

The Lord Lieutenant Townshend was disposed to reduce Catholic grievances, and so Eibhlín's resolve to seek redress from the king for the murder of Art may not have been just a literary conceit. After all, commentators from Swift to Burke had stressed that the Irish had equal rights with the English under a common crown. Her thinking is also in accord with received Catholic theology which taught that, when all other expedients had been exhausted, then and only then might it be moral to take the law into one's own hands:

> *Go dtiocfad ar ais arís*
> *Go bodach na fola duibhe*
> *A bhain díom féin mo mhaoin.*[31]

Until I come back again to the black-blooded churl who took my riches from me.

All through the lyric, the blackness of Art's enemies cannot match the sheer redness of his blood.

After the funeral, Eibhlín for once borrows a theme from her sister-in-law, explaining the absence of her own people, who would have attended had they heard her cry (a dubious assumption). However, she can at last recognize that the mill women (no longer 'dubha' [black] but now 'geala' [fair]) have shed real tears for Art. Her curse is now reserved for the betrayer Cooney. She marvels that he sought no bribe from her to pay for a swift horse (the implication being that he may soon need one) or to deck him in fine clothes. Her description of a bribed and prosperous Cooney sounds like a hollow counter-melody against the earlier account of Art, as if to suggest that he would only be a poor parody of his victim, a flawed imitation of the man he has given over to death. He would in short be like all the planters: a fake aristocrat whose suit of clothes would mock the man more than he became them:

> Ce gur mhór an trua liom
> Í fheiscint thuas ort,
> Mar cloisim á luachaint
> Gur boidhchín fuail tú.[32]

Even though it would be a pity for me to see it upon you, for I hear people whisper that you are a nasty churl.

The idea of Cooney as a botched impersonator of Art is in these lines: the suggestion is that the world is full of people who try to annex the part of another because they cannot truly play their own. Against that falseness, the dignity of Eibhlín's passion is striking. The authentic note of her grief exposes the off-notes of others, which the listener is intended to hear as such.

The widow's curse proved effective: Morris was found guilty of murder by a coroner's jury in June 1773.[33] Three shots were fired at him shortly afterwards. In 1775 he sold his property and went to England, but was dead in two months, perhaps from a wound sustained during the attack, which many believed had been mounted by Art's brother.[34] Nobody ratted on the assailant, despite a sizeable reward being offered for information. In the poem Eibhlín also curses Baldwin, her brother-in-law who gave up Art's mare to the authorities rather than connive in defiance of the Penal Code: she wishes for him a spavined gait but she exempts her own sister Máire from any curse.

Suddenly it is autumn and Art's lands are bountiful:

> Tá do stácaí ar a mbonn
> Tá do bha buí á gcrú . . .[35]

Your stacks of corn are standing, your yellow cows a-milking.

These lines conventionally assert the force of nature against death: for Eibhlín, on the other hand, there has been a breach in nature. The persistence of farm life, the ongoing harvests, all this seems inexplicable, as if nature has failed for once to conform to the poet's mood and continues about its own business in blatant disregard of the insult to the universe implicit in the murder. This lack of pathetic fallacy is an anti-romantic, modern perception, based on the notion that nature, despite human wishes, is neither sympathetic nor hostile – just *there*.

As she nears her ending, Eibhlín begins to speak like a *spéirbhean* in an *aisling*. The true prince has been supplanted by sly manipulators who fear to show their faces. Until Art returns, she will have no lightness of heart:

> *Go dtiocfaidh Art Ó Laoghaire chugam*
> *Ní scaipfidh ar mo chumha*
> *Atá i lár mo chroí á bhrú,*
> *Dúnta suas go dlúth*
> *Mar a bheadh glas a bheadh ar thrúnc*
> *'S go raghadh an eochair amú.*[36]

Until Art Ó Laoghaire comes to me there will be no end to my depression, which presses on my inmost heart and is shut tight, as a lock or a trunk for which the key has been lost.

There is an obsessive quality to the repeated *u* sounds, the metronomic terror of women beating out their grief in a series of sounds which seem, across two centuries, to anticipate those of Sylvia Plath:

> *And a love of the rack and the screw.*
> *And I said I do, I do.*
> *So daddy, I'm finally through.*
> *The black telephone's off at the root,*
> *The voices just can't get through . . .*[37]

In both cases the line functions as the unit of utterance, each line a heaving sob of sorrow. The *caoineadh* metre used may be even further from prose than were the syllabic quatrains of the *filí*, for their poetry, like all prose, was composed in sentences, whereas Eibhlín Dhubh, like Plath, composed in lines. In Eibhlín's case, the image of the heart as a locked trunk is a rare employment of simile in a lyric generally devoid of ornament.

Even as she insists that Art must come to her, she is turning away from direct address to the naming of him in the third person. In the very last lines, she still imagines him active, calling for drinks. But now her address is to the other keening women. She has changed rhythm herself and dropped her vocal register, so she instructs them to do the same. These subtle alterations, within the strict metrical scheme of the *caoineadh*, are appropriate to a work-in-process, for they hint at the fact that there can be no final perfection, none of that closure that is the refuge of the frightened. Here, with every line a sob, each phrase dies even as it is enunciated. Thus she resigns herself to his second burial in a consecrated place, Cill Chré monastery. The six months intervening between the first and second burials have, in effect, been one prolonged act of waking him: but the passing of time has healed nothing.

There is no reference at the close to any likelihood of consolation from Christian belief, nor any hint of a reunion in the next world. As in the last lines of Ó Rathaille, the mood is more stoic than Christian. Eibhlín says nothing about an afterlife: she simply wants her lover back *now*. Since this is impossible, she resolves to abandon her address to him, allowing him to move into the impersonal world of the dead. That move, from second- to third-person address, had been anticipated in the reported conversation at the mid-point of the keen, when Art had coached her in the new role of wife and martyr. As in the Deirdre legend, there is a strong indication that these doomed young aristocrats feel the need to nerve one another for the ultimate role. Here, however, there is also a hint that, for all their *hauteur*, the remaining members of the Gaelic upper class are in some danger of forgetting their assigned roles, which may in fact be useless ones, since the wider population no longer understands their ritual meaning. The dandy must remain impassive, despite the heart pounding within. The keeping up of appearances was now an immense strain, for if the fate of Ó Laoghaire proved anything, it was that the deliverer from Europe promised in the *aisling* would die and leave the *spéirbhean* widowed.

As Art Ó Laoghaire ceases to be spoken to and becomes just another one of those who are spoken *about*, his wife surrenders her own aristocratic voice to that of popular tradition, her own lyric enacting that very movement by submitting her individual talent to its anonymous protocols. Her lines have been filled with vivid personal details existing alongside the more ritual elements. In the late image of the corn stacks and milking cows, she appears to be seeing the farm all over again through Art's eyes. It is as if, in seeing that world incredulously but objectively, she sees herself fully and for the first time: a proud young woman who has stood alone against many traditions and conventions, but not finally against that of the *caoineadh*.

When J.M. Synge listened carefully to a keen on Aran, he was struck more by its communal than its individual elements: in it the consciousness of a people laid itself bare, he said.[38] Yet Synge was also well aware that every work of art is possible to only one person at one time and place.[39] *Caoineadh Airt Uí Laoghaire* is such an artwork: in the arrangement of images, in its variations of mood and metre, in its build-up of rhetorical power. Arguments as to whether it belongs more fully to oral or to written tradition seem beside the point. Seán Ó Súilleabháin considers it literature: Angela Bourke thinks it oral lore; and Louis Cullen suggests it was shaped 'in a complex relationship between manuscript and oral diffusion'.[40]

The plain fact is that the engagement with tradition within oral literature is not greatly different from the attitude to tradition taken by most modern poets outside the romantic movement. The revisions to the basic template were almost certainly initiated by Eibhlín Dhubh herself, on the basis that it wasn't just the text but herself that she was remaking. In all probability, the text grew longer because of the reworkings. The text is likely 'a close approximation to Eibhlín Dhubh's original lament', with later tellers adding 'a little'.[41] There is no reference in that text to either Art's father or his sister, and no real interaction between the three speakers: here as elsewhere in Irish literature, non-intersecting monologues masquerade as conversation, for the good reason that all were composed by the same person. The world of the 1770s is not so remote from the present as to suggest that authorship of a memorable lament could lose its attribution; and while the sheer prestige of the text might have made ambitious tellers want to add to it, it lived on primarily for its high art. Surrounded by death and dying, caught between two languages yet fully proficient in neither, many Irish people in the nineteenth century must have been struck by the fact that Eibhlín Dhubh had something to say. While most knew death as a weary numbness, here at least was a woman who could raise an articulate cry. The fact that most stanzas were composed after the event would not have unduly worried listeners, for most poetry fastens on emotions recollected in tranquillity.

In a powerful essay outlining the 'oral' element of the lament, Angela Bourke has shown how such performers 'make a new work of verbal art from materials already to hand'.[42] True enough – but modern writers do much the same. T.S. Eliot found that the best and most individual parts of a poet's work 'may be those in which the dead poets, his ancestors, assert their immortality most vigorously'.[43] The tradition which speaks through the good artist also encourages him or her to speak through it. This is, as it happens, exactly the balance of forces that Bourke finds in the *Caoineadh Airt Uí Laoghaire*: 'Originality consists in saying something that is new enough to be arresting and memorable, while remaining true enough to old patterns to be familiar – and memorable.'[44] Angela Bourke is right to suggest that a false polarization between tradition and inspiration disfigures some analyses of Irish-language writing, and that the unique qualities of the *Caoineadh Airt Uí Laoghaire* have been 'stressed to such an extent that her participation in a communal women's performance tradition is now almost forgotten'.[45] However, such a polarization has never been meaningful for modernist poets, who have sensed not alone the pastness of the past but also its presence.

If Eibhlín's *caoineadh* went into vibration with all its predecessors, the same is true of Eliot's poet: 'The necessity that he shall conform, that he shall cohere, is not one-sided; what happens when a new work of art is created is something that happens simultaneously to all the works of art which preceded it'.[46] Eibhlín Dhubh left a personal imprint on the received conventions of keening: hers was a developed sensibility rather than that of an untutored, raw genius. Her mind was in fact a perfect medium in which conventions and feelings could enter into combinations: and because she was a conscious artist, she could separate the woman who suffered from the mind which created. The conventions of the *caoineadh* had been held in suspension in her head (she had, after all, mourned an earlier husband) until the right combination of elements met to liberate them fully, to realize their genius. There is remarkably little circumstantial detail in the lament concerning the politics of the 1770s, or even about Art's death. That death freed energies which brought many other elements and themes together – aristocratic ideas of styles and audience; the relations between men and women; attitudes to the English; and so on. These spoke powerfully to the concerns of people, even after the original murder was all but forgotten. For instance, Eibhlín's rhythmic address to a dead man, designed to be less heard than overheard by others present, became in time a metaphor for much Irish writing and discourse, which pretended to be an internal dialogue of Irish persons but was often conducted with raised voices in hopes that some English well-wishers would get the message.

The lyric, in short, floated free of its enabling conditions: yet Eibhlín Dhubh Ní Chonaill's performance came to a beautiful fulfilment at the point where her desire to master the keening tradition called forth its most authentic nature. Had she sought absolute individuality, her words might have lapsed into autism and been soon forgotten: that she was able to strike a balance between tradition and talent ensured their immortality. Her lines do not so much express a clear response to the death as enact the very effort of her mind in formulating that response. A fear of that unappeasable mind led to various sorts of repressive analysis: some have wished to endow the author with the finished identity of romantic heroine, while others have tried to return her to the communal anonymity of a women's folk tradition. Neither does full justice to the achievement. The truth is that she had not so much a personality to express as a medium to perfect: but the unusual manner in which, within that medium, she brought off new combinations of elements indicated a deep individuality. Yet that personal note of grief must, as Synge noted, transcend even as it included the individual, and for a very good reason, which is at the centre of that text's understanding of the world: that extinction of personality which is always the accompaniment of great suffering and the consequence of death.

All through the *Caoineadh Airt Uí Laoghaire*, the notion of individual identity had been provisional, uncertain, easily usurped. The same was true of the various settings: one faded into another, as in cinematic dissolve. That was also how Eibhlín experienced time: she spoke in past, present and future tenses, but in a manner that suggested that none quite fitted the case.[47] Her search was for a tense suitable to one who feels that her significant life is over and yet still continuing – and there is no tense for that in Irish or in any other language. The world of the wake and funeral is a liminal one, existing 'outside time'.[48] In all her turns and twists, Eibhlín seemed to be trying to invent a new tense, beyond the time of linear history but in that 'woman's time' that Julia Kristeva has called 'monumental'.[49] In that version of time, there is no death, only changes of state, such as she dreams of for Art. If linear time presupposes identity, monumental time moves well beyond it to a more exploded and fluid notion of self. This connects in one aspect with 'archaic memory' (the conventions of ancient keening) and in another with 'marginal movements' (the Gaelic Irish under the jackboot of Penal Laws).[50] Eibhlín is one of those Kristevan women who refuse established power and create a parallel society.

Such women behave as if entering psychosis, but what they engage in is a disciplined performance, an act in a culture for which a word is also a deed.[51] They epitomize the knowledge that death lifts everyone outside of time, mourners as well as mourned. In those zones between life and death, anything is possible. Within Gaelic codes, there was always uncertainty about the precise moment of death: mirrors were held to the mouth of the deceased lest a breath moisten the glass. It might even be said that one function of a wake was to allow enough time to pass to ensure that the person mourned really was dead: hence the common fear, in a thousand stories, of a corpse that sits and speaks. Most fear such a moment, narrating the story of a death over and over again, the better to ensure a clear separation between dead and living: but deep mourners like Eibhlín cling to the liminal zone in hopes that the corpse really will come back to the living.[52]

The wake, even as it separated off the dead from the quick, also declared an ongoing overlap of their worlds. In some countries, people were not dead officially for a month after their passing: and the refusal of the authorities to allow Ó Laoghaire's burial in his destined plot effectively prolonged his wake to six months, keeping him liminal. That uncertainty also appealed to the mourners: in identifying so extremely with his in-between state, they also surrendered something of their own identities. Hence there is to be found in the *Caoineadh Airt Uí Laoghaire* the sharing of stanzaic form by living and dead or the mingling of lament formulae with the actual words of the survivors. Even as Eibhlín Dhubh fails to raise her dead husband, she succeeds by this mingling in making the past present: and by that success she ensures that both of them will live forever into the future. Their sharing of sentences, ideas, images may in one sense diminish their respective identities, but only because it enhances their love. In the words of the great English elegist John Donne: 'We two, being one, are it.'

12

Brian Merriman's
Midnight Court

'Be like me,' old masters told their pupils, 'but be not too like me.'[1] One of the achievements of Eibhlín Dhubh Ní Chonaill was the way in which, within an ancient structure, she created a new lyric sequence. Much the same might be said of Brian Merriman's *Cúirt an Mheán-Oíche*, written a few years later in Feakle, County Clare, about 1780. Here the old sovereignty myths of the *aisling* were well and truly parodied by a sophisticated intellectual of the Enlightenment, a man all too keenly aware that they had long been outmoded.

Merriman was a small farmer and a schoolmaster, born about 1750. Some claim he was a love child and that his mother later married a mason, who raised the boy as his son.[2] It has even been rumoured that his biological father could have been a local priest. Merriman was a resourceful farmer, winning prizes from the Royal Dublin Society for the quality of his flax. He was still a bachelor when he wrote the poem, apparently during a period of convalescence following an accident to his leg. No doubt he was tired of being asked by neighbours, 'When is the big day?" He was reticent in company and the poem is remarkable in that its narrator does not speak a word of dialogue at the court – a tactical silence which may well be the most satirical jibe of all. Other speakers there all agree that the Irish are in danger of dying out because of a reluctance to marry: yet the facts of demography show that the population rose steeply in the previous century.[3] Here again was an example of a people committed to the pretence that a living community was really at death's door. Merriman, with consummate intelligence, noted how little the forms of the *aisling* fitted the current feeling in Clare: and resolved to have his own subversive say.

The usual *aisling* began with a poet feeling tired and wan, often in a liminal zone frequented by fairies. Then a *spéirbhean* would appear in a vision, telling him that she was the land, awaiting the return of her rightful prince; often she made a prophecy of events yet to transpire. Some of the *spéirmhná* (or skywomen) promised not to sleep with a man until that return:

> *Is go mbeidh sí na spreas gan luí le fear*
> *Go bhfillfidh Mac an Cheannaí.*[4]

. . . she'll be like a dry branch and not lie with a man, until the merchant's son comes back.

The tradition had ancient roots, and the earliest versions were often less political than sexual in nature. Typically, their authors saw a world divided between two sorts of women: dark harridans and fair virgins. Always, a dark-haired hag initiated the sexual encounter with a shy male, who yielded to the overture, fell asleep after the encounter, and woke to discover that she was a rare beauty. She would then explain that she was really 'the sovereignty of Ireland' and he the true king. This story *might*, of course, be assigned a political meaning: often, however, the shape-changing women epitomized the psychic problems which would have to be overcome by any ambitious man if he were to attain his destined greatness.

Merriman wasn't the first eighteenth-century poet to parody these conventions: that had been done already by Ó Rathaille, Ó Súilleabháin and Ó Doirnín. But they stuck rigidly to a political format, implying that they no longer really believed in the return of a saviour. They could deface the old form, but not use it to create anything new or strange. Merriman alone managed to do that. Indifferent to the cause of nationalism in just those years when it was taking its modern shape, he transformed the inherited myth to propound radical ideas about the needs of the body for an unfettered sexual life.[5]

Those ideas had political implications in a rural Ireland that had been colonized by English puritans and by Irish priests preaching sexual abstinence. Even the strong women of the Celtic sovereignty tales had grown tame and domesticated in the eighteenth-century *aisling*. In it all agency was denied to the skywoman: 'the passive female is dejected and sad until a *male* poet brings her news that a *male* deliverer will free her from bondage'.[6] She must await the moment of liberation, allowing her body to become a site of contest between true and false lords, but taking no positive action herself. The passive, fainting, fair-haired virgin of Ó Rathaille's *aislingí* may represent the emerging eighteenth-century illusion of womanhood, but she had little enough connection with the older Celtic world. Merriman had mixed feelings about this genteel figure. His work begins with a sort of trick, a genre painting of the land around Loch Gréine done in an impeccably Augustan mode. Generations of schoolchildren have had to memorize these opening lines and have assumed that they must be representative of what follows, but they are tame and untypical. That may have been a deliberate tactic rather than a technical shortcoming, for Merriman is consciously pitting the genteel conventions of Augustan poetry against the more authentic Gaelic modes to follow.

What makes his lines sound Augustan, of course, is the fact that Merriman wrote in rhyming couplets, which varied the rhyme from couplet to couplet in a manner never attempted by his predecessors in Irish. This fact alone has led admirers to suggest the influence of Goldsmith, Swift and Pope, which is plausible given that Merriman had exposure to their work through his membership of the Royal Dublin Society. Even if his handling of the variable couplet is Augustan, however, the real source of his metre is the Gaelic tradition of *An Síogaí Rómhánach* (The Roman Fairy – a political poem of the previous century):

> *Lá dá rabhas ar maidin am aonar*
> *annsa Róimh ar órchnoc Céphas,*
> *lán do ghruaim ar uaigh na nGael san*
> *sínte ar lic ag sileadh déara . . .*[7]

One morning when I was alone on the golden hill of Cephas in Rome, full of gloom at the grave of those Gaels, stretched on a slab shedding tears . . .

Which is to say that Merriman infused older Gaelic forms with the techniques of Augustan writing: for instance, he achieved variation not only of rhyme but also in the sense of being able to write one line slow and another one fast.

There is something very new, as well as rather incongruous, about his fusion of Gaelic and Augustan modes in the opening lines:

Ar lachain 'na scuainte ar chuan gan ceo
Is an eala ar a bhfuaid 's í ag gluaiseacht leo,
Na héisc le meidhir ag éirghe in airde,
Péirse im radharc go taibhseach tarrbhreac,
Dath an locha agus gorm na dtonn
Ag teacht go tolgach torannach trom.[8]

The drifting of ducks on a bay without mist, and the swan
moving with them at their side; the fish gleefully rising on high
and a speckled perch in sight so vividly. The colour of the lake
and the blue of the waves breaking with a heavy syncopated
sound.

The long vowels capture the stately movement of the swan, while the
build-up of consonants (scuainte, bhfuaid) has a retarding effect on
the pace of delivery: the forward momentum of a conversational style
is briefly lost in a more 'literary' rendition. In the very next line, however, all speed is regained in a movement as precise and rapid as that
of the fish (with shorter vowels – e, i, – and fewer consonants). This
is the very technique employed by Alexander Pope in *Windsor Forest*:

See! from the brake the whirring pheasant springs,
And mounts exulting on triumphant wings . . .
Oft, as in airy wings they skim the heath
The clam'rous lapwings feel the leaden death . . .[9]

and it arises from the same in-feeling with animals. Sound and sense
combine perfectly in Merriman's description of the lake in the closing couplet just quoted: the *t* sounds capture the measured breaking
of waves on the beach, and the varied numbers of syllables in each
word helps clinch the effect:

tolgach (2)	*torannach* (3)	*trom* (1)
wave rising	highest point	breaks

A comparable effect is achieved in the famous line about the
mountains:

Ag bagairt a gcinn thar dhroim a cheile[10]

Tossing their heads above one another's backs

The *g* consonants seem to touch off the top of each rising peak, even

as the vowels move in a register (*a-i-e*) of ever-higher notes. One
critic has even suggested a possible source in lines from Isaac Rogers:

> *The tall hills yonder gently rise*
> *Nodding their heads across the skies.*[11]

That may well be so: but the deeper point is Merriman's parodic
thrust. The entire opening passage is written in the continuous past
tense (*aimsir ghnáthchaite*), as if to suggest that even the genre painting of the Augustans is now strictly outmoded and historical. The
bedridden poet may well be mocking his own immobility in the first
line ('I used to walk . . .'), but he is also suggesting that someone who
used to believe all the accompanying poetry-talk has now moved on
to a deeper wisdom. For the supreme joke of the section is clear: the
irruption of a fairy queen, Aoibheall, into the unlikeliest of daylight
Augustan settings.

Whatever about the dignity accorded the *aisling*, fairy stories
enjoyed only low status in Irish lore: yet they occupied a virtual
world which provided its own mirror on rural society: 'they share
space and time with the human population, but use both differently'.
The fairies, as Angela Bourke has explained,

> . . . are forever outside human culture, exempt from control by
> its rules. But they do hope to be saved, so instead of ranging
> themselves in opposition to human society, fairies are always
> prowling on its edges, looking above and below it, marking its
> boundaries, impinging on it from time to time with conse-
> quences that make the material of the stories.[12]

They are especially famous for abducting children unfortunate
enough to wander into those liminal zones that they frequent: but in
this poem it is the adult poet who is 'taken' from the area of Creag
Liath. By fusing this low-level vernacular fairy lore with the exalted
aisling and Augustan landscape traditions, Merriman is enabled to
subject the jaded higher forms to redemption from below.

The poet falls asleep by the side of a river, only to be visited in his
dream by a monstrous woman:

> *Do chonairc mé chúm le ciumhas an chuain*
> *An mhásach bholgach tholgach thaibhseach*
> *Chnámhach cholgach dhoirrgeach ghaibhdeach . . .*[13]

This was Brendan Behan's rendition of the lines:

> *I saw as I suddenly looked around*
> *A big-bellied bitch and her bottom gigantic,*
> *Fierce, furious, fearless, formidable, frantic . . .*[14]

The piling-up of adjectives, a tiresome conserving convention in the poetry of others, works here to great burlesque effect: and this woman, the bailiff, brings the poet to the Midnight Court ruled over by Queen Aoibheall, another harridan. Because Merriman is writing an anti-*aisling*, these women will never lose their monstrosity, even after the poet wakes.

At the Midnight Court, which is ruled entirely by women, Aoibheall outlines the problem: men are reluctant to marry, the population is falling, and the fairy host has mandated her to set up a court in place of the English ones and to propose a solution. The debate is split into three sections. At the outset, a handsome young woman complains that she has found no man to marry, even though she has worn the most fashionable stiletto heels and resorted to traditional folk remedies:

> *Níorbh áil liom codladh go socair aon uair dhíobh*
> *Gan lán mo stoca do thorthaibh fám chluasa,*
> *Is deimhin nárbh obair liom troscadh le cráifeacht*
> *Is greim ná blogam ní shlogainn trí trátha,*
> *In aghaidh na srotha do thomainn mo léine*
> *Ag súil trém chodladh le cogar óm chéile . . .*[15]

I never went to sound sleep at night without filling my stocking with apples beside my head; it's certain it was no hardship to perform holy fasts and avoid all food and drink thrice daily; my shift I washed against the stream's current, dreaming in my sleep of a whisper from a beloved . . .

– but to no avail. She is unable to sleep from sexual frustration, for those rare young men who do marry invariably pair off with old maids for the sake of their money. The ritualized contrast in the sovereignty tales between blonde young beauties and horrific harridans is maintained in this story of Clare, in however debased a form.

If the young woman seemed prematurely weighed down by the sadness of the world, the old man who now gives evidence is even more bitter. He accuses the woman of being a tart. The poor hovel from which she came was a very different place, but now she seems to have money for all the finery she wants. How did she get it? he asks. The vanity of young women has trapped many a good man into an unsuitable marriage to a flighty hussy. He offers himself as a sad instance, for his young wife bore him a child long before the due date:

> *Mo scanradh scéil, gan féith óm chroí air,*
> *Clann dá dtéamh dhom tar éis na hoíche,*
> *Collóid anfach ainigí scólta,*
> *Bunóc ceangailte is bean an tí breoite,*
> *Posóid leagaithe ar smeachaidí teo acu,*
> *Cainneog bhainne dhá greadadh le fórsa*
> *Is mullach ar láinmhias, bain bhia is siúicre,*
> *Ag Muireann Ní Chamliath, bainlia an chrúca.*
> *Bhí coiste cruinnithe ag tuilleadh dom chomharsain*
> *Chois na tine is ag siosarnach dhomhsa*
> *Scaoilid cogar i bhfogas dom éisteacht –*
> *'Míle moladh le Solas na Soilse!*
> *Bíodh nach baileach a d'aibigh an clóc seo*
> *Chímse an t-athair 'na sheasamh 'na chéadfa . . .'*[16]

My scary story, without any heartfelt reason for it, I had a family in just one night. The women fussed, snorted and scolded at the swaddled baby and sickly mother, and they preparing warm food by the fire, forcefully working on a bottle of milk, white bread and sugar for a full dish, made by Muireann Ní Chamliath, the midwife.

A further crowd of neighbours gathered by the fire, chattering about me. They whispered so my ear could catch it: 'A thousand praises to the light of lights, although the child came rather prematurely, I can see his father in each of his features . . .'

The midwife's name is a fair indication of the absurdity of the general situation: a conflation of *Muireann*, a virgin; *cam*, crooked or faulty; *lia*, a doctor. Accordingly the old man urges Aoibheall to abolish the marriage laws and allow procreation to proceed on a natural basis.

He closes his remarks with a paean to children born out of wedlock, in lines that insolently re-echo the words of the insincere women:

> *Is mó is is mire is is teinne is is tréine*
> *I gcló is a gclisteacht ná dlisteanaigh éinne . . .*[17]

He is bigger, faster, warmer, stronger, in shape and cleverness than a child of wedlock . . .

These lines have often been compared to 'The Bastard' by Richard Savage:

Blest be the Bastard's birth – though wondrous ways
He shines eccentric like a comet's blaze;
No sickly fruit of tame compliance he,
He stamped in Nature's mint of ecstasy . . .[18]

Merriman goes farther, causing the old man to argue that the practice of free love would lead to another heroic age of the kind enjoyed by the warriors of *Fiannaíocht* lore:

Cuirfidh an dlí seo gaois i nGaelaibh
Is tiocfaidh an brí mar bhí ina laochaibh;
Ceapfaidh sé com is drom is doirne
Ag fearaibh an domhain mar Gholl Mac Mórna . . .[19]

This law will bring strength to the Gaels, and wisdom will return to warriors; it will re-create the body, its back and fists, make the men of the world like Goll Mac Mórna . . .

The bounty of nature, which was once the sign of a rightful prince, is now presented as the effect of a vibrant, unconditional sexuality.

The young woman seizes the opportunity to reply with a defence of the old man's wife. She was indeed 'in trouble' when he met her, a beggar dependent on alms. All he did was to 'buy' her with promises of comfort and fulfilment, and then disappoint her sorely with his poor performance in bed:

Ba dubhach an fuadar suairceas oíche,
Smuit is ualach, duais is líonadh,
Luithní lua agus guaille caola
Is glúine crua chomh fuar le hoighre,
Cosa feoite dóite on ngríosaigh
Is colann bhreoite dhreoite chríonna . . .[20]

Grim was her manic search for nocturnal delights, dour and heavy, her prize was nothing, leaden sinews and thin shoulders and knock-knees as cold as ice; rotten feet burnt from the cinders and a sick, spent, wasted body.

She describes the poor woman's state as she tries to extract a flicker of life from the impotent old fool:

Is nár dom aithris mar chaitheadh sí an oíche
Ag fascadh an chriaiste 's ag seasadh 's ag síneadh,
Ag fascadh na ngéag 's an téadach fúithi,
A ballaibh go léir 's a déid ar lúthchrith,
Go loinnir an lae gan néall do dhubhadh uirthi
Ag imirt ó thaobh go taobh 's ag únfairt.[21]

It shames me to tell how she spent the night, grabbing the dotard and pulling and stretching, gripping the limbs and the sheets beneath her, her whole body and jaws palpitating, until break of day without a wink of sleep, but thrusting from side to side and sighing.

Too many young women are trapped in this way. Their problem is compounded by the refusal of the Catholic Church to allow robust, well-nourished priests to marry:

Is minic do chuala ar fuaid na tíre
Siosarnach luath dá lua go líonmhar
Is chonnairc mé taibhseach roinnt dá ramsa
Is uimhir dhá gcoinn ar shloinnte falsa.[22]

And often I heard around the country fulsome praise for a fit clergyman and I saw them rear a number of offspring under the surname of another man.

She therefore implores Aoibheall to allow priests to marry young women like herself.

The fifth and final section of the poem is the queen's adjudication, which fails to go as far as any of the litigants had wished. Marriage as an institution is not to be abolished, but young women who secure its institutional protection ('clóca') from older men should none the less be free to take lovers of their own age. As for clerical celibacy, Aoibheall says that they must all wait until the Pope has spoken. Her more immediate priority is the poet himself, a bachelor scandal at thirty years old. Just as J.M. Synge would be subjected to shrieks of derision by young girls on the Aran Islands for a similar offence, so the speaker (still silent) must submit to the punishment of lashes administered by a group of women led by the frustrated spinster. This reads strangely like a bondage fantasy by means of which the poet finally punishes himself for giving vent to some of the preceding anti-female outbursts:

Barr gach scola d'órdaigh an tsíbhean,
Báidh sa bhfeoil gach córda snaidhmeach,
Tomhais go fial na pianta is crua
Le tóin 's le tiarpa Bhriain gan trua ar bith . . .[23]

The whacks ordained by the fairywoman lash into his flesh with every bounden cord. Tenderly calibrate every cruel pain and whip Brian's backside without any pity.

The act is then signed by the queen and dated before the poet, who wakes all of a sudden from his sufferings.

Such a work posed many challenges to rather puritanical Irish revivalists at the start of the twentieth century. The conventional *aisling* they could admire as a nostalgic nationalist call for a return to the Celtic source, but Merriman's poem looked and felt different from these. It seemed rooted in its own Clare locality and utterly indifferent to all national narratives. As Frank O'Connor quipped: 'writing in Irish, Merriman had the advantage, which only a writer in Irish had, of not worrying whether what he wrote was Irish or not'.[24] The conscious savouring of natural landscape at the start seemed foreign as well as modern. A predictable corollary for some analysts was that Gaelic Ireland of itself could not have produced the poem, which bore the imprint of Rousseau, Voltaire and other precursors of romanticism.[25]

Another tactic used to deflect the radicalism of *Cúirt an Mheán-Oíche* was the suggestion that it was never intended to be taken seriously. Daniel Corkery read it as a *jeu d'esprit*. The critique of clerical celibacy and low satire were explained in similar terms by him: 'After all, in every society one meets a class who, lacking sensitivity themselves, raise laughter by shocking it in others – and one does not think of *all* this class as moralists.'[26] There are two difficulties posed by such a statement. First, enough is known of the circumstances of Merriman to suggest that he was a person of some sophistication: not only did he enter competitions of the Royal Dublin Society, but even in his Feakle days he was a resident tutor to some of the surrounding gentry.[27] Second, most laughter is not capricious, but raised to some sort of purpose: even the broadest laughter 'does not deny seriousness, but purifies and completes it'.[28] Ever since the *Aisling Mheic Coinglinne*, texts like this had offered a world of carnivalesque reversals of hierarchical order in opposition to officialdom: and the truly great works of Renaissance Europe had been those in which the saving energies of oral culture had been injected into the forms of high, written art. That process, which had in other countries produced Boccaccio, Rabelais, Shakespeare and Cervantes, in Ireland now threw up Merriman. The trivial comedy as always turned out to be for and about serious people. Though laughter might be its key method, it was a laughter dedicated to unmasking the violence of authority: for, as Karl Marx observed, the last phase of universal history must be comedy 'so that mankind could say a gay farewell to its past'.[29]

The monstrosity of bailiff and queen at the *cúirt* is of that kind (protruding bellies, huge noses, humps symptomatic of pregnancy and procreation) found at the core of carnival. There 'the monster death becomes pregnant'.[30] This is the method of the poem, which infuses various tired literary conventions with the pulsating life of the streets. For Merriman was an urbanizing, modernizing intellectual, who understood the implications of a moment when men and women reverse masks and roles, with the consequence that women become judges and men the ones judged. Connected to this was his strong sense that the ordinary people of Clare were employing whole spheres of speech that had never before been tapped for written literature. Indeed, the history of the *Cúirt an Mheán-Oíche* is the story of how various 'experts' sought to downplay those radical elements, either by explaining them away as vulgar localism or by regretting them as foreign intrusions.

Merriman was probably aware of the waves of liberal thought washing across Europe: a port like Kinvara or a prosperous town like Gort have been suggested as likely places for the transmission of such ideas.[31] However, these influences would have served mainly to confirm the conviction that for him the radical option was also the most traditional. All of the major features of his poem were already a vibrant part of Gaelic tradition, from the *chanson de la malmariée* of the young woman to the complaints of the betrayed old man.[32]

There remains the court framework. W.B. Yeats inclined to believe that the notion of a court in which each sex blames the other for the loss of love might have been taken from Swift's *Cadenus and Vanessa*, where the court frames the start and end of the exchanges as it does in Merriman's poem.[33] It is true that there had not previously been any Court of Love in Irish: but the implication of poetry with the actions of a mock court had long been a feature of the *barántas* lyrics. Moreover, the idea of a comic convocation that empowered those usually felt to be powerless had been the main conceit behind such seventeenth-century texts as *Pairlement Chloinne Tomáis*. In fact, an even closer precedent was to be found, almost a century after it, in *Párliament na mBan* (The Parliament of Women) by Dónal Ó Colmáin (1703). Although this was based on a

French original, the author used the device of a parliament ruled by women in a two-pronged assault, not only on the self-importance of parliamentarians (a common theme of Gaelic writers) but also on male chauvinism. The work described how thirty-two noblewomen met together and decided to build a 'cúirt mhór bhreá oirirc' (a big, fine, distinguished court) not in any city but in the countryside. To it they invited five hundred female deputies on 10 June 1697. They were addressed by their leader: she complained that their sex had lost much of its social power through enforced domesticity and lack of education over the previous century, 'agus sinn ag tréigean an uile ghnótha agus maithis phoibli, ag fanúint go cónaitheach ins an mbaile, ag tabhairt aire dár gcoigil agus dár maide sní, agus fós nach maith ins an mbaile féin mórán againn'[34] (and we forsaking all forms of business and public activity, resting sedentary in our homes, taking care of our distaffs and sewing boards, and even quite a lot of us not much good for that work itself).

Some ideas explored in the *Cúirt an Mheán-Oíche* might have sounded radical in the later eighteenth century and positively revolutionary in the nineteenth, but their liberalism was wholly in keeping with earlier Gaelic traditions. The old man who asserts that free sexual activity might herald a return of Goll Mac Mórna speaks perhaps the most central of all passages in Merriman's poem, which is really a none-too-covert call for a return to the ancient systems. According to one German student of the nineteenth century, 'the early Irish laws show a frankly astonishing concern for the dignity and individual personality of the wife in marriage'.[35] That is precisely what the young woman seeks. Under those laws, a woman could divorce a partner who was sexually unsatisfactory, impotent, sterile or homosexual, and priests had the right to marry, just as the young woman wishes. The old man would certainly approve also of a system in which there was no stigma of illegitimacy. 'With few exceptions', writes another historian of the period, 'children were regarded as legitimate and some women were only too anxious to father their children on members of the aristocracy in the hope of getting them a good start in life'.[36] This seems to have been the 'síolrú de réir nádúra' (natural procreation) for which the old litigant pines.

Perhaps the most striking aspect of that ancient society was the power and authority wielded in it by women. The wanton queen Medbh of the saga seems a precursor of queen Aoibheall, 'and we need not doubt that there were many like her in real life'.[37] The bailiff at the outset of the poem merely repeats a time-honoured idea when she suggests that the world would be a better place if it were brought under the rule of women. This, Merriman implies, is the

female version of the nostalgic *aisling*: but as a vision it is as impractical as the more pervasive male versions. For the bitter truth is that
'the natural development of these liberal customs was stunted to a
degree by the Norman invasion and cut off by the imposition of
English law on Ireland in the early seventeenth century. As a result,
in its attitude to women and their place in society, modern Ireland
enjoys no continuity with its Gaelic past.'[38]

It was the particular misfortune of Irishwomen that the great plantations of the seventeenth century coincided with the progressive
marginalization of their sisters to the domestic role in England. Even
writers who took their female readers with some seriousness, such as
the essayist Joseph Addison, seemed unable to avoid a facetiously
patronizing tone – he used it so often than Jonathan Swift was driven
to cry out in irritation, 'Let him fair-sex it to the world's end'.
Addison's attitude was more typical of the age, for which Lord
Chesterfield spoke in declaring that 'women are but children of a
larger growth'. If Addison warned women to avoid politics 'as there
is nothing so bad for the face as party-zeal', the Dissenter Daniel
Defoe wrote a treatise on petticoat government. In his *Essay upon
Projects* written in the very year of the mythical assembly of
Párliament na mBan, 1697, he strongly argued a case for the higher
education of women; and in 1702 he called in *Good Advice to the
Ladies* for a female presence in government, just a year before Ó
Colmáin completed his work.[39]

The refusal to take women seriously as political thinkers wounded
many of them. The convenor of the Párliament na mBan responds
with intelligent outrage:

> Do chítear daoibh go léir go mbíd a gcomhairlí agus a gcomh-
> thionóil ag na fearaibh go laethúil ag déanamh a ngnótha agus
> ag tabhairt aire do gach ní bhaineas riu féin, i gcás, an uair bhíd
> siad ag trácht orainne, gurb amhlaidh bhímid mar chaitheamh
> aimsire, mar chomparáid, nó mar stoc magaidh acu de ló agus
> d'oíche. Agus fós, ní admhaíd siad gur daoine sinn ar aon chor
> ar bith, ach gur créatúirí sinn do cruthaíodh in aghaidh nádúir,
> agus nach bhfuil ionainn ach *malum necessarium*, 'drochní is
> riachtanas do bheith ann'.[40]

It is evident to you that the menfolk had their meetings and
conferences on a daily basis, doing their business and taking
care of all that pertained to themselves – so that, whenever
they mentioned us, we were merely a pastime, a comparison, or
a source of mockery to them by day and night. And even still,

they will not admit that we are human at all, save only that we
are creatures created against the forces of nature, and that
we are nothing but a *malum necessarium*, a bad thing which is
necessary.

She therefore proposes the establishment of the sort of virtual assembly dramatized by Merriman about eight decades later. In the
intervening period, women's roles remained largely domestic.
Outside of the home, they were mainly decorative, driving Jane
Austen to complain at the end of the century that there remained
those 'for whom imbecility in females was a great enhancement of
their charms'.[41]

Over the eighteenth century women did win an increasing authority on matters of fashion and taste, but Merriman (like Swift) clearly
considered this to be no advance at all. Just like the Dean, he reserves
in the *Cúirt an Mheán-Oíche* a special loathing for the anglicized
fashions in clothing then being adopted wholesale by the more ambitious young women of the country. The few English loan words in
his poem are all placed in satiric contexts, referring to such new-
fangled apparel as 'cover', 'púdar', 'starch', 'húda' and the 'screw' on
the spiked stiletto heel. Like the women of the *cúirt*, he seems to have
felt a contempt for those women foolish enough to reify their own
bodies for the pleasure of the puritan male imagination. In the virtual
world of the *Cúirt an Mheán-Oíche*, the old view of women as
movers and shakers held good: but in the real world beyond Creag
Liath, women were still seen as amusing appendages to society.

The persistent popularity of the pagan–Christian debate in the
poems and songs of the people suggests that they were never fully
satisfied with Christian denials of the body. Merriman begins 'ar
chiumhas na habhann' (on the edge of the river), a free man open to
his own instincts (since water is a common image of the unconscious). He is devoid of responsibility, until fate takes a hand. The
debate that follows is not so much about frustrated love as about
unfulfilled libido. Hence the emphasis throughout on the workings of
the bodily parts. As far back as medieval literature, the body was
often taken as a metaphor for the community, and its health or lack
of it became a symptom of a wider condition. In repressive societies,
as Bakhtin argued, the orifices of the body are closed and strictly
policed: but in the virtual world of carnival the borders between
human bodies are broken down. The *Cúirt an Mheán-Oíche* celebrates not just the mingling of discourses but also the joining of the
male and the female body. It does this mainly by democratizing
laughter. The sustained realism of Merriman's descriptions – of the

young woman's folk spells; of the old man's humiliations; of the priest's chafing at the bit – might seem more at home in a comic novel than in the convention-bound world of Gaelic poetry, but that realism is the logical consequence of his laughter. This was what was so unsettling to nationalists of the Irish Revival and of the new Irish society that they created. They were as keen to protect bodies from intrusion as they were to secure the borders of the fragile new state.

Against that backdrop the poem was misread by many: but not by Piaras Béaslaoi, who took it to be an attack on the vices that derive from a suppression of natural instincts. His Merriman was a man who could clearly see how an unnatural doctrine like clerical celibacy was bound to lead to hypocrisy:

> He sees in nature not something hateful to be suppressed, but something beautiful to be understood and harmonised with the necessities of life. The old man argues against marriage, the young woman argues for marriage and against celibacy, but both rest their arguments on the forces and processes of nature.[42]

The poem asks whether it is possible to fulfil the instinctual desires of humans without destroying the social fabric.

That may be one reason why the court could hardly be called a Court of Love. If the Irish exponents of *dánta grá* (love poems) handled them with a pragmatism unknown to the makers of the *amour courtois*, the court of Merriman is positively empirical in its dealings with the body. Reading its debate, one is reminded of James Joyce's response to a young writer who asked for permission to kiss the hand that wrote *Ulysses*: 'No – that hand has done a lot of other things as well.' When Frank Budgen put his hand on his heart and began to talk of romantic love, Joyce demurred: 'The seat of the affections is lower down.'[43] Merriman would have applauded. The old man of the *Cúirt an Mheán-Oíche* marries in search of physical pleasure and the young women abandon old men who cannot satisfy their desires. Even those professional idealists, the priests, befriend young women not in order to give spiritual comfort but to secure physical consolation for their lonely lives. The young woman bitterly criticizes the old man not for a want of passion but for impotence. She and her sisters are arrant materialists who marry for wealth and comfort, only to encounter sexual stasis. In all that lies the central problem: how to satisfy everyone within a viable, cohesive society?

Frank O'Connor voiced disappointment that Aoibheall's final

judgement offers no answer to the questions raised: 'Clearly, this was intended to be the point at which Merriman would speak through her, and express his own convictions about life, but something went wrong.'[44] O'Connor suggests that the author really had nothing substantial to say in the end. Seamus Heaney goes further still, arguing that the conclusion is an attempt by a rather frightened poet to avoid the fate of Orpheus, who was dismembered by frenzied maenads for the liberties he had taken:

> The phallocentrism of its surface discourse can be re-read as an aspect of male anxiety about suppressed female power, both sexual and political; and the weakness of the conclusion, namely the deflection of the threat to Brian, this tidy outcome can be seen as the price that the satirical eighteenth-century mind was prepared to pay in order to keep the psychosexual demons of the unconscious at bay for a little while longer.[45]

It is as if, in this interpretation, the poet is left to punish himself for having taken too many freedoms.

Another reading may be possible, one that would accord greater respect for the verdict reached by Aoibheall at the close. True, her judgement lacks the radical rigour of a Rousseau, who would have done away with all forms of marriage. (The fact that the old, mean-minded man adopts this position may be Merriman's slightly caustic jibe against the *philosophes* of the Continental Enlightenment). On the other hand, the verdict is pragmatic in that it allows young people to fulfil their desires within the current social system. Aoibheall proposes to give the sanction of law to the double standard prevalent in the community – in effect to make unofficial behaviour patterns perfectly official. Under such a dispensation, the old man would no longer be ashamed if his wife slept with a youth, nor would children conceived out of wedlock face the taint of illegitimacy, because the philosophy underlying ancient Gaelic law would have been restored.

If Merriman was in fact a love-child, this resolution may have struck him as all the more compelling. He may not have felt disgraced at being born out of wedlock, since that was a natural occurrence, but the shame of illegitimacy in the eyes of the law must have tormented him. His poem doesn't propose to change human behaviour, but it does suggest an alteration in the law, which would bring the statutes into closer proximity to actual practice. That the change admitted seems to give legal recognition to the double standard rife among the community may shock idealists, but it is

precisely the sort of legal liberalization that was being widely discussed in Europe through the later decades of the eighteenth century.

Merriman may have had a personal investment in the pleas of the
old man. His praise of healthy bastards may afford a kind of vindication, but Seán Ó Tuama has contended that it leads Merriman
into contradiction: the old man denounces his wife for the freedoms
she took and then inconsistently urges the court to abolish marriage
and allow natural procreation. This may not be as contradictory as
it seems. The old man is angry with his wife because she broke a law
and so made a fool of him before the world. However, it is the legal
system that is to blame, for it promotes dishonesty and cynicism. It
is surely significant that the old man directs his plea not to the wife
or young woman but to the queen of the court. If love-children had
their proper status within the system, no law could have been broken
and he would not have been shamed. The double standard may be
regrettable but is so pervasive that it is wisest to submit to it. Then no
child need fear being illegitimate: on the contrary he or she might
take pride in their comeliness and vigour. The fact that this plea
alone is fully acceded to by the queen is indicative: she understands
that the issue is not so much philosophical as legal. Her pragmatic
solution is directed to a world built on libido rather than love. It is
based on the one analysis with which all speakers can agree: that the
law as it stands is an ass. Even the bailiff, long before the court
enters into session, says as much when she bemoans 'falsacht fear
dlí . . . dalladh le bríb, le fís, le falsacht'[46] (the falseness of the
lawyer . . . blinded by bribe, illusion and deceit).

If Merriman's natural father was a priest, this gives added savour
to the lines in which the young woman demands an end to clerical
celibacy. The frustration of some readers with the ending may be similar in kind to that of certain interpreters of *Caoineadh Airt Uí
Laoghaire*: they would wish for an author possessed of a clearer
identity and a declared agenda. Instead, Merriman teases with puns
on his own name and a canny distribution of his own likely opinions
across all the *dramatis personae*. Such restraint is utterly in keeping
with the rather mild-mannered mathematician that he seems to have
been. Unlike other Munster poets, he had no reputation for passion
and no inclination to write intense, short lyrics: rather he taught
himself how to construct a wholly integrated poetic sequence. The
writers of the Irish revival early in the twentieth century liked their
poets to be poetic and were somewhat dismayed by Merriman's manifest intellect and reason.

What critics once counted as a weakness may now be seen
as Merriman's virtue: his refusal of the 'poetry talk' of Munster

tradition. Realism impelled him to tell a good story through colourful characters caught up in an inherently stressful situation. Even Daniel Corkery is moved, against his better judgement, to grant Merriman that primary narrative gift, as in the passage where the young woman lists the folk spells:

> How downright it is, how clear cut. Yet convincing: the lady in the case might certainly have so spoken; the poet has not gone out of his way to help her out: each piseog, he has settled, is to get one line and no more.[47]

Merriman's genius lay in his capacity to write in a language very close to the everyday speech of his Clare, and yet somehow to infuse that speech with the rhymes and assonances of poetry. He understood, perhaps better than anyone, that Gaelic poetry had too often failed to trust the rhythms of conversational speech. If the court proposes that people should obey natural forces, its author clearly contends that poetry should base itself on *caint na ndaoine* (the speech of the people). The fact that Merriman belonged to no bardic school and did not consort with other poets left him very free to pursue his own modernizing agendas. It also reinforced in him a quality observed in many natives of County Clare: a sturdy independence of mind and of judgement.

Merriman existed on the Clare cusp between the literary language of Munster schools and the oral culture of Connacht, in the border zone between written and folk tradition. As with the fairy-folk of Creag Liath, the 'in-between' place often turns out to be the most exciting zone to occupy. That strategic location taught Merriman to be wary of a Munster poetry that often spilled over in an excess of self-cancelling adjectives. Such 'runs' he mocked once or twice in the *Cúirt an Mheán-Oíche*, as in the account of a skywoman who stands forth to make a complaint:

> *Bhí a gruag léi scaoilte síos go slaodach . . .*[48]

> Her hair was streaming loose and composed . . .

The words 'scaoilte' and 'slaodach' are at odds with one another, in the way that the epithets of an Ó Súilleabháin could often be. But Merriman understood that a truer literature would found itself on actual speech. For him poetry was a bargain struck when the currents of popular conversation could somehow be accommodated within the received metrical scheme.

Every text reads its readers. Even in the 1780s rural Irish society had witnessed the emergence of a Catholic middle class, whose families would show a growing desire for made marriages rather than matches based on mutual attraction. Merriman's poem has been read as an attack on this new policing of the sexual body. It is even possible that the author, a socially ambitious man, may have been spurned as not good enough by somebody like the young woman of the poem. He didn't marry until he was almost forty years of age (very old by the standards of that time) and his anxieties about male adequacy expressed themselves on the lips of his women characters as well as in the mouth of his old male speaker. The ending has something of the quality of a catharsis in the psychological process: a self-administered therapy. As his body is flayed, the poet comes to recognize that he is as guilty as anyone else of curbing his instincts: and with that recognition he is cured and fit to return to the world.

The mockery of English fashions in the text can be seen as a critique of the unnecessary complication of apparel in the eighteenth century. The woman's body was to the English planters a mannequin to be draped in costly clothes and seen to best advantage indoors. In Merriman's lines it is often undressed and in the open air, a statement of what people should look like. This was less a matter of transgressing the new English rules with all the swagger of a knowing dissident than of returning naturally to an older Gaelic code, which happened to come far closer to the 'free clothing' movement gathering power in revolutionary Paris.[49] If Merriman's lines were poetry in less formal rhythms and metres, the same might be said of the undressed quality of his human bodies.

One of the reasons why Frank O'Connor's spirited translation of the *Cúirt an Mheán-Oíche* is not a wholly faithful version may be found in its will to transgress, the very feature lacking in Merriman's words. O'Connor believed the poem to be one way of proving to puritanical nationalists that they had no real interest in a revival of authentic Gaelic traditions: and they duly obliged him by banning his translation, even as the original poem remained on sale in the government's own bookshop. Perhaps the censors were subtler than he recognized. The transgressive note in O'Connor's version excites only those minds whose self-censors have already been activated: it would have no meaning at all for someone wholly within the Gaelic tradition. This may be why Merriman's own version was never banned (a generation earlier, J.M. Synge had shrewdly observed that Douglas Hyde could in his books get away with effects in Irish for which Synge himself was roundly denounced when he reworked them in English).

Nowadays, the poem is less problematic.[50] Its critique of loveless marriage and its honest recognition that women have sexual desires might recommend it to feminist readers, already attracted by the notion of an all-female court: yet there are overtones of a more sexist philosophy in the old man's misogynistic outbursts and (more surprisingly) in the young woman's untroubled candour in listing all the wiles she employed in a futile attempt to trap a man. A strict feminist might wonder just how radical an advance it was to have a male poet produce an anti-*aisling* rather than the real thing. If queen Aoibheall herself were to return as a critic of the poem, she might laugh to scorn the very notion of a male poet such as the urbane Merriman ventriloquizing her voice and those of other female *personae*. Even in such striking later versions as Yeats's Crazy Jane or Joyce's Molly Bloom, the man who speaks through the voice of an implied woman is often found to carry an undertow of sexist attitudes into the moment of seeming liberation. If Jane and Molly prove more sharptongued and bitchy than some readers would like, that may because their authors' *anima*, kept below the level of consciousness until they were well into middle age, was bound to emerge from such repression in a raw, unforgiving mood. The same might be said of Merriman's poem, in which the old stereotype of the vengeful harridan is still vibrant, albeit in mockery. It was all too symptomatic of the limitations of Irish-speaking society that, at the end of the eighteenth century no less than at the beginning, its pleas for a frustrated womanhood should have been composed with success by a man.

That said, one shouldn't underestimate the immense technical problems posed for an artist like Merriman in his attempt to modernize a deeply conservative literary tradition. The success with which he managed 'to transform the mythological tie between the sovereignty of Ireland and a rightful hereditary king into a relationship between women and men' in the eighteenth-century countryside has only recently been fully described.[51] The fact that Merriman managed to express the new Enlightenment ideas of 'freedom and social mobility' in 'that contemporary emergent world' is an awesome technical as well as intellectual achievement.[52] In doing as much, he solved the problem that confronts all revolutionaries: how to express something unprecedented in a language that is by definition freighted only with ideas of the past? Just a decade later, French revolutionaries like Robespierre attempted a similar solution by presenting themselves less as radical innovators than as resurrected Romans: and so they had themselves painted in ancient togas. Their reasoning was transparent enough: launching a new departure into unknown territory, they themselves were probably not much less frightened than the onlooking citizenry, and it stilled the nerves of all parties to pretend that what was afoot was really a restoration of ancient democratic rights rather than an outright revolution. There would be time enough for the latent French meaning to emerge from beneath this layering of ancient Roman content after the deed itself was done.

Within the Irish context, the example given by Merriman was studied well. If he could portray his dream-world of polymorphous sex as a return to a desirable Gaelic order, by a somewhat similar technique James Joyce would manage to gift-wrap the most subversive prose narrative of the twentieth century in the outer framework of one of Europe's oldest tales, *The Odyssey* of Homer. In it, too, a passive, put-upon male would find himself submitting to the petticoat government of a masterful woman. Many of the developments in the further modernization of Irish culture by such intellectuals seem to connect powerfully back to Merriman's great poem.

It may also have been a sense of its once and future importance in the unfolding of the Irish story that caused a 35-year-old prisoner named Éamon de Valera to astonish his comrades by memorizing every single one of its lines during a sojourn in Lincoln Jail. A couple of days after he recited it word-perfect for his fellow inmates, de Valera was sprung by some of his comrades on the outside. He escaped by the simple enough device of dressing as a woman.[53] Merriman would have been amused, even if the forces of the crown were not.

13

Burke, Ireland
and Revolution

Edmund Burke was born in Dublin on New Year's Day, 1729. His mother was a Nagle from a distinguished family of Cork Jacobites, who looked down on the new Protestant planters in their area as upstarts and vulgarians. His father was a lawyer who, in order to secure his career, had made a tactical conversion from Catholicism to Protestantism.[1] The infant Burke may have been baptized a Catholic in a secret family ceremony – and for years his political enemies in England would brand him a Jesuit and a Jacobite – but in his self-descriptions to the world he invariably spoke as a Protestant Anglican. However, his schooling was a mingled affair, as befitted a boy of such composite background: from the age of six to eleven, he was taught at a hedge-school in Cork at which both Irish and English were spoken. Thereafter, he 'retained an interest in the Irish language and its literature'[2] to the extent of unearthing and saving manuscripts of both the *Book of Leinster* and the *Book of Lecan* (which he saw were returned from England to Trinity College Dublin).

The Nagles wished for a restoration of the Catholic Stuart dynasty, but Burke, always a respecter of actual circumstances, knew this was no longer possible. Yet he was forever haunted by the fate of his mother's proud people, who had lost lands and privileges after the Williamite victory. If he proclaimed himself a believer in God, his loyalty was more to Christianity in general than to any particular one of its churches. He took a BA at Trinity College in 1748, winning fame among its students for his oratory and powers of composition. These powers were revealed to the wider world in 1757 on publication of his *Philosophical Enquiry into the Origin of Our Ideas of the Sublime and the Beautiful*. In that year also he married Jane Nugent, the daughter of a noted Irish Catholic doctor. By then he had graduated from the Middle Temple, the great law school of London.

Burke soon became a political figure, a career which (he painfully knew) had been made possible only by his father's apostasy. He emerged as a defender of tradition, order and degree, but also as a ferocious critic of overweening power. Often, when it might have better served his immediate interests to remain silent, he denounced the Penal Code in Ireland: 'We found the people heretics and idolators; we have, by way of improving their condition, rendered them slaves and beggars.'[3] To a close political associate he wrote in 1773: 'I can never forget that I am an Irishman. I flatter myself perhaps; but I think I would shed my blood rather than see the limb I belong to oppressed or defrauded of its due nourishment.'[4] Accordingly, he offended the tradespeople of Bristol, whom he represented as member of parliament, by refusing to support their demand for restrictions on Irish trade (those same restrictions that had so incensed Swift). In 1778 he worked skilfully behind the scenes to secure the passing of the first measure to relax some of the Penal Laws. His contention was that they were designed to create perpetual insecurity and distrust, causing men to 'fly from their very species', so that 'all the means given by Providence to make life safe and comfortable are perverted into instruments of terror and torment'.[5] Conor Cruise O'Brien has argued that in doing all this, Burke may have been 'expiating the insult to his mother's faith, which his father had been obliged to inflict, in order to make possible his son's career. To discharge that debt, Edmund was in honour bound to subordinate that career, to a significant and costly degree, to the service of his mother's people.'[6]

Burke's fame today rests on two works that outwardly seem to have little connection with his Irish concerns – *Reflections on the Revolution in France* and his essay on the sublime and beautiful. In both he is an apologist for order and the *ancien régime*, yet he could not have offered so penetrating an analysis of the sublime terror of revolution were he not powerfully attracted to the very idea. In a letter to Lord Charlemont, he recalled the ambiguity of his early response to the revolution in France, as of one 'gazing with astonishment . . . and not knowing whether to blame or to applaud'.[7] Before 1789, Burke had praised French radicals so much that, when *Reflections on the Revolution in France* appeared, men like Tom

Paine pronounced themselves amazed that the book could come from so zealous a reformer as Burke.

The steady reform of society is one thing; the subversion of previous political hierarchies quite another. How did the French radicals come to hold such mistaken expectations of Burke? One answer might be his frequent declarations of support for England's Glorious Revolution of 1688, which some felt that they were simply extending to Paris. 'A positively vicious and abusive government ought to be changed', wrote Burke in 1789, 'and if necessary by violence, if it cannot (as is sometimes the case) be reformed.'[8] However, his view that James II intended to subvert the English constitution led him to cast the Whigs as reluctant rebels who, with infinite regret, resorted to force to protect the constitution and to reform major abuses. Unlike that of the French, theirs was a defensive rebellion to protect landed property and traditional rights, he said, rather than a modernizing insurrection that sought to loosen all ties of property, inheritance and aristocracy in order to replace them with a meritocracy. 'What we did was in truth and substance, and in a constitutional light, a revolution not made but prevented . . . In the stable, fundamental parts of our constitution, we made no revolution.'[9]

A second explanation of Burke's credibility among radicals was his campaign to expose the wrongs endured by the Catholics of Ireland. He saw his native country simmer with discontent, and the French terror later brought home to him just what the consequences of Protestant triumphalism might be. His writings on Ireland are, in effect, studies in potential revolution, as well as pleas for a measured amelioration of the appalling conditions. In these, his outline of the revolutionary situation often seems to take on a momentum of its own, far outstripping in its rhetorical power those passages that propose alternative methods. Not for nothing, therefore, has Conor Cruise O'Brien found in Burke's work a suppressed sympathy for revolution, for Burke had grown to maturity in a land raging against state tyranny.[10] The price of his successful career in England was the intermittent suppression of these sentiments, or at least their reformulation as a case for reform: but the early experience was none the less decisive. Burke did not need to travel to France to witness revolutionary conditions at first hand.

As his career in England developed, he could make his own comparisons between the competent administration of its affairs and the mediocrity and mendacity of government in the colony. England's representatives were really misrepresentatives, 'an ascendancy of hucksters' and 'a junto of robbers':

This protestant ascendancy means nothing like an influence obtained by virtue, by love, or even by artifice and seduction . . . It is neither more nor less than the resolution of one set of people in Ireland to consider themselves as sole citizens of the commonwealth; and to keep a dominion over the rest by reducing them to absolute slavery under a military power; and thus fortified in their power, to divide the public estate, which is the result of general contribution, as a military booty solely amongst themselves.[11]

The Anglo-Irish depended for their very identity on the Catholic Irish, whom they none the less consigned to the zones of nonexistence in law. This grave psychological contradiction filled some landlords with hatred for the natives, who yet had the temerity to exist.

It is possible in that context to read Burke's Irish writings in just the way that he read the events of 1688 – as studies in how to prevent rather than make a revolution. For the situation generated not only insurrectionism among the Catholics, but also (to some degree) a meritocratic philosophy among the more ambitious Anglicans. The very restricted size of the ascendancy, though a thoroughly unjust arrangement, had one positive effect among Anglicans: it allowed for careers open to talent, badly needed among such governmental mediocrity. This upward mobility was a feature of the Protestant community throughout the eighteenth century: as J.C. Beckett has wittily written, since it was invariably assumed that a gentleman was a Protestant, it became almost as easy to assume that a Protestant might be a gentleman.[12] This was the positive aspect of an 'aristocracy' whose members were often jumped-up tradespersons.

People today might admire such meritocratic arrangements, while regretting that they didn't extend to Catholics and Dissenters: but Burke did not admire them at all. To him such social mobility could only presage revolution and the installation of a new class whose power derived from cash rather than land. He constantly stressed the folly of any Irish campaign for national independence, since this would merely leave the Irish an easy prey to the designs of France. If compelled to choose between England and France, he knew which side he was on. He might rail against crazy English policies in his homeland, but this was the anger of a man who expected better things rather than the rage of one contesting England's right to be there. It was the frustration of a man who could foresee those policies creating in Ireland the same conditions that plunged France into terror: government from the barrel of a gun rather than with the consent of the governed.

The corrupt policy in Ireland, as in India and America, was beginning to poison domestic politics in England itself, unleashing many
adventurers with more money than taste. In 1796 Burke wrote to his
friend Dr Hussey that the reign of terror was as repugnant in Ireland
as in France:

> Shall you and I find fault with the proceedings of France, and
> be totally indifferent to the proceedings of Directories at
> home? You and I hate Jacobinism as we hate the gates of hell.
> Why? Because it is a system of oppression. What can make us
> in love with oppression because the syllables Jacobin are not
> put before the -ism, when the very same things are done under
> the -ism preceded by any other name in the Directory of
> Ireland?[13]

As late as that year, Burke still thought of Ireland as 'home'.

That strong language in castigating the French rebels can be translated with only a little strain into Irish terms. What the rebels did to
the French queen Marie Antoinette was to strip all her decent drapery away, leaving her to flee half-naked for her life. This is equivalent
to the Gaelic poet's notion of a rude male invader who took a female
Ireland by violence and then toppled her aristocracy, much as the
Cromwellians had extirpated Gaelic nobles a century earlier. Some of
the *filí*, such as Dáibhí Ó Bruadair, had berated their old lords for a
too-easy capitulation:

> *Nach ait an nós seo ag mórchuid d'fheara Éireann*
> *D'at go nódh le mórtas maingiléiseach?*
> *Cidh tais a dtreoir ar chodaibh Ghalla-chléire,*
> *Ní chanaid glór ach gósta garbh-Bhéarla.*[14]

Isn't this a strange habit amongst most Irishmen, who once
swelled with a vast pride? However warmly they pursue English
learning and art, they make no sound but a rough English
noise.

A similar yearning for a rooted aristocracy informed the writings
of Burke, who counselled the Duke of Richmond in 1772 to maintain the old *hauteur* and who consistently lashed those mandarins
who surrendered too easily to the mercantile class. Ó Bruadair, likewise, had sneered at the names of the puritan *arrivistes*, but in his
view the ultimate blame for their triumph lay with a culture that now
spurned learned men because, deep down, it had lost its faith in

itself. That loss is recorded in lines where jauntiness soon gives way
to a more melancholy note:

> Nach iongantach é mar theannta grinn
> In ionad na gcraobh 's an damhsa bhíodh
> Gan friotal i mbéal fán am so i dtír
> Ach gur chuireamar féin an samhradh i gcill.[15]

Isn't it marvellous (in a jocose kind of way) that in place of the
harp and the dances once known, there is by now no music on
the lips of any in the land? – for we ourselves have laid the
summer to rest.

The notion of original sin as the cause of such failure also underlay
Burke's rejection of eighteenth-century meliorism. Within himself he
could sense those darker instincts and desires that Shaftesburyan
England wanted only to wish away. That society lacked a vision of
evil and, because of its culpable naïveté, was capable of crimes far
worse than would ever be committed by those in closer touch with
their own deeper nature.

Burke's empathy with India under occupation was expressed in
terms that vividly recall the extirpation of Gaelic life by adventurers
and planters. Few people were as rooted in custom as the Indians,
but Burke complained that all this had been callously swept aside by
the East India Company. 'The first men of that country', 'eminent in
situation', were insulted and humiliated by 'obscure young men',
pushing upstarts who 'tore to pieces the most established rights, and
the most ancient and most revered institutions of ages and nations'.[16]
It was the selfsame humiliation known by the princely *filí*-turned-
beggars: and Burke saw in Warren Hastings the kind of profiteer
who ripped a social fabric. Affecting a mandarin style, these expro-
priators were *homo economicus* hell-bent on breaking Brahminism.
To those who worried that Burke might be overstating the case, he
replied in 1786, 'I know what I am doing, whether the white people
like it or not.'[17] Warren Hastings was in many ways the antithesis of
Burke. The former was a man born in an imperial power who went
to a colony in search of profitable adventure, while the latter was a
man born in a colony who went to the imperial centre to seek an
honourable career.

What Burke had to say against the 'junto of robbers' in Dublin
could have been said also of Hastings's men in India. They built no
schools or public utilities, being out for quick profit. They had the
boldness of young men who 'drink the intoxicating draughts of

authority and dominion before their heads are able to bear it'.[18] Burke was shocked by the complicity in all this of Indian middlemen, who prospered as stewards in much the same fashion as the bailiffs denounced by Gaelic poets. It was, however, for the fallen nobles of India that Burke offered his *caoineadh ar chéim síos na nuasal* (lament for fallen nobility). To the House of Lords he declared in 1794, 'I do not know a greater insult that can be offered to a man born to command than to find himself made a tool of a set of obscure men, come from an unknown country, without anything to distinguish them but an usurped power.'[19]

Whether the subject was England, India or France, the threat to traditional sanctity and loveliness was evoked by Burke in the image of a ravaged womanhood. In his *Reflections on the Revolution in France*, he describes how Marie Antoinette fled from a royal palace in which no chivalric hand was raised to defend her: 'I thought ten thousand swords must have leaped from their scabbards to avenge even a look that threatened her with insult. But the age of chivalry is gone. That of sophisters, economists, and calculators has succeeded; and the glory of Europe is extinguished forever.'[20] It wasn't hard for Burke to cast himself in a role made familiar by dozens of *aisling* poets, evoking a defenceless *spéirbhean* (skywoman) who would only recover happiness when a young warrior rallied to her defence. Where natural laws were transgressed, Burke believed, there could be nothing but pain and strife.

Burke's distrust of democracy hardened into opposition to any attempt to extend the franchise beyond the traditional elite. He disliked the imposition of popular will at the expense of educated reason, which he considered the preserve of the exceptional few. He held that governors should be held in awe as well as esteem, that mixture of dread and attention felt by persons in the presence of the sublime. His complaint, therefore, was not that Irish Catholics lacked a general franchise, but rather that they were denied the right to be represented by their natural leaders, the extirpated Gaelic nobility. He also had a shrewd pragmatist's distrust of any situation in which large numbers of men felt frustrated by a lack of occupations commensurate with their abilities.

It may appear at this point that there were certain contradictions in Burke's position.[21] He was against the spread of the franchise, yet proposed its extension to certain Irish Catholics; he was opposed to popular will, but bemoaned the fact that four-fifths of Ireland was unrepresented; he excoriated the middle class that ruled from Dublin, yet became by the 1790s the apologist for a Catholic middle class excluded from power. There were, in fact, two Burkes: an English

Burke who thought one thing (usually quite traditional), while the Irish Burke felt quite another thing (often covertly radical in tendency). Although Burke still has the reputation of a conservative, he is justly credited with being the first major thinker to grasp the long-term implications of the advanced ideas of his time. This is true in particular of his sense of the turbulence that might be unleashed by men of talent with no stake in the country, but provided with a disgruntled mass on which to rehearse their frustrations:

> These were all the talents which assert their pretensions, and are impatient of the place which settled society prescribes for them. These descriptions had got between the great and the populace; and the influence of the lower classes was with them. Without the great, the first movements in this revolution could not, perhaps, have been given. But the spirit of ambition, now for the first time connected with the spirit of speculation, was not to be restrained at will.[22]

That amazingly prescient passage foretold the major tension in nineteenth-century culture between the great traditional houses and the restless, speculative values of the cash nexus. The new, mobile hero and heroine would in time display an exploitative attitude to fellow creatures, a thirst for cash, a readiness to go from place to place, easily severing social ties and adopting a superficial approach to the life of the emotions. A novel such as Jane Austen's *Mansfield Park* would locate such attitudes in the charming but treacherous Mary and Henry Crawford, each of them a consummate actor able to don or doff a social mask at will: and it would play these off against the stable customs of the landed gentry, whose members were unadventurous but loyal, rural rather than urban in sensibility, trustworthy but often immobile to the point of torpor. Burke was the first to conceptualize this challenge of modernity, and he could give such a full account of these rival tendencies because he felt them so deeply in himself. His head might argue for order, but his heart kept reminding him of the disabilities of his own people 'at home'. In this, as in much else, Ireland was a more 'advanced' case than England, for the clash between big-house decorum and bourgeois energy had been enacted there in the 1600s, when the Cromwellians put paid to the Gaelic nobility. By the time Burke was a child in Cork, its effects were chillingly obvious in a leaderless and demoralized people, deprived of their traditional culture and consoled by no viable replacement. Sensing what was to follow in England from that experience, Burke was filled with foreboding.

If in the end Burke must be attached to either side, it might be more fitting to place him with the moderns. He was, after all, an expatriate careerist himself. Even more, as a theorist of revolution, he was just about the most modern thing anyone in his time could have been. Burke was perhaps the first in England to grasp the world-historical implications of the French upheaval, which he called in strikingly immodest language 'the greatest moral earthquake that ever convulsed and shattered this globe of ours' and 'the most important crisis that ever existed in the world'.[23] He conceptualized much that the French insurgents merely expressed at the level of action: and this was a most perilous exercise for a man so powerfully addicted to traditional values. For he always recognized that the foundations on which obedience is given to a state are not to be subjects of constant discussion without the state itself being jeopardized.

That other Burke, who spoke with an Irish voice, was quite the opposite of an upholder of received custom. His writings on Ireland prosecute that very discussion about the terms on which allegiance may be offered to a state – that debate he sought to discourage in England. It is in these works that one may find a not-very-suppressed sympathy for revolution. At times he even implied that violence might be necessary, if only to secure a hearing for moderation. In 1796, at a time of armed clashes and killings in Ireland, he wrote to Dr Hussey: 'dreadful it is, but it is now plain enough that Catholic *Defenderism* is the only restraint upon Protestant *Ascendancy*'.[24] Here again he offered cautious support for a defensive rather than modernizing revolution, but for revolution of a kind all the same.

If the English Burke was a political analyst counselling moderation, the Irish Burke was an artist, fascinated by the spectacle of the imagination embodied in human action. The notion of apocalyptic reversals had engaged artists from the days of the Old Testament: and Burke enjoyed the relative luxury of being able to study the French commotion at a safe remove. If the stable, ordered England of ancestral houses and neat plots of land seemed a trifle tame, it served none the less as a working definition of the beautiful: but for that sense of awe, dread and danger that he saw as elements of the sublime, a person need look no further than the revolution – terrible to be caught up in, but sublime when it was an experience of pain and danger, witnessed by one not in those actual circumstances.[25] Moreover, in offering an experience too vast and chaotic to be susceptible of intellectual control, it evoked wonder rather than pleasure, unease rather than serenity. It is hardly surprising that Burke denounced the sublime and endorsed the beautiful – but that, again, was the English Burke, perhaps because the Irish Burke, having grown up in a simmering land, had already had quite enough of turbulence.

Burke's essays on Ireland were not much publicized in his lifetime, but a collection was made and published by Matthew Arnold in 1881. The publication was an attempt to further Arnold's 'Union of Hearts' policy by increasing understanding between another English administration and an Ireland once again verging on rebellion. Arnold shared Burke's fear that the long-term implication of an Irish secession could be the break-up of the British empire.[26] Burke had suggested that a government proposal to tax Irish landlords resident in Britain would reduce what little commerce there was between the peoples. 'Their next step', he told Sir Charles Bingham, 'will be to encourage all the colonies – about thirty separate governments – to keep their people from all intercourse with each other and with the mother country.'[27] His only aim, as he averred in his Guildhall speech at Bristol, was 'to unite to this kingdom, in prosperity and in affection, whatever remained of the empire'.[28] Coded into that statement was another very modern understanding: on the need for hybridization, for an intensification of personality by a multiplication of identities. The English might seem lugubrious and the Irish fanciful, but taken together they could amount to something.

According to the sociologist Karl Mannheim, a traditional society is one in which the young are made to adjust to the codes of the elders, whereas a revolutionary society is one in which parents are usurped by children, husbands by wives, and so on.[29] Such usurpations were the telltale signs detected by Burke in Irish Catholic family life under the Penal Laws: the right of primogeniture being removed, a father would be forced either to divide his farm equally between all inheriting sons (leading to smaller, uneconomical units) or else he was made to hand over the entire farm to any son who conformed to the Anglican Church.

> The paternal power is in all such families so enervated that it may well be considered as entirely taken away; even the principle upon which it is founded seems to be directly reversed . . . Every child of every Popish parent was encouraged to come into what is called a Court of Equity to proffer a bill against his father . . . so that the parent has no security against a perpetual inquietude.[30]

In other words, there is a permanent revolution in personal relations.

Equally, Burke complained, if the wife of a Roman Catholic

should change her religion, from that moment she deprived her husband of all direction and management of their children. Burke spelled out the revolutionary potential of such a reversal: 'she herself by that hold inevitably acquires a power and superiority over her husband . . she deprives him of that source of domestic authority which the common law had left to him – that of rewarding or punishing by a voluntary distribution of his effects, what in his opinion was the good or ill behaviour of his wife'.[31] The sympathy there is not 'suppressed' at all, but it is a sympathy not so much for revolution as for those doomed to live their lives in a revolutionary situation. 'By the express words of the law, all possibility of acquiring any species of valuable property, in any sort connected with land, is taken away; and secondly, by the construction, all security for money is also cut off. No security is left, except what is merely personal.'[32] Which is to say that the autonomous, isolate modern self is born. Burke's account of Jacobin libertinism was strikingly close to his dire sketches of Ireland under Penal duress. Jacobin marriage was no more than a civil contract, he lamented, which could be torn up if either party sued for divorce. Mothers could now neglect children, and the old respect of youth for age would decline as 'children are encouraged to cut the throats of their parents'.[33]

All of these sentiments led Burke into a critique of that form of imperialism which employed religion to justify a material degradation of a people. He pointed to the self-contradictions, in purely religious terms, of such an enterprise. An Irishman could now be a Catholic with impunity, he scoffed, upon condition of living the life of a slave:

> We found the people heretics and idolators; we have, by way of improving their condition, rendered them slaves and beggars. They remain in all the misfortune of their old errors, and all the superadded misery of their recent punishment.[34]

This sustained irony was Swiftian, its ferocity similar to that of the Drapier. So also was Burke's love of paradox, by which the English invasion of Ireland, sanctioned by a papal bull of Adrian, is shown to be a strangely Catholic activity, and resistance to it, therefore, might be seen as a properly Protestant form of protest. The ultimate fear occasioned no playful irony at all. That was the prospect of a Catholic people bypassing Canterbury and turning to Dissenters for solace, precisely that conjunction preached by Wolfe Tone at the end of the century. This was predicted by Burke in 1792 in his letter to Sir Hercules Langrishe MP:

. . . if you force the Roman Catholics out of the religion of habit, education or opinion, it is not to yours that they will ever go. Shaken in their minds, they will go to that where the dogmas are fewest; where they are the most uncertain; where they lead them the least to a consideration of what they have abandoned. They will go to that uniformly democratic system to whose first movements they owed their emancipation.[35]

Burke's sympathy with revolution was suppressed because he was by nature a reformer. He believed less in abstract principles of absolute right and wrong than in the pragmatic reduction of abuses in the here-and-now. He berated the French rebels for their fear – as he saw it – of actual human complexities and their addiction to abstract ideals. In that degree, he was an early exponent of what has become known as 'the resistance to theory'.[36] The revolutionaries, he moaned, loved mankind but hated individual men. They asserted unconditional goodness, denied original sin and vented their fury upon a flawed humanity which could never hope to live up to such high-mindedness. Indeed, he accused them of employing the same twisted logic as that used by the apologists for the Penal Laws. They also applied the hateful notion that a machine of oppression could morally be imposed on a reluctant people simply because it was for their greater benefit in the longer run. As the Catholics were reduced to near-animality under the laws, he argued that the French, failing to attain perfection, would collapse into inhumanity at their inability to live up to such an enormous expectation. In pursuit of an imaginary perfection, legislators would justify all kinds of terror as a means to what they saw as a worthwhile end.

All this analysis was a version of familiar English arguments against partisan enthusiasms and religious zeal. These had been advanced ever since the Civil War and can be found in Swift's *Tale of a Tub*, the essays of Steele and Addison, or even in Restoration comedy. At their source was a desire to soften troublesome differences between Whig and Tory, Roundhead and cavalier, Protestant and Catholic: but what astonished Burke was the way in which such zeal still manifested itself in policy in Ireland, generating dangerous 'enthusiasms' in abundance. Contrary to English prejudice, he insisted that Irish rebellions sprang not from the discontent of the pampered but from poverty and ill-use. Indeed, he explicitly contrasted the French disturbance, which came from excessive speculation and fullness of bread, with the Irish kind, which was durable and rooted. The very wantonness that produced the French trouble might also serve to extinguish it, but 'the Jacobinism which arises from penury and irritation, from scorned loyalty and rejected allegiance, has much deeper roots'.[37] So, in his treatise on the Popery Laws, Burke attacked the misrepresentations of those English historians who perpetually cast Irish rebels in the parts of spoiled children. In telling the true 'interior history of Ireland',[38] he updated Céitinn.

Burke mocked the common stereotype of the Irish as a race 'more remarkable for determined resolution than clear ideas or much foresight';[39] he demonstrated, rather, the people's amazing self-restraint in the face of persecution. The following passage vibrates with his outrage and with the devious pleasure he seemed to take in imagining a London firebombed by vengeful terrorists:

> But though provoked by everything that can stir the blood of men, their houses and chapels in flames, not a hand was moved to retaliate, or even to defend. Had a conflict once begun, the rage of their persecutors would have redoubled. Thus fury increasing by the reverberation of outrages, house being fired for house, and church for chapel, I am convinced that no power under heaven could have prevented a general conflagration; and at this day, London would have been a tale.[40]

That may have been a forecasting image of the Fenian bomber in English literature, but it was also a veiled threat as well as a warning. It was an image of a kind that Burke would often deploy in his later years, as when he described the revolution in terms that recall Blake's Tyger:

> I can contemplate without dread, a royal or a national tiger on the borders of Pegu. I can look at him with an easy curiosity, as prisoner within bars in the menagerie of the tower. But if, by habeas corpus or otherwise, he was to come into the lobby of the House of Commons while your door was open, any of you would be more stout than wise, who would not gladly make your escape out of the back windows. I certainly should dread more from a wild cat in my bed-chamber, than from all the lions in the desert behind Algiers. But in this parallel it is the cat that is at a distance, and the lions and tigers that are in our ante-chambers and rooms.[41]

Confronted with a tax on landed estates in Ireland but not England, Burke said that this was 'a virtual declaration that England is a foreign country'.[42] A similar sentiment impelled him to support

American colonists in their rebellion against taxation without representation, a rebellion that he correctly foresaw would lead to independence. Even before the British empire was at its fullest expansion, he was a keen student of those tensions which would break it up. In his 'Letter to the Sheriffs of Bristol', he juxtaposed an England 'pampered by enormous wealth' with 'the high spirit of free dependencies'. The end of empire was already implicit in that formulation: and Burke thanked the insurrectionary Americans for 'making me think better of my nature'.[43]

Ireland, under the Penal Laws, was another glaring case of representation denied, as well as a misrepresentation of the true spirit of England. Burke went so far in his Guildhall speech as to dub the Protestant Association 'that libel on the national religion and English character'. The Irish Catholics he saw as victims of the Protestant betrayal of the idea of the *nation*, for the Protestants had 'divided the nation into two distinct bodies, without common interest, sympathy or connection'.[44] In his letter to Sir Hercules Langrishe, Burke described the transformation of the 'English interest' into an independent Irish interest among the Anglo-Irish in the lead-up to Grattan's Parliament of 1782. 'However,' he added, 'as the English in Ireland began to be domiciliated, they began also to recollect that they had a country' (a phrase to be used half a century later in a speech by Thomas Davis to his fellow students at Trinity College Dublin).[45] Burke freely admitted that 1782 was for many the Irish equivalent of 1688.

'The reproaches of the country that I once belonged to, and in which I still have a dearness of instinct more than I can justify to reason, make a greater impression on me than I had imagined,' he wrote to Thomas Burgh.[46] Protestant ascendancy was like Jacobinism, because in each case a single group substituted its own self-interest for the good of society as a whole. By this means the word *Protestant* was emptied of all its nobler theological meanings, becoming 'nothing more or better than the name of a persecuting faction'.[47] To Burke it was crystal-clear that the evils of Jacobinism would flow from those of ascendancy. Many Protestants answered him by insisting that they did not persecute on grounds of religion. He sarcastically agreed, saying that they used religion as a cloak for material greed and 'lust for lordship'. Consistently, he tried to expose this corruption to the London parliament, but by 1796 he had despaired, contending that if all the people of Ireland were flayed alive by the ascendancy, it would be next to impossible to have the matter debated in parliament. 'By a strange inversion of the order of things', he wearily concluded, 'not only the largest part of the natives of Ireland are thus annihilated, but the Parliament of Great Britain itself is rendered no better than an instrument in the hands of an Irish faction'.[48]

How can a modern mind explain the apparent contradictions between Burke's Irish patriotism and his support for certain forms of British imperialism, between his solidarity with Irish Catholics and his total opposition to rebellion by their leaders? One explanation may lie in his development of the idea of the *nation*, as a third term by which to reconcile conflicting claims of the individual and the state.[49] The twin tyrannies of modernity – anarchy and totalitarianism, in his view – he saw as being latent in Jacobinism and he feared one as much as the other, because of the ways in which they made men and women martyrs to abstraction. For Burke the nation was something concrete and tangible: it began with parents, friends, relations, and eventually the sentiments which it aroused extended to the entire community. The ascendancy which ruled from Dublin betrayed that ideal by claiming that Ireland was always on the verge of revolt, so that its members might retain their jobs. The House of Commons could, however, stop the rot if it acted with speed to extend the franchise, emancipating Catholics and welcoming their MPs. Burke saw no necessary contradiction between an Irish nation, sovereign in several respects, and a British empire to which it was affiliated by military alliance in defence of constitutional rights. In the eighteenth century, many (including the young Theobald Wolfe Tone) felt that there was no incompatibility between national sovereignty and membership of an empire.

There may, finally, be a more personal explanation of Burke's ambivalence in the face of revolution. In the eyes of the world, he was notable for almost everything *except* his Irish writings. Ireland was the place he came from, but which he kept well-suppressed in his past as he pursued a glorious career in England. In fact, the occasional Irish visitors to his home at Beaconsfield evoked only the embarrassed contempt of his English admirers, who winced at their thick accents. Like Oscar Wilde a century later, Burke used a golden reputation in England to repress some painful details from an Irish past; but every so often that past erupted into a self-assertion all the more potent for having been so often denied.

All this left Burke in the psychological predicament of a revolutionary who had repudiated his own background and usurped his parental inheritance. He would not have been the first or last Irishman in England whose self-invention left him filled with feelings of guilt and national apostasy. Hence his ambivalence on the subject of revolt, for he himself was a loving father whose own son became a leader of the Catholic Association of Ireland and, in a sense, his father's Irish conscience.[50] Because he could imagine himself in both roles, as father and as son, Burke never fully resolved his feelings as to whether the usurpation of fathers by sons was a good or a bad thing. His extreme anguish in old age at being predeceased by his son suggests that he believed that the old should ultimately make way for the young. Certainly, the notion of a rebel as someone who usurps the father, internalizes him as superego, and thereafter becomes even more repressive in turn, would accurately trace the evolution of Burke as honorary Englishman, the figure who imagined himself, accurately, as the progenitor of various traditions. However, the self-inventing son remains also present in the writings of Burke, a dishonoured Irishman smouldering with the unappeased anger of one who went to a hedge-school in Cork and never forgot it.

Burke was a traditionalist who offered a penetrating critique of the economism of the modern state (even before it had fully taken shape) and who prophesied the end of empire (even before the empire had fully formed). In one respect, that makes him the some-what surprising precursor of today's 'third world' theorists, who attack these twin phenomena in the years of their slow decline. Ireland provided Burke, as it would later provide many others, with a metaphor for the world beyond Dover. It offered points of com-parison, which helped to explain events in places as far-flung as India and America. The French terror, which he was certain that no English person could directly face, was available to him in a trans-posed account of life in post-Cromwellian Ireland, a hell in the grip of 'demoniacs possessed with a spirit of fallen pride and inverted ambition'.[51] The Irish had been told by Cromwell to go either to hell or to Connacht: but the hell of the Roundheads, so vividly described by John Milton, was now also visible and audible on the streets of Paris.

Burke transcended this tangled past, his all-too-powerful Catholic mother and his all-too-neglectful 'Protestant' father, by remaking himself in England. Over the years there, he seldom referred to his Irish background in private and never did so in public. (The tracts on the Popery Laws did not appear until after his death.) His enemies, of course, liked to play up his Irishness, his brogue, his allegedly secret Catholicism, his Celtic effeminacy (which led to suggestions that he was part of a homosexual circle). What they could not have known was that his real nightmare from the Irish past was his unsureness of his rather tepid father's love. Edmund sent each of his books as it appeared back to the old man, in order to show that he was now cut-ting a figure in the world. Insecure in the paternal relationship, Burke saw paternity as a myth to be established and ratified, whereas maternity was a biological fact and a mother's love could be taken as axiomatic.

His revolt was, in consequence, that of a radical conservative, in the sense that it took the form of a protest against the vacuum left by an inadequate and often absent authority. It was really a search for, rather than a destruction of, a code. In England Burke had no choice but to conceive of and father himself. That led him to adopt some rather radical postures. He argued that 'parents are made for their children, and not their children for them'.[52] He complained that parents thought too much of what children owed them, and not enough about what they owed to children. That painful truth was borne in on him when his only son drove himself to a fatal illness in his father's service.

Throughout his life, Burke tried to curb his own unfilial resentment against his father, fearing that it might only align him with those Jacobins ready to cut the throats of their parents. He was, on the other hand, also the man who told Dr Johnson that children owed parents little affection – 'nay, there would be no harm in that view, though children should at a certain age eat their parents'.[53] As an image of self-begetting, that could hardly be more graphic: and it would be repeated in many classic Irish texts from Edgeworth to Synge, from Moore to Joyce, sometimes in the context of a licensed patricide. It placed Burke, conservative though he was, in a revolutionary tradition that extolled the self-invented man.

From the moment when Arnold's edition of the Irish essays went into print in 1881, Burke's aesthetic became a dominant code of the Irish Revival. The idea of a son fathering himself was enacted by a masculine sublimity that coupled with feminine beauty in a true marriage of opposites. Ireland was sublime in its perturbation, wildness, force, to be revered like the forbidding father from a safe distance. England was beautiful in its order, proportion and gentility, to be loved in proximity like the fond wife. (Each land had also a deeper contrasexual side – Ireland as outraged female and England as predatory male, but these roles, he hoped, might be transcended.) Central to Burke's thinking was the need for a fusion of both attributes, if a whole personality was to be made – and in that he would be followed by Arnold. Burke's support for the Act of Union between Great Britain and Ireland made all the more sense in that context, as did his espousal of the cause of Irish Catholicism. Taken separately, each country seemed but a fraction lacking its integer. Taken together, they had the makings of an integrated being. The private wish-fulfilment in Burke's work was displaced and depersonalized, so that the writings could be received as art, without embarrassing an English reader who might have felt queasy about the latent desires therein. Irish readers, however, who uncover some of that hidden content do not in any way detract from the reputation of Burke as not only a prophetic thinker but also a very great artist.

14

Republican
Self-Fashioning:
The Journal of Wolfe Tone

If Theobald Wolfe Tone had never kept a journal, and if his wife Matilda hadn't gathered his texts together, it is probable that his life and death would not have the significance that now attaches to them. He died, like hundreds of others in 1798, fighting to create a republic, but it is because he left a moving and witty chronicle of his struggle that he is celebrated as the prophet of Irish independence.

Because that record is fragmentary, and because parts of it were lost by other people, it has the radiant quality of a romantic artwork. In it a man who has no sure sense of how events will turn out writes at the mercy of each passing moment, revealing a soul in all the vulnerability of its self-making. Tone's journal is the Irish *Prelude*, an account of the growth of its author's mind which by its very nature must remain unfinished, being a mere overture to something more interesting which will follow, the identity of a free citizen. The reader who knows how the tale ended must feel the poignant vulnerability of the writer in every line. The identity towards which Tone moves so gracefully is not the 'I' with which he began. It cannot, as it turns out, be written by Tone himself: and it is left to be inferred by his son William. He, one of the earliest intended readers, must write the introduction and fill the gaps in the broken narrative.

The extraordinary sense of involvement of all subsequent readers of the journal is due in great part to the space it leaves for a readerly role. The identity of Tone that emerges at the end is shaped as much by the attentive reader as by the patriot writer, defined from day to day amidst the fluctuations of the 1790s world in Ireland, the United States and France. Tone begins the memoir with some feeling of positional superiority over the more naïve, youthful fellow he was in the 1780s, and the chronicle begins with a sense of perfectly understandable self-division. Tone has not gone far before he is assigning pseudonyms to himself and his circle of friends, for whom everything, even revolution, takes on the quality of a great game. But this is a merely adolescent trying-on of various possible roles. What really captures the reader's imagination is the promise of an identity which will emerge in Tone from the very act of writing his life down. If his style represents a version of his current self, it contains the possibility of a richer personality yet to emerge out of the diarist's own self-division (for now Tone is 'Hutton' in the journal, 'James Smith' to the wider world).

At the start, Tone is so superior about his youthful self that he seems invulnerable in the present: but as the present moment approaches in his narrative and yields to daily journalizing, he loses that control. The text is turned over to the reader, who at once feels ashamed of knowing something its author could never have known: that the adventure of bringing the French to Ireland ended in his death. Yet somehow, Tone seems to have suspected that this was how it might all turn out, for his entries are written in the hope that some structure of future meaning will be discernible in the fragments of a chaotic life, a structure that is less imposed by the writer than discovered by the reader. In this, of course, he anticipates the gapped autobiographies and confessional narratives of W.B. Yeats and Samuel Beckett.

Edmund Burke emerges soon enough as the major antagonist of Tone in the journal, but had he known of its existence, he would probably have endorsed its method. He believed that the attempt to overcome modern fragmentation was *morbid*, leading only to a life-denying abstraction. Tone's refusal to reduce the journal to 'system', to a premature coherence, would have been applauded by him. W.B. Yeats also endorsed such an approach, for in his own *Autobiographies* (the plural title was deliberate), he observed their forward thrust: 'it is so many years before one can believe enough in what one feels to know what the feeling is'.[1] His description of Salvini, a great actor stuck with the bad part of the gravedigger in *Hamlet*, might well have been applied to Tone: 'when the world fails his ideal, as it must, and as he knows instinctively it must, he catches a glimpse of his true self before uttering his swansong'.[2] Tone's text too is offered as a promissory note to the future in compensation for a botched life.

Every autobiography is in some sense a confession of guilt. Ostensibly, Tone was expelled from his native Ireland in 1795 for writing a seditious letter to a French revolutionary agent; that was, in the eyes of some, his fitting punishment. He found the United States disagreeable enough: the life of a Princeton farmer humiliated his sense of merit, as did the prospect of seeing his children marry among boorish peasants. But his self-accusation is rather different: it is of abandoning his beloved family in the United States for a private mission as a secret emissary of the United Irishmen in Paris. If there is some residue of a Protestant 'search for evidences' in Tone's naked-ness before the moment, it may be found in his condition as a romantic solitary or wanderer, cast out from life's feast, a restless consciousness, travelling vast distances often incognito, unable to make normal social contacts with other people's families.

To experience Tone must now daily add the consciousness of it, as he submits to the humiliations of self-analysis. Like all romantic artists, 'he pleads to be forgiven, condoned, even condemned, so long as he is brought back into the wholeness of people and things'.[3] His attempt to describe seemingly indescribable experiences is the start of this re-entry process, for what Tone writes is a quest-romance. At the end should be the establishment of an Irish republic and the heaping of honours and comforts on his family as its first and foremost citizens, now rewarded for all their sufferings. All of Tone's pleasures are in that sense forepleasures, anticipations of a greater joy to come. Whether he is recalling the popularity of his young family on a ship to America, as they shared wine and food with other grateful emigrants, or an earlier moment when they climbed McArt's Fort on a lovely day with a community of like-minded Belfast republicans, Tone finds in such past experiences of solidarity a microcosm of the republic of the future.

The quest has, therefore, strong roots in past epiphanies, the memory of which is so potent that it triggers a wish for renewed ful-filment. The voyage to America is dangerous, but sweetened by the wine and cakes donated by the friends in Belfast and the gratitude of fellow passengers. The only discordant note is struck when the ship is boarded by callous captains of British frigates, who press some sailors and abuse the passengers. But the moments of solidarity seem all the more worthy of repetition, especially after such attack. The search of the romantic quester is for a society that will deliver him from the anxieties of reality, yet somehow contain that reality. His fear is self-absorption: hence the need for some grand ideal to serve. The danger is vanity, best avoided by strong doses of self-mockery and of real devotion to others. The search for enlightenment which was once the sole preserve of religion must now be conducted in a secular narrative because, for a modern republican, the only legitimate myth is art.

Tone wants a republic, but fears increasingly that he may have to find it first of all in himself. His journal becomes a virtual society, in which he trades quips and quotations with his wife, children, friends. It, at least, will fill the gap that is a result of his solitary mission to distant places. All this is one romantic author's attempt to come to terms with his own isolation: the almost unbearable poignancy is the knowledge that Tone, unlike the Ancient Mariner or the Leech-Gatherer, never did fully re-enter the human community. It is we eavesdroppers on his private conversation who must restore him, by a tender reading of his work.

Although a man of the Enlightenment, Tone was born late enough in the eighteenth century to be an early romantic. His memoir glosses quickly over his childhood in a distinctly Augustan fashion, which would have appalled Rousseau or Wordsworth. After that, however, he appears as a determined romantic, viewing his life as an experiment in living, worthy of analysis for the sake of those who come after. His emphasis is as often on the private as on the public world, for it is his own state of mind that provides the linking material between these disparate zones. Because the forms of autobiography are unique in each specific case, there can be no rigid rules. Everything is notionally admissable, for even acts of literary criticism or accounts of military manoeuvres may allow the writer to divulge some aspect of himself. The self and world, though apparently opposed, are fused in the consciousness by the very act of writing.

In that sense all writing – including his political pamphlets or memorials to the French government – becomes for Tone a version of autobiography. At the same time, he comes to recognize that any unmediated autobiography is impossible, though always desirable, for the *I* becomes a *me*, the subject an object, in the gesture of reportage, even as T.W. Tone becomes John Hutton or James Smith. The self isn't directly knowable in the conditions of modernity, nor should it necessarily seek to make itself available to outside decoders. It is known, rather, through its effects, from which its unknown qualities may be inferred. Like the poet John Keats, Tone knows that he can grasp only a part of the truth at a time: he too is the artist of half-knowledge, capable of living in doubts and uncertainties with no irritable reaching after fact and reason.[4] And, like Keats also in this, he leaves his texts as if they were traces which will not only survive his own death but be seen as a rehearsal for it. Compared with other rebels, Tone did very little, apart from fight gallantly when the

Hoche was about to be overpowered: we know him less through military action than through the consciousness revealed in the journal.

Living on the cusp between the eighteenth and nineteenth centuries, Tone understood that one really was an extension of the other rather than an alternative to it. For him the Imagination was not opposed to Reason so much as a heightened version of it. Imagination was the capacity to see things as they were; fantasy was the resort of those who wished to see them as they were not. Repeatedly in the journal he uses humour as a defensive wit, forestalling mockery of romantic idealism by another person. The perils of sincerity are never perils for Tone, because he is too continuously aware of his own multiplicity to make the mistake of stabilizing one identity over others. His choice of James Smith as a code-name seems almost a joke, for this most common name of Englishmen cries out to be seen through. Likewise, his playing at different roles – that of Irish roisterer, French lover, or American farmer – is done with an excess that borders on disavowal. Tone knows the dangers of singularity, for he has seen the word 'honest' become a term of abuse in the plays of Sheridan. The new Enlightenment protagonist was Diderot's Rameau, the man who knew that any one person has half a dozen selves to be true to. This was the spirit as praised by Hegel: 'to be conscious of its own distraught and torn existence, and to express itself accordingly – this is to pour scornful laughter on existence, on the confusion pervading the whole and on itself as well'.[5] There is a lot of that laughter in the journal, which never invests any entry with more emotion than it deserves from the reader.

The refusal of romantic artists to work in tired, old forms was based on a shrewd judgement of just how necessary it was for form to follow function. The object was to abolish the notion of art as a separate activity of a specialist caste, by substituting for it the example of autobiography as a complete expressiveness to which any citizen might aspire. Tone's journal is that of a dreamer, but one who is seeking to engage with real things; hence the fact that, like the notebooks kept by romantic poets and painters, it often takes the form of quasi-scientific note-taking, as if strange new ideas were being sketched or new forms essayed. 'The subjective emphasis is not egotistical,' says Jacques Barzun in *Classic, Romantic and Modern*: 'rather is it a condition of the search and the modesty of the searcher'.[6] Tone was imbued with the scientific spirit of experiment, but also with the idea that the role of language was to inform and to raise feeling. In so far as he contained within himself certain contradictions, he found in the nation a concept to reconcile individual energy and transcendent tasks, a notion vast enough to hold contrasting elements. He could conceive of Ireland as a nation uniting Catholic, Protestant and Dissenter because he himself had in a few years traversed the society: a coachmaker's son turned gentleman-scholar of Trinity College Dublin, a Protestant lawyer turned Catholic propagandist, a former empire man become a republican militant. Because he passed through so many levels of his society, he achieved an anthropologist's view of its codes; his diaries are proof that he could see it from an outside vantage-point, even as he continued to care passionately about what was happening within.

Tone had no compunction about applying the word 'romantic' repeatedly to himself and his siblings (most of whom travelled to the ends of the earth while young). Theatre posed for him in a particularly direct way the related problems of sincerity and authenticity. As a young tutor of twenty he found himself, like Rousseau, in the home of an aristocratic couple and promptly fell in love with the lady, Eliza Martin of Galway. She teased him mercilessly when they were male and female leads in a play called *Douglas*, during which he had to utter the lines

> *Her manifest affection for the youth*
> *Might breed suspicion in a husband's brain . . .*[7]

She was beautiful, influential and bored with her husband: and Tone knew it. 'Being myself somewhat of an actor,' he recalled a decade later, 'I was daily thrown into particular situations with her, both in rehearsals and on the stage.' His suffering was inconceivable, 'without, however, in a single instance overstepping the bounds of virtue, such was the purity of the extravagant affection I bore her'.[8] Some years later, Eliza Martin absconded with another man after a notorious affair: Tone came to feel that she had been simulating onstage an emotion which in his case was all too real ('an experiment no woman ought to make').[9] He was challenged by her acting abilities as well as her beauty, but he was a conflicted lover: 'Had my passion been less pure, it might have been not less agreeable'[10] – but not more either, for Tone had 'a puritanical attitude towards female virtue'[11] and would soon elope with the teenaged Martha (Matilda) Worthington on the rebound from Eliza.

Ever afterwards theatre haunted him, the cavalier in him delighting in its display even as the puritan worried about its insincerity. Despite these scruples, he could never abstain for long. Country house theatricals often posed such challenges. In Jane Austen's *Mansfield Park*, Sir Thomas Bertram bans them lest his daughter be enabled to express in her part onstage words of tenderness for the man she truly loves rather than for the one to whom she is engaged. All through the ensuing century men and women who acted in such theatricals were pronounced morally suspect by writers as different as Disraeli and Thackeray.[12]

Tone was histrionic and also something of a gallant. No sooner had he married Matilda and fathered children than he left them for a legal training in London. There he enjoyed dalliances because 'the Englishmen neglect their wives exceedingly'[13] and the wives were not cruel to willing substitutes. The thought that he might be similarly neglecting a loyal wife never seems to have entered Tone's head. On the other hand, the question of *trust* haunts him in early pages of the journal. The optimism of the Enlightenment tells him to trust appearances, yet all around is evidence of man's fallen nature. His own family are tied up by robbers in Kildare and he spends a terrible night bound and gagged, wondering whether his pregnant wife and his parents are dead. Yet with the intrepidity of a man, Matilda breaks free and bravely re-enters the house, freeing her husband. Later, when Tone agrees to work as secretary to the Catholic Committee (even though he has never met most of the Catholics before), he is a victim of two attempted robberies as he goes about its work by stagecoach. The more you trust, it seems, the more you are betrayed; and the more likely you are to betray those who trust you. All these scenes are, of course, screen versions of the anxiety that now assails the writer – the man who has no idea how much longer he'll live or what the future holds for Matilda and the children. Yet as always he resolves to trust the future, even as he abandons his family to the mercy of time's arrow.

Like Wordsworth in *The Prelude*, Tone recollects past emotion in present tranquillity, and he also is moved more by past or future moments than by present ones. So an early moment of revolutionary solidarity is to be found in the memory of happy days spent by his young family with Tom Russell of the United Irishmen in and around their small house at Irishtown. Tone recollects 'the delicious dinners, in the preparation of which my wife, Russell and myself were all engaged; the afternoon walks, the discussions as we lay stretched on the grass . . .'[14] This is an image of perfected community, whose men gladly assume domestic work and whose women partake fully in political debate. Neither Tone's wife nor his sister left the table, but were often joined for poetry-making and political repartee by Russell's old father. Such experiments offered the sort of plain living and high thinking that was sought by Wordsworth and Coleridge, a sort of Grasmere Cottage with sex: 'She loved Russell as well as I did. In short, a more interesting society of individuals, connected by purer motives and animated by a more ardent attachment and friendship for each other, cannot be imagined.' For Tone the personal is at least as important as the political, which is little more than an organized extension of the proper relations between individuals.

Tone had the eighteenth-century gregariousness made possible by an increase in leisure, as more people lived in towns. It is significant that his Irishtown epiphany should have been social in nature, whereas that experienced at the end of the nineteenth century by James Joyce across Dublin Bay on Dollymount Strand would be utterly solitary. As a moment, Tone's epiphany would repeat itself wherever United Irishmen gathered in a romantic setting – on Rams Island in Lough Neagh or at the summit of McArt's Fort, from which they looked down at the radical city of Belfast and vowed to subvert the authority of England in their country. It would be hard to over-state the importance of that recollected moment as Tone lay in the grass alongside his wife and best friend in Irishtown (the poor people's city parish by the sea). What is achieved in the recollection is an electric link between location and patriotic sentiment. The poignancy involves the possibility that such a golden moment may be recaptured and shared with the whole community. In this way Tone looks at once back and forward with something like the emotion that would be felt by soldiers dying for their land in foreign wars.

The linkage between *locale* and *self* also heightened an awareness of the significance of *time* in the construction of an identity. The Memoir was interpellated by Tone in the journal kept in France in September 1796, as if to emphasize the point. But the Memoir of his earlier life yields to the journal, kept intermittently from 1789 onwards. If the Memoir accepts the pastness of the past, the journal challenges it with the immediacy of each moment. Until the age of Rousseau and Tone, a life was assumed to be an accumulation of facts: the self of a writer and the self reported were assumed to be one and the same. Thereafter, an awareness grew of the effects of time as a form of experience on the making of an identity. People recognized that there was a personal past as well as a public past, even as they remained somewhat naïve in their confidence that they could recover past emotion. They soon discov-ered, like Wordsworth, that memory played many a trick and that the experience recollected was often usurped by the act of recollection, which itself became a more pressing alternative emotion. The real relationship was less between rememberer and remembered than between the subject and time. Tone was sophisticated in recognizing time as an opportunity as well as an enemy: perhaps the fact that he was writing at the end of a momentous century helped him to theorize time in this self-aware way.

It is his sharp awareness of tradition as an invention of the present that informs Tone's running commentary on the previous century of Irish writing in English, from Swift through Goldsmith and Sheridan, down to Burke. They (along with Shakespeare and Henry Fielding) are the authors most often quoted and they were not conjoined in this fashion by any text earlier than Tone's. He becomes in a sense the first Professor of Anglo-Irish Literature and Drama, a defender of that tradition, yet at the same time a fomentor of revolution. There is no necessary contradiction between these roles, for a similar ambivalence existed in Swift. Tone had no doubt of the moral of Swift's writing: 'that the influence of England was the radical vice of our government'.[15]

Tone's use of quotation is far more subtle than that of a clubman capping famous lines with a comrade over a frothy beer, for he often unfreezes the seemingly familiar aphorism, inflecting it with unexpected meanings in its new context. The entire journal might in fact be read as a parody of Swift's *Journal to Stella*, its coded names being a version of the 'little language' between the Dean and his friend. Early on, Tone jokes that his is 'a thousand times wittier than Swift's . . . for it is written for one a thousand times more amiable than Stella'.[16] As a parody, it is also an act of homage, but in neither role is it limited by its target. Tone is conscious of doing more fully what Swift *should* have done. In an essay of 1790 Tone had praised Swift for using *The Drapier's Letters* to question 'the imaginary dependence of Ireland on England. The bare mention of the subject had an instantaneous effect on the nerves of the English government.'[17] Yet even Swift, 'with all his intrepidity, does not more than hint at a crying testimony to the miserable depression of spirits in this country'.[18] The value of living after Swift is the chance to take up work that he left incomplete.

The code used in the journal is easy to crack: Tone is Mr John Hutton; Russell (a noted anticlerical) is the P.P. (parish priest); William Sinclair is the Draper; and Sinclair's native city of Belfast is Blefescu (sic). Relieved of their everyday identities and using this special code, the friends could be absolutely frank with one another in a mode of playful delight. Their masks were slippery and kept falling off or being confused with the face beneath, as happens so often with the devices used by Swift: but they allowed the comrades to play certain roles before themselves as a prelude to their attempt to strike the popular imagination. The theory of it all was based on yet another disavowal of sincerity: wearing his own face a man speaks with caution, but from the confines of a mask he may blurt out the truth, especially when tongues are loosened by drink. A recurrent theme is captured in Tone's entry from his early weeks in Belfast in 1790: 'Huzza. Generally drunk – Broke my glass thumping the table. Home, God knows how or when . . .'[19] Since the heyday of Sheridan, heavy drinking had been seen as a sign of sociability and libertinism – so much so that when a spy sent from London tried to keep up with Tone's progress through the hostelries of Dublin, he was soon paralysed with an excess of claret. The shared assumption of the members of his club is that revolution is nothing if it is not great fun:

> The Tanner (Mr Robert Simms) looks extremely wise and significant. Gog (Mr Keogh), Mr Hutton and he worship each other and *sign an article with their blood: flourish their hands three times in a most graceful manner (see Goldsmith's Citizen of the* World), and march off into town. *Ho, but they are indeed most agreeable creatures* (do.)[20]

Belfast in those years was a centre of radical activity, especially among its Presbyterian merchant class, who had little respect for inherited privilege. Tone loved the free-thinking ethos and reported it in his diary. One hairdresser, though a Presbyterian himself, had two children christened by a Catholic priest 'with a wish to blend the sects'.[21] Tone's own comments on the Catholic majority are filled with less warmth than Swift's. The ignorance of Catholics is 'a benefit just now as the leaders being few will be easily managed and the rabble are by nature and custom prone to follow them'. There is no affection in the reference, merely a clinical appraisal of the sheer force of Catholic numbers against the British.

What attracted Tone most of all to Belfast was its modernity, which allowed him to study the interactions between street and stage:

> Oct 17 1791: Came into town early, went to the theatre; saw a man in a white sheet on the stage, who called himself a Carmelite . . . NB A gentleman, indeed a nobleman, on the street in a white wig, vastly like a gentleman whom I had seen in the morning, walking the streets in a brown wig; one Mr Atkins, a player. QUARE Was he a lord or not? PP incapable of resolving my doubts; but one pretty woman in the house. Came home before the play was half over; the parties appearing all so miserable that I could foresee no end to their woes. Saw a fine waistcoat on the man who said he was a Carmelite, through a tear in the sheet which he had wrapped about him; afraid after all that he was no Carmelite, and that PP was right in his caution.[22]

Five days later comes a cryptic *sequitur*:

> Oct 22 Mem: Met the man who said on stage he was a Carmelite, walking the streets with a woman holding him by the arm; the woman painted up to the eyes; convinced, at last, that he was no Carmelite.[23]

The bad play *The Carmelite* allows Tone to make some points at a time when boundaries between street and stage have blurred and men behave like actors in order to be sociable.[24] Tone exploits that ambiguity in order to expose the aristocracy as no more than an unconvincing impersonation of 'gentlemen'. The other suggestion is linked: that Catholic priestcraft is also based on magical nonsense and on a similarly deceptive assumption of a falsely authoritative identity.

There is a lot of joking about Catholic ideas in the journal, and humour at the expense of their critics: 'See an apparition of Jordan, who is in London; find on speaking Latin to the said apparition that it is Jordan himself . . .'[25] On November 5 Tone pretends to see a vision of Guy Fawkes, who, on being questioned in Latin, turns out to be a policeman: none the less, with tongue firmly in cheek, Tone says that he sent for fire engines in his hotel bedroom. Like other United Irishmen, Tone believed in civil rights for all Catholics and that the arming of the citizenry would curtail clerical influence, 'so fatal to superstition and priestcraft is even the smallest degree of liberty'.[26] He questioned the widespread Protestant prejudice that Catholics were incapable of liberty: 'We plunge them by law, and continue them by statute, in gross ignorance, and then we make the incapacity we have created an argument for their exclusion from the common rights of man.'[27] Compared with the 'rights of man' argument, the limited freedoms and franchise of Grattan's Parliament (1782) were so much sham: an edifice of freedom built on a foundation of monopoly. 'Be mine the unpleasing task to strip it of its plumage and its tinsel, and show the naked figure.'[28] Again, his obsession with the difference between latent and manifest content, between appearance and underlying reality, emerges in these strictures. The common Protestant complaint against Catholics – that they judge only by surface imagery and neglect substantive content – is here deftly flung back in the face of a patriotic Protestant like Grattan by a thoroughgoing radical.

Tone believed that Catholics must be freed from their sense of dependence on the British government, and Presbyterians from their fears of enfranchising Catholics. The Catholic Relief Bill of 1793 was a minor relief, he admitted, but it was accompanied by a gunpowder act. Edmund Burke had been advising the British government on the need to ameliorate Catholic grievances and to drive a wedge between the emerging Catholic and Presbyterian radicals. The setting up of a national seminary for Catholic priests at Maynooth in 1795 did not impress Tone one jot: he foresaw that the clergy rather than the laity would gain control of the educational institutions thus allowed. Towards Burke himself, Tone was ambivalent. He was fascinated by his aesthetic theories and recognized the greatness of his writing. Although Burke affected to be a great defender of traditional privilege, Tone was aware that he was in fact a *parvenu* in England, who had used his immense abilities to win the favour of the mighty and powerful. His career, though glittering, constituted an act of national betrayal. Yet the sense of engagement with Burke in the journal goes well beyond the political into the personal, as if he is the real antagonist, the man to beat. Burke had been a precursor of Tone at Trinity College Dublin, also an auditor of its debating society and a man of burning ambition like himself. His *Reflections on the Revolution in France* (1790) had turned British people against the Jacobins, as Tone bitterly observed, by playing upon their competitive feelings towards French power and commerce. Ireland, however, was a different case (in Tone's view 'an oppressed, insulted and plundered nation'),[29] but this didn't deter Burke from fearing rather than encouraging a revolution in that country.

Burke had launched his beloved son Richard on a political career in the lucrative post of Secretary to the Catholic Committee in Ireland, but he proved incompetent. By 1792 the committee was paying him off to make way for Tone: but the father continued to woo members of the committee on behalf of his son. Tone's diary for 5 September is written with cryptic eloquence in the sort of interior monologue later made famous through Joyce's Leopold Bloom:

> Sad. Sad. Edmund wants to get another 2000 guineas for his son, if he can: dirty work. Edmund no fool in money matters. Flattering Gog (Keogh) to carry his point. Is that *sublime* or beautiful?[30]

In contrast to the self-seeking of the Burkes, Tone believed that his own actions were purged of all self-interest and were solely for the welfare of the Catholics. He believed that Burke was in the pay of the British government, and the award of a Civil List pension in 1794 only confirmed this suspicion.

In Tone's mental landscape, Edmund Burke occupies a position as

polar opposite to Tom Paine: the one a reactionary, the other a radical. While Burke is smooth, emulsive and eloquent, Paine is jagged,
challenging and awkward. After reading Paine, Tone can only
marvel: 'His wit is, without exception, the very worst I ever saw. He
is discontented with the human figure, which he seems to think is not
well constructed for enjoyment. He lies like a dog . . . He has discovered that a spider can hang from the ceiling by her web, and that
a man cannot, and this is *philosophy*.'[31] By his own admission not
the handsomest of men, Tone none the less took delight in all bodily
pleasures. After his arrival in Paris in 1796, he noted how drapes
were removed from windows, even as women adopted a *negligée*
appearance in the streets, which were to be places without masks.
Tone's own diary worked to a similar aesthetic of casual undress: its
body also was revealed in its basic lineaments. The Augustans had
sought to distort and conceal the body's natural shape, but now the
French were willing to expose it in all its vulnerability. Of the French
soldiers Tone observed: 'every one wears what he pleases; it is
enough if his coat be blue and his hat cocked'.[32] In the Conseils des
500, he noted the refusal of parliamentarians to dress up. As so
often before, he felt conflicting thoughts about this. The puritan in
him endorsed those French lawyers who forswore wigs and gowns,
but the dandy missed them.

The mockery of Paine's distrust of the body has, then, strong roots
in Tone's experience of the streets of post-Thermidorian Paris. He
met Paine in Paris in 1797 and they fell to talking of Burke. As so
often when caught between the claims of two charismatic men, Tone
couldn't help voicing some fellow-feeling with Burke, even as he
repudiated his politics. Once again, the defender of feeling against
intellect could strike Tone where he was most vulnerable – on the
subject of family feeling. Paine attributed Burke's depression to the
success of his own *Rights of Man*, but Tone knew that it had more
domestic roots:

> I am sure *The Rights of Man* have tormented Burke exceed-
> ingly, but I have seen myself the workings of a father's grief on
> his spirit, and I could not be deceived. Paine has no children?
> – Oh. my little babes, if I was to lose my Will, or my little
> Fantom![33]

Tone was amused by Paine's vanity, and certain that Burke's mind
had been shattered by the sudden death of his son.

Even in the 1790s, the passage in Burke's *Reflections on the
Revolution in France* about the flight of Marie Antoinette was

famous. A band of 'ruffians', Burke wrote, had invaded the bedroom from which she fled 'almost naked', the very image of the
newly freed bodies in Parisian streets; but for Burke this was not liberation but disenchantment: 'All the decent drapery of life is to be
rudely torn off.'[34] He might have expected ten thousand swords to
leap from their scabbards in vengeance but no, the age of chivalry
was dead, making way for an age of sophisters and calculators. The
Tone of the journal is as haunted by that passage as anyone. Visiting
Versailles, he is struck less by its majesty than by the *ennui* of a confined life in its *château*.

The central issue raised by Burke's passage is an ideal of womanhood. Tone admired women possessed of 'manly' spirit and men
capable of 'womanly' virtues, in keeping with the androgynous styles
promoted by the French revolution. Yet Paris proved to him that
truly democratic women were few and far between: most were secret
royalists. Nor was he fully sure that he admired the new freedoms.
He had failed to respond to the promptings of Eliza Martin in
Galway: now in his lodgings in Paris he rejected the advances of a
pushy landlady who wanted to take him to bed: 'I have no great
merit in my resistance, for she is as crooked as a ram's horn (which
is a famous illustration) and as ugly as sin besides; rot her, the dirty
little faggot, she torments me.'[35] On such a subject, he was more
ambivalent than ever, the puritan and cavalier cancelling one another
out. Tone's landlady is a further image of the revolution, a sort of
comic alternative to the tragic Burkean narrative of Marie
Antoinette, for she invites invasion of the bedchamber, being at once
ugly and aggressive. The treatment of the image suggests that Tone
had more in common with Burke than he cared to admit.

Burke had seen the France of the revolutionary terror as sublime
and peacetime England as beautiful. Though haunted by the immensity of the former, he settled gladly for the latter, but not without
struggle, for as an *arriviste* himself he would always harbour some
smouldering resentments towards those who inherited rather than
earned their privileges. Burke was shrewd enough to recognize that,
as an outraged Irishman, he might easily have identified with the
rebels, as Tone did. Tone in the journal repeatedly compares the
Parisian Terror with the current British policy of suppression in mid-
1790s Ireland: and so the possible equation is clear. What Ronald
Paulson has written of Burke – 'the ambivalence of the rebel towards
the act of revolt is both because it is an aggressive act and because the
object remains beyond comprehension'[36] – might apply also to
Tone's feelings about his French landlady.

For Burke the women in the mob that dragged Marie Antoinette from her bed were monstrous: an example of the 'false sublime' in their awful energy even as the outraged queen was beautiful. Mary Wollstonecraft argued against Burke that such turbulent women were badly needed to tear away the *in*decent draperies and reveal to men the true nature of the world – an image of stripping already used by Tone of Grattan's Parliament. In *A Vindication of the Rights of Women* (1792) she argued that women should seek power not over men but over themselves: the state of widowhood was an ideal model, she suggested, allowing women to double as father and mother in one.[37] This was exactly the situation of Matilda Tone in all but name, and after 1798 she would be a famous revolutionary widow for many years. Her husband may have shrunk from the advance of one unaccompanied woman in fear that the one he had abandoned for the sake of the revolution might feel her own situation to be no different from that of the landlady.

It could be said of Tone that he makes a clean breast of his flaws, while being careful to admit only likeable ones. There are moments when he seems anxious to present himself as a man attractive to women but one who never falls, and yet he was frank enough in confessing the London amours of his student years. The overriding impression conveyed, as in Rousseau's *Confessions*, is of a search for absolute transparency, 'a true republican frankness'.[38] Tone was an *honnête homme* but one who realized just how disintegrated a modern consciousness could be. He was capable of playing the rake, chatting up a Dutch beauty in a carriage, but he was also a child of the age of sensibility, and so rebuked Lord Chesterfield for encouraging his son to sleep with happily married women (including his best friend's wife). In such passages of the journal, the revolt of the laughing as opposed to the satiric comedy is re-enacted. Tone was fond of the sentimental comedies of Sheridan: a great grievance in Paris is that he may never see *The School for Scandal* in an English theatre again. The French production irritates him because the soliloquies are not uttered to the self, as in romantic rumination, but to the gallery. Worse still, the singing of civic airs at plays seems often done without real sincerity: after a few short years of revolution, the new rituals have already grown perfunctory. Yet the French retain the power to intrigue, removing the bloody conclusion of Shakespeare's *Othello* for a more uplifting closure: 'I admire a nation that will guillotine sixty people a day for months, men and women and children, and cannot bear the catastrophe of a dramatic exhibition.'[39]

'The catastrophe of a dramatic exhibition': the phrase is telling. Though Tone frequented the playhouses as a cure for his loneliness in Paris, he could not help feeling the theatre 'trivial', almost unworthy as a subject: 'but I must write something to amuse me'.[40] His reservations are puritanical in basis – acting encourages people to assume personalities not their own and to usurp those of others. Many passages of the journal are devoted to detecting and exposing imposters: swindlers in hotels, mountebanks in carriages, and so on. When, finally, Tone meets the ambitious French naval leader Lazare Hoche, the seaman says that 'he got me by heart' and Tone wonders what he means: if he has mastered the detail of his Memorials (political analyses of Ireland prepared for the French government), fine, but if he is pretending to have plumbed Tone's character to the depths, that is not so flattering and probably untrue. The French revolution, even as it sought transparency in human exchanges, nevertheless insisted that no citizen was obliged to possess a personality that was 'believable' in traditional terms. The new simplicity of dress added to the 'mystery within'. Tone, already possessed of one name and two pseudonyms, has no desire to be too easily read or decoded.

For him, the theatre was at once an immoral institution, which encouraged persons to simulate emotions they did not feel, and a glorious utopian zone in which a person might throw off the constraints of a jaded role and assume a new, altogether unprecedented character. By the time he reaches Paris, Tone can hardly conceal his excitement at being able to attend Racine's *Iphigénie* at the Grand Opera. The period costumes are utterly accurate and the muslin *negligée* dresses of the heroine beyond praise, 'entirely in white, without the least ornament'.[41] The ballet *L'Offrande à la liberté* was even more striking; and Tone deliberately uses a Burke-word to describe it: 'All this was at once pathetic and sublime, beyond what I had ever seen, or could almost imagine.'[42] This is the only moment in the journal when Tone feels that words cannot fully render what he has seen. For one majestic instant onstage, the gap between a reality and a representation of it has been closed, as the symbolic and real meanings coincide. In a stroke, those moral scruples touched off in him by theatrical performances have been resolved and the degradation of all actors – from the Carmelite in Belfast to the ham soliloquists in Sheridan – has been removed. 'What heightened it beyond all conception was that the men I saw before me were not hirelings acting a part; they were what they seemed, French citizens flying to arms to rescue their country from slavery.'[43]

What Tone felt in those moments was something rather like what Jean-Jacques Rousseau had recommended years earlier in his *Lettre à M. d'Alembert sur les Spectacles*. He also felt his self to be multiple and was aware of the problems this posed for the potentially sincere man: he had concluded that hope lay in the dedication of the honest soul to a transcendent task outside the self. Such a task was the creation of republican virtue: and the only entertainments worthy of a republic would be those in which the citizen was no longer just a spectator but also a participant:

> People think that they come together in the theatre and it is there that they are isolated. It is there that they go to forget their friends, neighbours and relations in order to concern themselves with fables . . .[44]

Rousseau's ideal spectacle was a memory of an impromptu communal festival during his childhood, a memory not unlike that of Tone of the Irish Volunteers linking hands in the Phoenix Park. Rousseau recalled 'the unity of five or six hundred men in uniform, holding one another by the hand and forming a long band that snaked about in rhythm and without confusion'.[45] While the original moment witnessed by Rousseau had a beautiful spontaneity, the attempt to describe it thereafter in programmatic fashion for others might seem forced, even insincere. Tone himself was quite scathing about the unconvinced rendition of civic airs at the Opéra, as has been seen.

At another military spectacle, *Serment de la Liberté*, at the Opéra on 13 March 1796, Tone watched as a procession of beautiful women presented a line of youths with their sabres, each man saluting his mistress and kissing the sabre on receipt:

> I do not know what Mr Burke may think, but I humbly conceive from the effect all this had on the audience that the age of chivalry is not gone in France. I can imagine nothing more suited to strike the imagination of a young Frenchman than such a spectacle as this . . .[46]

The context of the diary animates this analysis: for the journal is written by a man who seeks only the good opinion of his wife, referring all his thoughts, hopes and judgements back to her. If Hector's bravery against Achilles owed much to his desire for approval from the Trojan women, human nature hasn't changed over three millennia: Tone sees himself as gripped by the same emotion, such as was appealed to by Fielding's Lady Bellaston in working upon Lord Fellamar. The journal is, in fact, daily testimony that chivalry has never been stronger than in the new revolutionary world, though Tone is honest enough to include within its range the comically reduced anti-heroes of Fielding as well as the more austere heroes of Homer. There is, he sees, a demonstrable link anyway between the comic and heroic. The idea that a man may be laughed to scorn can only have meaning in the wider context of his dignity as a viable possibility.

The sheer pace of change in the 1790s amazes even Tone. Rereading entries from the previous winter, he is 'very curious to see what pains I took to prove fifty things which are now regarded as axioms'.[47] That sense of movement makes him all the more aware of how much he lives from moment to moment: the significance of events is often lost at the time of their happening. In the absence of any wider sense of significance into which things might be cast, it seems to him wiser not to impose even the beginnings of a pattern on entries: 'but as that would be something approaching to system, I despair of ever reaching it'.[48] The work of piecing together the shreds of an integral personality can safely be left to others: his task is simply to show how he came to be the man he now is.

Although Tone never accuses himself of deserting his family, and therefore never seeks formal forgiveness, the whole journal is composed with that implicit object. Proceeding more by implication than by statement, he trusts that the narrative of his exile will suggest a truth he is too modest to assert. His absence is, in fact, but a sign of his deep love. He removes himself from his family for a great task, but is forever present to them through his written words. They are all exiled from Ireland (the others in America, he in France), but then so is the truth that his country needs but cannot yet see. In this his dilemma is identical to that of Rousseau in the *Confessions*: 'To hide without writing would be to disappear. To write without hiding would be to give up the idea that he is different from other people . . . The goal is to be recognised as a "noble soul". He breaks with society only in hopes of making a triumphal return.'[49] The willingness to undress the soul before the world's tribunal is tantamount to an assertion of republican virtue, for a person so free of dissimulation, a character so *unrehearsed*, cannot have any sin to repent of. On the contrary, he will expect to be given credit by every single reader.

The mesmeric power of Tone's candour to later generations is straightforward enough in its origins: readers give credence to an image of Tone that they have largely constructed for themselves. His truth seems to come without mediation, unobstructed, even as his language hardly draws attention to itself. The self is so engrossed in itself that it gives little thought to the medium or to the techniques of sincerity. The prose, though beautiful, is deliberately styleless, suggesting a self not exceptional, just one man speaking to others in a search for the conditions in which that self might further grow. The reader has to help in the release of that future self and bring the story to its completion of that unfinished business. One consequence is that for almost two centuries Tone's journal has not even been treated as a work of literature. Like the Bible in the days before the higher criticism, it was a point of origin, the word unmediated, holy writ. Its theme was grand: being itself. And the challenge posed was not to be like Tone but to awaken every reader to the artist-hero who lies within himself or herself.

So far is Tone from notions of warrior-heroism that he repeatedly quotes Fielding's Parson Adams ('I do not desire to have the blood even of the wicked upon me'), and Sheridan's Bob Acres ('that I could be shot before I was aware').[50] Much of his time in France is spent – like that of his illustrious successor Beckett – pondering the meaning of waiting for something that may never happen: in this case a naval expedition. The arrest of Russell in October 1796 is traumatic news, leading to the collapse of the code: suddenly, revolution is no longer a game. As one expedition is cancelled and another aborted, Tone is on an emotional roller coaster, unsure whether he will live as an Irish citizen or French officer. Although he never discusses the medium of language as such, he often ruminates upon the processes of his own mind. A journal is a daily process, whereas a book would be only a finished object: Tone is less interested by the object than by the ways in which an imagination can reach out to an object. For him, meaning isn't preformed: rather it emerges in the process of the search, the mind being attracted and excited by the pleasures of that search itself. In the virtual society of the journal, he regrets that so many good ideas are lost for want of an interlocutor to make them seem real. As the day of departure for Ireland draws near, the *anomie* brought on by prolonged isolation astonishes him. The expedition may 'change the destiny of Europe', emancipating three nations and opening the seas. Before either Karl Marx or James Connolly, Tone could see that Ireland might be the Achilles heel of the British empire, but somehow he is underwhelmed:

> The human mind, or at least my mind, is a singular machine. I am here in a situation extremely interesting and, on the result of which, every thing most dear to me as a citizen and as a man depends, and yet I find myself in a state of indifference . . .[51]

Tone monitored his responses with the precision of a brain surgeon, and was astounded by what he found. On his first expedition to Bantry Bay in December 1796, he was on the ship that stood becalmed within a few yards of Ireland, utterly unable to land. It was a moment like that, months earlier, in which he had looked down with his friends from McArt's Fort on the townscape of Belfast. In Tone's writings, distance is always the necessary condition of love. Only those who can stand back from a city, a family or a nation, and conceive of it, can know precisely what it can be made to mean. Yet estrangement is also a condition of that intensity. A few years later a solitary romantic soul would define itself against the void on a mountain peak or at the lonely prow of a ship facing into storm, but for Tone such moments are ultimately *social*. His hope was always to make the inhabitants of Ireland share in that developed consciousness: 'Poor Pat . . . who knows what we may make of him yet?'[52] Nevertheless, when he finally reaches the desired moment on the Irish coastline, all he feels is an unexpected estrangement:

> I am now so near the shore that I can in a manner touch the sides of Bantry bay, with my right and left hand, yet God knows whether I shall ever tread again on Irish ground. There is one thing which I am surprised at, which is the extreme *sang froid* with which I view the coast. I expected I should have been violently affected, yet I look at it as if it were the coast of Japan; I do not, however, love my country the less, for not having romantic feelings with regard to her.[53]

Nothing, in fact, could have been more romantic than such an attitude. The landscape is no longer seen here as a mere backdrop to the human drama, but as a wholly unknown world with a mysterious life of its own, full of redemptive possibilities, but essentially inscrutable. In that respect it is akin to the Catholic masses, defined and defended but never really animated in Tone's writing. What Rainer Maria Rilke wrote of the strange disconnection of landscape from human figure in the *Mona Lisa* might be invoked in this scene:

> It had been necessary to see the landscape in this way, far and strange, remote and without love, as something living a life within itself, if it ever had to be the means and notion of an independent art; for it had to be far and completely unlike us – to be a redeeming likeness of our fate. It had to be almost hostile in its exalted indifference, if, with its objects, it was to give a new meaning to our existence.[54]

Because Tone had been so intently monitoring the workings of his inner self, the landscape had become estranged. This would be a characteristic experience of four generations of romantic and republican militants afterwards in Ireland: the same sense of tragic separation from the very people in whose name they risked their lives, and the same sense of the remote, ungraspable beauty of the landscapes through which they moved on their dangerous errands. *On Another Man's Wound*, Ernie O'Malley's account of the War of Independence, may be the consummation of a tradition that had its source in that paragraph of Tone. What was thought to be the discovery of a new intensity of feeling in the face of a natural setting was revealed in the entry to be really the revelation of a loss: the sense that nature, far from being in harmony with the human mood, was unspeakably other, indescribable, unavailable to ready meaning. The Tone who, when he became secretary to the Catholic Committee, could admit to never having known a single one of its Catholics, was in the same predicament as the romantic protagonist who finds himself standing *before* a landscape rather than *in* it.

Tone was born to be estranged, for he was a play-actor: even the revolution for which he gave his life was but another role. However, he was estranged for a very good reason from the world as he found it: his 'true' self, the one that would signal an end to all the acting, lay up ahead. His autobiography, like Rousseau's, confronted taboo subjects in seeking to make that better self. Written like many subsequent diaries of Irish republicans in conditions of quarantine – one thinks of John Mitchel's *Jail Journal*, Máirtín Ó Cadhain's *As an nGéibheann* or Brendan Behan's *Borstal Boy* – his journal was a plea for understanding and forgiveness. Of another Irish autobiographer, James Clarence Mangan, it would be said that he had two personalities, one well known to the Muses and the other to the police.[55] The greatness of Tone's journal is that it renders the life of both, of Theobald Wolfe Tone and of Citizen James Smith. It gives the *auto*, the life of the mind, even as it chronicles the *bios*, the experience of the body.

Yet, precisely because he could divulge such a range of public and private sentiment, and at the same time control that sentiment, Tone remained to his readers as mysterious as the shores of Bantry Bay were to him. His readers, like his biographers, help to construct him, but soon realize that they are simply indulging a fantasy of the romantic performer and of what he might really be like.[56] To some he is a rationalist patriot, to others a colonial outsider; to others again he is a conflicted romantic whose ideas were less original than he took them to be. There is nothing especially false about any of these partial interpretations, but they all ignore one salient fact: Tone was an artist. He was so good an artist, so adept at using art to conceal art, that for all but two centuries he convinced his readers that he was no more than an interesting diarist. 'As to literary fame', he recalls of his London days in the Memoir of 1796, 'I had *then* no great ambition to attain it.'[57] That sentence is as near as he comes to admitting that the autobiography will constitute his present attempt.

Tone finally landed on the shores of Lough Swilly (from which the Gaelic earls had fled in 1607) in 1798. He was captured, identified by a Trinity College classmate, and arrested to be tried for his life. He wounded himself in the throat and died after some days of terrible pain. Whether he was attempting suicide or seeking to delay the hangman remains uncertain. He wanted to be shot like a soldier, not hanged like a dog. 'I am sorry that I have been so bad an anatomist,' he said.[58] He was only thirty-five. His enemy and likeness, Edmund Burke, had died of old age just the previous year, still desolate after the death of his son. Burke was so terrified that Jacobins would dig up his remains and vandalize them that he carefully choreographed a secret burial. Tone was buried at the family home in Bodenstown. So defeated were republicans that his grave was not properly marked for half a century, until Thomas Davis helped his widow to raise a black slab.

It was unveiled at a private ceremony in order to prevent embarrassment to Daniel O'Connell, the Catholic emancipist.[59] Since those days, however, it has become a place of annual pilgrimage for political parties and revolutionary cadres of modern Ireland. Tone refused to recognize the received identities of Catholic, Protestant and Dissenter, challenging their supporters to reimagine themselves under the 'common name of Irishmen'.[60] But he did more than that. In his journal, he left a model of how such a freed consciousness might move through the modern world.

15

Native Informants:
Maria Edgeworth and
Castle Rackrent

Castle Rackrent was published in 1800. A full century later the glamorization of the houses of the landed gentry was initiated by W.B. Yeats, a middle-class outsider to that world. In promoting that glamorization, Yeats risked casting himself in the role of Thady Quirk, the seemingly loyal but brainless retainer who laments a fallen family in Edgeworth's novel: but even as the poet was constructing his myth of the eighteenth century ('that one Irish century that escaped from darkness and confusion'),[1] the figures of Sir Patrick, Sir Murtagh, Sir Kit and Sir Condy Rackrent could be cited as the very antitheses of Swift, Goldsmith, Berkeley and Burke.

Edgeworth's portrayal was highly influential. The English king, having read it, said 'I know something now of my Irish subjects.'[2] A later prime minister, Robert Peel, may have derived from it his sense of the Anglo-Irish landlords as a hopelessly irresponsible class, aware only of the rights of property but woefully ignorant of its duties. The feckless Rackrents, though located by Edgeworth in the eighteenth century, were in some ways even more typical of the nineteenth, after the Union had robbed landlords of influence and a parliament. By the 1840s the issue of the landlord–tenant relationship was being treated in Britain 'primarily as a peasants' rather than a proprietors' problem'.[3] The British public had grown weary of hapless Anglo-Irish landlords, whose troubles were largely of their own making. *Castle Rackrent* is one of the earliest attempts to trace that decline.

Maria Edgeworth's own family was very cultured and long established: the Edgeworths had been Longford landlords since 1583. Her father Richard Lovell Edgeworth was a man of the Enlightenment, who had read Rousseau and supported Catholic emancipation; he had the children of Protestant and Catholic families educated together in the school on his estate. Unlike others of their class, the Edgeworths did not deride France, and they were wary of the English tendency to stereotype other nations, the Irish as well as the French. When invading French forces, allied to the Irish *jacquerie*, came within miles of the Edgeworths' home in 1798, the family members were compelled to flee for their lives to Longford town: but it is a measure of their independence of thought that, far from finding safety there, Richard Edgeworth was almost lynched on suspicion of being a French spy.[4] It was hardly surprising that the book published by his daughter two years later, just after the Act of Union, should have been open to more than one interpretation. Although she wrote as a Protestant and as a member of the landed gentry rather than as an *arriviste*, her text has one surprisingly remarkable point of similarity with the writings of Edmund Burke: a not fully suppressed sympathy for revolution.

Edgeworth presents herself as a sort of Gibbon on speed: one who will document the decline and fall of a whole phase of civilization, but whose evidence will be drawn more from the private than the public world. This is not necessarily a female perspective (her book was published anonymously) so much as a serious insistence on the importance of the personal element in constituting a world. Edgeworth understood the ways in which individuals may bear the marks of social forces. In this she anticipated the epiphanic methods of James Joyce, who shared her belief in those careless gestures 'by which people betrayed the very things they were most careful to conceal'.[5] In her Preface, Edgeworth avers that it is from men's 'careless compositions, their half-finished sentences, that we may hope with the greatest possibility of success to discover their real characters'.[6]

That substitution of one thing (the personal) for another (the public) will become a central technique of *Castle Rackrent*, whether a slate is made to replace a broken window or, indeed, the form of the English novel is replaced by that of the Irish anecdote as more appropriate to a makeshift world. If Gibbon and Fielding produced epics in tragic or comic mode and at appropriate length, here is an oral *glissade* which will narrate the history of four generations in scarcely sixty pages. It is, however, produced in the conviction that literature should attend to the doings 'even of the worthless and the insignificant'.[7] What is left deliberately unclear is whether these words refer to the teller (Thady Quirk, family retainer) or to the Rackrent lords and ladies (of whom the tale is told). That early ambiguity is crucial, for it opens up multiple ways of decoding the tale.

A native informant like Thady might seek to dupe the editor or reader of his story, by impersonating just the sort of humorous, hopeless retainer they want him to be: but the act may be reciprocated. After all, the focus is not on the poor but on the life of a big house: and, even though the narrative asks to be read as coming from Thady, its real author is a representative of big house culture, mimicking the natives who so often (behind her back) mimic her peers. The colonial laboratory that was Ireland was an echo chamber of competing mimicries: Edgeworth's adoption of a servant's persona may have been 'a sort of defensive strategy',[8] a mimicry of mimicry, in that resounding context. If mimicry is the site of ambivalence, the zone in which all claims to final authority are lost,[9] then there is a demonstrable link between that dispossession and the politics of eighteenth-century Ireland which before 1782 (the period in which the work is set) and again after 1800 (the date of publication) found itself divested of any control of its own fate.

Seamus Deane has astutely noted that all of Edgeworth's characters, utilitarian gentry as well as feckless peasants, are 'only a hairsbreadth removed from caricature'.[10] This may be because each is acting a part, whether that of 'master' or 'servant', yet neither can be convinced of or convincing in their role – the former because they know in their bones that they are usurpers and the latter because they can never forget that they were the ones usurped. The 'fawning' act of Irish servants is much discussed in literary histories, but the possibility that the masters were also theatricalized is less often entertained. The rather cramped dimensions of Castle Rackrent (its kitchen is scarcely three paces in length; its doors open directly onto the village street) suggest a middle-class dwelling masquerading as a castellated ancestral seat. Edgeworth knew that the bourgeois planters were unconvincing aristocrats. In the political vacuum of pre-1782 Ireland, there was little to do except elaborate a personality, for neither master nor servant had hands on levers of significant power.[11]

Almost all readers assume that 'honest Thady' is too stupid to understand the meaning of the tale he tells, but that is more an ethnographic fallacy than an alert act of criticism. The fact that 'it was with some difficulty that he was persuaded to have it committed to writing'[12] is hardly a mark of his stupidity: the same reluctance would be displayed by the Blasket storytellers, as well as by Synge's friends on Inis Meáin. Just as African natives feared that a photograph might steal their souls, these informants may have understood all too keenly the logic of Sir William Wilde's contention that the best way to uproot old superstitions was to print them in books.[13] One possible implication is that Edgeworth's committal of Thady Quirk's tale to paper is a half-conscious attempt to extirpate, or at least expose, it in this fashion. But the motive may only have been half-intended: for the other half of her consciousness seems to have been complicit with his intentions. And for very good reason.

What is enacted in *Castle Rackrent* is a form of reverse anthropology. The Rackrents are far too gone in drink and dissipation to represent themselves, and so they must be represented, by one who can survey their lives from start to finish – and that person is Thady. What is often alleged of Thady – that he cannot construe the meaning of the experience narrated – is actually true of them. Yet the irony of ironies is that this tale will none the less be footnoted by a representative of that very class whose members are exposed as utterly unable to narrate.

It is in that uncertain context that one reads Maria Edgeworth's account of how the voice of a family servant, John Langan, came as she took pen in hand and assumed control. The word she uses is 'dictate', as if the future reversal of landlord–tenant relationship in the politics of landholding is rehearsed initially at the level of literature:

> The only character drawn from the life in *Castle Rackrent* is Thady himself, the teller of the story. He was an old steward (not very old, though, at the time; I added to his age to allow him time for the generations of the family). I heard him when I first came to Ireland, and his dialect struck me, and his character; and I became so acquainted with it, that I could think and speak in it without effort: so that when, for mere amusement, without any idea of publishing, I began to write a family history as Thady would tell it, he seemed to stand beside me and dictate; and I wrote as fast as my pen would go, the characters all imaginary. Of course they must have been compounded of persons I had seen or incidents I had heard; but how compounded I do not know: not by 'long forethought', for I had never thought of them till I began to write, and had made no sort of plan, sketch or framework . . .[14]

The insurgent counterappeal to the values of the natives, latent in the writings of Swift, becomes fully overt here, in a manoeuvre as exemplary as it is audacious. By it, a clever noblewoman discovers what life is like when one is poor, papist and old, and she can do this without being a traitor to her own class and family.[15]

Even more daring and exemplary is her 'crossing' of gender lines: by assuming the voice of a male servant, she invokes her own *animus* as a source of creativity in exactly the way that later male artists like Yeats, Joyce and Beckett would draw upon the *anima* for the compulsive monologues of Crazy Jane, Molly Bloom and Winnie. Edgeworth's is perhaps the earliest example of a process whose uncontrollability and suggestiveness was experienced by male authors who underwent a similar sort of possession afterward. Her audacity was, if anything, greater than theirs, not just because it came so much earlier, but also because by it she effectively crossed class and cultural divisions too. Coming from a Protestant Ireland whose penal enactments had for over a century pretended that no such thing as an Irish Catholic existed, it was something to give such complex life to one of them in literature.

The story Thady delivers is one that will demonstrate how the very idea of a noble family is more an illusion than a reality. That illusion is the creation of Thady himself, who simply asks each of his masters to live up to it, offering to coach them in their 'time-honoured' roles. This form of nobility hardly comes via primogeniture and a family tree – in fact, only Sir Murtagh inherits by that means. It comes rather when a proud retainer tells a blow-in like Sir Condy exactly what is expected of him by tradition, though the 'tradition' is a case of instant archaeology, nine-tenths improvised by the servant to meet the needs of a moment. What masquerades as a feudal relationship of reciprocal courtesies, whereby lord and tenant coexist in a happy collaboration, is really a system of exactions, which allows the underlings to receive roof-straw less as gift than as tribute. When Sir Condy, at the end, finds that he has no fortune left, he also discovers himself to be bereft of followers. In this way does the voice of Thady enact what Wilde would later call 'the tyranny of the weak over the strong – the only tyranny that lasts'.[16] No wonder that Edgeworth felt 'dictated' to.

The subversive potential of Thady's monologue has posed a problem for Edgeworth partisans ever since, beginning with herself. Her later books on Ireland are more didactic and less covert in implication, as if she had so unnerved herself by the freedoms permitted in *Castle Rackrent* that the animus must thereafter be kept under the strictest control. Her biographer Marilyn Butler seems to regard novels like *Ormond* and *The Absentee* as far greater works of art and to see *Castle Rackrent* as a piece of mere transcription, hardly a novel in any achieved sense. For her Thady Quirk is less a native informant than a vocal usurper, the sort of raucous underling who, given his head, might have barracked a Jane Austen into silence. Butler has no doubts as to where the roots of the problem are to be found: 'Her motives in taking to fiction were not to act as an amanuensis to John Langan; on the contrary, the viewpoint she wanted to adopt was English and forward-looking.'[17] On the contrary, it is in fact Edgeworth's openness to the disruption of English authority by Langan's voice that makes this a very modern book, at once more and less than a conventional English novel, ambivalent in form as it is undecidable in attitude.

The first attempt to curtail the ripples set off by the tale may be found in the learned footnotes and glossary, which repeat insistently the claim of the Preface that 'the race of the Rackrents has long since been extinct in Ireland'.[18] The subtitle marks the terminal date 1782, the year of Grattan's Parliament, which was also the year that Richard and his family returned to live on the estate in Ireland. The evidence seems almost deliberately flimsy: 'long since' would hardly cover a mere eighteen years, least of all in a land where 'long' means really long in the historical memory. The suggestion that drunkenness, profligacy and irresponsibility have disappeared among the gentry in the 1790s is patently ludicrous – as is the implication that popular superstitions have been erased among the peasantry.[19]

There seems a satiric thrust here at the insistence among proponents of the Union that Ireland is now indeed a case for cultural parity of esteem: for the more the notes seek to explain Irish customs in terms that make them comprehensible to English readers, the more they emphasize the underlying difference between the cultures of the two countries. A narrative that calculates the number of man-hours lost to the Irish workforce in attendance at wakes is clearly confronted with two utterly opposed mindsets.

The Union itself would soon run into a similar set of contradictions – for in Ireland nothing could be left to the initiative of local justices of the peace, whose relation with tenants was far less happy than that which obtained in England: the result was that everything in Ireland from the constabulary to the educational system was centralized, whereas most of these things remained localized in England.[20] Local Protestant landlords were not trusted by Pitt to run affairs in Ireland, with the consequence that everybody from county surveyors to prison officers was soon appointed by national authority. Ireland thus became 'modern' and 'national' in its daily workings decades before England; the early emergence of the 'national novel' from the pen of Edgeworth was of a piece with this. This case of nationalization *avant la lettre* meant that there was a state-of-Ireland novel decades before there was a state-of-England novel: and *Castle Rackrent* was its name. Terry Eagleton has contended that even when the state-of-England novel was pioneered by Dickens, that country was seen as a site of problems but never as constituting a problem in itself.[21] The Irish case was always different.

The obsessiveness with which Edgeworth insists on that Irish modernity in her notes seems so over-the-top as to be a disavowal. She is mocking the official pretence that a land as traditional as Ireland is ready for all this rationalization. A centralized system would keep power out of the hands of righteous Catholics and rascally landlords, but she may well have wondered whether it could ever be made to fit the conditions she knew. Her father was conflicted on the Union, supporting it in principle but voting against it in the event, because of the bribery with which it was secured from Irish landlords, who voted their own parliament out of existence. In the notes (her father's work as well as her own), Edgeworth parodied the tidy delusion of the modern mind that holds nothing to be more remote than the recent past: by 1800 the rites of landlords in the early 1780s must be made to seem positively prehistoric. The manic Irish race for modernity had already begun: and the Edgeworths, who had believed in the theory, were somewhat less assured when practice was imminent.

One consequence of that conflict is that the first state-of-Ireland novel threatens, even in its Preface, to be also the last: for a true union with Britain may herald not just the extinction of the Rackrents but of the Irish race itself:

> When Ireland loses her identity by an union with Great Britain, she will look back with a smile of good-humoured complacency on the Sir Kits and Sir Condys of her former existence.[22]

The subscription of the date 1800 under that passage is an act of savage irony. But so is the very opening remark of the passage ('Nations as well as individuals gradually lose all attachment to their identity . . .'), with which the date stands in a sort of tension. The beginning of the new century marked, if anything, the emergence rather than the erasure of national and ethnic identities all over Europe. Even if quite a number of these were responses to the increasing rationalization of economic and political arrangements, there was something inexorable about the process by the year 1800. The subtextual implication of what follows in the passage is clear: if there is any great controversy about these contentions, it will be a sign that the entity known as 'Ireland' still persists.

The text proper begins with Thady Quirk's clearance of his throat: the slow build-up of clauses indicates a watchfulness, a vigilance and an almost legalistic caution hardly suggestive of family passion:

> Having, out of friendship for the family, upon whose estate, praised be Heaven, I and mine have lived rent-free, time out of mind, voluntarily undertaken to publish the *Memoirs of the Rackrent Family*, I think it my duty to say a few words, in the first place, concerning myself.[23]

The words 'rent-free' prepare for the swerve from perfunctory, dutiful obsession to actual self-interest which is the wider trajectory of the chronicle, and the phrase 'of the Rackrent Family' is comically inexact, indicating that Thady is no longer really identifying with the family (since it is dissolved), but is rather the agent of a literary takeover to parallel his son Jason's financial and land appropriations. Yet the voice of the speaker is seductive and compulsive: so much so that Edgeworth drowns it out with an extended footnote which lasts far longer than the text has done up to this moment of interruption.

That note refers to Thady's greatcoat, worn down the generations, as a throwback to the Elizabethan plantations. The book covers just four generations, but the coat is of a kind mentioned by Spenser. The note, though learned and genteel in contrast to the wildness of the main text, is scarcely reassuring: for Spenser saw such a coat as a sign not of nature but of the *enemy* who might hide a weapon under its cover. It approximates Thady to an ancient native tradition, but one which is ambivalent. The suggestion of the Preface that private zones may disclose deeper public meanings takes on a more sinister tone: Thady may well be another smiler with a knife beneath the cloak. Back in the main text we read that this ineffectual man is – though one might never guess it – father of a high attorney Jason Quirk (who 'never minds what poor Thady says').[24] Here pride in the Quirk achievement comes before self-exculpation.

The mantle is incongruous in more ways than one: for it is as obsolete in the era of the cutaway coat as is the oral anecdote in the era of the novel. In a world filled with substitutions, where Sir Tallyhoo Rackrent thinks a car the best gate to mark the entry-point to a field, the text itself may be another stopgap. Yet the discrepancy between the old oral and modern written codes worries more than Thady. Sir Patrick Rackrent dies of drink, a man ruined by debts which are the result of his generosity to the tenantry. The law empowers agents to seize his body until debts are discharged, but his son Sir Murtagh refuses to pay. He is as tight as his father was profligate, and his wife (*née* Skinflint) lives down to her name. Though Thady may be a beneficiary of the wealth they extort from the peasantry, the language he uses to describe the new lady is exact and unsparing: 'She had a charity school for poor children, where they were taught to read and write gratis, and where they were kept well to spinning gratis for my lady in return.'[25] Sir Murtagh has one weakness: an addiction to litigation, which is his version of gambling. Observing its corrosive and wearing effects, Thady 'thanked my stars I was not born a gentleman to so much toil and trouble'.[26] The legal suits cost hundreds every year, says Thady, 'but he was a very learned man in the law, and I know nothing of the matter, except having a great regard for the family'. The sense of reservation grows ever stronger, even as he parrots the line indicating the supposed ignorance of servants in such matters.

On one subject only is Thady emboldened to offer countervailing advice – against the digging-up of a fairy mound – and on that he is roundly rejected: but Sir Murtagh 'had no luck afterwards'.[27] Like many peasants, Thady combines a sceptical empiricism with a real respect for the things of the spirit, and, believing in a both-and syncretic culture, he sees no major contradiction between analytic reason and false belief. Edgeworth, of course, enacts that very contradiction in the division between her text and her notes. The notes are written in the voice of impersonal scholarly authority: they order and survey, and what they survey is the speaker of the main text. But they also manage to convey the impression that his may be the better method: for the fairy lore is revealed to have, hidden within its magic rituals, a shrewdly practical set of purposes. The fairy mounds often contained riches or property, and the stories forbidding their destruction meant that they were more secure fortresses than banks; the waking of the dead, while it might be a means to offer company to the soul of the deceased, was also an unofficial 'kind of coroner's inquest'.[28] The Act of Union implied, however, that the voice of impersonal 'realism' in the scientific notes should finally override and erase that of Thady, which has room also for 'magic'. The separation of the two by Edgeworth blocks off the possibility that a literate Thady might in the next generation produce a novel in the mode of magical realism, which would be the logical outcome of his narrative method. But the very mastery of the codes of print might kill off that 'superstitious' possibility too.

The Rackrent graph is one of rise and rise, followed by a sudden, unexpected fall: 'out of the forty-nine suits which he had, he never lost one but seventeen'.[29] A note explains the underlying technique: 'An astonishing assertion is made in the beginning of the sentence, which ceases to be in the least surprising, when you hear the qualifying explanation that follows.'[30] A slow build-up of clauses gives way to one that is downbeat and defeated: 'I never saw him in such fine spirits as that day he went out – sure enough he was in ames-ace of getting quit handsomely of all his enemies; but unluckily, after hitting the tooth-pick out of his adversary's finger and thumb, he received a ball in a vital part, and was brought home, in little better than an hour after the affair, speechless on a hand-barrow, to my lady.'[31] The emotional rhythm of Rackrent living is enacted in the hopes and delays of that sentence, which portrays their life as a long preparation for a consummation that never quite happens. The sentence is full of rapid incident, but its energies portend no more than a sudden collapse.

Sir Kit, that ill-starred duellist, is a profligate who inherits by mere propinquity. One consequence is that he feels no personal investment in the Rackrent holdings, a fact hinted at in another of Thady's seeming bulls which carries a lethal underspin of moral reservation: 'though he had the spirit of a prince, and lived away to the honour of his country abroad, which I was proud to hear of, what were we the better for that at home?'[32] Some commentators have seen in Edgeworth's resolute indictment of absentee landlords a convenient mask for her failure to criticize the whole colonial system which made them possible:[33] but the intelligent sarcasm of Thady's rhetoric ('honour', 'proud') seems to dismantle the notion of a feudal order that could ever have been 'noble'. If Sir Murtagh's policy of extracting forced labour from tenants prevented them from properly improving their own holdings, the rapacious middlemen left in charge by an absentee like Sir Kit were even worse.[34] At the textual surface, Edgeworth seems to concur with Burke that people such as the Rackrents are a sham aristocracy of weaklings. If no man is a hero to his own valet, then Thady has the wit to attack the point of vulnerability of the capitalist–colonial system in its feeble sponsors, the Rackrents.

Though he offers periodic disclaimers of 'my son Jason' (the possessive laying claim even as the surrounding sentence denies it), Thady works with him to secure the lost inheritance. Of course, neither son nor father allows himself to conceive of this plan of campaign as such, until it is already more than half-delivered. Thady's words in describing Jason's takeover leave no ambiguity: 'with this the agent gave me a hint, and I spoke a good word for my son, and gave out in the country that nobody need bid against *us*'.[35] Soon the boy once intended for a priest is involved in a wheedling correspondence with Sir Kit.

The landlord returns with a rich young bride whose money will, he hopes, solve all the estate's problems. She alights from her coach by night, says Thady, and 'I held the flam full in her face',[36] hardly the act of a loyal footman but an intrusive invasion of personal space such as he enacts on a basis of privileged proximity all through. The new lady turns out to be a 'Jewish', an ultimate outsider who finds Ireland to be a botched, inadequate version of the England from which she has been snatched. Its trees are really just shrubs, its landscape mere bog, suggesting that the official hope of the Act of Union – that Ireland can be a convincing facsimile – is doomed by the very facts of Nature itself.

Thady, who keeps his reservations about the Jewess to himself ('for I had a great regard for the family'),[37] can't help enjoying the stressful efforts with which the newly arrived lady attempts to make real this patently unendurable setting. Looking at the familiar terrain through the eyes of this new wife, Sir Kit may have felt a little *frisson* – it was, after all, as if the Anglo-Irish themselves were new arrivals on the rural scene after decades of denial that such persons as Irish Catholics had any legal existence. When the wife refuses to give up a valuable gold cross in her possession, Sir Kit locks her in her room. The very possibility of a rift between them, hinted at in a footnote on the previous page, is now acted out in the main text, a technique used all through which confers on the footnotes an oddly predictive power, as if they are really what drives the story. A single mind drives the entire production and Thady is the instrument by which Edgeworth imagines the native indictment of a wasteful system. When Sir Kit dies, his horses are distributed among his friends, but the promised payments are never made. Thady has reasons of family loyalty to notice this – but loyalty to which family?

The greatest of all wastrels is Sir Condy, 'ever my great favourite', ostensibly for guileless goodness of heart but perhaps also because his wasteful virtues ensure Jason's ultimate takeover. The pincer movement to take out Sir Condy begins early: at home Thady dandles him on his knee, filling him with nonsense about the family's *flaithiúlacht* (generosity), while at school Jason sits beside him, 'not a little useful to him in his book-learning, which he acknowledged with gratitude ever after'.[38] Thady knows that other noble families view Sir Condy as a fool: the underground rumour machine among servants ensures that. When Miss Isabella, the daughter of the lord of

Mount Juliet's Town, falls in love with Sir Condy, the servant 'who waited that day behind my master's chair was the first who knew it'. Edgeworth could literally see how the lower orders were storing information in their memories against the day when they might assume control. The serving classes act more like undertakers than underlings of this system: when Sir Condy and Lady Isabella run short of candles, they must borrow some from Jason.

All that can save Sir Condy is election to parliament in Dublin, which would leave him invulnerable to debtors. Getting elected costs a fortune, but that must be borne. Perhaps the clearest sense of Thady's distance from his master is conveyed by his snappish response to the bailiff who arrives to dun Sir Condy at the very moment of his triumph:

> 'You belong to him?' says he. 'Not at all', says I: 'but I live under him, and have done so these two hundred years and upwards, me and mine'.[39]

Not even two centuries of service can induce Thady to use the preposition *with* rather than *under*.

The cutting intelligence that uses words to imply volumes is manifest in the explanation of Sir Condy's unaccountable vitality in the face of all his ruin:

> 'When a man's over head and shoulders in debt, he may live the faster for it', says I . . . 'just as you see the ducks in the chicken-yard, just after their heads are cut off by the cook, running round and round faster than when alive'.[40]

This might be read as Maria Edgeworth's forecasting image of Anglo-Ireland after the Union, its head or parliament cut off by a wily 'cook', in a scene that comes straight out of the political unconscious: but it is, on a more literal level, an image of those MPs who did as they were told in the parliament in Dublin in the years before Union. Only in the years of Grattan's Parliament from 1782 to 1800 did head and body seem to produce one person in healthy working order.

The politics of the period that brought Grattan's Parliament to a close are clearly hinted at in the fate of Sir Condy:

> . . . he was very ill used by the government about a place that was promised him and never given, after his supporting them against his conscience very honourably, and being greatly

abused for it, which hurt him greatly, he having the name of a great patriot in the country before.[41]

By 1796, when this section was written, Grattan's Parliament was already in danger of dissolution and it was clear that votes for a possible union would be bought by all kinds of bribes and promises. The phrase 'supporting them against his conscience very honourably' is less a bull of Thady's than his sardonic mimicry of the self-deceiving rhetoric employed by crooked landlords in squaring this circle.

Through all these twists and turns, even after his name was joined with that of the bailiff on the *custodiam* (to provide local authority), Jason 'looked down' on his father Thady. Yet the old man kept up a constant supply of information and action crucial to the takeover (much as Nelly Dean, the narrator of *Wuthering Heights*, would facilitate the expropriation of Thrushcross Grange and its personages by Heathcliff). As the end of the Rackrents draws near, Thady is pictured more and more often inside the house: while the master and mistress are away in Dublin, he feels intense loneliness, but he also has the house to himself, as if in rehearsal for his son's succession. The ultimate collapse of the Rackrents may be found in the fact that, in their absence, a broken window is not filled with a canvas or slate substitute: a stopgap kept up at least a semblance of order, but the refusal to make shift indicates surrender. That window, marking the boundary between the private zone of the Rackrents and the outside world, is no longer functional. Public and private worlds have collapsed in upon one another, as when Lady Isabella insists that a long passage be called the 'gallery'.

Being no artist, Lady Isabella cannot build an alternative world through style or language: and so she gives notice of her decision to quit. Sir Condy is anything but vengeful: he seems in fact relieved, offering an unsolicited settlement of five hundred pounds out of the estate after his death. By now Thady is eavesdropping on as many of their conversations as he can. 'This is very genteel of you, Sir Condy,' she responds, merely adding, 'You need not wait any longer, Thady.'[42] Lady Isabella's intuition is sound. She understood that colonial personages are already conflicted even before they assume office: and so she remained open to the possibility that Sir Condy secretly longed to abandon control even as Thady subconsciously longed to see his son take it up.

Commentators have often remarked on the paradox that Thady, though rich in language, is an empty person, describable in no set of clear principles. John Cronin calls him 'a magnificently realised slave, a terrifying vision of the results of colonial misrule'.[43] That is true, but it could also be said of his Rackrent masters, who seem also to be unpersons. All are caught up in a world of mimicry, where everyone can play every part except his own: Sir Condy will happily move into the servants' lodge at the close, even as Jason moves into the landlord's house. Their problem is that even their new lives will be acts, for 'mimicry conceals no presence or identity behind its mask'. Ultimately, Edgeworth herself is a victim of a process in which 'the look of surveillance returns as the displacing gaze of the disciplined'. For mimicry – 'a difference that is almost nothing but not quite' – will turn to menace – 'a difference that is almost total but not quite'.[44] As the mimics are swept aside – Thady and Maria Edgeworth – the name of that indescribable menace is Jason Quirk.

The Quirks enact the ambivalence that is the colonial predicament, dividing it on a social level between loving father and vengeful son: but the backdrop is itself so complicated that these bifurcations are also internalized within Thady's personality. As Sir Condy begins to crash, he can disclaim Jason ('we have scarce been on speaking terms of late'),[45] while still talking with Jason's father about the master's belated codicil favouring his estranged wife. To Jason such an undisclosed measure is ill-use of a gentleman (i.e. himself, the term now used of an ex-bourgeois without any self-irony). But Thady implies that Sir Condy knew exactly whom he was defrauding by the time he changed his will: by then the real script of the Quirk plot was known to all. This is not to deny Thady's grief at Sir Condy's fall – he is 'sick at heart for my poor master; and couldn't but speak'.[46] Such searing, inarticulate feeling can exist as an aspect of ambivalence, now that the moment has come: but Jason is not so conflicted. Sensing that his father's signature as a witness might only draw attention to the secret history of their collaboration, he suggests that Thady is too old for such work.

The meaning of the takeover has been much debated. It can be portrayed as a restoration of the mere Irish, but that reading is complicated by the fact that 'everybody knows' that the Rackrents were really descendants of the O'Shaughlins, scions of the last high king Maolsheachlann. Clearly, they turned Protestant to protect their holdings under the Penal Code, while maintaining private practice of Catholicism at home (a maid is punished for breaking the Lenten fast, for instance). So their removal represents in one sense a repetition of colonial expropriations of previous centuries even as, in another key, it signifies the long-delayed revenge and return of the natives. The tension is too much for Thady. His question to Jason about what people will think when they see 'the lawful owner turned out of the seat of his ancestors'[47] seems to endorse the first reading (a repeat of the colonial expropriation), even as his opening account of Jason as an esteemed gentleman buttressed the second (a revenge on colonial power by the underlings).

Sir Condy deflects such heavy concerns in drink and scenes of low farce. 'I've a great fancy to see my own funeral before I die,'[48] he tells Thady, who duly stages it. In this, at least, Sir Condy is keeping faith with the Gaelic Ireland of his ancestors, who proclaimed their own deaths in bardic poems of such power as to throw the sincerity of the claim into question. Sir Condy, like monks who sleep in their caskets, has been sleeping in the coffin of Castle Rackrent for a long time, on the somewhat Adornian principle that 'whoever occupies a period house embalms himself alive'.[49] Even before the Georgian mansions of Dublin declined into tenements, Edgeworth was willing to explore the possibility that every big house might be a slum. Feigning death, Sir Condy discovers (like all players of such tricks in later plays by Boucicault and Synge) that he is not as well-loved as he'd hoped: the old bardic notion of a fame that survives the ruler's death on the lips of the people no longer holds good. Instead, the servants spread the information that Lady Isabella isn't expected to survive a crash in her carriage. This prompts Jason to buy her jointure at a knockdown three hundred guineas.

The ending of the tale is a masterpiece of cool, clinical observation, with the sympathies of the reader being aroused and defeated in all directions. The seemingly good-hearted Judy Quirk, who once loved and was spurned by Sir Condy, now sets her cap at her cousin Jason. She displays the parasitic mentality of the tenantry, explaining to Thady that this is better than 'following the fortunes of them that have none left'.[50] This suggests that Thady's collaboration with his son has gone unnoticed outside the environs of the big house. His final act for his master is to fill the horn from which Sir Patrick drank: but the draught is fatal, and Thady, who administered it, weeps most of all.

The coda sets the tale in the context of the Union. Edgeworth remarks that only recently have the Irish become known to the English, but soon her passage lapses into cynical mockery:

All the features in the foregoing sketch were taken from the life, and they are characteristic of that mixture of quickness, simplicity, cunning, carelessness, dissipation, disinterestedness, shrewdness, and blunder, which, in different forms, and with various successes, has been brought upon the stage, or delineated in novels.[51]

So a work that opened with pretensions to scientific accuracy ends with an assertion that it has been shaped from first to last by previous exercises in stage-Irish mode. Now it becomes clear that the editorial voice of impersonal authority is just as compromised as any within the tale: readers' doubts about the strange complicity between the writer of footnotes and the author of the main tale are vindicated. The science of anthropology, like the practice of history itself, is shown to be one conducted at the prior mercy of literature and of its available forms.

Having destroyed the epistemological foundations – of realism and science – on which the Union was based, Edgeworth finally admits to uncertain feelings as to whether it will 'hasten or retard the restoration of this country'.[52] The few learned men among the Anglo-Irish will return to England now that their authority has been signed away, and the best hope for Ireland is that they will be replaced by energetic British manufacturers. The problem is obvious – various waves of middle-class merchants from England have already been planted to no great effect: they soon found themselves drinking whiskey and adopting slatternly Irish ways. The doubts raised by the Jewish lady's inability to imagine wind-beaten shrubs as sturdy English trees are merely reopened in the closing questions: 'Did the Warwickshire militia, who were chiefly artisans, teach the Irish to drink beer? or did they learn from the Irish to drink whiskey?'[53] There could hardly be a more jocular or corrosive stay to the glibness of Union thinking. The thinking, like the date 1800, was too neat by far.

Is *Castle Rackrent* another *caoineadh ar chéim síos na nuasal* (lament for fallen nobility)? On its publication English readers considered it so, sometimes missing the rather satirical treatment not only of 'honest' Thady but also of the Rackrents, whose irresponsibility seemed mitigated by their energy and humour. The sheer pace with which the four stories were told prevented readers from lingering too long over any painful scene, for tears soon gave way to laughter in the usual 'Irish' way. So cryptic and condensed were some scenes that the book reads more like shorthand notes towards a novel than a finished extended narrative: hence the widespread view of it as a storehouse for much that was to follow. Patrick Kavanagh's ideas about tragedy as underdeveloped comedy seem to draw inspiration from this method. Seen up close the struggles of the Rackrents might appear tragic; but viewed from a distance made possible by virtue of the sheer pace of narrative, they appear more comical than sad. Yet there is material here for many tragedies to come. The Jewish is, after all, the first 'madwoman in the attic', even as Thady is a distant precursor of Conrad's Marlow and Fitzgerald's Nick Carraway.

Edgeworth may have thought of her book as a comically debased *caoineadh* rather than as a novel. An extended footnote in the glossary speaks sadly of the decline of the bardic *crónán*, which 'fell into a sort of slipshod metre amongst women' and which 'cannot boast of such melody' as the male bards once achieved.[54] This is a Gibbonian theme, of degeneration and decline, but one that is played in a light key. That there are few to mourn Sir Condy is a further sign of the decline, but his self-regarding attempt to witness the outburst of popular emotion on his death makes its absence more ludicrous than lamentable. What Edgeworth is really writing is a *caoineadh ar chéim sios an chaoinidh* (a lament for the fall of the keen):[55] yet the collapse of the conditions enabling a fully felt keen may herald those for the rise of the novel.

This is the real meaning of Edgeworth's, as well as Thady's, preoccupation with the personal over the public. The novel may provide a suitable form for Edgeworth's own feeling of ambivalence, for in it the account of the collapse of a heroic civilization becomes the master narrative of the middle-class culture that supplants it. She was smart enough to sense that, before it leaves the stage of history, every social class must disgrace itself utterly; and she was artistic enough to intuit the comic potential of such a changing-of-the-guard. Hence her refusal to slow up her tale or mourn too deeply over its casualties. The elderly beggars of Ireland, as she marvels in a footnote, solicit money for their own funerals, attempting to assert at their deaths a semblance of the control that eluded them in life. The Edgeworths, as children of the Enlightenment, disdain to dramatize a death. Richard Lovell Edgeworth insisted on being buried in as private a way as possible, for no excessive man-hours should be lost in carrying on the work that he left unfinished.[56]

In its time, *Castle Rackrent* was treated as a *conte* rather than a novel of manners, as a sort of philosophical fable in the Enlightenment mode which might yield good counsel. Because the narrative is turned over to Thady, it has been taken to lack a didactic element, but the negative verdict on the Rackrent world could not be artistically more obvious without being morally less effective. It is the *failure* of Thady to judge them in moral terms that is the most scathing indictment of the culture to which they subscribe. The fact that Edgeworth describes no 'virtuous' character does not mean there is no moral. In the end, she refuses the Rackrents' raffish charm, though not without a struggle.

Not all readers see it this way. 'If the novel is that which indulges the vices of a depraved upper class', writes Terry Eagleton, 'the form she deploys is complicit with the conduct she seeks to reform.'[57] As a genre, however, the novel tends to indict rather than indulge Old Corruption, so that can hardly be the issue here. The real problem lies elsewhere – in the virtual absence of a middle class from the narrative. The oncoming British manufacturers are as yet but a glint in Edgeworth's eye, and the sinister figure of Jason Quirk, though centrally present in most of the decisive scenes, remains generally speechless and unarticulated (though we may assume him to have been utterly articulate). Jason is the Great Silence that broods over Castle Rackrent and a further reason why Edgeworth's repudiation of the Rackrents is attended by some regrets – for Jason, rather than British industry, may embody the worse that is yet to come. His main asset is his efficiency, yet he remains more mysterious and unknowable to Edgeworth than the peasantry (who are far less fully described than some commentators seem to think). It is clear that she does not like the little of him she sees: already the later hardening in Edgeworth's attitude to a risen Catholic middle class is apparent, despite the fact that a leader such as Daniel O'Connell could claim, as validly as she, to be an Enlightenment utilitarian. At root, her book is a howl of civilized protest against Jason, and by inference against the corrupt big house irresponsibility that made his accession not just possible but inescapable.

Edgeworth's readers were, in the main, the literate middle classes of Britain. She would soon master the art of supplying them with figures of exemplary utilitarian virtue in forms that could only be called novels; but in *Castle Rackrent* she raised the possibility that, given the deforming conditions in Ireland, such figures were more likely to be characters of exemplary viciousness and terror. All she could do was marvel at such cases of demoniac possession. She knew that the novel was to be the quintessential form for chronicling middle-class life, yet she felt obliged to produce something rather different as she protested against the emergence of this silent, shadowy merchant class. Its members – rather than the mob of peasants – are sinister, unavailable to the narrative of *Castle Rackrent* which is half-oral, half-anthropological, rather than a blend of both modes in the form of a viable novel. They can no more inhabit her *conte* than Sir Condy can survive in the big house: his move to the gate lodge is a belated recognition that his family can no longer bear the heroic discipline of aristocratic life. Henceforth, characters such as he will be fully available to the modes of the novel.

But what of Jason Quirk? Edgeworth was able to write of Irish country people only by maintaining an 'attitude of research'. This was the necessary protective barrier which prevented that fatal seduction that left the Rackrents, like the Warwickshire militia, more Irish than the Irish themselves – subject to all the fecklessness which 'going native' implied. The vices indicted in the Rackrents are, after all, attributed as much to their Irishness as to the colonial situation: and the banshees, which lament only native families, make no mistake in calling on them. But the attitude of research has a capital value in this context: 'it permits the Anglo-Irish writer to approach the native community without suffering disabling anxiety and without the threat of losing his or her distinct cultural, class and self-identity'.[58] Such an attitude, of course, works only so long as the natives remain illiterate, for once they begin to read, they will take issue with what is written about them and may resent being the subject of research at all. It is at this point – when a Jason Quirk may be imagined to snort with indignation at the foregoing narrative – that anthropology collapses into literature. It is, of course, greatly to Edgeworth's credit that she had by her mockery of the notes and glossary foreseen and even fore-enacted this collapse.

Yet the field notes were necessary, because native informants were by definition 'unreliable' and the culture they embodied was so rapidly becoming a thing of the past. In that sense Edgeworth is a latter-day Céitinn. Just as he, a representative of the Old English, sought in his *Foras Feasa ar Éirinn* to do proper justice to the Gaelic aristocracy before they (and possibly Ireland too) went out of business, so she makes her case that the way of life about to be erased had its redeeming and even noble qualities.[59] But the new Irish protagonist is Jason, and he will write his own narrative and footnotes in a proper conflation. The problem for Edgeworth is that, though she can convincingly describe the forces (landlord and peasant) that will combine to make the new middle class, she cannot know or report on that class itself – only on its making.

Her novels of Ireland after the Union are schematic affairs, painting by numbers but not by life. To her the emerging middle class *were* the mob, dark, unknowable, ferocious. The ambivalence she held in some sort of check in the cunning structuration of *Castle Rackrent* was an ambivalence which that middle class would live out on its pulses. Its members were the future, the unknown whose meaning might be grasped through the known, their more decipherable fathers like Thady. In any normal European society they would have been a novel's natural subjects, but because Ireland was Ireland, they became first of all its 'antagonists'.[60] If anthropology patronizes, literature distorts. There can be no reconciling their disparate claims in a linear narrative: at least, not until one of the emerging middle classes takes pen in hand and decides to write the experience directly from within.

It is now a commonplace to denounce Maria Edgeworth for her failure to stand outside the colonial nature of the Anglo-Irish relationship and indict it. However, she did something far better: she exposed the pathetic inadequacy of its inner workings. The big house of Castle Rackrent is shown to be an incongruous and ridiculous form in which to enclose the social energy and verbal excess of traditional Irish culture: it fails to harness those energies as dismally as the inherited form of the English novel itself. If Sir Condy finds it something of a relief to move to the gate lodge, Edgeworth herself may feel a similar sense of liberation in opting for the folk narrative rather than the print novel. Coded into such manoeuvres is a series of suggestions as to why the Act of Union may never work: it is based on the understanding that Ireland will forget characters like Sir Condy, whom Edgeworth has shown (for all their chaotic nature) to be unforgettable.[61]

Put simply, the discourse of Union was founded on ignorance of the realities of Irish life. 'The domestic habits of no nation in Europe were less known to the English than those of their sister country,' wrote the Edgeworths in their 1801 'Essay Upon Irish Bulls'.[62] That essay is in effect an accusation of something worse than colonialism: downright racism. It suggests that the Irish are unique in having their occasional blunders interpreted by English commentators as the basis of a 'national character': instead of a value-free anthropology, there is, in short, a loaded *animus*. The loaded gun was a logical corollary. One of the most admirable features of Edgeworth's writing is her refusal to stereotype nations: but, believing like Burke in the shaping power of local conditions, she sensed that English civil society was as non-transferable to Ireland as Burke thought French revolutionary practice was non-transmittable in England. What worked in England might in Ireland lead only to chaos: the Penal Laws had been proof of that. That woeful experiment in theory had not so much restricted the rights of Catholics as excluded them from citizenship itself:[63] it was asking a lot to expect a people thus deformed to learn in two or three years those civic virtues that the Sir Kits and Sir Condys had failed to assimilate in a century. So in the 'Essay Upon Irish Bulls', having retailed a rather excessive English compliment, the authors add acerbically: 'it will, we fear, be long before the Irish emerge as far from barbarism as to write in this style'.[64]

Nevertheless, as utilitarians, the Edgeworths well understood the virtues of forgetfulness for those who wished to take effective action in the secular world. Just as the Preface to *Castle Rackrent* rather breezily – too breezily? – accepted that nations might lose identity in the drive for economic rationalization, so the 'Essay Upon Irish Bulls' happily reports the spread of a more standard English across the community. In the process, it mocks the outdated preconceptions of an English visitor who, encountering neither howls nor brogue nor bulls, 'found that the stories I had heard were tales of other times'.[65] Generations of later researchers, from Jeremiah Curtin to W.B. Yeats, would find to the contrary, but no matter: the Edgeworths were pursuing an Enlightenment agenda which called for a true parity of esteem to match the new reality of two countries joined in 'equality' under the Union. Hence their canny demonstration of the links between English racism and the 'unreason' feared by all exponents of enlightenment.[66] The parody of English ethnocentrism is ferocious:

> We must not listen to what is called reason; we must not enter into any argument, pro or con, but silence every Irish opponent – if we can – with a laugh.[67]

Deep down the Edgeworths were well aware that, even after the Union, the relation between the peoples would remain an imperial one. In fact, as Irish numbers dropped after 1840, they fell away from being one-third of the population of Britain and Ireland to a minuscule fraction by 1850. But the Edgeworths' insistence that the same laws of courtesy and debate obtain for inhabitants on both sides of the Irish Sea was tonic.

By representing the main text of *Castle Rackrent* as an *objet trouvé*, Edgeworth was enabled to filter many Enlightenment ideas through the somewhat surprising consciousness of one of the natives. In this way she offered readers, especially English readers, a priceless insight into the unofficial story of Ireland hinted at in Burke's tract on the Popery Laws:

> But there is an interior History of Ireland, the genuine voice of its records and monuments, which speaks in a very different language from these historians, from Temple and Clarendon; these restore nature to its just rights, and policy to its proper order.[68]

The *Monthly Review* of London justly observed that 'many striking conclusions' might be drawn concerning the Act of Union from *Castle Rackrent*, but the writer did not care to specify what precisely they might be.[69] Like model landlords, wherever they went the

Edgeworths found the book universally admired – even Pitt loved it. On their travels they were told that 'it was a representation of past manners which should flatter the present generation'.[70]

In fact, they were too late. Ireland was now a 'national' entity and in the struggle for its leadership, the few improving landlords who refused to return to Britain were on a hiding to nothing against the Jason Quirks. As far back as 1792, amid the first fears among the 'junto of robbers' at the new radicalism and the rise of Catholics to some prosperity, the Chief Secretary, Hobart, had uncompromisingly said that 'if you are to maintain the Protestant Ascendancy, it must be by substituting influence for numbers'.[71] By then, Catholics could buy and bequeath land or become attorneys. Later, the Lord Chancellor, Fitzgibbon, called for a halt to such concessions if Pitt wished to have his support in passing the Union. The choice now confronting them all was phrased in language as downright as Tone's: either to maintain the Protestant ascendancy in power or to lose the island at a time of looming war with France. Pitt was told that Irish Protestants, faced with all the uncertainty, preferred a Union to equality with Roman Catholics, and that Catholics, for their part, found a Union preferable to continued degradation under the junto. 'The violence of both parties might be turned on this occasion to the advantage of England.'[72]

That was precisely what happened. English ignorance of Ireland was not broken down. No attempt was made to share power between Catholic and Protestant. Apart from one or two intrepid intellectuals like the Edgeworths, nobody bothered to define what the Union might mean: instead of being fully integrated into the British scheme of things, Ireland remained semi-detached under a viceregal system.[73] The promised British manufacturers never came, and Irish agriculture and industry remained undercapitalized.

In each succeeding decade, opinion grew more and more polarized. By the 1820s, Maria Edgeworth confessed to a hardening of her own views.[24] She had never liked Jason Quirk when he was silent and what was O'Connellism but Jason Quirk in militant mode? By 1834, she told a correspondent: 'It is impossible to draw Ireland as she now is in a book of fiction – realities are too strong, party passions too violent to bear to see, or to look at their faces in a looking-glass. The people would only break the glass and curse the fool who held the mirror up to nature – distorted nature, in a fever.'[35] Later writers such as James Joyce and J.M. Synge would, in contemplating that mirror, learn just how prophetic and astute Edgeworth was, both in what she said and in what she refused to say.

16

Confronting Famine:
Carleton's Peasantry

In the year 1818 a young man from a farm in Clogher, County
Tyrone, walked south to seek his fortune. He had been trained by
a hedge schoolmaster at a classical academy and so he tried to find
work as a tutor along the way. His efforts were not very successful.
Work was sporadic and poorly paid, and people seemed watchful
and nervous, for it was a time of famines and uprisings by local
bands of Ribbonmen in many parts of the land.

William Carleton had himself been sworn into the Ribbonmen,
bound to oppose Orange hegemony 'before I had time to pause or
reflect upon the consequences'.[1] But as he walked through Louth
that balmy autumn, the consequences swung in tar sacks from high
beams of wood along the road:

> There was a slight but agreeable breeze, the sack kept gently
> swinging backward and forward in obedience to the wind, and
> I could perceive long ropes of slime shining in the light, and
> dangling from the bottom.[2]

Inside that particular sack were the remains of one Paddy Devaun.
He had led a crowd of Ribbonmen in burning a family which refused
to join them; and now the county was studded with gibbets, set up
outside the residences of the convicted men. Their flesh fell off in the
autumn heat down to the bottom of each sack, whose tar melted in
the sun, and the morbid mass that oozed from the sack was the

shiny rope twinkling horribly in the light. Through the whole of that autumn, the inhabitants of the county, though often hungry, avoided eating fruit, for the flies that feasted on the gibbets expired in millions. It was, though the young man could not have known it, an image *in parvo* of what would later happen to humans.

On he went, further south, reading the signs of a society under stress. A priest who should have been kind to him, on the basis of a family connection, gave no help in Dundalk; but casual sailors and a serving-man in Drogheda were generous with money. In Navan, while staying with a poor cottier's family, he came upon a copy of *Castle Rackrent* in their pile of books. Wherever he went, he seemed to find books, even in the homes of the illiterate. These were in English, of course, despite the fact that the older people in the cottages would have spoken Irish: but under the approving eye of the elders, such books were 'most carefully laid up, in the hope that some young relation might be able to read them'.[3] Carleton read them all. Eventually, he reached the great Catholic college of Maynooth, only to find no place or work for him there. Later, he got employment as a tutor and writer in Dublin.

The experiences of that journey would stay with him forever: the gibbets, the casual cruelty and unexpected kindness, the sense of frustrated aspiration. But most of all *Castle Rackrent*. He called it inimitable,[4] which meant that of course he would emulate its achievement: after all, despite his ragged schooling, he had one great advantage denied to Edgeworth – he was himself a countryman and could write about the peasantry from within. And he would write about them with utter accuracy, so that the young people in the cottages, on taking up his books, would confirm their truth. For Carleton could see all around him something that Edgeworth scarcely surmised: the peasantry would soon be construing the narratives that purported to construe them.

'I found them a class unknown to literature,' he later observed, 'unknown by their own landlords, and unknown by those in whose hands much of their destiny was placed.'[5] They were also in an even deeper sense as yet unknown to themselves. Few enough of them had ever travelled far beyond their immediate parishes; but now, with a developing system of transport, it was possible for an entire community, perhaps even a nation, to know itself as such. Part of Carleton's achievement as a writer would be his rendition of a social panorama, a cross-section of peasant types, and above all his gift for capturing an individual moving through a vast crowd. With a population of perhaps seven million, Ireland was very crowded in those years. Soon it would not be crowded at all . . . and then his stories would have the poignancy of pictures of laughing, happy persons taken on the eve of some terrible holocaust which destroyed them utterly.

To write about his people at all, Carleton had to remove himself from them. This process began in the course of a pilgrimage to Station Island, Lough Derg, in 1817. What he saw 'detached me from the Roman Catholic Church, many of whose doctrines, when I became a thinking man, I could not force my judgement to believe'.[6] Carleton's portrayal of priests and bishops emphasizes their materialism. Ever since the enactment of Penal Laws, they had functioned more as practical leaders of their communities than as religious visionaries: a fact illustrated by the popular Gaelic sermons of James Gallagher, which say little about the mystery of the Trinity and a lot about how to keep a hygienic home or procure a steady job for a son. Carleton's own father was a devout Catholic, and his somewhat bemused son veered between praise for his 'unaffected piety and stainless integrity of principle' and later castigation of his 'superstitious kind of piety'.[7] Having converted to Anglicanism and married a Protestant, Carleton himself would remain in that faith, preferring its more low-key claims and rational theology. But he was never a lover of Protestant ascendancy. His conversion happened despite the reservations he felt about the injustices of Orange magistrates in their dealings with papists.

Writing is one alternative to violence, but in order to write one may have to go into exile. Success at such work can then seem like a form of betrayal, removing the writer further still from the very people whose lives he wishes to report. That carries its own double bind: those centrally located in Carleton's world yearn to utter themselves but cannot, while those who can write are already out on the edge, more outside than inside their subjects. As a youth in Clogher, Carleton had fallen in love with a girl named Annie Duffy, but he never told her; she returned his love, but never told him. Much of his later ambition to write was rooted in a desire to show her that he could amount to something in the world: but it was only years later, when both were happily married to other parties and he was a celebrated author, that he discovered that his feelings had been reciprocated. Only when the emotion had passed was Annie Duffy 'not ashamed to say it'.[8] Those who can feel in Carleton's world cannot immediately express, while those who can express may have lost much of the capacity to feel.

That dilemma was posed again and again along his path to fame. As a young man newly arrived in Dublin, he felt acutely the failure of its citizens to recognize his gifts with a proper post. Discovering the existence of a *doppelgänger* William Carleton, the owner of a shop, he decides to call for help, but is unable to speak when first he meets the man. A little later he is employed as an amanuensis by a journeyman tailor named McDonagh, but only because the man is inarticulate. McDonagh is of course a screen-version of Carleton himself, as is made very clear in a description of the tailor that drips with self-irony: 'The great foible of his character, however, was a wish to be looked upon as a man of genius, who had by some unaccountable decree of Providence been placed in a wrong position in life.'[9] The tailor asks Carleton to write down his life experiences, but this man, so fluent in conversation, stumbles even in dictation, with the result that Carleton feels entitled to imbue the bare facts 'with an easy spirit of fiction'[10] and his own choice of words. The tailor is none the less delighted with the outcome of their work:

> – Now, did you imagine me capable of such things? Tell me the truth.
>   I looked at him, to ascertain whether his vanity had led him so far as to suppose that *my* work was his *own*.[11]

That scene might be an exemplum of Carleton's artistic aim, to produce a writing that seamlessly renders the experience of a whole, hidden people. It is perfectly fitting that the man should think the work his, done without mediation. The scene is also paradigmatic in that the ungrateful tailor disappears without keeping his promise to pay Carleton's rent. Only much later is it revealed that he vanished to attend his mother's funeral in the west. The artist goes in effect unpaid and unthanked, by a people who preferred to re-enter their own narrative and bury the past themselves, in their own way.

The question of articulacy and inarticulacy is central to Carleton. For over a century, the Penal Laws had supposed such a person as an Irish Catholic not to exist. Though these people teemed in their millions, they had almost as little standing in English literature as in English law. Now, in the nineteenth century, they were beginning to disappear, through emigration and famine, but they were becoming a major concern of reformed laws and a new kind of literature. For Carleton, the pilgrimage to Station Island revealed not only the impossibility of a vocation to the Catholic priesthood but also the urgency of his vocation to writing. Thereafter, he was 'someone to whom experience was incomplete until he'd written of it'.[12] His very determination to write was both a response to and defiance of the thinking that had informed the Penal Codes, for their aim had been to reduce the peasantry to almost total silence. In Carleton's world, the happy life is the life expressed. The more literature there is, the less bitterness and grief: and a nation only achieves happiness and self-definition when, along with its eminent men and women, it also generates a literature of self-explanation.

Yet such a writing comes with certain costs. A literature which tries to explain and justify a culture may all too easily lapse into apologetics, into defensive demonstrations that such a thing as a native culture exists. Carleton makes few claims for his art, resting content with the conviction that his portrayals are accurate. One aspect of their representative status, however, is their recognition that these people have achieved fluency in English only by remaining all but dumb in Irish. If an Irish literature in English is a myth of consolation erected upon the grave of the Gaelic tradition, this may prompt a still more radical thought: that expression may compound the deeper sense of desolation. The more the people master the English language, the more meaningless and painful is that mastery without a similar access to English law, careers, capital and freedoms. If the unexpressed life is bad, the expressed life may be even more humiliating, because to poverty is added the consciousness of it as such. This was a truth long ago hinted by a broken Gaelic poet:

> Ní ins an ainnise is measa linn bheith síos go deo
> Ach an tarcaisne a leanas sinn i ndiaidh na leon . . .[13]

The worst thing is not to be sunk forever in misery, but to face the insult that follows us, now that the princes have gone . . .

The books by Defoe and Smollett kept in peasant cabins were supposed to be promissory notes against a future culture, which would replace the ebbing Gaelic one, but that culture never really seemed to come or to fulfil its rich potential.

To Carleton's ear, Irish eloquence in English was suspect, a sign of a people who might congratulate themselves on being fluent without ever really becoming articulate. The baroque language of hedge-schoolmasters might gull credulous parents, and might even be an implied rebuke to the utilitarian values associated with English, but it was hardly a vehicle for the pressure of real feeling. Moreover, it could never be an adequate replacement for the steely, classical precision of Irish. In that chiselled idiom, a whole people had hoarded words like misers with rare coins: now in English the hedge-schoolmasters spent them like drunkards throwing other people's money all over the place. Carleton linked the new long-windedness to the fatal pretensions of the ambitious peasant boy to the priesthood: he wrote about such a self-deluded comic buffoon in 'Denis O'Shaughnessy Going to Maynooth'.

In that story, the notion of literature as a displaced form of aggression is manifested early, during Denis's wordy contests with his father before all the neighbours on the village green. Intended for the priesthood, Denis resolves 'to begin 'atin wid a knife an' fork tomorrow'.[14] His parents try to bribe the parish priest with a valuable animal, if only he will persuade the bishop to send him on to Maynooth. At first their ruse fails; a second attempt succeeds. However, the bishop urges Denis to use plain words and give up his hedge-school polysyllables. Carleton uses this *Bildungsroman* to describe the sort of man he might have become, had he stayed in Clogher. The bishop's verdict might, after all, be applied also to his own English: 'his translations are strong and fluent, but ridiculously pedantic'.[15] Yet the problem faced by Carleton as translator was real enough: how to explain the elements of Gaelic culture in an English understood to be utterly alien to that culture? Often in Denis's story, he makes the common error of translators, explaining one word in the source language by reference to another: 'Now, a *scowdher* is an oaten cake laid upon a pair of tongs placed over the *greeslaugh*, or embers, that are spread out.'[16]

Such an explanation would hardly have been necessary for an Irish audience, but Carleton is assuming that much of his readership may be English or Scottish. In another comic *Bildungsroman*, 'Phelim O'Toole's Courtship', he offers even more intrusive commentaries, often patronizing his subjects. At the story's start, a childless couple pray for issue at a Pattern and Carleton is anxious to stand back, as it were, from his rudimentary characters: 'Such is a hasty sketch of the Pattern, as it is called in Ireland.'[17] The voice is scientific-judgemental: and the ritual stations are not seen as cleansing the pain of sin so much as constituting a silly exercise in masochism. A child named Phelim is, however, born to the overjoyed couple, who proceed to spoil him rotten, despite his smallpox:

——Doesn't he become the pock-marks well, the crather?
——Doesn't the droop in his eye set him off all to pieces?[18]

In a more sophisticated text, these lines could be read as a covert mockery of the attitudes towards Ireland adopted by many English readers and even policy-makers, but here they function as a sign of invincible parental ignorance. Carleton is painfully aware of how badly parents, and indeed all members of any impoverished community, need to live vicariously through one or two of their 'exceptional' children.

Phelim is a finished example of the lying native – he tricks three local women into engagements to marry him. Carleton maintains a note of arch superiority with references to the 'mansion' of a half-acre farm. When Phelim courts one girl, Molly (whom he may genuinely desire), we are offered an extended description of the bed, dresser, mats, roost, pots, stools, crockery and animals that make up a sixteen-feet-by-twelve homestead. Yet, even as Carleton amazes and convinces by his command of detail in keeping with the modes of 1830s realism, he is also apologizing to the English reader that his catalogue will not seem as impressive as it should:

> This catalogue of cottage furniture may appear to our English readers very miserable. We beg them to believe, however, that if every cabin in Ireland were equally comfortable, the country would be comparatively happy.[19]

The modes of European realism seemed hardly calibrated to such a world, for they were modes fashioned to describe the interiors of a prosperous middle class.

Carleton often bemoaned the lack of such a mediating social group in an Ireland that seemed to be divided only between the very poor and very rich: 'if this third class existed, Ireland would neither be so political nor so discontented as she is'.[20] The period between 1820 and 1850 was the heroic phase of the middle class elsewhere in Europe, that period when its members founded industries and companies. But Ireland produced not so much a middle class as its caricature: the middlemen, the consumerist parasites. In other lands, the bourgeoisie not only acted as a buffer between poor and rich: they also helped to referee the very conflict between them. In Ireland, however, the middleman class simply fed like leeches off such conflict and had, in fact, a vested interest in its exacerbation. Through much of the eighteenth century, there had been a native, improving class of rising Catholic merchants and resident Protestant landowners; but in the nineteenth, after the Union, such persons were greatly demoralized, and the few intellectuals to emerge from that group headed as soon as they could for England, where they joined other 'micks on the make' (in Roy Foster's phrase) in the world of publishing, politics and the professions.[21] As early as 1815, the students of Trinity College Dublin were reportedly transferring in large numbers to Oxford and Cambridge.[22]

Phelim O'Toole, however, being poorer, stays on the make at

home. The dénouement to all his trickery occurs at Sunday mass, when the wily priest 'calls' his banns three times in front of the entire congregation. Phelim believed that he would enjoy better luck once he married ('this is another absurd opinion', tuts Carleton, 'peculiar to the Irish'),[23] but the chance never comes. Inveigled into delivering a message to the local police, he is promptly arrested and transported as a Ribbonman. On interrogation, he is found to know no Christian doctrine and becomes a warning against those who resort to Ribbon violence, 'whatever the grievances of the people are, whether real or imaginary'.[24]

The nervous, almost hysterical quality of such flourishes suggests that Phelim's tale, like Denis's, represents a there-but-for-the-grace-of-God self which Carleton felt he had the luck to abort. It is as if in writing such superstitions down, the author hopes to liquidate that vivacious but disreputable phase of national life, as well as all conceivable versions of what he might otherwise have been. Nevertheless, the control of tone is jerky, because so much that is personal is at stake. Carleton had got his first publishing breaks by working for a Protestant proselytizer, Caesar Otway, and he knew that there would be many among his own people to call him a turncoat.

The uncertainty of tone arises directly from his own strategic positioning. He is never quite sure who exactly his audience might be. In his younger days, it was clearly a Dublin-based, Protestant, even proselytizing group. Thereafter, it seemed to expand in his mind to embrace enlightened readers in England and Scotland. Ultimately, in his late autobiography, he implied that his subjects had finally 'caught up' with the texts which represented them, and that the urbanized country people of Ireland could now enjoy a picture of what they once were. Gifted with powers of 'unconscious observation', Carleton saw himself as an Irish Wordsworth, writing for those who had migrated into cities and towns. His stories are filled with deliberate echoes of Wordsworth.[25] One of his collections was dedicated to the poet, and for his own portrait he sat in the selfsame posture as his exemplar. There is a definite touch of 'Tintern Abbey' in his claim that 'those who had forgotten that period in other and busier scenes of existence, meet again in the pages of Carleton the living personages of long past days, like friends returned from a distant land after an absence of many years.'[26]

Had Carleton been born as early as Wordsworth, he might have written in the poetic form; had he been born as late as Trollope, he would certainly have achieved a greater mastery of the novel – for each of these was the prestige mode of its period. As matters stood,

Carleton became a master of the lyric anecdote, the story representing a trait of peasant culture. Some, like 'Phelim O'Toole's Courtship' and 'Denis O'Shaughnessy Going to Maynooth', are halfway between short story and *Bildungsroman* – as such, they presage books like *Dubliners* and the trilogy of Beckett, being neither one thing nor the other, books not of a made society but of one still in the making. The choice of the longer short story was shrewd on Carleton's part, for the form was appropriate to the 'submerged population group'[27] that was the peasantry. He never achieved in the novel form the sort of convincing textual detail established in the stories and for good reason: a novel presupposes a made society and Ireland was hardly that. The anecdote fitted conditions better, because 'in its refusal to develop beyond a single incident, it is a symbolic rejection of progress'.[28]

But Carleton believed in progress, or at least he thought he did. That is the point of all those fussy scientific disclaimers and footnotes, which distance him from the folk beliefs of his people. All the same, there is something strained about such gestures, and that strain may be rooted in his uncertainty about the value of 'progress' itself. Caught between his peasant material and his educated readership, he is in a cleft stick. If he keeps his eye on the audience, he risks betraying the material; but if he keeps his gaze fixed on the material, he risks losing the audience. If every Irish writer must choose between expressing material or exploiting it, Carleton was rather unusual in trying to do both at once. He was in truth a literary equivalent of the despised middlemen, as surely as some of his predecessors among the Anglo-Irish had been literary versions of the absentee landlord. In the General Introduction to his work, he observed:

> Our men and women of genius uniformly carried their talents to the English market, whilst we laboured at home under all the dark privations of a literary famine . . . literary men even followed the example of our great landlords; they became absentees and drained the country of its intellectual wealth precisely as the others exhausted it of its rents.[29]

Now, he believes, he has proven that an Irish writer can be successful without having his work published in London: and this is the necessary basis for a national literature.

Carleton's idea of self-representation is severely limited and does not even extend to the political zone. 'A greater curse could not be inflicted on the country', he said, 'than to give it a parliament of its own making.'[30] His own rather heavy authorial intrusions into his narratives suggest that he had similar reservations about allowing his subjects permission to narrate themselves. He may have *known* more about the peasantry than Edgeworth, but he was far more fearful than she about giving unmediated liberation to their voices. Compared to hers, his censors work overtime, even in the main text.

There is a demonstrable link between the warm intimacy of his renditions of country life and the cold, judgemental tones of the footnotes: and that is his awareness that the dishevelled world of the peasantry needs to be contained and controlled. His interventions are those of a middleman, at once close to and distant from the people. He can never quite permit a character full expressive freedom, but must condescend, even phrasally, to these feckless, fluent chaps. He isn't exactly an anthropologist: rather he writes like a peasant who has read some books of anthropology and knows how the trick is done. His interventions are always writerly, volunteering to control the chaos of an oral world, just as his panoramic scenes feed the illusion that the peasantry can be surveyed and therefore controlled. Yet these interventions also vouch for the truth of much that might otherwise appear unbelievable. Ultimately, having given so much away in the game of exploitation, they nevertheless lodge a countervailing claim for the undeniable virtues of the peasantry: generosity to visitors, recovery from depression, and strong domestic sentiment.[31]

It is sometimes said that a single Carleton sentence seems to have been written in two very different styles by two very different men. The General Introduction to *Traits and Stories of the Irish Peasantry* reads at times like a justification of the very people whose vices are too often mocked in the texts. Like all introductions, it was written last and so may contain an element of retraction. 'System' was a dirty word in Carleton's lexicon and he was blithely untroubled by allegations of inconsistency: he appears to have written at some stage for every side in the Ireland of his time. Various groups from the proselytizing Protestants of the 1820s to the Young Irelanders of the 1840s tried to claim him as one of their own, but he resisted final assimilation. Some grew contemptuous, seeing in his multiple selfhood not the aggregate of a whole people but the base flexibility of an invertebrate. In his defence, it might be said that the very contradictions of his position left him more representative of Ireland than other, perhaps more principled, persons could be. Most of the leading intellectuals admired his writing. A petition to the British government in 1847 for a pension on his behalf was supported by Orange leaders, John O'Connell (the Liberator's son), Maria Edgeworth, Sir William Wilde and the President of Maynooth College.[32]

Thomas Davis, the Young Irelander, said that 'no man, who does not know the things he tells, knows Ireland'.[33] He could say this, despite the fact that he was a nationalist and Carleton a British empire man. Davis praised Carleton for detailed reportage of an Ireland already historical: 'the fairies and the banshee, the poor scholar and the Ribbonman, the Orange Lodge, the illicit still, and the faction fight are disappearing into history',[34] wrote Davis with touching optimism in a review of *Traits and Stories of the Irish Peasantry* in the year of his own death, 1845. This wasn't really true, of course, but Davis as a modernizing intellectual wished to believe that the Ireland of the recent past had been liquidated, and Carleton's work gave him permission to think such a thing.

The General Introduction to the *Traits and Stories of the Irish Peasantry* makes it very clear that their author is no republican, for he presents his peasants as 'an interesting portion of the empire'[35] He inserts the national experience (courtesy of the Union) into a system of global implication – and the ploy worked, for his stories were consumed by a global readership. 'As the son of an Irish peasant,' wrote Karl Marx to Friedrich Engels, urging him to read Volume One, 'he knows his subject better than the Levers and Lovers.'[36] Though the peasant has much to offer the British empire, says Carleton, he has been a victim of absurd prejudices, many of which are based on the distinctive use made by Irish persons of the English language: 'From the immortal bard of Avon down to the writers of the present day, neither play nor farce has ever been presented to Englishmen, in which, when an Irishman is introduced, he is not drawn as a broad grotesque blunderer . . .'[37] The implication is that the superior opportunities for subtle psychological portraiture offered by narrative prose will set much of this to rights.

Even the despised 'bulls' are shown to have been deliberate rather than unconscious, purposely employed to put hearers in a good mood. And the Irishman who was compelled to impress 'the idiom of his own language upon one with which he was not familiar' should not have been ridiculed, for he was the very sign of the modern, a hero of the transitional phase in the passage to modernity:

> The language of our people has been for centuries, and is up to the present day, in a transition state. The English tongue is gradually superseding the Irish. In my own native place, for instance, there is not by any means so much Irish spoken now as there was about twenty or five-and-twenty years ago.[38]

'Transition' was also a Davis word and the entire General Introduction reflects many of the patriot's ideas on Irish modernization: that

English, where accepted as the general vernacular in Ireland, is spoken with greater precision than in England (the Lower Drumcondra Principle, as mockingly enunciated later by James Joyce); that stage-brogue, like the stage-bull, was falsely attributed to the recesses of private and domestic life; and that the mockery of Irish-English had created unfriendly feelings between the two countries, but that these were happily disappearing. Once the English gain a truer account, they may begin to respect Ireland more. Nowhere, however, does Carleton more acutely reflect Davis than in his belief that modern science will draw peoples closer together. 'The progress of science, and the astonishing improvements in steam and machinery, have so completely removed the obstructions which impeded their discourse,' he wrote.[39] It is poignant to think of such a sentence written in 1842, for not even the steam engine was able to save one million Irish from death shortly after.

Yet, for all that, famine haunts Carleton's Introduction. The export of good writers, like good grain, led to 'all the dark privations of a literary famine'.[40] His real theme is underdevelopment in all its forms: economic, political, moral. His thesis is that the dire effects of the Penal Laws remain long after their repeal, for the same causes would have produced identical effects in any country. There is no essentialist feckless Irish character, merely Irish characters who are the logical product of crazy, asocial forces:

> . . . the Penal Laws rendered education criminal, and then caused the unhappy people to suffer for the crimes which proper knowledge would have prevented them from committing. It was just like depriving a man of his sight, and afterwards causing him to be punished for stumbling.[41]

Under far less provocation, the English would have resorted to outrage and war upon all authority, but most Irish bore their pains with mute patience – an echo of Edmund Burke. The crimes that now disfigure rural Ireland, says Carleton, should in many cases be attributed to the moral profligacy of bad landlords; and many political crimes 'are perpetrated by men who possess the best virtues of humanity, and whose hearts as individuals actually abhor the crime'.[42]

Whilst it may be hard to reconcile such rational analyses with the rather different accounts of Paddy Devaun or Phelim O'Toole in the *Traits and Stories of the Irish Peasantry*, the logic of Carleton's argument is compelling: 'the period, therefore, for putting the character of our country fairly upon its trial has not yet arrived'.[43] It will be time enough to return a verdict thirty or forty years hence, when education will have done its work.

The problem was that the great test of Irish mettle came not in thirty or forty years but in three or four. Carleton may not have been as surprised as others by the Great Famine. Through his adult life, the country had suffered from recurrent hungers: in 1817 when he walked to Lough Derg; in 1818 when he walked south; again in 1821, when he could see its effects even in Dublin; in the winter of 1837–8 when two and a half million souls faced starvation; and again in 1842 as he wrote the General Introduction with its cryptic reference to 'literary famine'.[44] Overt in that introduction was a thesis concerning the underdevelopment of the economy and of social mores. But this was a *covert* thesis of many of the *Traits and Stories* themselves: that the old Irish culture, which had functioned as a supportive myth of explanation for the peasantry, was dead, and that the new English culture, as contained in those mostly unread books stored in peasant cabins, had yet to take hold. The poignancy of the stories is not just that they offer glimpses of a vivacious people soon to disappear, but that they may contain within themselves some of the hidden reasons for the immensity of the catastrophe when it came.

A century earlier, in 1740, famine had left a quarter of a million dead, which as a proportion of the whole population was not much less than that which would die in the 1840s. Yet the stricken population sooner recovered its vitality.[45] The onset of yet another famine in 1845 probably caused little surprise, for nobody knew just how terrible its effects would be. A year later, however, Carleton decided that it was time to write a famine novel, *The Black Prophet*, 'to awaken those who legislate for us into something like a humane perception of a calamity that has been almost perennial for a century'.[46] *Almost perennial for a century*. If that is so, it may be possible to read the signs of that failure, cultural as well as economic, in the *Traits and Stories of the Irish Peasantry*. The consensus view is that they translate the vivacious but disorderly life of a largely Irish-speaking pre-Famine countryside into the discourse of modernity, via print and the English language: and that, in doing so, they help to save for posterity the shreds of a culture that might otherwise have passed out of sight. However, what was saved was little enough.

All commentators concur on one point: that there was a breakage. Some blame this on the Famine, some on emigration, some on the virtual collapse of the Irish language. The 1840s have been identified as the cut-off decade. The cultural gap that opened between an Irish-speaking past and an English-speaking present has been dramatized in various ways.

Fr Peter O'Leary wrote in his autobiography *Mo Scéal Féin* (My Own Story) of a contrast in temperament between the pre- and the post-Famine child. The former was alert, humorous and quick to respond ('dána gan a bheith droch-mhúinte': bold without being bad-mannered), while the latter was hesitant, surly and furtive ('droch-mhúinte gan a bheith dána': bad-mannered without being bold).[47] He attributed the difference to schooling under the English system, but the toll taken by the Famine on self-confidence was also a major element in the situation. The social commentator Raymond Crotty has argued that the steady emigration of young people and the resulting loss of their energy and talent must take much of the blame: for even after the hunger abated in the 1850s, the patterns of emigration, once established, could not be broken, despite the fact that the material conditions to which many went were arguably worse than those at home.[48] There is even a political version of the 'gap' theory, promulgated by Carleton himself, which lays blame for the loss of integrity in peasant life on the wheedling speeches of Daniel O'Connell, who told his listeners that they were the greatest people in the world. Before his onset, alleged Carleton, the mass of people were sincere, honest and truthful, but afterwards they became double-dealing and corrupt. The writer was probably jealous of O'Connell's rapport with the peasantry, a rapport that won him global acceptance as their representative.

The gap theory posed great problems for nationalists. If the old culture was dead, then in the name of what culture could the claim for political independence be lodged? Here the shreds of Gaelic that survived in the pages of Carleton would be turned to use. Hence the vital importance of the word 'transition', and the value assigned to writers whose knowledge of Irish enabled them to effect a translation. Modernity needed to preen itself just a little by marking itself off from the recent as well as the ancient past: for without them, it was not modernity at all. But those elements carried over from that past could themselves be made the basis of a national claim.

The problem with this version of culture was that it seemed to wish the gap that was the Famine away. It occluded a horrific event of the recent past, as surely as a later generation of revival writers would surpass and thereby occlude the achievements of the mid-century figures. Yeats would take over from James Clarence Mangan as the national poet, Joyce from Carleton as the great prose master, and Synge from Boucicault as the essential Irish dramatist. Each somehow managed to turn his forerunner into a sort of botched, incomplete version of himself, much as Tone had done with Swift.[49] Occlusion, not silence, is the real condition of mid-nineteenth-century Ireland. There was no silence about the Great Hunger in the literature of the period. Irish language poets, in the tradition of the seventeenth-century political artists, could not bring themselves to accept a merely scientific explanation for all the suffering in the failure of one vegetable plant: what they saw, instead, was the hand of God terribly testing a people before their inevitable triumph and justified deliverance from bondage.[50] This was, in its way, a version of the emerging national myth – the idea of a culture that was almost dead but still possessed of a great future. As a notion this went right back to the *filí*: the idea of a national sin that must be atoned for before it could be transferred to its ultimate bearers, the English.[51]

Famine memories were occluded, of course, for many reasons. The traumatic scenes witnessed were bound to create a sort of denial in many who felt guilty simply for having survived a holocaust that left so many loved ones dead. The American visitor, Mrs Asenath Nicholson, seemed to suggest that if it had gone on much longer, a wholly new language would have had to be invented to account for the world.[52] As always, there were some Irish who profiteered from the pain of others, buying the land of evicted neighbours at knock-down prices: they also had reasons for forgetting much that had been done. All commentators agree that whereas the people recovered after the earlier famines, this one was different. 'It was not that it made them that lived after poor,' said Malachi Horan, one farmer in the Dublin hills, 'for God knows they were used to that – but it made them so sad in themselves.'[53]

It is possible, however, that the Famine was simply a fearful, final symptom of a prior cultural failure. The woman spotted by Maria Edgeworth on the edge of her family estate 'too much stupefied by hunger and despair' to notice that the child she carried on her back was already dead,[54] may be a truer image of Ireland's broken tradition in the second half of the nineteenth century. Even in the Dublin of earlier decades, Charles Maturin had noticed the marks of terminal decay. 'Its beauty continues,' he wrote of the deposed capital after the Union, 'but it is the frightful lifeless beauty of a corpse, and the magnificent architecture of its public buildings seems like a skeleton of some gigantic frame, which the departing spirit has deserted.'[55] If the sense of collapse out in the countryside was 'almost perennial', that may prompt a rather different reading of Carleton from that usually offered.

It is not really true that the *Traits and Stories of the Irish Peasantry* enact the evolution of the folk tale into the modern short story, or that in them 'the declining culture of Gaelic Ireland is painfully translated into a self-consciously literary English'.[56] The folk tale is a tightly organized narrative, often filled with supernatural interventions and narrative formulae, and told in a language of real concentration.[57] It is about as far from Carleton's loosely organized anecdotes of domestic manners in the countryside as it could possibly be. Although Carleton used token Gaelic phrases as guarantors of his authenticity – perhaps he was the real pioneer of the *cúpla focal*, the couple of words – he did not deeply translate anything. In his stories, the enfeebled culture of Ireland after the Penal Laws, already in English, is revealed in all its poverty. Because he came from Irish-speaking parents, he was more acutely aware of the scale of that degeneration, about which he seems to have heard almost daily. His mother, for instance, refused a request to sing 'Bean an Fhir Rua' in English. 'I will sing it for you,' she said, 'but the English words and the air are like a quarrelling man and wife: *the Irish melts into the tune, but the English doesn't.*'[58] Already the people themselves had effected the translation to a 'modern' discourse, and on the basis of that very experience, they had already become theorists of translation themselves. What Carleton's mother said (in Irish) would be repeated (in English) by W.B. Yeats, in his castigation of the 'ungainly' appearance of Irish song material when fitted out in 'English garb',[59] and by an Aran islander who told Synge that 'a translation is no translation unless it will give you the music of a poem along with the words of it'.[60]

In the General Introduction, Carleton concedes that as a youth he was often guilty of perpetrating horrors of mis- and overtranslation. A bombastic pedant, he raised the coefficient of Hibernicisms to undreamed-of heights: 'not a word under six feet would come out of my lips, even in English'.[61] This mockery of his younger self recognizes the awful plight of a peasantry caught between two languages, yet full masters of neither. Carleton in his childhood 'had seen weddings with one party speaking English, the other speaking Irish, only with difficulty understanding each other'.[62] He noted that while the people seemed apt only for comedy in English, they attained the dignity of the epic and tragic far more often in the native tongue. 'I will speak to her in Irish,' says Carleton's Poor Scholar on returning to his mother. 'It will go directly to her heart.'[63]

By the time his stories were being published in the 1830s and 1840s, their Irish readers in towns could congratulate themselves on how far they had advanced from the linguistic disorder of their youth. In the countryside, it was a different matter. There parents spoke Irish and children English, and some of the more naïve children were unaware that these were different languages. When

Douglas Hyde asked a country lad, 'Nach labhraíonn tú an Ghaeilge?' (Don't you speak Irish?), the reply came back, 'Isn't it Irish I'm speaking, sir.'[64] A defendant, appearing at Kilkenny assizes during the 1850s, refused a liberal judge's invitation to conduct the case in Irish. 'I see how it is,' groaned the judge, as soon as the man began to plead in broken, incomprehensible English. 'You are more ashamed of knowing your own language than of not knowing any other.'[65] By then the pride that Carleton's mother had felt was no longer widely shared: Irish had become, in Matthew Arnold's phrase, the badge of a beaten race.[66] If anything, the incidence of Irish speakers was underreported in the Census of 1851, which recorded just 23 per cent of the population as Irish-speakers, despite the fact that about four million (or 46 per cent) had been registered in 1845.[67]

The use of Gaelic loan words by Carleton's peasants or by himself is seldom due to an inability to find an equivalent word in English: rather it may be seen as a nostalgic attempt to hold onto one or two shreds of a fast-dying culture. Those who must give up a lot will understandably try to hold onto what little remains. What is hard to accept as authentic in Carleton is the baroque usage attributed not just to scholars and clerical students like Denis O'Shaughnessy but also to simpletons like Phelim O'Toole. Perhaps, one might see in such style a conspicuous consumption of words utterly impossible at the level of things – and a savouring of language for its own sweet sake rather than for its use value. The problem is that it was hardly typical of what country people spoke to one another. The more knowing among them might conceivably speak in a rather 'literary' style to English visitors. However, the evidence gathered by Synge on Aran suggests that recent 'converts' to English rarely spoke in that way to one another. The heedless verbiage of a Phelim O'Toole was really a confession of inadequacy on the part of a speaker no more able to control his language than his political fate.

When, late in life, Carleton came to write his autobiography, the style he chose was precise, cool and even somewhat withheld, utterly without self-display. It was also perfect standard English, purged of Irish localisms. Even though most of his compatriots spoke at that time some form of Hiberno-English, he did not share the radical view, soon to be advanced by W.B. Yeats, that such a dialect ought to be made the idiom of newspaper editorials, church sermons and university lectures. He thought of it not as an instrument for analysing the life of country people but, at the very most, as an aspect of that life which might be analysed. The dialect is deliberately framed by the 'learned' discourse, with which it must never be confused. In every contrast of that kind, Carleton feels obliged to re-enact his own saving exile, in time and in territory, from the Clogher of his child-hood. Yet the Act of Union, whose theory underpins his adoption of Oxbridge English, has clearly failed his subjects: so that his political solution – a better sort of landlord – carries only a wan conviction. Nevertheless, he dedicated the 1843–4 version of *Traits and Stories of the Irish Peasantry* to Isaac Butt, the Member of Parliament who still tried to make the word 'landlord' mean the same thing in Ireland as in England: a responsible, protective presence fully committed to the well-being of his local community.[68] It was the duty of good landlords to work, as Swift had, for an equal relation between England and Ireland. Such an enlightened unionism was what Carleton had in mind when he called himself 'a liberal conservative and, I trust, a rational one'.[69]

The culture Carleton had to report was already translated by its practitioners, but because he grew up in a period of bilingualism, he seems to have evolved his own theory of *diglossia*. Of the *Traits and Stories of the Irish Peasantry* he remarks:

> I heard them as often in the Irish language as in the English, if not oftener; a circumstance which enabled me in my writings to transfer the genius, the idiomatic peculiarity and conversational spirit of the one language into the other, precisely as the people themselves do in their dialogue, whenever the heart or imagi-nation happens to be moved by the darker or better passions.[70]

A translator in such conditions need not be a traducer. Carleton dis-covered with pleasure the added value acquired by the carry-over to English. A phrase like 'm'anam istigh thú' (my soul within you) could, even after so literal a translation, capture the tender energies of love in the target language. Had Carleton's ideas been widely adopted, country people might have continued to speak Irish in the home and personal life, while reserving English for occasions of busi-ness, professional or political activity.

What happened was rather different. A people normally keen to synthesize the old and the new opted, on this one occasion, to do away with the old almost entirely. Unlike other European peoples, they did not wait until they had migrated to a new land, but instead taught one another English at home. The best explanation was given by a Connemara man to a visiting nationalist: 'Is beag an mhaitheas a dhéanfaidh sí duit, nuair a théas tú thar an Teach Dóite' (It's little use to you once you've passed beyond Recess).[71] Parents encouraged children to learn English as the language of modern com-merce and international scholarship. At a time when the importance of the state both as administrator and employer was becoming clearer, a knowledge of the language was useful. Even the case for political separatism was designed not just to be heard in Ireland but also to be overheard in England. Carleton often complained that he had lost money and readers by staying in Ireland; but for that very reason, he was keen to use tones that might be audible in England as well. That was the price of founding a national literature in a land not oversupplied with readers. For much the same reasons, when he addressed large crowds of Irish speakers, Daniel O'Connell spoke English in hopes that his sentiments might be understood and endorsed by the editorialists of London and Manchester.

For centuries the English in Ireland had, at least in theory, been trying to erase Irish and promote their own language. Until the growth of a significant state apparatus in the later part of the eighteenth century, the policy had little effect. Given that colonialism has always worked off a line of demarcation between colonizer and colonized, and that in Ireland the people looked exactly like the occupiers, it may well have suited the English over centuries to have most of the natives Irish-speaking. Then, with remarkable suddenness, those natives decided not to speak their own language and, within a couple of generations with only limited institutional help, effected a complete changeover. This wasn't necessarily an act of apostasy. The desire to master English might be seen, in at least some cases, as an attempt to thwart this cultural version of the 'colour bar', a form of sly, subversive civility about which postcolonial commentators have written. Far from maligning those who learned English, nationalists of later times might have recognized their immense intellectual achievement: after all, the attempt to reverse the policy, with far greater institutional support over the eighty years of an independent Irish state, has hardly been so effective. Yet acceptance of Irish as the major medium of Irish nationalism seemed to undermine the very basis of the separatist claim, for if the distinctive Gaelic culture was all but gone, then the 'Irish question' could be treated as one more economic than political in nature.

That is one reason why Irish was never wholly abandoned. In 1840–1 Carleton voiced alarm that the folk artisans of Tyrone in an earlier generation – the *seanchaithe*, pipers, thatchers, matchmakers – might soon pass away and the next generation know nothing of them. So he printed stories in the *Irish Penny Journal* on these traditions. Yet, a full century and a half later, the poet Seamus Heaney has devoted many fine poems to a celebration of the same 'disappearing' crafts, and for much the same reason. The tradition has been dying for a very long time: and the publicizing of that threat of extinction seems to be the very thing needed to keep it alive. The Great Famine was important because it made that threat seem all the more formidable.

Nevertheless, Irish was given up by most people, and few enough in the population seemed to consider it worthwhile to prolong the sort of *diglossia* observed by Carleton in the Clogher of his childhood. For all their verbal gifts, the Irish emulated their occupiers in displaying a real reluctance to speak a second language. This is one of the unexplained mysteries of nineteenth-century history. It is one thing to learn a modern international language for the sake of material success; it is quite another to act as if that decision also necessarily involves abandoning one's own tongue. Why did that happen? Carleton never directly addresses the question, but then nobody did. None the less, his stories imply an answer, for they are studies in a dying culture, one whose exponents no longer really believe in its value as a code for survival in the world. These people have given up Irish, while not yet enjoying the full expressive potentials of an achieved English-language civilization. Yet the decision was motivated not by any sense that Irish was deficient in expressive power (all testimony supplied by Carleton suggests the opposite), but because the society that was Ireland after the Penal Laws seemed inadequate to their modern needs. Those laws robbed the people of their natural leaders, leaving the way open for the Catholic clergy to fill the vacuum: but they also made English, for the first time on the island, the language that would ever afterward be identified with the prestigious classes. When an Irish soldier in a 'Wild Goose' regiment was asked by the French king why he never spoke his native tongue, he explained, 'Sire, in Ireland only the lower classes speak Irish.'[72]

In a world still built on social hierarchies, such attitudes counted for a lot. The contempt for Irish among what remained of a Catholic uppercrust had a massive effect. When the national seminary was founded at Maynooth in 1795, English was at once instituted as the language of instruction by bishops keen to prove loyalty to England and gratitude for relaxations of the Penal Laws. The graduates of the seminary became a force for anglicization.

It was in the late eighteenth and early nineteenth centuries that emigration really took hold, not necessarily because people were fleeing poverty so much as because they sensed that the very fabric of the old culture had been torn and broken. At their annual conference of 1874 the National Schoolmasters passed a resolution condemning the failure to teach Gaeltacht children Irish:

The peasants in Irish-speaking districts have not English enough to convey their ideas, except such as relate to the mechanical business of their occupation. Hence, they are not able in any degree to cultivate or impress the minds of their children (though often very intelligent themselves), who consequently grow up dull and stupid if they have been suffered to lose the Irish language or to drop out of the constant practice of it.[73]

The confusion of people caught between two languages, which Synge found in the west at the end of the nineteenth century, had marked the eastern parts at its start. A semi-literate countryman explained the plight to Douglas Hyde:

> The people that is living now a days could not understand the old Irish which made me drop it altogether their parents is striving to learn their children English what themselves never learned so the boys and girls has neither good English or good Irish . . .[74]

Synge attributed emigration not just to economic deprivation but to a collapse of cultural self-confidence. 'One feels', he concluded in a series of articles for the *Manchester Guardian*, 'that the only real remedy for emigration is the restoration of some national life to the people.'[75]

Against that wider backdrop, it can be seen that the culture on which Carleton reported was maimed and enfeebled. It afforded him his material, yet it also distorted and weakened his own very considerable talent. It lacked inner consistency, self-conviction, coherence: and those lacks are to be read in his endless shifts of political allegiance and jerkiness of style. Even in his flaws, however, he was a true representative of his people's condition. The gap that opened in Irish culture long predated the Great Famine and the ultimate challenge, when it came, simply exposed the inability of the cultural code to meet and overcome it. Of course the material facts are crucial: a chronically undercapitalized economy, exorbitant rents extracted by clients of the British for their mutual profit, lack of leadership from many landlords, the export of grain while many starved. Recent theorists have argued that in an era of easy transport, it is not so much a want of food as a lack of money to send the food to those who need it that creates scarcity. Undercapitalization may be the chief culprit and the Great Famine an early instance of this modern phenomenon. Yet five times more grain went into the country than went out, and the proportion starving was no greater than it had been in the 1740s. While it would be wrong to exculpate irresponsible leaders and landlords, it is clear that the severity of the 1840s famine exposed a new vulnerability in people, a want of *teacht aniar* (resistance). Some of the explanation for this may be cultural, in the sense that a people so sorely tested may have wondered what exactly they had to live for. 'It was not until the Famine struck', writes Seán de Fréine, 'that the active sociocultural edifice was revealed for the barren shell it had become.'[76]

De Fréine argues that the Great Famine was the first major crisis to affect the country following the widespread rejection of Gaelic tradition. 'It revealed for the first time how Tradition had been undermined. The sense of utter helplessness and loss which followed broke the hearts of the people.'[77] They had made a desperate gamble for modernity by giving up their language, and modernity had failed them. Small wonder that most subsequent Irish writers, from Yeats to Joyce to Beckett, rejected the idea of history as a straight line progressing to some evolutionary goal and thought instead in terms of circles of eternal recurrence. Yet, to the more extreme Malthusians in England, the Great Famine was progress, the final erasure of a feckless, hopeless, premodern peasantry. There were even some Irish commentators who would, in time, come round to that opinion.[78]

Carleton's novel reflecting the catastrophe, *The Black Prophet*, has been castigated for its melodramatic plot, which is accused of undermining rather than embodying its central theme. The suffering of people in the 1840s cannot be treated directly in the unfolding tale and so it has to be traced back to an unresolved crime committed twenty years earlier. This has been regretted as a vain attempt to find a sense of chronology, a long-term sense of cause-and-effect, even a hand of God, where there may have been none.[79] Carleton is also accused of writing around the central crisis of the peasantry rather than embodying it in his plot. The search for some prior shame to account for current suffering was as old as the Gaelic poets of the 1600s: but Carleton's instincts may have been shrewder than those of his empirically minded critics. The Great Famine was not some *acte gratuit*. Rather it was an event long in gestation, and the plot of his novel, like his *Traits and Stories of the Irish Peasantry*, attests to that fact. If the hunger itself finally defeats his powers of language, that is scarcely surprising. Few writers of the time even submitted their language to the attempt.

17

Feudalism Falling:
A Drama in Muslin

To write a convincing novel about the land revolution of the 1880s was almost impossible. One could have written a novel of manners focused on the Anglo-Irish ascendancy, for manners would soon be all that its members had left – but what of the insurgent masses and landless labourers beyond the castle walls? Their lives were all but unimaginable to a writer of ascendancy background.

George Moore went closest to solving this problem. His theme in *A Drama in Muslin* (1886) is the fall of feudalism and the birth of the modern, not just among the peasantry but, more specifically, for the educated ladies of the big houses, notably his heroine Alice Barton. Moore centres on the plight of the 'muslin martyrs', those girls in white dresses who attend the Castle Ball in Dublin each year knowing that there are no longer enough men to go around. Alice Barton concludes that her class is doomed and makes a leap of imaginative faith and fellow-feeling with the peasantry before the end of the novel. As a last gesture of humanity before leaving Ireland, she asks her new husband to pay the rent of a starving family which is about to be evicted. In the preceding narrative, Moore cannily interposes four or five passages which at least manage to hint at how that other half has lived. Though he centralizes the upper-class society, he includes in his novel the essential criticism of its code, raising his narrative above social apologetics to the level of art.

He could do this because of his own rather complex class position. Although himself a landlord, inheriting a huge estate in County

Mayo, he was also a Catholic by upbringing. This set him at an angle to the Protestant gentry, allowing a certain objectivity in his treatments of it. Moore was by temperament a bohemian, at home in the studios of Paris and London. He was close enough to the life of the aristocracy, however, to know that its decline had been a long time coming. By 1886, he could show that there is something strained and hysterical about the high spirits of the men and women who collapse into a drunken stupor at the end of a big house dance in Galway arranged by May Gould during the Land War. She has explained to her guests that since no *very* unpopular landlord has been invited, there is little danger of the building being blown up. Alice cannot help noticing the 'vague forms' staring in at all the finery – or the fact that her sister Olive's good looks are not matched by much intelligence:

> She was in white silk, so tightly drawn back that every line of her supple thighs, and every plumpness of the superb haunches was seen; and the double garland of geraniums that encircled the tulle veiling seemed like flowers of blood scattered in virgin snow. Her beauty imposed admiration; and murmuring assent, the dancers involuntarily drew into lines, and this pale uncoloured loveliness, her high rose seen and her silly laugh heard, by the side of her sharp brown-eyed mother, passed down the room.[1]

By inserting just one false note – the phrase about the 'silly' laugh – Moore warns how fragile all this social decorum really is.

He writes of the dance as if he were a social anthropologist caught among a strange, barbarous people whose customs baffle him. News comes through that a marquis has been shot nearby, but nobody wants to notice; his brother, 'the newly-made marquis had to fight his way through women who, in skin-tight dresses, danced with wantoning movements of the hips, and threw themselves into the arms of men to be, in true kitchen fashion, whirled round and round with prodigious violence'.[2] Again the one false note – 'kitchen fashion' – suggests that the young people are simulating aristocracy rather than achieving a true *sprezzatura*.

At her high-toned Catholic boarding school, St Leonard's in England, Alice had encountered a real meritocracy, where girls of character and intelligence could win deserved acclaim; here in the improvised dance hall of a rural building, only those pretty girls who devote themselves unreservedly to the pleasing of a man are admired. By the end of the ball, given by spinsters in desperate hopes of finding some interesting men, 'one couple had gone down splendidly before him, another had fallen over the prostrate ones; and in a moment, in positions more or less recumbent, eight people were on the floor'.[3] When a tipsy youth begins to knock over each drunk who passes, the chaperones and mothers ring for the carriages: and, as they leave, the sharp-eyed Alice notes how the places of the daughters on the young men's knees have been silently but effectively taken by the housemaids. The housemaids seem to be having a lot more fun.

The Anglo-Irish are shown to lack the capacity to act with a single will, receiving news of each atrocity as an isolated incident affecting only the immediate victim. Alice's artist father, Arthur Barton, epitomizes their will-less state, contenting himself with paintings that hint at a greatness never actually achieved. He allows an elderly local roué to bed his wife, and generally shrugs his shoulders at the state of the world. Influenced by the ideas of Darwin, who is often mentioned as part of Alice's reading, Moore sees the Anglo-Irish as examples of devolution rather than evolution, descendancy rather than ascendancy. The emptiness of the mother has been re-created in the beautiful Olive. She epitomizes one possible meaning of the whiteness of the muslin dresses, for white is strictly no-colour, in keeping with her pale, uncoloured loveliness. Moore is unsparing:

... it was easy to see that, from the imaginative but constantly unhinging intelligence of the father, the next step downwards was the weak feather-brained daughter. In what secret source, lost far back in the night of generations, was this human river polluted?[4]

Moore was (like Arthur) a painter of limited talent, but he can see that Olive's appeal lies in her pretty emptiness, which permits the onlooker to read whatever he or she most desires to see there. The white muslin dresses seem to repeat the seductive technique – in some places they might be the colour of mourning, but here at the balls they signify the awful emptiness of the life in store for the martyrs, 'the resultless life, the life of white idleness that awaited nearly all of them'.[5] At that life's end, for each there will be a muslin curtain, through which a coffin will pass.

Interestingly, it is with white muslin curtains that Alice's story begins. On leaving the convent school, she returns to her parents' home to prepare for coming-out, only to find that her mother had by skilful arrangement 'created the idea of a playful purity and daisylike candour' in her room, from whose ceiling meekly fell the 'white curtains'.[6] Even the wood has been painted white, in keeping with the fashion of the time, for what Mrs Barton seeks is not so much innocence as the image of innocence, such as may entrap a man. Moore finds this whiteness chilling and will later write a scene in which Olive almost dies out in the snow. He would prefer some reassuringly human flaw to set off Olive's beauty, but she has no flaw of body – yet she is as morally worthless as her mother, a 'personality'. Alice has many visible flaws, but also a depth of principle, being a 'character'. Because of that character, she revolts against her mother's contrived 'white death', fearing that it may come to symbolize for herself and her friends a lifelong sterility, since they are all forbidden to marry below their station, yet can find no suitable man of their own exalted social rank. The attempt to induce a whiteness of soul at the convent has not worked, for Alice, as a keen student of Darwin, has no real religious belief:

> Was she impure? She did not wish to be, but she trembled to think of her life pure from end to end – pure as that plain of virgin snow. Then the sorrow that rose out of her soul became part of the sorrow of others; and, pale and lonely as the glittering trees that raised their faces to the sky, she saw the girls she had seen at the ball passing stainless and sterile through the generation of which she was but a single unit. The moon had risen out of the clouds, and hanging like a night-lamp, blanching the draperies of the distant woods, the land was flooded with so divine an effulgence, that in the disordered imagination of the girl it seemed to be the white bed of celibacy in which the whole county was sleeping.[7]

This account of Galway as a county of perpetual virginity is a vision of mourning. The long passages through the novel detailing Alice's innermost thoughts stand in marked contrast to the very few single-sentence references to the fleeting thoughts about men and dresses that pass through Olive's feeble imagination. It is almost as if Moore is suggesting that she has no inner life, no capacity for introspection, no conscience at all.

A recurring image is that of the chase, and the attempt by Mrs Barton to marry off Olive to Lord Kilcarney is presented in terms of a huntress and her quarry. Moore is appalled at the way in which hunting seems to be all these people know of culture – yet Alice is an exception, described as a keen reader and writer. She reveres the work of George Eliot and Jane Austen and is infatuated for a time by the free-thinking novelist and journalist Harding, whom she meets at the

Shelbourne Hotel. By the end, she will have used her gift of writing to save the social skin of her breezy friend, the pregnant May Gould, in an act of heroic self-sacrifice. 'I spent the winter reading,' she tells Harding at the Shelbourne; and he, who knows the true reputation of the aristocracy, asks, 'Because there was no hunting?'[8] Fox-hunting may have been banned, lest Land Leaguers assassinate local lords, but Moore's deeper point is that the hunt continues by other means in the ballrooms of Dublin Castle. His technique brilliantly conflates ideas of Darwin on the evolution of animal species with the metaphors of hunting and being hunted:

> In the ballroom as in the forest, the female is most easily assailed when guarding her young; and nowhere in the whole animal kingdom is this fact so well exemplified as in Dublin Castle.[9]

The aristocracy, in the words of Benjamin Disraeli, wanted to be seen as angels but feared that they might only be apes: and Moore makes no bones as to where he places them on the ecological scale.

Yet the show put on in Dublin Castle was impressive. Each year the Viceroy and Vicereine received over six hundred guests from the nobility and professional classes. The dresses had three yards of train. Carriages had to wait for an hour outside the Castle Yard in Dame Street, where the poor rubber-necked and some felt free to offer cynical commentary.[10] The really well-to-do were spared this ordeal and allowed the use of a side gate at which there was no humiliating wait:

> 'I wish they would not stare so', said Mrs Barton, 'one would think they were a lot of hungry children looking into a sweet-meat shop. The police ought really to prevent it.'[11]

With her gift for connection, Alice is reminded instantly of the uncouth faces pressed against the windows at the Galway Ball: and she can tell that the onlookers truly are hungry. She also notes the huge disparities of wealth in Ireland. If in the countryside a hundred little houses work to keep one big one in sloth and luxury, here the contrasts of the urban setting are even more bleak. Dublin is described as a sick city, its plaster falling like scabs from a diseased body, its clothes rotten in fetid confusion, its labourers battered. When the carriages come to a standstill, 'sometimes no more than a foot separated their occupants from the crowd on the pavement's edge'.[12]

It is at this stage that Moore produces some of the most over-written passages of the book. Dublin is to him a second-hand city, whose characters 'strive to strut and lisp like those they saw last year at Hyde Park'.[13] The savagery of these passages may arise from the fact that Moore was refused an invitation to a Castle dinner, which he had sought as a reporting artist.[14] His view of the young men, for whom the muslin martyrs vie, is that they are not worth the winning. He sees in them mere instruments of the colonial power, as manipulated by the women as by their political masters in London who seldom consult them about anything important. 'Teacups were sent down to be washed, and the young men were passed from group to group.'[15] Unlike Yeats, Augusta Gregory and others, Moore displays little sentiment about the decline of the Anglo-Irish, a class which for him has no redeeming virtue. As a Darwinian, his heart is with the risen people: and so he describes a thunderclap 'so terrible that it seemed as if the heavens were speaking for the freedom-desiring nation, now goaded and gagged with Coercion Bills'.[16] In that context, the reference to the hunt in the dance hall as a Darwinian struggle for existence is somewhat jocose, for the real battle for new forms of life is being enacted in the streets and valleys outside.

Had Moore gained entry, he might have found the Castle ball a ritual more suited to social comedy than political satire. For example, the old Viceroy Lord Spencer was expected to kiss each debutante as she was presented. He had a flaming red beard, but it soon turned snowy white from all the face-powder deposited on it by blushing girls. He was expected to start the dance, behind a silken cord which was then let down to allow others join in. The State Steward was notorious for falling asleep (sometimes on his feet) at these occasions. His job was to deal with formal complaints, as when a dispute arose because the Earl of Clonmel had sat down heavily on the lap of a lady dowager, drunkenly mistaking her for a well-upholstered arm-chair.[17] Moore, however, was too intent on social satire to find much redeeming comedy in this group . . . and this despite the fact that he was almost killed in the summer of 1880, when he and his land agent tried to drive across a wooden bridge that had been sawn through by rebels. Unlike other landlords, he did not hate Gladstone, the prime minister who in 1881 offered fair rents and fixity of tenure to tenants. (In some of the big houses could be found chamber pots with Gladstone's image on the inside, so that the lord of the manor could urinate on the hated prime minister whenever so moved.)[18] The Anglo-Irish felt utterly betrayed by London, something that Moore scarcely brings out: nor does he bother to emphasize the fact that by the 1880s most landlords felt themselves to be as Irish as any of their tenants.[19]

They were especially sensitive to criticism by visiting English people.[20] Alice Barton's delighted response to Harding would have been untypical of her class, whose members would have viewed him as a jumped-up journalist. For Moore, however, he is a version of himself, a freethinking novelist who is convinced that a republic is the best form of government. His evolutionary ideas are echoed by Moore's description of those who followed Michael Davitt: 'out of the slime they crawled in strange and formless confusion, and in the twilight of nationhood they found the obscure and blind battle of birth'.[21] Moore thereby links nationalism, as well as ideas of woman's independence, to the fact of evolution. If poets are the unacknowledged legislators of the world, novelists are its unadmitted historians: and Moore as social historian links the landless peasants to the doomed debutantes as common victims of a corrupt system:

> The history of a nation as often lies hidden in social wrongs and domestic griefs as in the story of revolution, and if it be for the historian to narrate the one, it is for the novelist to dissect and explain the other; and who would say which is of the most vital importance – the thunder of the people against the oppression of the Castle, or the unnatural sterility, the cruel idleness of mind and body of the muslin martyrs who cover with their white skirts the shames of Cork Hill?[22]

Harding as evolutionist has predictive powers and foresees that Alice will end up in progressive Kensington. Though he impresses her with his daring talk, he does not manage to bed her, much less win her heart. That palm goes to Dr Reed, for his goodness and honest ambition. His response to the suffering of the poor has been to do what he could to lessen it; and over the prostrate body of a feverishly ill Olive, now lost forever to her marquis and abused by her beau, the two fall in love. This is arguably the weakest part of the novel, in that it is not fully 'earned' as a reconciling moment. The doctor is wheeled on at a rather late stage by an author who seems keen to finish everything fast. It turns out that Dr Reed has whiled away his time on the northern bogs writing a successful medical treatise which allows him to buy a modest London practice – and, better still, that he has been reading George Eliot. At the terrible revelation that she is to lose her one true friend to marriage, Cecilia Cullen (Alice's former classmate and confidante) announces suddenly that she will convert to Catholicism and undertake the life of a nun.

For Moore, who himself dreamed of converting to Protestanism, this is a final demonstration of Cecilia's defeat and derangement. He has suggested that her interest in Alice might have a lesbian dimension: but now it is to be frustrated. Moore regarded Catholicism as much further back on the evolutionary chain than either Protestantism or its successor, liberal humanism. Ireland was still caught in the great sleep of Catholicism, he complained, and the proof was that throughout the whole nineteenth century the national seminary at Maynooth had not produced a single theologian of international stature.[23] Moore's account in the novel of the Bartons' progress to Sunday mass recaptures many of his own youthful difficulties with religion. Once the darling of the nuns at St Leonard's, Alice is saddened by how little she identifies with the mystery at the heart of the mass. All along, this failure to tell the nuns honestly that she did not believe has been her one weakness. It is this defect that allows her to live a lie, that links her to the other young women of the story, in that they all to a greater or lesser extent betray their inner instincts. Most do that to please men. Alice does it to please the nuns. All, however, end up impersonating the sort of women other people want them to be. And the nuns, however meritocratic the school may be, are implicated in the other deception, since they train girls to be fitting brides for men of title. At that level, they are scarcely better than Mrs Barton or those other women who, denied authority in life, seek power by strategic linkages with men. Even Alice is not immune to this flaw, paying too much attention to Harding's ideas, 'because his personality seemed to her of such paramount importance compared with her own'.[24] He tells her that the ideas of Aquinas are risible and that Bethlehem and Nazareth will be subjects for future vaudevillists.

The decline of religion is another of Moore's obsessive themes. He begins his book with an image of the church which once commanded the heights but is now obscured by a greater enlightenment: 'The grey stone cross of the convent-church was scarcely seen in the dimness of the sun-smitten sky. The convent occupied an entire hilltop, and it overlooked the sea.'[25] The play Alice stages there should have been a study in ideals and mutual fulfilment between a high-born man and lowly woman. Instead, the acting of her classmates reduced the king to an arrant sensualist and the maid to a clever hucktress. The strategy of Moore's realism is to show Alice gradually awakening from various illusions and stripping away the false veneer of a religion that is now more a matter of social decorum than of true belief.[26]

Most of the book renders the world as it appears to Alice. In adopting the tones of an anthropologist visiting a primitive tribe, Moore uses Alice's consciousness to expose the crazy conceits (as he sees them) of Catholicism. When she walks into Sunday mass, Moore doesn't simply write 'she blessed herself on entering'. Instead, he offers an exact physical description of what happened as it would appear to the eye of a half-baffled outside observer:

> Then they entered a large, whitewashed building. In the middle of the earthen floor there was a stone basin filled with water into which each person dipped a hand, and therewith blessed themselves.[27]

As she sits through mass, Alice feels estranged from its rituals, an uncomprehending observer rather than a participant:

> Alice watched the ceremony of mass, and the falseness of it jarred her terribly. The mumbled Latin, the by-play with the wine and water, the mumming of the uplifted hands, were so appallingly trivial, and, worse still, all realisation of the idea seemed impossible to the mind of the congregation.[28]

Perhaps, like Nietzsche, she is coming to the conclusion that there was only one Christian – and they crucified him. At all events, the narrative moves from studied objectivity to a more frankly satirical tone: 'the long slim fingers held the gilt missals with the same well-bred grace as they would a fan'.[29] The proof of all this theological deadness for Alice is the fact that the rich do not follow Christ and give their wealth to the poor.

Her loss of illusion is not an impoverishment, however. When, at the end, she does decide to marry Dr Reed, she is not so much inundated with uncontrollable desire (as she was, briefly, for Harding) but quietly convinced of her new partner's decency. The low-key quality of the writing is, in part, what makes the ending seem so strange. Alice is as cool about leaving her native country as she is about loving her man. Like Moore, she feels little sentiment on leaving – only a sense that the real work of the world cannot be done on a landed estate. Her partner's lack of good looks is more than compensated for by the excitement of taking her own free decision, wedding him without parental approval or attendance. This is at the core of Moore's thesis – that the Viceroy and Christ share the crutch between them and know no scandal so great as a free individual. While Davitt, as leader of the Land League, might hope that democracy would rule in Ireland, Moore was more sceptical. Power was indeed passing from the Viceroy, but only into the hands of a peasantry that would abjectly defer to bishops. In such a context exile was the only option for a civilized person.

If part of Dr Reed's attraction for Alice is that he has earned rather than inherited his modest wealth, it is a point no less important in this scheme of things that she is utterly self-supporting, by virtue of her writing. In other words, she who was taught by her mother that you can get nowhere without making yourself dependent on a man, now shows that you can win no worthwhile man's love until first you learn how to depend on yourself. This means, of course, that the love between them has no ulterior cash motive, such as complicated so many of the earlier liaisons in the story. Alice has awakened from her dream of dependency, much as Ireland is ending its dependency on Dublin Castle. Though the Castle was important as a court in *A Drama in Muslin*, Moore was aware that for the Irish it was also a place where rebels had been tortured and even executed.[30]

Such a knowledge, however, did not lead him to sentimentalize the peasantry. The ferocity of his writing may be intended as a corrective to earlier novels and plays that depicted the rural people as lovable, lyrical rogues and the landlords as handsome, high-spirited bucks. There was a ready market in London for rollicking Irish tales, but Moore steadfastly refused to offer it any comforting news. His Ireland is the very reverse of whimsical, being largely colourless and often brutal. His Alice learns how to do something and then gets out in order to have some chance of doing it. She may in that guise be a projection of the author himself, for he too felt undervalued by his parents, and then surprised his mother with his literary abilities.[31]

If the somewhat arbitrary and low-key nature of the ending is part of the novel's point, so also may be its refusal to describe the insurgent peasantry in any but the most general of terms. We are as far as page 39 when a carriage full of Bartons causes a peasant 'surlily' to step aside. A bare-legged woman, surrounded by half-naked children and half-peeled potatoes, gazes after this rolling vision of elegance before uttering a single sentence: 'Shure there misht be a gathering at the big house this evening.'[32] Mostly, the peasants seem as silent as they are shadowy; the narrative often breaks off whenever this is mentioned, as if such people are indescribable, possessors of an unspeakable truth. At the spinsters' ball in Galway, 'there were hedges on both sides, through which vague forms were seen scrambling'[33] . . . but no more than that. Even when the cottiers bargain over the rent with a landlord (while Mrs Barton in a cinematic scene is bartering on the marriage mart with a suitor for Olive) they seem to lack all reality, speaking in the crudest cliché. Moore, who as a realist prided himself on getting every detail right, could surely have written more had he wanted to. His reticence on this point can only be deliberate. The peasants are real enough to him, but are unreal in their anger and suffering both to the landlords and to their daughters. This was the tragic flaw of the Anglo-Irish: to have lived without any sense of connection to the surrounding people. Ultimately, theirs was a failure to *trust* the people of the land in which they found themselves, despite the fact that (in Moore's own words) 'every chicken eaten, every glass of champagne drunk, every silk dress trailed in the street, every rose worn at a ball, comes straight out of the peasant's cabin'.[34]

Although Moore knew that the future was with the risen peasantry, he did not believe they would do any good for their country. They might have justice on their side and the energy of a valid resentment, but for him they lacked all charm and had absolutely no understanding of art. In *Confessions of a Young Man* he wrote:

That some wretched farmers and miners should refuse to starve, that I may not be deprived of my *demitasse* at Tortoni's: that I may not be forced to leave this beautiful retreat, my cat and my python – monstrous.[35]

He had sufficient sense of justice for his tongue to be somewhat in his cheek as he penned those lines, but only somewhat. Since the Irish problem was almost impossible, he shrugged, the wisest way of dealing with it might be to sink the island into the sea for twenty-four hours and then inspect what kind of life was left when you hauled it back up.

One of the strongest shared elements in the life of Alice Barton and Dr Reed, as they embark on life in London, is a passion for the novels of George Eliot. The English novelist might be said to have provided them with the very code in which they conducted their courtship. Eliot's greatest novel *Middlemarch* is, like Moore's, a study of provincial life. But what do these writers mean by the word 'provincial'? For Moore, it is the taking of ideas and values from some distant metropolis at second hand: 'see the young men – the Castle bureaucrats – how they splutter their recollections of English plays, English scenes, English noblemen'.[36] His case against the pathetic mimicry of a distant London authority is that it is catching: the underlings of the Castle bureaucrats must, in a sort of knock-on effect, derive their opinions from *them*. 'Dublin is a city without a conviction, without an opinion. Things are right or wrong according

to the dictum of the nearest official.'[37] The real significance of the
Land League in such a context goes well beyond agricultural reform:
for its new Ireland is a place that longs again to be metropolitan to
itself, the source of its own meanings. The whole movement for
Home Rule was an attempt to restore the deposed capital of Dublin
to its position of centrality, a position last enjoyed in the years of
Grattan's Parliament before the Act of Union of 1800.

Moore's own career as artist was bound up with the search for a
similar centrality. As a young man, he headed for Paris which has
been well described as 'the capital of the nineteenth century'. He was
painfully aware from the outset that his strange appearance was
against him, making him look like an uncouth provincial. When
Manet painted Moore, he gave him 'the look of a broken egg-yolk'
and showed that 'the sides of his face were not aligned'. Other
descriptions of him were equally unflattering – 'a boiled ghost', 'an
over-ripe gooseberry', 'a man with champagne-bottle shoulders'.[38]
When Manet's portrait was revealed to Parisians, they thought it
was that of a drowned man taken out of water. Writing was Moore's
means of answering such ridicule, of seizing power, of proving himself a smiter rather than one of the smitten. Likewise, his rage at
Maynooth for not producing a deep thinker was the anger of a man
who wanted Irish intellectuals to be more original and self-reliant.

His critique of Irish provincialism had an immense influence on
the later writer Patrick Kavanagh, who observed: 'Parochial and
provincial are direct opposites. A provincial is always trying to live
by other people's lives, but a parochial is self-sufficient.'[39] The nervous imitation of distant fashions is the very reverse of self-mastery or
self-government. Moore suggests that this is the real flaw of Mrs
Barton and the muslin martyrs, who are compelled to play at being
what men want them to be. His image of society as a great web was
borrowed from George Eliot – and a web is a device without an
absolute centre, an indisputable core point. What it offers instead are
many, varied nodal points: and at each of these, as Eliot laughingly
observed, foolish persons often mistakenly believe that they are at the
epicentre. This is the worst form of provincialism of all: a narrowness of mind that leads a person to think that all of civilization ends
at the perimeter of his or her own townland. If some of the provincialism of the Anglo-Irish in Moore's novel is rooted in a derivative
set of nervous imitations, yet more is to be found in the absolute,
invincible certainty of many characters as to their own rightness.
The results in either case are much the same: a people lacking any
sense of its own presence, of how it might appear to a wider world.

Eliot in *Middlemarch*, by ironical citations of Milton's *Paradise*

Lost, explained why it was impossible for a heroine like Dorothea Brooke to live according to epic values – for England was already made. Had she been born in another country – say Ireland or India – George Eliot might indeed have turned her novel into the story of the birth pangs of a nation: and there might have been a lot more for a Dorothea Brooke or a Tertius Lydgate to do. The shadowy figures lurking in hedges and undergrowth outside the windows of Moore's big house would in fact produce – were already producing – the conditions for such an epic literature: and in the century that followed, all those risen peoples whose countries were still being invented would produce epic poems and prose. In James Joyce's *Ulysses*, there is a scene set in the National Library, which bears amusingly on the theme, when someone suggests: 'Our national epic has yet to be written. Moore is the man for it . . .'[40]

Moore *might* have been the man for it, but he had too low an opinion of his people for that. Ireland, he diagnosed, was a disease, fatal to Englishmen and doubly fatal to Irishmen. Its religion was superstitious and its native language baffled him, despite repeated efforts to learn it.[41] Besides, Moore was far too impressed by the form of the English novel to feel any need to challenge it in ways that would eventually produce the sort of epic written by Joyce. Whereas Joyce would seek freedom from the English novel, Moore still sought freedom within it. If the available form wasn't fully suited to Irish society, that was a comment on the inadequacies of the society rather than on the limits of the form. So, although he knows that the ragged peasantry which appears intermittently in his story might, if he concentrated more fully on it, allow him to write a very different sort of narrative, he chooses not to do that, preferring to investigate just how far a version of *Middlemarch* can be written about Ireland.

With her plain features and high intelligence, Alice Barton might indeed be a George Eliot figure, for Eliot only discovered society as an entity after the collapse of her childhood belief in Christianity. When a society fits a person like a glove, that person is never conscious of it as such, because things are really studied only when they start to malfunction. Alice Barton finds that it is her own loss of religious faith which makes the society all around her seem the more pressing. Its true masters, she observes, are those who have the gift of living most fully in the present moment.

The Casaubon figure in Moore's book is Alice's grandfather Barton, who 'spent fifty years in his study, imagining himself a Gibbon, and writing unpublishable history and biography'.[42] The Ladislaw figure is his son, also a painter of limited talent, who has the same difficulty in settling to a career and who prefers to be a puzzle rather than a personality. In both books the tenantry exist on the edge of the consciousness of a minor aristocracy, the main difference being that the English tenants are as likely as their masters to resist reform, whereas the Irish tenants are all crying out for it.

In both works there is a strong, almost Darwinian, emphasis on the influence of the environment in curtailing human possibility, but Moore is somewhat more optimistic than Eliot on this point. Having read Schopenhauer, he believes also in the power of exceptional wills to challenge and transform the given conditions. Alice Barton, unable to change the subject, is able at last to change the country. By her literary gifts, she wins more freedom than Dorothea Brooke ever knew, that Dorothea who once despised women for not shaping their lives more but sadly abandoned the effort. Moore's Dr Reed is, of course, a less-than-dashing Lydgate, although he does possess some of Lydgate's intellectual abilities as a medical scholar and is free of those flaws that lead Lydgate to discount Dorothea as 'a fine girl – but a little too earnest'.[43] It is precisely Alice's earnestness that attracts Dr Reed.

In some ways, Moore is rewriting the end of *Middlemarch*, imagining what might have happened had a Lydgate figure married Dorothea (a reading possible if we take the Harding character who eludes Alice as an equivalent to the charming but somewhat frustrating Ladislaw). The word 'martyr' recurs in both novels as a description of the female condition. Dorothea's theoretic and idealizing mind was likely 'to seek martyrdom': and Alice, who cries, 'give me a mission to perform' is forced to consider 'the martyrdom which was awaiting her'.[44] To the reader who notices all these cross-references, it can hardly come as a great surprise when George Eliot is herself raised as an issue in Moore's text – and raised most surprisingly by Mrs Barton. She mentions Eliot to Alice, but only to disparage her as an incomplete ideal of womanhood:

> Don't waste your time thinking of your books, your painting, your accomplishments; if you were Jane Austens, George Eliots, and Rose Bonheurs, it would be of no use if you weren't married.[45]

The moral worth of the characters in *A Drama in Muslin* is infallibly gauged according to their attitude to George Eliot.

Like Eliot, Moore was radical in his view of writing as a serious career, and not just an ornament or mere avocation. Even the weaknesses of *A Drama in Muslin*, as when certain passages seem overwritten or out of register with one another, may be put down to his restless experimenting with styles, his propensity (as Oscar Wilde joked) to conduct his own education in public. Wilde held that it took Moore seven years to master grammar and another seven to learn the art of the paragraph; but by the time Moore was fully educated, he had become one of the great prose stylists of the age, capable now of joking about the flaws in other men's writing. The prose of Proust, he laughed, was that of 'a man trying to plough a field with knitting needles'; of his even more famous compatriot Irishman he remarked that 'Joyce has invented a language that only Joyce can understand'.[46]

Moore adopted in his dress and lifestyle the pose of a dandy, which is to say a courtier without a court, an appropriate role for an aristocrat on the skids. He knew that part of the dandy's art was to keep his external composure, even as his heart pounded amidst all the social upheavals: to betray no trace of feeling or sentiment. Moore had never been completely happy about being cast in the role of a landlord receiving unearned income, and on more than one occasion he equated that with the role of an artist who cannot create a real work, a conflation of roles re-created in Arthur Barton. This was probably his portrait of what he feared he might have become, had he not found fulfilment in art. By the very act of becoming a professional and productive writer, Moore thus set himself adrift from the Irish landlord class, a class that seemed quite incapable of reforming itself from within. He was so professional in his approach to his art that he constantly persecuted publishers for accounts of his sales and earnings. He was a man with a mission, and he wanted readers. In this, too, he became a prototype of later writers of the Irish renaissance, most of whom craved bestseller status. They realized that the distrust of the market by bohemians was itself a legacy of the old aristocratic snobbishness, which deemed a gentleman to be one above common toil. So it was perfectly consistent of Moore to use his novel to articulate a critique of aristocracy and a defence of hard work. *A Drama in Muslin* is one of the first serious artistic representation of the fall of feudalism in Ireland.

18

Love Songs
of Connacht

'If that is the sort of thing we are to get in Irish, the sooner it is dead the better.' So wrote Fr Peter O'Leary on 7 October 1895, following a talk by a Gaelic Leaguer on the love songs of the people:

> Abhráin ghrádha a bhídh ar siubhal aige – cuilínidhe agus buachaillidhe agus clann tabhartha agus neithe den tsórt sin, os comhair na cuideachtan.[1]

Love songs he was discussing – girls and boys and illegitimate families and things of that sort, before the assembly.

Fr O'Leary would have preferred healthier topics than such 'polluted' materials: he worried in particular what damage might have been done to the Gaelic League, had the talk been delivered in English. He strongly suggested that the Gaelic League should adopt a strict rule 'not to print a word in Irish that would not be fully appropriate to print in English'.[2]

The Gaelic League had been founded just two years earlier to protect the Irish language and to promote its distinctive culture. Already the conservatives in its ranks seemed intent less on articulating the Gaelic mindset than on producing an Irish-language version of Victorian prudishness. But Fr O'Leary was too late. For 1893 was also the year in which one of the founders of the Gaelic League, Douglas Hyde, published the book titled *Love Songs of*

Connacht, a set of Irish-language texts with English versions in both poetry and prose. He would later publish other songs – religious, political, drinking songs, as well as lyrics attributed to Anthony Raftery and Turlough Carolan. They were seized on gratefully by artists and by the young.

More than a decade after Fr O'Leary's letter, an audience at the Abbey theatre in Dublin broke up in disorder at the use of the word 'shift'. In an interview the playwright J.M. Synge made a comment that showed that Fr O'Leary's worries had some justification:

> Mr Synge said it was an everyday word in the West of Ireland, which would not be taken offence at there, and might be taken differently by people in Dublin. It was used without any objection in Douglas Hyde's *Songs of Connacht* in the Irish, but what could be published in Irish perhaps could not be published in English?[3]

Synge was discovering a bitter truth: that to be Gaelic was not at all the same thing as to be Irish in 1907. Yet his offending masterpiece *The Playboy of the Western World*, like other great works of the Irish revival, was essentially an act of translation, an attempt to render the psychic state of Gaelic culture in English, a language not expressly of that culture. It is not an exaggeration to say that without *Love Songs of Connacht* and the tradition of translation that lay behind them, the play would hardly have been written in the language or forms that ensured Synge's immortality.

The attempt at translating Irish into English was as old as the Anglo-Irish relationship itself: but for most English speakers, the literature and culture of Gaelic Ireland remained a sealed book. All kinds of crazy things were believed by the colonists: that Irish promoted vice and licentiousness, lewdness and ribaldry. Back in the 1590s, Edmund Spenser could at least recognize the beauty in some Gaelic poems, but by 1899 the professors at Trinity College Dublin could seriously suggest to the Committee on Intermediate Education that 'it was almost impossible to get hold of a text in Irish which is not religious or that is not silly or indecent'.[4] The professor of Old Irish opposed the school study of texts, lest they give young ladies a shock from which they might not recover for the rest of their lives.[5]

A century earlier, one young lady had not been quite so badly affected by such exposure. Charlotte Brooke, a noblewoman of Cavan, produced in 1789 *Reliques of Irish Poetry*, a major anthology of Gaelic texts with verse translations. She was, however, a little apologetic about her gender ('Why does not some Ajax in genius step forward?'), lamenting her own 'comparatively feeble hand', while insisting that it could at least, like the hands of Roman ladies, 'strew flowers in the paths of these laurelled champions of my country'.[6] There was astuteness in her maidenly bashfulness, for she presented Ireland in female role *vis-à-vis* male England, cleverly complicating the cliché with the suggestion that Ireland was the elder sister in the relationship:

> The British Muse is not yet informed that she has an elder sister in this isle; let us then introduce them to each other. Together let them walk in cordial union between two countries that seem formed by nature to be joined by every bond of interest and of amity . . .[7]

For Brooke, translation was a version of union: she wished to make Ireland a little less exotic in English eyes and ears.[8] Her belief was that the English language might gain new energies from the cross-fertilization, even as the long pedigree of Gaelic civilization would be established for sceptical English readers. On her father's estate in Cavan, she often heard one of the servants reciting from a manuscript in a hayfield: and she began to collect songs from family retainers. When James Macpherson's *Fragments of Ancient Poetry* (1760) came into her possession, she was astonished to discover that many of his songs carried strong echoes of those sung every day in fields around her home. So she resolved to publish a book that would provide the basic sources which, in the famous Ossianic controversy, Dr Johnson had failed to elicit from the enigmatic Scot. Learned people in Dublin and Belfast had been enraged by Macpherson's claim of his faked-up ballads for Scotland, so Brooke was keen to stake a rival claim for Ireland. She hoped also to challenge with it the common English view of the Irish as a barbarous, uncultivated people, and to clear the reputation of her own Anglo-Irish class as an ascendancy of muscular dullards. Above all – for her book was published in Dublin – she wished to remind her compatriots of a noble heritage.

In her Preface, she offered a concealed rebuke to English people's ignorance, followed by an invitation to blend the Gaelic tradition with their own, if they wished to administer a united and peaceful land. These high hopes were dashed by the sectarian hatreds unleashed before and after the 1798 rebellion, but the collection continued to sell well, offering versions of 'Éamonn an Chnoic', 'Bean Dubh an Ghleanna', Carolan's lyrics, and so on. The sort of union in which Brooke believed was not the Union that Ireland got in 1800. Like

Maria Edgeworth, she wished to bring an enlightened rigour to bear on the political crisis of the time, believing that the scientific spirit of the English could induce the lively Irish to modes of civility, even as the English were themselves enriched by Irish feeling in a relationship of true equals. She felt, however, that much of the 'sublime dignity and rapid energy' in Irish utterance could never be fully translated into English, nor, for that matter, into any modern language.

Brooke emphasized one quality of the poetry: 'manners of a degree of refinement astonishing at a period when the rest of Europe was newly sunk in barbarism'.[9] This would be a theme song of succeeding translators. James Hardiman, a Catholic supporter of O'Connell as well as an Irish-speaker, denied the 'wild', 'effeminate' strains attributed to a tradition that he saw as stately and refined: this was all in keeping with his belief in a people ready for sober self-government. It was left to a Protestant unionist, Sir Samuel Ferguson, to attack Hardiman's translations in *Irish Minstrelsy* (1831) for being overgenteel.[10] By the 1830s, the Act of Union had served only to heighten the Irish sense of cultural distinctiveness; but, though Hardiman sought to capture this identity, he was at pains to assure everyone that his two volumes contained 'no verses of even a doubtful tendency'.[11] The fear of libertinism was extensive among the emergent Catholic middle class. The translators who worked for Hardiman produced work that read fluently and easily in English, but Ferguson, wishing to lay greater stress on the native difference, opted for versions that, in being more literally true to the Irish, notably disrupted the target language. Even he, however, felt it necessary to reassure his audience that in Irish love songs there is 'nothing impure, nothing licentious in their languishing but savage sincerity'.[12]

Why were the translators so nervous of Irish sexuality? The answer may lie in the very nature of the translation enterprise itself, for it presupposes a crossover of boundaries and a blurring of identities normally kept in strict separation. If England wished to maintain rigid distinctions in Ireland between planter and Gael, it may have suited the authorities not to have translations, other than those conducted among the ruling elites. The fear may have been connected with a terror of miscegenation, in the event of sexual encounters between settler and native. The seductive charm of Irish culture had left many of the predecessor colonists more Irish than the Irish themselves: and the leaders of the colonial community were forever on guard against just the sort of hybridity that Charlotte Brooke had called for. The fear of the sexually potent native shaded into a fear of the hybridized human personality, in which opposite elements might cancel one another out, reducing the individual to mere barbarism as a prisoner of instinct. In that context, the translations offered by a Brooke or a Hardiman or a Ferguson, whatever the political views of their makers, once they achieved wide circulation amounted to a challenge to the prevailing order. Love songs, in particular, might function as siren songs, disturbing the sexual decorum of members of the ruling group, especially since their powerful appeal was based more on the heart than the head.[13] The fear of contamination by native love song may also have been rooted in a denial of sexuality itself.

Against the backdrop of that century-long debate, the publication of *Love Songs of Connacht* in 1893 was tantamount to a subversive act. It was an instant bestseller, bringing fame to its compiler, especially among young women. 'Douglas Hyde, with his strange dark face, seemed a prehistoric Celt or one of those the history books called Firbolgs, rolling off rapid Irish through his long black moustache.'[14] So wrote one youthful admirer, Mary Colum (née Maguire), who cared little for the drawing-room lyrics of Tom Moore but longed for poetry that sprang directly from Gaelic inspiration, that of Brooke, Mangan, Ferguson. For her, Hyde's volume had all the force of an explosion, permitting her generation, raised on strict standards of Victorian gentility, to reconnect with the vibrant sexuality of pre-Famine Ireland:

> These anonymous West-of-Ireland songs were mostly women's love songs, and they were unlike any love poetry we read in other languages. They had a directness of communication, an intensity of emotion which, I think, is the special Celtic gift to literature. It was odd that in a country where romantic love was not part of the social organisation, where it was even mocked at, where marriages were arranged and were even a sort of deliberate alliance between families, there should have been poetry of such a high kind. We read these songs in the original and in the striking translations so often that we knew them by heart.[15]

Colum said that the songs moved because they were in the voices of youthful yearning and because they were 'the special expression of the women of the race we belonged to, women who were married to men whom they barely knew, who took it for granted that marriage was a destiny they had to accept, but love was an aspiration of the heart and spirit to be expressed in beautiful words by people who had never handled a book except a prayer book'.[16]

If some of Hyde's songs evoked the freer modes of pre-Famine Ireland, others expressed the frustrations of loving couples who could not marry because the brutal imperatives of landholding and land acquisition after the Famine prevented their union. The great evil to be avoided was the uneconomic holding, and many farmers imposed matches on their sons and daughters, or forbade other matches, solely for material reasons.[17] Mary Colum voiced surprise in her autobiography that a book that rekindled the fire of youth, 'setting everybody on fire with the desire to have a national literature and to revive a national life', did not prompt any response from a colonial administration which proscribed Land League meetings and threw Irish politicians into jail: for the forces unleashed by Hyde were 'bound to develop towards another and more determined fight to throw off the English yoke'.[18] Hyde's collection was equally subversive of native Irish mores and cultural practices.

By far the most popular song in the collection was 'A Óganaigh an Chúil Cheangailte', to which Hyde gave the title 'Ringleted Youth of My Love', which, though 'greatly broken up, and the whole not in it',[19] seemed somehow all the more radiant for being in fragments. As a scholar of bardic poetry, much of which came down only in broken texts, Hyde well knew the experience of such painful remembering, 'the painful putting together of the dismembered past to make sense of the trauma of the present'.[20] That trauma, merely hinted at by Colum, was the denial of sexual choice to many young Irish people of the 1890s. A major reason for the popularity of the Gaelic League was the opportunity it gave to young men and women to mingle freely at weekly meetings and at summer schools conducted in romantic areas along the west of Ireland. The young James Joyce, for instance, despite his coolness towards Gaelic revivalism, attended Gaelic League classes run by Patrick Pearse in hopes of meeting girlfriends; the league refused repeated calls from the Catholic clergy to segregate the sexes in separate classes (arguing that such a move would be so expensive as to bankrupt the organization).[21] Such was the power of the clergy in most towns that only those civil servants who were in the Gaelic League (protected by their government posts from economic threat or boycott) could lead the opposition to this: when one shop assistant in Portarlington did so, he was fired from his job in 1906, following a refusal to apologize to a local priest.

The reading of 'Ringleted Youth of My Love' in this charged context was an exciting challenge, for the made marriage was by the 1890s under full-scale attack by young people:

A ógánaigh an chúil cheangailte
  Le a raibh mé seal i n-éinfheacht
Chuaidh tú 'réir an bealach so
  'S ní tháinig tú do m'fhéachaint.
Shaoil mé nach ndéanfaidhe dochar duit
  Dá dtiucfá, a's mé d'iarraidh,
'S gur b'í do phóigín thabharfadh sólás
  Dá mbeidhinn i lár an fhiabhrais.

A's shaoil mé a stóirín
  Go mbudh gealach agus grian thú,
A's shaoil mé 'nna dhiaigh sin
  Go mbudh sneachta ar an tsliabh thú,
A's shaoil mé 'inna dhiaigh sin
  Go mbudh lóchrann ó Dhia thú
Nó gurab tú an réult-eolais
  Ag dul romham a's mo dhiaigh thú.

Gheall tú síoda is saitin dam
  Callaidhe 's bróga árda,
A's gheall tú tar a éis sin
  Go leanfá tríd an tsnámh mé.
Ní mar sin atá mé
  Acht mo sgeach i mbéal bearna,
Gach nóin a's gach maidin
  Ag féachaint tí m'athar.

Hyde attached a verse translation in parallel text:

Ringleted youth of my love,
  With thy locks bound loosely behind thee,
You passed by the road above
  But you never came in to find me;
Where were the harm for you
  If you came for a little to see me?
Your kiss is a wakening dew
  Were I ever so ill or so dreamy.

I thought, O my love, you were so –
  As the moon is, or sun on a fountain
And I thought after that you were snow,
  The cold snow on top of the mountain;
And I thought after that, you were more

Like God's lamp shining to find me,
Or the bright star of knowledge before
And the star of knowledge behind me.

You promised me high-heeled shoes,
    And satin and silk, my storeen,
And to follow me, never to lose,
    Though the ocean were round us roaring
Like a bush in a gap in a wall
    I am now left lonely without thee,
And this house I grow dead of, is all
    That I see around or about me.[22]

Hyde's immediate object in publishing these songs, first in magazines and then in a book, had been to popularize the study of literature in Irish, and of the Irish language. The translations, though graceful enough, were included for learners, but the demands of fidelity to the original form, along with the rather biblical language ('thee'), can make them seem stilted. Nor are they always literally faithful: the final lines should read, for instance, 'every noon and every morning, looking out on my father's house'. In order to help learners further, Hyde added at the foot of some pages a prose crib. As an example, he offered the following prose version of the first two stanzas above:

O youth of the bound black hair, With whom I was once together. You went by this very last night, And you did not come to see me. I thought no harm would be done you If you were to come and to ask for me, And sure it is your kiss would give comfort, If I were in the midst of a fever.

And I thought, my storeen, That you were the sun and the moon, And I thought, after that, That you were snow on the mountain, And I thought, after that, That you were a lamp from God, Or that you were the star of knowledge Going before me and after me.[23]

These lines struck with the force of a revelation. For W.B. Yeats they were 'as they were to many others, the coming of a new power into literature'.[24] To Augusta Gregory, on reading the volume, came the realization that 'while I had thought poetry was all but dead in Ireland, the people about me had been keeping up the lyrical tradition that existed in Ireland before Chaucer lived'.[25] The lesson both drew from the experience was that the real reason for the poor state of poetry in 1890s Ireland lay in the sudden changeover from one language to another. In Yeats's view, one justification for the revival of Irish was that it might presage a revival of poetry. At the end of the decade he contended that 'the mass of the people cease to understand any poetry when they cease to understand the Irish language, which is the language of their imaginations'.[26]

Hyde's book did lead to the emergence of a strong literature in Irish. Its success emboldened the Gaelic League to move from a policy of mere preservation of the language in areas where it was still spoken to an attempt at its restoration countrywide. It would be hard to overstate the decisive influence of the collection. Michael Cronin in his *Translating Ireland* captures the changing nature of Irish–English translations as practised by Hyde.

> They mark a transition from translation as an act of exegesis to translation as an agent of aesthetic and political renewal. Translations no longer simply bore witness to the past; they were to actively shape a future.[27]

The fact that Hyde ended his Notice to the 1893 edition with the familiar nationalist prayer 'go saoraidh Dia Éire' (may God free Ireland) suggested that 'the political caution of the antiquarians is no longer in evidence'.[28]

Yet, for all its success, Hyde's volume was in some ways self-defeating. Though intended to popularize Irish, it had the effect of making a national literature in English seem all the more plausible. When Yeats praised its 'new power', he at once pointed to the 'prose parts of the book' as the source of that power.[29] In the intermittent prose cribs done in Hiberno-English, Yeats found the literary dialect that might enable a cultural revival, to be conducted in an English that was about as Irish as it would ever be possible for that language to be. The concreteness of image in Hyde's songs did much to dispel the shadowy poetry of the Celtic Twilight, opening the way for a more Irish lucidity in the verse of Yeats and others: and so, in preferring the prose to the poetic translations, Yeats may in fact have been engaging in a sort of auto-critique. The poetic versions have some charm, but even one of Hyde's greatest admirers has conceded that the 'forced rhymes, inversions and poetic diction' are 'out of tune with the simple directness of the originals'.[30]

1893 was Hyde's *annus mirabilis*. By its end he had married his German sweetheart and seen the foundation of the Gaelic League. His speech on deanglicization which underpinned the League's philosophy had ended with a call for 'the use of Anglo-Irish literature instead of English books':[31] so, at the outset, he may not have been

unduly disappointed to see what to him was the least important part
of his collection become the basis for a new literary movement. But
by the next decade, when J.M. Synge and Augusta Gregory were
publishing their masterpieces in Hiberno-English, Hyde was committed to the exclusive promotion of Irish as a living language, and
so the ambiguity of his achievement in *Love Songs of Connacht*
must have become painful. Subsequent literary history was to
emphasize the cruelty of his predicament. In one sense, he was the
leader of the movement to save Irish; in another, he was the first
exponent of the Anglo-Irish literary revival. It was unfortunate for
him that the twenty-year-long campaign to save Irish should have
coincided with the emergence of a group of Irish geniuses destined to
write classics in English. This is not to suggest that any of them
could have written powerfully in Irish (although George Moore did
rather arrogantly assert that, if he had learned Irish, the language
would soon have been restored).

One reason, perhaps, why Moore never made a sustained effort
was his claim that those who translated Irish word-for-word into
English were in any case producing poetry.[32] The claim might have
been excessive, but the deviation of Hiberno-English could seem
poetic to an ear tuned to the standard language. And poetry might be
gained, as well as lost, in the act of translation. A striking example
was the phrase 'réalt eolais' (star of knowledge) from 'A Óganaigh
an Chúil Cheangailte'. This was glossed by Hyde in a Hiberno-
English commentary:

> It is making us understand, it is, that there be's double knowl-
> edge and greatly increased sharp-sightedness to him who is in
> love. The love is like a star, and it is like a star of knowledge on
> account of the way in which it opens up our senses, so that we
> be double more light, more lively and more sharp than we were
> before. We understand then the glory and the beauty of the
> world in a way we never understood it until that.[33]

Thomas MacDonagh remarked that the phrase, almost formulaic in
Irish, becomes 'unexpected and exciting in a strange language of different metaphors and different logic'.[34] He thought many of Hyde's
versions were actually finer than the originals. This led MacDonagh
to advance a thesis that would not have pleased Hyde one bit: he
contended that such translation was natural at that particular
moment of literary history, but once all the emotions already in Irish
had been converted into English, 'this literature will go forward,
free from translation'.[35]

Yet MacDonagh was also the man who insisted that 'all of us find in Irish rather than in English a satisfying understanding of certain ways of ours and the best expression of certain of our emotions. So we are expressing ourselves in translating from the Irish.'[36] He knew that every translator is really a character in search of an author, in whose texts he can identify aspects of his innermost self.

The playwright J.M. Synge had made secret diary entries in Irish to record youthful infatuations with girlfriends;[37] and he proved especially responsive to the 'réalt eolais' image. In the song the beloved is the star of knowledge, but in Synge's *The Playboy of the Western World* the star is an attribute of Pegeen: 'Amn't I after seeing the love-light of the star of knowledge shining from her brow?'[38] Such a use of the image crops up elsewhere in *Love Songs of Connacht*. In 'Teig and Mary' 'a love-spot thou hast on thy brow'[39] is one of many instances in which lovers carry a *ball seirce* (spot of love) on their foreheads. Synge fuses this idea with the star image to brilliant effect, for he replaces the *ball seirce* with the star of knowledge on the beloved's forehead. This newly wrought image is invoked at the climax of the play, when Christy feels betrayed by Pegeen: 'But what did I want crawling forward to scorch my understanding at her flaming brow?'[40] The reference is all the more powerful for being oblique: taking the idea of the brightness of the star, it compounds it with the suggestion of a heat that becomes intolerable if one ventures too close. In the scenes, Christy Mahon resorts to the time-honoured imagery of the uneasy lover in Irish love song.

Writers believe that the test of a good artist is not whether he borrows but how he uses those borrowings. In yet another of his plays, *The Shadow of the Glen*, Synge makes further use of the last lines of 'A Óganaigh an Chúil Cheangailte'. The female speaker complains in Hyde's song that she is left alone on her father's farm like a bush in a gap, but in Synge's play this statement is cleverly and resourcefully deployed by the defiant wife of a cruel dotard, as she spurns another possible partner: 'soon your head'll be the like of a bush where sheep do be leaping a gap'.[41] Because of such skilful alterations, Synge may be called a Gaelic traditionalist, who did not simply emulate but developed classic conventions.

All across the countryside people were still thinking in Irish while using English words: Hyde's prose was, perhaps, the first occasion on which that merging dialect had been committed convincingly to print. London writers of the 1890s routinely lamented the fact that literary English was now enfeebled by cliché, but England's difficulty might once again be Ireland's cultural opportunity, in so far as Hiberno-English seemed more fresh and supple than either of the two standard languages between which it had emerged. By allowing English usage to be drastically disrupted and remoulded by the syntax of Irish, Hyde had helped to effect something like a linguistic revolution. Yeats hoped that writers would learn the lesson and praised Hyde's prose cribs as 'that beautiful English of the country people who remember too much Irish to talk like a newspaper'.[43] In *Samhain*, the theoretical journal of the national theatre, Yeats called for the ratification of that dialect – which, after all, was the language now spoken by most Irish people – through its use in prestigious activities like church sermons, newspaper editorials and university scholarship.[44] However, the people's minds were so conditioned by the prevailing colonial theory that they could understand only the imitation of its Oxbridge language and not the fact that of themselves they had created another.

Some Irish-language purists were among the strongest proponents of standard English and standard Irish, zealously opposing any hybrid growth. In a review of Hyde's collection, Tomás Ó Flannghaile praised the author for his commentaries on the poetic images. He saw the existence of such criticism in the Irish language as a welcome reversal of centuries of ethnocentric anthropology, which had been performed in English on the dying traditions of a Gaelic peasantry:

> To have an Irish commentary on anything will be new to many readers, and it is a pleasant sign of the times. It makes one feel that he is not dealing with dry bones – not moving through the chill corridors of a museum of dead antiquities.

But the same critic was moved almost to apology for the halfway house of Hyde's Hiberno-English prose, all too suspiciously like the lingo of the peasantry:

> And if at times his English has a singular turn, we must remember that the 'Craoibhín' thinks in Irish, and his thoughts therefore, expressed in English, can scarcely help having the picturesque Celtic idiom stamped on them. Considering the determined and persistent efforts adopted to make us all English, body and soul, it is a proof of Celtic tenacity to find Irish ideas still flourishing so vigorously in Ireland, and the expression of them so purely Irish.[45]

There is a manic quality to the lust for a national essence in the final sentence. Those who insisted most loudly on extirpating all traces of Englishness from Irish identity were often the very ones who sought an exact native equivalent for each defining element of Anglo-Saxon culture, standard English being top of the list. For them, no matter how admirable Hyde's project might seem, his way of working was dangerous. Ó Flannghaile, for instance, regretted the decision to print incomplete versions of the songs in all their brokenness, rather than attempting 'to restore these lyrics to their original simplicity and consistency'.[46]

Synge brought *Love Songs of Connacht* on visits to the Aran Islands, where he was able to note the similarity between Hyde's prose commentaries and the sort of English spoken by recent learners of that language. He noticed also that the islanders' versions of some songs differed from Hyde's.[47] What struck him most, however, was what had already amazed Carleton: the fact that the people were themselves already consummate self-translators and, as such, healthily critical of the translations produced by others. One old sailor confided to Synge that Archbishop MacHale's Irish-language versions of Moore's *Melodies* were unsatisfactory and he offered his own alternatives, based on his contention that 'a translation is no translation unless it will give you the music of the poem along with the words of it'.[48] In similar fashion, Synge's young friend Michael objected to the phrase 'gold chair' when, he said, 'golden chair' would be much nicer.[49]

Synge's own translations were based on methods very like Hyde's. Because he was still learning Irish on Aran, he translated with a word-for-word literalism, much as the islanders themselves were doing. He was well aware that previous translators during the nineteenth century had found some compound words untranslatable in a word or two. Undaunted, he tried to capture the music along with the words, without adding anything. The Hiberno-English emerged in the work of Synge and Hyde as a consequence of hearing the dialect spoken, but also as a result of their exercises in translation. Even Hyde's analytic commentaries contain elements of it: 'it is not in Munster alone it is' with the use of 'it is' to emphasize the words immediately following; the use of 'and' for 'when' as in 'and hard and ruined melancholy upon them'; the employment of alliterated double words, as in 'mixed up and mingled with other bad verses'; 'in it long ago' for 'living long ago'; and so on.[50]

The problem with most translations before Hyde had been obvious: the foolish attempt to translate the concrete, homely idioms of Irish into the false 'gentility' derided by Ferguson. Like most translations from a minor into an imperial language, these had proceeded from a bad premise, attempting to convert Irish into English rather than allowing English to be massively remoulded by the source language. In *Die Krisis der europäischen Kultur*, Rudolf Pannwitz diagnosed: 'The basic error of the translator is that he preserves the state in which his own language happens to be instead of allowing it to be powerfully affected by the foreign tongue.'[51] Hyde's claim to have 'courageously', if 'ruggedly', reproduced Irish idiom is a recognition that the songs of country people should never have been put into well-bred Tennysonian metrics.

Hyde had found a way of deterritorializing Irish and English, by freeing each from their traditional lineage in a zone where old contents and forms separated and regrouped. Irish and English burrowed into, as well as borrowed from, each other, as an orchid is possessed by the bee which it also possesses, leading to 'the capture of a fragment of the code and not the reproduction of an image'.[52] Neither Irish nor English is ratified by this becoming, which is so different from earlier nineteenth-century translations: both codes are disrupted, as English gets turned into Irish in all but words. Synge's own *The Playboy of the Western World* might even be seen as a comic version of the process, with its attack on all fatherly codes and its demonstration of how a 'dying' Irish can strongly remodel the English language, even as the dead Old Mahon revives and catches up with his son. Hyde's example had shown just how necessary it was to open up new, unofficial routes into language.

Synge agreed. Reviewing A.H. Leahy's *Heroic Romances of Ireland* in 1905, he suggested that, although a literal prose version can sometimes be unattractive, the odds against a verse translation of poetry were even greater: 'it may be doubted whether . . . almost the whole mass of English translations, from the time of Pope down, is not a dreary and disheartening exhibition of useless ingenuity which has produced hardly anything of interest for those who care most about poetry'.[53] The problem was the anxiety of influence: the voices of predecessor poets tended to infiltrate versions in English, drowning out the impulses from the original. Gaelic poetry, said Synge, is full of individuality and charm, but 'there is probably no mass of tawdry commonplace jingle quite so worthless as the verse translations that have been made from it in Ireland during the last century'.[54] Yeats concurred, complaining that the worst carriers of the virus were the Young Ireland poets, who borrowed English forms to sing of Irish wrongs. Their technical problem was akin to that of Carleton's peasantry caught in the no-man's-land between two languages: 'Their work was never wholly satisfactory, for what was

Irish in it looked ungainly in an English garb and what was English
was never perfectly mastered, never wholly absorbed into their
being.'[55]

Strong though that denunciation might seem – and it must be
remembered that Yeats was repenting of a youthful enthusiasm – it
was mild when compared with Ferguson's put-down of Hardiman.
His translations were 'actuated by a morbid desire, neither healthy
nor honest, to elevate the tone of the originals to a pitch of refined
poetic art altogether foreign to the whole genius and rationale of its
composition'.[56] It would have been better to have stayed faithful to
'the poetic fact of the original'.[57] Over seven decades later, Synge felt
compelled to repeat the stricture, treating Leahy's pastiche as a
deplorable misrepresentation of the concrete charm of the old verses.
To explain the point, he cited Hyde: 'Those who know no Irish can
get some idea what Gaelic poetry has suffered in this kind of treatment by comparing the beautiful prose translations which Dr
Douglas Hyde wrote of the *Love Songs of Connacht* with the verse
translations – in themselves often pleasing enough – which he put in
the same volume.'[58]

Both Hyde and Synge had a genius for translation, working most
finely in the manoeuvre between two languages. Their own poems in
English seem wan imitations of favoured Victorian modes, whereas
their brilliant versions – whether of Irish or some other language –
convey a real sense of the men themselves. In that sense, there is a
Nineties quality to their writing, based on the Wildean notion that
man is never himself except when speaking through a mask. That is
why the translator really is a character in search of an author, even if
that author is Anon., the voice of folk tradition. There may, of
course, be an element of blood-sucking about such transactions, a
possibility not lost on James Joyce who vampirized one of the most
beautiful lyrics in Hyde's collection, which is to say that he identified
the Nineties mode into which the scholar had cast his version. In the
third section of *Ulysses*, Stephen Dedalus composes a poem which is
a parody of 'My Grief on the Sea':

> Here. Put a pin in that chap, will you? My tablets. Mouth to
> her kiss. No. Must be two of 'em. Give 'em well. Mouth to her
> mouth's kiss.[59]

Only five sections later is the resulting poem exposed:

> *On swift sail flaming*
> *From storm and south*

He comes, pale vampire,
Mouth to my mouth.[60]

The speaker, as in Hyde's poem, must be female; the implication is that the four lines scarcely justify the immense theoretical framework of the 'Proteus' episode that gave rise to them.

Perhaps Joyce is mocking the derivative nature of Stephen's little lyric, but he is more likely suggesting that translation from the Irish is a vampiric act. If the potency of Hiberno-English derived in great part from the imminent death of Irish, then it was a feeder off corpses: and the 'deader' Irish became, the more vibrant Hiberno-English would seem. But, then, some feeding may be more parasitic than other kinds. In the 'Scylla and Charybdis' chapter of *Ulysses*, Joyce parodies the version of a bardic *deibhidhe* metre (seven syllables in a line ending in a word of one syllable: then seven syllables in a line that ends on a word of two syllables) with which Hyde concluded *The Story of Early Gaelic Literature* in 1894:

Bound thee forth, my booklet, quick
To greet the callous public.
Writ, I ween, 'twas not my wish
In lean unlovely English.[61]

In the chapter, a Gaelic enthusiast named Haines is reportedly keen to buy *Love Songs of Connacht*, provoking some derision in the cosmopolitan John Eglinton: 'The peatsmoke is going to his head.' However, the mystic poet George Russell suggests that 'people do not know how dangerous lovesongs can be. The movements which work revolutions in the world are born out of the dreams and visions in a peasant's hearth on the hillside.'[62] This may not be as parodic as it might seem: Joyce's own love song was, after all, sung to a woman from Connacht.

The original song that gave rise to all this commentary majestically survives parody and remoulding, because of its integrity of form and language. An old woman named Biddy Crummy, who lived on a Roscommon bog, gave Hyde this miraculous lyric:

Mo bhrón ar an bhairrge
  Is é atá mór,
Is é gabháil idir mé
  'S mo mhíle stór.

D'fhágadh 'san mbaile mé

Déunamh bróin,
Gan aon tsúil tar sáile liom
Choidhche ná go deo.

Mo léan nach bhfuil mise
'Gus mo mhúirnín bhán
I gCúige Laighean
Nó i gcondae an Chláir.

Mo léan nach bhfuil mise
'Gus mo mhíle grádh
Air bord loinge
Triall go 'mericá.

Leabuidh luachra
Bhí fúm aréir,
Agus chaith mé amach é
Le teas an lae.

Tháinig mo ghrádh-sa
Le mo thaebh
Guala ar ghualain
Agus béul air bhéul.[63]

Even in English the lines capture the rhythm of seawaves beating
sobs of sorrow out upon the shore:

My grief on the sea,
How the waves of it roll:
For they have come between me
And the love of my soul.

Abandoned, forsaken,
To grief and to care,
Will the sea ever waken
Relief from despair?

My grief and my trouble.
Would he and I were
In the province of Leinster
Or county of Clare.

Were I and my darling –
Oh, heart-bitter wound –
On board of the ship
For America bound.

> On a green bed of rushes
>   All last night I lay,
> And I flung it abroad
>   With the heat of the day.
>
> And my love came behind me –
>   He came from the South;
> His breast to my bosom,
>   His mouth to my mouth.

Hyde first encountered this piece in 1871, and all versions subsequently heard were from the lips of women. Yeats praised the lyric for closing the gap between art and life. 'Sheer hope and fear, joy and sorrow, made the poems', he wrote in *The Bookman* of October 1893, 'and not any mortal man or woman.'[64] After an age of specialization, in which the well-springs of art had been removed from life, he was yearning for a moment when the sources of an art, neither literary nor knowing, might again be found within the community . . . and the community might be a place where every man and woman could be an artist. Yeats was less interested in a specialist caste of seers than in awakening every man and woman to the potential artist within themselves. On that understanding, he infused his own ballads with the impersonal authority of folk tradition. Once, when walking with Hyde past a field in which haymakers were singing one of the scholar's songs, he was filled with the desire to see his own words pass into popular lore.[65]

In saluting the naturalness of the songs, however, Yeats may have underestimated the conscious artistry of those who created them. The proliferation of variants has left scholars disinclined to submit them to formal analysis, yet 'Mo Bhrón ar an bhFairrge' has a Blakean beauty of clarified structure. Its theme is the separation caused by emigration after the Famine: a girl laments the leaving of her lover for America. The immensity of the ocean that divides them is evoked, along with the bleak realization that she will get no call to join him. All she is left with is the power of her imagination to transcend time and space by wish-fulfilment: and so the speaker reduces the appalling distances to more manageable ones, imagining herself in holiday locations of Ireland or aboard ship with him bound for America. Then comes a sort of reverse *aisling* vision, in which a male appears to a female dreamer, who sleeps on a green bed of rushes, taking her by surprise from behind, before the kiss of homecoming. There is, however, a note of dismissal, even before the kiss is re-enacted, in the words 'chaith mé amach é' (I flung it abroad), as if the speaker knows that this is all impossible fantasy. For, utterly unlike the *aisling*, this male is no deliverer but an abandoner, travelling not closer but further and further away. The theme of frustrated love may connect, of course, with a wider set of resentments about those who emigrated after the Famine, leaving the country not just eerily silent but devoid of youthful hope: Maud Gonne would go so far as to accuse such emigrants of national apostasy.[66]

The singer of 'Mo Bhrón ar an bhFairrge' may be imagining a more liberal sexuality of pre-Famine days. A restoration of the older code would not only bridge the chasm in time, but also throw the new system of land inheritance based on primogeniture into question. Since the songs were communal, they assumed a common ownership of culture and land. Like many drinking songs, the love songs captured the carnivalesque and vernacular energies of older communities. The young clerks and shopgirls of the Gaelic League who sang them at early performances of the Irish Literary Theatre, to the astonishment of Synge, were reconnecting with those energies, so different from those on display at the Gaiety or Olympia theatres, whose audiences came to listen passively to stage professionals. The communal singing at the Literary Theatre carried the promise of a restored community . . . not the willed, abstracted nation of Davis's balladry, but the concrete solidarity of bodies pressed together in the auditorium of a national theatre, sharing the same structure of feeling. Synge reported this for a French audience: 'On venait de sentir flotter un instant dans la salle l'âme d'un peuple' (One could sense for an instant in the chamber the soul of a people).[67]

Synge learned that evening about the collaboration that might link author, actor and audience into a continuum. One of the plays was Hyde's *Casadh an tSúgáin* (The Twisting of the Rope). This dramatized one of the Connacht songs concerning a sweet-talking poet named Hanrahan, who beguiles the girls of a village before being expelled by a trick. The women have him twist a hayrope, which grows so long that he must walk out the door, but then it is closed in his face. The playlet gave 'a new direction and impulse to Irish Drama',[68] said Synge, with its idea 'of poet expelled by people'.[69] His own dramas would develop the concept at greater length. Augusta Gregory would also make much use of the theme, publishing a song-version of Hyde's playlet in her *Poets and Dreamers*. Yeats's Red Hanrahan also derived from Hyde's song and story.

Love Songs of Connacht as a publication was based on the same philosophy of 'self-help' that animated other Irish organizations after the Parnell tragedy. As the Gaelic League sought to promote Irish industry with the first St Patrick's Day parades, Hyde urged his readers to contact the publisher, Gill, with promises to buy further editions. The regional emphasis on Connacht was itself in keeping with the growth of local government and local pride in a decade that had, once again, seen the nationalist narrative stutter to a halt. If Cromwell had notoriously told his victims to go to Hell or to Connacht, here was the cultural antidote: the western province announced itself as the repository of all energies which the puritan imagination had failed to tame. John O'Daly had published, decades earlier, *Songs of the Munster Bards*, but Hyde wanted to stake a claim for Connacht, since there was as yet no standardized language. The growth of the rail system had heightened awareness of regional identities. While Munster by the 1890s was seen as the home of strong-farmer nationalists, the poorer land of Connacht had produced a more marginal but subversive ideology, less affected by English structures of thought.

Hyde's collection was an attempt to wrest Gaelic culture from the conformism threatening to overtake it. Much of the mainland had been so anglicized that what passed for a Gaelic revival was no more than a translation of Victorian values into the Irish language (the Munsterman, Fr Peter O'Leary and his conservative supporters being prime carriers of such attitudes). The pre-Famine past and the strong Celtic woman might flash forth in the 1890s to radical effect. Hyde's book subverted everything – and, ultimately, the intentions of its own author.

The 1890s was the decade of crusading journalism against university elites, the era when the notion of adult education took hold. The Gaelic League was at the forefront. *Love Songs of Connacht* was no exercise in academic anthropology with an eye on an English readership, but an act of popular reconnection. If the Famine had constituted a challenge to sexual energy and the life-force itself, this was some sort of response. But the period of high idealism in 1893 and after was brief enough. By 1907, some Gaelic Leaguers were leaders of the protest against Synge's *Playboy of the Western World*, objecting in particular to the allegedly salacious and titillating nature of love scenes (whose images and ideas were drawn, it turned out, from Hyde's collection). Many reasons have been adduced for the *Playboy* riots, and Synge's mockery of Celtic notions of heroism would feature on most lists, but one unconscious cause never mentioned might be the fact that his play demonstrated the viability of Hyde's material, and therefore of a national literature, in English. By 1907 Hyde and his followers no longer believed that a national literature in English could ever be enough. Hyde told Augusta Gregory that he would prefer to write one good verse in Irish than a whole book in English.[70] He had shown that

Hiberno-English could be put to higher uses than the farcical, but his aim was to make Irish again a living literary language. Yet Hiberno-English was, if anything, under as great a threat as Irish. Synge was right to see *Love Songs of Connacht* as a breakthrough towards 'a nearer appreciation of the country people'[71] and their idiom: but these people would soon purge their speech of localisms and Gaelic traces in the drive towards respectability. The landless labourers who spoke the dialect without shame would be the very ones transplanted to London and Boston, while the larger farmers who survived educated their children in standard English.

Catholic priests, especially the 'young dandies' who graduated from Maynooth, were mostly the sons of strong farmers and so a major force for anglicization and embourgeoisification. In that context, Hyde's keenness to pack Gaelic League platforms with priests who spoke Irish was his way of attaching to the language the prestige of men of the cloth. It was also his method of counteracting the 'Victorian Gael' within Catholicism itself,[72] by appealing to a more popular church of local saints and holy wells. As in Latin America today, there were two versions of Catholicism – a 'modernizing' but theologically conservative ecclesiocracy which had in the main turned its back on Irish, and a popular but theologically radical church which still honoured folk tradition.

The spread of literacy in English had brought with it a promotion of the conservative values of the ecclesiocrats, with women in particular being encouraged to defer to Victorian codes. The numbers of women at work dropped through the later nineteenth century, and daughters came to rely on dowries offered by elderly fathers for approved marriages. The historian Joseph Lee has observed:

> As the Irish language declined, however, and Gaelic values were eroded, prudery seeped through Irish society, and came close to being equated with morality itself. The physical realism of Irish love poems as late as the eighteenth century, for instance, was notably absent from the sentimental slush that passed as love songs in English in post-Famine Ireland. Indeed, the clergies in Ireland improved on the English model. The poorer classes in Britain generally rejected middle-class morality. The Protestant poor may have rejected it to a certain extent in Belfast also. But in the rest of Ireland the clergies captured the lower orders among their congregations for the farmers' values.[73]

Love Songs of Connacht was an attempt to recruit the forces of literacy to underwrite the more radical, oral culture of pre-Famine

Ireland. Hyde, whether he quite knew it or not, was waging a war of position: and the debate internal to the Gaelic movement was far more robust than that conducted with outside groups.

The Irish-Ireland element within the national movement soon became as suspicious of translation as of Hiberno-English. The latter was denounced as a halfway house between English and Irish, and many priests contended that Gaelic ideas just could not be expressed in so unsympathetic a medium as English. They feared that purity of diction and thought would be lost in a situation of uncontrollable translation and retranslation. The gender-bending in Synge's *Playboy of the Western World*, which featured manly women and womanly men, distressed many nationalists. It may also have been taken as a metaphor for the endless 'crossover' of English and Irish verbal energies in unconditioned cross-fertilization. Once unleashed, the urge to translate was unstoppable, a form of polymorphous perversity to some, as when George Moore planned to write a play on Diarmuid and Gráinne in French, have Tadhg Ó Donnchadha translate that into Irish, and Augusta Gregory then put it into English. Hyde, by his female impersonations, had merely started a fashion, which would flourish again in the Crazy Jane poems of Yeats, the Molly Bloom monologue of Joyce, and the speeches by Winnie in Beckett's *Happy Days*. The fact that Synge's plays translated easily and persuasively back into Irish simply added to the sense that they amounted to a subversion of all attempts to impose a single code of language or gender as official. If the Victorian Gael was devoted to an ideal of hypermasculinity in an undefiled ancestral Irish language, Synge's celebration of androgyny disrupted that agenda: but only in ways that Hyde's collection had already done.

By offering readers three texts of some lyrics, Hyde effectively removed the claims of any one to absolute centrality, enacting in this way the estrangement of the nineteenth-century Irish from all official languages. He also drew attention to the need for self-translation among a people, so that inherited language and texts are made even more fully their own. He believed that it was more crucial to translate than to interpret past moments and texts, so that they might combine with present ones, renewing lost potentials of their own and releasing new energies in the here and now. He was less interested in understanding the songs in their lost original contexts than in releasing their powers in the current context he knew so well.

The rediscovery of the love songs might be taken as a feat of involuntary memory, triggered by associative mechanisms. Yet the past so revived remained strange even to Hyde, who rendered that sense of its foreignness in the very literal-mindedness of his prose versions. As Friedrich Schleiermacher has written of a similar sort of myopic translation:

> The attempt seems to be the most extraordinary form of humil-
> iation that a writer, who is not a bad writer, could inflict upon
> himself . . . for who would gladly consent to be considered
> inept by studiously keeping us as close to the foreign language
> as his own language permits, and to be blamed, like those par-
> ents who place their children in the hands of acrobats, for
> putting his mother tongue through foreign and unnatural con-
> tortions instead of exercising it skilfully in the gymnastics of his
> own language?[74]

Hyde had little compunction about putting a mother tongue like English to such elastic usage, for in his case the disruptive 'foreign' tongue was his native Irish. The more foreign Hiberno-English could be made to seem, the more likely he felt it that some day he and his followers might break for home. Hyde was one of the first of the Revival generation to realize that only radical gestures of subversion and defiance could protect and restore elements of Gaelic tradition. He was, to that extent, another Tory Anarchist, another innovative traditionalist.

19

Anarchist Attitudes: Oscar Wilde

The Wilde family were social anthropologists by nature. If Sir William did his research among the dúns of Aran, his famous son studied a rather different set of prehistoric ruins, the English upper classes. Oscar Wilde anatomized his host society with its own favoured instrument, the Higher Criticism. He employed figures drawn from that class as *dramatis personae* in his attempt to imagine a utopian community, much as Synge would use the peasants of the Aran Islands a few years later. Synge is rightly praised for exposing himself to poverty and physical hardship, but Wilde was also a broker in risk, attempting to sketch the lineaments of an ideal society out of such unpromising materials. Both men were in flight from the chloroformed world of Protestant Dublin's professional classes; but in the course of their paths through utopia they discovered some surprising affinities between the Irish peasantry and the English aristocracy – a love of leisure, a heightened sensitivity to the promises of language, a belief in beauty above utility, a sense that there is always plenty of time.

The drawing-room figures of Wilde's drama are really the shaughrauns and rogues of nineteenth-century Irish writing brought indoors and civilized: and the play is the zone where the values of the old Gaelic and modern English aristocracies meet. What is under attack in both literatures is the imaginative narrowness of the new middle class. For the exponents of 'lying', wickedness is just another myth concocted by puritans to account for the curious attractiveness of others.

If medieval tyrants had the rack, the puritan bullies of the nine-teenth century employed the press to enforce conformism. By documenting its collective follies with such clarity in print, that middle class made Wilde's work so much easier: 'by giving us the opinions of the uneducated, it keeps us in touch with the ignorance of the community'.[1] His own witticisms are often no more than 'the inversion of the language of the press', a way of annoying the newly literate public.[2] His counter-aphorisms ('all bad art springs from genuine feeling') are mockeries of English sincerity made in an oral style that wars on the decorum of the merely writerly.

One example of this false decorum was the manner in which fairy tales had been transformed, within a couple of generations, from a subversive, underground, largely oral lore directed at adults to sen-timental, overground, printed narratives aimed at the moral improvement of Victorian children. Wilde's fairytales are intended, perhaps mainly, for adults – but for children too. He had heard some of them from poor women, patients of his father in the Dublin sur-gery: unable to pay in cash, they offered a good story instead.[3] What the tales have in common is a strong sense of the subversive nature of the story of Jesus, especially when taken literally by children. The equation of the Irishman with the child in Victorian thinking was based on the fear of the inner child within many adult males. It was this that had led to a ferocious disciplining of their offspring.

Nobody in Ireland has ever accused Wilde of plagiarizing stories like 'The Happy Prince', 'The Selfish Giant' or 'The Fisherman and His Soul', in the same way that English critics have routinely accused him of pilfering plots and dramatic devices. And for good reason. A moral code that enjoins that possessions be given Christlike to the poor is hardly in a position to issue such a rebuke. For Wilde, ideas and plots were made to do the rounds. As a believer in oral culture, Wilde thought of art as the individual enunciation of a collectively owned set of narratives.[4] He cheerfully offered his own plots to others in the knowledge that he had no originary claim on any of them: and, as a student of Proudhon, he supported the contention that all property is theft.

His own quips and paradoxes have become part of the folklore of modernity, being repeated in conversation or printed on calendars without attribution. By a somewhat similar process, his children's stories – first tested on his own young sons – have re-entered the Irish tradition through the astonishingly similar childhood parables of Patrick Pearse. Pearse's story 'Íosagán' has obvious roots in 'The Selfish Giant', with its idea of a Christ-child bearing redemptive mes-sages to a fallen adult world. Indeed, it would not be fanciful to suggest that the *mentalité* which lay behind the Easter Rising of 1916 – that he who loses life will save it by a Christlike combination of goodness and social rebellion – is traceable to this thinking. Pearse was hardly the only rebel who had been moved by the tales of Oscar Wilde, which saw in Jesus a conflation of artist and rebel, scapegoat and scapegrace.[5]

For all their differences of temperament, Wilde and Pearse shared something very fundamental with artists such as Synge and Joyce: a conviction that the modern world was a conspiracy against the individual. Wilde put it best:

> Most people are other people. Their thoughts are someone else's opinions, their life a mimicry, their passions a quotation. Christ was not merely the supreme Individualist, but he was the first in History.[6]

The possibilities opened up by Jesus were now being destroyed by public opinion. A frustration with that process explains the strange blend of cultural traditionalism and social radicalism in Irish modernism. Because they were committed to the expressive freedom of the individual, the artists drew upon more ancient traditions in their war upon the mass-produced philistines of the new bourgeoisie. Yeats loved old tales of kings and queens, and even Joyce spoke of a desire to enter 'the fair courts of life'.[7] They were all types of the radical dandy, so radical, in fact, that they could not countenance conventional Victorian ideas of progress. The Famine had made such glib beliefs impossible. Cyril Connolly succinctly revealed their dilemma as 'that of the revolutionary whose manners and way of life are attached to the old regime, whose ideals and loyalties belong to the new, and who by a kind of courageous exhibitionism is impelled to tell the truth about both'.[8]

The radical dandies donned the mask of the bohemian, deploying their witticisms as a wedge against national chauvinism, racial prejudice and, ultimately, the very forces of the literary market itself. Wilde always said that he would favour the social system most hospitable to art: but soon he despaired of the aristocracy. In his eyes, the dandies of the 1890s were the only real aristocrats left and, like the *filí* faced with the collapse of their bardic patrons, had no choice but to sell their wares (with appropriate irony) on the open market.[9] Just like the *filí*, Wilde soon began to denounce a pusillanimous aristocracy no longer committed to a defence of artistic standards. He lashed them hard.

It was inevitable that such a complex set of impulses would lead the more intrepid artists towards anarchism. Yeats said that, although no gentleman could be a socialist, he might be an anarchist.[10] The young Joyce immersed himself in the writings of Italian and Russian anarchists.[11] Synge attended the lectures of Sebastian Fauré in Paris, his initial ambivalence ('trés interessant, mais fou')[12] giving way to an enthusiasm discernible in every section of *The Aran Islands*. But Wilde's involvement was arguably the deepest of all.

Anarchism attracted because of its denial of the state. After the Act of Union, for most of the nineteenth century the Irish had been compelled by the power of the British state to live like an underground movement in their own country: and well Wilde knew it, for his own mother had had many brushes with the despised law, not least after her 'call to arms' on behalf of the Young Irelanders in 1848. The shock tactics used by anarchists in exposing the conflicted nature of authority appealed greatly to a dandy like Wilde, who said that 'the form of government that is most suitable to the artist is no government at all'.[13] This put him at odds with the Fabians, for they believed in the state as the deliverer of social democracy and gradual reform. They also opposed the doctrine of workers' revolt, but in Wilde's eyes civil disobedience was the first social virtue. He did not accept Marx's theory that social change would bring about a transformation in persons. Rather, he contended, all change must begin with the individual, and the role of art in such a transformation was crucial.[14]

These ideas were outlined in a long essay, 'The Soul of Man under Socialism', published in the *Fortnightly Review* of 1891, just three years after a translation of the *Communist Manifesto* had become widely available in England. Its flippant tone dismayed orthodox socialists, and Friedrich Engels pooh-poohed a socialism that 'has actually donned evening dress and lounges lazily on drawing-room *caseuses*'.[15] That sentence is a perfect description of Wilde's tactic of bringing the shaughraun figure into a high-society setting, but it utterly misunderstands the underlying motive.

Such debates on the far left interested only a minority. The main effect of the publication was 'to create feeling against Wilde among the influential and moneyed classes'.[16] They took some consolation from the flippant tone, but smarter readers knew from the outset that this was one of the dandy's techniques: 'the pleasure of astonishing and the proud satisfaction of never being astonished'.[17] Wilde was Exhibit A, the living proof of a system which would encourage every person to become an artist: and he was never more serious than when he was most flippant, for he knew that there was something of heroism in being sufficiently master of oneself to be always witty. For

him, the great evil of Victorian society was its remorseless specialization of realms. Under its dispensation a few privileged souls were
allowed to develop their individuality to an extreme degree, as poets,
artists, scientists or governors, while everyone else suffered as wage-
slaves, living a life just short of starvation. Now, the problem of
slavery was being addressed in a mass culture by the foolish remedy
of amusing the slaves. The old Roman palliative of bread and cir-
cuses had found a modern counterpart in the Society of the
Spectacle.[18]

The real remedy was to hand. Machines could be the new slaves,
freeing persons to perfect themselves as individual works of art. This
self-perfection is the goal of all of Wilde's artistic creations. Dorian
Gray stands before his picture in a locked room in search of such
integrity, a spectator of his own selfhood. Such figures might seem
smug, yet they represent an Eastern ideal found by Wilde in the writings of Chuang Tsu.[19] Shaw might scoff at the quietism of Eastern
philosophy, but Wilde dedicated himself to uncovering an Eastern
undertow in Western religious thought. He had always read Saint
Augustine's *De Civitate Dei* as a description of an ideal state, free of
governmental coercion, in which all were at liberty to enjoy the
pleasures of holiness without stint. Likewise, his Christ is the very
reverse of a Victorian do-gooder: when he advises a young man to
give to the destitute, 'it is not of the state of the poor that he is
thinking but of the soul of the young man'.[20] Under Wilde's
Christian scheme, there will be no contradiction between helping
the poor and becoming oneself: to do one will be to do the other.

Socialists and anarchists have always held that private charity can
be no substitute for organized justice. As long as unequal relations
based on private property persisted, charity would degrade both the
giver and receiver. In such a system of savage inequality, the only
immoral thing would be to remain acquiescent. If people revolted
against industrial tyrannies, they would restore personal affection in
place of contractual relationships, and personal pleasure would again
become a shared social experience. William Morris had said that
man 'must begin to build up the ornamental part of life – its pleasures, bodily and mental, scientific and artistic, social and
individual',[21] to such a point that art would be merely the expression
of a person's joy in labour.

Wilde agreed, arguing that men should be free to choose their
work, which might then take on the creative character of play. Both
he and Morris insisted that, far from deferring to public taste, artists
should hold forth higher ideals, towards which people would
inevitably subscribe once the cult of pleasure and the love of beauty

had been restored as replacements for utilitarian values. If all were lovers of beauty a poor, squalid being would be obnoxious, an unbearable rebuke to all who met him: and all would know what to do, if only out of self-interest. 'Living for others' in acts of programmatic charity was no way to create a society of Chuang Tsus and Augustines. It was ignoble because it assumed that egotism was man's natural condition (Mathew Arnold's 'doing as one likes'), and that it could be transcended only by woeful self-discipline. At its centre was a wholly Protestant gloom about one's natural instincts, but Wilde sought to counter this bleak, mechanistic philosophy with a world in which all shared a good life, whose primary basis was the imagination rather than political activity. To make men socialists would be no achievement if one form of coercion was replaced by another, but to make socialism human would be a real breakthrough. Then a false egotism (each person marooned in the prison of seemingly selfish desires) would make way for a true individualism (by which personal pleasure became socially available). 'I hope', says Gwendolen to Jack in *The Importance of Being Earnest*, 'you will always look at me just like that, especially when there are other people present.'[22]

The figure in whom Eastern serenity and Western kindness were reconciled was the Jesus of the Middle East: but Wilde could find such blending also in an anarchist like Peter Kropotkin, 'a man with the soul of that beautiful white Christ that seems coming out of Russia'.[23] Jesus, however, was the ultimate rebel against tyranny over body, soul and mind. His insurrectionary programme had been without precedent. The Christ whom Wilde celebrates is the rather Catholic mystic of Ernest Renan, a true artist rather than the breaker of false images beloved by Protestants. Less a didact than guru, he was not a model for imitation so much as an example of self-becoming. His soul scarcely existed apart from his senses. Wilde's is the outcast Christ celebrated in the popular spirituality of the rural Irish tales and proverbs heard from peasants in Wilde's youth.[24]

James Joyce interpreted Wilde's apparent conversion to Catholicism as 'the repudiation of his wild doctrine',[25] but that is hardly true. Wilde had always been something of a cultural Catholic. If there is one element of his art that is even more subversive of late-Victorian London culture than his anarchism, that may well be his ever-strengthening Catholicism. He had, of course, considered converting in his Oxford days, at a time when the bells-and-smells wing of Anglicanism was becoming interested in the seemingly richer store of imagery and ritual of the Catholics. To his English contemporaries, that may have seemed like a way of embarrassing parents, but to an Irishman it was a serious act of solidarity with a peasant people who had endured poverty and death rather than worship a God in whom they could not believe.[26] Wilde was struck out of his half-brother's will and said to a friend: 'you see I suffer good deal from my Romish leanings, in pocket and mind'[27] – for his punisher was deeply intolerant of such tendencies. His forbearance may have been connected with the recollection of being brought as a four-year-old boy by his mother for a second baptism at the Catholic church in Glencree, County Wicklow. (The desire for second baptism voiced by a character in *The Importance of Being Earnest* may have arisen from that experience.) Lady Wilde had taught her children to admire the Catholic Church, which was the major patron of the arts in Victorian Ireland. Oscar never forgot their attendance at masses in Glencree, and its affinities with classic drama inspired him: 'it is always a source of pleasure and awe to me to remember that the ultimate survival of the Greek chorus, lost elsewhere to art, is to be found in the servitor answering the priest at mass'.[28] At Trinity, his classics teacher J.P. Mahaffy tried to distract Wilde from Romish involvements with the seductive alternative of pagan Greece, ignoring the obvious fact that the pupil's paganism 'merely reinforced his attraction to the sensual elements of Catholicism'.[29]

Although Catholics had been emancipated in England for most of the nineteenth century, they found it very hard to penetrate such core institutions as the law, the military and the police. As with the Jews, there was an unspoken implication that they were not fully integrable to the progress of the English middle class, their ultimate allegiance being imagined to be to a transnational force. This was especially true of Catholics with an Irish background: the invention of the 'Celt' as a category to account for Irish unreliability was consolidated after emancipation in 1829, when Catholicism could no longer be openly invoked to explain aberrant behaviour and when racial theories became ever more fashionable.

The young poetic rebels of the Rhymers' Club (a group that met through the 1890s in the Cheshire Cheese pub off Fleet Street) expressed their distrust of the ruling Protestant ideology and their commitment to beauty. The culture of 'manliness' had created intolerable pressures for many sensitive men, who responded with spectacular conversions to Catholicism. Its communal rituals seemed also to heal the awesome loneliness of Protestant self-election. Such conversions were even more subversive of the social consensus than was Catholicism itself: the word 'pervert', for example, had been used of converts to Catholicism long before it was applied to homosexual persons (though, of course, as far back as Edmund Burke, the implied equation between Catholicism and homosexuality had been effected by those keen to break Irish careers in England). Wilde's cultural Catholicism was, therefore, an aspect of his subversion: and he shared Arnold's belief that sooner or later every decent English person must recognize the honorary Celt within himself.

For many intellectuals, Catholicism had the lure of forbidden fruit. Even the books of Cardinal Newman (the most famous convert of all) carried in their sinuous prose a *frisson* which Wilde openly acknowledged. The fear that secret agents in the Catholic interest might stealthily insert themselves into the social and political process was widespread: and the not-very-hidden Catholicism of Wilde's fairy tales might seem an inspired example of such programming, since it was aimed (at least in part) at a deeply susceptible audience – young children.[30] Wilde had once mocked his adult readers by saying to them, 'you give the criminal calendar of Europe to your children under the name of history': but his stories, with their strange blending of Irish and Oriental settings, might function as an antidote.[31]

He was, after all, concerned with the human soul. The implied conflict between 'soul' and 'socialism' in the title of his essay is dissolved in its actual argument. The Christlike figures of his children's stories embrace poverty, shame and social ostracism (as if their author foresaw his own final tragedy). There is a martyr cult at work here, somewhat reminiscent of Saint Sebastian, whose story always haunted Wilde. For him the only way to get rid of a temptation was to yield to it. If Protestantism seemed to repress impulse by the power of its spiritual disciplines, Catholicism might allow a person to act them out in a different kind of moral tale. The zones of Protestantism were the zones of common sense: its adherents had a sturdy distrust of surface ornament, whereas Wilde believed that only shallow people do not judge by appearances. Catholicism had multiple attractions for a Tory Anarchist, appealing at once to his love of gorgeous traditions and to his belief in rebellion. The Catholic Irish, in remaining true to the faith of their fathers, had attained the glamour of the outlaw in his eyes. In this he agreed with John Henry Newman, who defended the moral right of the Irish to rebel, if only to uphold their traditions.[32] In the case of England, Newman said that Catholics would be justified in telling 'moral lies' in defence of their faith. Charles Kingsley accused him of assuming a 'style of dishonesty' while preaching what he considered 'truth'. It may be no accident that such lying and subterfuge became ploys of the Wildean dandy, who often pretends to be evil while secretly being good.[33]

The art of Bunburying, as practised in *The Importance of Being*

Earnest, is based on the theory of *felix culpa*, the fault that is 'happy' because it becomes the basis of Augustinian self-correction and self-education. If experience is the name that a man gives to his mistakes, then Catholicism may well be the proper religion for a man who is willing to go wrong in order to go right. On this aspect of Wilde's experience, Joyce got the balance with great accuracy:

> He deceived himself into believing that he was the bearer of the good news of neo-paganism to an enslaved people. His own distinctive qualities, the qualities, perhaps, of his race – keenness, generosity and a sexless intellect – he placed at the service of a theory of beauty which, according to him, was to bring back the Golden Age and the joy of the world's youth. But if some truth adheres to his subjective interpretation of Aristotle, to his restless thought that proceeds by sophisms rather than syllogisms, to his assimilations of natures as foreign to his as the delinquent is to the humble, at its very base is a truth inherent in the soul of Catholicism: that man cannot reach the divine except through that sense of separation and loss called sin.[34]

That is in fact the link that Joyce could not otherwise find between the earlier and later works. If Bunburying is all about the educative effect of studying one's mistakes, then so also is *De Profundis*, the great letter to Lord Alfred Douglas written from jail. Douglas, whom he called 'Bosie', had been Wilde's lover and nemesis in the months before his fall. The famous play is comic, the letter tragic. The Christ in 'The Soul of Man under Socialism' is the same Christ extolled in *De Profundis*: an innocent man whose sin was the full artistic expression of himself. In the later text, he remains a guru rather than a preacher: 'he does not really teach one anything, but by being brought into his presence, one becomes something'.[35] The self-perfecting figure of the early essay is evoked again in *De Profundis*. 'To live for others as a definite self-conscious aim was not his creed,' Wilde writes: '. . . when he says "Forgive your enemies" it is not for the sake of the enemy but for one's own sake that he says so.'[36]

The redemptive potentials of the child, uppermost in the fairy tales, are seen as providing a rare exception to the refusal of Jesus to enforce a direct moral: 'he held them up as examples to their elders, which I myself have always thought the chief use of children, if what is perfect can have a use'.[37] This is but another way of regretting that the old-fashioned respect for the young is fast dying out. At the core of *De Profundis* is a recognition of the tragic contradiction in Wilde's earlier thought: he had, after all, declared himself indifferent to society, but had then committed the unpardonable sin (for an anarchist) of appealing to society for vindication in his conflict with Douglas's father, the Marquess of Queensberry. He was the first to admit the poetic justice of condemnation by a law that once he had flouted and then appealed to. Even after his conviction, he could, of course, have fled straight to France, but his mother expected that as a gentleman he would stand his ground and take what was coming to him. Perhaps Wilde had a half-conscious desire to continue his reverse anthropology in new and more testing zones. Prison might be the ultimate university, where the weaknesses of a host society were most fully concentrated and exposed.

Wilde never portrayed himself as a gay martyr, least of all to Bosie. 'I am here', he tells him in the letter from jail, 'for having tried to put your father in prison.'[38] (Wilde had sued the Marquess of Queensberry for libel). The artist's whole treatment of the Marquess seems an almost formulaic inversion of Anglo-Saxon racism. Whereas the British upper class had considered the Irish reckless and criminal, Wilde now reversed the charges, seeking to subvert the father/son relation on which the aristocracy based its claims of lineage. In court he effectively tried to drive a legal wedge between the Marquess and his heir. Hundreds, possibly thousands, of homosexual men occupied powerful positions in the London of the time.[39] Wilde did not go to jail for homosexuality (except in the most technical sense). His real crime was, in the words of Mary McCarthy, 'making himself too much at home' in English society.[40] He was the ultimate social nightmare, a self-invited guest who had to be barred.

Jail revealed to the writer the soul of man under capitalism, allowing him to 'see people and things as they really are'. It also confirmed his prior hunch about the educative effects of sin. To Bosie he writes: 'Suffering – curious as it may sound to you – is the means by which we exist, because it is the only means by which we become conscious of existing.'[41] The experience also ratified the argument in 'The Soul of Man under Socialism': that the punishments inflicted by the good were far more immoral than occasional outbreaks of crime, and that children were the major victims of such brutalization. It also proved that work under such a regime, far from rehabilitating the person, would cause him to dread all labour forever. In jail Wilde endured a hard pillow and plank bed. 'If this is how the queen treats her convicts,' he told one warder, 'she doesn't deserve to have any.'[42] Solitary confinement was the worst of all punishments. Designed to make offenders confront the nature of their sin, it was in fact a cynical device to destroy the sense of camaraderie with fellow inmates.

In the prison sick-bay, Wilde so entertained inmates with quips and stories that a guard was placed by his bed, under strict instructions not to answer if the prisoner spoke. It was as if the whole process was designed to disconnect him from all possible audiences.[43]

Yet the audience of fellow lags was the one that, by now, he wanted most. Despite the official policy, he achieved deep friendships with the convicts, and told Bosie:

> The poor are wise, more charitable, more kind, more sensitive than we are. In their eyes prison is a tragedy in a man's life, a casualty, something that calls for sympathy in others. They speak of one who is in prison as of one who is 'in trouble' simply. It is the phrase they always use, and the expression has the wisdom of love in it.[44]

The secret life of a London homosexual had inevitably led to clandestine contacts across the social divide with procurers and rent-boys, but these had always had a transgressive element (and some may have been frankly and horribly exploitative). In prison, on the other hand, the camaraderie was entirely sincere.

The extended letter to Bosie was Wilde's defiant response to the attempt by the authorities to prevent all but the most rudimentary communication. It was a viable and useful alternative to the madness that overcame many men in solitary confinement. The Christ who appears through its pages is an artist notable for his gift of giving voice to the lives of all who have been silenced; yet he transcends even that representative capacity, appearing once again as a wholly unconditioned being. At just that point when he appears to be about to project a knowable, believable personality, he eludes definition: 'To recognise that the soul of man is unknowable is the ultimate achievement of wisdom. The final mystery is oneself.'[45]

From his prison library, Wilde borrowed the works of Saint Augustine and Newman. One book for which (very wisely) he did not send was John Mitchel's *Jail Journal*.[46] He had met the author of that classic at his mother's soirées and commended it with mighty enthusiasm to his American audiences in 1882 during a lecture tour. Even as he wrote *De Profundis* (which he called *Epistula: in Carcere et Vinculis*), Wilde must have been aware that his text would take its place in the long tradition of Irish prison literature. He had always favoured the republican form of government as that most advantageous to art, but had heard throughout his life of the appalling sufferings of those Irishmen jailed for acting on republican principles. Stripped of even a name in his prison cell, he was set to picking oakum (a useless, unsaleable commodity), as Michael Davitt, the leader of the Land League, had been some years earlier. When Wilde was released, one of his first actions was to initiate a campaign for reform in the treatment of imprisoned children: Davitt was among the first people he contacted as he tried to drum up support. He also asked him to intervene in defence of a maltreated prisoner: 'No one knows better than yourself how terrible life in an English prison is and what cruelties result from the stupidity of officialdom, and the immobile ignorance of centralisation.'[47]

Wilde was open-hearted enough to recognize that warders also were brutalized by living close to so much hunger, insomnia and disease. One, Warder Martin, a Belfast Protestant, who had been especially kind to him, was dismissed – Wilde later found to his horror – for giving biscuits to an anaemic child. Here was another terrifying example of the stupidity of stereotyped, rule-ridden systems, another proof that authority destroyed those who exercised it as surely as those on whom it was exercised.

The poem which came out of these tribulations was 'The Ballad of Reading Gaol'. It is not a great work, being far too long at one hundred and nine stanzas, each of which the author felt was necessary if he was to shake public faith in the system. Its rhythms capture – some would say reproduce – the tedium of prison life. Yet many stanzas have a whiff of greatness about them and the ballad as a whole does not fail to live. It lacks the sophistication of Wilde's earlier works, but that is because it is addressed to a different audience, taking its place as proletarian literature. On its completion Wilde asked the publisher to invite Michael Davitt to write a preface: 'it would add to it very much'. He suggested that it be placed in *Reynolds' Magazine*, because 'it circulates widely among the criminal classes – to which I now belong – so I shall be read by my peers – a new experience for me'.[48] That is a breathtaking statement, suggesting as it does that every one of his previous writings had been received only by his enemies.

The author of 'The Ballad of Reading Gaol' was named only as 'C.3.3', carrying Wilde's theories of poetic impersonality into a new dimension of communal ballad-making. Despite its intermittent bathos and too-obvious looting of Coleridge's 'Rime of the Ancient Mariner', it creates the very feel of a virtual community among prisoners as they await the ritual hanging of one among their number. That sense of community is only strengthened by their shared understanding that the average citizen outside the walls has no inkling of what is going on:

He does not feel that sickening thirst
  That sands one's throat, before
The hangman with his gardener's gloves
  Comes through the padded door,
And binds one with three leathern thongs
  That the throat may thirst no more.

Over fifty years later, another Irish republican, Brendan Behan, would know the nightmare of proximity to an official execution. His play *The Quare Fellow* owes much to these lines of Wilde in specifying the effect on the mind:

We sewed the sacks, we broke the stones,
  We turned the dusty drill:
We banged the tins, and bawled the hymns,
  And sweated on the mill,
But in the heart of every man
  Terror was lying still.

'The Ballad of Reading Gaol' is a plea against Law and for Tradition. It questions not just the corrective value of punishment, but also the very use of physical confinement as a strategy for dealing with dissidents:

This too I know – and wise it were
  If each could know the same –
That every prison that men build
  Is built with bricks of shame,
And bound with bars lest Christ should see
  How men their brothers maim.[49]

The crime at the centre of the poem was one of passion: 'CTW' had killed his wife on discovering her infidelity. Hence the line 'each man kills the thing he loves'. A rebel against social norms, the criminal is here depicted as a man helpless in the grip of a force far greater than that of the individual, a force as implacable and inexplicable as storm or sea. Hence the refusal to identify either author or subject, since neither has real agency, being at the mercy of impulses that transcend the purely personal. A paradox ensues: the Wilde who could boast in *De Profundis* of having made the drama as personal a mode of expression as the lyric here seeks a sort of displaced social authority for the ballad.

In prison all property – including letters and papers – is regarded as communal: it provides the means by which an underground community can piece together the shreds of a lost narrative. Wilde was never accorded special category status of the kind reserved for some political offenders. His transgression was treated as a common crime, so that the existing order might proclaim its invulnerability. Nor did 'The Ballad of Reading Gaol' seek special category status as literature. Its avowedly proletarian ideas and images are aimed at the working class, in this fable of a man and community whose only crime is to have loved not wisely but too well. In it the masks and artifices by which the upper classes were allowed to speak their own condemnation are all removed: and the ordinary man and woman, the implied but unseen heroes and heroines of his earlier writings, finally emerge as speaker and audience. They are united in the image of that Jesus who abominated private property, gave up family ties, and moved among his people. In 'The Soul of Man under Socialism' Wilde had suggested that 'he who would lead a Christlike life is he who is perfectly and absolutely himself'.[50] That was now his own condition. Deprived even of contact with his two sons, he who had mocked all notions of parental succession in his plays (a handbag being the nearest thing to a progenitor in *The Importance of Being Earnest*) was free at last to derive only from himself.

The surrender of a name and an identity in the cellular life of Pentonville or Reading was not, after all, so very different from the disciplines of the religious life offered by Catholicism. That creed continued to interest Wilde. On the day of his release he asked to be taken in at a Jesuit retreat house in London. He had just confided in Stuart Headlam: 'I look on all the different religions as colleges in a great university. Roman Catholicism is the greatest and most romantic of them.' The Jesuits' response was jesuitical: they *might* accept him, but only after a year's deliberation. At this he broke down.[51]

Three years later, safer now and happier by far in France, he said that the Catholic Church was the place for saints and sinners (and in his own mind he was both). 'For respectable people,' he jocosely added, 'the Anglican Church will do.'[52] To the very end he regretted that his father had not allowed him to practise as a Catholic, although his own intellectual scruples might, on deeper reflection, have held him back anyway, for in his younger days he had felt that a code which denied supremacy to intellect was unlikely to last. By nature a rebel, he could only have submitted with difficulty to any rigorous creed: but the appeal of Catholicism to his senses only grew with the passing years, as his impatience with the intellect became stronger. At his death, he was given conditional baptism, absolved and anointed by a Dublin Passionist father, Cuthbert Dunne. Just a few weeks before, in the summer of 1900, he had sensed that not much time was left to him: 'If another century began, and I was still alive, it would really be more than the English could stand.'[53] For just once, he did what the English wanted.

20

George Bernard Shaw:
Arms and the Man

'I am an Irishman without a birth certificate,' George Bernard
Shaw told a visitor on hearing of the bombardment of the Four
Courts in Dublin during the Civil War.[1] He did not seem to feel
greatly disadvantaged by this predicament. By migrating from Dublin
to London as a young man in the 1870s, he had shrugged off his
nation and class, and after that he thought it wise to enter no other.
Instead, he became a sort of jocular analyst at large in England,
showing up the arbitrary nature of all its signs and the absurd spectacle of its class system. The separation of the latent content of
society from its manifest content was a technique made familiar by
Marx (whose *Capital* Shaw read in the British Museum), but he was
one of the first major artists to realize its potential for comedy.
Marx's use of official government statistics to press a case against
governments became a favoured tactic of Shaw: to give as accurate
and unillusioned an account of English society as he could and then
to stand back and view the results with greatly raised eyebrows. It
was also a method practised by the new anthropologists, who
patiently assembled evidence from native informants before going on
to offer a very different rearrangement and reinterpretation of available facts.

Shaw liked to compare Ireland to one or other of the exotic South
Sea islands then studied by anthropologists. His bohemian mother
Lucinda, far from being a disciplinarian, 'was much more like a
Tobriand islander as described by Mr Malinowski', because she
possessed 'so complete a disregard and even unconsciousness of

convention'.[2] Born in 1856, 'Sonny' was a gleeful product of her relaxed regime. He sometimes claimed that his native island was an asylum of happy instinctualists to which stern Englishmen should be sent for a spell in order to learn flexibility of mind.[3] But, for the purposes of his own studies, the larger island to the east suited very well. Perhaps because of the lack of parental discipline – his father was an alcoholic – the young boy was painfully shy in Dublin. Only by starting all over again, with a rigid programme of self-discipline as a public speaker in London, did he manage to conquer this timidity. He did so not by conforming to the social consensus, but by making a virtue of the fact that he was already so much at odds with it. Socialism became a substitute for shyness.

Because Victorian England was the host society for many refugee intellectuals, a good deal of 'reverse anthropology' was being practised on it by many displaced revolutionaries, social analysts and cultural critics. They would in time form a significant element of Shaw's circle, as well as a natural audience for one who felt himself 'a sojourner on this planet rather than a native of it'.[4] If the members of this community included many actors and often gave the impression of acting a part, that may have been because they felt obliged like him to create 'a fantastic personality fit and apt for dealing with men, and adaptable to the various parts I had to play as author, journalist, orator, politician, committee man, man of the world, and so forth'.[5] That persona of 'GBS' left little room for Sonny Shaw. It proved that acting was the immigrant's, as well as the shy person's, revenge.

The challenge for Shaw as artist was akin to that confronting him as socialist prophet: how to convince his audiences to free themselves of their unexamined preconceptions and adopt a scientific attitude? One method was to write plays in which for England was substituted another, distant society, which could then be submitted to clinical and comical analysis. The principle of substitution had been perfected by Sonny in his history classes at the Central Model School in Dublin. There the textbooks ignored Ireland and glorified England, so the young Fenian 'always substituted Ireland for England in such dithyrambs'.[6] The mapping of England onto Bulgaria or medieval France became a device of some of the greatest plays: but the analogies were kept unclear and covert until a fairly late stage of each work. Audiences were thereby tricked into laughing at a slightly skewed version of their own society: and the refusal of the playwright to offer a clear-cut ending or take-away moral became a major means of opening English audiences to the prospect of some kind of self-analysis.[7]

Opposed in principle to endings, Shaw preferred anticlimaxes, a taste inherited from his father. George Carr Shaw had told his son endless stories of idealism followed by deflation. As a mere lad of fourteen, the father had saved his own brother from drowning and – he darkly concluded – 'to tell you the truth, I was never so sorry for anything in my life afterwards'.[8] Another set-piece concerned the Bible, fulsomely saluted as a masterpiece of heroic literature and stylish prose, before the inevitable put-down, 'the damndest parcel of lies ever written'.[9]

The technique of passionate initial involvement followed by withdrawal for a sober re-estimate became the trademark of Shavian comedy. There are some who say that he carried it all just a bit too far. R.J. Kaufmann finds 'something of the vengeful provincial in his subversion of all dignity. His generalised kindliness cannot wholly conceal the gleeful Irish sniggerings of one who is never taken in . . .'[10] Which is simply to say that the Irish make natural anthropologists as well as artists. This may explain why Shaw never returned to live in Ireland: 'They would find me out in a week.'[11] The national reputation for mockery was rooted in that self-estrangement that comes from living for centuries in a contested space, a land without final settlement.

One of the abiding conceits of the Anglo-Irish was that they were aristocrats who would rule in perpetuity. Some even built majestic homes to give expression to that illusion. By the time the conceit had passed down to George Carr Shaw, however, it had become a tiresome affectation. He liked to think of his family as aristocratic, but Sonny had no such compunction, cheerfully admitting to being a downstart, 'as I call the boy-gentleman descended through younger sons from the plutocracy, for whom a university education is beyond his father's income, leaving him by family tradition a gentleman without a gentleman's means or education, and so only a penniless snob'.[12]

In England, Shaw was attracted to anarchism, though he feared that its precepts might be impossible to implement. He fully endorsed its diagnosis of the state as 'a huge machine for robbing and slave-driving the poor by brute force'[13] and its belief that private property corrupted human relationships. His analyses owe something to Swift and to Proudhon:

Property is theft; respectability founded on poverty is blasphemy; marriage founded on property is prostitution; it is easier for a camel to go through the eye of a needle than for a rich man to enter the kingdom of heaven.[14]

Shaw as Tory Anarchist shared Swift's conviction that whatever survived his corrosive mockeries would offer a bedrock of social wisdom. The critique he offered of liberal capitalism sounded radical to those used to left-wing diatribes against 'liberalism' but it was radical only in the deepest sense of being rooted in much older traditions. Eric Bentley has captured this element in an essay of which Shaw himself approved:

> Far from trying, after the fashion of unconservative or lunatic revolutionaries, to impose upon society ideas not native to it, Bernard Shaw took a stand *for* society *against* 'modern ideas', including liberalism and science.[15]

At the base of capitalism's evil, in Shaw's view, is its inability to create citizens devoted to the public service. Like Swift, he took the inherited ideal of a gentleman with such literal-mindedness that he became a dissident in style even as he enforced the oldest Christian virtues. To that degree, at least, he was George Carr Shaw's son.

In *The Sanity of Art* he depicted anarchism as a form of applied Protestantism. The exercise of private judgement must mean a decline in dependence on all systems external to the individual. The problem was that the working class lacked revolutionary fervour: its members were mostly happy parasites of the capitalist system and would, if pushed, fight to uphold it. All that was possible was a slow but pervasive transformation of every aspect of society. In this Shaw was at odds with his friend and fellow-dramatist Wilde. By 1885 he was writing as a reformed Fenian and conscientious Fabian:

> If socialism be not made respectable and formidable by the support of our class – if it be left entirely to the poor, then the proprietors will attempt to suppress it by such measures as they have already taken in Austria and Ireland. Dynamite will follow. Terror will follow dynamite. Cruelty will follow terror . . . If, on the other hand, the middle class will educate themselves to understand this question, they will be able to fortify whatever is just in socialism, and to crush whatever is dangerous in it.[16]

That is the wisdom of an Irishman whose chosen career in England proceeded upon something of the same lines as Edmund Burke's. Having seen the effects of injustice and violent resistance in Ireland, both consistently warned about the dangers of a similar commotion in England and attempted in their writings to help the English to stave it off.

The real war was not of one class against another, but of the life force against hypocritical moral codes invoked for their own protection by naked profiteers. The poor were not inherently more virtuous than the rich, for if they were that might be a good reason for keeping them poor. Shaw's real agenda was to put them out of business, so that all could partake of success and achievement. In 'The Soul of Man under Socialism' Wilde had joked that any man would sympathize with failure, but that it took a person of superior refinement to take pleasure in someone else's success. Both men had come from a country where failure was too often proclaimed heroic, and where every success was begrudged as something that could have been won only at the expense of too many losers. The life force announced in *Man and Superman* called for a new form of sympathy, not with misery, poverty or starvation so much as with joy, love and happiness.

Shaw believed that the developing ideas of the godhead indicated man's steady evolution. Under feudalism, the Old Testament god was an autocrat. Under capitalism, he was an arrant sentimentalist. Under anarchism, he or she would be devoted to self-perfection. The human will would in time raise all persons to this level of godly consciousness, a perfect consciousness, with no need of sexual activity or excremental function, but complete in itself. Marx and Darwin were sound analysts of social conditioning and environmental influences, but each had omitted one crucial factor from their equations – the transforming power of human will. The clashes in Shaw's plays are between exponents of human willpower and the representatives of a dreary mechanism. Although Shaw endorsed the scientific method, he recognized that in itself it was incomplete. Ultimately, all matter would be co-opted by the life-force and death would have no dominion. The life force was even stronger than science – trees grow beautifully without scientific help, unlike people.

For merely scientific socialists, all the huffing and puffing behind the Shavian system seemed an unnecessary prelude to a programme for simple self-help. Alick West was distressed by the *laissez-faire* element in its workings and mocked it in *A Good Man Fallen Among Fabians*: 'By some beneficent, pre-established harmony, the release of individual impulse in perfect anarchism will work for the good of all.'[17] This was why, he jeered, the socialist had to be resolutely unsocial, for Shaw insisted on seeing a proletariat which cannot save itself, and needs deliverance at the hands of a saintly superman like 'GBS'.

The high Tories were just as unimpressed as the orthodox socialists. In England Shaw was allowed to elaborate his theories because people were certain that only a minority of crackpots could ever take them seriously. Because he was witty, a public which mistook dullness for profundity concluded that he wasn't fully serious. His fame as an entertainer was global: but his influence in England minimal. Like Wilde, he identified with the mystical strain of the Christian tradition, and saw himself as a holy fool or Erasmian clown. That role he blended to singular effect with that of the roguish Paddy. All the time, he was well aware of the English tendency to dismiss Irish critiques as mere whimsy. He made a point of taking Wilde seriously and was grateful when his fellow-dramatist repudiated the English estimate of Shaw as a jester. But he could never get many others to do the same: 'Being an Irishman, I do not always see things as an Englishman would. Consequently, my most serious and blunt statements raise a laugh and create the impression that I am intentionally jesting.'[18]

Shaw probably asked too much of his host country. Like those anthropologists who visited even more exotic locations, he had a tendency to meddle in the social arrangements which he found. Many owners of country houses found him a monumental busybody, who tried to redesign everything from their daily diets to their front curtains. He failed to recognize that if England was to be reformed, English people themselves would do the reforming. In Ireland, by contrast, his influence was far, far greater than he ever seemed to realize. His plays were much admired not just by intellectuals but by trade unionists: many artisans, like the father of Brendan Behan, memorized whole speeches from the plays and paragraphs from the prefaces. To them, he was the scourge of all learned professions, which he called conspiracies against the laity. They revered him for asserting the interdependence of learning and labour, as opposed to the notion of a knowledge that is the preserve of a specialist elite. They were moved by his proposal that everyone could become a sort of gentleman in a greatly expanded middle class; and that, once that happened, the interests of that class and society itself would be one and the same, and the old world of ranks and hierarchies at an end.

Arms and the Man is an early confrontation with these themes. Written in the early 1890s, in the wake of the great success of *The Golden Bough*, it takes up some challenges posed by Sir James Frazer's anthropology. Frazer had contended that, although the contemporary savages of Africa were more cultivated than his own European ancestors, nevertheless a majority of Europeans was 'still living in a state of intellectual savagery with the smooth surface of society sapped and mired by superstition'.[19] Shaw's way of exploring that possibility was to set a Swiss down in Bulgaria (and, by his usual technique of substitution, he may have reflected something of his experience as an Irishman 'set down' in England). At all events, the techniques of an archaic, hierarchical culture are to be studied by the more 'sophisticated', democratic methods of another. The emerging science of anthropology was leading to similar kinds of novel. In this, two cultures are tested one upon the other, in order to see whether the result will be a sickening conflict or an enriching confluence and to investigate whether what unites men may be more important than what divides them. Frazer's own model might be termed optimistic, since by establishing those features held in common one could define the funadamental elements of a human nature. His successor, Bronislau Malinowski, was more struck by cultural differences and sounded a note of realistic caution about such universalist pretensions.

In more recent times, Claude Lévi-Strauss has blended these approaches, accepting that what is universal must be the essence of human nature, but contending that people can learn valuable ways of improving themselves through the systematic study of techniques employed in distant cultures. That method is, of course, utterly at variance with the gospel of high imperialism, whose sponsors saw themselves as having nothing to learn from others: but it was the method adopted by Shaw when, after a trip to communist Russia, he used the attributes of that society as a basis for a critique of England. He was also adept at making such reproving comparisons across the ages, pointing out (for example) that the Inquisition was more open to counter-argument than the General Medical Council. That would be the precise approach recommended by Lévi-Strauss:

> . . . while not clinging to elements from any one particular society, we make use of *all* of them in order to distinguish those principles of social life which may be applied to reform our own customs.[20]

In *Arms and the Man* Shaw tried to map Swiss culture onto Bulgarian, with the intention of pointing the way to a better social order. His hope, also, was to subvert the well-made Victorian melodrama and to substitute for it a new kind of anti-romantic comedy. He chose the term 'anti-romantic' *after* the success of the play in 1894, because of his conviction that it had been seriously misunderstood. Early audiences had been so beguiled by the comedy that they failed to pay much attention to its exposure of the self-deceiving romantic imagination. Shaw had, after all, written a work of Fabian propaganda against the posturing of the upper class, adding a dimension of humour to sugar the pill. He was dejected by the number of admirers who licked off the sugar and left the pill intact.

That first production 'brought the misunderstanding between my real world and the stage world of the critics to a climax, because the misunderstanding was itself, in a sense, the subject of the play'.[21] The heroine, Raina, tries to live her life according to the conventions of opera. She is stagey, and the progress of the drama will be the progressive unmasking of her aristocratic delusions. Critics routinely accuse Shaw of creating unreal, overschematic characters without a credible basis in human psychology, but his complaint is that life keeps doing that anyway, despite his best efforts. So his plays offer a deflation of persons who have so simplified themselves, along with an account of their return to a more complex self-understanding. This gradual revelation of self-deception is not only a staple of ancient comedy but the working method of the modern socialist critic, who substitutes economic explanations for specious, high-flown moral claims. By this means, Shaw becomes one of the few major writers to achieve a reconciliation between socialism and comedy.

As a self-declared Protestant anarchist, Shaw was committed to remoulding the forms of comedy, in which there is usually a clash of wills, a series of mistaken identities and a final relief in knowing the world for what it really is. Catholicism, placing less emphasis on the will to transform the world, may be more geared to a tragic sense of life. Yet, because of its suspicion of impersonation, the radical puritan intellect is hostile to most forms of theatricality, believing that it is a lifetime's task to learn how to play one's own self (and that time should not be wasted in false imitations of the identity of others). So Shaw reserves his deepest mockery here for the posturing of Raina, who fatally confuses art and life. At the root of that mockery is his healthy desire to keep literature in its place (as he sees it), a sauce but not a staple of life. What Shaw is therefore implying of the London reviewers of *Arms and the Man* is a failure similar to Raina's and thus an inability to understand the main point of the play.

The action is set in 1885, when the need to repel Serbian onslaughts has transformed the Bulgarians into heroic defenders:

> . . . but beginning to work out their own redemption from barbarism . . . or, if you prefer it, beginning to contract the disease of civilisation – they were very ignorant heroes, with boundless courage and patriotic enthusiasms . . . Into their country comes a professional officer from the high, democratic civilisation of Switzerland – a man completely acquainted, by long practical experience, with the realities of war. The comedy arises, of course, from the collision of the knowledge of the Swiss and the illusions of the Bulgarians.[22]

So, when the soldier Bluntschli explains to Raina that a cavalry charge is the least romantic thing on earth (like slinging a handful of peas against a window-pane), he evokes her disbelief, much as Shaw evoked the incredulity of a generation raised on memories of Balaclava and Tennyson's 'Charge of the Light Brigade'. To have the mystique attaching to war destroyed by a real soldier, and a mere Swiss at that, was more than some viewers could bear.

The neutral, peace-loving Swiss had, as a paradoxical consequence of their objectivity, become identified as soldiers *par excellence*, mercenaries who would fight for anyone because their own country stood for so little. The clash of rival nationalisms provided the internationalist Shaw with a suitable backdrop against which to position Bluntschli as a new sort of anti-hero, motivated only by intelligent self-interest. As soon as he stumbles out of the line of fire, onto the stage which is Raina's bedroom, he warns her that all soldiers are frightened to death and that the more sensible ones prefer to carry spare chocolate rather than cartridges. This must have shocked audiences which believed that it was a sweet and noble thing to die for country – and would still in the main believe it in 1914. Writing twenty years earlier, Shaw had his work cut out for him, precisely because the romanticism of the Bulgarians was not substantially different from that of the contemporary English. As he later recalled, 'Captain Bluntschli, who thinks of a battlefield as a very dangerous place, is incredible to the theatre critic who thinks of it only as a theatre in which to enjoy the luxurious excitements of patriotism, victory, and bloodshed without risk or retribution.'[23] The subsequent adoption of the term 'theatre' as a euphemism for battlefield by military commanders of the twentieth century was all too symptomatic of the mind-set Shaw was deploring.

Bluntschli comes from one of the least literary peoples of Europe, in keeping with the play's anti-literary theme. Shaw's Bulgaria, on the other hand, is a thinly disguised version of nineteenth-century England, beset by the same problem – that 'Byronism' exuded by Sergius, the gallant military lover of Raina:

> The clever imaginative barbarian shows an acute critical faculty which has been thrown into intense activity by the arrival of western civilisation in the Balkans. The result is precisely what the advent of nineteenth century thought first produced in England: to wit, Byronism. By his brooding on the perpetual failure, not only of others but of himself, to live up to his ideals: by his consequent cynical scorn for humanity: by his jejune incredulity as to the absolute validity of his concepts . . . he has

acquired a half-tragic, half-ironic air, the mysterious moodiness . . .[24]

The Victorians harped so incessantly on notions of gentility as to throw serious doubt on their achievement of it: and so it is with the Bulgarians. Raina's family owns the only library in the country and will not permit anyone to forget this major cultural fact. Their house furnishings dramatize the contradictions of those caught between a rich Bulgarian traditionalism and cheap ersatz Viennese. Gorgeous Oriental textiles hang alongside hideous Western wallpaper. Raina's mother, who would look splendid as a mountain farmer's wife, is hopelessly determined to play the Viennese lady. Such listlessness may be found in any society on the verge of modernity but still rooted in traditional values – and it can produce barbarians who are restrained by the codes of neither but fall into the chasm that opens between them. People who are half-savage are, for that very reason, anxious to embrace a sentimental code of gallantry, just as semi-illiterates are the ones most impressed by the power of literature and the associated arts.

Shaw's Bulgaria is corrupted by this vice of a half-formed civilization. Raina derives most of her ideals from rare trips to the Viennese opera. There is, however, a lack of conviction about the way in which Bulgarians adopt foreign styles: and Shaw extracts much comedy from their adoption of soap and water. When Bluntschli refrains from shaking Raina's hand because his is still grimy after battle, she deduces that he must be a gentleman: 'Bulgarians of good standing – people in our position – wash their hands nearly every day. So you see I can appreciate your delicacy.'[25] Her father will later account for his wife's recurrent sore throat by the fact that she washes her neck every day: a disgusting foreign habit, he complains, imported from the filthy English, whose climate leaves them so dirty that they have to be perpetually washing themselves. 'I don't mind a good wash once a week to keep up my position,' he adds, 'but once a day is carrying the thing to a ridiculous extreme.'[26] That philosophy was, of course, expressed even more pithily decades later in Brendan Behan's ringing aphorism 'only dirty people have to wash'. Shaw said it was a matter of record that by 1885 'the Bulgarians were adopting the washing habits of big western cities as pure ceremonies of culture and civilisation, and not on hygienic grounds'. He opined that a cockney 'by simple exposure to the atmosphere becomes more unpresentable in three hours than a Balkan mountaineer in three years'.[27] Some cockneys, nevertheless, might have been shocked by the lines of the play.

All of which shows how constricting are the conventions of any society – or of any literature. Excessive adherence to matters of form in literature will lead to restrictions of human possibility in life. 'Why,' exclaimed Shaw, 'you cannot even write a history without adapting the facts to the conditions of literary narrative, which are in some respects much more distorting than the dramatic conditions of representation on the stage.'[28] For him half the humour and most of the pain in life arose from the persistent attempt 'to found our institutions on the ideals suggested to our imaginations by our half-satisfied passions, instead of on a genuinely natural history'.[29] It is such a history that Shaw provides in Bluntschli. Raina, on the other hand, violates his ethic by asking life to follow art. She does show a certain uneasiness in her adoption of foreign literary modes, which suggests that she is salvable. Delight that her fiancé Sergius is a war hero is grounded not so much in his steely character as in the fact that 'it proves that all our ideals were real after all'. Even to raise the fearful possibility that she may have picked them up at the Viennese or Bucharest opera is to admit that she herself is already pained by that gap between books and the world. She is already a potential sceptic, by virtue of being a woman, allowed only to praise famous men but not to be brave herself.

Bluntschli compels her silence by threatening her with a revolver (it is in fact unloaded). Later he secures her cooperation by confiscating her cloak, safe in the knowledge that she would never dare to allow a soldier into her room to arrest Bluntschli while she was attired only in her underwear. His joke about the cloak – 'this cloak is better than a revolver, eh?'[30] – shows just how conservative Raina is. The conventions of gender may be superficial, but she observes them sedulously. So Bluntschli must begin her re-education. He assures her that all good soldiers are scared: and he is himself utterly kind. When loud knocking on the door suggests that he is done for, he returns the cloak and drops his intimidating manner, admitting to a nervousness that leaves him on the brink of tears. This audacity, in daring to reveal his sensitive nature, strikes Raina as the ultimate in bravery. She finds irresistible that combination of courage and delicacy. Being a manly woman she is drawn to this womanly man: 'though I am only a woman, I think I am at heart as brave as you'.[31]

The serving woman Louka is another emergent New Woman. When Sergius, returned in triumph from battle, tells her that he is never sorry for what he does, she responds, 'I wish I could believe a man could be as unlike a woman as that. I wonder are you really a brave man.'[32] Her implication is that the operatic misreading of heroism is part of a wider misunderstanding of gender roles. By the play's end, the war hero Sergius will be exposed as just another fallible youth, while the chocolate cream soldier Bluntschli will triumph because of his modest refusal to pose. 'What a man!' Sergius will exclaim in tribute, adding a final afterthought about the limits of masculinity: 'Is he a man?'[33]

Androgyny was part of Shaw's programme for transcending mere sexuality, and he believed that a perfected humanity would one day derive from the mind the pleasures once associated with sexual orgasm. In keeping with that programme, he explained the secret of the deep knowledge of women displayed in his plays: 'I have always assumed that a woman is a person exactly like myself, and that is how the trick is done.'[34] Although Raina and Louka might prefer men to be utterly different from women, a shrewder instinct tells them that this is not so – and that it is a form of neurosis to behave as though the sexual identity of a partner should in all respects call forth a diametrically opposed sexual identity in oneself. What seems an opposite might on inspection be revealed as a secret double.

Bluntschli's early conversation begins, for Raina, the slow unmasking of Sergius as a martyr to *machismo*. He led his suicidal cavalry charge 'like an operatic tenor', provoking derisive laughter among enemy soldiers, until they were informed that their ammunition was false and that they were done for. Bluntschli thereupon fled, with as many others as could escape. His thoughts on the matter are clear: the chap who led the charge should be court-martialled for rank amateurism, or else he was a sound tactician who, on hearing of the fake cartridges, knew that his charge was safe. This causes Raina to fear that Sergius is being branded a cowardly pretender. As yet, she is incapable of seeing the whole thing from Bluntschli's professional point of view.

One question-mark hangs over Raina's behaviour. If she is a Bulgarian patriot, why is she harbouring this enemy of her people? She offers flimsy excuses drawn from the opera *Ernani*, as to how a guest is always afforded immunity in a nobleman's house, even when that guest is an enemy soldier. The real explanation is that Bluntschli's confessed vulnerability allows her, for the first time in her life, to act purposefully rather than be acted on. She has developed 'a sub-conscious dislike for Sergius' under the strain of their idealized relationship. In Bluntschli she has at last found a man who does not want to be passively admired but one who can be actively helped in a reciprocal relation.

The battle of the sexes in *Arms and the Man* is complicated by the war of the classes: and the two sometimes overlap. Louka in Act One grimaces on being advised by Raina that 'we' must do what we are told. By the start of Act Two, she is smoking cigarettes and threatening to rebel against her mistress. Falsely, she convinces herself that knowledge of skeletons in the Petkoff family cupboard will leave her invulnerable to dismissal; but her fiancé, the shrewd servingman Nicola, insists on discretion since the higher-ups have the power to make or break them. Although Louka and Nicola represent the lower orders in this socialist play, they are not by that virtue its hero and heroine, any more than the proletariat is cast in a redemptive role in Shavian theory. Far from it: their most pressing desire is to enter the bourgeoisie. As a Fabian, Shaw had a strong desire to make bourgeois lifestyles available to all. Yet the strange thing is that although there is really just one middle-class figure onstage, Bluntschli's cathartic effect is to bring out the bourgeois in all those around him. When not maintaining his heroic posture before impressionable ladies, Sergius delivers himself of many home truths which bear out Bluntschli's commonsensical ideas on soldiering: 'the cowards' art of attacking mercilessly when you are strong, and keeping out of harm's way when you are weak'.[35] Indeed, he singles out for praise the pragmatism of a horse-dealing soldier who turns out to have been Bluntschli, 'a commercial traveller in uniform, bourgeois to his boots!'.[36] This is said with a mixture of awe and contempt, but by the play's end the final tribute from Sergius's lips will be less ambiguous.

Sergius's account of the subsequent fate of that soldier – whom he still doesn't know to have been Bluntschli – includes the tale of how he was saved by a young lady in whose bedroom he found refuge. Raina rather hypocritically rebukes Sergius for repeating such a coarse story: literature, even as oral narrative, should not be tainted, it seems, by squalid details of everyday life. 'If such women exist,' choruses the mother, 'we should be spared the knowledge of them.'[37] Yet why should literature be exalted over life? The masks of pretence are being slowly loosened, but they are still being deliberately worn – yet the strain is starting to show. In the next scene, Sergius is depicted as a knight protesting his unworthiness to Lady Raina. Such higher love is too fatiguing to keep up for any length. As a performer of these roles, Sergius fears that he may have six different 'acts', none truly his own. The real Sergius may indeed be the 'lower' man who finds himself caressing Louka, but she knows just how dishonest both he and Raina are on matters of sexual fidelity.

The reasons for that hypocrisy are clear to Louka, who can sense the difference between the acts they perform for one another and the manner of a real lover. Within the stereotypes of *amour courtois*, Sergius has almost as little freedom for fulfilment as Raina. His *droit de seigneur*, exercised over a maidservant, was a classic sexual opportunity of a closed society. 'Economic control seemed to guarantee erotic control,' wrote Mary Ellmann, 'and for the sadistic, exceptional rights of discipline lay in the relationship of employer and employee.'[38] Thus the cliché. Shaw's major refinement is to show how the higher orders might turn to the lower not for easy sex but for a fuller relationship. Raina's mother Catherine seems more erotically attracted to Sergius than is Raina herself; and it soon becomes obvious that his real interest is in Louka, who alone has the capacity to educate him, while at the same time allowing him to feel in certain respects superior. All he could ever feel for Raina was the unworthiness of a courtly lover: unlike Louka, he knew no other Raina, just as Raina knew only the spotless military hero. The discrepancy between their ideal and real identities is the sort that caused Freud to insist that there are four persons in every sexual act: the two actual people and the fantasies entertained by each of the other.

When Sergius learns that Raina may have been untrue to him, this is of no interest as an insight into her character. His only query is: 'Who is my rival?'[49] Thinking solely in terms of aristocratic honour, he reads the whole of life in such narrow categories. Being an idealist, he judges all forms of behaviour as either higher or lower than they may in reality be. For example, the conduct of Nicola strikes him as either the finest heroism or the most abject baseness, but it is never seen for what it is: a pragmatism somewhere in between. Sergius needs to worship absolutely or not at all. The false, melodramatic choices which he professes to face all around him are really a projection of his inner nature, split between an idealism so vast as to be inhuman and a realism so disappointed as to become a lethal cynicism. Sergius is nothing but a set of attitudes that do not as yet add up to a coherent personality, whereas Bluntschli, however varied the situation in which he finds himself, is still recognizably the same man. Returning to Raina's house with her father's borrowed coat at the end of Act Two, he is, though well brushed and restored, still unmistakable, the bourgeois integer confronted with a set of aristocratic fractions.

In Act Three, that coherent fellow shows himself capable of massive amounts of work on behalf of the Petkoff family, while the Major and Sergius, being desiccated nobles, lounge uneasily in the absence of a suitable war. Here again is evidence of Shaw's Protestant anarchism. Like such predecessors as Swift and Goldsmith, he despised the idleness of the aristocracy and wished to substitute for it a thoroughly Protestant commitment to the work ethic of the middle class. The joke against Petkoff's library of coffee-stained paperbacks seems like a rerun of Goldsmith's jibe against the Anglo-Irish expenditure on books: and it is complemented by the timidity of Petkoff's mind. So craven is this man that he brings his own wife to keep discipline among the soldiers. Meanwhile, Raina's act as an operatic heroine is wearing thin. To her teasing claim that he has insulted her, Bluntschli coolly responds, 'I can't help it. When you strike that noble attitude and speak in that thrilling voice, I admire you; but I find it impossible to believe a single word you say.'[40] Her response is not anger but amazement at being found out, and the ensuing relaxation of being known by a man for what she truly is.

This approach was revitalized in European theatre at the end of the nineteenth century in the time of suffragism, especially by the Scandinavian authors Ibsen and Strindberg. The latter's *Miss Julie* seems a palpable influence on *Arms and the Man* in its portrayal of an insurgent servant class, whose highest dream would be to imitate Bluntschli and open a hotel in Switzerland. In the plays of both Strindberg and Shaw, that aspiration is corrupted in two ways – by the idea not of participatory democracy but of peremptorily ordering people around, and then by the realization (as Louka says to Nicola) that 'when you set up shop, you will only be everybody's servant instead of somebody's servant'.[41] Moreover, Shaw follows Strindberg in suggesting that, although the class war may be resolved, the battle between the sexes will rage on. Louka knows that if Nicola becomes everybody's servant in his shop, he will compensate for this by playing lord and master at home. To his assertion that he will be master in his own house, she acerbically replies: 'You shall never be master in mine.'[42] Shaw finds bourgeois ideas admirable as far as they go, but recognizes that for a newly freed womanhood that may not be far enough.

Nicola pragmatically senses that as well. He suggests that it might be better for Louka to marry Sergius and become one of his prized customers, instead of just being his wife and costing him money. Advising an aristocractic reticence, he suggests that she show no touch of familiarity in her dealings with him. This is the Fabian–Shavian solution again: endless upward mobility for all. Even at the best of times, this would be a dubious prospect except for those of unusual ability and willpower. The problems consequent upon such merito-cratic policies are well known: they deprive the working class of natural leaders and are little more than mildly reformist, since they point a chosen few to 'inclusion in the dominant structures rather than at a revolutionary transformation of social relations'.[43] In the heyday of the Fabians, R.H. Tawney complained that meritocracy was really just a parody of democracy, since 'opportunities to rise are no substitute for a general diffusion of the means of civilisation' and of the 'dignity and culture' needed by all citizens.[44] The Fabian cult of experts was no real answer to earlier elites founded on social hierarchy or inherited wealth: they were simply people who offered to do the living and thinking of servants for them.[45] This was an unresolved contradiction in Shaw's thought, for he believed in a democracy where the entire people understood politics and culture, taking full responsibility for them, and yet he found himself supporting Sidney Webb's idea of a new form of aristocracy, a managerial elite more socially just than its predecessors, but an elite none the less.

Sergius voices the aristocratic philosophy of the exceptional individual. Displaying contempt for soldiers who follow like dogs, he says 'Give me the man who will defy to the death any power on earth or in heaven that sets itself up against his own will and conscience.'[46] There is as much of Shaw in that line as in any uttered by Bluntschli. The playwright heightens the radical implications of the growing romance between Bluntschli and Raina. Sergius cannot confess love for a servant just yet, so Louka seizes the chance to show that her menial tasks degrade him as much as they degrade her. This is not just an observation on the psychological damage wrought on one class by its exploitation of another: it is also a feminist statement about sexual relations. If Louka were the Empress of Russia, she would marry the man she loved, something that no queen in Europe has yet had courage to do. She would dare to be the equal of her inferior, much as Bluntschli has already dared to weep before Raina.

Although class feeling is depicted as stronger than sexual instinct, Shaw uses Louka to suggest that it may be more superficial and so more easily redirected. Sure enough, Sergius's notions collapse at the news that Raina will wed the Swiss. He challenges Bluntschli to a duel, himself choosing sabre, the Swiss a machine gun: when Raina asks Bluntschli why they are about to fight, he shrugs, 'I don't know, he hasn't told me.'[47] This throwback to a late scene in *The Rivals* is also a deflation of the authoritarian personality which always manages to exalt the fight over the thing fought for. No sooner is the duel arranged than Sergius withdraws because Bluntschli, being no gentleman but a professional soldier, is an unworthy opponent. Far from being insulted, Bluntschli is delighted by this show of pragmatism, that pragmatism which informs the man courageous enough not to fight. 'But now that you've found out that life isn't a farce, but something quite sensible and serious, what further obstacle is there to your happiness?'[48] he asks Sergius. This is the moment of happy disillusionment to which all Shaw's comedies move. The technique appealed to his sense of anticlimax, in a play that is all about the ways in which that feeling assails those living at the fag-end of the nineteenth century, in the backwash of romanticism.

Raina, for example, is outraged to discover that Sergius has been unfaithful: 'Oh, what sort of God is this I have been worshipping?'[49] He meets her gaze, says the stage direction, with sardonic enjoyment of her disenchantment. This fascinates Shaw: the manner in which the disillusioned one sets about exposing and savouring the ensuing disillusion of others. The problem with this 'characteristic form of modern pride' is that it may become an end in itself and that the undoubted pleasures of diagnosis may never make way for a more positive set of prescriptions. That objection can be made to many of Shaw's dénouements, but not to this one, in which Bluntschli powerfully commends a cheerful, life-enhancing pragmatism.

Of course, disillusion – once it takes hold – can be catching among those for whom the gleeful excitements of unmasking are the sole pleasures left. 'The world is not such an innocent place as we used to think, Petkoff,'[50] remarks Sergius on the revelation that Bluntschli – and not Sergius – is the chocolate cream soldier. Petkoff instantly snorts against the early-morning hypocrisy of his wife and daughter who considered the story of the chocolate cream soldier too vulgar to be told. Sergius now holds that even the lower orders should be exposed: so, having caught Louka eavesdropping at the door, he invites the ultimate unmasker Bluntschli to judge the snooper. 'I mustn't judge her,' is the response: 'I once listened myself outside a tent when there was a mutiny brewing. It's all a question of the degree of provocation. My life was at stake.'[51] Throughout the action, in fact, Shaw has sought to justify the behaviour of menial persons caught in compromising situations. Louka is rewarded not by punishment but by marriage to the man who has just tried to expose her.

Sergius finally accepts Louka and receives the congratulations of Bluntschli for bringing his ideals and realities at last into alignment. Whereas in other Shavian plays, the world of dream and fact veer pointlessly apart at the close, here they usefully interlock. Bluntschli offers the best wishes of a good republican. In that he is joined by Raina, who wins her chocolate soldier not by an ostentatious surrender of her virtue, but by a shared sense of human vulnerability. Shaw being Shaw, of course, could never leave it all at that. So, in the final moments, Bluntschli, that stripper of illusions, is disclosed as an incorrigible romantic. He confesses that it was a romantic disposition that led him to run away with the army as a boy, and later to return with the coat to Raina's home (rather than simply send it by mail).

His version of events is presented only at the end. He had returned, hoping perhaps for a mature love affair, only to find in

Raina an attitudinizing adolescent girl. The photograph sent by her with the legend 'Raina, to her Chocolate Cream Soldier' is taken by him as proof that she is just a player of a schoolgirl game in a matter of life and death to him. This is Bluntschli's own moment of disillusion, wrought to comic effect. Raina tears up the photo, not in repudiation of her shallow behaviour but in anger at his failure to register the serious nature of her earlier overtures. She, the seeming diva, turns out to have been the pragmatist all along, wooing within the constraints of her womanhood, for what else could she have done? He, the apparent debunker, was a romantic fool, mistaking for a schoolgirl's crush the sincere suit of a woman of twenty-three. Bluntschli is stupefied to learn her true age and Sergius savours the moment: 'Bluntschli, my one last belief is gone. Your sagacity is a fraud, like everything else. You have less sense than I.'[52] Perhaps that is a little unfair. Bluntschli may have been too literal-minded to imagine that someone so much younger than he could fall in love with him: or perhaps he was using the imputed age of seventeen as a ploy to compel the woman of his dreams to disclose her real age.

We can never know, for Shaw's art, far from being heavily didactic, is committed to a serene description of the world as it is. The radical indecision of audiences at the close is a return to the method of the Shakespearean problem play, such as *The Merchant of Venice* or *Measure for Measure*. Every character is permitted a reasonably high self-image and nobody is utterly destroyed. Shaw's clowns are often specialists and professionals; but their blindness about nine-tenths of reality affords them a piercing insight into the other one-tenth. The playwright is willing to honour his characters and to see each as he or she sees themselves. It is this that makes him a consummate artist. His many warnings against the corrupting effects of art worship are issued simply because he feels the artistic impulse so strongly in himself. It is his art, even more than his socialism, that leaves him classless and able to observe life with a measure of freedom: and that condition of cheerful estrangement is rendered easier by his outsider status as an Irishman in England.

By the close, Bluntschli has proved himself one of the most docile, passive and tractable male heroes in literature. In this, he is no more than an extreme version of the other docile men in the play, Petkoff, Nicola and Sergius – and he, being the most tractable, wins the masterful woman. Here has been enacted yet another domestication of epic values by an Irish author, another attempt to supplant the naked militarism of a predatory aristocracy with the more bourgeois virtues of civility. The 'counter-bidding' scene between Sergius and Bluntschli presents that conflict in terms of high opera, justifying

W.H. Auden's claim that Shaw's plays achieved 'an effect nearer to that of music than the work of any of the so-called pure writers'.[53]

Shaw had been a music and opera critic before becoming a playwright, and he tried, like Wilde, to fill his stages with verbal operas in which the over-the-top pretensions of the *ancien régime* could be comprehensively documented before being ultimately exploded. He faced some difficulty, as he later admitted:

> In a generation which knew nothing of any sort of acting but drawing-room acting, and which considered a speech of more than twenty words impossibly long, I went back to the classical style and wrote long rhetorical speeches like operatic solos, regarding my plays as musical performances precisely as Shakespeare did.[54]

To his chagrin the actors preferred to underdo their parts, lest they be considered stagey, and he had to fight to make the operatic nature of his works manifest. Again and again, scenes of his plays resound to the counterpoint between a bass and high tenor, as in Sergius's verbal duel with Bluntschli, the former offering his partner twenty horses and three carriages, the latter two hundred horses and seventy carriages.

Behind this tomfoolery, a serious statement is being made about the rise of the middle class and decline of the aristocracy. Shaw's own family could boast a baronet, but they had no money. One grandfather was so clever at carpentry that he could build boats and design house interiors, but being a country gentleman he was 'forbidden to make money by his gift of manual dexterity', despite the fact that 'for the management of his landed estate, he had not the smallest aptitude'.[55] As the young Sonny Shaw grew to manhood, he could not help noticing the fact 'that my father's tailor had a country house in Dalkey, a yacht in Dalkey Sound, and could afford to send his sons, much better dressed and equipped than I, to expensive preparatory schools and to college'.[56] If the Petkoffs represent the lesser aristocracy in decline, Bluntschli is the new kind of male protagonist. The Swiss in Bulgaria is a little like the 'micks on the make' in England, marrying (as did Shaw) a woman from a declining social caste.

The play was a great success, but more fastidious souls like W.B. Yeats (whose *Land of Heart's Desire* was the rather unlikely curtain-raiser) felt hatred as well as admiration: 'It seemed to me inorganic, logical straightness and not the crooked road of life, yet I stood aghast before its energy.'[57] Shortly after, Yeats was haunted in a nightmare by the image of Shaw as a clicking sewing-machine. The problem was that Shaw's appeals to the intellect and to feeling seemed to have been somehow disconnected. Viewers treated the play either as a sentimental melodrama or as a heartlessly mechanical comedy, whereas his intention had been to conduct a mutual critique between both discourses. Shaw knew that there were two constituencies in London audiences and he described how cleverly Wilde played to them – the subversive one-liners aimed at the intellectuals, while the traditional plots kept the sentimental majority satisfied. His own technique was to take the well-made comedy of exposure and then to turn its own techniques loose on the very form itself in the later scenes. The audience should have realized that he was mocking its satisfaction with the resolutions his play seemed to be proposing, but most of its members didn't. When one man shouted 'Boo', Shaw seemed momentarily encouraged: 'I quite agree with you . . . but what are we two against so many?'[58] Yet his method of presenting a radical new form of art in the exterior trappings of the old commercial drama did not go unadmired. He was, in his way, an early exponent of that Irish modernism that would delight in playing off the archaic against the hypermodern.

For all his well-publicized differences with Wilde, Shaw adopted astonishingly similar ideas and tactics. Both welcomed science but warned against the danger of making it a new religion (which would induce just a new form of dependency). For both, the only viable religion was art, the only threat to the established morality of the law would be a new dispensation of anarchist artists. Shaw said the laws, 'instead of making society better than its best unit, make it worse than its average unit, because they are never up to date'. An attack on their laggard morals might bring real salvation. Workers were too stupefied by grinding labour to see their true predicament, but artists could create a fuller awareness.

This utopian lament linked both Shaw and Wilde to the story of Irish modernism. They chose to dispose of what was no longer useful in tradition, the better to reassert the claims of whatever survived their scorn. Ultimately, their project was as religious as it was aesthetic: to re-enchant the world after a necessary phase of disillusion, and to do this in ways that freed the religious imagination from all dying creeds and social systems. Morality to them was no more than a rationalization of the self-interest of the ruling class. Its twin enemies in the struggle for a better world would be socialism and religion. What was wrong with the Victorians was that they had too many morals and not enough religion. Shaw and Wilde did their best to illustrate just how injurious a prim moralism had been to the interests of real religion, but their critique of that moralism has too often been interpreted as a denial of the sacred itself.

21

Somerville and Ross:
The Silver Fox

George Bernard Shaw was neither the first nor the last writer to note a strange combination of athleticism and cowardice in the life of the Anglo-Irish, especially when they engaged in the hunting of foxes: 'This way of producing hardy bodies and timid souls is so common in country houses that you may spend hours in them listening to stories of broken collar-bones, broken backs, or broken necks, without coming upon a single spiritual adventure or daring thought.'[1] The 'unspeakable in pursuit of the uneatable' became a working description not just of English gentlemen but of their Irish counterparts too.

Edith Somerville and Martin Ross were too fastidious to blind themselves to the force of such reservations. In *The Silver Fox* they write of one Major Bunbury: 'Although he hunted six days a week, he kept a soul somewhere and his sister knew where it was.'[2] The two authors loved the hunt, while regretting many of the hunting *types*: and much of their social comedy springs from that inner tension. Their mockery of the country-life set is far wittier than that of either Shaw or Wilde, because it is based on an intimate knowledge. Yet, for all its sharpness, it is a good example of their desire to find a mode of existence for their critical attitudes within the prevailing social system.

They were acutely aware of the threats posed to that system. Although she ended her days as a not unwilling citizen of an independent Irish state, Edith Somerville began as a frustrated loyalist.

Born in 1858, she grew up the first of seven children at Drishane House, Castletownshend, in Cork. Her early adult years were marked by the Land League unrest: many a landlord was shot, and even the more benevolent ones might find their lands poisoned or barbed wire traps left in the path of their hunt. To the Somervilles, however, the main lesson of the period was that of betrayal by Westminster: simply, the English could no longer be relied upon to support their people in Ireland. Later, she would recall how her parents

> . . . pulled through those bad years of the early 'eighties, when rents were unpaid, and crops failed, and Parnell and his wolf-pack were out for blood, and the English Government flung them, bit by bit, the property of the only men in Ireland who, faithful to the pitch of folly, had supported it since the days of the Union.[3]

Such feelings may account for the steadfastly critical portrayals of the new kind of middle-class English Victorians to be found in the duo's books: but no less intense for Martin Ross (whose real name was Violet Martin) was a sense of betrayal of the old feudal code by the Irish themselves. She was born in 1862 to a landlord family in Galway, where the rapport with the tenantry was so relaxed that her parents cheerfully permitted beloved foster-mothers to have each newborn child surreptitiously baptized by the local Catholic priest, after the 'official' Protestant ceremony: 'It was done for us all, and my father and mother knew it quite well, and never took any notice. I was baptised by Lord Plunket in the living-room at Ross, so the two Churches can fight it out for me.' Yet, in 1872, such easy relations came to an end when the tenantry voted for a Home Rule candidate and against their master, who never recovered from the blow: 'It was not the political defeat, severe as that was; it was the personal wound, and it was incurable.'[4] He died a broken man. In 1872 also, the family abandoned the estate as unviable and went to live in Dublin. Much later, in 1888, Martin would return to Ross and use her literary earnings to restore the house, but the old *noblesse oblige* had endured a mortal wound.

The pair had met for the first time in 1886, when Somerville was twenty-seven and Martin twenty-three. They became fast friends and within three years close literary collaborators. 'For most boys and girls the varying, yet invariable, fluctuations and emotional episodes of youth are resolved and composed by marriage,' recalled Somerville: 'To Martin and to me was opened another way, and the flowering of both our lives was when we met each other.'[5] In the later decades of the Victorian period, such intense relationships between intellectual women were widespread, especially among those for whom marriage was not necessarily the most attractive option. In a period when many aristocratic husbands spent much time away from their wives and when wives were expected to be deferential child-bearers and domestic hostesses, this was hardly surprising. To seek out spiritual companionship with another trusted young woman might be for a certain kind of person the only hope of intellectual growth. Some relations of this kind developed a strong physical dimension, but there is no clear evidence that Somerville and Ross explored that option.

Nor did they ever consider setting themselves up as an alternative to the structure of the inherited family: rather they wrote their books in order to earn the money that might secure their family inheritances. They were well aware of the frustrations of living in such families and could use a scathing wit at the expense of the male hearties who dominated big house life. In a letter to her partner, Somerville pointedly captured the boredom of endless tennis four-somes at Castletownshend, when all she wished to do was compose:

> To attempt anything serious or demanding steady work is just simply impossible here, and I feel sickened of even trying – we are all so tied together – whatever is done must be done by everyone in the whole place and as the majority prefer wasting their time that is the prevalent amusement.[6]

Helpless availability to intruders was not just a humiliation known by the occupants of Dublin tenements: it also disfigured the lives of society ladies. One of the profounder achievements of Somerville and Ross is their dramatization of the mortified female consciousness when it finds itself among disagreeable or unsympathetic people. There had, of course, been precedent for this in the novels of Jane Austen and Charlotte Brontë, but the pair added depth and intensity to the loneliness felt by women, even those who managed outwardly successful marriages. 'Men's professions, whether great or small,' wrote Somerville, 'invariably remind them of their position as part of a community, while the persistent effort of hundreds of generations of husbands has been to isolate and insulate their women.'[7]

Somerville had been in love with a charismatic engineer named Hewitt Poole, but her family forbade marriage because he had no money. Her books return obsessively to a thwarted love and to later meetings between a once-willing woman and her never-to-be-had

man. The self-reliance she developed through her writing and management of the Drishane estate may have been a response to this
early and demeaning example of female dependency: she had fallen
for one man (the engineer) and been stymied by another (her colonel
father). The mood of 1890s Ireland was anyway for self-help: after
the political frustration of the Parnell tragedy, the Gaelic League
attempted in 1893 to promote Irish culture and crafts in an atmosphere of self-reliance. If no help for Irish causes was to be had from
Westminster, it was up to Irish people to help themselves.

Somerville and Ross were caught up in the new enthusiasm. The
1890s were the golden years of their collaboration, a sort of Indian
summer of the ascendancy after the agrarian outrages of the previous
decade but before the crises of the new century. 'If there was a hint
of future trouble in the air', says Conor Cruise O'Brien, 'it was no
more than lent tang and tension and distinction to the lives of high-
spirited people like Somerville and her cousin [Ross].'[8] Somerville
attended Irish-language classes, and both women supported the
suffragist movement in the belief that, since every man judged
women by those whom he knew best, 'it rests with each of us to form
that opinion'.[9] Somerville half jocularly suggested that her suffragism
had been born in the moment when a company of English dragoons
in Castletownshend gave her brother a ride on their horses but
ignored her. Her suffragism placed a premium on intelligence, which
she found abundantly in her literary friend: 'The outstanding fact, as
it seems to me, among women who live by their brains, is friendship,
a profound friendship that extends through every phase and aspect
of life, intellectual, social, pecuniary.'[10]

Yet, for all that radicalism on cultural questions, the pair remained
until Martin's death in 1915 fundamentally conservative on the
national question. Here was yet another case of Tory Anarchism.
Both women campaigned for the Unionist Alliance in 1895, in the
conviction that the destruction of the landlord system would lead to
the collapse of all civil society in Ireland. A similar ambivalence
seems to have existed in Somerville's attitude to something as practical as money: she had to be careful, since the house was expensive to
run, yet every so often she would submit to an impulse of wild
extravagance.[11] Likewise ambivalent was Martin's attitude to the
peasantry: she had as a child happily followed her foster-mother
into weddings, wakes and even masses said in Irish, yet when push
came to shove she felt compelled to support the landlords against the
very people whom she had come to love. Such tensions help to
account for the most powerful scene they ever wrote – at the climax
of *The Silver Fox*, a novella of true genius.

That work was published amidst the general calm of the year 1897. There is in the handling of the tale a delightful wit and lightness of touch, which bespeak the optimism of the period and the renewed openness of the gentry to native codes. 'The 'nineties, for Anglo-Ireland', wrote Elizabeth Bowen, 'were a decade of fine consciences, and an humour that was uncombative, mellow and disengaged. Protestantism became less bigoted.'[12] In keeping with that mood, a gentle mockery is made in *The Silver Fox* of those more proselytizing Protestants who seek to convert pantry-boys to the true faith or to berate the popish tendencies of clergymen who say the creed while facing east. Even more notable – perhaps the word should be astounding – is the ferocious criticism of all things English which sounds in the story from beginning to end. Just three years after the publication of Douglas Hyde's lecture on the need to deanglicize Ireland, the writers produce a tale to that precise description, for in it an openness to rural folk belief will be combined with a coruscating critique of the crass commercialism of modern England. The loyalist duo, recalling their frustrations with London during the previous decade, took the chance to voice disapproval of the new order in books whose readership was mainly English; yet in that very process they were, ever so quietly, placing themselves in alignment with the cultural revival being led in Ireland by Hyde, Gregory and Yeats.

On a furtive visit to the Irish Literary Theatre in 1901, Martin beautifully rendered in a letter to her partner the strange tangentiality of their position in terms of her seating in the auditorium some rows behind W.B. Yeats: 'I daresay the Irish Literary Revival was quite disastrously unaware of my presence in the shades at the back.' She was astute enough to note 'the strange mix of saga and modern French situations' in *Diarmid and Grania* well before the conflation of heroic and novelistic modes in *Cuchulain of Muirthemne*, yet she remained caustic about some of the more preposterous personalities of the revival. The actor Benson was not convincing: 'in his love-making he moaned over Mrs B's face like a cat when a dog comes into the room'.[13] The *dramatis personae* in the auditorium were even worse: Maud Gonne's 'huge mop of curled yellow hair crowned her big fat body' so that 'one look at her would be enough for anyone to form an opinion'. Yet Martin's account of Yeats was kind: 'a cross between Dominic Sampson and a starved R.C. curate – in seedy black clothes – with a large black bow at the root of his long naked throat', but for all that every inch 'a poet'.[14] In reading such accounts, one gets the feeling that the frustrated empire loyalists had sent a scout deep into enemy territory with the intent of seeing whether it might not be the right time to change sides.

The bankruptcy of the alternative English culture is well exposed in the opening pages of *The Silver Fox*, set on the Hurlingham estate at mid-winter. Lady Susan French carries herself with invincible selfishness, blocking the fire with her hunting boots from Slaney Morris, before asking whether such things as riding boots have ever been heard of in Ireland. Unable to summon a brilliant retort, and ashamed of her own boots (which were made in an Irish country town), Slaney blushes, already at a moment of social disadvantage in the midst of outwardly confident 'cultured' people. But the narrative voice soon enters Slaney's consciousness, with the suggestion that English self-confidence amounts to nothing more than bluster. Looking out of the frame-window at distant skaters on a lake, she thinks of them as marionettes on a wire, *types* without any redeeming element of the individual:

> Even at that distance they seemed to Slaney over-dressed and artificial. No doubt they were screaming inanities to each other, as were those other English idiots in the room behind her. How ineffably stupid they were, and how shy and provincial they made her feel. How could Hugh have married into such a *pack*?[15]

The echoes of the hunt evoked by 'pack' are damning enough, but the insult to a vulnerable feminine intelligence is absolute. Lady Susan has indeed married Slaney's brother Hugh, whom she suspects of experiencing softening of the brain after a fall from a horse. Slaney knows nothing of that suspicion. 'She had sat, inwardly scornful and outwardly shy, in the midst of a conversation whose knack she did not catch, and whose purport she thought either babyish or vulgar.'[16] Lady Susan, a creature of sheer surfaces, has had her hair dyed 'as red as a fox now' on her passage through Paris: compared with such style, Slaney cannot compete. Yet her blushes become her, so that the onlooking Major Bunbury (revived as a joke from Wilde's *The Importance of Being Earnest*) finds her almost handsome.

In that opening scene, Slaney is amused to note the selfishness that governs the other characters. Finding no meal prepared, Lady Susan commandeers the waiter's dinner, yet as soon as she is satisfied, she gives the remains to a cat. It is a more devastating portrayal of the English than may be found in any nationalist tract of the decade, and it marks an immense shift in the depiction of Anglo-Irish attitudes.

Earlier writers such as Swift had attempted to show up the appalling discrepancy between English order at home and misrule in Ireland, the bad administrators in the smaller island being woefully mediocre and corrupt misrepresentatives of an intrinsically admirable home culture. But the slack-jawed villa vulgarity on display in this scene suggests that the English may now also be odious at home. True nobility may, by a curious paradox, be found only in remote outposts of Ireland, while those who live in England constitute the abominations of a once-proud code of service, selfless gentility and beautiful manners. Slaney is the authentic aristocrat, whom these vulgarians can only play at being, yet she is Irish to the core, named (after all) for a Wexford river with strong connotations of the 1798 rebellion.

She attempts to regale the company with a 'rum' story of a cultural clash in her home townland between ancient Irish and contemporary English codes. An engineer named Glasgow has been building a railway and is in need of gravel, so he has bought a hillside tract from old Danny Quin: but when the sand is blasted, a silver fox appears:

> They say that there is an old prophecy about the bad luck that is to come when that hill is thrown into Tully Lake. They believe that the fox is a witch or a fairy, and that it will bring the bad luck.[17]

Hugh's pragmatic response would be to kill the fox and, with it, the problem.

Next, we learn that Danny Quin is dead, following a fatal fall over the sandpit. He had been racked with guilt after the sale, but Glasgow would not annul it. The mourners agree that had he refrained from the deal, he would have been fine. Over eight pounds in silver has been subscribed to help the poor family with funeral expenses; the custom, we are told, 'combines the politeness to the dead man and his family, with a keen sense of the return that will be made in kind when it becomes the donor's turn to have a funeral'.[18] The echo of Maria Edgeworth is deliberate, for Somerville admired her as 'the last to write of Irish country life with sincerity and originality'. Edgeworth 'had the privilege, which was also ours, of living in Ireland, in the country, and amongst the people of whom she wrote'.[19] Like her, the collaborators were aware that there was invariably a sound, practical explanation for all the 'irrational' lore and superstitions of the peasantry.

The complacency of the new English in Ireland is epitomized by Glasgow, now pictured surveying his handiwork with approval and the mourners with distaste: 'What swine they are.'[20] The violent language is shocking in so modulated a story, all the more so given Slaney's romantic feelings for the ritual. Quin's own son calls Glasgow an 'English hound' (a metaphor that equates the Irish with the pursued fox). As tears runs down his hairy cheeks, he accuses Glasgow of precipitating his father's death. Glasgow, who has been trifling with the affections of Slaney, has designs on Lady Susan. Lamenting that her husband Hugh can not make a horse 'go', he suggests that women are sometimes more adept at this than men.

The hunt now functions as a metaphor for sexual desire as well as for landlord–tenant antagonisms: and it will be further complicated in the unfolding narrative. Lady Susan is amused by Glasgow's compliment:

> 'Oh, I say, that's what they call blarney over here, isn't it? We call it humbug in England, you know.'
>
> None the less, her opinion of Glasgow rose, and, so much is there in the manner of saying a stupid thing, he was pleased by the approval and did not notice the stupidity.[21]

The manner of these conversationalists is all. In total contrast, Slaney lacks style but attends to core values. When she rides a horse, she uses it solely 'as a means of transit, very much as people use omnibuses'. Contemplating her, Glasgow repents of his invitation that she ride out with the company, and turns instead towards Lady Susan. Yet Slaney still treasures his copy of Swinburne's *Atalanta in Calydon* given on loan, and she finds some of the passages that he marked 'the mouthpiece of his soul'.[22] Slaney, like Hugh, is all inwardness and spirit: the others are all exterior bravura. In this tale, there is an inverse relation between self-confidence and intelligence, with the consequence that while Hugh 'almost hated his wife for the easy confidence in him that he knew he did not deserve',[23] the comment on his fear of riding after his fall works strongly in his moral favour.

One of the many paradoxes of the tale is that 'modern' England has a rather constricted view of women, whereas 'traditional' Ireland provides a setting more conducive to the New Woman of the Nineties. Slaney can not only read works of high literature, but in her dealings with tenants can subvert the codes of professional males, practising medicine in its unofficial form. She had 'the turn for doctoring that is above all things adorable to the Irish poor, whose taste for the contraband finds in a female quack a gratification almost comparable to "potheen-making"'. Since her childhood – like Violet

Martin – she had attended their deathbeds and funerals, showing innate sympathy with their fears. The Widow Quin now confides in her the awful tale of how the dead Danny saw the silver fox, which made him feel 'a wind from the say coming bechuxt his skin an his blood':[24] and now their son Tom is similarly demented. Slaney innocently offers to have a reassuring word with him, but the widow craftily suggests that she might have a word with Glasgow. Whatever about the intellectual limits of the poor, their instincts remain shrewd and their brains alert. All the romantic hopes of the Slaneys and Glasgows seem crystal-clear to the underlings, even before their sponsors have learned how to formulate them.

From the tongue-tied girl of the opening, Slaney grows in stature with every passing scene. Now she impresses even Lady Susan and Major Bunbury, for context has changed everything. In England her natural refinement was ineffectual and lost: in Ireland it is pervading and subtle. Lady Susan mentally promotes her from the ranks of the 'non-combatants' (a reminder that the hunt is also war prosecuted by other means); it is at this moment that Major Bunbury decides that his sister (who liked Carlyle and Scarlatti) should know her. As Glasgow's interest wanes, theirs waxes, a hint that they may yet be redeemed. Lady Susan in particular sees real value in Slaney's rapport with the peasantry: by it, she hopes, the young woman may persuade the huntsman Danny-O to cut the gorse at the controversial railway channel.

Once again, an occasion is provided for the authors to offer an anthropological explanation of a seemingly bizarre custom: but as the narrative voice urges the internal logic of the system, it tilts audibly towards the viewpoint of the natives:

> It cannot be called superstition – being neither ignorant dread nor self-interested faith; it seems like the possession of another sense – imperfect, yet distinct from all others. She had seen and heard – between the sunset and the dawn – things not easily accounted for; she herself accepted them without fear, but she knew – as everyone who knows well a half-civilised people must know – how often a superstition is justified of its works.

The religious echo here (of belief justified by works rather than by faith alone) suggests a form of knowledge with the glamour of the forbidden to the Protestant mind; the repeated dashes emphasize the excitement of the discovery.[25]

In conversation with Glasgow, Slaney offers to share that wisdom in ways that might benefit his project. 'I often think', she says, 'that it isn't much good to go against the country people in these things.'[26] But he is unmoved: that self-confidence which made him attractive to lesser intelligences is unruffled. So he prefers to flirt, meaninglessly. Soon after, as Slaney reads his copy of *Fortnightly Review*, a letter in large handwriting falls out whose lines her eye cannot choose but see: and her good opinion of him is lost forever.

Yet Glasgow cannot yet know that. At the next hunt, while she takes new note of his baldness, he responds to her attractiveness and approves his own chivalry in recognizing it. The huntsman Danny-O refuses to go into the covert and Tom Quin offers a figure of abject desolation to the hunt. The silver fox materializes on cue. Slaney is filled with a sudden onset of energy and rides with passion. This is the central symbolic meaning of the tale: the fox, which immobilizes and destroys some characters on both sides of the social divide, has the effect of energizing others:

> Her courage repelled the shock to her instinct but her under-
> standing had taken a 'list' to the unknown and the impossible,
> and in spite of the morning sunshine and the candid blue sky,
> she did not altogether right herself.[27]

That list had already been taken by the narrative voice itself, as if in preparation for this epiphany.

As Glasgow's horse clears the stones, it is hit by a stick bran-dished by Tom Quin. Slaney urges Quin to go home. The scene is a throwback to the 1880s, describing 'that inarticulate futility of rage that is not good to see'.[28] The transitions of tone, from social comedy to intimations of a darker tragedy, are managed with a faultless ease which seems to contain within itself the hope that painful social ten-sions might yet be overcome: yet the situation is not at the sole command of the Anglo-Irish who might achieve this end. Rather, the blunt Englishman Glasgow seizes the initiative. To Slaney's protesta-tion that Tom doesn't know what he does, Glasgow responds brutally: 'He knows now.' Tom was a hunter for whom the hunter became the quarry, but he has been restored to his traditional posi-tion as the hunted one.

Meanwhile, Slaney has begun to ride like a woman possessed, 'in a dream-like rush'.[29] At this moment Somerville and Ross release all their love of the pleasures of the hunt, now that a heroine of real intelligence can be shown to be caught up in it. Lady Susan, asking where she has gone, likens the quiet young woman to the fox who vanished. 'Is *she* a witch too? I think she must be to have got that old crock along as she did.' The women seem more open to the numinous than the men, and all the more intelligent for that. Hugh's self-disgust at his lost nerve as a horseman leads him to shy away from a frank exchange with his wife. The want of intellect among a hunting set which worships only physical prowess leads to moral failure:

> Passionate admiration, turning to passionate jealousy of her flawless courage, and self-contempt, and knowledge that his eyes would never again meet hers without consciousness of failure: all these because a good little average man had but two ideas in life, and when one was taken from him, the other sickened like a poisoned thing.[30]

Technically given all the social advantages, men are shown here to be victims of the very system that enthrones them. Hugh as a sensitive soul is one potentially tragic version of that victimage, but so in a more comic mode is Major Bunbury:

> Major Bunbury was reading a newspaper with that air of serving his country that belongs to men when they read papers. No woman can hope to read the *Times* as though it were a profession: it is a masculine gift, akin to that of dining.[31]

There is a flash of real anger behind the comedy, but the final effect is of a mellow hilarity.

Even though a cad like Glasgow may be freed to treat as a passing fancy a moment unforgettable to Slaney (their kiss), somehow her own life seems far richer. She is in fact the real New Woman whom the smoking, henna-dyed Lady Susan pretends to be. Major Bunbury, considering Slaney's versatility, 'wondered how it was that so many impossible things were possible in Ireland'. While he is falling in love with her, she is far too busy falling out of love with Glasgow to notice. Glasgow's fatuous attempt to paw her under a blanket as they ride homewards by carriage recalls the famous carriage ride in Jane Austen's *Emma*, where the difficulty of escaping disagreeable people without rank discourtesy becomes a real issue. Slaney simply has herself reseated next to Major Bunbury, and as Lady Susan and Glasgow connect, the others hold 'a conversation lame with the consciousness of what it tried to ignore'.[32] That night, the near-psychic Slaney hears a strange sound beneath her bedroom window. Once again, the silver fox is brushing against her world.

The clash between the power of new money and the securities of rural tradition was a staple theme as early as the *fili*: and in the retelling of Somerville and Ross it becomes again a contest between nobility and mobility:

> The ring of the trowel travelled far on the wind across the heather, a voice of civilisation, saying pertinent, unhesitating things to a country where all was loose, and limitless, and inexact. Up here, by the shores of Lough Ture, people had, from all ages, told the time by the sun, and half-an-hour either way made no difference to anyone; now – most wondrous of all impossibilities – the winter sunrise was daily heralded by the steely shriek of an engine whirling truckloads of men to their work across the dark and dumb boglands.[33]

This might seem like the irruption of the capitalist code into the countryside for the first time, were it not for the authors' honesty in conceding that the Anglo-Irish were themselves originally a middle-class group. French's Court, they had written some pages earlier, had nothing to be said for it in aesthetic terms, being 'of as Presbyterian a gauntness as its tribe'.[34] The victory of technology over tradition, of cash over culture, attempted now by Glasgow, had already been effected at the Flight of the Earls. Or so it had seemed. But no victory in Ireland was ever unqualified, no new order ever quite achieved the status and sanction of a tradition. After eight months of remorseless effort, Glasgow is still trying to fill the Bog of Tully, but only the local workmen know how futile his attempt is. The clearing has water running under it and will never be secured. The folk superstition surrounding the area, far from being a piece of crazy foolishness, was the local warning that here was treacherous, unreliable ground: as always, a core of pragmatic good sense lay behind the 'superstition'.

Glasgow is building on sand and his workmen now go unpaid. The lines he liked to quote from Swinburne take on the contours of a death wish, 'foreknowledge of death'.[35] Major Bunbury, noting suddenly how mediocre he is, worries that Lady Susan may be losing her head about him. As others wilt, Slaney grows clairvoyant, sensing that the Major's silence 'was vexed with misgiving about Lady Susan'.[36] Yet the deeper the lady falls into the vortex of emotion, the more real she seems to Slaney. Somerville and Ross here add a delicate, sisterly touch: 'It was against all theories of womanhood, yet the fact remained that Slaney liked Lady Susan.'[37] Every character is shown, by such sudden turns in the narrative, to have mysterious, unexpected potentials. Even as Major Bunbury is revealed to have been silently critical of Glasgow all through, so Slaney is found to be a secret admirer of Lady Susan's quest for a life of some 'heart'.

The effect of the story is exactly that of a hunt chase, with a rise in energy and speed towards the close. After a stroll in the woods, during which Glasgow makes off with Lady Susan on a brake-van, Slaney and Major Bunbury must rush in a ballast-engine to catch them up. Suddenly, pursuers and pursued are faced with a dark obstruction: rock and gravel have fallen from the hillside onto the railway line, as if nature itself is declaring a limit to the confident expansionism of the English.

Moments earlier, Lady Susan had seemed as 'fast' and progressive as the new railway. She had been flirting with Glasgow in the rail station, yet even then the landscape all around had seemed too immense a background for her 'powdered cheek' (a beautifully ambiguous phrase). The land seems holy, yet Glasgow's belief in order leaves no room for the ineffable. In the end, his business fails because it is just too businesslike:

> . . . he had based his brilliant and minute calculations on the theory that cheap Irish labour would accomplish as much in the day as costly English, and the fact that it had not done so was obviously beyond the sphere of rational calculation.[38]

Although Slaney had come closer to death than Lady Susan at her moment of danger, she had been less frightened. Major Bunbury can only admire her pluck. As he teaches her to ride a bicycle, she finds it as hard as Hugh found it to ride a horse – but the Major feels that days spent without her would now be meaningless.

Tom Quin drowns in the lake, having lost his wits – and the story turns sombre in scenes of the sort at which Violet Martin excelled. They depict a suffering among the natives so great as to induce terror even in those unafflicted. The twice-bereaved Mrs Quin curses Glasgow: and the widow's curse is the most feared of all. Those who try to restrain her flow of invective are pulled back, lest the bad luck fall on those who interfere with her curse. Lady Susan, now much weakened, turns for comfort to Major Bunbury (and Slaney feels a pang, for she senses that the woman is 'expecting no quarter from a girl' – another sign of her own desire for sisterly solidarity). To Glasgow's jibe that these scenes are a result of encouraging superstition, Slaney mildly responds that they may be the result of discouraging it. He concludes that honest, sane people should give up all dealings with the Irish. 'Do you mean English people?' she asks: 'They certainly have not been eminently successful so far.'[39] They have been, in point of fact, about as ineffectual in Ireland as Slaney was in England.

Hearing her clear-sighted analysis, Glasgow can only wonder how he ever found such a woman attractive: a fair summary of England's own feeling about Ireland in 1897. Slaney fears that Lady Susan is in the snare of a fowler and chooses the moment to remind him of the letter that fell from the *Fortnightly Review*; as he wonders why she would bother to mention such a trifle, she asserts her fondness for Lady Susan:

> In the silence that followed it seemed to her as though she had thrown a heavy stone into deep water, without hope of result beyond the broken mirror and the flagging ripple.[40]

The writing is wonderfully modulated, with technique as precise as that of an imagist lyric, presenting 'an intellectual and emotional complex in an instant of time'.[41]

Hugh now receives a letter of complaint about the damage done in his absence by his hunt: the anonymous writer nastily links his wife to Glasgow. The prose has the exactitude of an Augustan couplet: 'His belief in her was falling with the fall of a strong and shading tree; he clung to it even as it fell; and all the while she stood and buttoned the glove across her white wrist.'[42] As he joins the hunt for the fox in the covert, Hugh sights an unknown man, pursuing him through the mists. All the while, he fears that he may be going mad. What he is seeing is really the ghost of Danny Quin and, though the moment is terrifying, in it he becomes the first of the gentlemen to open himself to an encounter with the numinous:

> Then, quite unexpectedly, his knees began to tremble, and the breath of the unknown entered into him, cowing the conventions and the disbelief of ordinary life.[43]

At that moment he has no flash of illumination but the prospect of an always unhappy future.

Yet he also has that same spirit of defiance that transformed Slaney from being smitten to becoming a smiter, after her encounter with the fox. It is as if the very fate of the Anglo-Irish as a race is defined in his action, caught between death-wish and a summons back to life. Set against the rather acerbic treatment of Church of Ireland services by the authors, this celebration of the spiritual dimension is comparable to that of W.B. Yeats in the same decade.[44]

Hugh resolves to show his wife (now on Glasgow's horse, of course) that he is as good a man as his rival; and so he rides like a madman past the druidic stones, to which the ghost had alerted him.

Calling out to try to save his imperilled wife, he is thrown onto his head. Meanwhile, Maria Quin, daughter of the dead Danny, leaves her brother's wake and sees the fox on a nearby wall. She has no difficulty in acknowledging the 'power of unseen things that had worked together to her brother's undoing' but, being also a strict Catholic, 'she cast herself on a higher protection, half doubtful as she was of its right to intervene'.[45] Her Sacred Heart scapular may, it is hinted, be no match for the silver fox. As the hunt approaches, she is enraged by the unfeeling gentry who 'for their own amusement, had wrecked the fortunes of a family, and now came to gallop past the house of death, guided by that grey and ill-omened thing'. In other words, by her reckoning the Anglo-Irish are the evil incarnate in the silver fox. Yet, in their eyes, the natives are the 'Arctic' quarry. The symbol could not be more ambiguous.

The hunt is an equally open symbol. The dethroned Gaelic aristocrats of 1600 had also followed the hunt, as is recorded in the beautiful song 'Seán Ó Duibhir an Ghleanna'; they also had been culpably impervious to the sufferings left in its wake:

> Is bean go dúbhach sa bhealach
> Ag áireamh a cuid géan . . .

> And a woman left sadly in the way
> counting her geese . . .[46]

The hunt had always expressed the sovereignty of an upper class. In the guise of exterminating a noxious animal from their holdings, local lords reminded the tenants who the rulers of that land really were.[47] Such 'sports' had often been suspended during the 1880s because of attacks by Land League activists, and their resumption in the 1890s sometimes had a hysterical quality in evidence here. The energies unleashed on these outings 'masked a nostalgia for dominance that would never again be satisfied in reality'.[48] When Lady Susan's horse plunges over the cliff to instant death, leaving her trapped in an overhanging tree, it is a proleptic image of what may be in store for the ascendancy. The horse, being faithful to his masters, faces a dignified but definite death, while the natives, now mutinous, set out to dictate a new set of terms to the hunt.

Maria Quin is an articulate rebel. When she comes at the height of her blazing anger upon the dangling form of Lady Susan, it is as if the gods have made her retribution easy: all she has to do is to push the silly member of a parasite class to her death. The scene may well be the greatest that Somerville and Ross ever wrote, for in it Maria suddenly has a fellow-feeling with another headstrong woman who has been used to voicing her thoughts without constraint. By refusing the easy revenge, Maria asserts the prior claims of that sisterhood to which Slaney Morris in her moments of grace aspired. And this is seen as an example of the sheer goodness of the ordinary people: 'The peasant heart struggled in the grave-clothes of hatred and superstition, and burst forth with its active impetuousness and warmth.'[49]

Maria rescues Lady Susan who promptly weeps for her horse in a moment worthy of Swift's Gulliver; for one who has just shown such grandeur of soul, Maria does not spare her the rough edge of a practised tongue: 'Little ye cried yestherday whin ye seen my brother thrown out on the ground by the pool . . . you that's breakin' yer heart afther yer horse.'[50] The writers of the scene recognize its meaning from both sides. For Lady Susan, it is dreadful to cry before an 'inferior'. For Maria, it is an outrage to find horses worth more than humans in the moral balance of other persons. But the language of anthropology soon gives way to that of emotional identification with the native culture, as the force of a felt experience supplants the pose of scientific explanation:

> The Irish peasant regards the sorrow for a mere animal as a childishness that is almost sinful, a tempting of ill fate in its parody of the grief rightly due only to what is described as 'a Christhian'; and Maria's heart glowed with the unwept wrongs of her brother.[51]

The imputation of childishness to the landlord class is a precise reversal of that ascendancy stereotyping that saw the peasantry as wild and childlike: but it perfectly captures Shaw's complaint about 'boyish' immaturity.

Had Lady Susan listened only to local lore, she would not have imperilled her life. 'But sure what are you but a sthranger?' explains the baffled but forgiving Maria. 'Oh, God help ye . . . What does the likes o' ye undherstand about the likes of us? It wasn't wanting to desthroy us ye were.'[52] Maria feels on sure enough ground now to complete the 'saving' of Lady Susan, by advising her not to make little of herself with Glasgow. They shake hands.

Even the greatest admirers of Somerville and Ross have sometimes failed to appreciate the implications of this scene, in which the authors do something most commentators considered impossible to the Anglo-Irish:[53] they detach themselves from the values of their class, and their work is enriched accordingly. Their general attitude was rarely quite so open: doubtless the threat to those values was so acute as to trigger many defence mechanisms, which precluded unlimited sympathy for the peasantry. The *de haut en bas* attitude was the more usual one, as Shaw complained when he accused Somerville of more usually treating the poor as figures of fun and forgetting that they were human beings.[54] Conor Cruise O'Brien has suggested that the duo 'had to look down on people in order to see them at all' and has found the peasants in even their best work 'a collection of grotesques envisaged bleakly and without sympathy'.[55] Maria Quin is no grotesque, however, and the implications of *The Silver Fox* are the same as those spoken in the famous Preface of Charlotte Brooke: the English must achieve a real understanding of the native Irish culture if they wish to administer a happy and prosperous island. The strong suggestion, in the 1890s as in the 1780s, is that they aren't up to the job.

Lady Susan finds her husband unconscious, with an anonymous, accusing letter connecting her to Mr Glasgow dangling from his pocket. Instantly, she resolves to tell all about her dealings with the *arriviste* and to seek forgiveness from a husband who is not straitlaced. As she awaits help, the face of the insensate man tortures her with mute reproach, and she kisses the cheek, 'knowing for the first time the dreadful kiss that is so much more to one, so much less than nothing to the other'.[56] This is a perfect leitmotif, repeating in a kind of tragic parody the earlier empty kiss of a then impassioned Slaney by the affectless, uninvolved Glasgow.

It is to Glasgow's house that Hugh's body is carried. There a surprise awaits the rescuers: a woman with a nasal, cockney voice and 'an air that irresistibly suggested the footlights' tells them that she is Mrs Glasgow, come over to auction her husband's remaining holdings. The repudiation of England and Englishness with which the tale began now reaches a crescendo, with its suggestion of a dreadful middle-class vulgarity about the revealed woman:

> Her hair was straw-coloured, and drooped in a nauseous picturesqueness over her coal-black eyebrows; her face was fat and white; her dress was a highly-coloured effort at the extreme of the latest fashion but one; the general effect was elderly.[57]

This description (admittedly one of the lesser subtleties in the book) stands in contrast with the account, at the outset, of Slaney's admirable indifference to fashion. By contrast with her genuine insouciance, the helplessly botched attempt by Mrs Glasgow to keep up with trends seems abject. Her large and heavy handwriting has been seen before by Slaney, in the wifely letter that fell like an accusation from the pages of the *Fortnightly Review*. The coda is almost predictable: Glasgow meets his foretold doom in a mineshaft in the Argentine Republic; Hugh and Lady Susan are reconciled; and Slaney happily weds Major Bunbury.

In the final pages may be found just the sort of insurgent counter-appeal that animated the pages of Swift and Edgeworth. The problems of big house decline could not, in the judgement of Somerville and Ross, be attributed mainly to an insurgent peasantry: they were mostly internal to the gentry itself. The writers' posture towards the ascendancy is highly critical, yet, for all that, sympathetic and even elegiac. What saves the Anglo-Irish in their view is their intelligence and ambivalence: pulled forever in contrary directions by the English and Irish, they can at their best achieve, like Slaney, a richly responsive sensibility that combines the best of both traditions. The time-honoured virtues of the English are, however, by the 1890s in abeyance and a code of mercantile values is taking their place. Confronted with the self-confident masters of that new regime, the intelligence of the Anglo-Irish can seem socially disabling; but, when placed in alliance with the instinctual integrity of the Irish poor, it has the makings of a genuinely comprehensive code. Though English confidence is largely external and assumed, people of lesser intellect may fall for it: but the defiant refusal of the Irish to give it *any* credence is part of their subversive charm and abiding wit.

In its unfolding, this novella has the effect of a musical score, with certain singular notes sounded at intervals through the story. That score calls for constant reinterpretation by the upper-class participants, for whom each new revelation dictates a rereading of all past exchanges; the natives, however, bereft of (say) the documentary evidence of Glasgow's turpitude, can none the less scent an imposter when faced with one. The repetition of certain revelatory scenes – like the kiss given to an unfeeling body – adds depth and complication to the score. The gravel that breaks upon the railway line seems a rather blatant image of a possible break in the tale of English progress in Ireland.

That break came, of course, in 1916, just a year after the death of Violet Martin. In her diary, Somerville wrote simply 'December 21. Tues. EOES. 1915', as if she herself had passed on; for months afterward she was numb to the world. Then came the rebellion at Easter, followed by the executions which seemed to prove just how unfitted the English were to understand Irish conditions. On 9 May Somerville had issued in the *Times* of London the only published letter of the period to plead for clemency for the rebel leaders. Her argument was straightforward and, in some ways, a disguised version of her own experiences in the 1890s. The impulse for deanglicization had run 'like an epidemic' through Ireland since that decade, eventually transforming even cultural movements like the Gaelic League 'from its ingenuous programme of jig-dancing and warbling passe treason in modern Irish' and setting them 'to more effective issues'.[58] A government that had allowed such movements to flourish could hardly now hang or condemn to life imprisonment those young products of these movements who risked all for their country. With brothers in the British forces, she well understood how the rebels might seem to many critics deserving of the traitor's automatic fate, but she protested strongly against the policy.

Perhaps her years of activism in the Munster Women's Franchise League had opened her eyes to the idealism of the young in Ireland. After all, what she had said of the oppressed condition of women could have been translated with no strain to apply to the national situation:

> Want of power causes want of interest, and want of interest causes stagnation, a sodden acquiescence in things as they are, or a peevish and uncomprehending acceptance of reforms that are imposed by main strength, as by Masters upon Slaves.[59]

After the rebellion, her move towards the ranks of separatist thought gathered speed and conviction. During the Black-and-Tan terror, she expressed her new-found conviction to the composer Ethel Smyth in an image taken, appropriately enough, from hunting circles:

> In all these centuries of disaffection and disappointment, one simple thing has never been tried – giving Ireland what she asks for. If I said I wanted to go hunting, I shouldn't be consoled for a refusal by a ticket for a Sunday concert in the Albert Hall.[60]

22

Undead in the Nineties: Bram Stoker and *Dracula*

It was said that, when the body of Parnell was brought back to Ireland at Kingstown pier in 1891, a comet flashed across the sky. Soon after his burial, rumours began to circulate to the effect that the casket had not contained his corpse, being filled instead with stones. The Chief was still alive, away in the hills, so the stories went, biding his time before a triumphant return.

The myth of eternal return was attractive to the Irish. Up in Donegal, folk narrators reported sightings of the ancient hero Cuchulain at work laying tracks on the new railroads. In one sense this was no more than the fulfilment of the dream of Standish James O'Grady that the ancient hero would become once again as real to Irish people as they were to one another. The spirits of the dead would be made current among the living. Throughout the 1890s, the ghosts of famine victims featured increasingly in folktales and prohibitions. A long series of commemorations of past events was a sign of public nervousness about the approach of a new century, the last of the second millennium. People began to project their anxieties onto powerfully symbolic dates. 1896 was the centenary of Hoche's ill-fated French expedition. 1897 was the fiftieth anniversary of the worst year of the Great Famine. In London it was greeted as the near-miraculous jubilee of the reigning queen, Victoria. The Irish, not to be outdone, countered in the next year with a commemoration of the rebels of 1798. In the course of this, Maud Gonne denounced Victoria as the 'famine queen' and distributed delicacies to schoolchildren, a riposte to similar gestures of munificence offered to mark the English queen's jubilee. With the revolutionary socialist leader James Connolly and the assistance of the poet W.B. Yeats, Gonne organized a vast demonstration at which a coffin was carried.

Such empty coffins were commonplace in Irish nationalist demonstrations: after the execution of the Manchester Martyrs in 1867, three empty coffins labelled 'Allen', 'Larkin' and 'O'Brien' in big white letters were carried to the republican plot at Glasnevin Cemetery. The memory of the dead would never be allowed to fade, and many strongly suspected that the dead would come again in glory. The decade that in England marked a set of endings (of the Victorian era, of imperial expansion and of industrial power) was seen in Ireland as a time of beginnings, of movements for self-help and cultural innovation. If in England the New Woman threatened an end to male power, in Ireland the rediscovery of the Celtic Woman portended a whole new social order. If English as a literary language seemed tired and clichéd, Irish was coming back to life. Talk of degeneration among social anthropologists in England, alarmed by the debility of a fading aristocracy and the alleged moral delinquency of the urban proletariat, was answered by news of regeneration in the Ireland of the Gaelic League, the Co-operative Movement and the Literary Theatre.

These contrary movements – towards debility and towards renewed strength – were linked emphatically in the vampire figures of Bram Stoker's *Dracula*, published in the middle of 1897. The oscillations of Lucy Westenra, between falling ill and getting well, seemed to reflect the uncertainty of the age as to whether the decade marked an ending or a beginning. Even if Stoker had never committed his mythic masterpiece to print, the decade would have been remembered for its fondness for vampiric images. Although he grew up a Protestant in middle-class Dublin, Stoker understood just how potent was the memory of the dead in Ireland. He was born in 'black '47', and his mother Charlotte had clear memories of a cholera plague in Sligo during the previous decade. She wrote an account at his request in the 1870s. As if anticipating the curse of Dracula, she told him of how 'one house would be attacked and the next spared',[1] with the result that the town became a place of the dead. Each day an undertaker knocked uninvited on hall doors to ask whether coffins were needed. In the end, five-eighths of the townspeople died. Some living were buried with the dead in mass graves, because no medical orderly could get close enough to them to confirm or deny life.[2]

The Great Famine brought home to everyone – and not just Irish nationalists – the parasitism and irresponsibility of the 6,000-odd absentee landlords who owned eight million acres of land. The London *Times* of 26 June 1845 pronounced the hunger man-made and blamed 'blood-sucking landlords', whose avarice for rents led to the export of food that might have saved many lives. As a youth, Stoker was a supporter of the British empire, but he regarded the absentee landlords as delinquent. What was needed, in his view, was a vibrant middle class. When it became clear that this could fully emerge only when the landlords had been expropriated, he became an ardent admirer of William Gladstone. In the 1880s Gladstone tried to set up federal parliaments in Ireland, Scotland, Wales and England.

Stoker's father provided the best education for his children, with the consequence that he was strapped for cash. Bram studied science at Trinity College Dublin, where he was not only an outstanding scholar and athlete but a figure so popular among his fellows that he was elected President of the University Philosophical Society and Auditor of the College Historical Society. The 'Hist' was the oldest university debating society in the world: previous auditors had included Burke, Davis and Tone. In his inaugural address of 1872, Stoker expounded the thesis of decline and renewal that would loom large in *Dracula*: 'everything sinks and falls in time but nothing is eternal but Truth and Progress'.[3] Confronting the ills of society, he averred that 'the only hope which remains for its regeneration is that we may be able to carry into it some of that personal purity which still exists within individuals'. But the youthful Stoker also had a tender view of the masses. While others feared the forces for degeneracy and disruption among the teeming millions in cities, he tended to see the crowd as vulnerable rather than predatory, threatened rather than threatening.

After graduation, Stoker worked in the Fines and Penalties section of Dublin Castle and later in the Registry of Petty Sessions' Clerks. The work was dull but he tackled it with energy, eventually producing a book on *Duties of the Clerks of the Petty Sessions in Ireland* (1879). Intended to promote efficient practice across the empire, it might seem a strange debut for the author of *Dracula*, but there is a demonstrable link between the streamlined administrative world of Dublin Castle and Stoker's interest in the supernatural.

Precisely because of his scientific training, Stoker was more willing than most to establish its outer limits – the zones of life for which it could provide no full explanation. After all, Dr Van Helsing in *Dracula* is a most advanced scientist, yet he uses sacred hosts, crucifixes and garlic to ward off evil. Irish Protestants might pride themselves on 'right reason', yet many felt themselves forever at the mercy of the occult. In a notebook kept in the 1890s, John Millington Synge mischievously noted that even R.C. Trench in his *Study of Words* (1851) had made the link: 'Ascendancy – shows belief in astrology.'[4] In later decades of the nineteenth century, the evangelical wing of the Church of Ireland waged a campaign against 'all traces of sacerdotalism and "Romanism"' in their prayer book and sacred rituals. Their reforms ran deep. Not only was the use of candles or holy wafers discouraged, but the placement of a crucifix on the communion table was said to be wrong. Communion, it was stressed, was not a physical consumption of the body of Christ but 'taken only in a heavenly and spiritual manner, through faith'.[5] Yet these revisions seemed to unleash only waves of further irrationalism: it would not be fanciful to list them as major causes of the literary Revival, which saw so many men and women of Protestant background embrace peasant spirituality.[6]

There was a radical irony in that embrace, because the same forces that sought to rationalize Protestant practice were sometimes invoked by the Roman Catholic bishops in their drive to combat 'superstitions' of popular devotionalism. So the belief in unofficial local saints and their healing potential was often discouraged by a hierarchy keen to see the emergence of a modern Catholic middle class: yet these were the very elements celebrated in the writings of Yeats, Augusta Gregory and Douglas Hyde. It was another case of the return of the repressed. Even within Protestant Dublin's professional elites, there was a remarkable market for fortune-tellers, phrenologists, mesmerists and so forth.

This helps to account for the attraction of Gothic for Irish Protestant authors from Maturin to Stoker, from Le Fanu to Yeats. Over in England, once the Roman Catholic minority had been emancipated, interest in Gothic began to subside. Catholics after the 1820s were considered somewhat 'safe' and 'integrated' at last into civil society: they would not become fully subversive again until the aesthetic adventure of the 1890s, at which moment, most significantly, London and Dublin authors would reconnect in explorations of the mode. One benign version of a literary Catholicism calculated to appeal to young Protestants was to be found in Hyde's editions of the songs of Connacht, and later in Augusta Gregory's *Book of Saints and Wonders*; but the more challenging version was unleashed in Gothic, with its medieval castles, feudal protagonists and cult of the paranormal. For such members of the Protestant ascendancy as remained, the mode was a way of embodying social fear. In Ireland those who haunted the nightly dreams of aristocrats might not even be dead spirits but live bodies of mass and weight, armed to the teeth outside demesne walls. There was inevitably a link between 'possession of land' and 'possession by spirits',[7] a link that may explain Synge's wicked joke about astrology.

The Gothic encouraged a besieged Protestant elite to dramatize its fears and phobias in a climate of inexorable political decline. The Gothic was what they had instead of historical novels in the mode of realism practised for the British by Walter Scott. There, past history was considered to be well and truly over. In Ireland, however, the past wasn't even properly past: it kept erupting into the present, and so the Gothic seemed the appropriate form for a society that would move from folklore to modernism without a sustained intervening phase of verisimilar realism. When Dracula shatters a mirror, that is a melodramatic fulfilment of Maria Edgeworth's 1834 prediction that the modes of literary realism would not serve in Ireland. He is literally unrepresentable in the mirror and says, 'Away with it!', shattering it into a thousand pieces.

The historian Roy Foster has argued that a wanderer like Dracula epitomizes 'a sense of displacement, a loss of social and psychological integration, and an escapism motivated by the threat of a takeover by the Catholic middle classes'.[8] There would be, of course, a more benign version of the wanderer, in the vagrants of Yeats and Gregory or the learned tramps of Synge and Beckett. But the changing-of-the-guard was well and truly begun: by 1870 the Church of Ireland had been disestablished and Catholics now controlled three major rail companies, a number of banks, and large tracts of the urban property network. An insecure middle class of Protestants might, as Foster suggests, seek 'refuge in the occult': but it may be equally true of other sorts of Protestant that the ghosts of the past were precisely what they wanted to escape from.[9]

This was still a transitional society, of course, with every post hotly contested: but few could doubt who the ultimate winners of the numbers game were going to be. Gothic, with its aura of feudal grandeur and ruined glories, may have appealed to a once-proud, now-marginal, Protestant elite – much as it would appeal to decayed landowners of the American South. For it is indeed about 'possession' in every sense of that word, and especially when possession may turn out to be more of a liability than a blessing. Yet terror at all the crucifixes and incense of Catholicism gave way to fascination among many Irish Protestant authors, a fascination that makes the cultural Catholicism coded into the children's tales of Oscar Wilde far more subversive than his one-liners against the upper class. Here was another case of the insurgent counterappeal, first experienced by

Swift and Goldsmith as a growing identification with an exploited peasantry, but now felt by Stoker and Wilde in the seductive majority religion of the risen people. Many Dublin Protestants with a hankering after the supernatural scorned to submit to the superstitious faith of the peasants up the road: hence the oft-repeated turn towards Eastern religion. The pursuit of occult studies was of a piece with this. 'For a Catholic, religious authority provided the arbitrary,' explains Roy Foster, 'but an Irish Protestant had to look elsewhere.'[10] This was literally true of Gothic, in the sense that power in its world would always exist somewhere else, but never in the surveyed society. The problem was that, deep down, many Protestants wanted less to compete with Catholicism than to Catholicize. Initial involvement with undergraduate Romanism or occult societies was often no more than an attempt to unmask the buttoned-down propriety of the parental generation; but these experiments could result in a deeper set of commitments to a Catholic symbology, of the kind indicated in *Dracula*, where the crucifix and communion wafer fortify professional people in their last battle with the Transylvanian monster.

The scale and scope of the Dracula myth have been so enormous as to obscure not only the author but the Irish world that made him. Some elements of the tale are clearly indebted to Sheridan Le Fanu's *Carmilla* and to Carleton's *leannán sidhe*, those unearthly women who draw vital energies from a wasting male, as the vampirellas enfeeble Jonathan Harker at the outset. The very notion of the Undead may derive from a discussion of the *neamh-mhairbh* in Seathrún Céitinn's *Foras Feasa ar Éirinn*. But there is no need to limit the resonances to Ireland. The fearsome power of the narrative comes from Stoker's refusal of specification – characters, locales and motives are all left terrifyingly open. A story about ultimate fears 'must of necessity combine fears that have different causes: economic, ideological, psychical, sexual'.[11] Nevertheless, the Irish resonances should not be ignored.[12] If Irish writing was done to be 'overheard' in England, then Irish writing in England was surely produced on the understanding that it might be read with a peculiar, probing intensity in Ireland. Such readers could decode the 'national' text without denying its other valencies.

Dracula begins with an apology for its spooky conflation of the embarrassingly archaic with the reassuringly avant-garde: the tale will be incredible, the documentation exemplary (by transcript, phonograph, newspaper cutting and diary, all coordinated in keeping with later modernist techniques of literary cubism). Its protagonist, a solicitor's apprentice named Jonathan Harker, takes pride in his diary: 'nineteenth century up-to-date with a vengeance'. The revenge of modernity on atavistic traditions will be difficult, as he later discovers, for these 'had and have powers of their own which mere "modernity" cannot kill'.[13] Harker is young, a professional of the middle class; the count whom he visits and eventually opposes is old, aristocratic, a vestige of a bygone age of heroes. Yet such is his force that Harker feels compelled to put the word 'modernity' in inverted commas. All the same, the age of heroics is over, though there will be times in the tale when Dracula's lament for lost greatness will sound like Standish James O'Grady's attempt to rally the fading gentry with the image of Cuchulain:

> Is it a wonder that we were a conquering race? . . . Bah! what good are peasants without a leader? . . . The warlike days are over. Blood is too precious a thing in these days of dishonourable peace: and the glories of the great races are as a tale that is told.[14]

As he voyages towards the count's castle, Harker senses a loss of Western order and control: trains grow less punctual. Every superstition in the world is found in the Carpathians. The forests around the castle function as sites of the unconscious, much as they did in English treatments of Gaelic Ireland, and accounts of peasant women who offer rosaries and crucifixes to the traveller seem transposed versions of travel in rural Ireland. The analogy with eastern Europe was a commonplace in the 1890s: it featured also in Shaw's play *Arms and the Man* which explored the same crisis of anxious masculinity and lost heroism. Stoker's brother George had found analogies of the Irish jig in Bavaria, and Bram had studied E.C. Johnson's *On the Tracks of the Crescent*, whose author found 'many points of resemblance to our friend Paddy' in the Transylvanian peasant.[15]

The analogies between the count and the Anglo-Irish aristocracy are even more suggestive. Harker, though feeling himself a prisoner of the castle, discovers Dracula making the beds, because in the absence of servants he must do everything. Meals are slovenly and served late, according to a Castle Rackrent-style flexitime. The count, an Anglophile, takes English magazines and papers, none of recent date. His excellent English, learned (like that of the nineteenth-century Irish) from books, has a strange intonation. Grammar and words are circumspect, in the manner of a colonial whose atlas falls open 'naturally' at England – that epitome of the human norm for 1897. Dracula plans a trip to England in order to allow himself to master modern technology. Whether he is to be seen as a type of the absentee landlord running out of soil may be open to doubt,[16] for his land at home is secure: but he does bear striking analogies to those ascendancy parasites who visited England in hopes of seducing society girls and sucking their financial blood.

Local peasants regard the count as an anti-Christ, but it scarcely matters whether he is pagan, Protestant or even Catholic, since aristocratic families (like the Rackrents) often contained amalgams of these elements. The point is that he is a diabolical aristocrat who can be fought only with a combination of the modern and the ancient, the typewriter and the crucifix. If ever there was a case of a fictional protagonist being educated in the protocols of a both/and philosophy, that figure is Harker. As an English churchman he had baulked at the crucifix offered by a peasant woman, but soon he is taking a more Yeatsian view. Still, he finds it odd that a thing he thought idolatrous 'should in a time of trouble and loneliness be of help'.[17] This is revising the Protestant revisionists of the 1870s to make way for the Catholicized Protestantism that would be a feature of Irish modernism from Augusta Gregory to Bernard Shaw. The peasant crucifix, made of rowan, is another powerful symbol which mere modernity cannot kill: yet Harker remains unclear whether the cross has force in itself or is 'a medium, a tangible help, in conveying memories of sympathy and comfort'.[18]

Harker needs what help he can get, for already he and the count (who would have made a wonderful solicitor, such is his attention to detail) are seeming to function as one another's doubles. Overcome by a wicked, burning desire to be kissed by the three female vampires, or vampirellas, of the castle, Harker forgets monogamy and his betrothal to Mina Murray: the fair-haired female arches her neck as the vampires lick their lips and line up to suck his blood. In this scene, Harker is passive as the women seize the initiative, only to hear Dracula countermand their desires: 'This man belongs to me.'[19] Dracula's desire is not exactly homoerotic, for he wishes less to penetrate than to transform his victim. He may even want to *become* his target, for soon he is wearing the clothes of Harker, so that any evil he does will be attributed by the local people to the Englishman. Dracula, envying Harker, wants to be more like him, a master of the bourgeois world: at the same time the solicitor's apprentice finds himself sleeping by day and deprived of those papers and timetables that would have located him confidently in that world. Already, the major characters of the book are deliquescing into one another. While Harker receives the propositions of the three vampirellas, back in England Lucy Westenra takes marriage proposals from three stalwart men. While he prowls by night around the castle, she sleepwalks through Whitby. When his energy fades, her health declines. The blood transfusions she later receives may be a kind of answer to her desire that a girl should be able to 'marry three men, or as many as want her',[20] but they certainly indicate the interchangeability of persons. The middle-class notion of the rugged, distinctive individual was already under attack in the social anthropology of the 1890s. The freedom once dreamed of for separate individuals by John Stuart Mill had turned out to be the freedom to be just like everybody else.

Even Dracula is not immune. What glamour he possesses derives less from innate qualities than from his capacity to mirror other persons. His own body may be unmirrorable, but that is because he is empty, a mere reflector of all other images. Pursued by the specialists of the 1890s world, he is largely speechless once he abandons his castle: and so he becomes a seductively open space into which they can read whatever fear or hope they wish. In the castle, he is terrifying, sleeping on newly dug grave-soil and offering three possible outcomes of his visit to Harker, in a nightmarish anticipation of the postmodern novels of Flann O'Brien. Harker, in fear and trembling, strikes at the grinning corpse-like body on the soil with a shovel, but to no effect. Dracula must live on to fulfil his mission of acquiring land in England, a land now under threat by this foreign body. Yet, even as Harker leaves for his return to that endangered place, one hears a note of defeated desire in Dracula's Hiberno-English lament: 'sad I am at your going'.[21]

Mina Murray's arrival by rail to visit Lucy Westenra at Whitby is a screen version of Harker's in Transylvania: the interchangeability of the referents defamiliarizes both. Henceforth, to the reader, far from being the norm at which an atlas falls open, England appears as an increasingly foreign land – as indeed it was to Stoker. There is a rare joke about this in an account of Harker's precipitate departure from the rail station in Transylvania: a kindly nurse reports in a letter that the attendants 'seeing from his violent behaviour that he was English . . . gave him a ticket'.[22] By the time he rejoins Mina, she also will have been challenged by abnormal experiences: a ship steered by a dead man will have arrived at the seaport and her friend Lucy will have sleepwalked into the arms of a monster. The non-specificity of the language used to describe that monster ('something') is indebted to Coleridge's 'Rime of the Ancient Mariner', as is the coffin-ship:

There was undoubtedly something, long and black, bending over the half-reclining white figure. I called in fright 'Lucy! Lucy!' and something raised a hand, and from where I was I could see a white face and red, gleaming eyes.[23]

Inadvertently, in fastening her protective cloak over Lucy's night-dress, Mina seems to pierce her friend's throat with a pin; after that, both adepts of Dracula seem half in love with the eastern cliff that was the scene of Lucy's violation. That violation was anticipated by the death of Swales, a local character who is slumped, neck back, on the public seat in the identical position taken by Lucy after her possession. Soon Lucy is reported as bloodless though not anaemic by one of her disappointed suitors, Dr Seward; the accepted man, Arthur Holmwood, gravely offers his blood for a transfusion. Then Seward offers his, as does his great Continental teacher Dr Van Helsing, who takes control of the case. But none of them does the trick. Lucy's mother has just died and, with a premonition, Lucy fears that it may be time for her to go too, since in folklore the Double often takes the form of the recent dead returning to claim a relation. Dr Van Helsing's last gamble is to infuse the blood of the other rejected suitor, the Texan Quincey Morris, for the Americans have the energy of the future and 'a brave man's blood is the best thing on this earth when a woman is in trouble'.[24] Nevertheless, Lucy dies.

At the centre of all these scenes is the crisis of masculinity in the 1890s. The American who can control his grief in the face of Lucy's death is saluted by the more diffident Seward as a moral Viking: 'if America can go on breeding men like that, she will be a power in the world indeed'.[25] But even in that country the decade was marked by anxiety that the great days of Daniel Boone were over: the forests were now cleared, the rails were laid down, and with no more continent to conquer, the days of the deskbound bureaucrat had begun. In an attempt to curb the 'damnable feminisation' of Yankee youth, a preacher named Billy Sunday was sent to tour Ivy League colleges promoting American football. He also preached a revisionist gospel in which the place of 'gentle Jesus meek and mild' was taken by a pugnacious saviour ('no lickspittle doughboy') who kicked the hated moneylenders from the Temple.[26] Henry James in *The Bostonians* (1886) had offered his own subtler reflections on the question. He allowed a Southern gentleman, Basil Ransom, to voice the fear that civilization was no more than a conspiracy of widows, aunts and spinsters: 'the masculine character, the ability to dare and endure, to know and yet not feel reality . . . that is what I want to preserve, or rather, as I may say, to recover'.[27] But James prefaced that speech with the warning that the young man was 'very provincial'.

Over in England, the fear ran just as deep and its name was Dracula. Deskbound professionals worried about being unmanned by their own tender feelings, by uncontrollable sexual desires, by nightmares, by polyandric females, but most of all by another male, who might seduce their women leaving them incapable of sexual fulfilment except in the seducer's arms. Harker suffers from recurrent bouts of debility after his encounter in Transylvania, but none of the other men considers him at fault. Indeed, Dr Seward sees his problems as the price paid for that manly courage displayed when going down on a second occasion to inspect Dracula's vaults, 'a remarkable piece of daring'.[28] The pressure under which Dracula places them all leaves the men vulnerable to breakdown: at various moments Dr Van Helsing bursts into hysterical laughter, and Lord Godalming (Arthur Holmwood, now a reluctant successor to his father's title) allows Mina (now married to Jonathan Harker) to stroke his head as a way of stilling his sobs. In a book where everybody turns into everyone else, Mina is expected to act the roles of lover, wife, mother and ultimate good chap in one and the same person. Likewise, Dracula, when he finally violates Mina, does so in a room where Harker is reduced to unconsciousness, but as she drinks from Dracula's bloody breast, he seems to discharge a function as much maternal as sexual.

The spectre of the New Woman haunts these scenes. Mina had raised the question early on, in recording that her own and Lucy's strong appetite for food after a seaside walk would have shocked the New Woman: and in her assumption that henceforth the modern woman would propose union to a man (another premonition of what the vampirellas were doing just then to her own fiancé). Such an active womanhood presupposes a passivity in the New Man. The 1890s male had in consequence a choice: if he repressed his own more sensitive aspect for the sake of manliness, he ran the risk that the repressed might erupt, reducing him to a blubbering baby or laughing hysteric. Stoker was attracted by older, Celtic codes of heroic manliness, but he knew that they were no longer negotiable. The problem was that, if a male gave vent to his softer emotions of *caritas*, he might be unmanned. Or else he might be compelled to adopt an even harsher front, for the *anima* thus revealed in him would cry out for proof that, despite the softness, he was still reassuringly male.

This had become an especially acute problem in Ireland, whose men had been typecast throughout the nineteenth century as effeminate and unstable. The very fact that Dr Van Helsing and Lord Godalming, the one a Netherlander and the other an English aristocrat, have to ride this roller coaster of human feelings, between a tear and a smile, is Stoker's mordant commentary on the limits of such a typology. By the 1890s, the Gaelic Athletic Association was promoting football and hurling as antidotes to the imputed unmanliness of the Irish male; but artists such as Wilde and Shaw had countered with celebrations of androgyny in the ideal man. Moving beyond the either/or binaries of the imperial mindset, they had instead devised a new set of categories, against which the limits of the masculine/feminine, English/Irish, good/evil polarities became apparent. Stoker clearly concurred in this, for it is the integrated, balanced and wholly androgynous figure of Mina Harker who takes control of his narrative in the end, being installed as his very muse. Her transcriptions of the men's narratives will take the place of Van Helsing's hopeless transfusions of male blood. This breakdown of polar thinking is one further reason why a purely Irish reading of *Dracula* can never suffice. For Dracula as character betrays features of both colonizer and colonized and, likewise, the tale owes at least as much to England as to the country of Stoker's birth.

As the story unfolds, Dracula is less and less physically present, disappearing entirely for long interludes. Yet he remains implicit in the growing sharpness of his victims' teeth or in his diabolic shape-changes, which may owe as much to Gaelic lore as to the Satan of *Paradise Lost*. If he is sexy, he is also strangely solitary, feeding off the sense of distance and the careful patrol of borders that were features of the Victorian world. If possession is power, then Dracula is cursed with the desire to own – land, houses, ultimately human beings. He is, however, less an intimate than a mesmerist: and that is one reason why he is largely silent in the novel once he has told his life's tale to Harker.[29] Lacking a confidant, thereafter he has no permission to narrate. Lacking a companion, he has none the less the capacity to drive other solitary souls into acts of organized friendship by which they may face him down.

One weapon they marshall against him is the talking cure of the 1890s, the power of narrative. This is an oddly self-cannibalizing book, in the sense that its contents must be constantly reread and reconsidered by its main protagonists, if it is to proceed and reach a satisfactory conclusion. Moreover, those contents are available to the participants only and exactly in the documentary forms already vouchsafed to the reader. It is as if all of human experience exists to become a transcript (if not a book). This is a necessary condition of living in the transitional, chaotic landscape of Gothic: its world is hardly *given*, but needs to be constantly validated, reconstructed from day to day by a process of rereading. *Dracula* is one book that we can imagine as already read by its protagonists before it is risked on the public; and precisely because its characters are so isolated, it offers 'the claustrophobia of experience without a world'.[30]

The privatization of space was at once the signal achievement and greatest curse of the nineteenth-century bourgeoisie. One consequence is that the professional pursuers of Dracula have few extended conversations. Their desire to understand the meaning of their experiences arises from a compulsion to make the present moment past, to reduce it to the level of documentary. So, rather than share many memories in conversation, they share them in a constant exchange of documents, records, archives, each compiled and read with the kind of concentration made possible by solitude and each avowedly a part which must by force of intellect be integrated into a total narrative. Yet, being questers at heart, the young people fret that their project reeks of the inauthentic, being encoded in mechanical typescript rather than in human handwriting, a story of types rather than traditional characters, which begins and ends with a regret that the evidence is not more immediate. Dracula, for all his faults, has an appalling authenticity which they feel themselves to lack; and, though he seeks to master their world of maps, timetables and legal deeds, he cannot transcend his primordial nature. One consequence is that the privatization of space means nothing to him: the bourgeois answer – enclosed rooms, locked houses, sealed coffins – is unavailing against the force of Death. Even the human body can be penetrated by such a shape-changer. The Englishman's home may be his castle and the Irishman's his coffin, but Dracula can slide in and out of them at will.

In another kind of story, Dracula would indeed have been the hero (at least in the way that Satan was in *Paradise Lost*). A hero, after all, is simply an exceptional being who has the courage to live out the consequences of his/her claim to heroism. Like Standish James O'Grady, Stoker was worried that modern society had no place for such figures; yet in the end, unlike O'Grady, he decided that the lack of such beings was a price worth paying for democracy. The ancient hero Cuchulain sacrificed himself so that others might live – his dying act, after all, had been to witness a raven alight on his shoulder and drink the last drops of his blood. The modern Dracula gorges himself so that others may die and he drinks their blood, creating a potentially endless cycle of consumers, each one incapable of creation. For Stoker, heroism is possible in the modern world only in that debased form, just as the authenticity of ancient dialects (whether Dr Van Helsing's absurd argot or the salty sailor speech of Swales) has to make way for Dracula's bloodlessly correct post-colonial prose.

The masses are, of course, the new heroes of the progressive mind, and so they must be protected. Confronted with newspaper reports of a 'Bloofer Lady' attacking children in public parks, Harker is

beside himself with fear. He knows in his heart that Dracula has
already arrived, for he has sighted someone very like the count staring intently at a beautiful woman in a Piccadilly crowd. His
frightfulness lies in the fact that he can hide in the innocent crowd
and then strike anywhere, anytime, violating the beautiful concord
between the individual and society. Near the end of the tale, Dr Van
Helsing describes the conflict between this proud individual and the
social consensus as a result of fast-forwarding a process that should
ordinarily take centuries:

> . . . the measure of leaving his own barren land – barren of
> people – and coming to a new land where life of man teems till
> they are like the multitude of standing corn, was the work of
> centuries. Were another of the Un-Dead, like him, to try to do
> what he has done, perhaps not all the centuries of the world
> that have been, or that will be, could aid him.[31]

The catastrophic onset of modernity, when forced at speed upon
uprooted peoples such as the post-Famine Irish, informs those lines:
but Van Helsing's analyses of the strange collusion of archaic heroics
and the modern mass move well beyond Anglo-Irish considerations
and into a more prophetic mode. He assures his followers that the
combustible elements of that modernist equation could lead straight
to autocracy:

> He would be yet – he may be yet if we fail – the father or fur-
> therer of a new order of beings, whose road must lead through
> Death, not Life.[32]

If Stoker concludes with some sadness that there is no place in the
modern world for old-style heroes, he has at least the courage to
explore the corollary: that there may be no role either for a thoroughly masculine male or a wholly feminine woman. The womanly
men survive in the end, as does the manly woman Mina. Quincey
Morris must die so that this new order can persist, and so also does
the voluptuous beauty Lucy Westenra. As the book's most spectacular vampire, she allows Stoker to register the tremendous
ambivalence felt towards a dead or dying thing. On the one hand,
her lover Arthur wishes understandably to bring her back to life, as
so many Gaelic revivalists hoped to resuscitate tradition; on the other
hand, Dr Van Helsing seems more anxious to end the intolerable
ambiguity of a life among the Undead by killing off the creature
once and for all. Those who revive her need to believe that she might

be dead; those who kill her fear that she might still have some bad life in her.

In her undead state, Lucy's loveliness had returned, that beauty that attaches to any threatened, expiring thing. Yet with that beauty always goes terror, for if anything is more frightening than being dead, it is the act of dying, and in her case that is prolonged over many pages. Struck by her loveliness, Arthur asks Dr Seward, in a line which will be reworked by Synge and many revivalists, 'Jack, is she really dead?'[33] Van Helsing speaks of her condition in a way that recalls Swift's Struldbrugs who could not die: like seemingly eternal tortoises or toads secreted in rocks for thousands of years, or Indian fakirs who are burned yet rise again. The one analogy he doesn't mention is that of Jesus Christ, whose blood was drunk before he rose from the tomb: the tradition that inspired that of the Irish revival. Yet Lucy's coffin, when the men visit it, is empty, as empty as Parnell's was said to be. It is as empty as the shroud made for Gaelic tradition, whose revenge also lasted over centuries, for the Undead are strong with the accumulated strength of blood sucked from many other expirers.

Anthropologists who have studied Irish attitudes to the dead often point to covert feelings of aggression beneath the acts of ritual tenderness: the dead are punished in the first instance for dying and so breaking up the intact human community. One way of coping with this is to deny death's ultimate dominion with assertions of surviving life: another is to join forces with the dead. Arthur Holmwood's desire to kiss his dying Lucy is a variant on both approaches, but it is forbidden by Van Helsing, who senses that she would by this kiss merely recruit another for the Undead. Strangely, this is the moment when Lucy's polyandry vanishes and she wishes only for a monogamous eternal love: 'Come, my husband, come.'[34] Survivor guilt is always a factor in approaches to the dead, mingled also with survivor fear that the dead one may have outstanding claims yet to be pressed home. Dr Van Helsing has seen one death borrow another and wishes to break the series.

However, this complex expresses itself in an awesome aggression visited upon the undead corpse of Lucy. The lover who could not kiss her is allowed instead to plunge a rod through her orgasmic, expiring body, 'driving deeper and deeper the mercy-bearing stake'.[35] Permission is given by Dr Van Helsing for the moral discharge of technically illegal impulses. The scene amounts to a gang-rape based on the central law of all pornography: that the erasure of a woman's sexual identity in coercive intercourse can climax most thrillingly in her death. Likewise, Van Helsing refuses to bring one of the children attacked by the 'Bloofer Lady' to a nearby police station, lest he and his band be asked to explain their activities in the cemetery, which culminate in the removal of Lucy's head and the filling of her dead mouth with garlic. This is done to end 'the curse of immortality', as if Lucy's inability to die were a nightmare version of Tír na nÓg, the land of the young.

In the eerie graveyard is re-enacted that primal Celtic scene when Patrick, the saint, routed Oscar, the Fenian son of Oisín, with the aid of the sacred host. 'I brought it from Amsterdam,' explains a breezy Dr Van Helsing. 'I have an Indulgence.'[36] He uses the host to bless and seal the tomb. Knowing that the Pope is effectively now a co-conspirator with them, the Protestant Dr Seward feels appalled but compelled to cooperate. The writing of the scene is spectacularly awful, yet part of the book's appeal is the power of a myth to survive even execrable prose. Besides, there is often but a millimetre separating the very good from the truly awful in writing. A word misplaced here or there will do the trick, and Stoker very often obliges.

By now it is clear that Dracula can only be defeated by a committee. In effect, Stoker recruits the Clerks of the Petty Sessions against the bloodsucker. Perhaps, this is his way of recognizing that heroic individualism has by the 1890s grown piratical. The currency in which Dracula trades – blood – has a transnational market and his own reign of the Undead is no respecter of boundaries. The Irish Land League radical Michael Davitt suggested a connection between blood-sucking and high capitalism, embodied in those 'cormorant vampires' called landlords.[37] In the book the syndrome is global. Dracula may lack servants but he can buy or beguile whomever he wants. When the cloth of his coat is torn in a knife attack, a shower of gold and banknotes falls out. The image of uncontrolled capital as a form of life-threatening disease was widely used in the decades after *Dracula*, notably in Ireland by James Connolly. But Karl Marx had already made the comparison: 'Capital is dead labour which, vampire-like, lives only by sucking living labour, and lives the more, the more labour it sucks.'[38] Against its transnational depredation, Dr Van Helsing and his band assert the force of human solidarity, as Mina Harker observes in her journal: 'So as we all took hands our solemn compact was made.'[39] She reports Van Helsing as reminding them all that they had 'the power of combination'. It sounds in one sense like an anticipation of the Five Find-Outers, Enid Blyton's secret club of young detectives sworn to eternal loyalty on a secret mission: and in another aspect it recalls the Irish Literary Society of 1890s London, composed largely of socially conscious civil servants and respectable Home Rulers.

As in so many advanced clubs, the question of woman's member-ship is soon raised. The initial impulse of the men is to exclude Mina, on grounds that she should not be burdened with the terrible secrets of their mission, but this proves impossible. As soon as Dracula stains her white nightdress with his blood, she must be admitted to their confidence. For one thing, she now has a telepathic insight into the enemy's mind and thinking; for another, her brain is far too pow-erful to be lost to the club. She is, despite her earlier mockeries of the type, a New Woman; and her own psyche is at the level of the indi-vidual a further example of the power of combination. Dr Van Helsing, in explaining that psyche, recurs to the word: 'She has man's brain – a brain that a man should have were he much gifted – and woman's heart . . . so good combination.'[40] Once this is said, it is obvious that, far from dying, she will be the one who saves the world from a monster. Dracula may wish to drink more male blood from her body, the nearest he can get to implementing his desires. She, on the other hand, will use her 'male' brain.

She can do this because she hardly sees Dracula as monstrous at all. He is less a devil than an incomplete human. All of her hus-band's faltering attempts to understand Dracula as a sort of doubling of himself are now clarified in Mina's sober description of their task:

> . . . it is not a work of hate. That poor soul who has wrought all this misery is the saddest case of all. Just think what will be his joy when he too is destroyed in his worser part that his better part may have spirit and immortality.[41]

The shadow-side must be integrated and the miscreant understood. The clairvoyant Mina can, with the aid of hypnosis, offer a diagno-sis of the one with whom she shares a blood-flow.

The count is a criminal type, according to the classifications of Nordau and Lombroso, two fashionable anthropologists of the decade, and so his brain is undeveloped. In effect, though Mina doesn't say it, his brain is smaller than hers. He may have caused a scar to appear on her forehead – a sort of anti-love spot – but his game is up. Mina's insights into her dark double permit the club to track him across Europe to his lair in Transylvania. There the three vampirellas are located, their graves are cleansed and their bodies are staked, before they can recruit Mina to make up a foursome. There also the great count is put down, even as Quincey Morris dies in the battle. America may hold the keys to the future, a fact signalized in the naming of the Harkers' first-born son after their dead comrade.

Dracula is a fable of how feudalism falls, but one that shows that not all of its favoured symbols may fall with it. Priests and vicars are oddly absent from a tale saturated in religious symbolism. However, it is made very clear that without the cross and host, the pursuers of the count would have been doomed. The Victorian moral order relies on such things, whatever Protestant revisionists may say. As a blood-drinking vampire, Dracula may appear to be a horribly literalist exponent of the Christian mystery, but those who can read that mystery on a more metaphorical level are saved. What saves such people is in part the very scepticism with which they hedge their religious commitments. The appeal of the tale is to a Nineties combination of occultism and scepticism which allowed a reunification in Dr Van Helsing of that Renaissance code that saw alchemy and science as two sides of the same coin. W.B. Yeats, after all, spent much of the decade seeing visions as a member of the Order of the Golden Dawn: and the rest of it being expelled for questioning them.[42]

Like the writings of Yeats, *Dracula* is a version of Irish modernism in that it recruits the forces of popular spirituality, as well as the typewriter and phonograph, against the past. The new professional middle class (joined by a decently adjusted aristocrat) move with the new technology against the bloodsucker, in a mode of benign interventionism. Yet, as they move, they find out that they must employ some of the older codes against their beneficiaries. If Dracula attempts to master an administrative world of wills, newspaper reports and legal documents, only to discover that he cannot overcome his atavism, those born into that comfortable settled world feel the need for a little of the older rituals. The lesson is obvious: what is repressed will always return, so it had better be in a non-toxic form. England has become an eternal suburb of painted villas, so Dracula must return to his mountain home in the forests of the unconscious. Despite his efforts, the new morality is encroaching even there, rooting out wild sexuality and replacing it with bourgeois marriage. Mina Harker might seem like a form of the revolutionary monster to come, but in truth she is the New Woman already tamed, a sober blend of old and new. She is one of that legion soon to be mocked in G.K. Chesterton's quip that 'millions of women said they would not be dictated to, and promptly became stenographers'. She may carry a large-bore revolver into Transylvania, but solely to enforce the new order. For, like Kate in Shakespeare's *The Taming of the Shrew*, she offers herself as a version of that ultimate male fantasy: the strong woman who will ideally tame herself.

In fact, she tames everything and everybody. The quivering intensity of Dr Seward's voice on the phonograph will be transformed by her into the impersonal authority of a typescript. She writes her own memories into diaries so that she has permission to forget the details, lest Dracula by reverse hypnosis seek to uncover the contents of her mind. Already, she is halfway to the objective of becoming a modern journalist, with powers of near-total forgetfulness. Stoker's mother Charlotte had written back in 1863 that 'a self-supporting woman is alike respected and respectable',[43] a line that might serve as a summation of Mina Harker. Yet not *wholly* respectable – for if Dracula can perforate her body, she has the rare ability to penetrate his mind, in an act of counterinvasion leading to ultimate victory. This was, says Mary FitzGerald, another ploy of the nineteenth-century Irish turning weakness to strength.[44] Such a counter-invasion would become characteristic of many liberation movements of the twentieth century, whose exiled adepts clustered in large cities rehearsing the terms of a revolution. Benedict Anderson has likened them to photographers who recorded there a black-on-white negative, which could only later be used when they went back to the site of oppression and there printed the final picture out of the darkroom of political struggle.[45]

Dracula shows that the past is never completely done with: and that the bang-up-to-date must go forth disguised in its trappings. The Fenian bombers who rocked Manchester in the 1860s might have been reminders of the primeval beast in man (especially to readers of Darwin), but they were also harbingers of that modern phenomenon, the urban terrorist. Phrenologists and anthropologists might seek to console the Mina Harkers and Van Helsings with the contention that the Irish, like the criminals, were recognizable *types*: but Harker honestly faced the terror that even a Dracula could skulk unrecognizable in any British city.[46] Dracula's lineage might be ancient, but he was by virtue of that very fact an essential component of modernity, a means by which the young professionals could mark themselves off as different – civil, sober and modern.

If Protestant Dubliners like Stoker began by sensing their own mythical propensities in a revolt against the limits of reason, they came to recognize and celebrate their own rationality through an involvement with the atavistic aboriginal. The dialectic was unending: the more streamlined the world became, the more primeval urges asserted themselves. That oscillation is brilliantly captured in the movements common to all the characters of the story, from periods of prolonged stupefaction and sleepiness to sudden bursts of sharp action. Such patterns were coded into an Ireland which in the nineteenth century had swung from sullen torpor to spasms of defiance, calling forth in British imperial policy a corresponding alternation between coercion and conciliation. But the code was lodged even more deeply in the national psyche. Writing about the ancient Irish hero Cuchulain, one of the leading literary men of the period, George Sigerson, noted how his progress through life was marked by phases of 'long inexplicable debility' followed by phases of sudden arousal as in the fabled *riastra* or battle-rage.[47] Such a sentence, published in 1907 a matter of weeks after the riots against Synge's *Playboy of the Western World* and a matter of years before the Easter Rising, was very well judged.

There could hardly have been a more curious anticipatory illumination of that rebellion, with its strange assortment of typewriting suffragists, reluctant aristocrats, religious symbolists and determined professional men than Stoker's enigmatic tale. Its influence on the discourse leading up to the Rising was so pervasive as to pass unnoticed, as if a fact of nature itself. The plays of Synge would be filled with suggestions of voices speaking from the dead, offering ironical reassurance that 'a man that's dead can do no hurt'.[48] Similarly, the writings of Joyce in the period were all structured around one idea: the flow of the past through the present. If in Synge's *Riders to the Sea* a drowned fisherman returns to claim his living brother for the next life, in *Dubliners* the first story opens with the image of a dead priest and the last story carries an account of monks who sleep in their coffins. W.B. Yeats and Augusta Gregory would imagine Cathleen Ní Houlihan as a very Irish sort of vampire: 'They that have red cheeks will have pale cheeks for my sake, and for all that, they will think they are well paid.'[49]

Ultimately, the idea of a 'latency' in a past moment when linked to a present moment could not be confined to literature. At the grave of Jeremiah O'Donovan Rossa in 1915, Patrick Pearse, soon to lead the Easter Rising, laughed at the 'fools' who thought that they had pacified Ireland. His words were to be as evocative in this context as in many others: 'But the fools, the fools, the fools. They have left us our Fenian dead, and while Ireland holds these graves, Ireland unfree shall never be at peace.'[50]

23

Augusta Gregory's
Cuchulain: The Rebirth
of the Hero

In 1902 Augusta Gregory published *Cuchulain of Muirthemne* in London, having failed to interest any Irish publisher in her project. She was acutely aware that people might ask whether a woman of little fame was equal to the heroic challenge, but the tradition of female apology for such undertakings was by then well-established in Anglo-Ireland. Charlotte Brooke had, after all, exculpated herself for abandoning needle and pianoforte to compile the *Reliques of Irish Poetry* with a similar explanation – the failure of the existing male scholars to produce a text.

In her 'Dedication of the Irish Edition to the people of Kiltartan', Gregory assumed less a national than a local audience, among the people of her own parish of Kiltartan. Many had lost touch with the old legends and now she offered to reconnect the tales and the community from which they had once come. Douglas Hyde had warned that only a scholar should do such work, but Gregory demurred.[1] Like the warrior queen Medbh, she set herself to man's work, chiding the scholars of Trinity College Dublin in the process:

> And indeed if there was more respect for Irish things among the
> learned men that live in the college at Dublin, where so many of
> these old writings are stored, this work would not have been
> left to a woman of the house, that has to be minding the place,
> and listening to complaints, and dividing her share of food.[2]

What the villagers made of this self-description by a lady of title can only be imagined: but she certainly saw herself as restoring not just the continuity of cultural tradition but the very idea of community.[3]

The professors of Trinity, on the other hand, had set their faces against the national revival, refusing to share their manuscripts with the wider society. One, Robert Atkinson, had lamented 'the smallness of the element of idealism', which he told a special committee on Intermediate Education in 1899 meant that it would be a mistake to encourage the study of Gaelic literature.[4] Gregory's aim, therefore, was to demonstrate ancient idealism. Another was to challenge the hegemony then acquired by conservative males in the field of Celtic Studies. They were already narrowing it into a linguistic discipline devoid of all interpretative audacity, and a discipline moreover that only the privileged few with a knowledge of Old Irish could master.[5] Even those who admired the old texts were somewhat mandarin in taste and attitude. By making the material available to the masses (and to young artists), Gregory had opened up debate. The wars of rival male specialists over infixed pronouns might continue, but the genie of Cuchulain had been let out of the bottle. This was conceded by the liberal Celtic scholar Eoin Mac Néill in a handsome letter of congratulation on 'the truest representation of the Irish heroic age, as our forefathers had it in their minds, that I have ever seen in English, and the Gaelic League will want to suppress you on a double indictment, to wit, depriving the Irish language of her sole right to express the innermost Irish mind, and secondly, investing the Anglo-Irish language with a literary dignity it has never hitherto possessed'.[6]

Augusta Gregory was in truth the Mina Harker of Celtic Studies. The versions of the heroic cycle available in learned journals lacked coherence, yet she welded them into a unity. When she told the clerk in the British Museum that she required material on Cuchulain, he asked whether the reading would take two hours. In fact, it took two years. As he tottered in with more and more volumes, he confessed that, although he knew all about Fionn and Oisín, he had never even heard of the Celtic hero. Cuchulain was indeed a very Irish phenomenon. Even his propensity to changes of shape might be construed as a reflection of the transformation of the landscape amid the instability of the local weather.

His origins were in the remote past, as the son of the sun-god Lugh, and a human mother, Dechtire. Caught thus between the divine and the human, his condition was precarious and vulnerable. The old gods, known as *sidhe* or fairy folk, lived still in mounds like Brú na Bóinne, and a semi-divine figure like Cuchulain could make contact with them on special occasions when he stood in need of supernatural help.[7]

Some scholars still give credence to the Trinity College view of the legends as 'coming from the youth of the world, before the heart had been trained to bow before the head':[8] but even those commentators stress their imaginative power. Most, however, consider them to be deliberated artistic works of learned Christian authors with specific aims: for instance, to mock the past pretensions of the province of Ulster to power and authority. The stories were told to illuminate contemporary themes. The misogyny of the monkish scribes might be inferred from the treatment of Queen Medbh, whose dangerous usurpation of male prerogatives leads her to precipitate a wasteful war between her own province of Connacht and the men of Ulster. There may even have been a Pauline warning here 'on the dangerous potential of the sovereignty myth to privilege the female at the expense of the male',[9] for Medbh's claim to have had a string of lovers is really a not-very-hidden reminder that she holds the sovereignty of Ireland.[10] The moral enunciated at the end by a dying Cuchulain – 'conscar bara bith' (anger destroys the world) – would enforce a pacific, Christian code. Some have even considered the provincial war as an allegory of the contest between traditional and reforming clergy for control of the archdiocese of Armagh (symbolized by Emain Macha), with the reformist author siding strongly with Cuchulain.[11] One thing is very clear: the tale was yet another example of ways in which the interests of the present moment determine a people's way of looking at history.

This, more than anything, is what characterizes all treatments of the Cuchulain story: 'a technique of exploring contemporary issues by means of narratives set in the past'.[12] That past was sufficiently remote to be tractable to present agendas: and this would in time explain the attraction of Cuchulain for Anglo-Irish writers of English, for he belonged to a period before splits into sectarian and political turbulence. Some went astonishingly far back in treating the theme. Standish James O'Grady began his *History of Ireland: Heroic Period* (1878) with an account of the ice ages and early development of the planet: it was only in his second volume, of 1880, that he dealt fully with Cuchulain. By reaching back to a time before the hero, he could justify his reach forward into a heroic future. His technique, however, was fanciful and outrageous: at one point, he has Cuchulain visit Dublin, a city that would not be founded for hundreds of years. Yet it contained a poetic truth: the past understands the needs of the present, a present that by definition it can know nothing of. Which is to say with Claude Lévi-Strauss that even as men fancy themselves to be thinking the myths, myths think themselves out in men without their knowledge.[13]

O'Grady's hero was to serve as an example of nobility to the class of delinquent landlords who appeared on the verge of extinction under the land reforms of the 1870s and 1880s. However, O'Grady's was a voice in the wilderness: he had to pay for publication of *History of Ireland* out of his own pocket. The landlords confirmed all his worst fears, causing him to erupt in 1886, 'Christ save us! You read nothing, know nothing!'[14] His case against them was that their penny-pinching selfishness had brought on the revolt of their tenants: if they had behaved with the largesse of real aristocrats, all would have been well. Their weakness was manifest also in a willingness to negotiate with their enemies, 'this waste, dark, howling mass of colliding interests, mad about the main chance'. O'Grady's fervent hope was that these wild, untamed people needed rule by natural aristocrats, just one or two or three Cuchulains, who 'will refashion her, moulding us anew after some human and heroic pattern', and so heading off 'evolutionary anarchies'.[15]

Nobody answered this call, although for a period O'Grady suffered from the delusion that Lord Randolph Churchill might be the hero who could face down 'this absurd Irish democracy'. Churchill disappointed his hopes. Offered no more promising material than the wily player of the Orange card, it was understandable that O'Grady should have concluded that the ancient hero should not be impersonated by humans at all. When he heard that George Russell (whose pseudonym was AE, from 'aeon', as befitted a mystic poet and political pragmatist) wished to stage a production of the Deirdre tale, he was appalled, urging writers to 'leave the heroic cycles alone, and not bring them down to the crowd'.[16]

For all his outbursts of male hysteria, O'Grady had a point. The heroes and heroines of Greek myth had lost some of their aura through frequent enactments in stage plays, whereas those in Irish myth, existing only in prose, were the more richly available to the individual imagination. One feature of epic is its refusal to describe protagonists in a merely physical way – intimacy is assumed in a known world of oral narrators, a tradition honoured even in Joyce's *Ulysses*, where characters like Leopold Bloom, despite the minute depiction of their consciousness, are never physically described. The shock of many Joyceans on seeing the actor Milo O'Shea play Bloom in Joseph Strick's 1968 film was probably very like that felt by O'Grady on hearing of AE's drama. AE pleaded that nothing could be a nobler vehicle for the treatment of ancient heroes than the speaking human voice; given time, however, he would conclude that O'Grady had been right.[17]

O'Grady was really a finished example of the Victorian Gael, someone who had the addiction of the age to what was vast or grandiose in scale. Lacking any rigorous knowledge of Irish, he worked from translations by Eugene O'Curry and other nine-teenth-century figures. To young artists like Yeats and Russell his books were a glorious revelation: but the prose in which they were written was overblown, baroque and even hysterical. Ultimately, the texts owed as much to Thomas Carlyle and his book *On Heroes, Hero-Worship and the Heroic in History* as to the ancient Celts, for with the waning of religious belief in the age of Darwin had come a search for Eminent Victorians, a conviction that the world might yet be saved by an exceptional man or woman who knew how to take the place of the lost gods. Cuchulain obviously might perform that signal office. The problem with O'Grady's figure was the difficulty that attended all figures from the Celtic past: they invariably seemed on closer inspection to be disguised versions of the British imperial present. Cuchulain was noted for combining a propensity to pagan violence against enemies with a Christlike sensitivity: but this was exactly the combination much praised in the muscular Christians of Eton and Rugby. The suspicion arose that all such exemplary figures might be nothing more than public schoolboys in drag.

The problem, hinted at in O'Grady's displeasure with dramatic enactments, lay in the very Victorian idea of mimetic or imitative heroism. One theologian of the period became so impatient with injunctions to emulate the virtues of Jesus Christ that he told his students, '. . . on the day of judgement, Jesus won't want to know why you weren't more like him: but he might ask why you weren't more like yourself.'[18] The doctrine of self-becoming established itself as a major nineteenth-century theme, and institutions came under attack for treating as heresy the very idea of a free individual. 'People are afraid', Kierkegaard had written, 'that the worst will happen as soon as the individual takes it into his head to comport himself as an individual.'[19] Soon Cuchulain was being treated in the same way that Jesus was explicated by existential theologians, as a hero of self-analysis. He was a figure in whom a whole culture achieved expression by virtue of his willingness to enter and describe himself, thereby revealing to all the fundamental nature of man.

W.B. Yeats confessed that he would always owe a portion of his soul to O'Grady,[20] but his own Cuchulain had no pretensions to immediate social usefulness. For the poet and dramatist, Cuchulain was exemplary not for bravery in battle but for his willingness to enter into the abyss of his own self. Yeats did not ask people to impersonate Cuchulain: rather he urged them to abandon the impedimenta of Victorian personality and make contact instead with their own deepest energies:

> When the imaginary saint or lover or hero moves us most deeply, it is the moment when he awakens within us for an instant our own heroism, our own sanctity, our own desire . . . If we understand our own minds, and the things that are striving to utter themselves through our minds, we move others, not because we have understood or thought about those others, but because all life has the same root . . .[21]

This heroism of the subversive individual had ultimate antecedents in the religious experience: but it spread widely into many forms of cultural and political discourse in the 1890s, as a sort of protest against the Victorian urge to amass private property and personal sensations. The new culture-hero was remarkable less for what he had or did than for what he was: and Hiberno-English, like the Irish language, was greatly praised for its syntax, which placed emphasis less on actions than on states of consciousness (Tá uaigneas orm – There is loneliness on me), on *being* rather than *having*. Oscar Wilde in 'The Soul of Man under Socialism' regretted that so many individuals still had to be combative, wasting half their strength in friction: but his real villain was the 'English' system of private property which made gain, not growth, its aim.[22]

Wilde insisted that his ideas had clear implications for art. 'It should never try to be popular': instead, 'the public should try to make itself artistic'. As a result of public interest, he contended, both the novel and drama in England had been dragged down to woeful levels of tawdriness: but 'the arts that have escaped best are the arts in which the public takes no interest'.[23] Yeats and Gregory must have read those lines with real excitement at the thought that the very neglect of Irish epics through the nineteenth century now provided them with a priceless opportunity. They had not been 'retold' in sham novels suitable for grocers' assistants, as the classics of England had been emasculated for the dissemination of middle-class virtue. 'The public makes use of the classics of a country as a means of checking the progress of Art,'[24] snorted Wilde: but in Ireland this was not true, for there the old stories were truly subversive, surviving only on the very margins of society to which they had been relegated. Tradition in England might be the very basis of social tranquillity, but in Ireland it was identified with defiance, irrational-ism and commotion.

Wilde was fascinated by fairy legends, as much for their hidden practical meanings (a lost sword might symbolize impotence) as for their subversion of Victorian order. He had, after all, grown up in a period that saw the cultural loss of those traditions in rural Ireland, even as his father worked mightily to save some of them; he himself praised 'the innermost heart of the Celt in the moments he has grown to love through centuries of persecution'.[25] The virtual reality of fairy legend was what led Wilde to conclude that the real life is the life we do not lead: or, as Angela Bourke has written, 'Fairy-belief legend, an elaborate system of fictions through which a significant mode of vernacular thinking is articulated, was clearly in opposition to the modes of literacy, and became increasingly associated with poverty and marginality.'[26]

The great enemy of such a world was the drawing-room drama and realist novel – and the intellectual leaders of an 'improving' middle class, like the professors at Trinity College. When such people describe a work as immoral, said Wilde (perhaps thinking of teach-ers like Mahaffy and Atkinson), 'they mean that the artist has said or made a beautiful thing that is true'.[27] The novel had been divested of beauty by a public that denied self-expression to artists through the imposition of market expectations. Journalism had similarly declined into the retailing of ugly or disgusting facts in cliché-ridden para-graphs. If epic was one antidote to the novel, Hiberno-English might meet the challenge of jaded journalese: and so Augusta Gregory's *Cuchulain of Muirthemne* was the answer to which Wilde's essay provided the overwhelming question. One of Europe's oldest tales could also provide something utterly fresh and new, as a further case of radical traditionalism: and the fact that it was largely unknown and unused was the greatest virtue of all. It was a magnificent story extolling the energies of youth from the dawn of the world. The old-fashioned respect for the young might be dying in the England of the Victorian Sage, but in Ireland it was being reborn. Yeats could not contain his joy at the challenge:

In England I sometimes hear men complain that the old themes of verse and prose are used up. Here in Ireland the marble block is waiting for us almost untouched, and the statues will come as soon as we have learned to use the chisel.[28]

'The Soul of Man under Socialism' expresses the thinking of a rather aristocratic kind of socialist. It fears for an art debased by the exercise of popular sanction. At heart Wilde was a mythographer, who held that 'the work of art is to dominate the spectator: the spectator is not to dominate the work of art'.[29] If O'Grady could have brought himself to believe that this was how a play about Deirdre could work on the Dublin theatre audience, he might never have protested: but he had not that faith. Yeats shared the fear that the modern school of art 'finds the scullion in the queen, because there are scullions in the audience but no queens':[30] yet he and Gregory persisted in the conviction that if they went on giving what was good back to people, one day it would become truly popular again.

The modern novel was quite at variance with all this, because its writers tried not to realize an ideal of beauty so much as to bring about some social improvement. Wilde was scathing about such 'revolting sentimentality' which caused 'a mess of facts' to be thrown together by Ibsens and Zolas devoid of imagination.[31] Yeats agreed. In his view, the people of Ireland had never been fully socialized, and so their delight in the elaboration of personality called for a grander art. The problem with Ibsen and Zola was that there seemed to be less to their characters than met the eye. Wilde praised Renaissance art for bypassing social problems and busying itself instead with the full development of the individual. Far from indicating selfishness in artists, this allowed for a valuable distinction between the egotist (who makes claims on others) and the individualist (who will not desire to do that).[32] The property relations that are the itemized stuff of modern novels had, he believed, damaged the individualism made possible by the Renaissance.

As she worked in the British Museum on the texts that fed *Cuchulain of Muirthemne*, Augusta Gregory read nightly through one of the most famous nineteenth-century novels, *Bleak House* by Charles Dickens. She confessed to finding 'an immense relief, a sort of warmth and refreshment in its humour and its humanity, a reaction, no doubt, from those hours in the ancient world of heroism and dreams'.[33] Of course, there was more than relief at issue here, for she was aware that the narrative skills of a Dickens provided 'another thread to weave into the web' for her future readers. She was not the first or last to find the people of the heroic cycles rather hard to interpret as characters. Synge also found them remote and feared that they might 'loosen my grip on reality'.[34] Gregory, who found it helpful to compare a Cuchulain with Lord Talbot or Oisín with Sir Robert Peel, may have cannily employed *Bleak House* as a sort of reality-check as she proceeded. This was probably why she removed many of the grotesque or supernatural interventions by which

Cuchulain received assistance from the otherworldly *sidhe*. She knew that these would be hard for modern readers to accept. Yet she may also have read *Bleak House* to remind herself of the world of property and social class, which her book was intended to transcend. Art was art because it was not nature but an intensification of daily realities. *Cuchulain of Muirthemne* would have to retain that difference if it were to outsell competing novels.

Even as English writers sought to inject an epic strain into the novel, Gregory achieved the more difficult feat of re-creating novelistic elements in the epic. Her tactic appealed greatly to younger readers like Mary Colum, who preferred Gregory's books to O'Grady's rather stiff heroics.[35] Perhaps younger people could better sense the possibilities opened up for literature by Gregory's splicing of epic and novelistic modes. The ultimate outcome of this, after all, would be Joyce's *Ulysses*, which contains an approving commentary on the method. The potentials for epic in the modern novel had been all but lost in England, ever since the mock-heroic narratives of Fielding in books like *Tom Jones*. *Paradise Lost* had been in effect the last English epic, and after it the main use that writers had for epic values was to mock their high pretentiousness. Even the most ambitious of all nineteenth-century novels, *Middlemarch* by George Eliot, could only write out the impossibility of heroism in the reduced new context. The protagonist, Dorothea Brooke, wishes to be another Saint Theresa, a martyr and heroine, but finds that her society is a flawed medium through which to realize these values. The novel's subtitle is 'a study of provincial life' and it is provinciality of spirit that prevents figures like Dorothea from achieving their potential. The epigraphs from *Paradise Lost* distributed through the narrative serve only to remind readers that heroics are no longer viable in England.

The problem was obvious enough: epic treats of the birth or salvation of a nation, but England had been solidly established for centuries. Ireland, on the contrary, had almost disappeared in the decade of the Great Famine and stood forever in dire need of saving. Cuchulain, with his bravery and generosity, seemed just the sort of figure needed to bring the modern nation to a consciousness of itself. When the charismatic leader Parnell was lost in 1891, the need seemed more pressing: and the analogies with a hero who was sexually incautious yet utterly loyal to his people were not lost. A teenager named Patrick Pearse told a meeting of the Gaelic League in 1898 that 'the noble personality of Cuchulainn forms a true type of Gaelic nationality, full as it is of youthful life and vigour and hope'.[36] 'Vigour' and 'hope' were mantras intoned to ward off memories of a famine that had led Charles Gavan Duffy to conclude of his people after 1848 that 'it was hopeless to lead them to heroic enterprises'.[37] Pearse's attempt to reactivate the Cuchulain legend among Gaelic Leaguers was made as a deliberate antidote to the bickering of Irish politicians after Parnell. The people, he lamented, were 'sunk in apathy', while 'the men we call our leaders are engaged in tearing out one another's vitals'.[38]

Augusta Gregory could hardly have produced her volume at a more opportune time. For one thing, Cuchulain was a larger-than-life figure, who could inspire by the sheer scale of his exhibited energy. He also existed in a climate of prevailing torpor: and some of his bravest deeds had been done while the men of Ulster were laid low with the 'cés noinden', a sickness like that which assailed women on the childbed. A man who could vindicate honour while a torpor gripped his people was a useful icon as the century ended. Gregory chose to emphasize Cuchulain's skill in single combat, so clearly at variance with the team spirit promoted at the time in English public schools. Such individual contests showed that the object of fighting was not to annex the territory of enemies so much as to uphold social order and bonding among one's own people:[39] a true analogy for the aims of Irish nationalism.

Heroism, so defined, arose less from a desire to humiliate others than to live up to an ideal conception of the self, in the process of which one epitomized the cultural values of one's race. Cuchulain resolved the problem of how to reconcile self-fulfilment with the wider social good. In her own search for personal fame through writing *Cuchulain of Muirthemne*, Gregory also managed to combine self-gratification and social fulfilment. It was as if the Celtic hero were her own undiscovered *animus*, a secret self which had lain dormant for years beneath the exterior of the Coole wife and widow. The figure of Cuchulain also reconciled for her the visionary and secular dimensions, for he saw no contradiction between the things of this world and the next.

For Gregory, Cuchulain was a drag act in more ways than one. He allowed her to impersonate the sort of strong man she greatly admired, but also (as Thady Quirk had permitted Maria Edgeworth) to speak and write in the idiom of the common people. The project of collating all written versions with those she heard from the lips of neighbours was massive, but she took to the challenge with an intensity that surprised even herself. The superb self-concentration of the figure, strong enough to re-create the given world along the lines of his desire, seemed to connect with her own.

Being the child of multiple fathers, Cuchulain is compelled to derive ultimately from himself. Lugh's creation of him – he enters Dechtire disguised as a mayfly – is a beautiful illustration of the peasant adage that 'God possesses the heavens but covets the earth.' The hero-light that burns in his forehead when he is angry is a reminder of his divine origins and a sign that no mortal can surpass him. Such themes would resound through many texts of the Irish revival. The search of the human protagonist for the hero-light of his origins would become above all a question of psychology. The protagonist must look within and learn what it was in him that possessed such knowledge, if only he could learn how to use it.

The role of a hero such as Cuchulain is dangerous, precarious, unenviable, and hedged on all sides by human and divine sanctions, beginning with the prophecy by Cathbad the Druid at his birth. He will accordingly feel gratitude and anger towards those parents who give him life: and he will feel those things in about equal measure. A part of him will wish to return to the god, and another to deny his debt to a parent altogether. The myth of multiple fathers is one way of coping with this intolerable burden. It would be taken up by – of all people – George Bernard Shaw. Disappointed in his actual father, he reimagined himself as 'GBS', the self-invented child of his own writings, suppressing the names which linked him to his frustrating parent. Along with George Carr Shaw, he added to the list of possible fathers his mother's music teacher and his uncle Walter: 'Natural parents should bear in mind that the more supplementaries their children find, the better they will know that it takes all sorts to make a world.'[40] Joyce also invented in Stephen Dedalus a figure who became 'himself his own father': and Synge's Christy Mahon attempted to erase his parent so that he might conceive more freely of himself.

The psychologist Otto Rank, writing on the myth of the birth of the hero, observes that 'the extraordinary life-history of the hero can only be imagined as ushered in by a wonderful infancy'.[41] The *Macghníomhartha* or 'boy deeds' of Cuchulain provide such a setting. All his future deeds are latent in this early scene. Setanta routs the assembly of youths in Conchubor's court and kills the hound of Culan the Smith by mistake, thereby gaining its spirit, which is what will fill him with the later *riastra* or battle-rage.[42] (Warriors sometimes wore the heads of totemic animals, such as hounds.) As child of a sun-god, Setanta's mission is to scatter the power of darkness and to affirm the forces of vegetation and life. So, even as a child, he seems fully formed, a prodigy like the infant Jesus who taught the wise men of the Temple. He offers to take the place of the dead dog and is named Cú Chulain, the hound of Culan. So strong is he that he breaks all arms except those of the king when he puts them to the test. Cathbad the Druid had foretold that whoever did this would become champion of Ireland, but his life would be short. The tale is of energy and youth – and the great evil to be avoided is old age and slow death. The theme would recur from Wilde's Dorian Gray through Yeats's Oisin, to Synge's *Deirdre of the Sorrows*.

Cuchulain courts Emer, his future wife, by riddles, since he is also a great poet. The *riastra* may as easily produce beautiful images as blood on the field of battle, for poetry and violence are conjoint in this heroic world. 'I stood by the knee of Amergin the poet', he proudly asserts: 'he was my tutor, so that I can stand up to any man. I can make praises for the doing of a king.'[43]

Although Cuchulain will have many lovers – including a brief fling with Queen Aoife in Scotland – he begins as a bashful youth. Having slaughtered three challengers in combat, he returns to Emain Macha in the grip of the *riastra*, and the Ulstermen fear that he might destroy their capital with his vibrations and rages. They produce an Irish solution to an Irish problem, for they 'send out three fifties of the women of Emain to meet him'. Standish O'Grady had written that they were 'clad only in the pure raiment of their womanhood',[44] but Gregory's 'red-naked' is more touchingly blunt, true to the violence of the hero's latency period:

> When the boy saw the women coming, there was shame on him, and he leaned down his head into the cushions of the chariot, and hid his face in them. And the wildness went out of him . . .[45]

In some versions (though not Gregory's), he is passed through three vats of cold water (a classic remedy of British public schools), before the rage leaves him.

The virtues of Gregory's style are those of the Gaelic originals, for her narrative is written in a terse, pacy mode, with sentences that can seem even taut and elliptical.[46] Oral narrative tends, of course, to 'situate knowledge in the context of struggle', so that aphorisms and proverbs are used not only to store knowledge but as weapons of combat.[47] Fixed, rhythmic, balanced expressions form the substance of thought in a predominantly oral culture, whether in the paradoxes of Wilde, the proverbs of Leopold Bloom or the aphorisms of Cuchulain. Indeed, the recurrent violence of the legend may be connected with the structure of orality itself, for Walter Ong has said:

> When all verbal communication must be by direct word of

mouth, involved in the give-and-take of dynamics of sound, interpersonal relations are kept high – both attraction (fulsome expressions of praise) and antagonisms.[48]

This is why figures of heroic narrative bulk larger than life: and why George Russell had a point in emphasizing the capacity of the spoken voice of drama to manifest the *dramatis personae* to one another as conscious interiors.

If print isolates persons from one another, sound incorporates interlocuters into close-knit groups. Since the life of Cuchulain has the 'same root' as that of his audience, every speech made assumes that the speaker, as part of an orally driven community, is already in intimate communication with the person addressed, already inside that mind.[49] These qualities still enjoyed prestige in turn-of-the-century Ireland, where oratory and recitation were much-practised arts: so Gregory, like Joyce, could write her epic in the confident assumption that it would often be read aloud. Joyce himself insisted that any obscurities in *Ulysses* could be resolved by oral recital, and Yeats wrote in his preface to Gregory's book that 'if we but tell these stories to our children, the land will begin again to be a Holy Land'.[50]

Gregory reproduced the great set-piece scenes from the life of the hero: the moment when his indifference to pain and death won him the championship of Ulster; the battle with Medbh for the bull of Cuailgne; the jealousy of Emer; the combat with the son who came from Aoife in Scotland; and his foretold death. 'A great name outlasts life,' he tells his sorrowful mother at their last parting.[51] Already he is a world hero, famous for chivalry. He refused to kill Medbh, because it would be wrong to kill such a woman, for if he did he would be according her warrior status. The biases of Christian scribes may intrude here, as does their anti-war philosophy, which sees the Ulster victory in the cattle raid as pyrrhic, since the two great bulls (the wealth of two provinces) lie dead. Likewise, the defeat of his friend Ferdia in single combat at the ford, and the awful pain it brings to Cuchulain as victor, may be a warning against civil strife. The crushing of the woman-warrior Medbh is explained in moralistic terms by Fergus: 'And it is following the lead of a woman has brought it into this distress.'[52]

Yeats saw in Cuchulain's openness to the *sidhe* the vestiges of ancient fairy-faith, which not even the Christian scribes thought it wise to suppress; but Gregory actually removed many accounts of supernatural help from the *sidhe*, so emphasizing the heroism of the protagonist in purely human terms. Yeats believed that the fairy-faith was a little like Gaelic tradition: '. . . it will, perhaps, in Ireland at any rate, be always going and never gone.'[53] As a student of *The Golden Bough*, he saw Cuchulain as another fertility god who had to die in order to regenerate an entire people. Gregory's account of the death is in keeping. When a Druid threatens to put a bad name on Cuchulain, the hero throws his spear at the Druid: this protects Cuchulain's reputation but at the cost of leaving him impotent. His enemy Lugad then takes the spear and gives Cuchulain his deadly wound. He stumbles over to a lake for a drink, as if returning like a vegetation god to waters whence he came; then he fastens himself to a pillar-stone, 'the way he would not meet his death lying down, but would meet it standing up'.[54] A bird comes and settles on his shoulder, sensing carrion (in some versions the bird drinks Cuchulain's last drops of blood). Even after death, however, Cuchulain seems always going and never gone, for 'the three times fifty queens that loved Cuchulain saw him appear in his Druid chariot, going through Emain Macha; and they would hear him singing the music of the Sidhe'.[55]

Cuchulain of Muirthemne did bring fame to Gregory. The more literal-minded Celtic scholars such as Kuno Meyer regretted her decision to remove the description of the heroine's naked body in 'The Wooing of Etain', but most understood that she did this to undercut the Trinity professors so that they could 'no longer scoff at our literature and its "want of idealism"'.[56] The international acclaim drowned out the Atkinsons and Mahaffys. York Powell praised 'a beautiful piece of English as well as a beautiful story and subject',[57] endorsing Mark Twain's verdict that 'The Fate of the Sons of Uisneach' contained the best images of all. Although George Moore satirized the limited syntactical range of Gregory's Hiberno-English (which he rudely called 'a Kiltartan three-hole whistle'),[58] a far greater exponent of that dialect, J.M. Synge, saluted her: 'I had no idea the book was going to be so great. What paltry pallid stuff most of our modern writing seems beside it. Many of the stories, of course, I have known for a long time, but they seem to gain a new life in the beautiful language you have told them in.'[59]

Although Yeats drew on the stories in plotting the plays of his Cuchulain cycle, it was Synge who put them to the most detailed use. In a review in the *Speaker* of June 1902, he denied Yeats's claim that Gregory had 'discovered' a dialect already used in Hyde's *Love Songs of Connacht*: and he conceded that strict students must still rely on German scholars, 'who translate without hesitation all that has come down to us in the manuscripts'.[60] Synge enthused about the book to the great Celtic scholar Henri d'Arbois de Jubainville only to find that he took the scholarly rather than the more liberal view. In her

Dedication to the local villagers, Gregory had said, 'I have left out a good deal that I thought you would not care about for one reason or another.'[61] Synge fully decoded her reasons, implying a critical verdict on the professors of his *alma mater*: 'I hope that her book will give new impetus to many lukewarm Irishmen who have been unsympathetic towards their country because they were ignorant of her real tradition.'[62]

Two years later, Synge was telling Gregory, '*Cuchulain* is still a part of my daily bread.'[63] It provided him with a model of the alliterative prose he would perfect in his plays. Yet the performance of Yeats's Cuchulain cycle led Synge also to question the possibility of 'a purely fantastic unmodern ideal breezy springdayish Cuchulanoid National Theatre'.[64] He may have begun to suspect that O'Grady's opposition to humans impersonating ancient heroes was correct. *The Shadowy Waters* produced only 'a half-empty room with growling men and tittering females'. If *he* were to use Cuchulain, it would be in a mode that allowed for the embodiment of such reservations in the treatment.

The Playboy of the Western World was an occluded parody of Gregory's work, evoking the heroic cycle in order to mock the reduced life among peasants who still told the tale. Christy is a mock-Cuchulain, but the mockery cuts both ways, also calling into question the pretentious cult of ancient violence. The ideals for which Cuchulain died were never fully defined, despite Gregory's best efforts: sometimes it seemed as if he were dying for nothing more than the idea of his own heroism. Even Gregory's biographer regrets the 'limited set of ideals' in a hero whose story 'made the Irish people more willing to fight for freedom, but contributed to making them less fit to govern'.[65] As a rebel who bucked all social systems, Cuchulain might encourage mindless loyalty but also a want of 'political realism'. Something of the same problem has been identified in Yeats's version of a hero who is never an egotist, but 'the altruism of whose pugnacity remains vague'.[66]

Synge sought a dialectical exploration of the relation between ancient heroism and a rural Ireland in which such tales lingered. His point-for-point parody of *Cuchulain of Muirthemne* has been fully described,[67] but the amusing detail in which he recast some of its plot gives some sense of his dialogue with Gregory. The scene that apparently ignited the riot in 1907 was intended as a mockery of the red-naked females on the plain of Emain. Christy, also filled with battle-rage after his exertions at sports on the beach, tells Widow Quin that no woman but Pegeen can satisfy him now: 'It's Pegeen I'm seeking only, and what'd I care if you brought me a drift of chosen females, standing in their shifts itself, maybe, from this place to the Eastern World.'[68] In the typescript, Synge had the women 'stripped itself', but was advised (probably by Yeats) that the puritanical nationalists of the Abbey audience could not abide such candour. The advice was poor. Every pornographer from Petronius to Hugh Hefner attests to the fact that a scantily clad woman can be even more inflammatory than a red-naked woman to the jaded male imagination. Cuchulain was permitted the vision of bare-breasted women before he blushed and tried to hide in his chariot: but the latter-day disciples of Cuchulain could not tolerate the vision of a peasant boy whose fury was soothed (if only in his imagination) by women standing in shifts. The word 'shift' had been used in Hyde's *Love Songs of Connacht* without controversy. That the audience should have broken into disorder at its use on stage was deeply ironic.

The rioters, mainly male, felt that Synge was impugning their virility: and they reasserted it in traditional fashion. Like all mythological figures, Cuchulain was notably androgynous, praised not only for his strength but laughed at by young men for his too-smooth skin. When Synge re-created such qualities in Christy's nuances of phrasing and dainty feet, he showed how a more virile womanhood might be entranced accordingly: the womanly man was attracted by and attractive to the manly woman. This gender-bending did not please an audience dedicated to the construction of a heroic Irish male: their violent response served only to increase Synge's scepticism about the thinking that underlay it.[69]

So his last play, *Deirdre of the Sorrows*, is filled with phrases that ironically echo the Hiberno-English of Gregory's versions. She had shown how ancient royalty could speak like latter-day peasants while remaining heroic; but Synge inverted the pastoral norm, and instead treated his characters as peasants who imagine themselves to be aristocrats. In this way, he emphasized the human qualities of the protagonists, the sense that they are participants in a crisis of human relations. 'For the present, the only possible beauty in drama is peasant drama,' he had written,[70] against the idea of a literal attempt to stage the heroes of the past in an exalted language. So his Deirdre and Naisi, rather than act under *geasa* (strict injunction), make flawed decisions under the pressure of the moment: for instance, they resolve to return to Emain from Alban rather than face the decay of their love, only to dissolve at the edge of their grave into the very bickering this sacrifice was designed to avoid.

Synge's treatment is a critique of the notion of a fated narrative, a foredoomed tragedy. His choric figure Lavarcham rejects the idea that the old familiar story must necessarily be re-enacted in the time-honoured way. The only hurt in growing old is not old age itself, but the prospect of seeing beloved youth turn itself into a martyr to received texts. Deirdre is, however, already posing fatally for posterity: 'and a story will be told forever'.[71]

In calling *Cuchulain of Muirthemne* his daily bread, Synge was shrewdly hinting at the many Christian analogies in the epic. Gregory, herself a devout Christian, was alert to these, but Synge was much more subversive in his use of Christian images. He delighted in the playing-off of biblical language against pagan moments, as in the wedding ceremony of *Deirdre of the Sorrows*: 'by the sun and the moon and the whole earth I wed Deirdre to Naisi'[72] reads like an aggressive mimicry of the sign of the cross. Such subversive potentials could be exploited far more seriously by Patrick Pearse, who found in the story of Cuchulain an unconscious prophecy of Calvary, a symbolization of the redemption of man by a sinless God.[73]

What struck Synge most forcefully of all, however, was the Deirdre tale's exposure of the bankruptcy of the aristocratic code. The lovers in it die less through any fault of their own than because their trusted friend, the messenger Fergus, has been duped by the dishonest king Conchubor. Synge had said that the very use of swords on stage was 'babyish' and that to revive such legends was to risk reviving the unreal. In final confirmation of that fear, his Fergus throws the sword that was supposed to epitomize warrior honour into the lovers' grave. This is Synge's last repudiation of a discredited aristocratic code incapable of keeping its word. Here is yet another case of a mandarin class that must learn how to disgrace itself utterly before going out of business.

The sword of light, the *claidheamh soluis*, symbol of the Gaelic League, survived this indignity: and so did the cult of the hero. Even as Synge raised his difficult questions, Patrick Pearse was proposing the most literal and radical re-enactment of all. In 1908 he founded St Enda's College, named for the saint of Aran but based on the heroic ideals of the *Macghníomhartha*, 'to help as many boys as possible become good men'.[74] On its first anniversary, the boys performed a dramatization of that early phase of the story. The intention was clear: 'we are anxious to send our boys home with the knightly image of Cuchulain in their hearts and his knightly words ringing in their ears. They will leave St Enda's under the spell of the magic of their most beloved leader.'[75] A frieze sculpted by Edwin Morrow in the school building showed Cuchulain taking arms over the most famous line from the 'boy-deeds': 'I care not though I were to live but one day and one night provided my fame and my deeds live after me.'[76] It was small wonder that one of the pupils, Desmond Ryan, wrote later in his reminiscences that 'at Enda's Cuchulain was an important if invisible member of the staff'.[77]

Pearse had vast reserves of self-belief and he needed them, at a time when a policeman was paid more than a schoolmaster. But he was an inspiring teacher. His schoolrooms were lively, boisterous places where children learned to express themselves, and the freer spirits among Dublin's citizenry were soon sending their children to him. Even 'Big Jim' Larkin, the socialist and trade unionist, insisted that his boys attend St Enda's (before later being packed off to Moscow). Pearse saw all this as perfectly in keeping with 'the old Irish tradition of the boy-corps of Emain Macha, the band of children of the famous who sat at the feet of their king and teacher and learned how to construct a happy and united society'. His aim was 'an Irish school in a sense not known or dreamt of in Ireland since the Flight of the Earls'.[78] The cult of youth was uppermost, placing Pearse at odds with Victorian themes of discipline and control.

The more violent potentials of the cult were not lost on some boys. One was amazed on prize day to receive as a reward from his headmaster not a book or bible but a gleaming new rifle. This could point only one way. The image of Cuchulain dying strapped to a pillar, defending his people while a sickness paralysed them, mingled with the story of Jesus. It was also a central complex of imagery in Pearse's play *The Singer*, which ends with a famous injunction:

> One man can free a people as one Man redeemed the world. I will take no pike. I will go into the battle with bare hands. I will stand up before the Gall as Christ hung naked before men on the tree.[79]

The discourses of paganism and Christianity became even more mingled in Pearse's rhetoric than they had ever been in Synge's. In his autobiography, Synge had employed a strangely Pearsean phrase, speaking of how faith in the 'Kingdom of God' had given way to faith in the 'Kingdom of Ireland'.[80] Christianity was the gloved hand with which they reached back to even deeper national traditions. Synge shared with Pearse an impatience with the pseudo-liberalism of the English world at the turn of the century, with its novels and plays of social realism. He had lost all belief in traditional Christianity and his writings all suggest that he viewed it as a thin over-layer on a far more rooted pagan code in Irish culture. Pearse was provocative in his use of Christian terms, but provocative in a different way: he was a leader within Catholicism of those dissidents in opposition to an ecclesiocracy that disparaged folk spirituality and excommunicated republicans. He remained a devout believer and regarded the echoes of paganism in Irish Christianity as proof of the fundamental continuity of Irish spirituality. He found that Christian ideas had grown somewhat clichéd in the modern context, but might glow again with a strange beauty in a pagan context. He was forever describing the heroic and Christian in identical terms:

> A love and a sense of service so excessive as to annihilate all thought of self, a recognition that one must give all, must be willing to make the ultimate sacrifice – this is the inspiration alike of the Story of Cuchulain and the story of Colmcille, the inspiration that made the one a hero and the other a saint.[81]

This complex of feeling was less Irish than Pearse thought, for 'a preoccupation with self-sacrifice' in the neighbouring island also found expression in the first years of the twentieth century in the figure of Peter Pan – 'the Englishman as the eternal adolescent'.[82] That movement had roots in Matthew Arnold's theory that access to the canon of an English national literature (the best that has been thought or said) could be achieved only by students willing to suppress their daily selves for the sake of a higher self, to be delivered by great books. This was a late-imperial strategy which saw inner division as the key to canonical power and which was widely employed in the colonies from Ireland to India:[83] but Pearse proposed to adapt it to alternative Irish purposes. The study of Irish-language literature would produce 'manly' values, for it would combine the arduous, character-forming linguistic discipline of the classics (Greek and Roman) with the national virtue found by the English in *Morte D'Arthur*. It was in much the same mode that Augusta Gregory had managed to be both the Irish Shakespeare and the Irish Tennyson.

The central ideals of *Fiannaíocht* poetry ('glaine 'nár gcroí, neart inár ngéag, is beart de réir ar mbriathar': cleanness of heart, strength of limb, and deeds in accord with our words) were, as it happened, identical to those propounded by Dr Thomas Arnold for the boys of Rugby School: 'What we must look for here is, 1st religious and moral principles; 2nd gentlemanly conduct; 3rd intellectual ability.'[84] Cuchulain would have fitted this ideology perfectly – and did. The long peace had allowed all boys to glamorize distant wars, and *Cuchulain of Muirthemne* was read avidly by many English boys as well as by their Irish counterparts.

The homoerotic traditions of the English public schools were not a thousand miles removed from the *Blutsbrüderschaft* of the heroic world: Cuchulain's intimate enmity with Ferdia has an intensity surpassing any of his transactions with women (an intensity that would become well familiar to students of the English novel of the time from Forster to Lawrence). However, despite the attempt by one or two of Pearse's biographers to read a homosexual subtheme into his writings, it is far more useful to follow Seamus Deane in reading him as an Irish Arnold.[85] Pearse's Gael was an exponent of the 'Celtic element': nature-loving, hero-worshipping. His texts for boys were carefully purged of all reference to 'private parts': Conan Maol, for instance, loses skin not from the buttocks but from his heels. But Pearse's heroic values are the Gaelic antitheses of the philistinism of the new middle class. His aim was to produce a cadre of the national elect from whom the leaders of a renovated land might emerge. This minority would be composed of persons superior in culture, bravery and analytic intellect to the masses: for the Cuchulain myth had always been oddly dependent on the torpor of the masses for its syndication, a truth that Synge worriedly sensed and dramatized. It was a mark of the desperation of the Mayo villagers in his *Playboy of the Western World* that they should have been able to turn a clown like Christy into a hero, a moment not unlike that mocked in Marx's portrayal of a buffoon-turned-leader in *The Eighteenth Brumaire of Louis Bonaparte*. Pearse did not share these doubts: his theory assumed that heroism was catching and that eventually it too would be socialized, with the people acting as its own Messiah. All that was needed was an elite corps, like the Fianna or Red Branch Knights or Committee for the Pursuit of Dracula, and the job was half done.

Cuchulain, therefore, replaced even Wolfe Tone in Pearse's pantheon: and heroism like his must be validated in each generation. O'Grady's objection to the dramatization of legend in Dublin theatres was based on a shrewd anticipation of what it might all lead to – the revolutionary seizure of installations in 1916. With uncanny precision, he predicted that the cultural movement would be followed by a political one, and that this would give way to a military uprising.[86] Many exponents of Gaelic revivalism had remarked that their texts were even more potent than bullets and had been surprised that no attempt was made by the authorities to block their dissemination. Perhaps the authorities thought that all this was no more than another version of the 'Let Erin Remember' tradition and so a suitable case for tolerance – perhaps even a safety valve for the release of otherwise more lethal energies. Or maybe they were subconsciously willing the natives to revolt. Augustine Birrell, that most enlightened of Chief Secretaries, wrote long after the Easter Rising of how it had taken him completely by surprise; and yet he conceded that the events which went into its making were precisely what had distracted him: 'Irish literature and drama, and Messrs Maunsel's list of new Irish publications, and the programme of the Abbey Theatre, became for me of far more real significance than the monthly reports of the Royal Irish Constabulary.'[87] If O'Grady's words of warning had failed to alert him, then nothing could have.

The Easter rebels were deliberately emulating a Cuchulain who had faced hopeless odds. Pearse, Connolly and their comrades sacrificed their lives with the aim not alone of freeing their country but of demonstrating that heroes and heroines might still be possible in the modern world. Stoker's anxieties had been more than fully answered.

24

Synge's *Tristes Tropiques*: *The Aran Islands*

Like *Gulliver's Travels*, J.M. Synge's personal documentary on the Aran islands is composed of four parts, each devoted to a separate voyage: and each more fragmented and problematic than its predecessor. The self which narrates its adventures grows ever more uncertain as a direct result of what has been experienced. In each work the author asks a question: are animals worth more than humans? What Synge found in the writings of Pierre Loti about Breton fishermen – 'a terrified search for some sign of the persistence of the person'[1] – may also be found in his book. There can be few more harrowing scenes in Irish writing than that funeral described in *The Aran Islands* at which a woman snatches the skull of her dead mother from an opened grave and begins a loud keen as she cradles it in her lap.

The subsistence economy of the islands might seem to deny their inhabitants the chance of becoming individuals, in a culture that has both dead and living sharing the same limited repertoire of phrases, clothes and equipment. Synge's even more terrifying discovery, however, is that there are no persons persisting on the mainland: only those *types* mass-produced by a thoroughly anglicized society. His visits to Aran, ostensibly to discover the island culture, will prompt him to deliver a fierce critique of a mainland that is losing contact with its own dynamic traditions, to make way for a double-chinned vulgarity.

He wasn't the first member of his family to go to Aran. His uncle, the Reverend Alexander Synge, established a Protestant mission there in 1851, hoping to combat the 'dirt and ignorance' of the people.[2] The mission failed. When John Millington Synge set foot on Dún Aengus in 1898, he came with a different agenda: to learn Irish and to take instruction from the people. He was no day-tripper, much less a hot-gospeller. Each Sunday, while the inhabitants of the middle island called Inis Meáin attended mass, he climbed the local Dún to meditate. This prompted the visiting priest to joke over breakfast; 'If ever you go to heaven, you'll have a great laugh at us.'[3] Synge shared the life of the islanders, the dangers of the sea and the vulnerabilities of a world without a doctor or nurse (a real risk for a chronic asthmatic, as Synge was).

Being shy, he brought with him a fiddle and a camera, hopeful that these could provide talking points with local people. The box camera was the first ever used among them, causing some to marvel at how the photographs allowed them to see themselves as if for the first time. One of the younger men, who taught Synge Irish from books, quarrelled with the photographer, wishing to appear in his Galway suit rather than the homespuns 'that become him far better'.[4] Synge was, in fact, an exponent of that left-wing pastoral that in later decades would go by other names: sociology and anthropology. There are basically two kinds of pastoral. The first is that in which a leisured aristocracy plays at being poor in a spurious attempt to wish real class differences away; and the second is the more radical sort, in which a real peasantry may be depicted as having qualities thought peculiar to aristocrats. *The Aran Islands* fascinates because it draws simultaneously on both traditions, for its upper-class author discovers among the poor values of a lost Gaelic aristocracy.

Synge's spiritual autobiography is written into the narrative in a familiar Orientalist mode, involving all the usual elements: a romantic landscape as a backdrop to the play of the writer's own consciousness; a betrayed friendship with a sensitive local youth; an infatuation with a native girl who leans innocently across his knees admiring the photos; and a sad, melancholy withdrawal from a place that seems more and more lost in a dream.[5] The scientific, objective element in Synge's personality, which led to his agnosticism, is evident in his claim of 'inventing nothing, and changing nothing that is essential'. The same blend of old-fashioned romanticism and sceptical empiricism would be found in many other left-wing pastorals of the twentieth century, from Orwell's *The Road to Wigan Pier* to Roddy Doyle's novels of the 1980s Dublin poor.

Synge's photography displays that same ambivalence. It runs the obvious risk of exposing him as a mere 'tourist in other people's reality'[6] and one, moreover, who may have the effect of reducing the islanders to tourists in their own. Some of the islanders, admiring his pictures, seem to have decided that a world of representations may be somehow superior to the real world itself. The young man who shuns homespuns wants to look more like the sort of youth who should normally appear in a picture album: already, he inhabits a landscape where nothing is finally real until it has been photographed. That is why traditionalists in such communities feared that a camera might take their souls away. Most of the people of Inis Meáin came to suspect that most representations were misrepresentations.

On an island where everyone seems to be an artist, there can be no need for art with a capital A. Pat Dirane, the old carrier of local tradition, creates a comical scene which is at once a representation of mockery and a mockery of representation:

> Today a grotesque twopenny doll was lying on the floor near the old woman. He picked it up and examined it as if comparing it with her. Then he held it up: 'Is it you is after bringing that thing into the world', he said, 'woman of the house?'[7]

The portable camera, by a similar miniaturizing of experience, runs the risk of transforming it into mere spectacle, by ripping each moment out of its wider social process; and a truly artistic photo may be beautiful but deeply untruthful, indicative of the gap that can exist between a fine image and a painful reality, 'between a gallous story and a dirty deed'.[8] This is why the poet Charles Baudelaire was so shocked by 'Daguerre's cheap method of disseminating a loathing for history'.[9] He feared that such pictures would take the place of memory and rob persons of a capacity for judgement, leaving them in the grip of sensations rather than experiences. That is the anxiety that haunts the younger islanders once they enter the culture of the mainland in Galway – that they will forget their own kindred. The fear of forgetting is so deep in the character called Michael (actually Synge's best friend Martin McDonagh) that, when he sees Synge in a Galway street, he is too shy to accost him immediately in the crowd, 'so I followed you the way I'd see if you remembered me'.[10] In other words, his natural assumption is that even friendly persons from a modern society do not necessarily have a developed capacity to recall old comrades.

Synge was aware of the dangers posed by the camera, but to someone who felt himself a mere interloper among an island people, the machine helped to register that mingled sense of intimacy and estrangement. As Susan Sontag has observed:

It offers in one, easy, habit-forming activity, both participation and alienation in our own lives and those of others – allowing us to participate, while confirming alienation.[11]

The risk of succumbing to conservative pastoral was obvious. The *flâneur* of the boulevards walking solitary among scenes of Parisian blight in the 1890s might transfer himself to the islands, where his photographic eye might survey all with a bohemian detachment. However, Synge did not succumb. By providing each photo with a context of other photos and also with the text of *The Aran Islands*, he returned each snapshot to its developing history. In many ways, the narrative technique of the volume is photographic, a fast succession of briefly realized scenes, each overlaid on the previous one. The sequencing is so richly layered as to render the intensity of a deeply felt experience. Walter Benjamin argued that this was the best way to undo the violence of photography: with other photographs and with words.

The pictures taken by Synge do not have an invasive quality, for it is clear that they were done only with full permission of their subjects, such as a mother and daughter at a cottage door or a man scutching straw on a stone. Moreover, they show that Synge saw himself not just as a reporter to the rest of the world, but 'as a recorder for those involved in the events photographed'.[12] He incorporated the pictures into a communal memory. It could even be argued that, as some islanders had their few possessions seized during evictions, these snapshots might be one of the few things remaining in the world to ratify the reality of their past lives.

Synge also brought the first alarm clock to the islands. He left it with the McDonaghs, prompting one of them to boast that no two cocks could equal it.[13] Before that, the general understanding of time had depended on shadows cast by the sun through open doors (for there was not even one sundial in the place).

The Aran Islands is a study of the onset of modernity, for after Synge's departure people will count off the hours and learn to show their facial profile to greatest advantage. However, this is a modernity that the author and most of the islanders largely deplore. Synge's one serious breach of trust occurred when he published one of Martin McDonagh's letters without permission in *The Gael* of April 1901. Those like Martin who existed on the cusp between tradition and modernity were sensitive to possible ridicule: and they were angry with Synge for quoting the non-standard English of the letter in this way. The row was an early instance of an immense problem in both ethnography and literary modernism: the removal of cultural artefacts, whether African statuary or Latin American music, from their original settings and their republication in Western works of art. Synge was much troubled by such activities. Early in *The Aran Islands* he records a local storyteller's remark that Jeremiah Curtin earned f500 for a book of that teller's own stories. The islanders, however, seem unbothered by money-relations among themselves, seeing cash as an affliction of the outside world. One old man even encourages Synge to take out an insurance policy on his life in Dublin and earn himself £500 on it – the exact amount gained by Curtin for retailing the local lore.

What the people whose cultural artefacts were appropriated in this manner actually thought of such usage remains a mostly unrecorded chapter in the history of modernism. Those who travelled far enough to discover what had been done were often as angry as Martin McDonagh. For his part, Synge sought forgiveness and by February 1902 was told he would be welcome back for a fifth visit.[14] All the same, he never returned after that last trip.

In his own mind Aran was a world elsewhere, his version of what the later anthropologist Claude Lévi-Strauss would call the *Tristes Tropiques*. Again and again in his narrative an 'eastern' note is sounded. The recital of ballads on Inishere 'has the general effect of a chant I once heard from a party of Orientals',[15] while the red petticoats of the women project 'a glow of almost eastern promise'.[16] Synge's documentary is also Orientalist in being an anthology of selected texts, parts taken as exemplary of a whole in the manner of nineteenth-century samplers. The elements identified by Edward Said in *Orientalism* are all present. Apart from those already listed, there is also the sense that the visitor can feel more for the natives than they may feel for him. The writer is mocked for being over thirty and unmarried (as Edward Lane was ribbed in the East[17] and Brian Merriman in *Cúirt an Mheán-Oíche*). The confused moods of a listless young European sophisticate are brought into objective clarification by the spectacle of a 'primitive' world laid out before him. The underlying suggestion is that the old place is debilitated and wan, like a beautiful but depressed woman, who can only be restored to vitality by a male deliverer – a truism which interestingly links the *aisling* to the Orientalist.

Most striking of all, however, is the intertextual nature of such writing. What seems a first-time discovery of a pristine world turns out to be 'a form of copying'.[18] The main template for Synge was an essay called 'The Isles of Aran', published by Arthur Symons in *The Savoy* of 1896. Even the opening account in Symons's essay, the sighting of 'a grey outline',[19] is repeated in Synge's 'dreary rock'.[20] For Symons the attraction lay in 'the most primitive life, of any part of Ireland':[21] in Synge the ante would be upped to 'the most primitive that is left in Europe'.[22] Symons found the Inis Meáin people more charming than the inhabitants of Inis Mór, the largest island, a view echoed by Synge, who called them 'a simpler and perhaps a more interesting type'.[23]

'There is not even a policeman,' Symons had written, 'so sober, so law-abiding, are these islanders.'[24] Symons was especially struck by the red petticoats and blue shawls, drawn closely about their wearers, 'as women in the east draw their veils closer about their faces'.[25] All that would be recycled, as well as Symons's perception that shyness and eagerness impelled the women and children in about equal measure. The upright carriage of the men was attributed by both Symons and Synge to the light pampooties (island shoes) used among the rocks. Symons imagined a prehistoric setting – 'the long-oared galleys of ravaging kings'[26] – and also an affinity between natural and human moods. Likewise, he met in sequence with the two storytellers, Old Mourteen on Inis Mór and an old man on Inis Meáin (who told of how a murderer from Connemara had been sheltered on the islands).

Apart from Symons, the other textual influence appears to be Wilde's 'Soul of Man under Socialism'. Symons in 1896 had judged the islanders so law-abiding that there was no need of a policeman. Two years later in *The Aran Islands*, Synge finds that his predecessor had got things the wrong way round: it was not crime that brought the police but the police who had brought with them the idea of crime. One islander has sold his 'honour' for money (by acting as a bailiff) in a straightforward confrontation between the new English law and the old Irish tradition. Knowing that the sort of eviction his own brother had sanctioned on their family estate was now to be carried out against defaulting tenants, Synge feels 'a strange throb'[27] to see the boats being lowered. What he is about to witness is the primal fall, the colonial occupation of Ireland re-enacted. His use of the word 'civilisation' is now as nauseated as was Symons's:

> After my weeks spent among primitive men this glimpse of the newer types of humanity was not reassuring. Yet these mechanical police, with the commonplace agents and sheriffs and the rabble they had lured, represented aptly enough the civilisation for which the homes of the island were to be desecrated.[28]

The outrage to the family hearth is the catastrophic onset of modernity. The scene-painting is done in broad brush-strokes. While the police sweat and gasp, the islanders walk about as cool and fresh-looking as the gulls.

A few pages on, Synge recalls another parable of law versus tradition: that story of the murderer who was protected by the people and then spirited away to America. Succour was offered not only because the English law was despised, but because the people (never criminals, though always capable of crime) knew that 'a man will not do wrong unless he is under the influence of a passion which is as irresponsible as a storm on the sea':

> If a man has killed his father, and is obviously sick and broken with remorse, they can see no reason why he should be dragged away and killed by the law.
>
> Such a man, they say, will be quiet all the rest of his life, and if you suggest that punishment is needed as an example, they ask, 'Would any one kill his father if he was able to help it?'
>
> Some time ago, before the introduction of the police, all the people of the islands were as innocent as the people here (on Inis Meáin) remain to this day.[29]

The ethic here is existential: one is punished less *for* one's sins than *by* one's sins.

To that liberal critique of capital punishment (adumbrated, of course, by Wilde) is added a rooted distrust of the corrective effect of state institutions. Synge declares it absurd to apply the same laws to the islanders as to the criminal classes of the cities. Caustically, he observes that the introduction of police has brought an increase of crime to Inis Mór. Worse still, the old faction fights, which used to be waged to a self-regulating code, are now liable to lead to endless litigation, as law displaces tradition. There was a time, he reports, when a miscreant islander could be entrusted with a letter to his mainland jailer – a story which exposes the silliness of incarceration. Even further back, in days when Galway had no jail, a criminal might be sentenced to a month on Aran, but once or twice the islanders returned the compliment, by sentencing pests to a month on the mainland.

All of this connects powerfully with the major contentions put forth in 'The Soul of Man under Socialism':

> The less punishment, the less crime. Where there is not punishment at all, crime will either cease to exist, or if it occurs, will be treated by physicians as a very distressing form of dementia, to be cured by care and kindness.[30]

Wilde was sickened not by the crimes committed by the weak so much as by the punishments inflicted by the virtuous. He suggested that society is often more brutalized by punishment than by crime. In writing as much, he may have been coping with a distressing memory of Irish evictions, or with accounts of such recalled by his nationalist mother. 'English law has always treated offences against a man's property with far more severity than offences against his person,' he lamented, 'and property is still the test of complete citizenship.' The real perfection of persons lies not in what they have but what they are. Just as the culture of money leads an islander to sell his honour, so the law of property 'has made gain not growth its aim'.[31] On the more 'developed' island of Inis Mór, Synge is appalled by the effects of the new money economy on even the look of men's bodies:

> The charm which the people over there (on Inis Meáin) share with the birds and flowers has been replaced here by the anxiety of men who are eager for gain. The eyes and expression are different.[32]

The Aran Islands might be read as a document in the history of 1890s anarchism, with the community on Inis Meáin presented as a version of the commune, a utopian zone where most of the discontents of civilization seem to be annulled. The journey out is a voyage back in time: 'It gave me a moment of exquisite satisfaction to find myself moving away from civilisation in this rude canvas canoe of a model that has served primitive races since men first went on the sea.'[33] Synge is introduced to islanders as a man who was in France 'a month from this day': though the Commune there may be only a memory, on Inis Meáin it clearly flourishes. Art has ceased to be a decadently specialist pursuit and, instead, every man and woman 'in this simple life where all art is unknown' can realize the impulses of artists. Each item of furniture has a personal character and even canoes or baskets, being made of local materials, exist as a natural link between the people and an unalienated environment.

Wilde had questioned whether the full expression of a personality was now possible on anything other than the imaginative plane of art: and his remedy was that the public should try to make itself artistic. This is the state already enjoyed (but without deliberate effort) by the people of Inis Meáin, who live against a majestic seascape:

> The continual passing in this island between the misery of last night and the splendour of today, seems to create an affinity

between the moods of these people and the moods of varying
rapture that are frequent in artists, and in certain forms of
alienation.[34]

It is almost as if the artists and alienists of Montmartre have found
at last a spiritual home. Even the danger of life at sea and on rock has
called forth a grace of bodily movement 'which makes it impossible
for clumsy, foolhardy or timid men to live on the islands'.[35] The
storytellers, like Wildean dandies, 'can tell as many lies as four
men',[36] which is only to say that stories have strengthened their
imaginations.

Work in a communal setting has none of the character of sweated
labour, being instead 'full of sociability'.[37] The thatching of a cottage
roof is more like a festival, and the man whose house is being redec-
orated is seen as a host rather than an employer. There is no
contractual trade relationship. The energies of art seem to animate
the people, who are perfectly unaware of the modern world of specialist endeavour, a world in which each employee discharges the
same tasks over and over. Not so on the islands, where people
become strong individuals (despite poverty) through the sheer versatility of their activities:

> It is likely that much of the intelligence and charm of the people
> is due to the absence of any division of labour, and to the cor-
> respondingly wide development of each individual, whose
> varied knowledge and skill necessitates a considerable activity
> of mind. Each man can speak two languages. He is a skilled
> fisherman, and can manage a curagh with extraordinary nerve
> and dexterity. He can farm simply, burn kelp, cut out pam-
> pooties, mend nets, build and thatch a house, and make a
> cradle or a coffin. His work changes with the seasons in a way
> that keeps him free from the dullness that comes to people who
> have always the same occupation. The danger of his life on the
> sea gives him the alertness of a primitive hunter, and the long
> nights he spends fishing in his curagh bring him some of the
> emotions that are thought peculiar to men who have lived with
> the arts.[38]

Such versatility is repeatedly contrasted with the monotony of industrial culture. When he encounters a suit of miserable black clothes
among vibrant islanders, Synge is sure that it has come from the
mainland.

In a predominantly oral culture, there is little abstraction of speech. This is a noun-centred language of concreteness, in which each word clings to its uniquely appropriate object. Such an idiom has the childlike directness that Wilde expected to find in a wholly realized personality of a kind like Synge's, which delights to describe a thing or person as if either is being seen for the first time. In his love letters to the Abbey actress Molly Allgood, Synge claimed to be able to see her as no man ever had or would, a sentiment voiced also by Martin Doul in *The Well of the Saints* as he sweet-talks the ravishing Molly Byrne. Yeats had such moments in mind when he praised Synge for writing as if he were Adam and this the first morning of creation.

A concrete language assumes a strong sense of context. A pig is never just a pig but 'the pig with the black feet', and a rope is 'the rope was bought in Connemara'.[39] Words become part of the object they render, and that object is utterly attached to its proper word. That is why the islanders, despite Synge's own doubts, can never imagine that Irish could die out, for in their minds potatoes cannot be planted nor hay saved without the magical words that allow those things to be done. 'They have only the Irish words for all that they do in the fields,' explains one man, before articulating why Irish must seem to die before being perpetually reborn: 'It can never die out, and when the people begin to see it fallen very low, it will rise up again like the phoenix from its own ashes.'[40] That is a paradigm of island life, for Synge never feels himself more vibrant than when he is dicing with death, buffeted by massive, rolling waves in a frail *currach*.

That heightened sense of life is conditional upon a constant experience of shock and disorientation. A world filled with jeopardy and sudden death calls forth an answering assertion of life. Hence the flaming red petticoats of the women, which stand out against the monochrome grey tints of rock and sky. Another example is the poteen: this brings 'a shock of joy to the blood' and 'seems predestined to keep sanity in men who live forgotten in these worlds of mist'.[41] The poteen is often taken before men submit themselves to the terrors of the sea. For Synge himself, the ultimate shock (of which these are but minor echoes) was the enigma of arrival on Aran: the sense that here was a world founded on a philosophy of life utterly at variance with any he had previously known.

It was strange for a young man who knew Dublin and Wicklow to walk across a landscape bereft of trees: and stranger still to cross an island without a single wheel in use. Even more shocking was the cheerful indifference of the inhabitants to all traditional Victorian distinctions – between a thing and a name, between feeling and reason, between pagan and Christian. Soon after landing, Synge is amazed to learn that far from attacking the fairy-faith (as most priests on the mainland were now doing), the people of Inis Mór had effortlessly assimilated it to Catholicism. They held that when Lucifer saw himself in a mirror (again that bogy of representation), he declared war on God and was thrown out of heaven, along with the bad angels. As they fell towards hell, an archangel interceded asking mercy for some, 'and those that were falling are in the air still, and have power to wreck ships, and to work evil in the world'.[42] Not only do the islanders refuse to separate pagan and Christian notions, but they 'make no distinction between the natural and the supernatural'.[43] The dead are as present to them as the living. One island girl regards Synge's ability to fan the flames of a fire by the trick of holding a newspaper against the mouth of the chimney as a sure sign that he is a sorcerer. 'It's to hell you'll be going by and by,' she worries.[44]

No distinction is made either between the scientific and the magical. The one is simply the other, for anything the people cannot understand is assumed to be the work of fairies or spirits. If pagan belief can be assimilated to Christian, that process can be reversed, as when the *De Profundis* prayer is recommended to ward off evil spirits. The ethos of Dracula prevails, even to the extent that a child taken by the fairies is replaced by one with 'a wound on its neck' and it dies some days later. The locals understand that Protestants do not believe in such things 'and do be making fun of us'.[45] Nevertheless, they steadfastly assume that a child so 'taken' was away in body and soul, with a surrogate deposited in its bed, much as Cuchulain, in the heroic tales, was replaced by his fairy-father when he took a rest in mid-battle with the men of Connacht.

By placing himself in such a setting, Synge as an ascendancy gentleman is deliberately exposing himself to all kinds of shock. Even the distinction between animal and human – so precious to the Victorians after the revelations of Darwin – is soon broken down, and in very strange ways. The islanders strike Synge as animalistic, yet for all that, rather aristocratic as well, a surprising combination:

> The absence of the heavy boot of Europe has preserved to these people the agile walk of the wild animal, while the general simplicity of their lives has given them many other points of physical perfection. Their way of life has never been acted on by anything more artificial than the nests and burrows . . . they seem in a certain sense to approach more nearly to the finer types of aristocracies – who are bred artificially to a natural ideal – than to the labourer or citizen, as the wild horse resembles the thoroughbred rather than the hack or cart-horse.[46]

Once again the implication is anarchist: only those beyond the world of wage slavery can enjoy a life where work is play because play is work, a life free of the discontents of civilization. In the heroine of *Deirdre of the Sorrows* – a girl placed by the high-king in the wild woods as preparation for the noble calling to be his queen – Synge re-created that unusual mix first encountered on Inis Meáin, where 'a touch of the refinement of old societies is blended, with singular effect, among the qualities of the wild animal'.[47] Down at the seashore, the young women with red bodices and white-skinned legs seem to have the beauty of tropical seabirds.

Soon the narrator embraces the possibility of becoming animal himself. He finds companionship in cormorant and crow: 'their language is easier than Gaelic, and I seem to understand the greater part of their cries'.[48] For him a full expression of any personality demands a recapitulation of all experience from prehistoric man to modern living. It is the attempt to re-enact that evolution that is one of Synge's major reasons for sojourning on the islands. Yet the tragic knowledge he must accept on this journey is the inculpation of his own people, the Anglo-Irish. It is they who have precipitated a fall from communal living into a world of private property, a lapse from the majesty of tradition to the pedantry of the law.

In the third section Synge begins to realize that if humans have animalistic qualities, animals may in moments of vulnerability seem sadly human. The pigs of Inis Meáin shriek 'with almost human intonations'[49] as they are loaded for export to England. A kindly woman strokes a particular pet to keep it still while the boats are launched. Synge recognizes with a guilty start that he is witnessing yet another version of that primal scene, the fall from grace which would lead inexorably to eviction and emigration. The pigs are all too human, all too Irish: 'They seemed to know where they were going, and looked up at me over the gunnel with an ignoble desperation that made me shudder to think that I had eaten of their whimpering flesh.'[50] Too honest to deny the truth, Synge knows that his very presence as visitor to the islands is paid for by eviction scenes such as this. In a notebook which he kept on the islands, he penned a black dedication: 'to the little Irish pigs that have eaten filth all their lives to enable me to wander in Paris, these leaves are dedicated with respect and sympathy'.[51]

Synge often seems to conspire in turning Inis Meáin into a version of the Latin Quarter of Paris. He takes pleasure in teaching French phrases to learners. The newspaper trick at the fireplace prompts him to tell the incredulous young woman of 'men who live alone in Paris and make their own fires that they may have no one to bother them'.

Her response is 'They're like me so' and 'would any one have thought that?'[52] The island women remind Synge of those self-sufficient women whom he had known as dancers and writers in Paris: but those of Aran are 'before conventionality', unlike the bohemians whose freedom is more knowing and 'who have freed themselves by a desperate personal effort from the moral bondage of ladylike persons'.[53] None the less, the affinities startle Synge, who finds that the island women 'share some of the liberal features that are thought peculiar to the women of Paris and New York'. The Paris Commune had been put down in 1871, the year of Synge's birth, but it was still a living memory to many of the intellectuals with whom he mingled in the city. They would have recalled figures like Louise Michel, the natural daughter of a *châtelaine*, who wore a wide red belt with a gun and travelled under cover of male disguises to Versailles, just to demonstrate to colleagues that the trick could be done.[54]

When Arthur Griffith accused the author of *The Shadow of the Glen* of blending hedge-school folklore with 'the decadent cynicism that passes current in the Latin *Quartier*',[55] he may have been a poor literary critic of a good play but his antennae were picking up its main cultural codings. All the same, Synge was hardly one to promote sexual licence. In *The Aran Islands* he writes rather admiringly of the delicate balance between the sexual instincts and family feeling: 'The direct sexual instincts are not weak on the island, but they are so subordinated to the instincts of the family that they rarely lead to irregularity.'[56] People have struck an enviable compromise between the moods of romantic love and the impulsive life of the savage. When he visits Michael in his new life in the city of Galway, Synge is impressed by the refinement of his nature, which leaves him as unaware of the presence of half-naked women on a Salthill beach as was the young woman who leaned innocently across Synge's limbs to study the photographs quite unaware of the visitor's sexual interest. The islanders seem like perfectly balanced androgynes who are well on the way to transcending all consciousness of gender.

Nevertheless, life on the islands exacts a psychic cost, especially from the women. The maternal feeling is so strong that it imposes a life of torment on many, who raise children only to lose them to the sea or to the emigrant ship. They have only two redresses: to curtail their feelings towards their children in life, and to articulate them with ritual intensity when their offspring are lost. Out of the experience of mortal loss come the *mná chaointe*, those wailing women whose voices seem to call forth a thunder-clap over an island funeral. Each of the women, taking up the recitative of the *caoineadh*, seems momentarily possessed by a cosmic grief, of the kind voiced in her famous lament by Eibhlín Dhubh Ní Chonaill:

> The grief of the keen is no personal complaint for the death of one woman over eighty years, but seems to contain the whole passionate rage that lurks somewhere in every native of the island. In this cry of pain the inner consciousness of the people seems to lay itself bare for an instant, and to reveal the mood of beings who feel their isolation in the face of a universe that wars on them with winds or seas. They are usually silent, but in the presence of death all outward show of indifference or patience is forgotten, and they shriek with pitiable despair before the horror of the fate to which they are all doomed.[57]

Much later, in Part Four at the funeral of a young man, Synge observes that 'the keen lost a part of its formal nature, and was recited as the expression of intense personal grief by the young men and women of the man's own family'.[58] This alteration is in keeping with Eibhlín Dhubh's treatment. Synge may have overstated this gloomy feature of island life, reading intimations of his own early death into fishermen, each of whom he believed to be under 'a judgement of death':[59] but he was careful to recognize also that wild jests and laughter too allowed people to express 'their loneliness and desolation'.[60]

Another text of the 1890s that influenced Synge was *The Golden Bough* by James Frazer. When Synge remarks that a needle is recommended on Aran to ward off evil spirits, the explanation comes straight out of Frazer's book, augmented by a Breton memory: 'Iron is a common talisman with barbarians, but in this case the idea of exquisite sharpness was probably present also, and, perhaps, some feeling for the sanctity of the instrument of toil, a folk-belief that is common in Brittany.'[61] This would all be incorporated into that scene of *The Shadow of the Glen* in which a tramp advises the wife of a dead man: 'there's great safety in a needle'.[62]

Synge was also indebted to Frazer's overall scheme. The old man who believed that Irish could never die, since it was used by those who named and sowed potatoes, was applying a principle that Frazer dubbed 'contagious magic'. 'It proceeds', Frazer said, 'upon the notion that things which have once been conjoined must remain so ever afterwards even when quite dissevered from each other, in such a sympathetic relation that whatever is done to the one must similarly affect the other.'[63] Many of Frazer's categories – measurement of time; puberty and marriage; magic; murder – are seen to recur in Synge's narrative.

Was Synge in fact an anthropologist *avant la lettre*? Like the anthropologists of Cambridge and the Collège de France, he followed tracks first beaten by Christian missionaries like his uncle Alexander or antiquarians such as Sir William Wilde. Frazer had argued that there were three phases in the history of civilizations: the magical, the religious and the scientific. Synge viewed the islanders as caught between the first and second stages, for they converted even his rational explanation of how the newspaper fanned the fire into the terms of magic.

Frazer considered himself an evolutionary scientist: from that privileged vantage point, he could study more 'primitive' peoples. He worked from his armchair at Cambridge University, employing his categories to 'fix' the primitives of the globe as satellites around a still centre of Western science. These people were 'a spectacle surveyed and dominated by the viewing taxonomist'.[64] Synge's approach was different. He worked and wrote in the field, carrying notebooks, camera and typewriter wherever he went. He was radically disoriented by what he found: and *The Aran Islands* shows that he asked as many questions as he answered. If there is an implied 'Western' norm at the start of Part One, it is well and truly broken into fragments-without-commentary by the end of Part Four.[65] Just as he recognized the ways in which the islanders' Irish permitted them to disrupt the syntax of standard English, so Synge also exposed himself willingly to the shocks of inconceivable ideas. His was not only an Orientalist practice, but also a sort of reverse Orientalism, which accepted the capacity of the 'Orient' to intervene in the 'West'. Although he continued to write the standard English that he himself spoke, it takes up less and less space in each part of his book: and the Hiberno-English spoken by islanders emerges instead as an idiom well suited to a study of mainland culture in an act of anthropological reversal.

In the decades after Synge, anthropologists would find that there were basically two ways in which to report a landscape: as a moody backdrop to the writer's self-fashioning or as an objectively documented world. In the first mode, the ego often risks overwhelming the world. In the second, the danger is that the world will annihilate the self which reports. The brilliance of *The Aran Islands* is its astute interweaving of both methods: passages of spiritual autobiography or vivid dreaming are followed by island recitals or accounts of actual conversations. Sometimes, the two styles are employed in the same paragraph, with the empirical used to undercut any excessive tendencies towards romanticism:

Yet it is only in the intonation of a few sentences or some old fragment of melody that I catch the real spirit of the island, for in general the men sit together and talk with endless iteration of the tides and fish, and of the price of kelp in Connemara.[66]

Synge said that whatever is highest in poetry is always reached where the dreamer is reaching out to reality, or where the real man is lifted out of it.[67] Those are the techniques at work in *The Aran Islands*. Near the close of the first part, he recounts a dream in which his body seems to dance involuntarily to a siren-sound and he loses the distinction between self and soul. It is a characteristic Nineties moment, Dracula-like in intensity, when 'I knew that if I yielded I would be carried away to some moment of terrible agony',[68] but his limbs move in spite of him and he surrenders himself. The predicted agony and self-disgust follow, and then the cryptic sentence, 'I am leaving in two days.' This return to the real is fitting punishment. But is the dreamer really culpable? After all, the dream seems unwilled, a proof of the psychic memory that plays itself out in certain locations.

In saying as much, Synge has effectively signed away his pretensions to scientific rigour and willingly conscripted himself back into the world of magic. Who now is the true primitive? Later anthropologists would ask the same of Frazer, whose own tendency to taxonomize everything in triads seemed a form of white magic, 'as if the evolutionist sought mythical solutions to the problem of myth'.[69] Synge at least remained open to the possibility that he might be no more than another dreamer reaching out to another reality. His imagining of Inis Meáin as a woman anticipates Bronislau Malinowski's relation to the Western Pacific as a female body, 'beautiful but odious to the touch'.[70] Here is Synge:

> With this limestone Inishmaan however I am in love, and hear with galling jealousy of the various priests and scholars who have lived here before me. They have grown to me as the former lover of one's mistress, horrible existences haunting with dreamed kisses the lip she presses to your own. The thought that this island will gradually yield to the ruthlessness of 'progress' is as the certainty that decaying age is moving always nearer the cheeks it is your ecstasy to kiss. How much of Ireland was formerly like this and how much is today anglicised and civilised and brutalised?[71]

That passage was suppressed from the published book, perhaps because it hinted at a truth, portraying Synge as a necrophiliac and re-enacting the one shock that truly terrifies him: the fall into colonialism. Malinowski suppressed *all* semblance of colonial experience from his texts in the attempt to render the primitive life as it was before that intervention. In effect, Malinowski wished away the very project of which his own anthropology formed a part. There is thus a strange congruence between the agendas of anthropologists and those of certain nationalist or Anglo-Irish writers, all committed to the recovery of a pre-invasion identity. Synge was more honest, including in his published text two graphic accounts of this fall (the pigs and the evictions), both emphasizing the barbarous ways in which the new dispensation was imposed.

If Synge employed a quasi-religious vocabulary (pilgrimage, glory, radiance) to describe his voyage to Aran, that may have been suitable to introduce his withdrawal from the 'big world' for a period of penance and struggle in the wilderness. The anthropologist is among other things a latter-day ascetic, who may have a conversion experience in the waters and the wild. Susan Sontag observes in her essay 'The Anthropologist as Hero':

> It is mainly poets, novelists, a few painters who have *lived* this tortured spiritual impulse, in willed derangement and self-imposed exile and in compulsive travel. But there are other professions whose conditions of life have been made to bear witness to this vertiginous modern attraction to the alien.[72]

Her subject is Claude Lévi-Strauss, but she might equally be describing Synge. He also exposed the few ideas that survived his youthful clashes with religion to an island code which challenged and corroded them to an extreme degree. The heroism is of the usual kind, calling for physical courage and endurance, as well as a vigilant intelligence, and, beyond these, a willingness to heal one's alienation from society by completing it utterly.

The anthropologist solves his alienation by becoming a nomad, a stranger to his own people. Synge took a similar stance. An artist should, he said, never be like his country's idea of itself and should in fact become one of its foremost critics. The price is never to feel at home anywhere and it is paid on Inis Meáin by a young island woman who has spent time on the mainland before returning. 'The disillusion she found in Galway has coloured her imagination,'[73] he notes, even though she is still a teenager. When he asks whether she would prefer to return to the mainland town, she answers with the fellow-feeling of another lonely soul whom life has made an anthropologist: 'Ah, it's a queer place, and indeed I don't know the place that isn't .'[74]

Synge's identification with this figure of romantic estrangement is absolute. For him she *is* the enigma of the islands: 'at one moment she is a simple peasant: at another she seems to be looking out at the world with a sense of prehistoric disillusion'.[75] Synge fell in love with this woman, whose consciousness seemed more developed than that of other islanders. She is the one who considers that the lonely men in Parisian apartments (including the writer, of course) are 'like me so', and yet she is also the one who thinks that his fire stunt will send him to hell. In her ambivalance, she embodies his own conflicted feelings about Aran, a deep fascination but also the sort of repulsion felt at some point by most anthropologists from the primitive itself.

Some anthropologists deluded themselves into thinking that the native always lacked the self-awareness of the visitor. In *The Aran Islands*, on the contrary, this is a consciousness which many people have to an acute degree, whether Michael in Galway or the returned Yank or that girl who left the mainland. What they also display, however, is a willingness to anthropologize the mainland, in that mode of defamiliarization favoured by literary modernists, to the point at which the mainland reader feels less and less comfortable in his/her culture. The islands which began in peripheral vision eventually become *normative* by Part Four.

All anthropologists seek to record the moment when the techniques of 'our' society are brought to bear in a study of 'theirs': but the interest that draws a person towards the study of a culture may in the end cause that culture to overwhelm many aspects of the self. That is what happens gradually through Synge's narrative: yet the minimal self that survives at the end is supposed to be purified and, therefore, narratable. As the documentary disintegrates into fragments, the autobiographical portions grow less and less, and the more objective sections take precedence. The encounter with the island girl comes to nothing after she writes Synge off as a devil's apprentice. He was a translator of Petrarch and, as David Richards has wickedly suggested, 'there is something of the petrarchan lover about the anthropologist in his passion for a subject which cannot or will not satisfy his desire but leaves his questions unanswered'.[76] Synge knows that he will always be a waif and an eavesdropper, reading over the shoulder of an Inis Meáin youth those texts which belong more to the boy than they ever can to him. The *Love Songs of Connacht* really are the book of another people.

Many anthropologists, like Malinowski, kept personal diaries of their experiences, while drawing up their field notes in the publishable, official narrative. Synge bravely conflated the two modes of writing. If the autobiographical sections are imagined as removed from the earlier parts of *The Aran Islands*, what remains reads a little like the opening chapters of a nineteenth-century novel with its network of social relations, omniscient author and vision of an old world frozen before the irruption of outside forces, of whose existence the inhabitants are still largely ignorant. The attraction of the book for its first generation of readers, like the seductive charm of *Cuchulain of Muirthemne*, may have derived from its blend of the novelistic and the mythical.

Of course the methods of novelistic realism never seemed to fit such transitional communities. One reason was that 'realism' offered the semblance of actual experience, a stunningly exact version of a world known to most readers, whereas a place such as Inis Meáin interested them because it was the opposite of their quotidian location. Unlike Yeats, Synge was far too shrewd to attempt a full-blown Aran novel, but smart enough to employ some devices of the novel form – character study, reported conversation, chapter sequences – in order to win over the reader.

He used the primitive world of Aran much as Lévi-Strauss would employ that of *Tristes Tropiques*: as a basis from which to offer a critique of 'progress'. Whereas Frazer had been sceptical of ancient religion and a celebrant of progress, Synge took the opposite view.[77] The insurgent counterappeal from the native Irish had found another willing respondent from the ascendancy class, a process about which T.S. Eliot would soon issue a strong warning: 'in so far as the culture is *lived*, the student will tend to identify himself so completely with the people whom he studies, that he will lose the point of view from where it was worthwhile and even possible to study it'.[78]

Synge might have responded, 'if only that were so'. Ultimately, the anthropologist is a type of the hero, because what is attempted is in fact impossible. Synge recognizes that he can never fully know or narrate the islanders: and, at about the same time as he reaches this conclusion, he also begins to abandon the attempt to narrate himself. His own identity needs to undergo a period of reformulation, in the light of what he has learned, before it seeks further self-expression. He knows, however, that it would be folly to become yet another in the long line of mainlanders (including his fatuous uncle) who have tried to reform the islanders. It takes a heroic constitution to live out this tragic knowledge, as Lévi-Strauss avers:

The paradox is irresoluble: the less one culture communicates with another, the less likely they are to be corrupted, one by the other; but on the other hand, the less likely it is, in such conditions, that the respective emissaries of these cultures will be able to seize the richness and significance of their diversity.[79]

For that reason, Synge is driven back to the mainland, in the knowledge that what he has learned may be of help in improving his own society. His own is the only one that he can reform, as he now realizes, without destroying. He cannot claim the islands: rather, they have possessed him, and may yet speak through him, helping him to express a life of his own that has not found expression. Lévi-Strauss says that the anthropologist has no axe (Christian, Freudian, rationalist) to grind, for his real object is to save his own soul by 'an act of intellectual catharsis'.[80] That catharsis, like the conversions of ancient saints, occurs out in the field, where it is marked by a turning point and a revolution in the heart. For Synge as for Lévi-Strauss, that was the recognition that there was no real difference between mythical and scientific thinking: science was just the magic of the modern world.

Beyond the excitement of these discoveries lies a sense of tragedy for Synge which, no matter how he tries to deflect it with superb story-telling, keeps breaking into his narrative: the fall into colonial expropriation. It can only be undone if one pays the necessary price of abandoning all ideas of human progress, those crazy ideas that had brought the police and tax-collectors to the islands. Appropriately, Synge refuses to append a map – that tell-tale device of a colonial surveyor – to his text. The only way to free the Aran Islands is to vacate them and to recognize the spot as the no-place or utopian commune which it is for most of those who still live happily enough on it. 'It is not drawn on any map,' observes Herman Melville of a similar spot in *Moby-Dick*: 'True places never are.'

25

W.B. Yeats – Building
Amid Ruins

The greatness of Yeats lay in his constant capacity to adjust to ever-changing conditions. He began in his teens writing poetry of octogenarian senility, yet ended his days creating passionate celebrations of the human body. 'When I was young, my muse was old,' he later explained with a glint, 'but now I am old my muse is young.'[1] As the years passed, he grew simpler in expression, using shorter lines dominated by monosyllables, with more nouns and fewer adjectives. He said himself that a poet should think like a wise man, but express himself as one of the common people.[2] That sounds rather like the plight of the *filí* after the collapse of the bardic system compelled them to seek a popular audience. The fascination of reading Yeats is in witnessing a poet whose understanding of culture was based on ancient, mandarin assumptions seeking to adjust to the violent, jagged modern world, and then having the courage to let that world flow through him.

He believed that he was, by right of inheritance, an Anglo-Irish gentleman of the lower aristocracy. The world, however, had a different fate in store for him. In 1874 at the age of nine, he prepared to leave Sligo for school in London and his aunt said to him, 'Here you are somebody. There you will be nobody at all.'[3] The great revelation of his early career was a meeting with Oscar Wilde, a talker unequalled in eloquence among the London personalities of the day. 'I never before heard a man talking with perfect sentences', he recalled, 'as if he had written them overnight with labour, and yet all spontaneous.'[4] It was only when he saw beads of sweat running off Wilde's drooping hand at a dinner table that the young Yeats realized how all the epigrams were the outcome of rigorous rehearsal. He learned three useful lessons from Wilde: on the value of wearing a mask; on the nature of art as concentrated utterance; and on the need to disguise all complications of thought in the most direct of language. Wilde had made many of the old aristocratic notions of pleasure marketable in an age of the bourgeoisie.

For Yeats, Wilde's *Intentions* was a wonderful book, since it confirmed his hunch that art, far from being representative of its age, is more often written against its prevailing spirit. Yeats, accordingly, was less interested in being read by his age than in providing his own strong, adversarial readings of it. Nor was his a version of the war of the nineteenth century against the twentieth (though, being thirty-five as the century turned, he might have been forgiven for taking that view). It was the sheer breadth of his perspectives on historical time that allowed him to look forward as well as back. Even the death of the old imagination might become the greatest challenge to forms of consciousness intrepid enough to imagine such a thing:

> *Shakespearean fish swam the sea, far away from land;*
> *Romantic fish swam in nets coming to the hand;*
> *What are all those fish that lie gasping on the strand?*[5]

Because he took long views, Yeats was able to see the disorder of the modern world as rooted in its foolish devotion to mere mechanism. In the early poems, he sought a relief from all this in a certain formlessness, but the new century had brought in its harsh geometry a drastic return to fixed structures. The search for a freer form had been answered by the old, familiar imposition. This sickness had its source in the Enlightenment, said Yeats, which reduced everything to quantities and fractions. Swift and Burke had foretold all this with distaste, but the rude mechanicians mocked by Gulliver were already carrying the day. However, since no victory was ever final, their time of humiliation and defeat would come.

Yeats knew that not even Swift was wholly 'clean' in this matter, since he was a nominal representative of that Anglo-Irish society which, three centuries earlier, had extirpated the *filí*. In their fate Yeats saw a prophecy of his own. Like them, he wrote a poetry of praise and blame: and he saw it as his duty to speak for an entire civilization which he felt to be under threat. Yet he soon tired of the bardic role, and often sought to shrug it off. In 'At the Abbey Theatre', upset by the fickleness of public taste, he all but appoints the populist

Douglas Hyde as national poet to a rather infantile people. This would leave Yeats free to pursue his own more mandarin art, in keeping with the deeper agendas of the *filí* – the production of that heroic verse now so unpopular with most Abbey playgoers. The irony of the poem is rich: Hyde, allegedly the sponsor of bardic values, will be given the leadership of the *vulgus*, while Yeats, the resigned national bard, will in fact keep a deeper faith with the underlying inheritance.

Much of that faith declared itself in a refusal to uphold low artistic standards. When bad poets began to imitate Yeats's style, far from feeling flattered, he voiced outrage and a disinclination to praise his imitators:

> *You say, as I have often given tongue*
> *In praise of what another's said or sung,*
> *'Twere politic to do the like by these;*
> *But was there ever dog that praised his fleas?*[6]

This is also a refusal to found a school of Yeatsian poetry. The poet who could not recognize Davis, Mangan or Ferguson as real progenitors of his own aesthetic of the Unconscious is resolved to be the first and last of his line, a sponsor of what he would elsewhere call (in a marvellous phrase) 'the tradition of myself'.[7]

The thinking behind the refusal is clear enough: imitation is suicide for any self-respecting artist. It is a point to which he returns in 'A Coat', where again he tries to disperse with savage mockery his growing band of disciples;

> *I made my song a coat*
> *Covered with embroideries*
> *Out of old mythologies*
> *From heel to throat;*
> *But the fools caught it,*
> *Wore it in the world's eyes*
> *As though they'd wrought it.*
> *Song, let them take it,*
> *For there's more enterprise*
> *In walking naked.*[8]

This is also a dismissal of his own earlier Nineties mode, literally of its 'embroidered cloths'. Now the outline is more stark and clear, in lines whose tight-lipped terseness amounts to a determination to confront reality, however distasteful. Even the broken rhythms of the close, and the half-rhyme between 'take it' and 'naked' point to the future and to a world no longer felt to be regular. Of the forty-five words in the lyric, thirty-nine are monosyllables, used with all the deliberation of a man who understands very well the force of Synge's prediction that verse would have to become brutal again before it could be fully human.

The situation of Yeats is very close to that of Baudelaire, when he describes the poet dropping his halo in a city street and preferring that some bad imitator should pick it up instead of its owner. The aura attaching to earlier traditions is now a bauble worn only by fifth-rate practitioners: it can be of no interest to those who walk naked. Yet the loss of the old halo forces Baudelaire into the marketplace, where he must sell his songs to whomever will buy. His way of imprinting himself on popular consciousness was to choose a drastically limited number of exemplary poses which made him instantly recognizable to the public. Yeats learned that lesson well and used his own images: hero, saint, sage, lover, fool. Yet the aim of self-renewal with which he sought to defeat the commodification by market forces of his styles was never wholly successful. Not only did Yeats repudiate earlier styles; he often rewrote entire poems, long after they had appeared in published books, prompting frustrated admirers to complain that they would never have a definitive edition of his work. His riposte was as radical as any delivered to his bad imitators:

> *They do not know what is at stake;*
> *It is myself that I remake.*[9]

No doubt – but the resale value of reworked poems in further volumes showed that even art for art's sake had its own cash worth as an aspect of the fashion system.

Driven to survive in market conditions, Yeats (like Wilde before him) had little choice but to sell himself as a commodity. Years of struggle in winning audiences for the high art of the Abbey Theatre reminded him of the realities of a world in which a *file* must find a purchaser for a poem, which in its lines would sell off what remained of the older values:

> *When I was young*
> *I had not given a penny for a song*
> *Did not the poet sing it with such airs*
> *That one believed he had a sword upstairs;*
> *Yet would be now, could I but have my wish,*
> *Colder and dumber and deafer than a fish.*[10]

The selling of penny songs in Yeats's youth had been done mostly by mendicants and beggars rather than by ruined noblemen with swords secreted in their wardrobes: but the point is fair enough. The songs were a link back to a lost world of heroism, grace and leisure: hence the discrepancy between the poet's memories and current condition. The tramp or wanderer in Yeats's poems is one who knows 'the exorbitant dreams of beggary', the relation between imaginative sumptuousness and material destitution. If Augusta Gregory was impressed on her visits to Galway work-houses by the contrast between the poverty of storytellers and the splendour of their tales, Yeats could see in these deracinated figures an image of Anglo-Ireland on the skids. So did Synge, who signed his love letters to Molly Allgood 'Your Old Tramp'.[11] So did Samuel Beckett whose tramps talk as if they possess doctorates ('How do you know they don't?' Beckett once asked an inter-viewer)[12] but whose clothes (dented bowler, shabby morning suit) told a story of the decline of a bardic class. 'You should have been a poet,' says Didi. 'I was once,' answers Gogo, looking down at his rags: 'Is it not obvious?'[13]

Yeats was often desolate at the thought of the world that had been lost and at the terrible demands of the new moment, but he never fully relaxed into the more modern versions of a national bard. 'Easter 1916' is the tell-tale poem that enacts his reservations. By tra-dition, it should name and celebrate the warrior dead and conclude that the land has been redeemed by their sacrifice. In fact it is a pro-longed deferral of that bardic duty, as the poet refuses to name anybody ('This man kept a school', 'that other', 'This woman's days') and asks some painful questions about the costs in human terms of such dreaming. By the time he submits to duty and intones the lead-ing names, the doubts of a private citizen have all but drowned out the confident, elegiac tones of a national bard: and the emphasis of the closing refrain is at least as strongly on the terror as on the beauty of what has happened. Yet the 'terrible beauty' is, none the less, proclaimed and, in being proclaimed, it is set up against the denial of all possibility of heroism uttered just three years earlier in the poem 'September 1913'.

This capacity for drastic self-renewal, for the transcendence of earlier modes and attitudes, is what makes Yeats a thoroughly modern poet, yet it is done in order to protect as much as can be pro-tected of the values with which the artist set out. The more fragmented and contorted the form, the more likely it is to deliver a defence of ancient wisdom or heroic nobility. Yeats was always fas-cinated by shape-changers in mythology, who adopted ever-altering guises in order to frustrate and defeat their enemies. One poem often inverts what has been said in another (without ever quite cancelling it out, since both exist forever after in a sort of suspension). The expectations set off by a title like 'The Second Coming' or 'Easter 1916' may be completely reversed in the texts themselves, which are likely to enact even at the level of the telling phrase ('ignorant goodwill', 'mere anarchy') a poet's obsessive quarrel with himself. Such relentless self-subversion should logically result in a disintegrated identity, yet somehow the word 'Yeatsian' survives the experience with added definition and force. The same is true of the word 'Swiftian' and for similar reasons, for in the forms of both authors all is conflict, yet the underlying themes do not change very much, repeating themselves obsessively from book to book.

In the case of Yeats, those themes include the denunciation of old age; the recording of the high cost of dreams; and the setting of the claims of 'dream' against the truth of the human 'heart'. In the first lyric of his *Collected Poems*, 'The Song of the Happy Shepherd', he warns against any hunger for truth

> *Lest all thy toiling only breeds*
> *New dreams, new dreams; there is no truth*
> *Saving in thine own heart.*[14]

This is also the theme of a late work such as 'The Circus Animals' Desertion', which pits the claims of the 'dream itself' (of art and love) against its sources in the human heart:

> *Now that my ladder's gone*
> *I must lie down where all the ladders start,*
> *In the foul rag-and-bone shop of the heart.*[15]

His handling of the theme is as repetitive as that of Swift. Yet because, like his predecessor, he can take a long, anthropological view of the cycles of history, he is never utterly dismayed by the immediate catastrophe, finding something redemptive even in the energies with which people live out a process of negation. That feeling may have its roots in the old satires of *filí*, whose 'delight in vehemence takes out of anger half the bitterness with all of the gloom'.[16]

It is impossible to write a pure satire in such conditions, for the pleasure in stating the worst very well becomes more real to the poet than the awfulness of the situation he contemplates. Indeed, the sheer extremity of the prevailing conditions becomes the measure of the greatness of an art that can somehow frame and articulate them. If satire sometimes undoes itself by the sheer excess of its enunciation, that may be true of other forms of art as well. Here the sheer heroism of Yeats's theory of art becomes most pressing, for it turns out that not only civilizations but also styles of poetry may contain within themselves from the very outset the seeds of their own destruction.

There is, as always, a much more beautiful way of phrasing that terrible idea:

> *Everything that man esteems*
> *Endures a moment or a day.*
> *Love's pleasure drives his love away,*
> *The painter's brush consumes his dreams;*
> *The herald's cry, the soldier's tread*
> *Exhaust his glory and his might:*
> *Whatever flames upon the night*
> *Man's own resinous heart has fed.*[17]

The self can destroy itself by the very energies that define its being, just as a poet can be mummified by being widely accepted:

> *Much did I rage when young,*
> *Being by the world oppressed,*
> *But now with flattering tongue*
> *It speeds the parting guest.*[18]

However Yeats is even more interested in the act of forming a self or a poem. If expression is loss, that is only because the artwork passes out of the poet's mouth and into the world, there to do a task of re-creation. Life always tended to imitate art and the world, as Wilde sighed, grew sad because a puppet like Hamlet had once been melancholy. Yeats believed that the loss of control over one's creation is the price an artist pays for seeing it reconfigure the world.

Where did the creative energy come from? If for Marx the accumulated labours of past workers were signified by money, for Yeats they appeared as moods. The invisible life of earlier times was intermittently manifest now in the fairy-world, or in those bodiless souls that descended into human forms as moods. These moods could characterize an entire period of history, such as the 1890s, or they could possess certain strong individuals, working to bring about momentous alterations for good or ill:

THE MOODS
Time drops in decay,
Like a candle burnt out,
And the mountains and woods
Have their day, have their day;
What one in the rout
Of the fire-borne moods
Has fallen away?[19]

Poetry in this conception is a form of trapped energy, saved from earlier generations: and it is the one tradition that may assist an artist strong enough to direct the available energies.

Amidst the ruins of the modern world, Yeats felt himself able to tap into the images and energies of a collective past long erased from official memory. The greatest sin would be to bring the work of dead predecessors to nothing: for those predecessors expected the later generations to press on their behalf a claim to a restored divinity, a claim which could not be made cheaply but which had to be lodged. The Enlightenment had divested matter of all spirit, leaving mere excrement instead. The failure of transcendence was obvious in the lack of any fit between human feeling and available form. For the first time in history man lived in an environment largely of his own making, yet he had never felt more estranged from his surroundings. That was because places and things needed to be emancipated just as much as people did, to be reanimated with spirit and rescued from mere ownership. The process must begin with the landscape itself. The argument in Ireland between landlord and tenant was about mere ownership, but the freeing of territory demanded a recognition that the soil on which people walked was holy ground. Only those who could really *see* the land for what it was deserved to possess it (the condition being that they were first of all possessed by its spirit). The *filí* had interpreted the justice or turpitude of a chieftain's reign by the evidence offered in the state of the landscape – and the modern poet must do the same.

Likewise with things. Things also had a spiritual history which only those whose imaginations had been impoverished by science could dare to ignore. The artist's task was to restore such autonomy to every object that it ceased to be a mere prop and regained the dignity of symbol. If the modern world was only a simulacrum of a more real world elsewhere, then one could never afford to deny the life in objects, a life that might at any time threaten to usurp this one. Yeats wrote a brilliant lyric on the theme, which inverts the situation described by Synge in *The Aran Islands*, when a family derides a

newly delivered doll as a poor, botched imitation of humanity. In
'The Dolls' that trajectory is reversed as a prelude to that moment
when the real and illusory are so confused as to seem to present just
a choice of illusions:

> *A doll in the doll-maker's house*
> *Looks at the cradle and bawls:*
> *'That is an insult to us.'*
> *But the oldest of all the dolls,*
> *Who had seen, being kept for show,*
> *Generations of his sort,*
> *Out-screams the whole shelf: 'Although*
> *There's not a man can report*
> *Evil of this place,*
> *The man and the woman bring*
> *Hither, to our disgrace,*
> *A noisy and filthy thing.'*
> *Hearing him groan and stretch*
> *The doll-maker's wife is aware*
> *Her husband has heard the wretch,*
> *And crouched by the arm of his chair,*
> *She murmurs into his ear,*
> *Head upon shoulders leant:*
> *'My dear, my dear, O dear,*
> *It was an accident.'*[20]

Even objects have their vanity and can take exception to being
mocked or marred by bad copies. To those who actually inhabit the
world of art, life itself may appear a paltry imitation. The husband,
disturbed by sounds, stretches expectantly, as if he may be about to
make another baby: but his wife murmurs into an ear (whether the
husband's or the doll's is left beautifully unclear) that it was an accident. She may be humouring the dolls or deceiving him.

It is a strange lyric to find in a volume titled *Responsibilities*, but
Yeats's epigraph explains that it is in dreams that responsibilities
begin. The dreams of the present generation may be the responsibilities of the next, who will seek to make them flesh. The idea is similar
to a famous formulation of Walter Benjamin: 'Each epoch not only
dreams the next but also, while dreaming, impels it towards the
moment of its waking. It bears its end within itself and unfolds it – as
Hegel already saw – with cunning.'[21] A redeemed world might well
be one in which dolls have speech and feeling, and in which mankind
awakens from history's nightmare to a higher level of consciousness.

A remarkable number of Yeats's greatest poems are about such a moment of awakening from the enclosed mindset of one era into the starker realities of another. 'The Second Coming' might provide the classic instance:

> *The darkness drops again: but now I know*
> *That twenty centuries of stony sleep*
> *Were vexed to nightmare by a rocking cradle,*
> *And what rough beast, its hour come round at last,*
> *Slouches towards Bethlehem to be born?*[22]

Those lines come as the climax to a volume and an oeuvre that have been centrally devoted to the idea of waking up. The *r* sounds at the start of the poem are repeated in a hypnotic fashion, as if the speaker has been mesmerized by a vision that emphasizes the poverty of his vocabulary to describe so immense an experience. Yet the link back to 'Easter 1916' is clear enough: the subject is the awakening from dream to a sense of reality, precipitated by a momentous event which happens in the world outside the speaker, who is unhappy but also deeply moved. The same might be said of other lyrics in the volume *Michael Robartes and the Dancer*. 'Solomon and Sheba', 'An Image from a Past Life' and 'Towards Break of Day' all describe experiences in which a newly-wed couple struggles, upon waking, to extract some significance from dreams. One might be forgiven for thinking this the organizing principle of the volume, until one recalls how often Yeats's earlier poems dealt with identical situations. 'The Stolen Child' asked what happened to the world abandoned for the dreams of fairyland: and 'The Song of the Happy Shepherd' warned against 'new dreams' which could only baffle the awakened heart.

'What is highest in poetry', wrote Synge, 'is always reached when the dreamer is leaning out to reality, or where the man of real life is lifted out of it, and in all the poets the greatest have both these elements.'[23] That was especially true of Yeats. Hence the utopian thrust of his declaration that the arts lie dreaming of what is to come. Within each artwork is concentrated an intense form of consciousness of things past, and of a future that will be admirable to precisely the extent that it is hard to imagine in the present. Even 'The Second Coming' ends with a surge towards the future which, despite its terrifying problems, brings the poet new images and themes. The claim still made by the past carries, folded within it, a demand on the future. Yeats's thinking was profoundly dialectical. For him the demand to abandon illusions about a situation could be nothing other than the demand to abandon a situation that might feed off such illusions. But he had no illusion about illusions: he knew just how valuable they could be in charting a way forward to the higher state in which they might not seem so manifestly inaccurate an account of reality. That was one aspect of his thought shared with an unlikely fellow traveller, Karl Marx, who said, 'the world has long possessed in the form of a dream something of which it has only to become conscious in order to possess it in reality'.[24] Those are indeed the responsibilities that begin in reveries.

For Yeats the shock of waking up was linked to the idea of remembering a world before its fall into mechanism. The bad dream, in other words, was what Shaw's Peter Keegan called 'the wicked dream of efficiency'.[25] Received wisdom of the scientific world could only continue to blinker mankind to all the invisible signs of the spiritual world: but better dreams might raise a sense of responsibility to man's deeper potentials. This brings us, of course, to the point at which Yeats broke with those Marxians who saw history as a locomotive speeding steadily towards a definite goal. He had once been jolted on a tram over Dalkey Bay in a comic outing with Oliver St John Gogarty. The famous poet was posing (as usual), remarking on the splendour of the view and on his willingness to give up half a lifetime, if only he could be vouchsafed five minutes in which to contemplate 'the Naples of Ireland'. Quick as a flash, the trickster Gogarty pulled the emergency cord and said, 'Yeats, you can have it right now for five pounds' (the 'penalty for improper use'). It was a useful, if expensive, lesson, for it taught Yeats to entertain the possibility that revolution might not be the moving train so much as the reaching of humanity for the emergency cord (all uses of which carried some penalty). Walter Benjamin took the same view and likened such moments when life's flow is brought to standstill to those scenes in classic drama when fleeing warriors pause for a review of the action.[26] Such was the 'image from a past life' that flashes into the present at a moment of danger to jolt all dreamers awake: but that was as likely to be an old story or symbol, without a clear use-value in current contexts, as the memory of some lost lover. As a collector of old lore, Yeats often fastened upon material that had been long out of circulation, reintroducing it to the cultural stream.

Such a dynamic traditionalism was in fact the ultimate in literary modernism, a ploy which would in time be taken up by the surrealists. They also wished to awaken a sort of thought in despised objects and, by embracing all that was rejected in an overmanaged society, to reconnect with earlier versions of the collective unconscious. *A Vision*, with its automatic writing and stylistic rearrangements of experience, is a wholly surrealist text: and its critique of mere reason, as well as its images of a recovered sense of communal utterance, is also indicative. Most of the surrealists from Paris or Berlin had to travel great distances to primitive parts of the world in order to locate such raw materials: but Yeats was able to find all the necessary elements at home. He was in fact a surrealist *avant la lettre*, for his early obsession with the wish-potentials of dreams, along with his discovery that modernity was but the latest form of mythic consciousness, anticipated by decades the work of Breton, Aragon and others. Their roots were to be found in two very different, even discordant, movements of the 1890s to which Yeats, with his genius for reconciling seemingly opposed ideas, managed to belong: the aesthetes and the anarchists. Both were fused in the surrealists, who tried to liberate the perfected forms of a pure art back into the social mainstream: but they had already been fused in Yeats's own work. As early as 1901 he had praised the idea of William Morris that 'permits even common men to understand good art and high thinking, and to have the fine manners these things can give'. England, by creating great wealth for the few alongside vast poverty for the many, 'has already made the understanding of the arts and of high thinking impossible outside a small cultivated class'.[27]

Yeats had long taken the view that genius was a process by which the buried self was joined to one's everyday mind: it was that deeper self that restored the old, wild energies of a lost pre-Enlightenment world. Dreaming was one way of restoring contact between the conscious and unconscious elements of a person, but the great artist was one who could achieve that while still awake. Every dream constructed itself, however, on the understanding that such an awakening was the outer limits of its organizing wish. Freud had joked that the sleeper abandoned himself to the ranks of the dead with high hopes of a daily reprieve.[28] This was the very paradigm of all poetic creation for Yeats and the explanation of his much-abused Celtic Twilight phase. The wavering rhythms of his earlier poems were intended to render a world caught in the zones between wakefulness and sleep.

Poetry as imagined by him took the form of a near-death experience, indefinitely prolonged. His earlier lyrics tended to evoke fading and tired life on the edge of unconsciousness, and his later poems captured the experience of waking up. Whatever their direction, they were validated by the nearness of the sleeper's brush with death. It was that which heightened their celebration of life: 'we begin to live when we conceive of life as a tragedy'.[29] Yeats followed the *filí* who found that a closeness to death might give an even more compelling shape to what they had to say. The breath-poems of Yeats, which confer a vertical structure upon a single grammatical sentence, are spell-binding examples of this: and in their involutions they demand an exhalation of breath that feels like an expiration:

> THAT THE NIGHT COME
> *She lived in storm and strife,*
> *Her soul had such desire*
> *For what proud death may bring*
> *That it could not endure*
> *The common good of life,*
> *But lived as 'twere a king*
> *That packed his marriage day*
> *With banneret and pennon,*
> *Trumpet and kettledrum,*
> *And the outrageous cannon,*
> *To bundle time away*
> *That the night come.*[30]

These lines commemorate the intensity of a death-wish which held life always at the point of drama. The *sprezzatura* of the woman's performance is repeated in the throwaway epigram of the lyric, which manages to see death as something achieved rather than endured. Likewise, in another poem Yeats celebrates the playwright John Synge, who 'dying chose the living word for text'.[31] There is a lesson in these great ones who make their destitution their glory. It is given a more extended elaboration in 'The Wild Swans at Coole', whose lines lament the death of friends and the loss of creative powers, but in words of such eloquence as to belie the very suggestion. As always, out of the moment of near-defeat, Yeats seizes the potential for self-conquest.

In Yeats's aesthetic theory, all creation was implicated in a sense of compromise and loss, for incarnation was crucifixion. This applied in the first instance to the ultimate creator. It had been an act of drastic self-limitation for a perfect God to create a flawed world through which to realize a plan: and the artist–creator could not expect to escape a similar humiliation. That was why for Yeats also 'the finished work is the death-mask of its conception'[32] in at least two senses – first, the frustrations of a damaged form and, second, the prospect of its imminent death. The return to God was really a longing by the creature for its own destruction, 'like the moth's desire for the light'.[33] Even love might be no more than a desire for those things that come after death.

Art might be an agent of destruction. 'Is not all history but the coming of that conscious art which first makes articulate and then destroys the old wild energy?'[34] Yeats's advice to Synge – to express a life that had never found expression – while ill-judged concerning the tradition of art on Aran, was a true enough account of the way in which his own poetry worked: he himself could create only while in the grip of forces not yet fully uttered or known. 'Literature can never be made by anything but by what is still blind and dumb within ourselves':[35] hence the strange desire to be colder and deafer and dumber than a fish. That is why an achieved, smoothly transmitted and self-confident culture would have been an oppression to Yeats, for it would have marked the end of a tradition. All that could be handed over of that would have been a beautiful, mummified corpse. Better by far to have a troubled passing-on of a broken but still breathing thing.

What was most radical in Yeats's idea of culture was also what was most ancient: his conviction that real culture was a shedding of knowledge and illusions rather than an accretion of them. Hence his wonderful assertion that culture consists not in acquiring opinions but in getting rid of them: withering into truth.[36] In that, at least, he had something in common with the thinkers of the late nineteenth century, who saw their task as the unmasking of the superficial trappings of a society to reveal the core of unadorned truth beneath. But Yeats included science in the list of superfluities to be removed. He praised Tennyson for 'the shedding of hopes based on mere mechanical change and mere scientific or political inventiveness, until at last his soul came near to standing, as the soul of a poet should, naked under the heavens'.[37] That almost Lutheran moment of nakedness under the skies is evoked in 'The Cold Heaven' as the judgement that comes just after death:

> *Ah! when the ghost begins to quicken,*
> *Confusion of the death-bed over, is it sent*
> *Out naked on the roads, as the books say, and stricken*
> *By the injustice of the skies for punishment?*[38]

Art simply hastened that moment. It was an attempt at that 'furious impartiality' with which an intrepid soul may step outside its given culture and become an unillusioned witness of itself. To that extent, the artist and anthropologist have something in common with the god of the final judgement. The stark, death-haunted plays of Synge, with their talk of skeletons and ghosts, were 'a perpetual Last Day, a trumpeting and coming up to Judgement'. In this they were exemplary:

All art is the disengaging of a soul from place and history, its
suspension in a beautiful or terrible light to await the
Judgement, though it must be, seeing that all its days were a
Last Day, judged already.[39]

Yeats's fascination with old age is that it brings such a moment
closer, the moment when the real value of his poetry might be
known.

Once, during a visit to a zoo, Yeats speculated aloud as to whether
or not monkeys might be 'degenerate men' – hence (he felt) their look
of wizened age.[40] He became a sort of inverse evolutionist, in the
sense of one who believed that past cultures always amounted to
something more than present cultures which did away with them.
What called itself a civilization might be just a tenable illusion,
imposed by those willing to exceed in savagery the barbarism of
predecessors. Each succeeding illusion was a much lesser thing than
that which preceded it:

Science is a criticism of Myth. There would be no Darwin had
there been no book of Genesis, no electrons but for the Greek
atomic myth, and when the criticism is finished there is not
even a drift of ashes on the pyre . . .

His conclusion was bleak, Beckettian, but exhilarating for all that:

There is no improvement: only a series of sudden fires, each
though fainter as necessary as the one before it. We free ourselves from delusion that we may be nothing. The last kiss is
given to the void.[41]

The only hope of humanity was to break out of this diminishing
series of cycles by recasting life on an altogether higher plane of consciousness.

Possessed of ideas like these, Yeats was honour-bound to tap the
energies of the dead, whose memories he believed to be the very
source of human instincts. Those energies worked most potently in
the present through persons who were often unaware of the forces
that animated them. Here was an involuntary memory at work
among the community, as well as at the level of the individual: the
significance of a moment passed over in youth might only become
clear in old age. The ageing process might be welcomed, as a
reminder that apparently lost moments were redeemable. So also, on
a communal basis, images from the past, uttered and then lost by one

social group, might be embraced by another, perhaps their very underlings, who might locate their unused potentials. In this way, the incompleteness of past moments could be redeemed and, say, an asocial hooligan like Cuchulain could become a virtual revolutionary.

To submit to that process was to concede that one was building amid ruins. The great lyric sequences of 'The Tower' are knowingly created as ruins by an artist who conspires with the process of time's decay from the outset. He hopes that the blasted structure which remains after his efforts will endure for some considerable time. In their sheer fragmentation these works are intended to be radiant. Since the traditions Yeats inherited were gapped from the start, the chosen forms had to reflect that, conveying the impression (at one and the same time) of being unfinished and used up. *Ulysses*, the other great example of Irish modernism in the 1920s, was built to similar specifications. In that same decade in Germany, Walter Benjamin said that since it was impossible to erect a building that would resist the corrosion of centuries, the creation of a ruin as such was the shrewdest way of overtaking catastrophe.[42]

Yeats seemed to agree, and to endorse the linked idea that criticism, embodied in a work of art, may help to complete the work even as it seems to destroy its potential for totality. Engineers and architects had, after all, to blast the walls of a building in the very act of completing it: and so Yeats in his lyric sequence sees both the completion and destruction of the tower as virtually identical. The building itself, which Yeats occupied at Thoor Ballylee with his young family in the early 1920s, was already ruinous, 'half-dead at the top' as well as very damp. It was a bleak confirmation of the aphorism that 'whoever purchases a period house embalms himself alive'.[43] But a poet who was willing to work in a variety of ancient stanza forms from ancient English tradition was not to be daunted, especially when he could splice them with ideas and images from the Gaelic tradition of Raftery. The old man, recovering from illness, finds in Raftery's celebration of the beauty of a peasant girl named Mary Hynes a reminder of all the characters he created in his youth, beginning with Red Hanrahan:

> *Good fellows shuffled cards in an old bawn;*
> *And when that ancient ruffian's turn was on*
> *He so bewitched the cards under his thumb*
> *That all but one card became*
> *A pack of hounds and not a pack of cards,*
> *And that he changed into a hare.*
> *Hanrahan rose in frenzy there*

And followed up those baying creatures towards –
O towards I have forgotten what – enough![44]

This breaking of the formal structure arises from a forgetting that may be functional – as if the poet fears that he will be mastered by an image which once he seemed able to master. By calling attention to the blockage, he realizes the idea that one builds as one destroys, and that no totality is possible. Moreover, the poet can also vividly remember moments of past blockage:

Does the imagination dwell the most
Upon a woman won or woman lost?
If on the lost, admit you turned aside
From a great labyrinth out of pride,
Cowardice, some silly over-subtle thought
Or anything called conscience once:
And that if memory recur, the sun's
Under eclipse and the day blotted out.[45]

What fatigues the writer is the thought of old stanza forms not used to their full potential and of a similar failure to live the dream of existence that was intended for him.

'I shall be a sinful man to the end', wrote the aged Yeats to Olivia Shakespeare, 'and think upon my death-bed of all the nights I wasted in my youth.'[46] What aged a man was not his over-used instincts but his refusal to submit to them in youth. Proust has said that the wrinkles on a man's face were traces of the great passions that had called on him and gone unanswered.[47] Poetry for Yeats was a way of redeeming lost time. At the close, he compares his gathering of neglected forms and images to the birds who gather random twigs to build a nest in the ruined roof of the tower. Out of the crisis of that moment he finds it possible to sing like the swan before it dies.

'Meditations in Time of Civil War' enacts a similar set of gestures. It begins with images of serene beauty in the ancestral houses of the Anglo-Irish, but soon acknowledges the violence of the plantation:

Some violent bitter man, some powerful man
Called architect and artist in, that they,
Bitter and violent men, might rear in stone
The sweetness that all longed for night and day,
The gentleness none there had ever known;
But when the master's buried mice can play,

> *And maybe the great-grandson of that house*
> *For all its bronze and marble, 's but a mouse.*[48]

The images of harmony are deceptive, created to soothe the sensibilities of warlike founders with an illusion of civilization, only for the beneficiaries of a merely inherited glory to show a weaker bloom. Yeats is too honest to admire such beauty for long: and his sequence reinterprets the false image of a self-delighting fountain as a summons once again to found 'the tradition of myself'. This allows him to telescope the whole process of the rise and fall of Anglo-Ireland into a single career, to be the first and last of his line. A culture that is founded upon a successful barbarism will result only in emotional enervation, lapsing into the merely ornamental shells left after a more glorious past. Against that is pitted the heroism of a self-begotten man.

The more ruinous the tower seems, the more it becomes a site of breeding, fecundity and creation. Determined not to grow bitter in a time of carnage, Yeats notices how nature asserts its daily defiance of the death instinct. The disintegration of one edifice becomes the very condition for erecting another:

> *The bees build in the crevices*
> *Of loosening masonry, and there*
> *The mother birds bring grubs and flies.*
> *My wall is loosening; honey-bees*
> *Come build in the empty house of the stare.*[49]

Tempted by the idea of military action, the poet knows that it too would be no more than a devotion to another set of images. He does not claim to be exempt from the civilized hypocrisy of those whose culture is the product of an occluded violence which they can usually afford to disown: for he knows that the image-worship of his own poetry fed off past acts of violence, as well as deriving its power from the keeping down of *hysterica passio*:

> *We had fed the heart on fantasies,*
> *The heart's grown brutal from the fare . . .*[50]

The practice of self-criticism within the poem 'Nineteen Hundred and Nineteen' is a little like the action of the bees loosening the masonry of the tower. It alerts us to the real nature of the underlying process. It also prompts the thought that a truly perfected creation might vanish in its own first breath:

That were a lucky death,
For triumph can but mar our solitude.[51]

The energies unleashed in the disintegration seem to move Yeats at
least as much as those deployed in an act of creation and he has no
desire to deny the complicity of his own art with its Cuchulanoid
heroics in the collapse:

We who seven years ago
Talked of honour and of truth,
Shriek with pleasure if we show
The weasel's twist, the weasel's tooth.[52]

To take an anthropologist's view of a civil war in which his
own life was at risk (since he was a partisan of the new government
party) was a strange achievement: yet that war provided a bracing
test of the wisdom he had gathered. All that he could offer, he concluded, was a song before parting. It was as if he were but another
of those Talmudic angels created only to celebrate the glory of
God and to go back to nothingness just as soon as that is done.
The sheer pleasure taken in joyful utterance may be as near as man
comes to a divinity on earth, the joy of that poet who 'sang unnoticed like a bird'.[53] If at times Yeats's cult of aristocracy seemed
autocratic, that was no political statement by the poet, as much as
an unconcealed envy of those lucky persons who could still pursue
pleasure for its own sake. Little persists in the modern world of
that claim to pure self-expression, but nevertheless 'an aimless joy
is a pure joy' and 'only the wasteful virtues gain the sun'.[54] A
truly struck note might, after all, be as effective a way of awakening a consciousness in things as the pressing of live lips upon a
plummet-measured face.

To kiss a sculpture in 'The Statues' is to bring it back to life, much
as Yeats reanimates the despised husks of a discarded past. Ever vigilant, he realizes that no past civilization is ever wholly lost, for it has
its fifth columnists in the present dispensation: and he is surely one of
them. Just as Cuchulain had the magical capacity to draw strength
and guidance from his *sidhe* fathers under the ground, so Yeats can
draw inspiration from the last lines of Aogán Ó Rathaille in 'The
Curse of Cromwell':

And there is an old beggar wandering in his pride –
His fathers served their fathers before Christ was
crucified.[55]

Access to such sources may, of course, disable a man in the eyes of the living, but he is consoled by the virtual community:

> *That the swordsmen and the ladies can still keep company,*
> *Can pay the poet for a verse and hear the fiddle sound,*
> *That I am still their servant though all are underground.*[56]

That ground is like the buried consciousness of the community, a landscape of layered memories, any one of which might flash forth and bring the old world back, so that the ruins of the past would be truly illuminated in the present:

> *I came on a great house in the middle of the night,*
> *Its open lighted doorway and its windows all alight,*
> *And all my friends were there and made me welcome too;*
> *But I woke in an old ruin that the winds howled through;*
> *And while I pay attention I must out and walk*
> *Among the dogs and horses that understand my talk.*
> > O what of that, O what of that,
> > What is there left to say?[57]

Like the *fili*, Yeats was a mortician of the old culture, one for whom there would be only one radical novelty: death itself. His gift for perpetual self-liquidation had strong roots in his Protestant conception of selves, ever dying, being ever reborn, on a strenuous path to identity: 'A writer must die every day he lives, be reborn, as it is said in the Burial Service, an incorruptible self, that self opposite to all that he has named "himself"'.[58] However, it drew an equal sanction from a Gaelic tradition which, for centuries, had revolved around near-death experiences. The more one excavated dead bones or lost experiences, the more strength one drew from a past forever coming back to life. The earth preserved not just bodies but consciousness itself:

> *A brief parting from those dear*
> *Is the worst man has to fear.*
> *Though grave-diggers' toil is long,*
> *Sharp their spades, their muscles strong,*
> *They but thrust their buried men*
> *Back in the human mind again.*[59]

The dead spirits one embraced should always be those which filled whatever gaps were to be found in the present. The test of a civilization was its capacity to offer (or at least dredge up) antithetical images with which a person might unite. This was not the much-vaunted inner conflict of Romantic poetry, but a conflict with an identity which returned from outside the self, from the remote past.[60] A man might at first feel a deep enmity towards this destiny, and yet come to love nothing but that destiny, another name for which might be 'tradition' . . . the painted woman who comes out of the past to haunt his dreams. The discarded potentials of a lost past turn out to be the 'woman lost', encountered a second time as the literary tradition:

> When a man loves a girl it should be because her face and character offer what he lacks; the more profound his nature the more should he realise his lack and the greater be the difference. It is as though he wanted to take his own death into his arms, and beget a stronger life upon that death.[61]

Necrophilia, like nostalgia, might not be what it used to be, but Yeats had no compunction about resorting to it, for the image of the despised harlot had indeed been the Gaelic poets' own description of their inherited culture. What gave him the courage to record the collapse of one civilization was his confidence that such an account would be the very basis of its successor. After all, the *filí* had shown the way.

Yeats's conclusive meditation on the mysteries of such a handover is to be found in 'Long-Legged Fly':

> *That civilisation may not sink,*
> *Its great battle lost,*
> *Quiet the dog, tether the pony*
> *To a distant post;*
> *Our master Caesar is in the tent*
> *Where the maps are spread,*
> *His eyes fixed upon nothing,*
> *A hand under his head.*
> Like a long-legged fly upon the stream
> His mind moves upon silence.[62]

The suggestion is that great things are possible in moments of self-forgetfulness, when a person's mind has relaxed into pure contemplation after a period of prolonged attention to some technical problem. Attention of this kind seems like a form of prayer, in which the mind is emptied of mere knowledge for the sake of something higher. Nothing can be permitted to interrupt the contemplation, or else civilization will fall. In 'Leda and the Swan', Yeats has fretted that Leda, like the poet, was rudely possessed by a divine power over which she could exercise little control: but here he is happy with that possibility, believing that all great forces in life act through persons who are open to them without being fully conscious of them as such.

The moments of greatest blessedness are granted, therefore, to those who do not worry unduly about the sources of their insight:

> *That the topless towers be burnt*
> *And men recall that face,*
> *Move most gently if move you must*
> *In this lonely place.*
> *She thinks, part woman, three parts a child,*
> *That nobody looks; her feet*
> *Practise a tinker shuffle*
> *Picked up on a street.*
> Like a long-legged fly upon the stream
> Her mind moves upon silence.[63]

Helen had no deliberate intention of greatness. Like all of Yeats's beauties, she was ravishing by virtue of not taking thought, by the taking of pleasure in a dance for its own sweet sake. Her precious solitude, like Caesar's, was put in jeopardy and needed tender protecting, if a true culture of the feelings was to be preserved. As yet she had no inkling of her future fame, nor any desire to impress another party.

For the reader, Helen's life is long past; for her, it is all potential in the future. So Yeats's dialectical view of tradition emerges in a restoration to the past, seemingly trivial moment of the openness it once had. Without that protected openness, nothing illustrious would have been possible. The meaning of the long-legged fly may become more apparent in that context: for it is momentarily caught on the waters, like the human agent trapped in history, and yet it manages to tread the water in some sort of holding pattern, idly passing the moments like Helen in her shuffle.

The final stanza secures these insights:

> *That girls at puberty may find*
> *The first Adam in their thought,*
> *Shut the door of the Pope's chapel,*
> *Keep those children out.*
> *There on that scaffolding reclines*

Michael Angelo,
With no more sound than the mice make
His hand moves to and fro.
Like a long-legged fly upon the stream
His mind moves upon silence.[64]

The movements of the artist are deliberately kept until the last, for the artists are the makers of supreme fictions, the hypnotists of civilization. In order to attain that authority, however, their movements must be as mindless as the fly's gyrations on the stream. Michelangelo is painting in the Sistine Chapel an image of radical creation, the making of Adam, whose hand moves in obedience to God's electric current, much as the painter's moves across the ceiling. That original act of creation had been reported in the Bible as the spirit of God moving upon the waters, and so the long-legged fly may also be a part of the divine plan, the eternal shaping and reshaping of a world, predestinate yet free.

26

Ulysses, Newspapers
and Modernism

James Joyce's *Ulysses* can be read as a slow-motion alternative to
the daily newspaper of Dublin for 16 June 1904. Given that most
inhabitants of cities read only newspapers by the time of its publication in 1922, it might even be construed as an artist's revenge, a
reappropriation of newspaper methods by an exponent of the threatened novel form. By juxtaposing mythical and mundane elements,
Ulysses achieved something like the same effect as George Russell's
paper *The Irish Homestead*, in which columns listing the weekly
manure prices appeared alongside the editor's mystical poems. The
surrealist technique of aligning discordant contents was but an application to high art of the methods of the popular press.

Joyce's appropriation of those methods was not necessarily hostile. When he called himself a scissors-and-paste man,[1] he was casting
himself as editor-in-chief of the counter-newspaper that was *Ulysses*:
but his own apprenticeship as a writer of stories for *The Irish
Homestead* was a major factor behind his first collection, *Dubliners*.
The *feuilletons*, in which intellectuals wrote cameos of the urban
scene, were a sort of newspaper-within-a-newspaper. Joyce's early
stories such as 'After the Race' or 'Araby', with their traversals of
sections of the inner city, were written very much in the same style,
capturing in an urban shorthand impressions of evanescent
moments.

The progressive intellectuals of nineteenth-century Ireland from
Thomas Davis to Michael Davitt had promoted reading rooms and

libraries as part of their educational programme.[2] Douglas Hyde might inveigh against penny dreadfuls and shilling shockers,[3] but he himself first published the songs of Connacht in a popular magazine. And J.M. Synge, who never read newspapers, none the less managed to write a series of articles on the poverty-stricken areas of western Ireland for the *Manchester Guardian*, as well as making the laconic observation that 'every healthy mind is more interested in *Tit-Bits* than in *Idylls of the King*'.[4]

What set the Irish modernists off from their Continental counterparts was their marked willingness to engage with newspapers. Yeats's voluminous journalizing fills the two largest of his published volumes: *Uncollected Prose*.[5] Wilde might castigate the press as a latter-day version of the rack, but only for its misuse of the utopian potentials of the new technology. He himself edited a women's magazine. Along with Shaw, he was one of the first artists to use the media in building a cult of his own personality. The major debates of the Irish revival were conducted in the pages of the *Daily Express* and *United Irishman*. Contributing journalists belonged to a profession for which a university degree was not a prerequisite, which accounts for the democratic tone and suspicion of aristocracy in these exchanges. Many supported movements for 'self-help', whether in adult education or Abbey Theatre, on principles first laid down by Jonathan Swift. He had shown by his brilliant polemics that it was quite possible to close the gap between journalism and art. Overseas intellectuals, on the other hand, were far less trusting of the forces of an open literary market. 'The rabble spit forth their bile', jeered Nietzsche, 'and they call the results a newspaper.'[6] The 'rabble' were in fact the newly literate masses, many of them solid members of the bourgeoisie, but the fastidious recoil from mass culture might be found in aspiring artists from even the humblest social background. 'That everyone can learn to read will ruin in the long run not only writing, but thinking too,' remarked Nietzsche.[7]

Just as the displaced Gaelic *filí* had adjusted, however reluctantly, to the newer populist forms of poetry in the 1600s, so now three centuries later Irish artists tried to come to terms with ever-developing forms of technology. Painters could never hope to compete with the realism of a cheap photograph, but critics began to notice that many of the best photographs were painterly. If technology concealed its newness by a recourse to old image systems, the converse might also be possible – that older techniques of painting and writing might protect themselves against the new technologies by drastic innovations of form.

Joyce's early stories offered readers the pleasures of snooping from one cityscape to another, pleasures that had once been the preserve of idle *flâneurs* but were now possible to all citizens. In the early stories such strolling is unproblematic, enjoyed even by schoolboys. The ultimate commodification of the *flâneur* would be found in the sandwich-board men of Helys Stationers in *Ulysses*: and the very sight of humans pressed between hard boards would suggest a savage parody by Joyce of the commodification of the book itself. As Walter Benjamin wrote in *One-way Street*, 'Writing, which has found an asylum in the printed book, where it led an autonomous existence, is unavoidably cast out into the streets by advertising and subjected to the brutal heteronomies of economic chaos.'[8] *Ulysses* seeks through Bloom to recover the dignity of the *flâneur* as citizen – his strollings trace the form of a question mark rather than those straight lines that might have suggested a life reduced to mere mechanism.

By a complex dialectic, however, *Ulysses* also seeks to recapture the writing of the street between the hard covers of a printed book. So the major sources of news to Bloom as he walks the streets are posters, handbills, advertisements and glimpsed newspaper headlines. The book's formal complexity is the result not of any snobbery on Joyce's part – he avoided literary types like the plague and when he was finally forced to meet Proust, spent the whole session talking about chocolate truffles – but of his desire to resist some of the dehumanizing forces already at work in mass culture. The new technology had the power to liberate workers, but instead was too often used to degrade them. Wilde had insisted that the public must become artistic if it was to enjoy real freedom: and in *The Soul of Man under Socialism* art was presented as an image of what free persons might become rather than as something adapted to their degraded state. This was the real reason why Joyce made a point of giving presents of *Ulysses* to hotel porters and waiters: his book was *for* as well as *about* the common man.

Ulysses was written early enough in the twentieth century for its author to have high hopes of mass technology: and it remains at all times alert to its possibilities. Like a newspaper broadsheet, it juxtaposed discrepant reports and experiences, and it demands a similar technique of reading. In the words of Peter Fritzsche, 'mass circulation newspapers posed the real possibility that readers would be left to cobble together a world-view from a variety of unauthoritative sources'[9] – hence entire episodes like 'Cyclops' and 'Eumaeus' are entrusted to unidentified narrators who are patently hostile to Leopold Bloom. The qualities of watchfulness, scepticism and unshockability called for in persons who negotiated the crossings of city streets are demanded also of the scanners of a broadsheet page or of *Ulysses*. Like the city or newspaper, the book can be entered or quit at any one of its many points: one needs to have arrived and left by many routes before one can claim truly to know it. The meaning of a newspaper is largely a do-it-yourself construction on the part of the reader-as-stroller. Likewise in *Ulysses*, the juxtaposition of elements is a deliberate denial of older hierarchies of value, in a sheer excess of detail, much of which must be skimmed for the sake of the reader's sanity. Attempts to establish hierarchy within the world of the book by, say, the Viceroy are hardly successful: he is either misrecognized or ignored by most citizens. The lack of a fixed narrative voice mimics the absence of any universally recognized authority in the city. That Dublin is, after all, both a provincial outpost of empire and a national metropolis, whose statues indicate just what a site of contest the streets have become. A statue erected to Crampton, surgeon-general to her majesty's forces, baffles Bloom ('who was he?'),[10] while everyone knows about the spot designated for the yet-uncreated statue of Tone ('the slab where Wolfe Tone's statue was not').[11] Joyce liked to joke that there were only two kinds of statue in Dublin: the sort that held out a scornful arm as if to say 'In my day the dunghill was so high,' and the kind that seemed to entreat 'How do I get down?'[12]

Like most people, Joyce was fascinated by the seemingly miraculous production to a precise deadline of a daily paper. In the 'Aeolus' episode he began by linking that sense of schedule to the strictly timed departures of city-centre tramcars. Of all sections in *Ulysses*, 'Aeolus' is that most obviously modelled on a newspaper, with mischievously suggestive headlines like 'How a Great Daily Organ Is Turned Out'. Incidents early in the section seem to reduce all human activity and language to mere mechanism:

Gentlemen of the Press
Grossbooted draymen rolled barrels dullthudding out of Prince's stores and bumped them up on the brewery float. On the brewery float bumped dullthudding barrels rolled by grossbooted draymen out of Prince's stores.[13]

Headlines often seem here to have little connection with ensuing material, as if composed by someone other than the author proper (as happens usually in newspapers). The combination of cliché headlines with Joycean narrative suggests that journalistic mechanisms may become more real than the text on which they are imposed. For, as the section proceeds to its conclusion, Joyce has fun at the expense of certain American papers famous for long, portentous headlines over brief actual reports. Yet the narrative proper remains somehow uncorrupted by and impervious to the increasingly ridiculous head-lines.

In the offices of the *Freeman's Journal*, Joyce's narrative imitates the sound made by paper passing through machines:

> Sllt. The nethermost deck of the first machine jogged forwards its flyboard with sllt the first batch of quire-folded papers. Sllt. Almost human the way it sllt to call attention. Doing its level best to speak. That door too sllt creaking, asking to be shut. Everything speaks in its own way. Sllt.[14]

If humans are mechanized, machines can be humanized, and this one is a surrogate for Bloom's attempts to communicate to others in a half-articulate speech. He is, however, badly snubbed by Myles Crawford, the editor, whose office is filled with gusts of wind which Joyce wittily uses to evoke the flatulent rhetoric of much *Freeman* journalism. The paper took its *diktat* from the Archbishop's palace and from the desires of small advertisers. Bloom, for example, is seeking a puff paragraph in the news section in return for a formal advertisement taken by the House of Keyes. Yet, even though the treatment seems to deride a provincial press, Joyce knew by the time he published this section that the Easter Rising had begun in Dublin's General Post Office, just yards from the newspaper office. The rebels had ended all the torpor, in effect transforming a colonial city into a modern metropolis. They delivered on that promise of a confident modernity implicit in the timetabled arrivals and departures of trams 'In the Heart of the Hibernian Metropolis'.

As a book *Ulysses* assembles many of the raw materials that also filled out newspapers: snatches of overheard conversation, editorial commentary, government edicts, commercial advertisements, short stories. Assigning no priority to what was reported, it could treat a viceregal cavalcade and a private citizen's walk on Sandymount Strand as equally momentous and equally insignificant. As a collection of stories bolted with some strain together, rather than a smoothly linear narrative, the book does read like a newspaper. It may also be the first work of fiction to show that inhabitants can no longer understand the life of their cities without the aid of newspa-pers.[15] So many aspects of the action, from Bloom's love affair to his earnings, from his mourning of Paddy Dignam to his alleged win-nings on the Gold Cup, are mediated in some way through papers. His relaxed progress through various parts of the city imitates the browsers through a newspaper, taking in hospital reports, low-life vignettes and society occasions. By 1904 Dubliners no longer trod the confined beat of their own neighbourhoods but casually assumed the freedom of the entire city: its varied levels of reality generated countless anecdotes which broke in upon rather than complemented one another. *Ulysses* is one way of accommodating that turbulence, the *Freeman's Journal* another.

If Leopold Bloom's mind is a tissue of quotations from editorials, articles and jingles, Joyce does not mock him for that. Far from it. He respects instead the verbal resourcefulness of a character whose oral saws seem to invert old proverbs by comically tilting them towards the advertising slogan 'An Irishman's house is his coffin.'[16] Unlike Nietzsche or Lawrence, who feared and fled mass-man, Joyce showed how lovable and reassuring such a creature could be. Sensing that advertisements represent a society's unconscious, its hidden fantasy life, Joyce was writing at a time when the sociologists of the Frankfurt School had not yet depressed themselves about the ways in which technology could be used to flatten individuality and manufacture consensus, and so his treatment of mass media is more celebratory than critical. His implication (through Bloom's consciousness) that a printing machine might eventually learn to speak in a human tongue represents a utopian view of technology. The suggestion is that every single object has its own history and consciousness, albeit mute, and that it will yield a meaning if accorded the sort of loving attention that Bloom gives to things.

The advertising jingle for the bar of soap singing in Bloom's pocket is but another example:

> *We're a capital couple are Bloom and I;*
> *He brightens the earth, I polish the sky.*[17]

This manages at once to issue a reprimand to the self-importance of a humanity which sees itself as the source of all creation in the world and to combat the impression that everything in the modern city can be reduced to mechanism. In doing so, it out-Wildes Wilde. He had thought of technology as something to liberate workers from common toil, but had never considered emancipating things – merely controlling them. He had never questioned the priority of the knowing person over the thing to be known.

If nature had good intentions that only art could carry out, Joyce now seems to be updating Wilde's theory with the suggestion that art may have good intentions on which only technology can finally deliver. The man who opened one of the first cinemas in Dublin ultimately saw no distinction between technology and nature. The Great

War had simply demonstrated that as yet man had failed to liberate the potential of technology and had instead been martyred to it: once technology became the servant of the whole community, all would be transformed. Joyce was trying to understand the potentials of the modern media, much as Swift in his day had liberated those of print.[18] Bloom's comic fertility in inventing new advertisements through the narrative is Joyce's recognition that modern advertising may be even more alert than art to such potential. As Walter Benjamin said, 'the advertisement is the cunning with which the dream imposed itself upon industry'.[19] Even advertising was in its creative, early phase of development as Joyce recorded Bloom's thoughts on its associative methods (House of Keyes; Manx parliament; St Peter's keys to the kingdom; implication of Home Rule), and had not yet been fully subordinated to the dictates of consumerism. Besides, in Ireland a confident middle class was still only emerging and had not yet equated liberation with the freedom to consume: so Bloom's playful improvisations have the somewhat arbitrary quality of an artwork. Joyce felt freer than continental intellectuals to embrace such modern practices because the influence of Irish intellectuals had not been eroded by the emergence of an entrepreneurial elite. So, by minutely documenting the thoughts and feelings of persons like Bloom, Joyce showed that art might engage with the culture of the masses, whose profoundly democratic character offered a challenge to all attempts at social control.

Which isn't to say that Joyce was a naïve celebrant of newspapers or magazines. Early in *Ulysses*, Bloom wipes his bottom in the garden latrine with pages of newsprint, a moment derisively recalled at the start of 'Circe':

> *Moses, Moses, king of the jews,*
> *Wiped his arse with the Daily News.*[20]

There was something faintly shocking, and exciting, about the capacity of the printed word to expire on the very day of its enunciation. The sheer disposability of such texts leads Bloom into a painful confrontation with anti-Semites, who think that he has won money on a horse called *Throwaway*, when all he has really done is throw away a paper containing tips. Even more shocking – and thrilling – was the speed with which each new edition of a daily paper condemned the previous edition to the scrapheap: that was 'modernism' with a vengeance, since the succession of second, third, fourth and fifth editions denied final authority to any one (much like what has happened to the various editions of Joyce's own text).

These newspaper editions led to an obsessive focus on the present moment, a form of temporal provincialism which seemed to suggest that all previous history counted for little or nothing. This was reinforced by improvements in print technology, as a result of which the proportion of articles dealing with the previous twenty-four hours went in the four decades before *Ulysses* from about 10 to 95 per cent. The effect, says Peter Fritzsche, was to erase interest in the past and concentrate on the immediate moment.[21] By concentrating on a single day's news, journalists began to rip events out of their wider contexts in the emplotment of time: they denied the human capacity for considered experience and played up the love of sensation. The sheer immediacy, instantaneousness and disposability of newspapers were never better captured than in accounts of the poet Patrick Kavanagh tearing each page from the *Racing News* and throwing it to the ground (expressing also, perhaps, the latent hostility of the poet towards the journalist).[22] In that context, *Ulysses* may be read as a pondered answer to the problem posed by such rapid coverage, for the private ruminations of Leopold, Molly and Stephen do restore some sort of history to human lives: 'The ordinary is the proper domain of the artist', sniffed Joyce: 'the extraordinary can safely be left to journalists.'[23]

What he meant was that the capacity for news that stays news was being lost in a welter of sensation: people felt oppressed by an overload of information but in no way illuminated by it. 'Every morning brings us the news of the globe', wrote Walter Benjamin, 'and yet we are poor in noteworthy stories.'[24] The old oral tales came from afar, carried by artisans who conferred on them the authority of felt experience and the shrewd counsel that followed; but in the modern world the very communicability of experience, the possibility of handing on tradition, was being sabotaged. Newspapers, with their built-in obsolescence, were considered complicit in that sabotage, but *Ulysses* attempts to capture the day's permanence as no newspaper could. Joyce hoped by it to write for just one day out of all the lost, passing days an account of twenty-four hours that would live forever, unremarkable for anything other than the fact that he had recorded them. His book is really a collection of short stories in the drag of a novel and so it captures something of the old storyteller's authority, even as it harnesses the leaflets, papers and posters of the modern city. The double impulse of Irish modernism – to mask the modern in an outmoded form and to mask the ancient in a modern form – is thus honoured: but it is the Homeric structure that falls away and vanishes to make way for the newer one.

Most of the citizens of Joyce's Dublin had come in from the countryside, bringing with them a love of story. To commit such stories to
a book was a way of saving the culture of the past in a modern
form. It produced the art of *Ulysses*, its masquerade as an experimental novel while really being a collection of short stories. The
formula would be repeated by Beckett, Flann O'Brien and Máirtín Ó
Cadhain.[25]

Joyce's attitude to the past was ambiguous. He wanted to liquidate
it, but in the very act of doing so to make its energies current in the
present. He compared the progress of *Ulysses* to that of a blast, each
successive section leaving behind a burnt-up field (the previous
modes of the English language).[26] In that sense, its structure has
much in common with those newspapers that supplant one edition
by the next. It is a useful reminder that there may be no stronger tradition in Ireland than that which subverts all attempts to make a
tradition official. This quality makes Joyce appear more radical to
those who study him outside the Irish context than he really is:
within the native frame his approach is precedented.

The resemblance between that Irish methodology and the conditions of literary modernism is obvious. It is summed up in Irving
Howe's now-classic definition: 'modernism must struggle and never
quite triumph, and in the end it must struggle in order not to triumph'.[27] That is its necessary weariness, epitomized by the fashion
system in which a limited number of permutations must somehow
maintain the illusion of innovation. 'The same, only different' is one
phrase for a phenomenon also captured in Lenehan's quip 'expecting
every moment to be his next'.[28] That is his version of *Nacheinander*,
one damn thing after another:[29] and, although there is nothing
wrong with repetition *per se*, it troubles when it comes after a promise of newness. The commodities of fashion are all priced in the
text – Kino's trousers 11/-, Gerty MacDowell's knickers at 4/11d – as
a sign of how recent is this conversion to consumerism: but the
whore in the black straw hat who unnerves Bloom is both commodity and seller in one. Like the prostitutes of 'Circe', she is like a
corpse that has been beautified to seem forever young, in a ghastly
parody of Swift's Struldbrugs. The modern denial of death presupposes endlessly staged little deaths, much as the newspaper market
demands similar editions superseding one another, based on the
human need to stage repeated liquidations and revivals. The very
term 'Irish revival' may itself have been yet another denial of death:
for within the economy of *Ulysses*, where everything is recycled, the
burial of a man seems an excessive 'liberty'. Yet the book itself has
been complicit in the modern triumph over the ageing process: the

challenge Joyce poses, said Richard Ellmann, is that the reader learn how to catch up and become his contemporary.[30]

The whore is in that sense rather like the Gaelic tradition described by *filí*: 'teasing death, already becoming something else again, something new, as death looks about for her in order to strike her down'.[31] The Gaelic poets who simulated a corpse in order to survive are a little like the barmaids of 'Sirens': they enacted the iron law of a fashion which 'turns the body into a sexual commodity and knows to escape from death only by mimicking it'.[32] Fashion erases the individual to make way for a *type* (and the other meaning is important, also, in a text so fearful of mechanism). This is the real reason for the contrast between Gerty's consumerism and Molly's sturdy individualism. Molly is Joyce's evidence that there may be some persistence of the person, even in the zones of interior monologue.

The 'crime against coition' inveighed against in 'Oxen of the Sun' is the whore's final resort against ageing: to stay lovely she must make herself forever new, but a pregnancy and childbirth would jeopardize her very survival as a commodity. Joyce's harsh mockery of a labour without production, a belly without a baby, is his repudiation of a sexual act that assumes the guise of work rather than pleasure. The anarchists had seen a person's joy in work as an image of the urge to procreate, but a sexuality without that possibility struck him as the further reduction of pleasure to the level of grim duty, since pleasure was to be found in creation. No wonder that the doughty deed of the Purefoy couple is celebrated. An author born only decades after the Great Famine could hardly have taken any other position. The whole trajectory of *Ulysses* is in fact to rewind the reel of history from 1922 to 1904 and to reopen at that point one of the infinite possibilities then ousted or 'impossibilized'. It is literally an attempt to undo contraception by an act of re-member-ing. Joyce may have recurred to the date on which he first walked out with Nora Barnacle not so much to commemorate their coupling as to explore a set of different potentials that coupling ousted: a meeting with the Jewish citizen and a going home to his house, 'to be married by Father Maher'.

What contraception signifies is only that fashion that is a woeful parody of revolution, for which it substitutes a cheap simulation of mere novelty. Instead of all that, Joyce hoped that he might discover a language above and beyond tradition.[33] His view of tradition was that it should be first celebrated and then liquidated, so that life might move onto a higher plane. The problem was that the rich potentials of technology were not yet recognized. Joyce's generation was living at the very outset of the new technological civilization: hence the affinities he felt with the primitive phase of earlier forms of society, summed up in Homer. But the restless urge to press ahead with modernization may also explain his clear impatience with the art of his immediate predecessors, those realists like Flaubert and Zola.

When in *Ulysses* Bloom contrasts the photograph of his wife (which, though taken years earlier, 'did not do justice to her figure')[34] with the superb Greek statues of the female form in the National Museum, he speaks his author's death sentence on artistic realism: 'Marble could give the original, shoulders, back, all the symmetry . . . whereas no photo could, because it simply wasn't art, in a word.'[35] The claim of writers to capture surfaces seemed pointless in an age of camera and electronic recorder. Joyce was more impressed by the art of the ancients, so patently artificial, so clearly a world of its own and not a botched, incomplete imitation of this one. The fashions of the day-before-yesterday must always seem anti-aphrodisiac to the current generation, but never more so than in the decades when the world was changing so fast.

The pace of change was so great that new technologies often adopted the protective appearance of the older forms they were designed to overcome: railcars imitated stagecoaches, electric light bulbs were made to look like gas flames, and the novel mimicked the epic (much as *Ulysses* seemed to emulate the novel form). This was one reason why the potential of the new often went unremarked and unfulfilled. Another was that technology, intended as a means of fulfilling human desires, had been mistaken as itself their realization. (Even the Futurists were guilty of that error). Newspapers had not, for example, been harnessed to meet the expressive possibilities of their readers, most of whom were reduced to passive consumers rather than co-creators. *Ulysses*, however, is offered as a book that is co-authored rather than simply read: and it celebrates the desires of Leopold, Molly and Gerty MacDowell to become, although they are ordinary people, artists. The utopian element is manifest not just in Bloom's daydream of a suburban home, but also in those radical moments when a supernatural event occurs, as when Bloom is beatified or when he is assumed into heaven. The whole text is saturated in messianic possibility, a sense that Leopold Bloom himself might transcend tradition and achieve the blessedness of a new, reconciled state of being. The corollary is that the old form of the novel will be transcended by the emergence of a new one, as yet unnamed.

Walter Benjamin's submission that a major artwork contains all past and potential forms in itself seems apposite here: 'it will either establish the genre or abolish it – and the perfect work will do both'.[36] The latent possibilities are released by a focus within the form on its own processes, the better to awaken the form to full consciousness of itself. *Ulysses* accepts that there is no final order now, but that the longing for it indicates its likely re-emergence when humanity reaches a higher plane of being. The text is simply the hand with which the artist-child reaches for the moon and so learns to clutch a useful, but nearer, object. The sheer agitation of styles in *Ulysses* suggests a world made very new. But a book so constructed may as easily relapse into the fragments of a newspaper as move forward to the next stage – as happened, indeed, to Edna O'Brien's *The Country Girls*, a copy of which was torn into its separate pages which were passed like news-sheets around the author's own community.[37] By a sort of reversal of that dialectic, *Ulysses* might be seen as capturing some of the codes of the newspaper, in order to release the deeper possibilities of its forms.

It does no less with *The Odyssey* of Homer, which it treats as a botched *ur*-version of itself. As noted above, Joyce's attitude to the past is anything but respectful: he has no interest in reviving it in its own terms (as it was); rather, his interest is in destroying its structures and releasing their energies into the present. Bloom himself is completely unaware that he is re-enacting in the streets of Dublin the wanderings of Odysseus through the Mediterranean. For Joyce, heroism is never conscious of itself as such. This is another example of involuntary memory, the Homeric analogy irrupting into consciousness precisely when it seemed most forgotten. By creating a constellation between the very old and the utterly new, Joyce releases further impulses into an open future.

A cynic might see this as yet another case of the incorrigibly new taking on the protective coloration of the decently ancient, much as Bloom is encased in the respectability of a bourgeois home. Adorno's jibe about a period house embalming its owner alive may arise from the same kind of thinking that leads Bloom to conclude that an Irishman's house is his coffin.[38] But Bloom himself is cast out onto the streets, those zones of the collective, where he makes common cause with a range of fellow sufferers from Josie Breen to the blind stripling. Yet even there he is cased like the rare books in the National Library, which will only lose their intimidating aura of 'culture' when taken down by human hands. Here the casing is the black mourning suit, which he regrets and seeks to escape (knowing that this suit of the dying class will provoke awkward, useless comments all day).[39] Leaving the cemetery, he avers that there is 'plenty to see and hear and feel yet . . . They are not going to get me this innings. Warm beds: warm fullblooded life.'[40] He wishes rather, like Stephen, to realize the present, which might otherwise vanish before it is seized and possessed. This attempt to live deeply in the present was a feature of Irish revival art, and it based itself on the notion that things are most themselves just before the moment of their disappearance.

Yet the forms revived from the distant Homeric past have their value, since they are shot through with utopian longings, mostly unfulfilled. It is for this longing rather than for their objective qualities that they are revived now. Joyce's use of ancient Greece is rather like Robespierre's employment of ancient Rome – both served to glorify newness while at the same time creating the impression that it might be a reassuring revival of something quite old. The mask worn was but a temporary expedient. Beneath the mask of the past, the present protagonists relaxed enough to compose their own faces for the first time, and then to reveal them to an astonished world. Karl Marx's account of a revolution that finds its poetry in the future rather than the past describes this progression in terms that properly fit not only *Ulysses* but, more generally, what the Irish did in changing their language in the nineteenth century:

> It is like the beginner who always translates back into the mother tongue, but appropriates the spirit of the new language and becomes capable of producing freely within it only by moving about in it without recalling the old.[41]

The greatest sin, Yeats said, would be to bring the work of the dead to nothing: one had, in finishing one's own work, to bring theirs to completion too. His desire to retell the Cuchulain story is not really an attempt to bring back the past so much as to reconnect with its unfinished energies. Just as children whose bodies change so fast can demand the security of conservative, familiar food, so Joyce's and Yeats's evocation of ancient heroes, rather than constituting an exercise in useless nostalgia, was their response to being hurtled into modernity. The past is not to be repeated but *redeemed*, because it has the power yet to redeem the future: and the old stories are made more completely available one last time, before they are allowed to disappear. The past in such a form is no principle of stability, but a reminder of the impermanence of the modern forms just being perfected.

In this transaction, Joyce turns out to be as conservative as Yeats, even as the poet turns out to be as radical as the youth who worried that Yeats might be too old to be helped.[42] In their works both live and feel the past, but only to complete the rupture with it: and this is done by acknowledging the meanings not recognized in earlier periods – such as *The Odyssey* as a draft-dodger's charter. The posthumous life of an author will utterly alter the meaning of a work: Shakespeare, for example, 'was made in Germany . . . as the champion french-polisher of Italian scandals'.[43]

There is a crucial point at issue. It is only by abandoning the attempts to imitate the past and by devoting oneself utterly to the present that one allows the older images to return, unbidden but in all their fullness. Those images are likely to take their most powerful form at the moment of their disappearance into those that replace them. The past helps to define by reflection what is really new: without tradition there can be no modernity. But the price of this transaction is the disappearance of Homer into the interstices of *Ulysses*, for the titles of sections taken from *The Odyssey* were removed by Joyce from the final published text. This might be seen as paradigmatic of the way in which the Irish language also disappeared into Hiberno-English, there to live more potently for a majority of Irish people than it ever could in its own right.

In the same way, the traditional genre of the short story survives more powerfully for being central but implicit in *Ulysses* and in many other modernist Irish texts. Completion is achieved only at the price of liquidation.[44] The argument of plays by Wilde or Shaw undoes itself in the final twist: the finished work is the death mask of its conception. Each chapter of *Ulysses* dissolves the preceding style, as Joyce's series of blasts continues. The breaking of styles, like the blasting of a building, is a way of completing the essential structure: all that is mere cultural adornment is eliminated. Hence the auto-critical elements in *Ulysses*, its willingness to supply the criticism by which it can be illuminated. If consciousness can be awakened in a paper machine or bar of soap, then it may be found also in the self-reflections of Joyce's narrative. So Molly Bloom's final 'yes' is preceded by Stephen's more critical explanation that literature is the eternal affirmation of the spirit of man: and there are many paragraphs that hint at the Homeric parallel. These passages are motivated not by any desire to assert the self-sufficiency of the artwork but by the author's awareness of the need to train his audience in the protocols of the new reading: for a moment must be reached when the reader emerges as the true Odysseus, the real wanderer in the labyrinth.[45] Yet by exploring the ancient analogy in this way, *Ulysses* unleashed the corrosions of the passing ages upon itself. It absorbed its own chosen medium fully into its own sensorium, in precisely the ways that mankind needed to come to terms with the new technology. A new work can never be wholly intelligible without the critique implied by an earlier one: its completion and critical disintegration are one and the same. Indeed, without a death, the ambiguity of the experience that preceded it might be put into question, much as the little death of the whore is open to the allegation of being faked.

The effect of aligning *The Odyssey* and *Ulysses* is rather like that achieved by Sir James Frazer in *The Golden Bough*. Frazer's juxtaposition of pagan and Christian practices raises the possibility that Christianity is just another, more recent among the mythologies; and the collocation of ancient and modern by Joyce exposes the modern as just another form of mythological thinking. The French Revolution, which had purported to put an end to all myth-making, instituted instead the myth of modernity, the notion of perpetual renewal animating spirits as diverse as those of Ezra Pound ('make it new') and Leon Trotsky ('permanent revolution'). In Joyce's hands, the latest myth is aware of its status as fiction. This awareness is necessary for without it the Homeric means might be mistaken for the end, with the archaic posing successfully as the new. By insisting on his writing as work-in-progress, Joyce recognizes the job still to be done in bringing the world and the book much closer. The freedom known by his characters is solely inward, but there is no fit between such a liberated consciousness and the available social forms. Indeed, the very richness of the interior monologues is sometimes suspect: as if people are driven for consolation out of the world and into the head. They might all prefer, if given the choice, to have a more agreeable environment and a less rich inner life. The splendours of the interior monologues are a comment on the poverty of their social occasions. Where other major European novels have their plots propelled mainly by the dialogue, here the conversations are generally unsatisfactory; and where a city like Paris becomes the centre of the protagonist's aspiration in Stendhal or Proust, for Joyce Dublin is the centre of paralysis best left behind or else displaced by one's own superior inner landscape.

Joyce's tactic is perfectly surrealist. Even as *Ulysses* assimilates elements of everyday life, it also tries to make that life more artistic, by celebrating the ordinary man and woman as artists. That is the positive contribution of the monologues, which show how people may already be as artistic as Wilde wanted them to be. Joyce may have presented his work to lowly workers in order to strengthen their sense of expressive dignity, ratified now in a major work of art. It was, after all, aristocratic and bourgeois art that had been commodified in the later nineteenth century: and Mr Deasy's troves of Stuart coins and apostle spoons are fully cased in the book as a sign that those phases of civilization are coming to an end, a 'barbarian's booty'.[46]

Redemption presupposes a messiah, and Bloom (the new womanly man) is auditioned more than once for the role of Ben Bloom Elijah. Even the more banal scenes prepare for his estrangement and possible deification. In some of these scenes, he is cast in the role of amateur anthropologist, who observes the working rituals of his own people with a degree of incredulity. Eavesdropping on the mass at All Hallows, he anatomizes the devotional peculiarities of Irish Catholics and wonders how they explain them 'to the heathen Chinee',[47] whose horizontal Buddha might seem ill-sorted with a vertical saviour hanging on a cross. Bloom's mental notes on the reception of the sacred host are pure fieldwork:

> A batch knelt at the altar rails. The priest went along by them, murmuring, holding the thing in his hands. He stopped at each, took out a communion, shook a drop or two (are they in water?) off it and put it neatly into her mouth. Her hat and head sank. Then the next one: a small old woman. The priest bent down to put it into her mouth, murmuring all the time. Latin. The next one. Shut your eyes and open your mouth. What? *Corpus*. Body. Corpse. Good idea the Latin. Stupefies them first. Hospice for the dying. They don't seem to chew it; only swallow it down. Rum idea: eating bits of a corpse why the cannibals cotton onto it.[48]

The amazed analysis of the finer points of ritual is carried a stage further in 'Hades', where Bloom is at a loss to know the names of sacred objects:

> The priest took a stick with a knob at the end of it out of the boy's bucket and shook it over the coffin.[49]

Being a Jew in a Gentile city accounts for much of Bloom's estrangement, but he carries this further, becoming one with the stars and galaxies, looking down on life on earth, as if man had at last acquired the capacity to become an inhuman witness of himself. At this late stage, even the homely rituals of his own kitchen in Eccles Street are subjected to anthropological analysis. What had been in 'Calypso' a simple domestic chore:

> He scalded and rinsed out the teapot and put in four full spoons of tea, tilting the kettle to let the water flow in . . .[50]

becomes in 'Ithaca' an account given in a technical detail so literal as to suggest that the observer is utterly unaware of the meaning of the action:

> He removed the saucepan to the left hob, rose and carried the iron kettle to the sink in order to tap the current by turning the faucet to let it flow.[51]

The qualities that Bloom admires in water are laboriously listed, not least of them being universality and democracy, since nobody owns it. Enabled to take the long view of his own actions, he seems to see the world as a comedy of incomplete systems of classification. 'Ithaca' wants, in its catechism structure, to include everything, even those possibilities ousted by the activities embarked on in this book. But the project is doomed. The ensuing book would be as large as the world, or larger. This book becomes, in effect, an exercise in subverting the claims of anthropology, for it 'shuns the arbitrariness of any system of classification, either of the book or, by implication, of the world'.[52]

Bloom is largely silent in the kitchen with Stephen. He seems to have moved far beyond the experience of mortal man. The vividness with which the whole fallen world unwinds before his eyes in the long chapter of 'Ithaca' might seem to resemble the way a lifetime of images flashes before the eyes of a dying man. It is at this moment that the narrative is turned over to the reader for a final decoding.

The reader is the one who witnesses, and then completes, the book's own self-reflection. If art has good intentions, it is criticism finally that must carry them out, liberating its unconscious potentials. What Stephen reads in Shakespeare may be said also of *Ulysses*: that it can be compared only with itself and that the reader, in judging it solely by the apparatus it supplies, will thus complete the enactment.

This is at the core of Joyce's notion of tradition. He sees it less as a set of canonical texts than as the very transmissibility of ideas: it is a medium rather than a set of contents, a way of handing down rather than the thing handed. Irish revivalists who spoke of their longing for a Gaelic past were really, in his view, confessing to a breakdown in cultural transmission. If that past were really present to them, they would not have longed so deeply for it. The Great Famine and its aftermath had completed the break with the Irish past: it could never be restored as what it once had been, but elements might be remembered in the present. Sometimes, when that happened, the carriers of the past acted compulsively, without realizing that the past was repeating itself through them, as in Bloom's unawareness of Odysseus. But the reader's turn to be Odysseus, when it comes, is recognized for the repetition that it is, and that recognition is the first step to breaking the spell and ending the nightmare of history. Such awakening is true memory, but it is a memory of something that was not fully experienced first time around and so must be repeated before it can be bidden farewell forever.

Joyce wishes to free himself and his readers of future dependence on the past, by ensuring that the current moment is experienced in all its ramifications. His hope is for a heroic reader who will be as aware of media as of messages, and who will help the new forms to emerge. The great rapprochement between bohemian and bourgeois at the centre of his work is yet another feature that marks it off from other classics of European modernism, where the two were sworn enemies. The experimental artists who huddled into Montparnasse and Soho were not snobs, however, despite their fastidiousness: their hope was to perfect in their special surroundings new forms and new ideas, which might be brought back into the social mainstream. Joyce, never a lover of specialists, spurned such living: Ireland and not Bohemia was his native country. However, he attempted to bring forward in his work the moment of which even the surrealists dreamed: when the ordinary citizen and the artist would achieve an expressive ensemble. *Ulysses* maps out the zones of such a liberation, abolishing old distinctions between writer and reader, author and audience, as all are caught up in the process of tradition itself. Bloom was both observing anthropologist and the anthropologist observed: and Joyce, performing his own reverse anthropology in Europe, engaged in a mapping more radical than that done by a Shaw or a Stoker. Now in *Ulysses* instead of X (Bulgaria, Transylvania) really being Ireland, Ireland is really X – a test-case for the future of the world.

The loss of the Irish language in most areas in the decades before *Ulysses* is one of the test-cases. That experience was not worked through, even as the continuity of tradition was lost: and so it was bound to repeat itself in the shreds of Gaelic strewn through the book and also, even more potently, in its rich Hiberno-English. The ties to an unpurged past are the hardest of all to break. History is a nightmare because so little has been really transmitted. A society whose mythology is erected around experiences of shape-changing knows how forces that are versatile can cheat death in a thousand guises. No wonder that the youthful Joyce could proclaim death to be the highest form of life.[53] The lessons of Irish modernism had been clear for three centuries before he put pen to paper: nearness to

death created surges of immense vitality. Joyce himself was a futur-
ologist, a messianic artist, a utopian. He wished only to bury the
past, but in order to do that he discovered that he would first have to
dig it up: for all previous burials had been botched. His handling of
religion, language and nationalism prefigures the Belfast Agreement,
for he recognizes that each must seem to die before it can be reborn.
Likewise, in his hands, the novel is reborn as newspaper, before it in
turn is reincarnated as a truly open, collective narrative. While other
Irish writers fretted about the viability of epic, and while the surrealist avant-garde proclaimed that newspapers were already dead,
Joyce spliced the two forms. The assemblage that resulted still has no
name, but it was born in his hands.

27

After the Revolution:
O'Casey and O'Flaherty

'The birth of a nation is never an immaculate conception.'[1] More
Irish people died in the Civil War of 1922–3 than had been
killed in the War of Independence between 1919 and 1921: and
some of that killing was even more brutal than anything perpetrated
by the Black and Tans. At the time of the fighting, the issues raised by
the Civil War were imperfectly understood by the wider public. A
popular misconception was that the republicans were fighting a partitionist Free State as a protest against the ceding of six northern
counties to the United Kingdom in the Anglo-Irish treaty of 1921. In
fact, the more immediate concern was an Oath of Allegiance to the
crown demanded of all political representatives of the Free State. To
many people, this all seemed hair-splitting of the worst kind. Quite a
number who had fought bravely against the British up to 1921 did
not consider that the differences of opinion justified a civil war.

The legacy of all this was a distinctive conservatism in public life.
Those who survived to conduct Irish politics in the ensuing decades
proved, in the words of Kevin O'Higgins, 'the most conservative
revolutionaries in history'.[2] So much energy had been expended that
there was little left with which to redesign a society. The final decades
of British rule had been 'characterised by originality and independence of thought'.[3] With the bleakness of freedom came a different
philosophy. Deranged idealists were now blamed for provoking the
Civil War, and one consequence was a severe distrust of all exponents
of theory. Pragmatism replaced principle as a driving force behind

the public mood. The leaders of the new state asserted the importance of respectability in thought and action. Irish people must by their discipline show themselves worthy of the new freedom. In other countries the decade was known as the Roaring Twenties; but in Ireland, although it started with gunplay and revolution, it concluded with censorship of art and an attempt to police social morality. The tradition of Tory Anarchism was, after three hundred years, beginning to disintegrate, and placing all emphasis on the first word rather than on the second.

Sean O'Casey, a near-blind Dublin labourer in his forties, wrote a play that captured the mood: *Juno and the Paycock*. It proved hugely popular with Abbey Theatre audiences, and so it has remained. Its author was already linked in the public mind with James Joyce, for both wrote out of a conviction that the songs and stories of the past had celebrated the wrong people: the smiters of the world rather than the smitten. Their heroes were to be found not in militants who could inflict pain but in wily, anonymous citizens who, by showing grace under pressure, somehow managed to survive. For O'Casey such figures were most often women like Mrs Juno Boyle, who keeps her family intact as long as she can, under the intolerable pressure of a Civil War in which her son Johnny is unmasked as a coward by his republican comrades. Or they might be found in men brave enough to treat heroism as just another temptation best deflated by humour and mockery.

Juno and the Paycock is properly subtitled 'A Tragedy in Three Acts', despite the fact that comic situations account for almost two of its two and a half hours. For all its rich humour and vibrant language, it is arguably O'Casey's most negative play, an indictment of the selfish irresponsibility of almost everyone onstage and, by implication, of the offstage leaders of Ireland. The predicament of the Boyle family is an apt metaphor of the wider society, for the stock device of a legacy that turns out to be false is a comment on the bitter testament of Irish nationalism. That nationalism had promised workers reconquest of Ireland but delivered no more than green flags and green postboxes. Likewise, the familiar dramatic device of a vanished Englishman who leaves a decent Irish girl pregnant might be taken as O'Casey's indictment of the precipitate, unplanned nature of the British withdrawal.

The execution of Johnny Boyle as a traitor is an accurate image of a land sundered by civil strife, but for O'Casey the saddest feature was the pretension to respectability that led many of yesterday's rebels to see themselves as the new elite. In his autobiography he would be scathing about the way in which the fight for the Irish language was replaced by a scramble for collars and ties. That outbreak of middle-class morality is satirized in the figure of Captain Boyle, a man who once denounced the Catholic clergy for their suppression of revolution but who, on inheriting some wealth, begins to defend the priests and to denounce his daughter's friend, the trade unionist Jerry Devine. The inconsistency of Boyle's political philosophy may be taken as O'Casey's sign that nationalism rather than real republicanism has triumphed, and with it the self-interest of the propertied class.

An astonishing number of the play's jokes have a distinctly contemporary reference, which would have been utterly exciting for audiences used to plays with historical or peasant settings. Boyle's manifesto of conjugal independence is a case in point: 'Today, Joxer, there's goin' to be issued a proclamation be me, establishin' an independent Republic, an' Juno'll have to take an oath of allegiance.'[4] Here the family as metaphor for the state is clearly implied, but in terms that mock the Free State, then enforcing the controversial oath. An audience might laugh at Boyle's swagger only to realize that it was chortling at the fundamental contradiction that disfigured its own state. During the Treaty debates, one supporter had said, 'When a man gets married he promises to be faithful to his wife, which is very different from owing allegiance to her', but a heckler from the back had warned, 'Wait till you get married.'[5] O'Casey liked to suggest that the Irish had a gift for treating a joke as a serious thing and a serious thing as a joke. His technique was to grab the attention of his audience with a witticism only to turn it into something very disturbing indeed.

The Abbey audiences were still far too close to the painful events to be able to confront all these truths directly, and so actors tended to emphasize the comic elements and to deflect some of the darker implications. This has been a longstanding way of treating Irish dramatic classics: to remove the violence from Synge's work and emphasize the lyricism, or to edit out the painful silences from Beckett, leaving just the witty one-liners. But O'Casey was at pains to insist that his plays were not tragicomedies but tragedies. At bottom, he wished to shock his spectators and compel them to undertake a reassessment of their deepest convictions. This he often did by putting conventionally admirable words into the mouths of dubious characters, in order to expose the vulnerability of such sentiments. Captain Boyle's catch phrase ('The whole world's in a state o' chassis') is a telling example. At the obvious level it indicates a personality both self-righteous and self-deceiving: and the audience is from the outset invited to laugh at the sloppy verbiage of a man whose linguistic reach is greater than his grasp. People do laugh at the line again and again, for if anything is funnier than an unintentional slip, it is an unintentional slip endlessly replicated. Comic characters are by nature static and prone to repeating themselves, because of their ludicrous incapacity to learn from experience. The line ultimately backfires on Boyle. An educated audience which at first may find his 'chassis' charming will in the end become outraged by the moral self-deception that is shown to lie behind it.

He uses the word initially to castigate 'chiselurs who don't care a damn now about their parents',[6] but in the end he himself is revealed to be a parent who doesn't give a damn about his pregnant daughter, turning her out of his home rather than risk the disapproval of neighbours. The phrase he patented as an exposure of the contemporary world becomes instead a self-indictment. This suggests his inability to take responsibility not just for his language but for the values that language is expected to underwrite. Imprecision of language indicates for O'Casey a failure of thought. Used in a dire crisis for the fifth or sixth time, the phrase grows pathetic, a mark of an impoverished imagination. Boyle is fluent but hardly articulate, for he uses language to conceal a failure of thought and feeling. Raymond Williams put this brilliantly when he said that in the plays of O'Casey there is always a contrast between the language of those who confront experience and the language of those who evade it.[7]

Words become the best register of a character's moral stature in *Juno and the Paycock*. If Boyle's strike us as finally hollow, his wife's are creative. Even her moments of cutting sarcasm are redeemed by the sheer creativity with which she remodels a tired old sentence. 'To be sure, no bread's a lot better than half a loaf,' she observes to her daughter during the trade union strike of Act One; and when the pregnant Mary laments that her baby will have no father, Juno sharply retorts, 'It'll have what's better – two mothers.'[8] A concern with absent or inadequate fathers is to be found in the classic works of Irish modernism from Joyce's *Ulysses* to Synge's *Playboy of the Western World*: it is a sign of a society unsure of its own bearings. But the Oedipal revolt is less against the fathers for being tyrannical than for failing to provide any kind of lead at all. The desire is not for a subjugation of existing authority but rather for an authority of some kind to reveal itself. O'Casey's form of radical traditionalism is as old as that of Edmund Burke.

Boyle's repetitions are always lame and empty. By contrast, when Juno repeats a line (which is seldom), she does so to some point and purpose. She reworks the prayers of her bereaved neighbour, Mrs Tancred, and that shows not intellectual laziness but high moral courage. She is in effect confessing the guilt of her own failure to learn from her neighbour's words. Remembering how she had caroused and played the new gramophone, while Mrs Tancred mourned her murdered son, she repents and speaks for all of O'Casey's mothers: 'Ah, why didn't I remember that he wasn't a Die-hard or a Stater, but only a poor dead son?'[9] Then with a humble courage she repeats the woman's supplication to the Sacred Heart to take away the murdering hate and hearts of stone – an image that may well have been derived from Yeats's poem 'Easter 1916', in which fanatic 'hearts with one purpose alone' seem 'enchanted to a stone / To trouble the living stream'.[10]

In O'Casey's mind all -isms are wasms. As surely as Swift, he treats all theorists as madmen, and Juno is the vehicle of his satire. She speaks for all flesh-and-blood mothers when she tells her crippled IRA son, 'You lost your best principle when you lost your arm: them's the only sort o' principles that's any good to a workin' man.'[11] Yet the word 'principle' has a slightly hollow sound in her mouth, especially in the context of the working man, for it comes from the same woman who has just warned her daughter against coming out on strike in defence of a union comrade. 'When the employers sacrifice wan victim, the trade unions go wan better be sacrificin' a hundred': but Mary retorts, 'It doesn't matter what you say, how you may argue, ma, a principle's a principle.'[12] Principles won't pay the shopkeeper, says Juno. This same commonsensical dismissal of abstract ideals lies behind her greatest speech: her plea for the sacredness of life and her denial of all sectarian patriotisms that would divide the suffering mothers of the world from one another.

Through various stage directions and twists in the plot, O'Casey seems to endorse Juno's attack on all -isms, including scientific socialism (for which he substitutes a simple goodness of heart). Mary has been imbued by her socialist boyfriend Devine with his trade union principles, yet in the end he turns out to be as callous and intolerant as her father, for he spurns his sweetheart on discovering that she has been left pregnant by the Englishman. Just as Joxer is capable of disloyalty to Boyle ('that oul bummer'), so Devine abandons ideals of human brotherhood, lapsing into a narrow moralism that considers pregnancy out of wedlock an evil far worse than tuberculosis. 'It's only as I expected,' says Mary: 'Your humanity is just as narrow as the humanity of others.'[13] This is the selfsame point already made by O'Casey himself in a long stage direction introducing Devine to the play:

He is a type, becoming very common now in the Labour Movement, of a mind knowing enough to make the mass of his associates a power, and too little to broaden that power for the benefit of all.[14]

O'Casey stated, as early as the revolutionary year of 1919, that the trade unions could increase the amount of food on a working person's table (a good thing in itself), but that they could never broaden the mind.

If idealists are exposed as crazed theorists (usually male) who lack compassion, then the realists of this world are generally women who can feel for those in distress. But that contrast is never completely formulaic: even Juno is not flawless. Those who say that a principle's a principle emerge as cowards, traitors or (at best) self-improving careerists, while the homely realism of Juno seems finally less destructible. Her honest refusal to espouse any -ism makes her an inadvertent heroine. That is not, however, to absolve her of some responsibility for the awful predicament of her son. Earlier, she and her family seem to have encouraged his republican activities, whereas now they discount the rebels as mere 'die-hards'.

Under pressure of these inconsistencies, not to mention the loss of a limb for the 'cause', Johnny Boyle becomes confused. His republican faith is eroded and he betrays Robbie Tancred, who lives in the same tenement. His actions are those of an ailing child never given a clear moral lead by his parents. Boyle is even less consistent than Juno. In Act One he espouses the republican cause in condemning the priests, but in Act Two he praises the clergy and denounces republicans. As a parent, he fails Johnny, even as Johnny then fails a comrade. O'Casey strongly hints that the earlier encouragement of Johnny's involvement may have arisen from the family's desire to enjoy a higher social position in an independent Ireland. Juno falls as willingly as Boyle into the trap of consumerism, made possible by the promised legacy. She even encourages her husband in his new role of conservative paterfamilias and then, when the scheme explodes, hastily absolves herself of any responsibility for the mess.

In that limited sense, she is as guilty of irresponsibility as other characters. Even her radical daughter Mary partakes of this inconsistency. As a trade unionist, she well knows that it is the wealthier class that exploits and sacrifices her comrades, and she shows an honest contempt for the materialistic philosophy that makes her parents want to join that class. She herself desires to escape poverty and reads Ibsen for self-improvement: *A Doll's House*, *Ghosts*, *The Wild Duck*, 'buks only fit for chiselurs', according to her baffled father.[15] Yet in ditching her sweetheart Jerry Devine for the plausible schoolmaster Bentham (a utilitarian philosopher, if ever there was one), she

displays the same materialism as her mother, the only difference
being that she can cloak her ambition in more genteel images, in
terms of the leather-bound volumes of Ibsen rather than the strident
gramophone. In every one of these cases, whether the idealism is of
a materialist, socialist or bourgeois variety, it is a mask for self-
interest.

That is why this is O'Casey's darkest play. It indicates what he is
against, but is less clear in implying what in any worldly sense he
might be *for*. He affords his audiences a piercing insight into the
undeveloped conversations and analyses that are the result of the
crowded conditions of the tenements. He shows with compassion the
'helpless availability' which is the lot of those condemned to live in
such a setting. Yet he also registers the utopian longings: for a better
material condition, for more control over one's world, for a greater
scope of mind and amplitude of imagination. Indeed, it is often these
very longings that lead people to acts of heartlessness or carelessness
in the present: yet that does not discredit the aspirations. By a miraculous irony, it is left to Captain Boyle of all people to give voice to
this frustrated but lyric yearning. Even the most sceptical member of
the audience will endorse his halting attempt to explain his wonder
at the planetary system, and will regret that he lacks the vocabulary
to do any more than hint at the immensity of his feelings: 'I often
looked up at the sky an' assed meself the question – what is the
stars, what is the stars?'[16]

A different, but related, question concerns O'Casey. Is he as incapable as Boyle of developing or sustaining a dramatic idea? It is
sometimes said that he depicts the suffering of war without examin-
ing its causes. He can show the naïveté of the workers and the alleged
irrelevance of the nationalists to their felt needs, but can never take
that one step further to raise questions about the entire social system
which gives rise to so much blindness. That is only to say that he
refuses in the end to write a prescriptive socialist play. Yet, somehow,
the energy of his language, its surging desire to create in words a
sense of spaciousness impossible in the world, seems to endorse the
utopian thrust of the characters. Even as their situation grows ever
bleaker, the style carries the hope of a redeeming perspective on
things.

Juno becomes the agent of that desire onstage. Through her,
O'Casey issues a demand that the men abandon their idealist illusions. Juno assures her daughter that the disasters overtaking them
all have nothing to do with the will of God and everything to do with
the folly of man. 'Oh, what can God do agen the stupidity o' men?'[17]
In effect she is telling her children that they have the power to

remake their own lives, to become the subjects rather than the objects of history. Her call on men to abandon the illusions about their situation is real enough: but something prevents O'Casey from converting it into a call to abandon any situation that can feed off such illusions. Perhaps it is an artistic scruple that leads him to the belief that preaching is ineffectual and that there can be no more revolutionary art than the exact description of the state of things as they are. It may also be a canny awareness that the largely middle-class element in the Abbey audience had been pushed about as far as it could go in debunking ideas of national heroism.

Such explanations, though all feasible, seem partial. Ultimately, O'Casey may have aborted his incipient dialectic for reasons that had nothing to do with artistic tact or social timidity. He was after all a believing Christian: and in so far as he developed a dialectic, it was one that placed 'life' and 'religion' in a state of creative tension. Religion showed him the hollowness of life, but then life went and complicated things by suggesting the possible hollowness of religion. Like George Bernard Shaw, he never really got beyond that aporia. The stripping of the stage of its props and artefacts, its debris of consumerist aspiration, might be taken as a Marxian comment on the vanity of bourgeois wishes, but it is really something more. It is the enactment of a principle of disintegration that animates the whole play, a stripping away of artifice and illusion, a de-creation of ideals, all done in the hope of achieving a true exposure to the suffering of being. That is a Protestant imperative, of a kind that would inspire the young Samuel Beckett, who also saw the ideal stage as one divested of all props and images. In a world where every man is encouraged to become his own priest and take responsibility for himself and his language, that may be the point of connection between two comic nihilists of the modern stage.

The dilemmas which they face and which they set for their characters are not finally soluble in worldly terms. Neither Marxism nor existentialism would ever suffice. Hence their shared addiction to the off-key ending (inherited from Shaw) and to the anticlimactic line. They love to build up a scene or a speech for the even greater pleasure of pulling it down. What happens to the furniture in *Juno* is the same sort of asset-stripping enacted in the words uttered onstage. This gift for deflation and even bathos has remained very popular with Irish audiences, who enjoy 'slagging': but it may ultimately be traced to a distrust of the things of this world and to a refusal to take anything pertaining to this world overseriously. A similar sense of humour links Shaw and Joyce, a sense of anticlimax possible only to those who have been given excessive expectations of this world.

Joyce, when asked what he thought of the life to come, said that he didn't think much of this one; Beckett's retort in *Endgame* was 'Mine was always that'; and Yeats saw life as a long preparation for an illumination that never quite came.[18] Such an approach prefers wry fade-outs to noisy climaxes. This is all, no doubt, in some way a response to the difficult nature of Irish history, but also a sign of a religious consciousness which refuses to take anything, even suffering and unhappiness, with more seriousness than God would assign to it.[19]

The Civil War was a social tragedy which set brother against brother, but it was also a cultural tragedy in so far as it induced a suspicion of innovative ideas or theories as a basis for public policy. The conservatism especially afflicted the emerging middle class, whose sexual ethic was deeply puritanical. Watching these developments with some alarm from Paris, James Joyce told Arthur Power that in his young days the Irish had no responsibility for anything and so felt free to say or do what they liked, but that now they were gripped by a fear of freedom.[20] In schools, abstract learning (of Latin and classical studies) was prized over pragmatic modern disciplines (such as science or commerce), with disastrous consequences for the economy of the infant state. Those who now exercised responsibility for policy were often cautious, as well as keen to indict examples of 'irresponsibility' in others. Hence a pervasive theme of O'Casey's play, which ends with the removal of furniture that the Boyle family scarcely had time to enjoy. The ultimate indictment of the middle-class authorities is the fact that O'Casey never allows them onstage, as if they are not felt to be a force for disruption in his proletarians' lives. They may be unseen, but theirs is the dominant role. The right to consume (furniture, gramophone players etcetera) will be confined to the new bourgeoisie, which will not be itself productive but simply an extension of the state class. The poor people on O'Casey's stage may for the most part be unable to provide an analysis of their own exploitation, but they can feel its effects on their pulses.

O'Casey's plotting, which often seems crudely obvious on the page, can generate wonderfully theatrical moments onstage, because his dramaturgy is so rooted in trusted conventions. Like the plays of Sheridan, his are ever-popular and for similar reasons: their challenging ideas are encased not in radical new forms but in old-fashioned ones. Sheridan's republican ethic was well masked in his blend of satirical and sentimental comedy; likewise the social vision of O'Casey was implied by the use of such stock devices as melodrama, sketches, popular songs and routines. The gap between the heroic pretensions of Boyle and his actual practice is filled with a sense of comedy which chronicles his self-deception.

Liam O'Flaherty was the other major analyst of post-revolutionary disillusion in the mid-1920s, but his vision left no room for hilarity. Working more by instinct than by thought, he found the world a tragic place. Born in Inis Mór, the largest of the Aran Islands, he grew up in conditions of poverty that seemed to negate revivalist illusions of a pristine, intact Gaelic culture. Later on he would observe that 'the only civilisation to which the Gaelic conquerors of this country seem to have been addicted was fighting, drunkenness, incest and chess-playing'.[21]

Life on Aran was hard, and happiness for O'Flaherty was to be found in the degree to which the human will might master nature. His characters feel themselves estranged from society, but are often even more alienated from the limitations of human nature itself. Among the islanders, the Galway mainland was known derisively as 'The Continent', to emphasize its foreignness: and there is a sense in which O'Flaherty would always feel himself an outsider in that place.[22] (His *Tourist's Guide to Ireland* is accordingly written in a mode of incredulous anthropology).

Being a bright boy, he had been sent to Rockwell College and later Blackrock, in some hopes that he might become a priest: but after study at University College Dublin, he enlisted in the British army for the Great War. A bad wound in 1917 left him a victim of acute melancholy for years afterward. He took to a life of travel and in Rio de Janeiro in 1919 noticed a newspaper headline: 'Republica declarata na Irlanda'. He headed home. By the time he became fully involved, the great revolutionary programme of the First Dáil of 1919 was dwindling to the cautious conservatism of the Free State. In January 1922, at the head of a group of unemployed men, O'Flaherty occupied the Rotunda Building in Dublin and flew the red flag over it for four days. Across the province of Munster, trade unionists were setting up 'soviets' in flour mills, bakeries and factories: and O'Flaherty mistakenly thought that a revolution was imminent. Later, he fled to Cork. His involvement in radical politics, always marginal and unclear, was neither sustained nor disciplined, but it provided the material for his most famous novel, *The Informer*, published in 1925.

O'Flaherty took the view that the best writing was that which chronicled action without any kind of 'analysis'. On the basis of that aesthetic, he said that he would gladly exchange a whole shipload of Irish political martyrs for a solitary descriptive genius like Guy de Maupassant. By the mid-1920s he had befriended the

near-blind worker-playwright O'Casey. To his London editor
Edward Garnett, he wrote on 10 March 1924: 'He is an artist, unlike
the other bastard writers I met here. The play is a fine thing. It is
called *Juno and the Paycock*. A fine piece of realistic work but in my
opinion he spoils it with tragedy.'[23]

O'Casey's play had a major effect on *The Informer*, which was
written in the next few months. It was to be a tragedy unspoilt by
any comic relief, which is to say a thriller. O'Flaherty did not share
O'Casey's desire for popular acclaim and commented with amusement on the playwright's naïve belief that novels were
moneyspinners. He had hoped to recruit his new friend for a radical
group in Dublin that opposed the influence of the Yeats circle: but
O'Casey shrewdly resisted, later opining that there was something
touchingly humble about Yeats's arrogance (even as there was something arrogant about other writers' ostentatious humility).[24]
O'Flaherty admired the critique of embourgeoisification in *Juno and
the Paycock*, re-creating the aspirations of socialists to social
respectability in *The Informer*, whose Mary McPhillip seems a version of Mary Boyle. Soon, however, he was detecting similar
tendencies to embourgeoisification in O'Casey.[25]

He later joined in the attacks on *The Plough and the Stars*, which
he took to be a slur on the memory of James Connolly. There may
have been an element of compensation in that protest, as if he himself were attempting to atone for his indifference during Easter Week:
but he made the point that artists should always side with the weak
against self-constituted authority.[26] His own writings were attempts
to re-create the energy and spirit of the insurrectionists, 'for force is,
after all, the opposite of sluggishness . . . Ours is the wild tumult of
the unchained storm.'[27]

In *The Informer* that unchained storm is Gypo Nolan. He betrays
his comrade McPhillip to the police, who kill him. The action takes
only eight hours. Its author sought the effect of 'a sort of high-brow
detective story'[28] with a tale set among communist revolutionaries
in the early days of the Free State. By July 1924 he felt himself
utterly possessed by the unbeautiful Gypo, a hairy-ape type. His aim
was to induce in the 'mob' of second-rate readers a final pity for a
figure whom they would at first consider monstrous.[29] This would
be done by toying with their emotions. Gypo would develop from a
'brutal, immensely strong, stupid character' to 'a soul in torment'
and the style of narration would be transformed from harshness to
sympathy.[30] The plot reads like a somewhat revised version of *Juno
and the Paycock*, with a sick and ailing informer replaced by a vigorous and brainless man, in order to test O'Flaherty's ideas about

the role of energy, willpower and environment in the shaping of the person.

Although Nolan takes his twenty-pound reward from the police, he doesn't really go on to impress readers with the intensity of his remorse. His lack of intellect at the outset may ameliorate the reader's moral outrage, for Gypo can scarcely imagine what he has done until confronted with its effect on McPhillip's grieving mother: but it also reduces the scale of his self-arraignment, and that in turn severely qualifies the pity readers can feel for him. The emotional graph traced by O'Flaherty is not quite the one he intended.

Part of the problem is a movie-like reliance on sheerly external depiction, from which inner states are to be inferred. Sometimes this works well enough. The prematurely aged faces of the disappointed men disconsolately eating their food in the Dunboy Home at the start might be a convincing image of the already exhausted infant state: but the narrative often lingers over surfaces that are never more than that. McPhillip is dying of consumption after a spell living rough in the hills. His account of that experience is a bleak exercise in anti-pastoral, a deliberate reworking of some of Synge's darker speeches on the threat to sanity and health posed by wild nature. Only belatedly does Gypo offer some of his food to his friend: and this failure of sympathy seems to lead naturally to the moment when, confronted with his own poverty, he betrays McPhillip to the authorities. After that, the sound of human footsteps becomes 'menacing',[31] a word that may imply moral rebuke or may just evoke physical fear of revenge. Gypo's covert jealousy of McPhillip's more prominent role in the revolutionary movement may help to explain this rather arbitrary betrayal: but that is merely hinted at in B-movie lingo: 'Mac, you bite the easy side o' the cheese. I got to do all the rough work an' you do all the thinkin'.'[32]

As if by dumb impulse, Nolan turns to his girlfriend, the prostitute Katie (a figure who may in turn have influenced the presentation of Rosie Redmond in *The Plough and the Stars*). In the Dublin of the time, many whores were on terms of friendship with rebels on the run, offering them shelter and comfort. Some did this out of compassion, others out of a republican commitment. (When one of the famous brothels was closed by the new government, a famous harlot danced on the last night of business, her skirts rising higher until she revealed a petticoat, slip and knickers in the green-white-and-orange of the flag of the illegal republic).[33] Katie had been expelled from the revolutionary organization from which Nolan and McPhillip had also been dismissed: she for prostitution and they for killing a union official without prior sanction by headquarters. Hence her fellow-feeling.

Wandering the streets after a less than satisfactory encounter with her, Nolan has a sudden, involuntary memory of life long ago with his parents in a little Tipperary village:

> He stiffened himself, as if he were about to haul himself by sheer force back through the intervening years, of sin and sorrow and misery, to the peace and gentleness and monotony of life, in that little village at the foot of the Galtees.[34]

For all his tough exterior, O'Flaherty was a pastoralist at heart and the evocation of a pristine rural landscape against the backdrop of a fallen urban setting was a favourite device. By contrast, the streets of Dublin seem suddenly strange to Nolan, as if he had never seen them before. His obscure sense of guilt casts them in a new, unwelcome light, the sort of light that might be cast on them in close-up by an artist. Inarticulate though he may be, the informer is also a type of the artist.

McPhillip's mother, always gentle to Nolan, represents a further development of the *rus in urbe* theme, when he visits her family hours after her son's death. He feels no tenderness for former comrades present, for they had 'cut' him after his expulsion. In his view, their sole interest is in securing portentously titled jobs. The McPhillip family are presented as a variant of O'Casey's Boyles, and the assessment reads like one of the playwright's extended stage directions. The father wishes to improve their lot but is

> . . . a weak, nervous character, slightly hysterical, capable of committing any act on the spur of the moment, but incapable of pursuing a logical course of action resolutely. But his children were resolute. The son was resolute in his hatred of the existing conditions of society. He was a resolute, determined revolutionary, with his father's energy. His daughter was resolute in her determination to get out of the slums.[35]

Mary denounces her father for going back on his son's radical involvement, much as Boyle did with Johnny: and she asks Gypo to tell her who last talked with her brother. By this stage, the many echoes of the life of Jesus are beginning to form an emotional complex, with the coins that Gypo lets fall from his pocket in his confusion recalling the thirty pieces of silver for which Judas betrayed Christ. Gypo offers money to the mother.

The parallel is complicated, however. By rights, McPhillip should be the Christ figure, with his mother as Mary and Gypo Judas: but

O'Flaherty shifts the analogies at the midpoint, so that McPhillip appears more as a John the Baptist and Gypo as the suffering Christ. Gypo's subsequent trial by the revolutionary leaders recalls the appearance of Jesus before Pilate; his incarceration seems to hint at the time spent by Jesus in the tomb; and so on. While the symbolism may seem obvious, its handling is not: the equation of roles between Jesus and the informer requires considerable flexibility on the part of readers and is in fact O'Flaherty's challenge to received Christian orthodoxies. He had always mythologized himself as someone considered 'evil' by society, while in fact he was intent only on liberating humanity. His disrespect for passive suffering and his cult of the will led him to revise the figure of gentle Jesus, presenting him as a violent, simple-minded, lumbering giant. This may be an aspect of the author's own search for dishonour and outlawry. Far from deferring to popular ideas by his use of a Jesus-figure, he challenges them to a radical degree by making him a cross between the hairy ape and a Nietzschean beast.[36]

The Informer is O'Flaherty's attempt to wrest the meaning and interpretation of the Jesus story from the priests. Yet he always supported his mother's doctrine that all things which moved or sang had been created by God.[37] O'Flaherty's real complaint against Irish priests lay in their relentless intellectualization of a faith that he considered an appeal to instinct rather than intellect. Hence his strangely tender treatment of Gypo, whose ferocity was no more than that of nature itself. The effects of shell-shock on O'Flaherty in the Great War should not be discounted as an element in this portrayal: other writer-veterans of that combat also created a cult of violence around charismatic but inarticulate heroes, whose willingness to inflict pain was exceeded only by their capacity to endure it. There may even be a sort of displacement at work, as if the author is projecting onto the character a repetition of the war experience that otherwise he might fear having to endure all over again himself.[38] Ernest Hemingway is the obvious comparison here, for not only does he also cultivate a tough-guy exterior which never fully conceals a heart of gold, but he too questions the assumption that people are necessarily the centre of the natural world, preferring the suggestion that the land may be the only enduring hero.

There is little or no formal experiment with narrative in *The Informer*, as there are no new dramatic techniques in O'Casey's *Juno and the Paycock*. Each relies at times on rather crude and obvious effects: yet, for all that, they vividly render the doubts, the paranoia and moral disorder of the country in the months immediately after independence. O'Flaherty in particular captures the obsession, even among revolutionary groups, with the hunt for places and jobs: for example, the leader of the movement, Gallagher, tells Gypo that if he can identify the informer who ratted on McPhillip, he will get his old position at headquarters back again.

The writer also has some fun at the expense of the elitist thinking in such movements at the time. On the basis of Gallagher's rather flimsy offer of renewed employment, Gypo suddenly regards the rest of humanity 'with contempt'.[39] He uses his reward money for a series of expansive, patronizing gestures, purchasing fish and chips for the inner-city poor. The madame of a down-at-heel brothel, Biddy Burke, offers her own mordant analysis of the failure of the social revolution to visiting scouts from the movement who have come to investigate the veracity of Gypo's claims:

> Not that I didn't do me bit to help the boys, God bless 'em, but 'tisn't the boys that done the fightin' that get the jobs. So it isn't. It never is . . . They were talkin' about English tyrants, but sure nobody ever saw the likes o' these tyrants with their watches an' their raids, an' every divil's wart of a farmer's son that can pull on his breeches without his mother's help runnin' around and callin' himself a gineral.[40]

Gypo spurns the base pleasures of Biddy Burke's for a more up-market brothel, where he meets Connemara Maggie: in this unlikely setting, O'Flaherty unleashes a sexual pastoral with a fine suddenness. The longing in this bordello is less for a multiplication of sexual possibilities than for a return to bucolic values:

> She busied herself tending her man, just as if she had never left the purity of her Connemara hills and she were tending her peasant spouse after a hard day's work in the fields; instead of tending a casual lover in the sordid environment of a brothel. There was no hint of vice or of libidinous pleasure in her face or in her movements.[41]

A character named Rat Mulligan is tried for McPhillip's murder, on the basis of an accusation by Gypo. Gypo himself is also cross-questioned. Mulligan's alibi is obvious and convincing: but, despite his manifest lying, Gypo's own speech has the magnificence of an epic outburst. O'Flaherty resorts to heroic simile ('as a thunderstorm bursts over a calm sea on a sultry day')[42] to describe the response of his body and soul, as he is cornered by men wilier than he. He is condemned to death and held down during his protests by five men, like a Laocoön entwined with snakes. In his cell he remembers an escape plan hatched by McPhillip in their days of freedom (should such a ruse be necessary), and so he prises himself to liberty. Gallagher receives that news with cold fury. Even as he accepts the embraces of Mary McPhillip, he is thinking not of love but of the danger facing his organization if Gypo reveals its secrets to the police. But Gypo's mind is set. Even as he sneaks past the police, he forgets that as an informer he could put himself under their protection. To him they are still the enemy: 'To his understanding he was still a revolutionary. He was not at all conscious of being an informer, or a friend of law and order, a protégé of the police.'[43] There could hardly be a more astute dramatization of the strange blend of the conservative and the radical that characterized the Irish revolutionaries. O'Flaherty sensed it even in himself, confessing in May 1926 after the birth of his daughter that he might be a 'revolutionary conservative'.[44] In *Two Years*, an autobiographical study, he would write: '. . . socialists are the most conservative people in the world. Notice how they never seem to change the colour of their neck-ties.'[45]

The irruption of Gypo Nolan from his cell leads to the final movement of the book. He seeks escape from the city, but finds himself caught in its vicious circles and returns to the sanctuary of Katie's lodging, a room shared with another prostitute. Over their shared bed is hung a statue of Saint Joseph, not out of piety but as 'a blasphemous protest against the incompetence of the saint'.[46] Traced by his pursuers, Gypo runs into the nearby church where McPhillip's mother is attending mass. He is mortally wounded by bullets. He blesses himself with the holy water, begs and receives the woman's forgiveness, and, stretching out his arms so that his body lies cruciform, he dies.

Despite the blatancy of the final symbolism, O'Flaherty's book captured the national mood of bleak realism. Even the leaders of the earlier phase of the Irish revival – against whom much of the writing was aimed – got caught up in it. W.B. Yeats praised *The Informer* as 'too full of abounding life to be terrible' and 'full of that tragic farce we have invented'.[47] O'Flaherty had hoped to blast Yeats and his cohorts onto the scrapheap of literary history, but the poet shrewdly suggested that the 'new' realism wasn't so new at all. Rather, it was part of a continuum stretching back via Joyce to J.M. Synge:

> . . . after the agrarian passion we began to value truth . . . free discussion appeared among us for the first time, bringing the passion for reality, the satiric genius that informs *Ulysses*, *The Playboy of the Western World*, *The Informer*, *The Puritan*, and

other books and plays; the accumulated hatred of the years was suddenly transferred from England to Ireland.[48]

Despite Yeats's ploy, most commentators chose to bracket O'Flaherty with O'Casey and Joyce as leaders of a counter-Revival realism in art. By 1927 a writer in the *Irish Statesman* pointed out that urban slums had replaced idealized rural landscapes in art. He wondered, all the same, whether these seemingly opposed images might not be opposite sides of the one coin:

> Standish O'Grady would disown the child whose literary existence I surmise his Cuchulain made inevitable. That O'Grady's *Cuchulain*, that fusion of fire and gentleness, the inevitably heroic, should have for offspring *The Informer* will call forth endless repudiations. But the law demands it and logic accepts it for all the irony of the situation so created. If *Cuchulain* had not been so noble, *The Informer* would not have been so ignoble. If O'Grady had written stories with characters like Jane Austen's, does anybody believe that *The Informer* would have been necessitated as the logical reaction? As is the case with Yeats and Joyce, where the literary heredity is seen in the fact that both are stylists, so in the case of O'Grady and O'Flaherty, the character is common and the tendency in both is to action.[49]

The epic similes and thriller pace of *The Informer* had clear precedents, as did the intermittent outbursts of pastoral longing: the thesis has been met with its antithesis. O'Flaherty was in fact as much an idealist and dreamer as O'Grady had been, but he wrote in a different age, which subjected many of those ideals to dire humiliation. His violence was encoded less in the heroic ideals themselves than in the response of a disappointed man, who feared that he had been fooled into such initially dreamy postures. His immediate contemporary Seán Ó Faoláin rightly described him as an inverted romantic who 'swoops to see if there is anything worth his respect in what he has already destroyed and, screaming, flies away, unsatisfied'.[50]

O'Flaherty developed that talent in further books. *A Tourist's Guide to Ireland*, published in 1929, stripped away the Revivalist pretences in order to expose the underlying reality. That was of a poverty-stricken state which, instead of seeking material betterment and greater productivity, had installed as its leaders a parasitic class of publicans, priests and politicians, a class that knew how to consume wealth but not how to create it.[51] The besetting vice of this class was Yeatsian: 'the attempt to unite mysticism with reality'. Yet O'Flaherty, though a keen diagnostician, also seemed to catch this disease. By 1946, on his return to Ireland and to writing in Irish after a prolonged stay abroad, he proposed in an interview to make Irish 'as compulsory as English was in 1848', with horse-whipping and no votes for those who refused. (Perhaps his tongue was buried deep in his cheek as he said this, but his interviewer didn't think so.) The wonderful short stories of *Dúil*, his one collection in Irish published in 1953, might be praised for precisely combining a mystical intuition with a realist sense of social textures. They were set mainly in the countryside, unlike his later novels which sometimes had an urban backdrop.

Never a systematic thinker, O'Flaherty delighted in such contradictions, finding in them perhaps the secret sources of his art. His radicalism was in the end more Swiftian than socialist. 'A Cure for Unemployment' produced in 1931 suggested the adoption of poor people as domestic pets and it clearly owes a lot to 'A Modest Proposal'.[52] The Swiftian style, which O'Flaherty liked to think of as a deliberate stylelessness, was perfectly calibrated to draw attention to the subjects rather than to the flourishes of the writer. In so far as he ever evolved a philosophy, it was a strange blend of nihilism and Nietzscheanism. The inverted romantic became a sort of reverse evolutionist, increasingly unsure as to the possibility of progress at all. Sometimes, he suspected regress. All that he could admire without reservation were the energies displayed by humans, animals and nature itself in the working-out of this unfathomable process.

28

Gaelic Absurdism:
At Swim-Two-Birds

Not long after the foundation of the Free State in 1922, George Russell sent a letter reporting the new mood of pragmatism and realism to the American writer Van Wyck Brooks. He concluded: 'I would like to live for fifteen years more because I think we will react again to the imaginative and spiritual, and we shall probably begin a fight for spiritual freedom.'[1] The achievement up to 1922 had been awesome: an artistic renaissance had been followed by the extirpation from twenty-six counties of a great imperial power. Economic success might have been expected to ensue.

It was not to be. Global recession at the close of the 1920s was a prelude to the Economic War of the next decade, the major consequence of which was that Irish producers lost access to the lucrative British market. The state, which had come under ferocious attack in its first year of independence, became the be-all and end-all of the new elites. They worked to defend it rather than reshape it to the needs of the people. Many of those people – landless labourers, women, Protestants, Gaeltacht dwellers – were still so estranged from the official apparatus that they behaved like members of an underground movement in their own country.

Now the highest aim of many was a job for life in the civil service or the banking system. The blacksmith who had assured comrades in 1922 that 'we will in our arse have our own gentry'[2] had not reckoned with the new administrators, who showed a distrust of enterprise and risk-taking. The system of public examinations became the basis for recruiting the state class, whose ethos was more consumerist than entrepreneurial. The prevailing idea of a gentleman remained that of one who was 'not preoccupied in getting on in the world'.[3] Work was a necessary discipline for the poor and a minor irritation to other groups. The economy reflected this stasis. It was honestly run but it scarcely expanded, as wave after wave of young people left the ports forever. The political achievements were remarkable in their way – an orderly, democratic transfer of power from one civil war party to another in 1932–3, an authoritative role at the League of Nations, and in 1937 a written constitution securing citizens' rights – but they were not matched by economic modernization or by administrative reform. Ownership of the state, and not its very nature, seemed in retrospect to have been the primary point of contention between the Irish and the British.

Only in the field of literature did the continuing talent for experiment persist. The more staid the behaviour of the new elites, the more fantastic and improvisational did much of the writing become. In no artist's work is that disjunction captured more effectively than in that of Flann O'Brien (whose real name was Brian Ó Nualláin). By background and training, he held ideal qualifications for an exalted career in the new administration. He had grown up in an Irish-speaking family and had taken an arts degree at University College Dublin. His master's dissertation at UCD on Celtic Nature Poetry had to be resubmitted on two occasions before the professors would pass it: it applies the fashionable modernist ideas of T.S. Eliot and Ezra Pound in a celebration of the 'impersonality' of the lyrics treated. That conjunction of high modernist theory and ancient Gaelic verse may have been quite enough to raise the eyebrows of the examiners, for in those days Celtic Studies was largely an affair of linguistic rather than interpretative analysis: but in truth the dissertation is a dismal job which would hardly pass muster today. Its author, already widely reputed a genius, was clearly holding his best energies in check for writing of a more creative kind.

Ó Nualláin joined the Civil Service in 1935. Where other literary-minded recruits sought a post in the department of External Affairs (with the likelihood of a quick escape overseas), he chose instead to work in the department of Local Government. In his early years as a civil servant, he continued to labour part-time on an anti-novel which burst upon the literary scene in 1939 under the strange title *At Swim-Two-Birds*. Ó Nualláin saw his book as a potential bestseller, which might simultaneously appeal to highbrow and popular taste. He dreamed of the sort of comprehensive success enjoyed by Ethel Mannin, in a letter to whom he described the work as 'a belly-laugh or high-class literary pretentious slush, depending on how you look at it'.[4] Some have seen this as the mark of a defensive provincial insecurity. In truth, that desire is not only a personal wish but a key to the central meaning of the book.

The epigraph at the start from *Hercules Furens* means 'all things naturally draw apart and give place to one another'. It is an appropriately classical tagline for a set of fragmented narratives, drawn with astonishing eclecticism from Celtic Studies, cowboy novels, proletarian balladry, racing tipsters, encyclopedias and modernist literature. The maker of these plot-lines seems scandalized by the splitting of modern readership into so many discrepant constituencies. His work might be read as an attempt to restore a lost unity or at least to glue all the shattered pieces together as best he can.

The narrator is an unnamed student at UCD, who lives with his rather puritanical and censorious uncle, the holder of a 'third class clerkship' in Guinness's brewery. An obsession with class – classes of society, calibrations of administrative employment, sorts of persons – informs every phase of the work, suggesting a community that is utterly fissured by social gradations. The life of a student in such conditions is very attenuated and so he retreats instead into the imagination. He is writing a novel about a public-house owner named Dermot Trellis who, just like himself, spends most of the time either writing or sleeping. Trellis's work is a version of the fashionable Catholic novel of evil: he fills it with villainous exponents of those sins he wishes to condemn. With his colleague William Tracy, an author of Wild West romances, he has developed a scientific–literary device named 'aestho-autogamy', by which characters are created as fully mature adults. So one villain, Furriskey, is born at the age of twenty-five 'with a memory, but without a personal experience to account for it'.[5] This may be a jibe at the impoverished social life available to young people in 1930s Ireland: 'experience' was hardly the word. It is certainly a moment of self-mockery, for Ó Nualláin was himself a prodigy, who 'did not seem to have served his time' (according to his brother Kevin)[6] but 'burst on the scene fully equipped as a writer' (according to his friend Niall Sheridan, the Brinsley of the book).[7]

Usually, it is unnecessary for Trellis to invent characters, since he can borrow them from existing literary works: Finn MacCool from Irish legend, Shorty Andrews and Slug Willard from the cowboy tales of Tracy, Sweeny from a Middle Irish romance of a madman who fled a battlefield and went to live in the trees. Events turn against Trellis as author. Although his characters must conform to his designs while he is awake, they act according to their own free will while he sleeps, which is for twenty hours a day. Furriskey falls in love with the very woman whom Trellis had intended him to rape. They marry and live together as owners of a sweetshop for the twenty free hours, but are compelled by Trellis to perform immoral actions in the remaining four. In order to lead less trammelled lives, they drug their maker so that he will spend even more time in sleep. Just as Trellis loses control over his characters, he also loses command of himself. Having created Sheila Lamont as a paragon of beauty, he is so overwhelmed by her looks that he violates her himself. The child born of this act is named Orlick Trellis and he inherits his father's artistic bent. The other inhabitants of the Red Swan Hotel persuade Orlick to punish Trellis by writing a novel in which he will feature as a victim of awful pains and humiliations. After multiple torments, in which Dermot Trellis is confused with the deranged Sweeny, and in which he is defendant at a trial during which one of his accusers is a cow, he is saved from death. His servant girl accidentally burns the papers in which these rebellious characters solely lived, thereby putting an end to their assault. At the same time, the narrator passes his college examinations and returns to more friendly terms with his uncle.

Such a book has 'several planes and dimensions',[8] all of which intersect upon one another in its bizarre, trellis-like structure. Stories are constantly embarked upon, only to be interrupted by others before they can reach their appointed conclusion. One has the sense, when characters gather for conversation, that each is far more keen to perform than to listen ('Can't you listen?' implores one, to no avail).[9] The inability to tell or hear a story from start to finish may be a comment on the diminished sense of reality in the world depicted here: its characters seem to have sensations (mostly painful) rather than those experiences that make stories or even growth possible. Of Dermot Trellis it can at least be said that 'there's always a head and a tail on his yarns, a beginning and an end, give him his due':[10] but the same can hardly be said of Flann O'Brien. The plots, for all their fantastic complication, are secondary to that language which is the real hero of the book. Each of its stories falls apart, to make way for another. Yet there are subtle links: the cavity in Furriskey's molar seems to connect with the bad tooth of the narrator.

Early on, Brinsley suspects that each character might have an equivalent in real life: 'I hope that Trellis is not a replica of the uncle.'[11] The room in which the narrator writes is his only liberated zone, a fact resented by the uncle, who is a petty tyrant: 'I know the game you are at above in your bedroom.' (He may suspect masturbation or – worse – literary production.) The squalor of the Dublin settings is rendered in far more detail than in the writings of Joyce, but only because they provide the various narrators with a pressing excuse for a retreat into the mind. The aesthetic is Wildean, the real life being not the life they lead but the one they create in the imagination. Art exists mainly as a way of mocking the oppressions of the real world: if that oppression ceases (as it does at the end), the fictions die, for they are functions less of vision than of irritation.

The narrator, holed up in his bedroom, is a latter-day *file* at work: 'A contemplative life has always been suitable to my disposition. I was accustomed to stretch myself for many hours upon my bed.'[12] But the old culture is invoked only as a measure of current estrangement from it. No longer can the members of an entire community feel themselves represented by a single utterance: instead, the written literature of modernity has fragmented into specialisms. Those who read high modernism have no time for the Bard of Booterstown: and those who enjoy cowboy novels have no knowledge of the *Fiannaíocht*. Perhaps the greatest sadness of all may be found in the fact that the Gaelic poetry which once bound a people together as listeners is now the sole preserve of Celtic scholars. The poems uttered by Sweeny may be 'the real old stuff of the native land' and may have 'put our country where she stands today', but the proletarian-loving Shanahan has a question: 'the man in the street, where does he come in?'[13]

Lamont agrees with the implied diagnosis: 'there are people who read that . . . and keep reading it . . . and read damn the bloody thing else. Now that's a mistake.' Only one in a thousand can savour the Sweeny poems, but each does so at the cost of a dire specialism which allows him to savour nothing else. Ó Nualláin's brief, unhappy life as a Celtic scholar explains this thrust: but his hopes for a renewed confluence of literary cultures are reduced to the role of a parody which conflates the Sweeny idiom with that of the Booterstown Bard:

> When stags appear on the mountain high, with flanks the
>   colour of bran,
> When a badger bold can say goodbye, A Pint of Plain is
>   Your Only Man.[14]

That the blending of modes throughout the book should always be brutally parodic – as in Brinsley's mockery of *Fiannaíocht*: 'the neck to Trellis is house-thick and house-rough'[15] – suggests that there is little hope of recovery from the tragedy of a specialist modern world.

The rot began, of course, with writing. On that at least the characters agree. 'The voice was Number One,' opines Furriskey at a social gathering: 'Anything that came after was only an imitation of the voice.' As if to bear out that judgement, dialogue is by far the most entertaining aspect of the book, unchastened by any demands from the plot. Indeed, the Good Fairy indulges in a tirade against those who permit writerly codes to compress honest drawn-out dialogue into summary versions. His interlocutors all concur and can therefore pay Homer the ultimate compliment, for the writer of the *Iliad* was an oral poet:

——You have read it, Mr Shanahan?
——He was the daddy of them all, said Shanahan.[16]

Mr Shanahan has, of course, not read it. Books, in this order of things, are useful solely in that they provide raw material for conversation, oratory and oral performance: to read them might be going a little too far. The uncle's refrain – 'do you ever open a book at all?' – might be directed at anyone. The five shillings he gives to the narrator to purchase *Die Harzreise* is spent instead in the pubs, where conversation provides the makings of this student novel, filled with its own puns, fairytales, legends and epigrams.

Those who joke that all of modern literature is a footnote to Goethe's *Faust* do not go back far enough. Better the famous riposte by Patrick Kavanagh to the taunt that he was a derivative, second-rate poet: 'Since Homer we all are.'[17] The idea of belatedness weighed heavily on that post-Yeats, post-Joyce generation: one way of coping with it was to hint that this was a humiliation shared with the greatest artists of postclassical literature. In analysing how the integrity of the spoken voice was lost to literature, Flann O'Brien was retracing his own progress (or regress). Irish had been the language of his parents and siblings, among whom he was educated by home tutors until the age of twelve: 'he heard little English spoken for a number of years'.[18] His childhood reading was necessarily done mostly in English-language books, while his family conversations were conducted in Irish. One effect was that, when he finally got around to using English frequently in conversation, he may have employed a writerly brand of it. Most Irish persons who learned English in earlier centuries had done so with the aid of books: hence the rather exaggerated correctness displayed in their syntax, as if they were trying to master an official code, a discourse of power, from which they were still somewhat estranged. This was the source of O'Brien's rather hilarious usages, yet he seems also to have somewhat despised that very discourse in which he became so proficient.

He preferred, he said, the 'steely, latinistic quality' of Irish and its 'complete precision in the use of words'.[19]

All of which may help to explain why the versions of the Sweeny poetry, alone among the various styles reproduced in the work, remain exempt from O'Brien's corrosive parody. Even Finn MacCool is reduced to a butt of undergraduate comedy. The fustian in which he speaks is an exaggerated imitation of the Victorian translatorese into which Standish H. O'Grady put the stories of *Silva Gadelica*; and O'Brien, who clearly had his own problems in translating Irish into English, was merciless, recalling how the versatile hero was 'rummaging generous women, vibrating quick spears, and engaging in sapient dialectics with bag-eyed brehons'.[20] The gigantism of Finn's body ('Three fifties of fosterlings could engage with handball against the wideness of his backside')[21] owes much to similar passages in the 'Cyclops' chapter of *Ulysses*: and the humiliation of the hero, by making him a character in a debased, postmodern tale, might be seen as the *reductio ad absurdum* of that novelization of epic initiated in the modern period by Augusta Gregory. Gaelic scholars agree that O'Brien's concern was not with folklore but with literary texts, from *Fiannaíocht* to *Ulysses*, 'as a butt for his mockery and as a basis for his parody'.[22] The text bears them out, for its thrust is very much against the book as book: 'Who but a book-poet would dishonour the God-big Finn for the sake of a gap-worded story?'[23]

Many of the questions put to Finn are awkwardly obvious pre-texts for an already-composed poem. In that they have a lot in common with the riddles and puns shared by the undergraduates of UCD, whose conversation is a game in which occasions can be man-ufactured for the delivery of well-worn witticisms ('Your conclusion is based on licensed premises').[24] Some of these games are even reserved for the alert reader familiar with Hiberno-English ('Brinsley utilised an unclean expression in a random fashion and added that the weather was very bad, likening it, in fact, to a harlot' i.e. 'it's a hoor of a day').[25] But there is one kind of utterance for which the framing devices are supplied in no spirit of mischief and that is the poetic quatrains of Sweeny.

Most of these are literal translations, done with some help (per-haps) from the versions of J.G. O'Keeffe, but subjected to remarkably little revision or distortion. Although Niall Sheridan wrote off that portion of the book as 'dry filling',[26] O'Brien wanted to call the book *Sweeny in the Trees* and regarded it as central. His satires proceeded from the basis that there was one thing about which he could never feel satirical and that was Sweeny's nature poetry. The Middle Irish romance from which the poems were taken was really a loose, ill-fitted prose narrative retrospectively erected around the lyrics as a way of ordering and presenting them; in like manner the postmodern novel that is *At Swim-Two-Birds* might be seen as a pretext for the smuggling of these classic quatrains to the attention of the contemporary reader. This native tradition was 'the only source of inspiration that he acknowledged without qualification'.[27]

Some commentators have claimed that it attracted O'Brien because it was not just very beautiful but also quite useless for any modern purpose. But this is to overlook the sense of Sweeny's lyrics as striking a single, pure note amidst a cacophony of false sounds and broken intervals. In it a man of real experience is impelled to pure utterance from the depths of his being. By contrast, all that modern literature can offer is an account of various 'classes of persons' marooned in acts of specialist self-love. This is manifest in the narrator's inability to render other people as anything more than shadows on the fringe of his consciousness: a failure protested by Brinsley (himself unsatisfactorily depicted) who holds that 'true dialogue is dependent on the conflict rather than the confluence of minds'.[28] Yet Furriskey, Lamont and Shanahan have the makings of a plausible singular male . . . perhaps the author. He, however, is so self-obsessed that he can write only about a writing that takes on the quality of furtive, jeopardized masturbation. When the uncle comes to the bedroom door, 'hastily I covered such sheets as contained reference to the forbidden question of the sexual relations'.[29]

A specialist society, like a literature of specialists, turns out to be far more class-ridden than ever, for it is constructed around mutually exclusive categories and types. O'Brien believed that whereas once an entire community could gather round the Sweeny tale, now only drivel like 'A Pint of Plain' commands appeal in a mass culture. The more a modern culture subdivides its categories, the more it becomes a conspiracy against the truly individual. This is a world in which slaveys, 'the Ford cars of humanity', are 'created to a standard pattern by the hundred thousands'.[30] It is hard to imagine Joyce writing such a line. O'Brien remained, however, faithful to the spirit of Joyce's modernism: he attacked his immediate predecessor in the same spirit with which Joyce had mocked Flaubert and Zola. Like Joyce, he mingled many styles the better to mock the claim of any one to be definitive: but he included Joyce's own methods (catechism, mythic parallel, a portrait of a student-artist deflated by classmates) in the medley to be laughed at.[31]

The problem of language confronting an Irish author in English had not changed all that greatly since the time of Joyce. It might be summed up in the fact that all of O'Brien's debunkings of Joyce were parodies of a parody, since there was no definitively Joycean style. Educated English in Ireland really was 'educated', containing a sort of half-convinced imitation of polite English. When Gabriel Conroy in 'The Dead' says 'I'll engage they did,' he offers such an imitation: but when he says that his wife 'takes three mortal hours to dress herself', he is closer to the Hiberno-English of the folk.[32] Much of the trickery of Irish modernist authors is nothing more than the attempt to hit upon a viable expressive style: but each suffers from that tenuous selfhood that he discerns in his characters. O'Brien's Finn may sound somewhat Joycean in saying 'I am my own father and son,' but in the end he claims to be so many things that he is nothing, 'A hole in the wall.'[33] The exponent of the multiple self runs the risk of finally having none.

That authorial uncertainty is revealed in Dermot Trellis, who is easily usurped by his creations. The modern novel, says the narrator, 'should be a self-evident sham to which the reader could regulate at will the degree of his credulity'. Administered in private to solitary readers, it could in the wrong hands grow despotic: 'It was undemocratic to compel characters to be uniformly good or bad or poor or rich. Each should be allowed a private life, self-determination and a decent standard of living.'[34] In particular, it should be possible to change characters from one book to another, or from one plot to another (as here). The ideal novel would be largely a work of reference, made rather than written, perhaps even as a piece of technology. Ó Nualláin had told Niall Sheridan that the principles of the Industrial Revolution should be applied at last to literature, and a book made of various 'found' passages had a better chance of becoming a bestseller. ('That's not a plot,' Sheridan responded. 'It's a conspiracy.')[35]

One consequence of this literary democracy would be an end to overweening, omniscient authorship: in *At Swim-Two-Birds* Brinsley jokes that 'the plot has him well in hand'[36] – that is, the book is writing the narrator. Which was precisely the effect he had hoped in his theory to achieve:

> Most authors spend their time saying what has been said before – usually said much better. A wealth of references to existing works would acquaint the reader instantaneously with the nature of each character, would obviate tiresome explanations and would effectively preclude mountebanks, upstarts, thimbleriggers and persons of inferior education from an understanding of contemporary literature.[37]

That final sentence is a jibe at *The Waste Land*, but it is hardly a description of this book's method, which requires little more than a schoolboy's acquaintance with myth, cowboy tales and English literature. If Eliot's footnotes to his poem were critical of a world whose readers now needed such guidance, O'Brien seems rather to have manipulated disparate discourses so that they might fuse back together into a idiom characteristic of a pre-specialist world. His remedy is not to compensate for modern lack (like Eliot), but to exacerbate the mutual alienation of styles, until that can be resolved at a level (both postmodern and pre-literary) where the speeded-up circuits of an oral culture allow all people to know everything once again as parts of a shared culture. *The Conspectus of the Arts and Natural Sciences* (from which many extracts are printed verbatim) had attempted to achieve this synthesis in the Victorian period, but only in a multi-volume encyclopedia.

The democratic programme mapped out here is a protest not just against a narcissistic specialism but also against romantic glamorizations of the creative individual imagination, seen now by O'Brien as containing some seeds of modern tyranny. Three decades before Roland Barthes and Michel Foucault announced the death of the author, O'Brien had left this figure seriously wounded at the hands of his own creations. Even more radical was his suggestion that art might be largely a circuit of hatred and revenge, best broken. The punishment for the failure of understanding that allowed Dermot Trellis to create an original character is that the character soon gets out of control and undercuts Trellis's power. It is, after all, the invented characters rather than the recycled ones who initiate the rebellion.

Roland Barthes wrote in 'The Death of the Author': 'the text is a tissue of quotations drawn from the innumerable centres of culture . . . the author's only power is to mix his writings, to counter the ones with the others, in such a way as never to rest on any one of them'.[38] O'Brien does not go quite that far, although he might endorse Barthes's view that a masterpiece is now impossible, since only a lifeless but splendid language remains. O'Brien's understanding of Gaelic tradition provided a point of rest, a still centre in his ever-turning narratives. Hence, the title which refers to a world around the ancient monastery at Clonmacnoise, a place whose centre still held, a world whose inhabitants know the benefits of a Unity of Culture witnessed in the panoptic gaze of a flying Sweeny over Snámh-dá-én (Swim-Two-Birds):

. . . here the clerics were engaged at the observation of their

nones, flax was being beaten and here and there a woman was
giving birth to a child; and Sweeny did not stop until he recited
the full length of a further lay.[39]

Part of the power of this world is the anonymity of its creators, their
utter refusal to lay claim to personal merit in moments of making,
which are celebrations of communal tradition rather than outbursts
of individual talent. Real creation is taken to occur against a wider
natural backdrop of prayer, birthing and the production of crops
(rather than as a separate, specialist activity). And the reception of
Sweeny's artwork is possible to each and all who are active members
of that community. Far from using myth as an escape from the exile
of modernity, O'Brien combines the methods of myth and realism in
order to demonstrate the exile of Ireland from its own past.

By contrast, the uncertainty of the modern author, burdened with
romantic ideas of originality, is communicated like a virus to the
reader, who can never hope to locate in his or her personality a self
confident enough to choose a definite opening (from the three available). Yet the ultimate aim of this process is democratic: if multiple
possibilities opened by the book call for a new kind of protean
reader, they demand one who can finally stand by his or her interpretations. The wounding of the author will be the release of the
reader. Such a programme seeks to return to readers the kind of
interpretative freedom that might be expected under conditions of
liberal anarchism.

Ó Nualláin multiplied his own pseudonyms (Brother Barnabas,
Myles na gCopaleen, as well as Flann O'Brien) in order to confess to
a default in authorship. Conversely, in the novels of Jean-Paul Sartre
and Albert Camus, written at the same time as *At Swim-Two-Birds*,
such feelings of inauthenticity plagued only the characters in conventional narratives with a beginning, middle and end. It was the
honesty of O'Brien, as of Beckett and Brendan Behan, to show the
same uncertainty eating away at an earlier stage in the literary performance – at the very act of construction. What is offered in *At
Swim-Two-Birds* is an imitation of a novel by someone nervously
impersonating the role of author. From being a beautiful creation, literature becomes a partial birth; from being an art (whose maker's eye
was on the object), it becomes a performance (whose producer's eye
is on the audience). That eye is so trained because its owner is baffled
by a seemingly intractable variety of specializations, competing idi-
olects, fragmentation.

Confronted with such an uncertain situation, the writer is often
less anxious to say something new than to find a self that is capable

of saying anything at all. Some postmodern writers have appeared in their own works, as if in poignant demonstration of the very fact that they exist. O'Brien is too fastidious for such direct interventions, but his narrator does engage in nervous discussion of his work-in-progress with Brinsley and others, as if to verify contact with a real audience. Yet even in confessing itself a sham, the tale repeats the bad conscience of that Cretan who said 'all Cretans are liars'. The real world would offer not three openings, but many, many more. Exposing the deception, the show trial of Dermot Trellis as novelist actually compounds it. This may be unavoidable: for in the contemporary world the same audience will demand both fantasy and realism. It will seek to indulge its credulity while also reserving the right to eternal scepticism.[40]

Irish writers encountered that challenge earlier than most. Inheriting storytelling gifts in an age when all notions of fiction came under beady scrutiny, they had to find a mode of existence both for the gift and for the growing scepticism about it. Their predicament was like that of an old Galway woman who, when asked whether she believed in fairies, replied: 'I do not, sir – but they're there anyway.' The more each story in *At Swim-Two-Birds* is interrupted, dismissed or discredited, the deeper still runs the human desire for a viable narrative. O'Brien's audience can both enjoy the tales and be spared the vulgar charge of believing them.

It is a postmodern truism that if Chartres cathedral were to be rebuilt, this could only be an ironic performance, employing the pleasures of anachronism to throw into relief the cultural conventions of each succeeding age. That is the method pursued, with seriousness, by Flann O'Brien. It may be undercut by constant 'belly-laughs', as he conceded to Mannin, but something of it survives such mockery. The nostalgia is not so much for a modernist world in which art was given the duty of saving human souls, but for a much older Gaelic world in which artists took their appointed place at the centre rather than the edge of society. Even in nineteenth-century England, artists were still influential – Dickens worked as a political reporter and his writings led to social legislation, while Disraeli managed to combine a career as novelist with that of prime minister. It was only with the increasing specialization of roles that artists found themselves on the periphery, grouped in bohemian coteries, pursuing an art for art's sake, in such suburbs as Greenwich Village, Montparnasse or the Catacombs in Dublin. In their assaults on earlier art, they began to thumb their noses at a bourgeoisie that was often too philistine even to notice the gesture of revolt. When their cult of obscenity or obscurity failed to attract attention, they sometimes began to thumb their noses at one another. Hence Joyce's war on realism, and O'Brien's parodies of Joyce. Reverence was reserved for ancient art: Joyce's for Homer, O'Brien's for *Buile Shuibhne* (The Rage of Sweeny).

Art did not save mankind from the torments of World War One, and by the 1920s it was growing more relaxed in its claims, in keeping with the new effort-to-be-trivial mood. *At Swim-Two-Birds* could be read as an attempt to complete the liquidation of those humanist principles that still attached to literature in the period of high modernism. The stable ego is now thoroughly discredited, and so art can revert to mere 'performance', a probing into all those things a self might be. This would explain the rather adolescent quality of O'Brien's book, much criticized in the initial review in the *Times Literary Supplement*.[41] One of his tactics in this long war on modernism is to expose the exorbitance of the claims made for a specialist literature. Rather than prevent the exposure of art to the corrosions of popular culture, O'Brien followed Joyce in taking this confrontation as a given fact of contemporary experience.[42] Enter the Ringsend cowboys and Booterstown Bard, but also the Conspectus and racing tipster.

The resulting multiplicity of styles is itself an effect of the dissemination of higher education and of information through the mass media. When the fustian of Standish H. O'Grady competes in the bookshops with the cowboy romances of William Tracy, the illicit couplings made possible by the market cry out for new literary forms. *At Swim-Two-Birds* struggles to supply such a form, to catch up with the social process of a consumer culture: yet it also recognizes that the process, far from honouring tradition, cannibalizes it as an enemy of economic development. The university world is a reflection of these brutal realities. In it also each style is consumed by the next approved technique. Hence O'Brien in his handling of Gaelic material protests not only against its neglect by popular culture but also against its assimilation to the institutes of higher learning.

In the Ireland of the 1930s perhaps the most popular of all literary forms was the Wild West novel. It never fell foul of the Censorship Board and examples were read by remarkably wide sections of the community: even W.B. Yeats found these stories relaxing and, according to his wife, would often shout in his sleep, 'Don't shoot the sheriff! Don't shoot the sheriff!'[43] These books were glamorized by repeated Hollywood treatments, and since the Irish had the greatest number of cinema seats per thousand of any people in Europe, that meant something.[44] But there were more locally rooted explanations for that popularity. The Wild West tales ratified an essentially rural set of values, then under dire stress in an Ireland where families were being broken up by enforced emigration. The myth of the man alone against the system would have spoken to bachelor males in communities where women had long left for life in the cities. The war of independence was still a vivid memory for many: and the warrior experience of solitude in the countryside linked many westerns not just to the Gaelic lore of Finn and Sweeny but to the world of lonely comrades evoked in a 1930s bestseller, Ernie O'Malley's *On Another Man's Wound*.

For those men who now had family cares and financial worries, cowboy tales offered the fantasy of escape. That the actual life of American cowboys had been harsh, short and riddled with illness was a truth confronted more often in the books than in the films, but it was a truth with which many rural Irishmen could identify. The improvisations of life in a frontier society offered an interesting additional perspective on the world of *Fiannaíocht* and must have had a powerful appeal over those who were unable to adjust to the structures of the new state. So durable was it that it resurfaced again in the vogue for country-and-western music of the 1970s, as well as in the fondness for giving farmhouses a 'ranch' look with Texan-style driveways. The rugged individualist who could buck the system of official extortion (otherwise known as taxation) had strong appeal across a rural society where masses were still said by local priests in memory of the outlaw Jesse James.[45]

At Swim-Two-Birds picks up on much of this. The narrator and his friends are always 'boys'; their encounters with women are fleeting and rudimentary; and their long walks through Ringsend and Irishtown indicate a cowboy restlessness. Most fascinating of all is the *rus in urbe* motif, O'Brien's location of cowboys in an incongruously urban setting. Dublin 1930s was a city still dominated by a rural ethos. Cattle were routinely herded across O'Connell Bridge down to the docks for export; and a great number of civil servants, teachers, nurses and policemen who ran the city's affairs were migrants from the countryside. They brought with them many of the cultural values of their parents, with the result that Dublin felt less like a streamlined modern capital than like a collection of discrete villages, each with its own accent, personality and appearance.

Perhaps this was why Joyce had dubbed Dublin 'the last of the intimate cities'.[46] It would certainly explain the addiction of three very different Dublin writers – Joyce, Beckett and O'Brien – to an experimental narrative composed largely of micro-stories. If the city was really a stringing-together of villages, like beads along the necklace of Dublin Bay, their 'experimental novels' were – as has been shown in the case of *Ulysses* – disguised collections of short stories in the drag of a revolutionary narrative. The issue is raised during an energetic debate about Sergeant Craddock, who beat the champion jumper of Ireland. 'With all his faults and by God he has plenty', observes Shanahan sagely, 'the Irishman can jump. By God he can jump.'[47] The theory was widespread in the 1930s, following international success at jump and hammer-throw, that Irish people excelled in sports that called for short, sharp effort rather than prolonged discipline. This was a sporting inflection of the old Arnoldian notion that Irish artists excelled at brief lyric outbursts but not 'in the steady deep-searching survey'.[48] If Yeats's answer to such typecasting was the lyric sequence of *The Tower*, Joyce, Beckett and O'Brien came up with their own prose version, which assembled in a complex alignment a set of shorter tales and anecdotes. The very geography of Dublin, with its fiercely independent villages and suburbs, may have provided a template.

O'Brien's cowboys, Shorty Andrews and Slug Willard, are identified with Ringsend, a working-class suburb just south of the city centre along Dublin Bay. The hilarious incongruity of these persons and that place is exploited to the full in Shanahan's reminiscences of the 'rare life in Dublin in the old days', when men were men and knew how to threaten one another in words taken mostly from the movies:

> ——Come across, Kiersey, says I, come across with our steers and our black girls or down I go straight to Lad Lane and get the police up. Keep your hands up or I'll paste your guts on that tree.[49]

In court shortly after, 'the accused were described by superintendent Clohessy as a gang of corner boys whose horseplay in the streets was the curse of the Ringsend district'.[50] The strong implication is that a group of footloose UCD students have been terrorizing elderly villagers. References to the students repeatedly emphasize bouts of horseplay, assaults on unsuspecting women, mockery of working-class speech, and wild oath-taking – as if there were no more natural outlet for the energies of youth.[51]

Had those youths been born twenty years earlier, they might have found an alternative expression of their vitality on the streets of Dublin that witnessed the Easter Rebellion. Throughout *At Swim-Two-Birds* one has the sense of a post-heroic society: a people who had once asserted revolution or death now has to cope with the death of the revolution. The flying columns of the young have turned into sedate committees of the safe middle-aged, earnestly discussing whether the waltz is an unIrish dance form. The narrator's uncle, chairing the committee, insists that only points of order can be raised and that those who raise them must address the chair. All speak to one another as 'Mr', with the exaggerated deference of lower-middle-class shop assistants in a work by H.G. Wells. The search for a free Ireland has declined into a desire for such respectability. The compulsion to form committees was a feature of national life in the 1930s (and even *At Swim Two-Birds* might be read as a novel written by a committee).

All this was part of the bureaucratization of Irish life, a sort of half-conscious mimicry of civil service modes: but it was also a logical response to the experience of Civil War. Independence from Britain might lead some to seek independence from government itself, and then maybe from the very neighbours in the street. One response was committees to fill the social vacuum left by the fall of feudalism and the loss of many young people to the emigrant ship. One still jaunty member of the uncle's committee, Mr Connors, laughs out loud at a Mr Hickey who denounces waltzing and assures him that once he waltzed:

> When did I dance it? asked Mr Hickey.
> *Description of Mr Hickey*: Old, yellow, dark, lean. Pendulous flesh at eyes and jaws. Of utterance precise and slow. A watching listener.
> On a Point of Personal Explanation? asked my uncle.
> Yes, said Mr Hickey.
> Very well.
> Twenty-three years ago at the Rotunda gardens, said Mr Connors. Haven't I a good memory?
> You certainly have, said Mr Hickey.[52]

Twenty-three years earlier would have been 1916; and the Rotunda gardens was the place in which the republican insurgents were rounded up by the British enemies before being marched off to prison.

Much of the writing of the later 1930s – especially that done in Irish – laments the decay of the old revolutionary fervour into a world of paper-clips, memoranda and routine. In *Mo Bhealach Féin* (My Own Way, 1940) Seosamh Mac Grianna reports that even the Irish Republican Army has been reduced to bureaucratic activity and he castigates the torpor of those Gaels who have settled into tame domesticity, 'nár bhain agus nár chaill' (those who did not reap and did not lose out).[53] The ill-conceived IRA bombing campaign in English cities during 1939 was probably a desperate riposte to that tame new world of school examinations, language revival policies and campaigns against immodest language and literature, a world of 'terror without guns'. The gap between the banal, bereft real and the utopian ideal was by now massive, as great as that between the brutal facts and unreal dreams lamented a generation earlier by Shaw. The wine of the founders had evaporated, leaving only sediment at the base of the glass.

O'Brien himself was in the strictest sense a Free State author, disabled by that very culture that had nurtured him, yet strangely addicted to many of its practices. He was one of those law-abiding bourgeois souls who actually paid his rates in advance, and whose journalism was motivated by a concern that ratepayers get value for their pound;[54] but he consorted with the city's bohemian set in bars before slipping away to catch the bus home to Blackrock.[55] If the cultural debates of the time pitted Irish-speaking suburban inheritors of the national culture against the roaring dissidence of a Patrick Kavanagh, O'Brien found himself on the cusp between the two groups. The intellectual stasis of the civil servants was replicated in his art as surely as the formal energies of the bohemians. His own gift as a writer was to heal the breach by making the familiar seem wonderful, by releasing those exotic qualities that always lie dormant in the ordinary (a trick also done by the absurdists). Like the Irish intelligentsia of the period, he was unsure whether the artist should be a dissident anarchist or a Tory upholder of the establishment – so he became both.

His obsession with Tomás Ó Criomhthain's *An tOileánach* (The Islandman) was based on the fact that it came from a culture in which quotidian detail and formal exactitude could still be conjoined in a single style. Like *Ulysses*, it was an abiding influence.[56] The two books could scarcely have been more different, yet both took the quotidian as a unit to be celebrated and achieved a kind of poetry by the precision with which they rendered everyday things. O'Brien read *An tOileánach* on publication and was overwhelmed; as with Joyce, homage took the form of ferocious parody (in *An Béal Bocht*, The Poor Mouth). This was another case of belatedness, of being 'found' by earlier works, which seem at once to enlarge and constrict possibilities. And he took the parodist's revenge, converting the predecessor into an *ur*-version of himself.

That kind of subversion of the major achievements of the recent past was by then the strongest of all formulae in Irish writing: a means of marking off the hypermodernity of the present moment.

There is always a risk in that manoeuvre – the danger that, when all previous styles and authors have been unmasked, what remains will be only a levelling and pervasive scepticism about everything, tantamount to nihilism. What saved O'Brien from lapsing into postmodern nihilism was not his Catholicism which held that the world was a doomed and hopeless place,[57] but his respect for the prose of *An tOileánach* or the poetry of *Buile Shuibhne*, where language still did its appointed work.

Much of the book mocks the obsession with pensionable jobs and with the examination system that alone led to such plum appointments. The narrator and his uncle are, after all, reconciled at the end when by passing his exams he gains a place in the new state elite; and once this is done the uncle is no longer described as mean-spirited but as well-intentioned. At that moment also, the fiction which has been constructed on anger and satire simply consumes itself. O'Brien is, of course, never more satirical than at this phase: for he knows that literature itself has been co-opted into a system of rote learning for public examinations and that books are read less for their vision than as a necessary source of knowledge with which to face the examiners. A literature that once helped to shape a nation has been degraded to a device for the mere passing of tests.

No wonder that literary activities can seem 'spare-time' in a land where every other person seems to hold more than one job, each one worked for less than a full day under the gentleman-amateur dispensation. O'Brien may not have regretted this: after all, he combined the career of writer and civil servant for many years as his own protest against specialism. Most of the characters in *At Swim-Two-Birds* distrust excessive work: when Furriskey talks of taking up the violin, he is warned that that 'would mean practice' and 'practice means work'.[58] Work always runs the risk of turning a man into a specialist. On the other hand, the participants at Trellis's show trial manage to perform as judge, jury and witnesses in a fine rebuttal of professional decorum: and the guru to Dublin youth, Michael Byrne, is as versatile as Finn, being painter, poet, composer, pianist, printer, tactician and a student of ballistics. He redeems the old libel on Irish indolence by assigning it altogether more positive explanations: if the real life is the life of dream and imagination, then we should not sleep to recover energies lost in waking work but rather awaken on rare occasions to expel 'the unwanted energy that sleep engenders'.[59] Again, the thinking is Wildean.

Such an aesthetic informs the 'dream-work' of the book, placing a low premium on felt, waking experience. The shifting of narrative planes makes a virtue of the modern reader's inability to concentrate for long on any one, but it is itself a recognition that the pressure of actual experience hardly lies behind these stories at all. This is a comment on a land where all jokes are carefully vetted for cleanliness before they can be told. It was of those who did such things that Seán Ó Faoláin used the term 'apple-lickers', meaning persons who, if tempted in the garden of Eden, would have licked rather than bitten the apple. But that sort of prudishness was hardly confined to Ireland in the 1930s: the British recoil from the 'vulgarity' of *Ulysses* in the previous decade would be repeated by the London reviewers of *At Swim-Two-Birds*. (The Welshman Dylan Thomas loved it, but in ways that simply confirmed that prejudice: 'Just the book to give your sister, if she is a loud, dirty, boozy girl.')[60]

Far from being overshadowed by Joyce's work, *At Swim-Two-Birds* may have been a victim of Joyce's reputation, with his linkage to vulgarity working against his successor. 'Keep the fun clean' was a widespread motto in a decade of social idealism, which saw many novelists produce stylized accounts of proletarian virtue. That tradition is mocked to nothingness in the portrayal of Jem Casey, the poet of the pick, 'saying nothing to nobody but working away at a poem in his head with a pick in his hand and the sweat pouring down off his face'.[61] The cliché-touch is flawless, so deadly that Sean O'Casey may not have noticed the jibes at his own rhetoric:

> *In time of trouble and lousy strife,*
> *You have still got a darlint plan,*
> *You still can turn to a brighter life –*
> A PINT OF PLAIN IS YOUR ONLY MAN.

The monotonous, self-righteous sponsor of this tosh, Shanahan, has developed a matching aesthetic, which may be O'Brien's epitaph on the political novel of the 1930s: 'You have to remember the man in the street . . . Oh, by God you have to go very slow if you want *him* to follow you. A snail would be too fast for him.'[63]

At the other end of the spectrum is the snobbish Good Fairy, who is revolted by Casey's tendency to urinate in public ('it speaks very poorly for their home life').[64] The Good Fairy accuses the workers of crippling the country with strikes before crippling a card game with his own stinginess. The gap between the snob and the prole is filled by the other characters, who display a dread of immodest language. When Dermot Trellis, under threat of death, calls his assailant a black bastard, the Pooka laments such inharmonious colloquy which 'makes for barriers between the classes'.[65]

If some speak in Victorian fustian, others use a language which is almost a literal translation from the Irish: 'the first man in Ireland at the long jump in the time that's gone'.[66] English may be, as jumping Sergeant Craddock insists, the language of modern Ireland, but it is an English of a very peculiar kind. All of it is in some sense 'translated'. Some of it is really the work of minds still thinking in Irish, while using English words – the blatant example is the book's title, so literally rendered as to seem meaningless to English ears. This is the native Irish speaker's revenge on *Béarlachas*, that brand of Irish spoken and written by school students and administrators, in which the user thinks in English while using Irish words. Sean O'Casey was right to praise Ó Nualláin in a letter for recognizing in Irish 'that unknown quantity in us which enables us to transform the English language',[67] but he might have added that Irish itself could be similarly remoulded by English.

The civil service *Gaeilge Chaighdeánach* (Standard Irish) which had already taken hold as the official idiom of the state class, bore scant relation to any living dialect: but it produced in time an equivalent administrative English. Ó Nualláin was well aware that this was to be found in the 1937 Constitution, which proclaimed Irish the first official language (against all the evidence) but which had been devised in English. He pointed out that this meant that the English source would be prevailed over in the event of its having been mistranslated. The whole country was becoming addicted to officialese:[68] and even those who despised it voiced their scorn in endless conversational imitations of it. World War Two rapidly became known as 'the Emergency', a word that proved that the Irish could rival the ancient English gift for understatement any day of the week.

In later years a somewhat paranoid O'Nualláin liked to speculate that Hitler had started a war in order to torpedo the sales of his remarkable book. It required no fascist dictator, however, to slow its progress. Its immensely complicated structure was just too much for readers: and it sold just two hundred and fifty copies in its first year. Thirty years later, on its republication in the postmodern 1960s, it achieved global success as a cult classic. By then Ó Nualláin was dead, having departed this world (appropriately enough) on 1 April 1966. In later years he was (like one of his characters) 'a terrible man for the blankets'[69] and might not have appreciated that all too symbolic date: but his misfortune was, as Lenin said of the Easter rebels, that he rose too soon. He was an experimentalist who was way ahead of his time: only after his death did his readers learn how to become his contemporaries.

29

The Blasket
Autobiographies

The tiny islands off the west coast of Ireland fascinated writers and artists. For some, like W.B. Yeats, they epitomized pride, solitude and a sense of estrangement. For others, such as Synge, they provided the example of a commune, in which life was reduced to its fundamentals – mankind pitted against nature. Being isolated, they had not been greatly affected by Victorian culture or by the Catholic devotional revival of the nineteenth century. People still presented themselves to one another in their essential outline, and their language had a corresponding economy, with every clause and rhythm indicating a reality that underlay the words and seemed to proclaim itself through them. Some outside commentators – most especially Synge – felt drawn to the pre-Christian character of island life, as if hoping to find in it a common bedrock of Irish culture, before the sectarian splits of more recent centuries. There is certainly a stoic quality to much of the island philosophy: a sense that there is no point in grieving excessively for those who have died, because such grief can never feed the living. Intense sorrow is understandable, of course, but it may be seen if taken too far as a form of *hubris*, a sin against *toil Dé* (the will of God), and as such a form of sentimentality, because it may invest earthly things with more significance than the eternal powers would give to them.

The centuries-old life of the Blasket islands was already clearly doomed to pass away when Tomás Ó Criomhthain published *An tOileánach* (The Islandman) in 1929: but over the next seven years that culture achieved an extraordinary concentration of utterance in the subsequent autobiographies of Muiris Ó Súilleabháin and Peig Sayers. In each book, something of the tradition survived the lament for its passing; and the template that had been laid down by Synge in *The Aran Islands* was now seized by islanders themselves. In the act of making it their own, they provided a wholly new set of impulses which would animate subsequent Irish writing from the raucous parody of *An Béal Bocht* (The Poor Mouth, 1941) to the austere lyricism of *Amongst Women* (1990). All were, in that sense, examples of the energizing effect of a real homage to past culture: for in each text a deep humility before that tradition is accompanied by an invincible pride, and both characteristics shine through the pages. The islanders are scarcely part of the literate world, yet they speak a kind of elegant poetry. They live in a sort of socialist commune, where all share a common danger and poverty, yet they bear themselves with the beautiful reserve and considered manners of real aristocrats. They are the ultimate in radical traditionalism. The 'king' of the Blaskets is always elected.

Tomás Ó Criomhthain had learned how to read and write English at the island school in the 1860s, but, like almost all Gaeltacht people of the time, he remained illiterate in Irish. He only began to learn how to read and write Irish when he was convinced by visiting scholars – whom he was chosen by the king of the island to instruct in Irish – that a book of his experiences would be a thing of value in the world. By then, he was well over forty. The king had reasoned well, for he sensed that Ó Criomhthain's rich oral Irish could never be constricted or corrupted by the written protocols of the language: its bases were too securely laid by then. Ó Criomhthain possessed a wide vocabulary, but he was always restrained and exact in his choice of words.

His first student was a linguist named Carl Marstrander, a polevault champion from Norway who demonstrated his athletic prowess to the islanders (who had never heard of that particular skill) by using the oar of a *naomhóg* (coracle) to launch himself right over Ó Criomhthain's house. Another student was Robin Flower, an Englishman who worked in the British Museum.[1] The obvious reverence shown by both for the lore of the Blaskets helped to convince Ó Criomhthain that he should record that life. A schools inspector from Killarney named Brian Ó Ceallaigh had the bright idea of presenting him with a copy of the same book that had once intrigued Synge, Pierre Loti's *Pêcheur d'Islande* (1886). The story he eventually told would show just how accurate and honest Synge's impressions had been: it had the added advantage of coming from one of the people themselves, from within the communal experience.

An tOileánach begins in the 1860s and it ends in the 1920s. The world it evokes is almost medieval. The Kerry Gaeltacht was a two-day carriage-ride from Dublin and the islands were often inaccessible by sea. Daily life was inherently poetic: there were prayers by morning and night; work songs and proverbs to fill the hours of light; stories with verses and long narrative poems in the evenings as well as personal recollections by the fireside. Those who used words with terseness and wit were greatly admired: and the people loved to fasten on any new or remarkable image for description. The contrast between the material poverty of the islanders and the verbal richness of their tales could not have been greater: even their conversation – the chief entertainment on the Blaskets – was treated as an art form. This was a culture therefore which seemed to 'turn deprivation to positive advantage and to make limitations an enhancement of freedom'.[2]

Most of the tales that were learned by Tomás Ó Criomhthain had been given oral narration for centuries before they were written down: to that extent they were like those of Homer, not least in that terse understated and concrete idiom which seemed always to tremble on the brink of poetry. This was the view taken by two classicists, J.V. Luce and George Thomson, the latter of whom wrote:

> Gan amhras ní filíocht atá sna leabhra ná prós – ach tá prós na scéalaíochta Gaeilge an-ghairid don bhfilíocht. Tá píosaí sna leabhra seo agus ní mór ná go bhféadfá dánta a ghlaoch orthu, tá siad chomh fileata san.[3]

> Undoubtedly, what is in the books is neither poetry nor prose – but the prose of Gaelic storytelling is very close to poetry. There are passages in the books which you might almost describe as poetry because they are so lyrical.

The early passages of the autobiography, much influenced by Maxim Gorky's, present not just the writer's childhood memories, but the very way in which he recollected them – random, associative, even a little haphazard. Nevertheless, as the narrative progresses, a clearer outline is achieved, even as the associative method is developed and a fine metaphor grows out of a seemingly casual image. Ó Criomhthain is describing the youthful eating of an apple:

> Níor mhór an faraireacht a dheineas istigh nó go raibh m'úll meilte agam. Do bhí an muileann meilte go maith agam an uair úd, rud ná fuil inniu agam le rá leis.[4]

My work inside wasn't great until I had ground the apple. I had a good grinding mill in those days, something that I can't say of it today.

Like Synge's Araners, the islanders are caught between the moods of romantic love and the harsh necessities of subsistence farming: and Ó Criomhthain becomes a victim of their irreconcilibility. On a visit to Inis Icealáin with his uncle Diarmuid, he is supposed to be hunting rabbits but has gone there in reality to court a local woman with whom he is deeply in love. He walks out from a party with her into the stillness of the night. For that he is gently teased by the uncle (who is none the less a great advocate of the match). But the writer's family have other ideas: it is more practical for him to marry a woman from his own place, whose people might be of help in time of difficulty. So Tomás marries the local woman, much against his own inclinations. At the wedding feast this man (who usually never stopped singing) offers the company just one song, 'Caisleán Uí Néill' (O'Neill's Castle). This breaks register with the festive occasion, since it tells of a girl's hopeless love;

Mo shlán chun na hoíche aréir, is mo léan nach anocht atá
    ann,
Mo bhuachaillín séimh deas a bhréagfadh mé seal ar a
    ghlún:
Dá neosfainn mo scéal duit is baolach ná déanfa orm rún,
Go bhfuil mo ghrá bán dom thréigean, as a Dhia ghléigil
    as a Mhuire nach dubhach?[5]

My farewell to last night, and my pity it isn't tonight,
When my gentle fine boy would sweet-talk me on his knee:
If I told you my story, there's danger you wouldn't keep the
    secret on me,
That my fair-headed love is abandoning me, and o bright
    God and Mary, isn't that bleak?

There is no real description of the development of the marriage: perhaps this is the author's quiet protest at the system of made matches. Instead, he loses children to the cliffs, the whooping cough, the sea and even to America; and these deprivations are chronicled in rapid succession in a simple but amazing style:

Do saoluigheadh deichniúr clainne dhúinn ach níor lean an rath iad san, go bhfóiridh Dia orainn. An chéad duine riamh a

baisteadh liom bhí sé a seacht nó a hocht de bhlianaibh nuair a
thuit sé le faill agus marbhuigheadh é. As san amach níor
thapúla duine orainn ná dínn. D'imigh beirt leis an mbruitínigh
agus ní raibh galar d'á dtagadh ná beireadh duine éigin uaim.
Bádh Domhnaill d'iarraidh an bhean-uasal a thabhairt slán leis
ar an dTráigh Bhán. Do bhí buachaill breagh eile agam, ag
tarrac chugam. Ní ró-fhada a bhí an t-am gur tógadh uaim é.

Do ghoill buairt na nithe sin go léir ar an máthair bhoicht
agus tógadh uaim í. Ní rabhas dall ar fad go dtí san. Nár dhal-
laidh Dia sinn. Bhí naoidhneán beag i n-a dhiaidh – ach go
raibh cailín beag fásta suas a thug aire di – ní raibh sí ach fásta
suas san am gur glaodhadh uirthi chomh maith leo. An cailín a
thóg í sin do phós sí sa Dún Mór. Cailleadh í sin, leis, agus
d'fhág seisear leanbh i n-a diaidh. Buachaill amháin atá fanta
faram annso sa bhaile. Buachaill eile i Meirice. Sin é crích
d'imigh ar mo chlainn-se. Beannacht Dé leo – a bhfuil san uaigh
aca – agus leis an mnaoi bhoicht gur bhris a misneach d'á
ndeascaibh.[6]

Ten were born to us and they were not followed by any luck,
may God protect us. The first of mine to be baptized was seven
or eight years old when he fell down a cliff and was killed. After
that we no sooner had one than we lost one. Two died of the
whooping cough and there was no illness to come that didn't
take someone from me. Donal was drowned attempting to save
the life of a lady off the White Strand. I had another fine boy,
assisting me. It was not too long before he was taken from me.

The sorrow of all those things oppressed the poor mother
and she was taken from me. I wasn't blind completely until
then. May God never blind us. There was a little infant left after
her – only that there was a grown girl to take care of her – but
she was only grown herself at the time that she was called away
as well. The girl who reared her married in Dunmore. She also
died and left six children after her. One boy alone is left here at
home. Another boy in America. That is the end that came to my
own family. The blessing of God with them – those who are in
the grave – and with the poor woman whose courage broke for
their sake.

The choice of words is as careful and deliberated as ever. Nóra ní
Chatháin is remembered not as 'mo bhean chéile' (my wife) but 'an
máthair bocht' (the poor mother): and the rejection of the possessive
in favour of the article speaks volumes. So does the characterization

of the woman as a mother rather than a wife: the women of the island, perhaps as a result of the made matches, seem more interested in their children than in their husbands. This was exactly the situation Synge had found on the Aran islands, where the sexual instincts, though strong, were subordinated to the demands of family life, and where the maternal feeling, because it was so powerful, gave a life of torture to many women who reared their children only to lose them later to the sea or to the emigrant ship. The quiet understatement of the whole passage implies a great deal that is clearly being left unsaid. This is a stunning instance of that necessary separation which T.S. Eliot praised in all stoic literature between the man who suffers and the mind which creates.[7]

In Synge's *Riders to the Sea* the closing lines of Old Maurya, who has lost all her men to the ocean, have the same gravely reticent dignity: and in truth there are points of real contact between the two passages:

> I've had a husband, and a husband's father, and six sons in this house . . . and some of them were found and some of them were not found, but they're gone now the lot of them . . . There was Sheamus and his father, and his own father again, were lost in a dark night . . . There was Patch after was drowned out of a curagh that turned over . . . They're all together this time and the end is come. May the Almighty God have mercy on Bartley's soul, and on Michael's soul . . . and may he have mercy on my soul, Nora, and on the soul of every one is left living in the world . . . Michael has a clean burial in the far north by the grace of the Almighty God. Bartley will have a fine coffin out of the white boards, and a deep grave surely . . . What more can we want than that? No man at all can be living for ever and we must be satisfied.[8]

There is, however, one fundamental difference between the handling of the material. Synge's speech is placed at the climactic, conclusive moments of a taut one-act play, whereas Ó Criomhthain offers this rapid flash-forward in a central chapter of his book, removing in a single gesture most of the suspense and uncertainty from later chapters.

Why did he do this? One explanation might be found in his desire to enforce a note of fatalism in the second half of the book, as if its characters (rather like the fishermen who so moved Synge) are felt to be living under sentence of death. A more practical reason might be found in Ó Criomhthain's determination to divide up his narrative into separate thematic units, taken chapter by chapter. This is the chapter that deals with family tragedy: others deal with such matters as houses, work, games and pastimes, marriage and so on. The effect is to make *An tOileánach* appear, at least in its structure, to be a little like an anthropological textbook, albeit one written for an audience of secondary schoolchildren, imagined by the author as reading perhaps a chapter in each school week. Whatever the reason for this telescoping of a whole plethora of tragedies into two quiet paragraphs, the style of writing is of a piece with the mood of acceptance that informs the author's other chapters. There is little analysis of motive or psychology in *An tOileánach*: things just happen, as if under *geasa* in some hero tale, and the better part of wisdom is to live as gracefully as one can with an imperfect world rather than submit to the inexcusable vanity of seeking to challenge fate.

One of the great set pieces in Ó Criomhthain's book is his account of the day when the police came looking for rents and taxes. The lore of the islands was filled through much of the later nineteenth century with accounts of how such absurd intrusions by the ever-growing state institutions had been outwitted. Synge, for example, was told on Aran of how all the dogs of one island obligingly hid themselves away in a cave for a day so that their owners would not have to part with the licence fee; similar tales were told on the Blaskets. There is evidence of a good deal of unashamed Homeric boasting in such accounts. In a more sober description offered to a collector in *Seanchas ón Oileán Thiar* (Old Stories from the West Island), Ó Criomhthain talks of how the police came to the island, but were accompanied by landlords who, confronted with the dire poverty all around them, declared that it would be shameful to extract rents from so destitute a people. *An tOileánach* gives a rather different account, of how the island women rained down a hail of stones and rocks to prevent the search party from landing.[9] The climax of the anecdote is reached when the police appear just about to land successfully on the cove, as the women run out of available stones. All that one woman can find on the ground nearby is her own infant child:

'Mo chroidhe 'on diabhal go gcaithfead an leanbh leo,' ar sise.
'Dhera, 'dhiabhail óinsighe,' arsan bhean ba ghiorra dhi, 'ná téire as do mheabhair agus coimeád do leanbh.'
Thug sí rúideog faoin leanbh a chaitheamh ach do ghreamuigh an bhean eile é. Níor thúisce sin nó bhí bean ó'n dtaobh eile tagaithe agus bloc de scraithín caithte síos aici agus an bheirt thíos casta le fánaidh. Tá an leanbh úd a bhí le caitheamh leo thall i Meirice go lán láidir fós.[10]

'My heart to the devil but I'll throw my child on them,' she said.

'Yerra, you devilish idiot,' said the woman nearest her. 'Don't go out of your mind and keep your child.'

She swung the child to throw it but the other woman grabbed it. No sooner was that done than a woman from the other side had come and thrown a piece of sod that knocked them both down the hillock. That child who was to be thrown is over in America still, full and well.

This flash-forward technique is often used by Ó Criomhthain, for purposes of light, mocking humour. By nature a little aloof, he seems anxious to deflate all persons and situations that threaten to grow over-intense. Early passages in the book delight to recall how the youth whom he once elbowed in the ribs is now the king of the island. The technique can be seen as reasserting time's capacity to heal all wounds, but it runs the risk already noted of removing the suspense from an otherwise gripping story. Once we know that the child wasn't thrown and survived the incident, the tale of the rent collectors is effectively over.

The separation effected in Ó Criomhthainn's sensibility between the person who suffered and the mind which created seems to have been shared generally by the islanders, who were perfectly capable of praising a witty, astringent line even when they were the target of its attack. Speaking to a middle-aged woman named Síle, as she works in her kitchen on some fine-flavoured potatoes, he says:

'Ó tá do bhláth féin sleamhnaithe uait, nach mór an ní dhuit é a beith ar do phrátaí?'[11]

'Since your bloom has slid from you, isn't it a great thing that it's on your potatoes?'

– and the woman is delighted by the imaginative, audacious beauty of the conceit. Ó Criomhthain has the same capacity to detach himself suddenly from the flow of a felt experience in order to submit it to a cool, artistic appraisal, even as he narrates it. His humour is sceptical and implies a recognition that it is wise to reserve all final judgements, as a consequence of which he is sought out in the role of confidant by many neighbours who are keen to have the good opinion of a man known for his considered assessments.

Of nobody is this more true than the poet Seán Ó Duinnshléibhe, who comes to pester the author with a request to listen to some of his

songs. Ó Criomhthain has gone to the bog to harvest turf, but the
poet suggests that the noon of day is too warm for such work, which
is better done in the evenings. The author knows from personal
experience that manual labour and poetic aspiration rarely conspire
and, though he is reluctant to abandon his task, he does so. This is
not just done out of politeness, but from a very real fear that, if his
offer is spurned, the poet has the power to pen a vicious satire on
him which might raise blisters on the face:

> Ní rabhas ró-bhuidheach d'á chomhrádh ach gur bhuail náire
> mé gan suidhe 'n-a theannta. Rud eile, thuigeas, mara mbeadh
> an file buidheach díom, go ndéanfadh sé aor orm ná beadh ar
> fónamh agus mé i mbéal mo thugtha amach san am sin.[12]

> I wasn't too grateful for his conversation but I would have been
> shamed not to sit in his presence. Also, I understood that if he
> was ungrateful to me, he could make a satire on me that would
> be damaging and I about to strike out on my own at that time.

The result is that no work at all is done: Ó Criomhthain takes out
pencil and paper which, very mysteriously, he happens to have in his
pocket during an expedition to the bog. With these he takes down
the poet's song. Otherwise, they both understand, that song would
have died.

Yet the price of such artistic permanence is, in human terms, very
high. From that day forth, Ó Criomhthain begins to feel that the
practical affairs of the world go against him:

> Dhá ualach sean-asail de mhóin níor thuit le Tomás bocht an lá
> san go raibh an saothar mór beartaithe aige le déanamh; agus
> do bhí an lá úd ar na chéad laethannta riamh gur bhraitheas an
> saoghal ag teacht im' choinnibh, mar 'seadh bhí lá liom agus
> cúig lá im' choinnibh as san amach.[13]

> Two loads of old turf were not felled by poor Tomás on that
> day for which he had the great work planned: and that was the
> first day that I felt life coming against me, for after that if ever
> a day went with me, five went against me.

The composition of poetry leaves a man spent and empty, as
exhausted as the young Tomás felt himself after a hillside romp with
the local girls. Pádraig Ó Siochfhradha, the schoolmaster who edited
the text for publication, must have considered it necessary to make it

safe for the classroom: how otherwise can one explain his decision to excise the rather innocent but very poetic references to a wind that blew the girls' dresses so high that Ó Criomhthain could write: 'd'fhéachas isteach in áit nár shaighneáil an ghrian ariamh' (I looked into a place where the sun never shone before)?[14] The making of songs and poems is a little like sexual activity: pleasurable at the time, but ultimately dangerous. After these events, life seems a long anticlimax: the tide, which had once been brimming over the stones on the beach, now withdraws and goes slowly out.

In a foreword to his own excellent translation, Robin Flower remarked on the need for self-discipline in speech and action among a people who lived so literally on the edge of things. That may be another reason for the stringent humour and ironical cast of mind which permits Ó Criomhthain to keep a sense of perspective on a life that might otherwise overwhelm. 'There is always a narrow margin between these men and violent death,' observed Flower, 'and their faculties are keener for that.'[15] The same point had already been made by Synge about the perils of a life that made it 'impossible for clumsy, foolhardy or timid men to live on these islands'. The communitarian values endorsed by Synge at the start of the century were rediscovered in the Blaskets for the next generation by Flower: 'Such a life, without shops or specialist craftsmen, develops an all-round competence, a total physical and mental alertness.'[16] If the islanders were inadvertent poets, they were also instinctual anarchists. Synge, as has been shown, noted the versatility of a generally bilingual people who knew no division of labour, their work changing with the seasons from fishing to burning kelp, from cutting shoes to thatching houses, from building cradles to making coffins, in a way that kept them free from the dullness and monotony of industrial life. 'The danger of his life on the sea gives (a man) the alertness of a primitive hunter, and the long nights he spends fishing in his curagh bring him some of the emotions that are thought peculiar to men who have lived with the arts.'[17]

The young women on the Blasket, who knocked Ó Criomhthain over onto the long grass for horseplay, were in their manners very like the candid, free-spirited women of Inis Meáin, who had never (in Synge's view) submitted to the 'moral bondage' of 'ladylike persons'. The shared risks and pleasures of that life were so rudimentary and so essential that it came as a terrible shock for Ó Criomhthain to visit the mainland town of Dingle and there on the quayside to discover a social system characterized by the ugly injuries of class feeling:

Chonnac daoine uaisle ina seasamh ann agus slabhraí timpeall a mbuilg, daoine bochta agus gan a leath-ceart d'éadach orthu.[18]

I saw gentlefolk standing there, with decorative chains around their waists, and poor people without their sufficiency of clothing.

The islanders were egalitarians, but the mainland had been anglicized and overtaken by class snobberies. It was hardly an accident (though it was a high old irony) that English radicals such as George Thomson and Robin Flower should come to this outpost of an ancient civilization in flight from such anglicization.

Synge had made much of the intimate affinities between the moods of the Inis Meáin people and the changing moods of nature. Much of this had to do with the *carpe diem* philosophy of people who say, whether of sadness or of joy, 'níl ann ach lá dár saol' (it's only a day of our lives).[19] Whenever they have a little money, they do not fear to spend and enjoy it, believing that not to use God's gifts is itself a kind of sin against providence. After a successful fishing campaign, the men often go on a drinking spree in Dingle, much to the chagrin of Ó Criomhthain, who can't help remembering the hungry women and children waiting anxiously at home. For instance, he berates his uncle for abandoning his wife in this way, only to be told, 'Ní bean ró-bhreá í . . . Ní baol di' (She's not too fine a woman . . . She's in no danger).[20]

Ó Criomhthain understands the relief which drink brings to men who live close to death and danger. He concedes 'do dheineadh braon a thógaint croí a chur ionainn' (the taking of a drop would put heart in us),[21] much as Synge recognized the value of poteen, 'which brings a shock of joy to the blood' and 'seems predestined to keep sanity in men who live forgotten in these worlds of mist'.[22] But Ó Criomhthain also believes that the 'lá dár saol' philosophy should be applied to those periods when work can be profitably done because of a plentitude of fish or a period of good weather. Then also the day exists to be seized. Reluctantly accompanying a group of drinkers on a visit to Dingle, Ó Criomhthain finds that their return is further delayed by a sudden storm: and his description of the eerie silence after that tempest has about it the quality of a cosmic hangover, as he likens the mood of numb drunkards to that of the sea:

D'fhéachas ins na ceithre hardaibh. Bhí an spéir 'na tost tar éis an tórnaigh sin a chur di ar nós na ndruncaeirí a bhí istigh i dtigh an ósta nár bhraith síon na hoíche ná fós an lá ag teacht.[23]

I looked in the four directions. The sky was silent after the thunder she had emitted, like those drunkards who were in the guest-house and who could feel neither the storm of the night nor yet the day breaking.

Mainland people, who met the islanders on these sprees, falsely assumed that they were undisciplined hedonists, failing to recognize that for them the mainland was a kind of laboratory of the unconscious, in which people of immense self-restraint worked off their frustrations.

The writer John McGahern has pointed to Ó Criomhthain's sense of the life of a person being formed by a succession of single days: 'when he apologises for the waste of a day in Dingle in relief of hardship through drunkenness, there is a physical sense of the day being taken out of the succession of days and squandered like the actual coins in their pockets'.[24] The Blasket people eat only twice daily, at the start of work and again at the end: and each day is a wholly new, unpredictable unit, so that it is as futile 'to plan ahead' as it is madness 'to look back in regret'.[25] *Ní chothaíonn an té a imíonn an té a fhanann.* (The one who dies does not feed the one who remains). Yet Ó Criomhthain is somewhat more respectful of the wisdom of ancestors than are those neighbours who decide to drink and seize the day. *Is minic do hóladh cuid mhaith i measc na namhad,* he says (it's often that a lot was drunk among a man's enemies), making his own distrust of mainlanders all too manifest.

Yet it is in some sense for those mainland people, as much as for his own, that the book is finally written: and he is poignantly careful to emphasize that, but for the sacrifice of his mother who went to cut turf when he was eight, thereby freeing him to go to school and master the world of learning, this new book would never be in the reader's hands. He knows and recognizes that every achievement of civilization is won at a fearful cost and that it may be lost at any time. The precarious peace maintained with the old hag who lives next door is a perpetual reminder of the need to discipline the self and avoid futile conflicts, but the civility won is always under stress and sometimes in real jeopardy. Ó Criomhthain is anxious to demonstrate to a sceptical outside world just how heroic was the self-restraint held over centuries of awesome toil: and he is sufficiently aware of the norms of that outside world to know what elements of Blasket life will prove to be of deepest interest.

Much of this can be narrated in the mode of comedy. He offers a po-faced account of the terror touched off in Blasket children by the arrival of the first visitor with four eyes, namely, a schools inspector wearing spectacles. The fun is less in the scene itself – though that is hilarious enough – than in Ó Criomhthain's delighted speculation about how strange it will seem to the *reader*. Repeatedly, he addresses himself to that reader, of whom he forms a conception remarkably clear for a work written out of an essentially oral culture: 'mo gheall leat, a léitheoir, gurb 'in scéal ná fuairis le léamh roimis seo nó b'fhéidir faid is beo duit ach oiread'[26] (I'll bet, reader, that that's a story you never got to read before or perhaps as long as you live either).

Some sceptics – notably Máirtín Ó Cadhain – have found in the closing paragraphs of the final chapter a series of false notes. They believe that no islander could have recognized the imminent death of the culture or construed his own culture quite as definitively as Ó Criomhthain did when he bade farewell to the communal pleasures of his youth: 'Tá san imithe agus tá an mór-chroidhe agus an scléip ag dul as an saoghal' (That is gone and the high heart and fun are leaving the world).[27] In particular, such readers detect the hand of Robin Flower (or perhaps of the editor Pádraig Ó Siochfhradha himself) in the following passage:

> Do scríobhas go mion-chruinn ar a lán dár gcúrsaidhe d'fhonn go mbeadh cuimhne a mball éigin ortha agus thugas iarracht ar mheon na ndaoine a bhí im' thimcheall a chur síos chun go mbeadh ár dtuairisc inár ndiaidh, mar ná beidh ár leithéidí arís ann.[28]

> I wrote with minute exactitude about a lot of our doings so that there would be remembrance of some sort of them and I tried to capture the temperament of the people who were around me so that an account of us would be left after us, because our like will not be there again.

Two things might be said in defence of the integrity of the passage as a true statement of Ó Criomhthain's own project. For one thing it accords utterly with the kind of declaration with which Gaelic storytellers explained their narratives right back to the time of Seathrún Céitinn who wrote

> chuireas romham stair na hÉireann do scríobh . . . de bhrí gur mheasas nár bh'oircheas chomh-onóraighe na hÉireann do chrích agus comh-uaisle gach fóirne d'ar áitigh í, do dhul i mbáthadh gan lua ná iomrádh do bheith orthu.[29]

> I took in hand to write the history of Ireland . . . because I

thought it was not fitting that a country like Ireland for honour, and races as honourable as every race that inhabited it, should be swallowed up without any word or mention to be left about them.

For another thing Ó Criomhthain had always shown himself possessed of an artist's capacity to stand back from his life and appraise it through the implied eyes of another. That is why his book, though it may be the least self-conscious autobiography ever written (since it contains no interior monologue and no thoughts withheld from the wider community), is at all times supremely self-aware. He knows just how musical and even how unique is the narrative just completed: and that is why he is at pains to explain that he chose to write not a full account but one filled only with those events that interested him. Yet, lest there appear to be even a suggestion of elaborated personality in the selection of material, he makes it very clear that he wrote primarily to impart information, and because he considered himself a central representative of the values of his community: 'má bhí beirt dob fhearr ná mé, bhí triúr ba mheasa'[30] (if there were two better than me, there were three worse). Perhaps Robin Flower was aware that cynics were accusing him of interfering with the book's conclusion, for he himself wrote a definitive response in the foreword to his 1937 translation, published eight years after the Gaelic original:

He has always reflected on his experience and watched his fellows with a certain aloofness . . . his critical alertness is very noticeable in his use of the native language . . . He has told me that, in writing this book, he aimed at a simple style, intelligible to every reader of Irish, using none of the 'crua-Ghaoluinn', the 'cramp-Irish' of the pure literary tradition . . . But the style is none the less unmistakably his own, and to those who have known the man his whole figure and character is implicit in the manner of his writing.[31]

While Ó Criomhthain was writing his masterpiece, another young English scholar followed Flower to the islands. He was George Thomson and he arrived in August 1923, during the first election to be conducted in the Free State. The police in Dingle, ever watchful for trouble, feared that he might be a British agent of some kind. He was no such thing: just another radical classicist attracted by a culture that seemed to provide a link with the ancient world of Homer and, at the same time, with the more modern philosophy of communitarian living.

On the Blaskets, Thomson befriended a youth named Muiris Ó
Súilleabháin, who voiced a desire to write of island life. Born in
1904, he had been sent to an orphanage in Dingle at the age of one
following his mother's death; when he returned at six to the islands,
he found himself with no Irish. His grandfather, Eoghan Ó
Súilleabháin, a gifted storyteller, soon set that to rights, supplying
the youth with many of the tales and anecdotes that he would eventually stitch together into *Fiche Blian ag Fás* (Twenty Years
a-Growing, 1933). His first attempts at writing were unsuccessful,
but with the publication of *An tOileánach* in 1929, he found the
courage to try again. By then he was a serving policeman in the
Galway Gaeltacht; and when Thomson was appointed lecturer in
classics at the nearby university, this made possible a renewal of their
happy collaboration. An Gúm, the official government publisher,
refused to accept the book unless references to pint-drinking at the
Ventry Races were excised and an undertaking was given that there
would be no English translation. Ó Súilleabháin sensibly refused to
make either compromise and his book appeared along with an
English version by Thomson and Mona Llewellyn Davies to
immense acclaim in 1933. (The English version appears to have
been issued first.)[32]

Fiche Blian ag Fás is really a novelistic rendition of *An
tOileánach*, adapted to the needs and tastes of a younger, more literary generation. Its upbeat rhythms and affirmation of a happy
childhood spent on the island appealed greatly to the young, but
some of the older people, bred to a stricter Gaelic, privately preferred Ó Criomhthain's book. In his introductory note to the English
version, the novelist E.M. Forster marvelled at 'an account of
neolithic civilisation from the inside. Synge and others have
described it from the outside, and very sympathetically, but I know
of no other instance where it has itself become vocal, and addressed
modernity'.[33] That is literally true and in more ways than one. Ó
Súilleabháin attempts to encase the age-old rituals in a narrative that
provides just the sort of authorial self-consciousness in which his
predecessor steadfastly refused to indulge. But he also confronts
modernity in the sense that the second part of his book is an
extended account of how one islander, having moved, coped with
the challenges of mainland life. He goes to the police academy as a
trainee garda, crossing through Dingle *en route* to the great city of
Dublin. What is conducted in these pages is yet another form of
inverse anthropology, in the course of which he reports back to the
old women of the island on the strange sights and doings of an
exotic culture. The method is in fact anticipatory of some of the

great postcolonial novels like Tayib Salih's *Season of Migration to the North* (1969), which reverses Joseph Conrad's expedition to the African *Heart of Darkness* with a voyage into the European wastelands.

Before all that, however, there is the establishment of the Blasket civilization, by whose implied standards the other one will be measured. The author, being far younger than Ó Criomhthain, recalls the vibrant conversations among the island youth; and there is far more direct speech in a narrative that often permits conversations to continue for two or three pages on end. One of the many paradoxes of *An tOileánach* was that the master of oral tradition had little scope for extended conversation, and for good reason. Storytellers had always found it difficult to render in direct speech the talk of many different characters in a story. 'The danger', as James Delargy has pointed out, 'was that such speeches would become confused with the teller's own narrative.'[34] Most solved the problem by paring conversation to a telegraphic minimum (a technique carried over into the powerfully reticent novels of John McGahern). Ó Súilleabháin, at home in print codes, has no such difficulty, for his is a far more modern and writerly sensibility.

Whereas Ó Criomhthain had made a virtue of his own typicality as an upholder of social custom, the younger man not only seeks the exceptional experience but feels himself exceptional to begin with. He starts as an orphaned infant on the mainland, then returns and feels himself a somewhat alien presence on the island, only to find himself an utter foreigner when at last he returns to Dingle. There is an almost existential quality to his solitude: and on three separate occasions he cites *Robinson Crusoe*, that first in a long line of novels to deal with the alienation inherent in a capitalist society and to document, with the return of the protagonist, his sense of estrangement at the centre of a lonely crowd.[35] For this very reason, Ó Súilleabháin proves rather more adept than the older man at describing crowd scenes and social occasions, such as the American wake held before a young relation leaves for the USA. Hanging around the edges rather than continually caught up, he is better positioned to paint a full picture.

Although Ó Criomhthain seldom permits other characters (not even the poet) to impinge for long on his narrative or on himself, he chooses not to exploit that situation by revealing the inner resources of his own consciousness as an alternative field of force. He remains as reticent about himself as he is about others. His book may be an autobiography, but there is a steely, objective and external quality about its accounts. Ó Súilleabháin, on the other hand, chooses to splice the methods of autobiography with the techniques of the modern novel – he had read Loti's *Pêcheur d'Islande* as well as *The Aran Islands* – and so he produced his own portrait of the artist as a young man. There are plenty of characters in all his chapters – from Daideo the grandfather to his playful young friends – but the narrator often prefers to attend to his own inner thoughts in the midst of a social occasion. He laughs gently to himself in an abstracted way which sometimes dismays the grandfather who repeats obsessively, 'Mo thrua do cheann' (My pity for your head). Muiris's is an intrepid and active imagination. His slight outsider status permits him to offer his own psychological explanation of the real motives behind some of those ancient customs accepted without question by Ó Criomhthain. The universal praise accorded to the dead at wakes is, he insists, rooted less in genuine admiration than in a fear of being haunted by their uneasy spirits.

There are many rather knowing quotations from literature. For example, the first lines of *Cúirt an Mheán-Oíche* are repeated in a conscious savouring of the beauties of landscape such as was rare enough in native poetry. For Ó Criomhthain the landscape was beautiful too, but in his view there was little need to record something as 'given' as a shared setting. However, this youth who knows the sadness of estrangement is also cannily aware of the aesthetic pleasures it makes possible. All around him he sees external nature not just in itself but as potential art: 'an spéir ghorm narbh fhéidir a dath a phéinteáil' (the blue sky whose colour could not be painted).[36] As he sits contemplating the coming end of his youth, he feels a sudden affinity with the cries of a desolate seal, lamenting the loss of its baby to the ocean: a moment that may owe something to Synge's sad recognition of the keening gulls in *The Aran Islands*: 'their language is easier than Gaelic, and I seem to understand the greater part of their cries'.[37]

Some of the literary echoes, however, resonate back far further than Synge, Merriman or Defoe. From his grandfather, Ó Súilleabháin learned some of the great 'runs' used by the oral storytellers and singers of tales, to provide a respite for themselves in mid-narrative and to impress the crowded audience with the resources of their own language. Here is a classic description of the fall of night:

> Bhí sé ag éirí déanach. Bhí an ghrian ina luí in íor ne spéire, an drúcht ag titim go trom, mar bhí an taer ag fuarú, na cupóga ag dúnadh isteach ar a chéile i gcomhair n hoíche, éanlaithe na mara ag screadaigh mar thagaidís fé dhéin na ngearrcach, glór

ag na coiníní á bhaint as an raithnigh ag teacht amach as an
gcoinigéar dóibh mar ba ghnáth, gliosarcarnach na gclocha
scáil imithe as amharc, agus cuma uaigneach ag teacht ar na
cumaracha. – Tá sé ina oíche, a Thomáis.[38]

It was getting late. The sun was lying on the edge of the sky, the
dew falling heavily, because the air was cooling and the flowers
closing in upon one another for the night; the seabirds
screeched as they came towards their young; rabbits made
sounds through the ferns as they came out of their warrens as
usual; the shimmering through shadowy stones went from sight
and a lonely appearance overtook the valleys. – It is night,
Thomas, I said.

George Thomson likened that passage to certain nature poems in
Old Irish, during which the writer lists the signs of approaching
darkness, one after another in the same order in which they strike eye
or ear. The same verb is used repeatedly in the formula (Bhí . . .), or
else one such usage governs any number of sentences: and the whole
passage ends with a return to the opening idea, rather like the *cean-
gal* (or linking refrain) in poetry.[39] The rhythm of the writing has the
emphasis and accentuation of the oldest poetry, but the surrounding
context vitalizes and modernizes the effect, reflecting a modernist
agenda which was articulated by Edmund Wilson, who wrote: 'the
technique of prose today seems to be absorbing the technique of
verse – but it is proving itself equal to the work'.[40]

For some the charm of *Fiche Blian ag Fás* derives from the fact
that it was written without much thought of a wider public, being
intended mainly for the older women who remained on the island:
and this report back to them from the mainland has some of the fascination of a clandestine document produced by a secret agent. No
sooner does Ó Súilleabháin arrive in Dingle than his strange island
gait prompts a question from an old friend who fails at first to recognize him. That question is deep: who is he?

———Dar fia, arsa mise, nach aon Éireannach mé ach go
háirithe, cé go bhfuil fuil Éireannach ionam.
———Cathain a tháinís go hÉirinn mar sin, agus cad é an riab-
hach cuma gur phiocais suas an Ghaoluinn bhlasta atá agat?
———Dhera, a dhuine na n-árann, arsa mise, ná fuil togha
Gaoluinne againne?
———Agus marab Éireannach thú, ar seisean, cad é thú?
———Blascaodach, a bhuachaill, arsa mise.[41]

——Faith, I said, I am not any Irishman in particular, even though there is Irish blood in me.

——When did you come to Ireland then, and how on earth did you pick up the tasty Irish you have?

——Yerra, my good man, I said, don't we have the choicest Irish?

——And if you're not an Irishman, said he, what are you?

——A Blasketman, my boy, I said.

For Ó Súilleabháin, as for Ó Criomhthain before him, to arrive on the quay at Dingle is to experience all over again the fall of man from an anarchist commune into a world of social division and coercive state power.

The islanders discover to their cost that to be Gaelic is not at all the same thing as to be Irish. The mainlanders are part of the new project of state formation, and as such too Irish to be Gaelic – a fact obscurely hinted by the youth in his smart but mysterious response. He is himself about to be inducted as a trainee policeman and, therefore, a significant role-player in the protection of the new order. But he has read his Synge and knows that the introduction of police to the Galway Gaeltacht – where soon he will be posted – led only to a loss of innocence among the people. To underline that bitter irony, the friend who had alerted him to these jobs for Irish-speakers in the Garda Síochána was none other than George Thomson, the very man who had come to the Blaskets seeking not just the life of a commune but liberation from the very idea of the state as such. Friedrich Engels's grim prediction was coming true: the Irish were starting to act like strangers in their own country.

Ó Súilleabháin's progress from the moment he set foot in Dingle was a bleak confirmation of that diagnosis. So confused was he by the labyrinth of streets and the press of pedestrians through them that he preferred to remain at the railway station rather than risk getting lost in the throng and missing the Dublin train. Accordingly, he paid two boys of the town to buy and bring him bread and butter from a shop. The story is rather reminiscent of Bertrand Russell's account in his autobiography of how he was so embarrassed to ask any of the members of the Cambridge college in which he sat entrance examinations at the age of seventeen for directions to the nearest lavatory that he preferred to walk all the way back to the railway station every morning.[42]

Ó Súilleabháin for his part made it to Dublin and became a garda, but he never repeated the early success of *Fiche Blian ag Fás*, nor did he enjoy the duties of law enforcement. He married and settled in

Connemara, but drowned in shallow water off Salthill strand in 1950, perhaps of a heart attack. Thomson resigned his Galway lectureship following a refusal by the college authorities to sanction extramural courses in the classics, which he wished to teach in Irish to the people of Connemara. He moved to the chair of classics at Birmingham and became a leading intellectual of the British communist movement: but he never forgot his Blasket friends. In his masterpiece *The Prehistoric Aegean* (1949) he thanked them for sharing their culture with him: 'The conversation of those ragged peasants, as soon as I had learned to follow it, electrified me. It was as though Homer had come alive. Its vitality was inexhaustible, yet it was rhythmical, alliterative, formal, artificial, always on the point of bursting into poetry.'[43] He returned, invigorated, to the study of Homer, now convinced that he was a people's poet, writing out of a time when class snobberies had not yet created a split between rich and poor, and when there was still something like a common culture.

The third of the great Blasket autobiographers was Peig Sayers. She was born on the mainland in Dún Chaoin in 1873, but grew up in a house filled with conflict between her father (whom she loved) and the wife of her brother Seán. Eventually, to assist the household economy (but also for the sake of peace, since she also spoke her mind), she was put into service as a *cailín aimsire* (servant girl) in Dingle. There her health broke and she returned to Dún Chaoin. Her early memories were of the Land War and of the bold local rebel Muiris Ó Séaghdha, who composed songs to soothe his own loneliness in days and nights on the run from crown forces. When Muiris finally emigrated, Sayers's mother drank his health with a memorable toast at his American wake: 'Sid í sláinte Mhuiris, nár chuir leanbh a chomharsa riamh ag gol is ní lú nár tháinig go dtí an doras riamh le fearg chugam'[44] (That is the health of Maurice, who never set a neighbour's child crying nor ever came to my door in anger). The emphasis of the women, as on the islands, was upon their children rather than their husbands. Perhaps this was pervasive in the Ireland of the time, for the young Stanislaus Joyce noted how early his brother James had resigned himself to a marginal role as the partner of Nora Barnacle, not expecting to be the main interest of her life and recognizing that sooner or later children would take the place he had so briefly occupied.[45]

Peig Sayers's closest confidante was Cáit Jim. She was to go to the United States and earn enough there to provide passage money for her friend. The relationship was perhaps the most intense of Sayers's life, but it was broken early by emigration. The account of their farewell is deeply moving, but Sayers, like Ó Criomhthain, cannot resist the tragic flash-forward which dispels the sort of suspense that a more 'literary' composer would have maintained in the tale: 'Ba é sin an radharc déanach a fuaireamar ar a chéile' (That was the last sight we got of one another).[46] Sayers was unable to read or write Irish, but she was one of the greatest storytellers of her age. Her life was told in the first instance to her son Mícheál Ó Guithín, who wrote it down at her dictation; and she may have interpolated such a comment knowing that the fate of Cáit Jim (who injured her hand in an accident soon after arrival in North America) was well known to all her listeners. It is possible that Sayers wished also to disrupt the line of chronology with a more fatalistic view of time as an 'eternal now' of pain, for her version, unlike the men's, puts great emphasis on her own suffering and on the heroic reserves of patience with which she met it. She responds to the bad news from Cáit Jim, as so often, with a proverb: 'Níl leigheas ar an gcathú ach é a mharú le foighne' (There is no remedy for temptation but to kill it with patience).[47]

By all accounts Peig Sayers was a beautiful as well as a gifted young woman, but her father could offer no dowry, and so she had no chance of marrying a landed farmer. Instead, she wed Pádraig Ó Guithín of the Blasket and went to live with his people in a very crowded house. One of her nieces died on the day of the wedding, an event that seemed to sum up her own philosophy which held that good and bad forces in the world are always kept in some kind of balance. 'Thuas seal, thíos seal' (A time up, a time down) was the motto of the woman who said, 'Mara raibh bainis amuigh ar an tír againn, bhí bainis againn istigh san oileán' (If we did not have a wedding feast on the mainland, we had it on the island).[48]

Soon she came to value the character of the island people, and to question the outsider view of them as barbarians. In her autobiography, she seems at times to take up where her male predecessors left off, explaining the customs of the Blaskets to the people from whom she came. She is especially anxious to note those female customs over which the male authors may have too lightly passed, such as the welcome the islandwomen had for her after the safe delivery of her first child on the mainland:

Bhí a lán de na seanmhná istigh romham. Béas é sin a bhíonn ag seanmhná, agus dá bhrí sin, ní raibh seanmhná an Oileáin saor ón seanbhéas céanna.[49]

There were lots of old women inside (the house) before me.

That is a custom of old women, and for that reason the old women of the Island were not free of that old ritual either.

If anything, Sayers is keen to offer a normative interpretation of island life, integrating it ever more fully with the shared culture of the mainland. The ravishing beauty of the Blasket landscape helped to console her for the harsh conditions endured: four of her ten children died young, and it was twenty years before she had a home of her own. But greater solace still was found in her religious faith, the true source of her stoic philosophy:

> Bliain le duine agus bliain ina choinne, sin mar a bhí agamsa. Gach bliain mar thagadh, tugadh sí a hathrú féin léi, sólás go dtí duine agus dólás go dtí duine eile, agus d'éalaíodh sí mar a éalaíonn an taoide de ghaineamh na trá.[50]

> A year of luck with a person and a year of luck going against them, that's how it was with me. Every year that came, it would bring its changes, happiness to someone and sadness to another, and then it would escape just as the tide escapes from the sand on the strand.

The sense of time in such a culture is fully marked in terms of the sense of place, the one in a beautiful consort with the other. Humanity is like a well, with two buckets, one rising and the other falling: and for every symptom that is eased, another is made worse. Peig's son Mícheál returns (and that is a joy to her), but because of poverty (and that is a defeat for him).

The closure of the book is in the style made famous by Ó Criomhthain; but the formula had grown so predictable that it was by now ripe for parody. *Dublin Opinion*, a satirical magazine, had already depicted the Blaskets in June 1933 as a place resounding to the clatter of typewriters (though, in all likelihood, the only type-writers ever worked there were plied by visiting scholars): and in 1941 Myles na gCopaleen in *An Béal Bocht* would mercilessly mock those storytellers who had discovered that to proclaim the immi-nent death of one's culture was the smartest career move of all. Had Sayers known just how corrosive such mockery would become, she might not have laid it on quite so thick in the end:

> Anois táim i ndeireadh mo laethanta agus is dóigh liom nach mbeidh seanbhean chomh Gaelach liomsa ar an Oileán seo go deo arís.[51]

> Now I am in the end of my days and I suppose that there will
> never be an old woman as Gaelic as I on the Island again.

Ó Criomhthain had lamented the disappearance of the high heart
and sense of fun from the island world. That *might* have been taken
as a natural lament for the ebbing of energies as he passed his prime;
it would even, in a more sardonic interpretation, be seen as his covert
but dignified protest against the bowdlerizing of his text by puritanical nationalist censors. But his keen for a world that would never
repeat its rituals again had really been a sort of epic boasting, a way
of saying that the world would never seem so real to successors as it
had once to him. With Peig Sayers all metaphorical implications are
gone: and so she must find another, even more direct way of saying
that the mould is being broken and will never be remade. She shares
the desire to be remembered when she is gone 'ar shlí na fírinne' (on
the way of truth). However, she is not issuing posterity with any
Homeric challenge to measure up to the past: 'Ach ní bheidh ár
samhailne acu le fáil. Beimid sínte go ciúin – agus beidh an seansaol
imithe'[52] (And our sort will not be available to those who walk
above. We shall be buried in silence – and the old life will be gone).

She was right. By the time she died in Dingle in 1958, the Blasket
was quite empty. In 1987, by the sort of irony that would have
wrung the heart of George Thomson, it was offered for sale in the
pages of the *Wall Street Journal*.

30

Incorrigibly Plural:
Louis MacNeice

The greatest of all Irish poets was Yeats and his background was Protestant. Despite that, there is a widespread perception that the central traditions of northern Irish poetry are somehow less readily available to writers who grew up in the embrace of Protestantism. Why this should be so is not immediately clear: perhaps, it is merely a reflection of the premium put on the scientific disciplines by the teachers in northern Protestant schools and of the resultant stereotyping of Catholic schools as centres of artistic endeavour.[1] There is also the consideration that it is not in the nature of Protestant or even post-Protestant writers to form movements, much less traditions. The still, small voice of the individual often prefers to be heard on its own.

For that very reason the Protestant imagination can often appear to be isolate, sceptical of absolutes, and ever more wryly self-mocking. It treats poetry not as passionate public rhetoric but as the private discourse of an intimate group – and its prose is only slightly raised. Aware of the darkness and chaos that always threaten to snuff out the saving points of light, it finds in composure only a momentary victory. Elegance it no longer sees as a sign of decadence, but as an idea of order in a world verging on savagery. Far from embracing chaos as a sublime challenge, its notion of pleasure is linked intimately to order, which is no more than an assurance of control. But these moments of regular, satisfying impulses are precarious and always passing:

Time was away and somewhere else
There were two glasses and two chairs
And two people with the one pulse
(Somebody stopped the moving stairs):
Time was away and somewhere else.[2]

Louis MacNeice can recognise the sacred potentials of such an interlude of blessedness, but the claim is lodged in minimalist terms, as a whisper rather than an acclamation:

God or whatever means the Good
Be praised that time can stop like this,
That what the heart has understood
Can verify in the body's peace
God or whatever means the Good.[3]

The poise held at such moments is classical, a shared moment of individual pleasure (the poem is titled 'Meeting Point'): and the sweetness, though intensely private, is communicable to those kindred spirits who might recognize such an epiphany. MacNeice was but the most famous of a formidable line of northern poets whose professional training in classical scholarship helped to define a poetic mode: successors like Derek Mahon and Michael Longley share in that sense of amenity, rigour of form and clarity of outline, as mildly moral stays against chaos. In this lower-case setting, poetry is no longer seen as a false theatrics which erodes the integrity of the person, but rather as an urbanely amused attempt at the construction of a self. The classical inheritance allows for a temperate expression of stoicism, doubt, even cosmic pessimism; however, it is counterbalanced by a conviction of the redeeming possibilities of certain golden moments. Knowledge may be a knowing that we cannot know life's ultimate destiny, but it is none the less decent as well as desirable to experience moments of elation. If in the nineteenth century a classical British education was designed to enforce an imperial imperative, its effect in the twentieth was less to legislate for the world than to enable a quiet poise, in an art purged of all romantic or high-modernist superstitions about its own sovereign powers.

MacNeice was born in Belfast in the year 1907. His father was a clergyman in the staunchly Protestant seaside town of Carrickfergus, a liberal man who refused to endorse the divisive Ulster Covenant against Home Rule in 1912 and who always taught his children to love the west of Ireland, from which both he and his wife had come. Long before Louis had ever seen the western landscapes, he felt an active longing – a nostalgia, even – for their 'pre-natal' mountains. A similar curiosity overwhelmed him to enter and know the forbidden 'Irish quarter' of Carrickfergus, a place inhabited only by poor Catholics:

> I was the rector's son, born to the anglican order,
> Banned for ever from the candles of the Irish poor.[4]

At home, Louis was confined with his brother and sister to the rectory garden, where they spent delightful hours with their mother, who tried to prevent them from acquiring a strong Belfast accent (which MacNeice later found harsh but full of character).[5]

The children loved their Catholic nurse Annie from Tyrone and the local Protestant gardener Archie: both had a fund of vivid stories and anecdotes. But they were terrified of a dour Anglican governess, Miss Craig, whose puritanical edicts cast a gloom over the household. 'It came to be a point of honour', recalled MacNeice's sister Elizabeth, 'that we did not belong to the north of Ireland.'[6] Their roots must lie somewhere else. Louis MacNeice often joked about this *nostalgie de la boue*: 'for many years I lived in nostalgia for somewhere I had never been'.[7] He remained convinced that his birth in Belfast had been a kind of mistake, albeit one that could not be undone:

> Torn before birth from where my fathers dwelt,
> Schooled from the age of ten to a foreign voice,
> Yet neither western Ireland nor southern England
> Cancels this interlude; what chance misspelt
> May never now be righted by my choice.[8]

Yeats had revered those moments when chance and choice are one, but this poet can only know the more modulated pleasures of the near miss. The word 'interlude' is a rather low-key term to describe the intense experience of a childhood in Carrickfergus:

> But I cannot deny my past to which my self is wed,
> The woven figure cannot undo its thread.[9]

For all that, MacNeice carried into his later years the strong conviction that he was, by real inheritance, a western Irish peasant. It was of course a fancy and a conceit: but the very name 'Connemara' filled him with excitement. He believed that, had he not been sent to Marlborough and Oxford to study classics, he might well have ended up working in England not as an academic but as a building-site labourer. He wrote in a letter to a lover:

> I am a peasant who has gate-crashed culture, and when I say that I am a peasant this isn't a figure of speech or an inverted snob romanticism, it is just a statement of fact.[10]

He therefore felt able to claim an innate understanding of the lives of the poor, which far from seeming 'exotic' were utterly 'intelligible'. 'My relations', he explained, 'are still living in mud-floored cottages in the west of Ireland.'[11]

This might appear to be crass sentimentality, but for the Beckettian rigour with which even birth is treated as an early experience of exile. Derek Mahon has pointed out that whereas authors like Joyce and O'Casey felt themselves estranged from Ireland, MacNeice shared with Beckett the more radical notion of life itself as the first loss.[12] The pre-natal mountain of Connemara was for MacNeice less a definite, known spot than a version of the godly place surrounded by clouds of glory, from which Wordsworth also had been untimely ripped into this world. And the experience of childhood was, in essence, a confrontation with the loss of a perfect world. Those nursery rhymes told by a beloved mother would provide rhythms for the poem in which her grown son still mourned that death which snatched her from him in his early years:

> *My mother wore a yellow dress;*
> *Gently, gently, gentleness.*
> Come back early or never come.
>
> *When I was five the black dreams came;*
> *Nothing after was quite the same.*
> Come back early or never come.[13]

MacNeice carried a sense of guilt about his mother's death, which was due (so people said) to an injury incurred during his birth; but deeper still was the sense of having been abandoned.[14] It is even possible that the covert hostility which this induced in him was transferred to Ireland as a whole. If the west was the pre-natal mountain which he longed to re-enter, the other parts of the island might be the nauseous body he wished only to escape. Terence Brown has attributed his reserve, his suspicion of extreme commitments, and his philosophical scepticism to a 'fracturing of experience' inherent in his early years.[15] This would also help to account for his unhappy and repetitive experience of loving women who usually left him.

The fragmentation was not necessarily a negative thing, however. A more positive phrase for the process could have been 'achieved versatility'. What MacNeice came to love in Irish skyscapes was something he was soon discovering in himself: a capacity to change, and very fast, from dark monotones to scintillating points of bright light.[16] Charles Stewart Parnell had spoken in praise of 'the cursed versatility of the Celt' and Wilde had exemplified the truth that the intensification of personality lay in its multiplication. MacNeice could only concur.

Inevitably, the experience of being an Irish boy at Marlborough compounded this fragmentation of personality. While there, MacNeice mocked the Protestant bigots who spouted 'rubbish' on the Twelfth of July; later he felt cheap and mean for denouncing one of the traditions of his birthplace. His favourite teacher was a northern Irish Protestant, G.M. Sergeaunt, who inculcated stoic ideals. Even in his teens, the apprentice poet was writing in a style that was a mixture of Yeatsian lyricism and Thirties pylon poetry:

> *Come you away to the black peat bog,*
> *The driving sleet and the drifting rain,*
> *Where the wee folk weave from the path of the reed*
> *And the world is rid of financial greed*
> *And the guilty dance in a chain.*[17]

The elements may sound discordant and oddly jarring, but they were equally a part of his personality. By the time he reached Oxford, his problem in settling down was symptomatic. Asked to choose either the hearties, the aesthetes or the scholars, he felt an equal attraction to all three groups and so took to drink.[18] The pluralism and tolerance inculcated by his father had taken hold:

> *World is crazier and more of it than we think,*
> *Incorribly plural. I peel and portion*
> *A tangerine and spit the pips and feel*
> *The drunkenness of things being various.*[19]

Which is not to say that MacNeice could ever share his father's unquenchable Christian faith. Though Christian steadfastness was admirable, making the life 'more all of a piece',[20] it was impossible for the son to believe with certainty.[21] His own philosophy was, in the witty phrase of Terence Brown, that of 'unresolved disbelief'.[22] This was almost inevitable, given the tendency of

fashionable intellectuals like Freud to insist on a value-free analysis: people were not so much good or evil as products of their
given conditions. Speaking for the generation that grew to maturity after World War One, MacNeice said, 'because we learned to
account for the actions of others, we learned neither to praise nor
to blame them'.[23] This attitude was, in some ways, a return to the
Negative Capability celebrated by Keats, who had said that the
best way of strengthening a mind was to resolve on nothing,
simply letting it become a 'thoroughfare for all thoughts'.[24] The
rather rigid postures adopted by some 1930s poets may in fact
have been a terrified retreat into certainty, by those who had found
themselves unable to live long with doubt. MacNeice was never of
that party. As a liberal, he was shocked by the instrumental view of
human nature taken by the orthodox Marxist: 'he forgets the end
in the means, the evil of the means drowns the good of the end,
power corrupts, the living gospel withers, Siberia fills with
ghosts'.[25] A poet should stand against all propagandists, defending
the freshness and integrity of language: he should be 'a maker, not
a retail trader'.[26]

MacNeice always blocked the retreat to simple commitment,
regarding his detachment as a precious possession, which kept the
variousness of things intact. If he was a tourist in his own country, he
was that only because he preferred being a tourist everywhere, for he
felt most himself when either he or the object of his contemplation
was in motion. His pose was that of a dandy, affecting unsurprise at
the passing pageant, but there was mingled with it a strain of puri-
tanism, which could at any moment translate the tourist's travels into
a pilgrim's strenuous progress.

Given the *Letters from Iceland*, co-written with W.H. Auden in
1937, it might be tempting to claim that MacNeice worked at the
point of intersection between literature and anthropology: but if he
did, he was less interested than most anthropologists in the 'host' culture and far more committed to registering its effects on himself. His
motto might have been Victor Hugo's:

> The man who finds his homeland sweet is still a tender begin-
> ner; he to whom every soil is as his native one is already strong;
> but he is perfect to whom the entire world is as a foreign land.[27]

Having left Ireland, he was better able to assess it in comparison
with other lands: but he was also better equipped to assess himself.
Once again in this context MacNeice's strategy was Beckettian:
whenever he felt himself long enough in one place to register the

boredom of routine, he uprooted and exposed himself to the 'suffering of being' that was a new situation.[28] Although this might seem an option for perpetual estrangement, it was also a thoroughly Irish gesture: ever since the 1840s such uprooting and instability have been the lot of all Irish emigrants and, for that matter, of those who remained at home in a landscape made mysterious and strange by a new language.

The self, far from feeling deprived of lost settings, was a process: and it could only be defined as a direct result of such negotiations. Identity, as in Keats's scheme of things, lay up ahead, a possible reward for those who had the courage of their own versatility. Peter MacDonald put this astutely when he observed that for MacNeice there could be no self without displacement, because displacement made possible a bracing contest with new environments: yet displacement was also the condition of freedom.[29] In effect, the Ireland from which MacNeice had been severed was no stable entity, but a land whose flux and uncertainty exactly reflected the inchoate mind of a man still in the making.

In *Autumn Journal*, his masterpiece written late in 1938, MacNeice audaciously confronted his own addiction to a floating island of ever-changing light and shade:

> *Kathaleen ni Houlihan! Why*
> *Must a country, like a ship or a car, be always female,*
> *Mother or sweetheart? A woman passing by,*
> *We did but see her passing.*[30]

The writer of these lines had come a long way from his idealization of an unseen but anti-capitalist peasantry: his response to the western peasant was no longer Yeatsian, but more in the style of Joyce's recoil from the 'red-rimmed horny eyes' of a threatening figure.[31] For MacNeice that fear was increased by the awareness that this terrifying apparition was an aspect of his own buried self. There was but a thin line separating the peasant who gatecrashes culture and the poet-professor who gatecrashes the peasant reservation.

Was MacNeice's identification with the western peasantry completely fanciful? Perhaps not, for it answered his own ambivalence. His father did not bring the children to Donegal after the Civil War, saying, 'how can you mix with people who might be murderers without your knowing it?';[32] and even when the clergyman did eventually return, he remained forever struck by the beauty of the place and appalled by the backwardness of the people. For northern Protestants, the issue posed by the continuing neglect and decline of the west under the new state was stark indeed: and it must have especially troubled those liberals like John MacNeice who had favoured some form of Home Rule. In the period of national revival, the peasant had been proclaimed the repository of all that was best in the culture of Gaelic Ireland, yet under the new governments western communities continued to die. If this was how the authorities in Dublin treated a community that was widely recognized as the bedrock of national tradition, how would they deal in any reunited Ireland with the estranged tribe of unionists, whose very existence was anathema to their state? In the 'sophisticated primitive' of the west, one lost tribesman recognized another. Far from being 'grandiose monsters', the bowler-hatted Orangemen were sad anachronisms: 'If they were lost, they were lost with a small l.'[33]

This may explain the poet's recurring tendency to equate unionist nostalgia for the Siege of Derry with the revivalists' dream of a 'land of the Ever Young'. Both were yearners for an absolute which, however desirable, could never be attained: and so both offered lessons in how life should not be lived:

> My diehard countrymen like drayhorses
> Drag their ruin behind them.
> Shooting straight in the cause of crooked thinking
> Their greed is sugared with pretence of public spirit
> From all which I am an exile.[34]

These lines of 1936 might apply equally to northern unionists or southern nationalists: and 'Eclogue from Iceland' was a prime example of what one of MacNeice's contemporaries called 'his Irish habit of beating his nurse when he writes of his home country'.[35] Equally, many of the lines about Northern Ireland in *Autumn Journal* seemed deliberately framed in terms that might be considered true also of the southern state:

> A city built upon mud;
>   A culture built upon profit;
> Free speech nipped in the bud,
>   The minority always guilty.[36]

Even in his moments of distaste for it, the Ireland that MacNeice saw was coherent, even unitary: just as the relentless reciprocity in the north bound planter and rebel to rehearse the same narrow band of themes:

And one read black where the other read white, his hope
The other man's damnation.[37]

Autumn Journal is of course about much more than Ireland: but somehow the ideas and attitudes generated by his native background serve MacNeice in bringing to focus a wider range of themes. His indictment of Neville Chamberlain's appeasement of Hitler at Munich in the autumn of 1938 is informed by his incredulity at Ireland's own insularity of mind in the face of developments in the outside world:

Ourselves alone. Let the round tower stand aloof
In a world of bursting mortar.
Let the school-children fumble their sums
In a half-dead language;
Let the censor be busy on the books; pull down the
Georgian slums;
Let the games be played in Gaelic.[38]

MacNeice's own need, under pressure by propagandists of the left to join the communists, is to find a mode of objectivity that is somehow different from the somnolent indifference that seems to unite Chamberlain's England and de Valera's Ireland. Yeats is the obvious model here, for he also might 'envy men of action' yet ultimately settle for a more detached position. Like republican Spain, Ireland has a fatal lure for the intellectual because it promises 'that on this tiny stage with luck a man / Might see the end of one particular action': but the temptation is 'self-deception of course'.[39]

There is no escape from modernity, for Ireland is no different from the rest of Europe. At the centre of *Autumn Journal* is a moving description of the cutting down of trees on Primrose Hill: the change is necessary to make way for gun emplacements in case of war, but the poet feels it as a personal deprivation. His lament for that moment of deforestation recalls the Gaelic lyric *Cill Cais*, to which it may indeed be indebted, for Frank O'Connor had recently published an English version of the song, which was still sung by Irish navvies in Britain. Again, the implicit equation of the poet with such immigrants shadows the poem:

If it were not for Lit. Hum. I might be climbing
A ladder with a hod.[40]

Autumn Journal, like Yeats's great poems in *The Tower*, is an attempt to avoid bitterness in the face of political catastrophe: and to sing in spite of suffering. As MacNeice wrote in its later stages, the republican city of Barcelona in Spain was falling to the fascists:

> *Listen. a whirr, a challenge, an aubade –*
> *It is the cock crowing in Barcelona.*[41]

The cock is not so much the bird of morning as the biblical reproacher of a laggard betrayer. With the fall of the Spanish city went the hopes of all radicals in that generation. Their panaceas had not saved Europe and they were left to confront, as Yeats had, the unreformed world and a politics of tragedy. That the great poet should have died in the same short period simply reinforced his exemplary claim, for he, more than any other poet, had allowed the public themes of the modern age to flow through his personal lyrics (as in 'Easter 1916'). MacNeice's strategy in *Autumn Journal* was an inversion of this: he began with the personal and proceeded to read public events in terms of his autobiography, lamenting a lost, neglected love as a version of the irrecoverable and yet culpable innocence of the decade. In effect, MacNeice defended the primacy of private experience by submitting the public world to its challenges and interrogations.

Yet he followed Yeats in erasing the clear border between private and public discourse: which is to say that, as an Irish person, he recognized that such a distinction had little meaning for a people who found the personal in the political. It was in the months following these events that MacNeice wrote his astringent but finally admiring study of Yeats. This emphasized that poetry, far from being a refusal to make action urgent, is a wholly effective way of making its nature clear. Both men had, after all, grown up in a still oral culture, for whose participants every word had the status of a deed. By spring 1939, even Auden had come to conclude that they were right: the poet was indeed a man of action and his deed was the defence of language, keeping it clean and clear against the defilements of propagandists.[42] His wonderful elegy 'In Memory of W.B. Yeats', was followed two years later by MacNeice's fine book, which praised the Irishman's ability to elevate the occasional lyric to the grave dignity of a public poem.

Yeats's conception of the self as fragmented and multiple accorded well with MacNeice's. The latter had told his editor at Faber and Faber (another poet, T.S. Eliot) that *Autumn Journal* allowed for the dramatization of 'different parts of myself (e.g. the anarchist, the defeatist, the sensual man, the philosopher, the would-be good citizen)'.[43] Even the fluctuations between tender love and outright repulsion in his attitude to Ireland were something he had in common with his predecessor – a bardic willingness to praise or to condemn as the occasion demanded. Although Yeats had no formal training in the classics, he too was capable of looking at the west of Ireland and seeing – Greece. This tendency was shared with such writers as Stephen MacKenna, George Thomson and Pádraig de Brún.

Nobody accuses Yeats's poetry of lacking a core of belief and yet that allegation is repeatedly made against MacNeice. He is accused of the sort of 'evasive honesty' which constantly promises a disquieting illumination of a kind that is never actually provided.[44] Yet MacNeice never refused to take sides against fascism, telling Auden in a 1937 letter that such a stance was 'a more vital habit than the detachment of the pure aesthete'.[45] However, such commitments were best left implicit in a work of art. When MacNeice allowed his deep contempt for Ireland's policy of neutrality to show, the effect (though understandable given the loss of his dear friend Graham Shepard to U-boats in the Atlantic) was crude:

> *But then look eastward from your heart, there bulks*
> *A continent, close, dark, as archetypal sin,*
> *While to the west off your own shores the mackerel*
> *Are fat – on the flesh of your kin.*[46]

After World War Two, MacNeice grew more fond of Ireland and especially of Dublin, feeling more at ease there than in London or any other city. Dublin's indeterminacy seemed to connect with his own protean identity and to refuse any simple self-description:

> *She is not an Irish town*
> *And she is not English.*
> *Fort of the Dane,*
> *Garrison of the Saxon,*
> *Augustan capital*
> *Of a Gaelic nation . . .*[47]

The capital epitomized the plight of a man who wished that 'one could either *live* in Ireland or *feel oneself* in England':[48] but, even though he registered the seductive charm of a city 'appropriating all' who came to it, he resisted a final surrender. Dublin fascinated, however, because like MacNeice it was held in suspension between rival atavistic tendencies. He felt caught between his southern blood and northern upbringing, his classical tastes and Anglican training, his father's Home Rule philosophy and his own cosmopolitanism. The very versatility of elements that went into his making may have led him to suspect what he would never dare to assert: that, deep down, he was more Irish than most of those writers who had long ago been given a free pass into the pantheon. He was indeed a poet of surfaces, but one who lived the truth of Wilde's dictum that only shallow people do not judge by appearances. His method was that of the miscellany, when it was not the epic listing of beloved objects now threatened with the collapse of civilization itself. In that he was at one with the *filí*, whose words he never directly knew, except through the screen of translation. His insistence that poetry root itself in the dignity of everyday life (newspapers, politics, advertising, small talk) was Joycean: and, if Leopold Bloom had ever become a poet, his name might have been Louis MacNeice – the ordinary man who notices a lot and is never completely overwhelmed.

Like many London intellectuals who survived World War Two without suffering the indignity of occupation or the joy of liberation, MacNeice appears to have envied those continental counterparts who knew these strong experiences. After the war, his poetry continued his role of elegist, lamenting the loss of a more courteous world: but now it grieved for the collapse of those solidarities that wartime conditions had made briefly possible:

> *And nobody rose, only some meaningless*
> *Buildings and the people once more were strangers*
> *At home with no one, sibling or friend.*
> *Which is why now the petals fall*
> *Fast from the flower of cities all.*[49]

Instead, he sought significance in – where else? – Connemara. His lament for it might have been his keen for the lost tribe of Ulster Protestants:

> *From the bourne of emigrant uncle and son, a defeated*
> *Music that yearns and abdicates; chimney-smoke and*
> *   spinthrift*
> *Mingle and part as ghosts do. The decree*
> *Of the sea's divorce is final.*[50]

MacNeice had a philosophy, albeit a minimalist one. Denying the fashionable Marxian doctrine of history as a merely impersonal force, he found even in the trauma of birth grounds for some celebration:

For to have been born is itself a triumph
Among all that waste of sperm.
And it is gratitude to wait the proper term
Or, if not gratitude, duty.[51]

His position was a perfectly logical one: birth might be at once a terrible exile from the pre-natal mountain and a liberation into the flux of life. The catalogues from which his poetry derived so much of its momentum could be similarly dual in tone – either exalted exhibitions of the limitless possibilities opened up by the world or a grave naming of the details of a dying culture. The greatness of *Autumn Journal* is its rendition in some of its more powerful passages of both feelings at one and the same time.

MacNeice wrote *Autumn Journal*, as he wrote everything, at the mercy of his own historical period and without any of those certainties about the shape of the future that seemed to console communist and fascist alike. For that very reason, he saw more deeply into his own moment than those who took longer views. Because he devoted himself so utterly to rendering the surfaces of his world in verses of classic decorum, he has been accused of a glib facility without any strong ethical core; and because he took exile for a theme even in his own country, he has been decried as a listless cosmopolitan without a sense of authentic identity. Neither charge is true: yet even the accidents of a random, haphazard life seemed to corroborate them. Two anecdotes from MacNeice's two suddenly-entered marriages sum this up perfectly. First, when as a student he resolved to marry Mary Beazley, he asked a friend to send a reassuring telegram to his father. Somehow, it got scrambled in the transmission, so that it read 'can vouch for Louis's nationality' (rather than 'rationality').[52] That, at least, was a potentially positive development. However, many years later, when the poet and Hedli Anderson decided to marry, her parents sent her a worried telegram, asking simply, 'Who is Louis MacNeice?'[53] It was, in its way, a fair enough question.

31

Kate O'Brien:
The Ante-Room

How can you write a novel of manners about a society that has none? That notorious question asked of the United States in the mid-nineteenth century had also been raised in the case of Ireland. Artists would have liked to employ the novel to chronicle the quotidian life of the emerging Catholic middle class, but the social conditions were too inflamed to admit of such treatment. Ireland was a land of extremes, in which a few fabulously rich persons scarcely noticed the immiseration all around them, but it was hardly a land suitable to the middle range of human experience, which was the staple of most novelists. The form of the novel presupposes a made society: Ireland's was a society still in the making.

Some Catholic families made private fortunes in the period and lived a life of upholstered ease, which was an exception to the general rule. It was into such a background that Kate O'Brien was born in 1897, the fourth daughter of a successful breeder of thoroughbred horses. One of her uncles had taken out a patent on the modern lifeboat and was rich on the annual royalties that followed. Her mother died when Kate was only six years old and she was sent to board with the nuns at Laurel Hill School in Limerick, where she spent about thirteen years. It was run on 'European' lines and provided girls with a formidable education by the standards of the time. O'Brien was happy there. Subsequently, she embarked on the study of French and English at University College Dublin, just months after the Easter Rising. 'We were a hungry, untidy, dirty lot – we of

1917–1919,' she recalled. 'But did we enjoy ourselves? Did we read, did we think, did we loaf, did we argue?'[1] Graduating with honours in 1919, she later served as secretary to the director of de Valera's American campaign to raise bonds for Ireland. It was even rumoured that on one occasion the handsome young assistant had worn the Russian crown jewels at a social function (for these had passed by a strange sequence of events into the keeping of one of de Valera's aides).

O'Brien then worked for a time as a governess in Spain and wrote a number of plays before settling to the life of a novelist. Soon she had won a reputation as a somewhat scandalous recorder of the confined, claustrophobic world of the Catholic upper bourgeoisie from which she came. Laurel Hill girls were accused by nationalists of wanting nothing more than marriage to a colonial governor.[2] O'Brien, through her work for de Valera, had already set herself aslant from such a career: and the *risqué* nature of her stories caused one mother-superior to rebuke her in a letter which ended by asking why she wrote such trash. The artist answered by terse telegram: 'Pounds, Shillings and Pence.'[3]

There was more bravado than accuracy in the reply. While it was true that O'Brien deployed some of the methods of popular romantic fiction, she spliced them with those of the art novel in a fashion which ensured that she could never make much money. For hers was a fastidious, refined sensibility. In her books she presented heroines with a passion not so much for men as for the processes of the mind itself. Her mentors in art were George Eliot and Henry James and she stressed the crucial role of education as a means of liberating her heroines. Her own tastes remained rarefied. Despite a chronic shortage of cash through most of her writing life, she managed to affect the *hauteur* of a lady of title. In the report of one admiring but slightly shocked friend, 'the uses of Vim were unknown to her'.[4] In her house at Roundstone, Connemara, she entertained many exotic visitors, including the French scholar Enid Starkie whose mannish clothes amused the local people. Eventually, she found life there too expensive and moved to Canterbury, Kent, from where she wrote a legendary column for the *Irish Times* under the title 'Long Distance'.[5]

The narrow, intense world of genteel Catholicism to which she devoted her art was not destined to survive into the twentieth century, for it had set its face against that nationalism which was clearly bound to triumph. It was a world rendered with a loving but critical accuracy in *The Ante-Room* (1934), the book she rightly considered the greatest of her novels. The action is set in Mellick (her fictional name for Limerick) in 1880, and dinner parties echo with brief, baffled references to the Land League, Parnell and the political tactic of boycotting. These things have a whiff of the future about them, beyond the ken of Danny Mulqueen, the paterfamilias of Roseholm:

> 'This business with that unfortunate Captain Boycott now', Danny went on, 'what's the idea in that, will you tell me?'
> 'Actually', said William Curran, 'there is a good and natural idea in it.'
> 'It'll lead to trouble – that's what it'll lead to.'
> 'Probably', said Vincent, 'Most good and natural ideas do.'[6]

The world of Roseholm turns its back on Parnell, Davitt and their followers: it was, in the words of another writer, Eavan Boland, 'a selfish, limited, insular class' which, despite its Catholicism, 'had more in common with the oppressors than the oppressed'.[7] Its members found it easiest to remain mildly pro-British but effectively non-political. The situation in which Danny Mulqueen lives is not unlike that of Mr Brooke in George Eliot's *Middlemarch*, a novel set in the era of the Reform Bill: both are men of acquiescent temper and uncertain opinion, who just bumble along.[8] Danny Mulqueen, we are told, was worried by opinion or information, 'since they required a reaction'. Dr Curran is O'Brien's version of Dr Lydgate in the English classic: a brilliant young doctor with a European training, exiled to a backwater where his weaknesses of character seem to conspire with the mediocrity of his setting.

There is no real sense of a wider society in *The Ante-Room*, such as may be found in *Middlemarch*. O'Brien's focus is almost entirely on a single family, whose isolation from the world around it is, perhaps, its most notable feature. There is no suggestion that the Mulqueens might be a metaphor of Ireland or, even, of a comprehensive social class. Indeed, the alert reader may register a suspicion that the author herself has some difficulty in rendering the details of upper-class Catholic life. It is almost as if she has to invent whole parts of her world in the very act of reporting it, as if that social class is about to expire before it has come fully into being. The narrator has to keep reminding herself of the date and the characters ('This was 1880, and he was a small-town doctor'),[9] lest both might without such reminders suddenly disappear. The great set-piece dinner held to impress a visiting consultant from London seems to be structured around a sort of absence, as if its hosts are not used to holding banquets in such exalted company and not exactly sure how to behave. O'Brien brilliantly captures that uncertainty of tone, but it is an uncertainty that sometimes leaks into her own style. Her Eliotesque study of provincial life shows how painfully aware is the Catholic uppercrust of the possibly 'quaint' spectacle it might present to a visiting English dignitary: and how important it is to pass muster at such moments. The old days of making the visitors become more Irish than the Irish themselves have well and truly gone.

If George Eliot is a great exemplar, that is not only because of her incisive anatomization of provincialism, but also for her dignification of the novel as an instrument for measuring the moral growth of its characters. Most Irish writers before O'Brien and most after her too have treated religion in terms of its social effects. She is unusual in her alertness to the spiritual dilemmas posed for conscientious young intellectuals by its exacting claims. O'Brien wrote as an agnostic but as one who had a deep respect for the drama of the Catholic conscience, as deep indeed as that shown by George Eliot for the nonconformist mindset of her most rooted characters. 'I am a moralist in that I see no story unless there is a moral conflict,' she remarked in an interview;[10] and in her lecture on Eliot, delivered to the Royal Society, she stressed the writer's ability to confer even on weak or shabby figures the dignity of a struggle with conscience:

> She was always primarily concerned for the moral development of her characters whilst being able to expose their dilemmas with the purest possible detachment, yet tenderly. The right and wrong of each heart – its *own* right and wrong – was her quarry; and she would spare no trouble to catch up with it, and study it calmly in relation to its place and nature.[11]

That might be read as O'Brien's apologia and answer to those who accused her of being a sociologist rather than an artist. Her interest is less in recording Catholic belief as such than in the strenuous drama of conscience to which it gives rise in the sensitive young. 'What a refreshment it is to be concerned in a fiction with a young woman who is more cerebrally than sensually conscious,'[12] she said in her Eliot paper, saluting the achievement of *Romola*. If Joyce had presented in *A Portrait of the Artist as a Young Man* a young hero whose days were characterized by his passion for thinking, she did no less for her heroine Agnes Mulqueen.

Even the weaknesses of O'Brien's art are flaws she appears to share with Eliot. The 'wise woman' syndrome, which grated even on Victorians who had some tolerance for moralizing, is repeated in the Irishwoman's work, much enhanced (of course) by the intervening revelations of Freud and the psychologists. She has a tendency to tell rather than show, or at least to tell before (and again after) she shows a character in action. This leads the reader to fear – especially for her men – that there may be no more to them than meets the eye, and quite possibly a lot less. There is, along with the genuine complexity in the portrayal of many different characters, little sense of anything withheld, little awareness that figures so suggestively rendered may yet contain unknown depths or unsuspected intensities. 'The danger of the method', observed Vivian Mercier, 'is that the character is bounded by the author's explanation.'[13] However, it is only just to add that this may be almost inevitable in a novel that deals with intellectual themes. Similar objections have been lodged against writers like Simone de Beauvoir and Jean-Paul Sartre (although, interestingly, these objections are often less strenuously prosecuted against a male than a female author who tells readers what they may think).

The Ante-Room begins in the autumnal mood of a resigned and minimalist elegy. This is a world that is doomed to die even as it is revealed, and one which might be said never to have fully existed at all. That may be one meaning of the title: a condition of latency which turns out to bear no final fruit. In Ireland the emergence of a fully functional middle class was utterly belated; and by the time such a class began to emerge in any numbers (about 1934, in fact), it was clear that it had missed out on the heroic phase of the bourgeoisie in the early nineteenth century, learning how to consume rather than produce and being less a version of the European bourgeoisie than its caricature. The phrases with which O'Brien opens her tale proceed by negations and denials ('no high light', 'no wind about'), introducing a 'muted day' with only 'tenuous sunshine'.[14] That style of scrupulous meanness which a young Joyce had considered appropriate to Dublin's lower-middle class is here used of Limerick's uppercrust, as Agnes Mulqueen feels the daylight 'calling her back to things she did not wish to face'.

Her world will be divided into two sorts of person – those who can unflinchingly face their own experiences and those who steadfastly refuse to do so. Her bumbling father, her dissolute and broken brother Reggie (wasting at thirty-five from the effects of syphilis) and her dying but doting mother are all among the refusers. The mother, Teresa, has incurable cancer but cannot bear to submit to it, lest her hopeless son be left defenceless in the world; and he in turn cannot admit the terminal nature of her sickness, since her going would take his last prop away. Reggie is a failure who does everything in half-measure. Only half-desiring to play the piano well, he never gets to the end of his Chopin recitals, his creative impulse being always arrested; likewise he can only ever half-confront the misery of his own life. His love for his mother 'was almost heroism in its surrender of laziness to perpetual small exaction':[15] but in fact it is rooted in the shared selfishness of both mother and son.

Agnes is by contrast a facer of facts. She 'could not bear to see the eyes of a human being filmed against himself'. To her, Reggie's situation, with 'its long chain of small unselfishness founded on a mighty selfishness',[16] is hideous. The mother is aptly named Teresa, for she seeks just a single miracle, the prolongation of her own martyrdom, but this is a miracle that not even skilful doctors can grant. George Eliot had opened *Middlemarch* with a Prelude lamenting that 'later-born Theresas were helped by no coherent social faith which could perform the function of knowledge for the ardently willing soul'.[17] In effect, Eliot was warning that heroism might no longer be possible. The most that could be expected was 'a certain spiritual grandeur ill-matched with meanness of opportunity', a phrase that perfectly describes the plight of Agnes. She is a heroine who has learned the lesson of Dorothea Brooke and who will make no false attempt at self-glorifying heroics. Trained by her religion in modes of self-mortification, she is so subtle and self-aware that she is suspicious even of her own holiness:

> Prayer that should humble gave relief by self-inflation. Agnes often wondered how it was possible to accept and honour God and yet steer clear of heroics.[18]

Perhaps the rather ostentatiously borne suffering of her mother leaves the daughter alert to the dangers of a similar contradiction in her own piety: but the drama of the solitary soul in dialogue with God would in any case leave a humble spirit like that of Agnes overwhelmed with a sense of its own unworthiness. She is assailed by the selfsame doubts when she makes a confession. What should be an exercise in self-contempt becomes too often a version of personal pomposity in the face of an absolute mystery: 'To stage one's miserable narration in terms of distress and tragic uniqueness was nothing short of idiotic.'[19] Ever vigilant to the corruptions of the mind which is self-conscious rather than self-aware, she sees how every confession of a sin might merely compound it by a repetition of self-love. One of the attendant perils of Catholicism is its confessionalization of discourse, with the result that those who think they can know no further forbidden pleasure may discover a new *frisson* in the knowledge of pleasure.

Agnes is all of twenty-five but her ineffectual father calls her 'child', despite relying utterly on her management of the home. She feels far older than her years, being already inclined to 'melancholy reminiscence'. Her life, like that of her social group, seems at once over and scarcely begun. Obsessed with present duties to faith and family, she feels that her own past life away at school might well have been someone else's. Her own deeper self is the one true friend she has never made: for the present moment, it is as if someone else is living her life for her and she knows nothing at all about such a person. Her consciousness is disintegrated and modern: 'she wondered then if other lives had more unity than hers'.[20] What is lacking, above all, is a sense of linkage between one experience and the next, along the continuum of a coherent and believable personality:

> The lives she read about in novels were not like that. There one thing always led to another, whereas what struck her about her own span of experience was that no section of it seemed to have offered preparation or warning for the next.[21]

The old romantic notions of a singular, stable personality will no longer serve for Agnes: hers is the more stringent problem of authenticity, of being true to all her varied selves.

The need at a technical level is for a multiplanar narrative that will capture all the fragments of that experience: the passage just quoted from a very early stage of the book seems to cry out for a new method, as if O'Brien were objecting to the modes of the realist novel which she cannot ultimately transcend. *The Ante-Room* will contain brief passages of interior monologue set within the consciousness of most of the major characters, so that the precedent set by *Ulysses* is honoured: but the device is so sparingly and so cautiously used (even in dramatizing the thoughts of Agnes) as to constitute a regression to nineteenth-century modes. Given the degree of repression in this world depicted, it would be reasonable to assume a correspondingly rich inner life by way of reaction for many of the female characters. This constriction becomes emblematic of O'Brien's treatment of such themes as family and feminine consciousness: she points, like a true radical, to the limitations of received forms, yet also displays a canny awareness of their continuing uses. Her revolutionary notions are given the protective coverage of well-tried structures, even as her fascination with the possibilities of popular women's romance is well contained within the protocols of nineteenth-century novels as practised by Eliot and James.

Agnes has a guilty secret and it is only partly her intelligence. Her pretty older sister (whose life proved that 'beauty carried the surest weapons')[22] is unhappily married to a handsome Dublin heir, Vincent de Courcy O'Regan. He is himself a 'much disappointed' man and the principle of negation runs like a unstoppable dye through the book. Agnes's love for her sister is genuine and deep (Marie-Rose's worthiness of it is quite another matter). Her awful secret, however, is that she also loves Vincent O'Regan. Her first recognition of him within the economy of this taut, elegantly constructed book is appropriately less than ecstatic: she saw 'no demigod'[23] but a man who seemed older than his years. But love him she does.

His rival for her affections is Dr William Curran, a Lydgate figure and arguably O'Brien's most convincing portrayal of a male. He is practical, clever, well-informed, but also lacking in a certain warmth of personality or capacity for imagination. His long study of medicine in Europe makes him aware of just how expensive, exhausting and futile will be the visit of the London consultant to Roseholm: and so he warns Agnes against it. Like her, he is a facer of facts and so the polar opposite of his patient, Reggie. Yet such is the intricate moral patterning of the book that he is also revealed to have much in common with the dissolute invalid: both of them, it transpires, indulged their sensuality during their days in Europe, but Dr Curran, by virtue of his professional knowledge, was able to save himself from the ill effects of sexual disease by taking medical precautions. If he was 'loose' on the Continent, he is now continent in Ireland, and 'it seemed to him that the Catholic Church provided as good a system as might be found for keeping the human animal in order'.[24] His theory of life was that he was beyond the disruptions caused by amorous feeling, but once he meets Agnes he is struck during his daily consultations by her beauty and grace. In *Middlemarch* Dr Lydgate (whose fine mind was none the less marked by spots of commonness) fell in love with a vapid flirt whom he took at first for a profound and noble soul. In *The Ante-Room* Dr Curran (who tends to judge by merely material criteria) falls for a deep and conscientious woman whom he judged to be a startling beauty.

The passages in which Dr Curran registers that beauty are written in the charged, emotional style of romantic fiction: but the narrative lingers so long and so lovingly on its descriptions of the female form as to suggest that Kate O'Brien herself has a personal stake in these moments:

The long, narrow lines of her body, the girlish thinness of her

arms, the sweet young breast, the soft dark fall of her hair, her
profile, saved from perfection by too much length of bone, by
subtle irregularities of mouth and nostril and upslanting eye-
brow, above all by its exquisite mobility of expression – all
these beauties raised in him such a conflict of senses and spirit
as made victory and defeat alike unbearable. For if he won her,
what skill or right had he in such possession, and if he lost –[25]

The rhetoric of the connoisseur is at work in the scene, as if Agnes is
no more than a particularly fine vase to be added to the young
doctor's collection. That it is entirely guileless and innocent of the
cynicism usually associated with such epicures is soon made clear
when Dr Curran openly blurts his rather rudimentary feelings to
Agnes herself: 'it was no part of my plan to fall in love with a *femme
fatale*'.[26]
    She is so far from thinking of herself in such a role that his pro-
posal runs the risk of seeming ludicrous rather than searing: yet it is
part of his attractiveness that he has some saving sense of the idiocy
of the situation. A young woman who finds that her most heartfelt
prayers verge on self-inflation might be responsively aware of such a
problem. To a great extent the problem is one that also assails
O'Brien repeatedly through the book, and it can be summed up by
one of her mantra-words: setting. If she has difficulty in realizing her
characters in their chosen settings, that may be reflected in the rather
similar difficulty they experience themselves. Or so Dr Curran
finds it:

> How ludicrous, in black frock-coat, in healthy sweating flesh
> that covered healthy bones, surrounded by the reassuring
> decencies of mahogany and mantelpiece and ticking clock, to be
> unable to ask a decorous and personable young lady to do him
> the honour of becoming his wife.[27]

Poor Agnes is appalled by the spectacle of his suffering. 'Is no one
happy then?' she fiercely asks.
    The nurse who attends on Teresa Mulqueen is reputed to be the
best in Ireland: she is kind, professional, reliable and efficient. She is
also without a fortune and, though pretty, has now reached the age
of thirty without any prospects, for those doctors who kissed her for
fun were too shrewd to be entrapped. Nurse Cunningham's true
analogy in the story is Marie-Rose, the vain and comely sister of
Agnes, who is also a victim (but in a different way) of the market in
marriageable females. Both women are about the same age and,

though one was born to riches and the other to poverty, both are now in an emotional cul-de-sac, living as marginal figures in houses not their own. Even worse, both have become willing creatures of the male world, brightening visibly when an appreciative man enters the room. To all intents they exist only in their perception of and by men. Yet Agnes (for she is no paragon) can idealize her sister even as she despises the manipulative nurse. In this novel family feeling counts for a great deal: the memory of that distant moment when the charismatic older sister protected the young Agnes from the mockery of schoolmates will be replayed in every situation. Dr Curran, who worships Agnes, is baffled by her devotion and constantly searches in Marie-Rose for 'a reason beyond her charms why Agnes loved her'.[28]

Although O'Brien was, like George Eliot, an agnostic, her characters are orthodox believers, and this includes even those whose illicit love threatens to remove them from the embrace of holy mother Church. If the author's weakness was to turn for solutions to the very institutions that raised so many problems, this was also her greatest strength: unlike other artists, who celebrated the audacity of those who stepped outside the local codes, she more stubbornly tried to find a mode of existence for her critical attitudes within the received institutions. To challenge and subvert Catholicism from within its felt experience was not just stubborn, but the ultimate in theological sophistication. Throbbing with her private passion, Agnes resolves to make a good confession – her first in ten weeks – as a preparation for the triduum of masses planned by her uncle, Father Tom Considine, brother of the dying Teresa.

Faith is the cold 'fact' with which she will destroy 'fantasy'.[29] She confesses her sin with great moral rigour, even accusing herself of fearing the power of prayer to kill her love. Her confessor bluntly tells her that it is the fate of all earthly love to die – hardly a proposal in keeping with the words of Jesus who taught that love of the neighbour found its ultimate fulfilment in the eternal love of God, but a dogma that accorded with the life-denying Jansenism much favoured in 1880s Ireland. This coldness is forbidding, yet oddly seductive to Agnes. Her faith is 'a cold thing, a fact'. So is Vincent O'Regan, whose attraction for women seems to lie in his cool imperviousness to emotion: 'Born into an age not so much of feeling as of disseminated attachments and sentiments, he lacked the disposition to experience them.'[30] So he becomes a walking challenge to every woman to rekindle in him a sense of involvement with life. He had hoped by marriage to the pretty Marie-Rose to 'grow warm and confident enough to be himself, as he had been with his mother'.[31] Once again family feeling dictates all that is to follow in the life of the emotions, and with disastrous results. Vincent's needs have scant room for those of Marie-Rose, another vain and rather selfish person, with the consequence that the marriage fails. The disaster has, however, robbed Vincent of his former indifference to feeling, which now burns like a subterranean fire in the depths of his personality, while he relies on fine manners to 'carry him through a life he hardly noticed'.[32] Then the passion for Agnes erupts.

The passing reference to Parnell at a dinner party evokes the dangers for them both, should they break out of the social code. It is part of O'Brien's great achievement that she can at once record the value of that code, while at the same time raising the possibility that it may be perverse. Vincent continues to play the husband game with Marie-Rose, as both lie down at day's end for sleep together: 'a curious intimacy', writes a savage and sardonic O'Brien, 'which the world called natural'.[33] It would be too obvious to read this as a lesbian critique of orthodox marriage: it may be that, but it is also an aspect of O'Brien's attempt, through her characters, to imagine alternatives to the family structure. There are no happily married couples in *The Ante-Room*: even Danny Mulqueen, who still loves his dying wife, must implore her to speak to him, despite his pained knowledge that she has eyes now only for her adored son. Marriage is the trap into which women walk as a prelude to the discovery of their real desire. The work of the book is the attempt to know that desire, and to feel it, and then name it with the vividness of speech: and that project is well-nigh impossible. There may be other utopian possibilities that could replace marriage, but they are briefly intuited as implications rather than overt statements at fleeting moments in the narrative. For instance, when Vincent viciously dismisses the erotic overtures of his wife ('Go away'), she steals out of their boudoir and makes for her sister's room, 'and no cruelty would be allowed to touch her there'.[34] Vincent has no difficulty in imagining that scene: in truth the imagining of it greatly excites him, for his wife has now gone where he would most like to be, straight into the arms of Agnes. Agnes, who would want nothing better than to melt into his arms, will now (he knows) make do with the arms of the wife who so recently touched him. It is as if, unable to make love directly to one another, they can do so only at a remove, in the sharing of Marie-Rose – and so have the one through possession of the other.

Feminist critics of the book have marvelled at the apparent contradiction between its highly traditional paragraphs outlining feminine beauty of a kind that appeals to the male gaze and its radical search in the spaces between such moments for a more authentic sexuality.[35] But there may be no real contradiction between both sorts of passage. The narrative accounts of Marie-Rose's beauty tend to stress its auto-erotic, self-caressing quality: and this makes perfect sense if she is to be seen as a surrogate lover for both Vincent and Agnes, enacting on her body a set of gestures that they wish to perform on one another:

> In spite of weary lines about her eyes, she was looking – she could not but admit – delicious. She ran her hand affectionately along her smooth young cheek, and mused with an impartial pleasure upon the whiteness of her throat. The white frills of her nightdress, the flounces and niches of her white wrap, foamed delicately, and made a dramatic darkness of the shadows on which she sat.[36]

To say that 'the scopic representation of women as objects of the male gaze is very prevalent in O'Brien'[37] is not to say that she necessarily endorses it: after all, the treatment of Marie-Rose is generally critical, even dismissive. O'Brien is rather scathing about the fact that for her 'male society was bread and wine',[38] so that it is hardly surprising that she should view her body with the rapture of an approving male.

The technique had become graphic in James Joyce's portrayal of a similar tendency in Molly Bloom:

> . . . I bet he never saw a better pair of thighs than that look how white they are the smoothest part is right there between this bit here how soft like a peach God I wouldn't mind being a man and get up on a lovely woman O Lord . . .[39]

It is based on a recognition that even in moments of deep emotion, a woman may be accompanied by an image of herself, split quite literally in two. John Berger has written that woman, 'born into the keeping of man', is often an object to herself: 'whilst she is walking across a room or whilst she is weeping at the death of her father, she can scarcely avoid envisaging herself walking or weeping'.[40] To some this is a problem and a dire humiliation, but for others, such as Marie-Rose, it is a pleasure to impersonate the male fetish and to do so for her own pleasure as much as for a man's.[41] The scene quoted above is enacted in the solitude of her room, to be repeated many times in more social settings.[42] What O'Brien is doing in these scenes is submitting the traditional portraiture to the implied critique of the narrative, just as she deploys the modes of popular romance in order to raise questions that are ordinarily felt to lie well outside their limits.[43] Rather than mock or patronize those modes, she reshapes them for her own subversive purposes. In the space she occupies between high and popular art, she opens up a zone of ambiguity in which an unprecedented knowledge may become possible. Vincent O'Regan seeks precisely that kind of knowledge when, hearing his wife's jibe that Agnes may become a bluestocking, he ponders the idea of a salon under their joint direction: the virtue of the idea in his mind lay in the fact that 'it could not be family life in a family drawing-room'.[44]

Marie-Rose is undoubtedly a creature drawn from the world of popular melodrama. Viewing the scene before her in which Agnes does needlework while Vincent and Dr Curran hover, she thinks 'it would make a pretty moment in a play. But what a deadly play in which nothing was ever allowed to happen.'[45] Because no such play is conceivable, this narrative detailing latency must take the form of a psychological novel. Those who do not think, as Agnes laments, may acquire a sense of reality from the sheer certainty with which they act: but those who take thought are doomed to wait and to wonder. This is the 'non-reality' that Vincent wishes to make a central theme. In a tale of so many characters who refuse to confront reality, those who can bring themselves to face it find themselves confronting their own non-reality, as Vincent explains to Agnes:

> 'Today is an ante-room', he said dreamily. 'It's only this moment struck me, but that's what it is. That's what I feel.'[46]

The mass said by Father Tom has been celebrated in the ante-room to his sister's bedroom, and that might be a symbol of the robing-room for angels voyaging to heaven. In another novel, O'Brien writes of Ireland itself as 'Heaven's ante-room',[47] and in many of her works one has the sense of the country as a place from which a person might start out on an adventure but hardly one in which a transforming experience could happen. The ante-room that was Ireland in the 1880s would soon lead to the radical politics of Sinn Féin and the Gaelic League, but these were movements that would pass the Mulqueens, if not Dr Curran, by.[48]

The drama of waiting for an end that may make a beginning possible had been transcribed by Tone and Yeats long before O'Brien and Beckett were to make of it a central feature of the novel. But that sense of expectancy has for Vincent even deeper possible meaning, which Agnes queries:

> 'A mystical experience?' Her voice was ironical.

'It may be, but it doesn't require a name. It doesn't even need to be anything but an illusion.'[49]

Later, alone with himself, Vincent concedes that the image of Agnes was on the far side of *his* ante-room:

> Admit your meaning. Are you trapped by the inexorability of time? What was your meaning then?
>
> An ante-room – well, perhaps to truth, or fate, or any of those useful abstracts. And she was all of them.[50]

Vincent is a romantic and may well, in seizing upon the image, have been thinking of the poet John Keats, who offered in a famous letter his description of human development as a progress through a mansion of many apartments, only two of which the poet could describe: 'The first we step into we call the infant or thoughtless Chamber, in which we remain as long as we do not think.'[51] This is the state of rudimentary being outlined to Agnes at the dinner party: 'so X is only himself in so far as he doesn't think'.[52] But intrepid souls like theirs can never find that state enough, for as Keats continues in his passage:

> We remain there a long while, and notwithstanding the doors of the second Chamber remain wide open, showing a bright appearance, we care not to hasten to it; but are at length imperceptibly impelled by the awakening of this thinking principle within us – we no sooner get into the second Chamber, which I shall call the Chamber of Maiden-Thought, than we become intoxicated with the light and the atmosphere, we see nothing but pleasant wonders and think of delaying them for ever in delight: However among the effects this breathing is father of is that tremendous one of sharpening one's vision into the heart and nature of Man – of convincing one's nerves that the world is full of Misery and Heartbreak, Pain, Sickness and oppression – whereby this Chamber of Maiden-Thought becomes gradually darkened and at the same time on all sides of it many doors are set open – but all dark – all leading to dark passages – We see not the balance of good and evil. We are in a Mist.[53]

For Vincent, the problem is that he cannot leave the chamber of latency and grow to a fully adult life. His fidelity to Catholic doctrine holds him back, as surely as it troubles Agnes: but deeper still for both of them are the prior ties to family, his to his mother, hers to her sister.

The force of nature itself seems to demand their coupling. When they embrace, they seem grooved by heaven to take one another, 'as if the platonic spirit was mended here, and a completed creature stood united to itself at last'.[54] The old myth of male and female as broken halves of a once-full, now-fractured person is repeated, as if to suggest that real love is the return of two broken halves on earth to form a single being. However, that utopian possibility cannot occur on earth. Vincent had once looked Agnes over and passed her by, and so they must both live with the consequences: 'she knew that it could never happen, and that the wildest danger was not danger'.[55] In the end, it is not even their Catholicism that precludes the possibility so much as their familism. Vincent is fixated on his mother and openly admits that Agnes's attraction is that she reminds him of her: if the dead woman were alive, he would not need Agnes at all. That is a syndrome depressingly close to Reggie's, and lest there be any doubt, Vincent spells it out in a plea to Agnes: 'If you're ever the mother of a son, don't ever die until he's hardened to the idea.'[56]

Desire in *The Ante-Room* is invariably a displaced form of family feeling, which is usually 'mapped' onto a transitional object – by Vincent from his dead mother to Agnes, by her from her living sister to Vincent. Yet it must, in the stringent economy of the emotions, be returned to family in the end. Not even the incest taboo seems strong enough to overwhelm it. The ante-room is never really abandoned, except by Dr Curran who, for all his crazy notions of *femmes fatales*, can experience a truly selfless love for another person: 'Let her love anyone, his heart cried, so long as that anyone can take her love and keep it in fidelity and fruitfulness.'[57] Vincent clearly cannot. Instead, he shoots himself, thereby freeing his unhappy wife of their temporary arrangement, even as he plunges his beloved into an even deeper circle of pain. 'Darling mother. He pulled the trigger, his thoughts far off in boyhood.'[58] The histrionics of that final line are infantile, regressive: and they come out of a very different sort of plot from the one that began with so many modulations and resignations. The effect is as if an Ibsen problem play had been rewritten as a novel by Henry James: but that may be no weakness on the part of O'Brien so much as the logical consequence of the decadent romanticism that disables most of the men in this tale. Agnes has also thought of the possibility of her own death, but as of a freedom she has no right to expect, rather like a full consummation with Vincent: 'They are all alive, even Mother. But I'm dying. Vincent, if I could only die – oh,

Vincent, darling –'[59] However, such is her devotion to duty that the very notion of suicide would never even cross her mind.

The final two sentences of the book could, after all, function also as an epitaph for Reggie, now to undergo the charade of a marriage to Nurse Cunningham. His mother's smothering concern has ensured that he will never be a responsible, self-validating adult: and yet his parody of a heterosexual wedding must function as the answer to her prayer for a new protector to watch over her son after she dies. The romantic novel of nurses and sickroom romances has been provided here by O'Brien, but as a dire parody of the genre, whose truly silly plot is 'written' to a conclusion by Teresa Mulqueen. The nurse survives the casual tragedy as securely as will Marie-Rose, because both lack the sort of imagination and empathy that allows Agnes to describe the mock-marriage as horrible. Whether she can survive the sorrow of a dead lover to recognize the moral pressure of Dr Curran's claim is left open at the end: but by then a heterosexual marriage of this kind has been made to seem more like a trap than a reward for persons of some moral integrity. The comedy of manners that should end in a male–female wedding has become instead a sombre tragedy of conscience in which painful weddings are undone and a hollow marriage is greeted as a boon. The conclusion, for all the melodrama of the last line, is richly sceptical.

The great mid-nineteenth-century novels of Emily Brontë and George Eliot often centred on persons who were determined to carry the feelings of childhood into the powers of adult life: most ended in tragedies of arrested adolescence. In the hands of a Brontë, the treatment could be melodramatic. In those of Eliot, it was more subtle. Kate O'Brien takes up the theme, finding in the holy childhood of Irish Catholics a world whose claustrophobic narrowness is compensated for by a real intensity of feeling. The family romance among the upper class is, it seems, unending. So is the decisive impact of a religious formation: once a Catholic, always a Catholic.

Agnes and Vincent test their love against the accumulated wisdom of the Church simply because their religion, for all its flaws, is the only institution capable of expressing – if not solving – the mystery of existence. They feel no conflict between their love and the love of God: merely a sense that the one could be completed only in the other and that the earthly interpreters of God's law could never countenance the physical consummation of their love in marriage. The central mysteries of the faith are never questioned. There may be a crisis of conscience but there is no waning of belief. O'Brien, for all her agnosticism, wrote with tender respect for those audacious enough to place their belief in the central mystery of Catholicism, 'the quietest moment of their faith, a moment so still that bells must ring and sometimes guns must sound to make it humanly bearable'. She could feel this respect because she considered herself above 'the mighty lie of romantic passion',[60] and so she felt the need to afford human solidarities some institutional protection.

It is by no means clear that for her the family could ever function as such an institution. Although Agnes is driven back into it, this is made to seem a terrible defeat, a regression to infantilism and 'that night in Junior Recreation'.[61] Even O'Brien's staunchest admirers suggest that she finds the family a smothering but essential institution, 'always more real, more reliable, more lasting than the passionate attraction of mature adults'.[62] But there is no textual evidence to suggest that she approves of that observation in *The Ante-Room*, and plenty to indicate that she found it a tyrannical formula rather than a life-enhancing form. The characters in whom she is truly interested feel enervated rather than uplifted by the conventions of their inherited world, much as O'Brien herself was frustrated more than facilitated by the existing Anglo-Irish novel. Her title may also indicate her conviction that the novel of personal relations in Ireland has yet to be fully made, the house of fiction has yet to be built and entered.[63]

It would have been impossible for any Irish writer in 1880 to report such a tale, but even from the retrospect of 1934 the difficulties were immense. O'Brien needed to invent at least as much of the 'furniture' as she described, and also the emotional nuances of her characters: an exacting and exhausting challenge. English writers from the 1880s to the 1930s could take such settings and feelings for granted as part of their social 'given': all they needed to do was to colour them by numbers. But O'Brien was compelled to bring into being an entire social world before she could report it with conviction. All writers must invent a world, of course, but most have raw materials to hand out of which to re-create a personal version of that world. She, however, had little enough. That her world was enclosed and impervious was part of the problem: it would never be rendered in objective accounts by outsiders but its decline could be felt only from within and by those who knew that its doom was sealed.

Perhaps this is why John McGahern, another exponent of the novel as social elegy, has called her a poet working in prose.[64] Yet the people whom she describes are, for all their blindness, possessed of one claim to dignity: they are among the very few who are enabled by the privilege of upbringing and education to appreciate the poetry at the heart of the Catholic religion and to attempt to bring their behaviour into conformity with that imaginative vision, felt less as a matter of social propriety than as a deeply personal imperative. O'Brien's agnosticism is kept well hidden in her writings, but if she was in any sense a Catholic, she was one of a Continental rather than an Irish kind.

32

All the Dead Voices –
Cré Na Cille

Ils m'ennuient. On espère toujours trouver la paix dans la mort, mais la tombe ne semble pas encore être la mort. On ne trouve ici en tout cas, que de l'ennui . . .[1]

These might sound like the words of Beckett's Malone, but are in fact spoken by the French airman, killed when his plane crashed on Connemara soil, who was buried in Máirtín Ó Cadhain's mythical Cré na Cille (Graveyard Clay). His Gallic voice, shot through with disappointment and yearning, speaks for every denizen of that grave-yard, lamenting a life that is over but not yet ended, even after death. Gaelic folk wisdom proclaimed that the border between the living and dead was unclear, uncharted but undeniably there. Modernists from Beckett to Ó Cadhain have all but erased it, preferring to explore the liminal zones between. Whereas nineteenth-century romantic poets like Coleridge often described the experience of feeling dead while being alive, the moderns, more frighteningly perhaps, suggested that a person may die and yet go on talking. That theme was pervasive, from Gogol's *Dead Souls* to Edgar Lee Masters's *Spoon River Anthology* and thence to Borges's *Book of the Dead*. *Under Milk Wood* by Dylan Thomas is especially similar to *Cré na Cille*, which also might well have been a radio play. Under the baton of the First Narrator – whose tone is in the pompous, portentous mode of Stoc na Cille – the characters under Milk Wood gossip about village life, just as Ó Cadhain's do. There is no question of influence here, or if there were it would be of the influence of Ó Cadhain upon Thomas, for *Cré na Cille* was published in 1949 and the text of *Under Milk Wood* was completed only during the interval of its first performance in New York in 1953. It is simply that the idea of a 'text for voices' was developed simultaneously in a number of cultures, in the golden age of broadcast radio during the 1940s and 1950s.

Neither can it be confidently asserted that Máirtín Ó Cadhain came under the direct influence of Beckett as early as 1949. As contemporary writers, however, they treated remarkably similar themes, abandoned their readers to intractable materials, forsook traditional plot in favour of 'situations', and, most notably of all, subjected the institution of literature to a coruscating mockery. They did not exempt themselves as authors from this critique, being particularly scathing of all ideas of 'style'. Ultimately, both writers sought to install their readers in a dissolving, uncertain universe.

Although there is much talk in *Cré na Cille* about funeral rituals, about the quality of candles and crosses used at the characters' funerals, or about the number of priests who officiated, there is no reference to the consolations of Catholic belief or to the mercy of a compassionate God. As with Ó Rathaille in his farewell poem, as with Synge's Aran Islanders, so also with Ó Cadhain's village gossips. In this blessed cemetery, no corpse enjoys a wink of sleep or a moment's repose. The central character, Caitríona Pháidín, whose dream is to be reburied in a more expensive part of the graveyard, has occasion to ask plaintively at the outset:

> An beo nó marbh atá siad seo? Tá siad uilig ag cur díobh chomh treán céanna agus a bhí ós cionn talúna. Shíl mé ó chuirfí i gcill mé go mbeadh suaimhneas i ndán dom . . . ach cén chiall an chathaíocht seo i gcré na cille?[2]

> Are these dead or alive? They are all holding forth as strongly as they did over ground. I thought that once I was buried, my lot would be repose, but what sense is there to this bickering in graveyard clay?

It isn't long before her old friend Muread Phroinsiais explains:

> An saol céanna atá anseo a Chaitríona, agus a bhí san 'ould country' ach gurb é a bhfeiceann muid an uaigh a bhfuil muid inti, agus nach bhféadann muid an chónra a fhágáil. Ní chloisfidh tú

an duine beo ach oiread, nó ní bheidh a fhios agat céard is cor dó ach de réir mar a innseos na marbháin nua-churtha é.[3]

It's the same life here, Caitríona, that was in the 'ould country', but for the fact that we can see the grave we're in, and that we're not able to leave the coffin. You won't hear live people either, nor will you know what happens to them, except according as the newly buried tell you.

This condition resembles the anti-purgatory of Dante and Beckett, a murky zone between life and death, where the penitent is compelled to wait at the foot of the mountain, for exactly the same span which he passed sinfully in life, doomed to endure the indolence in which he used to indulge. According to both Beckett and orthodox Catholic doctrine, *that* is why there is no serenity to be found in the grave, for the pains of life will not suffice to expiate a person's sins.

Samuel Beckett wrote in *Malone Dies*:

And without knowing exactly what his sin was he felt full well that living was not a sufficient atonement for it, or that this atonement was itself a sin, calling for more atonement . . . he even wondered if it was really necessary to be guilty in order to be punished . . .[4]

Those caught in this state cannot grow or develop, even though their bodies continue to degenerate and disintegrate. Since they cannot move elsewhere, there is no great vitality in the narrating nor any clear plot-line in the narrative. As Al Alvarez has noted of *Malone Dies*, this is the aesthetic equivalent of impotence, this stasis between life and death, this purgatory suspended between paradise and earthly toil.[5] Doubtless it was such a liminal zone that Ó Cadhain evoked when he called each of his chapters an *eadarlúid* (interlude), an insubstantial setting which falls between two acts of greater moment.[6]

Beckett's contention is that death makes no great difference either to the dead souls or to their surviving companions. 'And when one dies', observes a terrified Malone, 'others go on as if nothing happened.'[7] So it is with *Cré na Cille*. Caitríona Pháidín retains her curiosity about those who are still alive over the ground, but what is remarkable in their conversation is the implicit refusal of any participant to admit that he or she has passed out of life. Towards the end of the book, and many years after Caitríona's death, Tomás Taobh Istigh (Thomas Inside) will still say: 'Ní thaobhaíonn duine uasal ar bith tigh Chaitríona'[8] (No noble person at all frequents Caitríona's house). Her death has made little difference to him: that building will forever be 'Caitríona's house' to him, as if she were eternally inside, peering out through its windows. Nor is that all. If Tomás thinks that she is still alive in this world, Brian Mór (Big Brian) makes it clear that he *knows* that she is still alive in the other world. An elderly man, Brian has an instinctive understanding of 'the other side', and so he casually remarks to Tom Rua (Red Tom), who is about to die:

> Má tá i ndán is go dtiúrfaidh tú an tour anonn, agus go gcasfar Caitríona Pháidín i do shiúlta leat, seachain a bhfaigheadh sí brabach ar bith ar do chuid cainte. D'athraigh sí go mór nó beidh sí ag tóraíocht béadáin.[9]

> If destiny has it that you take the tour 'over', and that you meet with Caitríona Pháidín on your travels, be careful that she does not make any profit out of your conversation. She has changed a lot if she isn't looking for gossip.

If the line separating living and dead has dimmed, that seems to weigh more heavily on the dead than on the living over ground. 'Aimsir! Am! Sin dhá rud nach gcuirfidh aon imní ort anseo'[10] (Tense! Time! Those are two things that won't cause you anxiety here), they ritually tell every newly interred corpse: but that is not strictly true, for it is clear that time is their sorest affliction. Ó Cadhain informs us at the outset that the time is 'eternity' and the place 'the cemetery': and in those words lies the crux of the problem. These people have died, but their death has changed little or nothing, and they have not attained serenity. Now they find themselves waiting impatiently for the day of judgement, that moment when time itself will be set at naught. 'Ní beo iad cuid de na daoine gan a bheith ag caint'[11] (Some of the people aren't alive unless they're talking), says Caitríona: and, one might add, some aren't dead either. 'Ní chreidfeá ach an mhaith a níos scéal nua do dhaoine anseo'[12] (You wouldn't believe the good a story does to people here), she adds by way of explanation. Talk, gossip, storytelling offer the only relief to time-tormented souls; and Caitríona concedes that time *is* an issue when she recalls that it has passed much more quickly for her since the interment of Jeaic na Scolóige (Jack the Student). There is even a bleak satisfaction to be had from sparring with rivals among the dead. One man comments to his antagonist, 'Féacha an sásamh atá agat ag géaraíocht anseo ormsa – céard a dhéanfá dá gcuirfí thú le stráinséaraí i mBaile Átha Cliath nó thíos in íochtar tíre?'[13] (Consider the satisfaction you have prodding me here – What would you have done, if you'd been buried among strangers in Dublin or in the lowlands?)

In order to deepen the satisfaction accorded by words, questions are ritually asked of every corpse on its burial, but the interrogators are in no hurry for a quick reply. They would prefer to fantasize about a matter than to know the facts immediately, something observed on the Aran islands early in the century by J.M. Synge. As a consequence, when one new arrival discloses that the schoolmistress has a recent lover, everyone – including her dead husband – starts theorizing about the possible surrounding circumstances:

Diabhal a raibh tú fuaraithe muis, a Mháistir, nó go raibh a súil cócáilte aici ar fhear eile . . .
    An Máistir Beag . . . Go deimhin, muise, ní hé a Mháistir . . . Máistir Dhoire Locha. Sin fear gnaíúil a Mháistir. An striog féin ní ólann sé. Tá sé féin agus deirfiúr an tsagairt phobail – an tsliseoigín ghágach dhubh siúd a mbíonn an treabhsar uirthi – le pósadh go gairid . . . Go deimhin, muise, ní hé an póilí rua é ach oiread. Tá plioma de 'nurse' aige sin ar stropa sa nGealchathair . . . ná fear na bhfataí . . . Tomhais leat anois, a Mháistir, tiúrfaidh mé cion do thomhaise dhuit.[14]

You weren't even cold, Master, before she had her eye cocked on another man . . .
    The Little Master . . . Certainly, well, it's not the Master . . . The Master of Derrylock. That's an able man, Master. He doesn't drink a drop. He himself and the priest's sister – that cracked, dark rasher who wears trousers – are to marry shortly. For certain, Master, it isn't the red-headed policeman either. He has a big hunk of a nurse on attachment in Galway . . . nor is it the potato-man . . . Guess, now, Master, and I'll tell you the value of your guess.

And so on. The final clarification of the mystery is postponed to another day, for the further amusement of the corpses, and of course for the further torturing of the master.

Although the dead souls are waiting for the moment when time is annihilated, it is obvious to the reader that life could go on like this indefinitely. That may account for Ó Cadhain's use of the dot-dot-dot sequence to end sentences or, more precisely, to defer the ending of sentences. In the *schema* given at the start, the author says that these triple dots indicate omitted speeches or phrases of talk. Perhaps these omissions are of significant material, or it may even be that the writer is redoubling the burdens of the reader, with his challenge to fill these gaps. There could even be a somewhat metaphorical explanation. The dead do not themselves wish to complete their own 'sentences', for they know that a conclusion will bring no relief, only a terrifying silence. After all, one type of ending, death, has brought no comfort: and it is just as likely that the end of a sentence or story will bring no relief either. For that very reason, they are happy to repeat the same conversations many times over, rather than shiver in the silence that is the only alternative. They are trapped in the same dilemma as Beckett's Molloy, who moans that his life is over and yet it goes on, and who is therefore driven to enquire, 'Is there any tense for that?'[14] Such a linguistic challenge is answered by Ó Cadhain's sequence of dots, which suggest to the reader that the sentence is over but not finished, that all has been said yet utterance continues. The double meaning inherent in the word 'sentence' becomes manifest: for these sentences, like the characters of the graveyard, cannot finally and definitively expire until time itself is abandoned: and that may never happen.

One can be certain that the dead souls really would like to die. In *Páipéir Bhána agus Páipéir Bhreaca* (Unwritten and Written Papers), a major critical essay, Ó Cadhain contended that everyone in this unsure world experiences a longing for immortality and eternity, and that nothing is more eternal than death.[16] Perhaps this reveals why Caitríona Pháidín and her fellow-corpses are so preoccupied with crosses. Ó Cadhain is here, as always, mocking rural notions of respectability – the people who boast that 'my death was announced in two newspapers' or 'there were four motor cars at my funeral' – and suggesting that Caitríona Pháidín is similarly afflicted in her fond hope that a green slab of island marble be raised over her grave. There may, however, be a force deeper than a desire for mere respectability at work here. In Beckett's trilogy, Molloy was detained by such worries: 'I wanted a Latin cross over my grave, with my name clearly marked on it and the date. But they would not let me.'[17] Molloy fears that he will lose his identity in the cemetery, unless his name and location are marked by a cross.

Caitríona also believes that a cross helps to chart the fuzzy margins between life and death, and that it helps to banish those spectral presences which monotonously hint that there is no sure border between the two worlds. In her view, the naïve, rudimentary organisms still living above ground fail to appreciate the benefit to the dead of a well-placed cross. They think of it as a costly and spurious homage, and are sadly unaware of the continuing importance of individuality to the inhabitants of a cemetery that has been incorrectly mapped:

> Tá siad á gcaitheamh síos i bpoll ar bith sa reilig fearach is dá mba putógaí éisc nó sliogáin fhaochan a bheadh acu ann. Mara bhfuil crois ós do chionn sa reilig seo, dheamhan lá san aer nach oscailte a bheas sé.[18]

> They are being thrown down into any old hole in the cemetery, as if they were no more than fish shells. Unless you have a cross overhead in this cemetery, one day your grave will be opened to the air.

This world and the next are so porous that the integrity of the person is under constant threat. At least a clear demarcation of graves is an aid to self-respect.

That was why Beckett's Malone wanted a marked grave. On the other hand, he did not wish to depart this life, lest he find no comfort in the grave: but, on the other, he says, 'it is also possible that I am dead already and that all continues more or less as it was'.[19] Nobody among those underground in *Cré na Cille* would dispute the latter contention: and, indeed, above ground one or two persons might also be found to confirm it: those who saw the ghost of the French aviator, or who still see the spirit of Tomás Taobh Istigh expelling farm animals from his plot of land every afternoon. If the margins between townland and cemetery were vague enough at the start of the narrative, they have all but disappeared by the end, as is clear when a newly buried corpse remarks, 'Chuala mise, a Chaitríona, nach dtug tú suaimhneas ar bith do Jeaic na Scolóige ó a thosaigh tú' (I heard, Caitríona, that you have given no peace to Jack the Student since your death).[20] Her spirit has been haunting the live man, seeking to summon him to the graveyard.

As a result of all these factors, there is a circular structure to both *Cré na Cille* and Beckett's trilogy. The characters cannot step out of time, but they are also incapable of growth. There can be no beginning, middle or end in the ensuing narration, only the perpetual repetition of the same range of sentences, petering out into a dot-dot-dot. The protagonists, though that is hardly the word, of Beckett's third volume *The Unnamable* have no identity, only a rotting body and a noisy voice. This is a state similar to Caitríona's: 'a little hell, after my own heart, with a few nice damned to foist my groans on'. Ideally, these protagonists would prefer a final silence: 'Ah, if only it would stop, this meaningless voice which just barely prevents you from being nothing.' He would like to conclude on one emphatic full stop: but Beckett, addicted to the indeterminacy of things, cannot record such an ending: 'the search for the means to put an end to things, an end to speech, is what enables discourse to continue'.[21]

Of what value is such a discourse to artists who have a consistently low opinion of the communicative powers of language? Oscar Wilde once joked that everybody is good until they learn how to talk, because to talk is in effect to lie. Beckett's anti-heroes found that words were inadequate to conceal what they felt. One challenge entertained in *The Unnamable* is the attempt to 'go without saying', to write sentences without saying anything at all. The narrator discovers, however, that language cannot even be relied on to fail fully in its expressive function. He would, baby-like, wish to say 'ba, ba, ba', but 'it seems impossible to speak and yet say nothing, you think that you have succeeded but you always overlook something, a little yes, a little no, enough to exterminate a regiment of dragoons'.[22] If discourse can neither conceal nor reveal, then its only function is to shorten the wait for the day of judgement, a day that may never come.

Since content is so inconsiderable, all energy must be invested in the notion of style. Ó Cadhain once said that words should be handled as carefully as new-laid eggs,[23] and he had no great opinion of the manner in which most people use them. One of his characters in *Cré na Cille*, Tom Rua, is so evasive in his cautious repetitions that the other corpses can extract no news whatever from him when he is buried among them:

Cé mar atá siad suas ansin?
   Cé mar atá siad suas ansin? Suas ansin. Suas ansin muis . . .
   Bréa nach dtiúrfá freagra ar an té a labhródh leat, a Tom Rua. Cé mar atá siad suas ansin?
   Cuid acu go maith. Cuid acu go dona . . .
   Slán an scéalaí. Cé tá go maith agus cé tá go dona?
   Is críonna an té adéarfadh. Is críonna an té adéarfadh cé tá go maith agus cé tá go dona.[24]

How are they up there?
   How are they up there? Up there. Up there now.
   Isn't it fine the way you won't give an answer to the person who speaks to you, Red Tom. How are they up there?
   Some of them good. Some of them bad . . .
   Good health to the teller. Who is good and who is bad?

It's a wise man who could say. It's a wise man who could say who is good and who is bad.

Ó Cadhain again raises the question broached in his short story 'Fios' (Knowledge). What does a conversation signify? How much of it is strictly meaningless? Is it a satisfactory mode of communication at all? He seems to have thought not. In *Páipéir Bhána agus Páipéir Bhreaca* he suggested that these questions had been asked and answered by Beckett:

D'fhéach Beckett leis an gceist a fhreagairt in úrscéalta agus i ndrámaí de chineál nár scríobhadh cheana agus anois tá na focla féin ligthe ar lár. Níl fanta ach cineál mím.[25]

Beckett looked to answer the question in novels and plays of a kind not written before; and now the words themselves have been left out. Only a kind of mime remains.

Ó Cadhain was concerned not just with the possible death of Irish, but with the death of language as such. He lashed out against those literary critics who were making fashionable use of a terminology in Irish – 'téatar' for theatre, 'caracatúr' for caricature – and said that they would be better employed playing golf. He understood the complexities of Irish usage, but equally, in *Cré na Cille*, he could mock the pedant who lost five hundred pounds in a crossword competition because he insisted that there should be five letters in the word 'teine' (rather than the modern 'tine'). More fundamental, however, was his conviction that attempts to use language for purposes of communication are seldom made and even less often reciprocated. *Cré na Cille* is punctuated not by genuine conversation but by collections of rival monologues, without interaction of any significant kind, as each speaker seeks to appease his or her monomania and to reduce all interlocutors to silence. As one is told, 'Síleann tú má d'airigh tú do sheanleaba féin crua, go bhfuil chuile leaba eile crua freisin'[26] (You think that, just because you found your own bed hard, everybody else's bed is hard as well). Similar monologues, disguised as conversation, recur repeatedly in Beckett's novels and, indeed, in sections of *Ulysses*.

If Ó Cadhain is dubious about communication, he is positively scathing about the alleged nobility of literature as a traditional institution and repository of value. As in the novels of Flann O'Brien, that significance assigned to literature by the high romantic philosophy is then methodically removed for the sake of a hard-edged, modern authenticity. The schoolmaster and his wife in *Cré na Cille* are made to speak an arty lingo, a jargon that is factitiously elevated; their high-minded acquaintances like Nóra Shéainin (Nóra, daughter of Johnny) cannot imagine their own lives without recourse to the clichés of the novelette – 'Ar chuala tú mar deir Kinks le Blicsín sa Chaor-Phóg é?' (Have you heard how Kinks speaks to Blixen in *The Noble Kiss?*).[27] Nóra's friend Dotie is the Gerty MacDowell of the Gaeltacht, and every time she utters another tearful lament that she was not buried in the better earth of east Galway, Nóra says sadly, 'Dotie! Maothnas! an óinsiúlacht arís!' (Dotie! Sentimentality! Womanly silliness again!)[28] When the schoolmaster speaks tenderly of his courtship with his wife, he receives a similar rebuke: indeed, an explicit contrast is made between his hyper-literary account of things and the more homely memories of those neighbours who spotted him through the schoolroom window: 'M'anam, i gcead duitse, a Mháistir, go raibh tú dhá cláradh istigh' (By my soul, and with your permission, Master, but you were fucking her in there).[29]

It is against this background of contending registers and tonalities that the narrative voice of Stoc na Cille is most clearly explicable. Daniel Corkery made an error in suggesting that these passages, at the start of each interlude, were no more than an awkward excrescence. He accused Ó Cadhain of foolishly attempting to add depth and amplitude to the book by recourse to a spuriously romantic, foreign-sounding voice. In a text filled with mockery of false archaism and purple passages, however, it is obvious that Stoc na Cille was an entirely playful, ironical invention. Ó Cadhain intended a contrast between his empty but self-confident tones and the irritable but authentic speech of the other corpses.[30] His object was to pare down the rhetorical cliché and to expose its practitioners, as Beckett had with Pozzo. If nothing can be fully expressed, then style becomes an ornament which can only draw attention to its own uselessness. Although Stoc na Cille constantly asserts, 'Ba mé an chéad chorp sa gcill. Nach síleann sibh gur cóir go mbeadh rud éicínt le rá ag sean-undúir na cille. Cead cainte dhom! Cead cainte! . . .' (I was the first body in the cemetery. Don't you think there must be something to be said by the old founder of the graveyard? Give me permission to speak! Permission to speak! . . .),[31] he has not a thing to say when given his chance at the end. Stoc na Cille is in fact a style without any underlying character or content. It interesting to recall in that context how Ó Cadhain's greatest critics often complained that, though he was a master of idiomatic Irish, he had no vision or philosophy.

He seems to have been well aware of this and to have identified his own voice with that of Stoc na Cille. In the final passages of *Páipéir*

Bhána agus Páipéir Bhreaca, he reverted, quite knowingly, to the Stoc na Cille style, conflating it with echoes of Pearse and Joyce:

> Tá aois na Caillí Béarra agam, aois Bhrú na Bóinne, aois na heilite móire. Tá dhá mhíle bliain den chráin bhréan sin arb í Éire í, ag dul i mo cheann, i mo bhéal, i mo shúile, i mo cheann, i mo bhrionglóidí.[32]

> I am the age of the Hag of Beare, the age of Bru na Boinne, the age of the great deer. The two thousand years of that tiresome sow called Éire I have coursing through my head, my mouth, my eyes, my head, my dreams.

If there is mockery of Stoc na Cille in the novel, it is also an auto-critique, a debunking of the cult of the author. Ó Cadhain shared in the contemporary distrust of omniscient authors who coerced or usurped readers' responses. He preferred to leave the reader free to assign meaning in the space provided by the dot-dot-dots; and he preferred this precisely because he had no philosophy, no assured wisdom to offer. If Stoc na Cille exemplified anything, it is Beckett's famous description of an art

> . . . weary of its puny exploits, weary of pretending to be able, of being able, of doing a little better the same old thing, of going a little further along a dreary road . . . and preferring the expression that there is nothing to express, no power to express, no desire to express, along with the obligation to express.[33]

Cré na Cille is an anti-novel in the Beckettian mode and its writer goes to great lengths to deflate the autocratic pretensions of the artist. Consider the following ludicrous injunctions to a would-be wordsmith:

> Má tá fút a dhul ag cumadh, a Chóilí, cuimhnigh gur geis leis an nGúm rud ar bith a chuirfeadh inín i bhfalach ar a hathair a fhoilsiú . . . Tá fonn scríbhneoireachta ort. Níl duine ar bith de lucht na Gaeilge nach mbuaileann sé tráth éigin. Is dualgas coinsiais ar gach Gaeilgeoir a fháil amach an bhfuil bua na scríbhneoireachta aige, go háirid bua na gearrscéalaíochta, na drámaíochta, agus na filíochta. Is coitianta go fada an dá bhua dheire seo ná bua na gearrscéalaíochta féin. Filíocht, cuirim i gcás. Níl agat ach tosnú ag scríobh ó bhun an leathanaigh leat

suas – san nó scríobh ó dheis go clé, ach níl sin baol ar chomh fileata leis an mbealach eile.[34]

If you are in a mood to compose, Cóilí, remember that it is impossible for An Gúm to publish anything which a daughter would hide from her father . . . You are in the mood to write. There is nobody in the Irish language movement who is not struck by it at some time. It is the conscientious duty of every Irish speaker to establish whether he has the writer's skill, especially the skills of the short story, drama and poetry. The latter two skills are a lot more widespread than the skill of short-storytelling itself. Poetry, for example. You need only start to write from the bottom of the page upwards – that or else write from the right to the left, but that isn't nearly as poetic as the other way.

This literary mentor is a sort of surrogate Ó Cadhain, for he reads passages from his own book as examples for study by Cóilí, the apprentice author. They are all purple passages, of course:

'Agus bhí grian bheag dhreach-chaillte ag dul i dtalamh ar chúla Chnoc an tSeanbhaile . . .' Sin é an tour-de-force, a Chóilí: 'grian bheag dhreach-chaillte ag dul i dtalamh'; agus ní miste dhom a mheabhrú dhuit nach mór an líne dheiridh tar éis an fhocail dheiridh a bheith spréite go flaithiúil le poncannaí, poncannaí scríbhneora mar a thugaimse orthu . . .[35]

'And there was a little mis-shapen sun going down to ground behind Knockshanbally . . .' That is the tour-de-force, Cóilí. 'A little mis-shapen sun going down to ground'; and I must remind you that the last line after the last word should be sprayed generously with full stops, writer's stops as I call them . . .

Behind this self-mockery, it is clear that this author too has nothing to say, since his intensity is reserved for sound rather than sense.

Rereading the early reviews of *Cré na Cille*, one notices something rather strange. Quite without saving irony, critics read and celebrated the book for its sounds, its style, its living language: 'píosa de theanga na Gaeltachta ná déanfar é a shárú go ceann i bhfad' (a piece of Gaeltacht idiom that will not be bettered for a long time).[36] An innocent student of the reviews might conclude that the book lacked ideas, being little more than a disguised encyclopedia of *cortha cainte* (turns of speech). It went without saying that the book went without saying, or as Beckett's Molloy would put it:

Not to want to say, not to know what you want to say, not to be able to say what you think you want to say, and never to stop saying – that is the thing to keep in mind, even in the heat of composition.[37]

Faced with the demand to hold to a single tense, Molloy opts for the same one deployed by Stoc na Cille:

I speak in the present tense, it is so easy to speak in the present tense when speaking of the past. It is the mythological present, don't mind it.[38]

If Beckett, Kavanagh and Flann O'Brien all came to prominence in the 1940s, offering explorations of underdevelopment, then *Cré na Cille* at the end of that decade was the logical consummation of their movement. Published in serial form in the *Irish Press*, it proved massively popular, despite its layered language and difficult vocabulary. Official Ireland, however, was less amused. Ó Cadhain encountered much the same critique that half a century earlier, had greeted Synge. The nationalist magazine *Ar Aghaidh* (Onward) wrote: 'Ní ar nós *Chré na Cille* a dhathaigh an Piarsach ná a chairde Gaeilgeoirí na Gaeltachta. Ní ag casadh míola ná sneá ar a chéile a chuir sé iad' (It wasn't in the manner of *Cré na Cille* that Pearse or his friends depicted the Irish speakers of the Gaeltacht. He did not depict them throwing lice and nits at one another).[39] Ó Cadhain had never claimed that his book offered a literal version of Gaeltacht life: he insisted, as late as *Páipéir Bhána agus Páipéir Bhreaca*, that the truth of art was not the truth of life. Like Synge's, his was no social documentary, but an account of the psychic state of a locality. He probably wished to contest de Valera's vision of a pastoral Ireland at a perpetual crossroads dance. If Kavanagh had redefined the peasant as one who lives an unexamined life below the level of consciousness, Ó Cadhain was in full agreement:

Ní peasants a chaomhnaigh an litríocht bhéil. Tá faitíos orm gur beag a chaomhnaíos peasants ach na claidheacha tórann agus an taisce sa stoca.[40]

It wasn't peasants who collected the oral literature. I fear that peasants collect little other than boundary walls and savings in the stocking.

That latter image reads like the account of the peasant given by

James Joyce's Stephen Hero, who conjured to the mind a weekly debauch, a weekly piety, and a weekly calculation of coppers in the stocking among a people 'as like one another as a peascod is to another peascod'.[41] Joyce was critical of the 'senility' of the folklore on which, he alleged, no individual mind had ever managed to draw out a line of beauty. He contrasted the imaginative individualism of European art with the anonymity of folklore.

By the late 1940s, American anthropologists had written extensively on communities in the west of Ireland. Some of their accounts were greatly idealized. In *Family and Community in Ireland* (1940), Arensberg and Kimball, for example, produced paragraphs of beautiful prose describing women in farmyard kitchens, statuesque in time-honoured rituals, as in a Dutch interior painting. Readers from within the community itself began to notice, however, that what the anthropologists rendered was a static, timeless world without process, seasonal migration or traumatic structural change. To capture the true nature of that society, one had to turn instead to contemporary writings by artists from within the community such as Liam O'Flaherty or Máirtín Ó Cadhain. Arensberg and Kimball had probably based their idealized vision on youthful reading of certain classics of the Irish revival, such as Yeats or Augusta Gregory: thereafter the eye of the social scientist saw only what the poet or playwright had trained it to see rather than what actually lay before it. Much of the writing in Arensberg and Kimball's work is majestic, but also euphemistic. If the social anthropologists were producing a form of pastoral literature, it was left to artists to deliver a more accurate form of sociology.[42] In doing so, they were linking up with the deglamorized version of western life, postulated against the Yeatsian version, by the young James Joyce.

Ó Cadhain concurred with the Joycean analysis, even to the extent of disparaging the folk mind. When an editorial in the folklore journal *Béaloideas* declared that unless writing in Irish reworked folk traditions, it would become dull and unvital, Ó Cadhain was quick with his rejoinder: 'Cén chaoi mar sin a néiríonn le daoine in áiteacha eile san Eoraip scríbhneoireacht a dhéanamh, d'uireasa béaloideasa, agus ar neamhchead leis?'[43] (How is it, therefore, that people in other parts of Europe can produce literature in the absence of folklore, and quite indifferent to it?). In that, he was simply repeating Patrick Pearse's injunction to Irish writers to move away from the 'cruach mhóna agus an carn aoiligh'[44] (stack of turf and pile of manure). Pearse objected to the impersonality of oral tradition, which he felt to be at variance with the individualism of major modernist writing. 'Style, after all, is only another name for personality,' he declared. Ó

Cadhain added a further element to that analysis: 'Ní dhéanann an béaloideas litríocht, mar is as aigne an duine a thagann sé amach. Maireann an litríocht ar phearsantacht a mhúnlaíos an tábhar'[45] (Folklore does not make a literature, which comes out of the individual mind. Literature lives on the personality that shapes its subject).

If Ó Cadhain did not describe the people of the west in the reverential manner adopted by Pearse, he did something more important: he answered Pearse's call for someone to bring a mind shaped by Gaelic tradition into contact with 'the mind of Europe'.[46] He learned much from his reading in French and Russian realism, more again from Kafka, but most perhaps from the talk and life of his own Connemara people. As he remarked, 'Ba inspéisiúil an rud é dhá ndéantaí staidéar ar scéalaíocht aon pharáiste amháin' (It would be an interesting thing to make a study of the lore of a single parish).[47] He claimed to spend most of his time walking around listening to the talk of half a parish echoing in his head. In that respect, as in so many others, he recalls his direct contemporary Kavanagh, who also elevated the parochial over the provincial. Kavanagh felt that the English-language writers of Ireland were obsessed with London and New York as centres of literary value, to the detriment of their own art and judgement. They should instead cultivate a stance of happy self-sufficiency.

This was exactly the kind of freedom that Ó Cadhain found in Irish. Writing in that language, he had the advantage (once enjoyed by Merriman) of being free of all worries as to whether what he wrote was sufficiently Irish or not: and he was free also of the editorial pressure from London or New York publishers that curtailed the possibilities of so much Irish writing. He was at liberty to express rather than exploit his material. Aware of the temptation to 'paddywhackery' which beset the writers of the 1940s, he found in Irish that same safeguard against stage-Irishry that Beckett found in French as he went in search of *le mot juste*. Each man could locate in either language that point of underdevelopment at which a margin of expressive integrity was possible. If Beckett had to cope with the language of exhaustion, Ó Cadhain had to find in himself the response to the exhaustion of a language. He did this by reviving ancient words from Old Irish, by borrowing from Scots Gaelic and Hiberno-English, and, if he found that the desired words did not exist, he followed the lead of Joyce and invented them himself. His blending of supernatural impossibilities with the methods of literary realism looked back to *Ulysses* but forward also to the 'boom' among the magic realists of Latin America in the 1960s and after.

There were many who believed that Ó Cadhain's graveyard, with its talking corpses, was his metaphor for the state of the Irish language: a sly innuendo to the effect that the argument was no longer about how to save the language as about who owned the embarrassingly vociferous corpse. Ó Cadhain had spent more than half of the 1940s in the 'underground world' of the Curragh internment camp as a republican prisoner and there he had had the opportunity to listen to officially dead souls in daily conversation. To read the book only in those ways, however, would be to miss much of its value. In the words of one of its more ludicrous characters, Nóra Sheáinín, *ars longa, vita brevis.* Ó Cadhain in *Cré na Cille* was already shoring against his ruins, looking forward to a time when his book would live on after his language might have died. The central *datum* of the novel is less a metaphor for the state of Irish than it is a metaphor of the fate of literature in a future world. For Ó Cadhain shared with Beckett the desperate, terrified hope that even after a language dies, the voices may continue:

> *All the dead voices.*
> *They make a noise like wings.*
> *Like leaves.*
> *Like sand.*
> *Like leaves.*
> *They all speak together.*
> *Each one to itself.*
> *What do they say?*
> *They talk about their lives.*
> *To have lived is not enough for them.*
> *They have to talk about it.*
> *To be dead is not enough for them.*
> *It is not sufficient.*[48]

The Irish language might finally expire, but even that would not be the end. The Hag of Beare, Mad Sweeny, lamenting Deirdre, Eibhlín Dhubh, Cuchulain, the young lovers of Connacht will all continue to speak and sing – and so will the voice of Stoc na Cille.

33

Underdeveloped Comedy: Patrick Kavanagh

The writer of a minor literature, according to Gilles Deleuze and Felix Guattari, 'feeds himself on abstinence' and tears out of language 'all the qualities of underdevelopment that it has tried to hide'. He tries to 'make it cry with an extremely sober and rigorous cry'. What these critics are defining is a place made sumptuous by destitution, in which writers 'oppose the oppressed quality of a language to its oppressive quality' in the attempt to locate those points of underdevelopment at which a new kind of art becomes possible.[1]

In these terms Samuel Beckett must stand as the pre-eminent resistance writer, as one who has always hated the languages of masters and who has tried to remain a stranger within his own language. First he sought impoverishment by writing in learner's French as an escape from the baroque excesses of the Anglo-Irish tradition, in which wit and wordplay were ritually expected by English readers of Irish users of their language. In French, Beckett could write with the myopic literalism of a careful student of a second language. For an Irish author to embrace French in this way was an act of linguistic self-denial.

Decades later, having achieved fame as a brilliant writer of that language, Beckett again rejected mastery, returning in works like *Company* to English, lest his 'stain upon the silence' seem made too easily. In that late period his works grew shorter, as if their maker was a kind of literary anorexic, straining for 'the blessedness of absence', for the point at which underdevelopment shades into silence.[2] 'This is becoming really insignificant,' laments a character in *Waiting for Godot*, only to be told, 'Not enough.'[3] The less Beckett had to say, the better he said it; the slimmer his texts became, the weightier the analyses they seemed to generate.

For most of his life, Beckett knew failure as others know the air they breathe, so when recognition and success came, they could not deflect him from his mission: he had breathed the 'vivifying' air of defeat too long to want to abandon it now. To be an artist was to fail, but to give that failure a form: and so Beckett, more than any other, deserved the description of one who gave a voice to the voiceless. Whereas Joyce had chosen enrichment, Beckett stripped everything down and took everything out. In a rare interview he offered Israel Shenker a piercingly lucid self-estimate:

> The kind of work I do is one in which I'm not master of my material. The more Joyce knew the more he could. I'm working with impotence, ignorance. I don't think ignorance has been exploited in the past. There seems to be a kind of aesthetic axiom that expression is achievement – must be an achievement. My little exploration is that whole zone of being which has always been set aside by artists as something unusable – as something by definition incompatible with art.[4]

The helplessness of one who lives where there is nothing to express, nothing with which to express, along with the obligation to express, seems a feasible description of the postcolonial artist. Reared in a cultural vacuum, fatigued by the representational naïveté of realist artists of the colonial power, and twitching with the urge to leave some trace behind him, he can feed only on abstinence.

Patrick Kavanagh, although Beckett's contemporary, is seldom mentioned in relation to him, perhaps because their backgrounds, talents and destinies were so very different: and yet they had a great deal in common, not least an obsession with the notion of expressive underdevelopment. Kavanagh embarked on a very Beckettian study of the mind of God, without the assistance of Christian mythology. This mythology had sustained him in youth, until he decided that it was just a beautiful fairy story:

> *No System, no Plan,*
> *Yeatsian invention*
> *No all-over*
> *Organisational power.*
> *Let words laugh*

And people be stimulated by our stuff
. . .
Beckett's garbage-can
Contains all our man
Who without fright on his face
Dominates the place
And makes all feel
That all is well.   ('Mermaid Tavern')[5]

The Plan is a Yeatsian invention, parodied by System with a capital S, but against this false literary project Kavanagh pits the author of *Endgame*. The reason there is no fright, despite the extreme situation, is that Beckett has found the healing release of laughter. He has taken failure, made it his subject, and laughed at it, just as Kavanagh could mock his own in the caustic 'If Ever You Go To Dublin Town':

I saw his name with a hundred others
In a book in the library,
It said he had never fully achieved
His potentiality.
O he was slothful,
Fol dol the di do,
He was slothful
I tell you.[6]

That might be Belacqua or Murphy or Malone, illustrating Beckett's contention that to be an artist is to fail as nobody else has failed – a point made even more poignantly in Kavanagh's self-mockingly titled 'Portrait of the Artist': 'A man of talent who lacked the little more / That makes the difference / Between success and failure'.[7] To one who saw Irish society as mere 'pastiche' with no 'overall purpose', Beckett's remedy, 'to put despair and futility on the stage for us to laugh at them', was the only option.[8] This strategy Kavanagh contrasted with that of 'academic writers ready to offer a large illuminating symbol . . . as if society were a solid, unified Victorian lie'. He thereby endorsed Beckett's 1934 essay on Irish poetry, which praised modernists and denigrated well-upholstered antiquarians.[9] Kavanagh also followed Beckett in asserting that the old-world certainties of Gaelic heroes had interest now for 'none but the academic'. The answer to the sense of doom was not to avoid tears, but to revert to laughter after they had dried. Otherwise a people would know only emotional and spiritual underdevelopment of the kind described a century earlier by a near neighbour of his, Carleton:

for, as Kavanagh put it in his Author's Note in the *Collected Poems*, 'tragedy is underdeveloped comedy, comedy not fully born'.[10]

It was just such an underdevelopment that Kavanagh explored in *The Great Hunger*. The world of subsistence farming he evokes in this long poem of 1942 shows us lower-case tragedy, according to Kavanagh, and not the upper-case kind that is underdeveloped comedy. It is a place of dire underdevelopment – economic, religious and intellectual. The poem is a fierce anti-pastoral which won the admiration of Cyril Connolly, Stephen Spender and W.H. Auden for its cultivated, banal repetitions and its slack line-endings. The title seems to promise a study of heroic nineteenth-century peasants, but the text delivers a nihilistic account of unheroic farmers in the twentieth. All this is framed sarcastically in the cinematic techniques of a curious First World anatomizing the Third.

The camera pans in on the potato-gatherers at the start, creating a sort of anti-travelogue: 'If we watch them an hour is there anything we can prove / Of life as it is broken-backed over the Book / Of Death?'[11] – but the voice grows increasingly impatient and caustic in its parody of pastoralism, for this is the voice of one who has read not only the rural landscape but William Empson too:

> *The world looks on*
> *And talks of the peasant:*
> *The peasant has no worries;*
> *In his little lyrical fields*
> *He ploughs and sows;*
> *He eats fresh food,*
> *He loves fresh women,*
> *He is his own master*
> *As it was in the Beginning*
> *The simpleness of peasant life.*
> *The birds that sing for him are eternal choirs,*
> *Everywhere he walks there are flowers.*
> *His heart is pure,*
> *His mind is clear,*
> *He can talk to God as Moses and Isaiah talked –*
> *The peasant who is only one remove from the beasts he*
> *   drives.*
> *The travellers stop their cars to gape over the green bank*
> *   into his fields:*
>
> *There is the source from which all cultures rise,*
> *And all religions,*

> There *is the pool in which the poet dips*
> *And the musician.*
> *Without the peasant base civilisation must die,*
> *Unless the clay is in the mouth the singer's singing is*
>   *useless.*
> *The travellers touch the roots of the grass and feel renewed*
> *When they grasp the steering wheels again.*[12]

The subject, as in Beckett, is how one dies a little every day; and the attempt in each section is to find a tense adequate to the plight of one whose life is ended but not yet over. The world of nature blooms and reproduces while Paddy Maguire looks impotently on, denied even the dubious pleasure of a climactic ending:

> *No crash,*
> *No drama.*
> *That was how his life happened,*
> *No mad hooves galloping in the sky.*
> *But the weak, washy way of true tragedy –*
> *A sick horse nosing around the meadow for a clean place*
>   *to die.*[13]

That final line is expanded to a slack endlessness, and the passage asserts what Beckett adumbrated: the impossibility of old-fashioned tragedy, with its moment of clarification, and its redefinition as a matter of everyday numbness. The plight of Paddy Maguire is at once absurd and Christian, absurd because it reflects the unexamined Christianity of a rural Ireland whose mothers tell their sons, 'Now go to Mass and pray and confess your sins / And you'll have all the luck'.[14]

The result is a man who never achieves even a rudimentary consciousness, a peasant in Kavanagh's anti-Revivalist sense of the species: 'Although the literal idea of the peasant is of a farm-labouring person, in fact a peasant is all that mass of mankind which lives below a certain level of consciousness. They live in the dark cave of the unconscious and they scream when they see the light.'[15] That is a description of a Joycean rather than a Yeatsian peasant, and a knowing throwback to the bare-breasted woman who beckoned across a half-door to the passing youth in *A Portrait of the Artist as a Young Man*, and who seemed to Stephen 'a type of her race and of his own, a batlike soul waking to the consciousness of itself in darkness and secrecy and loneliness'.[16] Like those Revivalist poets denounced by Beckett, Maguire never awakens to self-perception.

The Great Hunger is a reworking of Beckett's 1934 thesis: that the

failure of the Revivalists to explore self was the inevitable consequence of their resort for subject matter to an uncritical celebration
of peasant life. Kavanagh eventually concluded that his involvement
with the theme was so deep that he too had fallen into the trap of
excessive care. 'Not caring is really a sense of values and feeling of
confidence', he concluded: 'A man who cares is not the master.'[17]
Instead, such a man is the victim of the tragedy that is underdevelopment and of the underdevelopment that is tragedy.

The birth pangs of a developed comedy became, after *The Great
Hunger*, Kavanagh's abiding theme. In Joyce's equation of the artist
with the omnipotent God, high above his creation, paring his fin-
gernails, Kavanagh found his desired wisdom. Kavanagh remained
confident that the existence of a benevolent deity permitted man to
take himself far less seriously than did most modern intellectuals: to
anyone who really believed in God, the whole notion of man became
hilariously funny. Thus was born the philosophy of not caring.
Excessive solemnity became, within this new code, a form of blasphemy, or at least a vulgar sentimentality (since it was sentimental to
invest things with more significance than God gave them).

The remoteness that is the necessary condition for such laughter
allows the poet to question his own ridiculous pretensions to power
or majesty. In his poems Kavanagh seldom emulates Beckett in
making direct statements that mock the act of writing, but such declarations come frequently in the prose: 'Stupid poets think that by
taking subjects of public importance it will help their work to survive. There is nothing as dead and damned as an important thing.'[18]
Within the poetry these assaults are evident in a rejection of the portentous or the significant. Accepting that his duty is not to theorize
but to record, Kavanagh rejects the temptation to allegory, endorsing
Beckett's aphorism 'No symbols where none intended'.[19]

Above all, Kavanagh deflected solemnity by his delight in deliberate technical risk, by his attempt to write a looser and more prosaic
type of line that steadfastly resisted the seductions of Irish rhetoric.
Beckett called this the attempt to write without style. Kavanagh
explained the aspiration more colourfully, as the urge 'to play a true
note on a dead slack string'.[20] Where Joyce had tried to make prose
more poetic, Kavanagh would attempt to render poetry more prosaic. He believed that the delight of Irish talk lay not in exotic
Synge-song, but in ordinariness. So in his later poems he ran the
risk of banality, even cliché: absurdism and not caring became both
his subject and his technique in poems such as 'Lines Written on a
Seat on the Grand Canal, Dublin, Erected to the Memory of Mrs
Dermot O'Brien':

O commemorate me where there is water,
Canal water, preferably, so stilly
Greeny at the heart of summer. Brother
Commemorate me thus beautifully.
Where by a lock Niagariously roars
The falls for those who sit in the tremendous silence
Of mid-July. No one will speak in prose
Who finds his way to these Parnassian islands.
A swan goes by head low with many apologies,
Fantastic light looks through the eyes of bridges –
And look! a barge comes bringing from Athy
And other far-flung towns mythologies.
O commemorate me with no hero-courageous
Tomb – just a canal-bank seat for the passer-by.[21]

One could point to a dozen risks knowingly taken there, the most obvious being that a veteran of the 'Baggot Street Gallop' should ask for commemoration where there is water. Technically, one notes the use of repetition, as of a man forming and reforming in leisurely fashion the elements of a sentence – 'water . . . canal water, preferably' – until he gets it right. (This is the characteristic mannerism of Beckett's prose in much of the trilogy.) The use of the Dublinese -y conveys a sense that the adjective found is an approximation, not a true hit. The effect of one line reeling into the next, without end-stopping, is compounded in the last couplet by the use of a hyphenated word at the moment of transition, as if the poem were the work of a slightly tipsy man. 'Hero-courageous' is a relaxed, childlike composite, yet it topples into 'tomb'; and the off-key ending clinches the effect of poetic indifference to audience response: 'just' reduces the claims made for a poet's immortality, and the sentence collapses into silence on its last, awkward word 'passer-by'.

Darcy O'Brien has pointed to Kavanagh's eschewing of conventional rhyme (water/brother, roars/prose, bridges/courageous, silence/islands) in a poem that wreaks havoc with the sonnet, that strictest and most austere of forms.[22] The deflation of Yeatsian intensities is completed with that swan, shy rather than superb, and the use of Athy to mock that titular abstraction beloved of the great Sligo poet 'mythologies'. 'Lines Written on a Seat on the Grand Canal' was, literally and metaphorically, a watershed in Kavanagh's life, a moment when he discovered that 'my purpose was to have no purpose'. So the later Kavanagh could follow Beckett in admitting the futility of all knowledge: 'Making the statement is enough – there are no answers / To any real question'.[23] Beckett's *Molloy* had concluded

that the desire to know is a pernicious ailment that can be redeemed
only by the concrete experience of physical objects. This is also
Kavanagh's conclusion: some time in the 1950s he decided that great
poetry is simply an inventory of objects known and loved. So he follows Beckett's example and in 'The Hospital' he places his persons in
a hospital terminal ward, and then sets out on his loving inventory of
kitsch:

> *A year ago I fell in love with the functional ward*
> *Of a chest hospital: square cubicles in a row*
> *Plain concrete, wash basins – an art lover's woe,*
> *Not counting how the fellow in the next bed snored.*
>
> . . .
>
> *This is what love does to things: the Rialto Bridge,*
> *The main gate that was bent by a heavy lorry,*
> *The seat at the back of a shed that was a suntrap.*
> *Naming these things is the love-act and its pledge;*
> *For we must record love's mystery without claptrap,*
> *Snatch out of time the passionate transitory.*[24]

In this situation the poet is namer rather than beloved, and his devotion to objects gives him back a sense of his own reality.

The great difference between Kavanagh and Beckett – apart from
the obvious one between a major talent and an outright genius – lies
in their attitudes to God. Both assert the limits of human knowledge, reject pat symbolic systems, and warn of the limits of logic
and the vital necessity for mystery: 'If we go on in a logical way we
come to cage bars,' says Kavanagh. 'We must not ask the ultimate
question. "Why?" is God.'[25] This is rather like the absurdist's conviction that events simply happen and only a fool looks for causes.
A secular absurdist like Beckett is by no means sure that God is
there, but he continues to study and to curse him anyway. For
Kavanagh the value of God as an idea arises from the fact that
arguments about him cannot be proven. Beckett is suspicious about
the 'leap of faith', but he also yearns for an inscrutable to adore,
and so his Molloy seeks and finds mystery in the beautiful, incomprehensible patterns traced by dancing bees. Moran says with
rapture, 'Here is something I can study all my life and never understand.'[26] That is precisely what Kavanagh concludes about the
mind of God:

> *We have tested and tasted too much, lover –*
> *Through a chink too wide there comes in no wonder.*

. . .
Won't we be rich, my love and I, and please
God we shall not ask for reason's payment,
The why of heart-breaking strangeness in dreeping hedges
Nor analyse God's breath in common statement.[27]

Such analysis would anyway have proved impossible to a poet who sought to ravish the ineffable without the assistance of the available mythologies. For the Christian myth, Yeats had substituted *A Vision*, preferring to create his own system rather than be beholden to another's. Kavanagh rejected even this option as a questionable luxury. He chose to define himself without the props afforded by the system, and he often paid an artistic price for that loneliness, in bad poems and half-realized themes. It was of him that Brendan Kennelly said 'a man without a mythology is a man confronting famine'.[28] But Kavanagh at least had the courage to make that brave attempt.

As a critic, Kavanagh has been underestimated and misunderstood. He had a deep contempt for the wilful cultivation of Irishness in writing: 'Irishness is a form of anti-art', he wrote, 'a way of posing as a poet without actually being one.' He dubbed such pseudo-poets 'buckleppers' and defined the bucklep as follows:

> . . . an act performed by a man eager to display his merit and exuberance as a true Gael. He gallivants along some street in Dublin and suddenly he will leap into the air with a shout, causing his heels to strike hard against his buttocks. This is buckleppin'.[29]

All of this was explained in a voice close to that of his friend the Gaelic satirist Flann O'Brien, but it was also in part the voice of another exemplar, Samuel Beckett, who in the 1934 essay had dismissed those poets who tried to reproduce Gaelic prosody in English as antiquarians in flight from self-awareness.

This was Kavanagh's view too, detailed in his devastating essay on F.R. Higgins:

> Writing about F.R. Higgins is a problem – the problem of exploring a labyrinth that leads nowhere. There is also the problem of keeping oneself from accepting the fraudulent premises and invalid symbols established by the subject. The work of F.R. Higgins is based on an illusion – on a myth which he pretended to believe.
>
> The myth and illusion was Ireland.

One must try to get some things straight about the man: he was a Protestant.

He most desperately wanted to be what mystically or poetically does not exist, an 'Irishman'.

Nearly everything about Higgins would need to be put in inverted commas. All this was the essence of insincerity, for sincerity means giving all of oneself to one's work, being absolutely real. For all his pleasant verse Higgins was a dabbler.[30]

Part of Higgins's factitiousness lay in his attempt to build up Dublin as a theme, a stratagem Kavanagh called 'a gerrymandering of the constituencies of the soul'. Higgins failed to realize that Dublin derived its literary glamour from Joyce, not Joyce from Dublin.

It is hard, of course, to separate the anti-Protestantism from the anti-pastoralism in Kavanagh's criticism, but it should be emphasized that he was never theologically anti-Protestant. He was merely opposed to the use of pastoral formulae by Protestant writers who were foolishly trying to compensate for a self-diagnosed want of Irishness. When the editor who published the Higgins essay told Kavanagh that it gave the impression that he thought a Protestant could not be an Irish writer and asked him to make it clear in a footnote that this was not the case, what Kavanagh produced in response was far more interesting than a mere correction of a misunderstanding:

My immediate reaction would be: who wants to be an Irish writer?

A man is what he is, and if there is some mystical quality in the nation or the race it will ooze through the skin. Many Protestants, doubting that their Irishism would ooze, have painted it on from the outside. National characteristics are superficial qualities and are not the stuff with which the poet deals.[31]

Deep down, of course, Kavanagh did not believe in a national essence. On one famous occasion, he announced that while Daniel Corkery, Frank O'Connor and others were cranking out their 'Ireland' material, the real writers of contemporary Ireland were W.H. Auden and George Barker.

These analyses make complete sense only if removed from the constricting Irish context of the mid-twentieth century. Kavanagh was a genuinely postcolonial thinker, one who had emptied his mind of the categories devised by colonialist and anti-colonialist alike. He was the first to expose the ways in which Irish revivalism was complicit with its putative enemy, sanitizing slurs and reworking jaded categories – hence his charge that it was 'a thoroughgoing English-bred lie'.[32] Given his origins on a small farm, Kavanagh saw that what appeared to be essential traits of the Irish peasantry were to be found in most societies with little economic development and saw too that the notion of Irish essence was an ideological veil cast by a ruling class over its own self-interests. Why fetishize such a thing?

This analysis of revivalism was consistent with Frantz Fanon's account of the second phase of decolonization, when intellectuals begin to behave like foreign tourists in their own country, 'going native' in excesses of enthusiasm. Because he refused that role, Kavanagh remained as incomprehensible to most English critics as did Fanon to most French intellectuals. It was almost a point of pride to the man who was 'never much considered by the English critics' that Joyce's *A Portrait of the Artist as a Young Man*, when it appeared in 1916, got no review in England.[33] Neither Joyce nor Kavanagh had any truck with bucklepping Irishness.

Kavanagh was alert to the danger that certain 'radicals', in denouncing revivalist nationalism, might breathe new life into it by furthering the illusion that, three decades after independence, it still counted for something. Of such people he savagely wrote: 'They are not Lilliputian cranks as some outsiders scream / They are the official liberal opposition and part of the regime.'[34] The problem such pseudo-liberals could never face was the one Kavanagh confronted and solved: the fact that anti-nationalism is neither a political ideology nor a philosophy, but a neurotic reaction. He cited Sean O'Casey as a tell-tale instance of this neurosis and lamented his failure to transcend this fixation on Ireland: 'O'Casey is loved in Ireland because, however he attacks, he always accepts the theme of Ireland. To deny Ireland as a spiritual entity leaves so many people floundering without art.'[35]

Kavanagh mischievously noted that the anti-clericalism of many Irish Stalinists was much admired by the clerics themselves, because it fed the illusion that they were still important. Attacks on the Catholic Church had become almost *de rigueur* in a certain kind of play, a kind that posed challenges to audiences keen to demonstrate how far they had travelled in terms of sophistication in those early decades after independence. What Kavanagh wrote in 1954 of the contemporary scene in *The Bell* could have been repeated, without inaccuracy, for the next half-century:

You have plays in which barbarous characters are set up so that audiences can feel superior. The audiences which only yesterday were humble folk in the small fields have taken over the function of the idiotic ascendancy, and authors have turned up to invent a lower order that one can be superior about.

Great liberality is permitted towards these mythical characters in the case of murder, infanticide, drunkenness and outrageous brawling. The new middle class audience of theatre and books is falling backwards in its effort to prove itself broad-minded . . .[36]

That new class was stuck fast, repudiating its earlier nationalism but refusing, lest it be construed as an admission that native elites had the same weaknesses found elsewhere in the postcolonial world, to adopt the analysis that would have given meaning to that repudiation. They could have moved, in line with Fanon's analysis, from a revivalist nationalism to liberation: but did not make that option. Kavanagh was remorseless in his verdict on those evasions: but he was also one of the first poets in the English language to take up the theme of underdevelopment.

34

Anglo-Gaelic Literature:
Seán Ó Ríordáin

In 1899 an unknown teenager named Patrick Pearse wrote a denunciation of Yeats's planned theatre, likening it to the Trinity professoriate which had set its face against 'Irish' Ireland:

> The Irish Literary Theatre is, in my opinion, more dangerous because less glaringly anti-national than Trinity College. If we once admit the Irish-Literature-Is-English idea, then the language movement is a mistake. Mr Yeats' precious 'Irish' Literary Theatre may, if it develops, give the Gaelic League more trouble than the Atkinson–Mahaffy combination. Let us strangle it at its birth. Against Mr Yeats personally we have nothing to object. He is a mere English poet of the third or fourth rank and as such he is harmless. But when he attempts to run an 'Irish' Literary Theatre it is time for him to be crushed.[1]

In due time, Pearse came to have a higher opinion of Yeats, Synge and their colleagues: but the suggestion that an Irish national literature in English was a contradiction in terms won many backers over the following decades. It led to an artificial division between writing in Irish and English in the classrooms and literary journals of the independent state. Such a division ignored the growing band of bilingual artists who wrote well in both languages. The quality of the ensuing critical debate was attenuated and unreal: the Irish-language stories of Liam O'Flaherty were analysed without reference to the artist's re-creation of those themes in English. In neither case was a debate initiated on the choice between the two languages as creative medium. Nobody asked why O'Flaherty turned from Irish to English in the mid-1920s, only to revert to Irish following his return to live in the country in 1946. What artistic frustrations prompted that return? And why did this recovered enthusiasm fade after scarcely six years?

This question of choice is vital, for it is an issue that has been confronted by every bilingual writer on the island – not just practising bilingual authors like Brendan Behan or Flann O'Brien but also figures such as Pádraic Ó Conaire and Seosamh Mac Grianna, who are usually envisaged solely as Irish-language authors. As young men, they also were faced with the same dilemma. Ó Conaire began his career writing short stories in English under the influence of Dickens and the Russians, before a meeting with W.P. Ryan in London convinced him that he should work only in Irish. Similarly, Seosamh Mac Grianna was writing lyrics and stories in English, after the manner of Shelley and the English Romantics, when a reading of Ó Conaire's *An Chéad Chloch* (The First Stone) converted him to the Gaelic scheme of things. Seán Ó Ríordáin wrote sprung rhythms in imitation of Hopkins before he ever composed a poem in the native language. All of these abandoned English, but they did not forget the lessons learned from its masters: and it is impossible to do full critical justice to their achievements without some reference to English traditions.

Unlike the academic policemen of the classroom, most modern Irish writers did not succumb to the partitionist mentality in their art. Whatever about his youthful strictures as a critic, the artist Patrick Pearse wrote stories, poems and plays in both languages, many of them under the sign of Wordsworth and J.M. Barrie. Equally, on the other side, people like Yeats and Augusta Gregory made detailed studies of Gaelic lore, in the belief that the task now facing Ireland was a fusion of the two traditions. Lacking a deep knowledge of Irish, they produced work that was less an amalgam of the two streams than an incorporation of shreds of Irish into English: hence Pearse's complaint that Yeats's Cuchulain was a cross between a distrait Hamlet and a cockney corner boy.[2] Only Synge, among the artists of the national theatre, achieved a more profoundly bilingual work. He found it 'unfortunate' that the Abbey people wrote in English, unlike their Breton counterparts, who worked in their own language: but a return to Irish after a century of near-silence in both languages was not on, he felt.[3] So he opted to write in an English as Irish as it is possible for that language to be, re-creating Gaelic syntax, rhythms, images. Ignoring the division between the rival languages at his peril, Synge paid in the Ireland of his time the inevitable price. Those who might have admired him for his commitment to the native tradition denounced him for his belief in the higher claims of art. Those who loved his art could never fully appreciate the extent of his commitment to the native culture.

The same might be said of many Irish-language authors and their recourse to English traditions: and the case of Seán Ó Ríordáin is exemplary, given the high quality of his writing. An equivalent set of arguments might be advanced for such gifted authors as Ó Conaire, Mac Grianna, Máire Mhac an tSaoi, Máirtín Ó Direáin, and many more in the contemporary period. Ó Ríordáin was aware that the notion of modernist lyric in Irish might appear to be a contradiction in terms (to some admirers as well as detractors of the language), but he resolved to write an Irish as English as it could be, in terms of syntax, rhythm, and tonality. Doing that, he enriched the Gaelic mode, forging the most exacting body of poems since the work of Aogán Ó Rathaille, marked by levels of abstraction that had seemed to disappear from Irish at the outset of the eighteenth century.

Ó Ríordáin understood that a divided mind is the inheritance of every modern Irish person, running far deeper than the merely physical partition of the island. Though he regretted the political division, he gloried in the dual cultural inheritance. The imprint of Hopkins, and of such seventeenth-century Irish poets as Haicéad and Feiritéar, may be found through the Foreword to his first collection *Eireaball Spideoige* (A Robin's Tail, 1952). Here he became the first major writer in Irish to offer a sustained examination of the fractured nature of Irish culture. He was most certainly not the kind of Gael who assumed that the Gaelic element would 'absorb' all others. In fact, he was an Anglo-Gaelic poet in the most literal sense, recognizing that the spiritual hyphenation that had once characterized the Anglo-Irish now affected everyone on the island.

He was more aware of this hyphenation than most, caught as he saw himself between an Irish nature and an English culture. Daniel Corkery had already explored this crisis in his criticism: and Ó Ríordáin, in a lyric 'Do Dhomhnall Ó Corcora' (To Daniel Corkery), paid homage to his mentor's skill in re-creating the Munster poets of the eighteenth century in the vivid English prose of *The Hidden Ireland*:

> *Gur thit anuas*
> *De phlimp ar urlár gallda an lae seo*
> *Eoghan béal binn,*

Aindrias Mac Craith, Seán Clárach, Aodhgán,
Cioth filí.[4]

Until there fell down
With a bang onto the foreign floor of modernity
Sweet-mouthed Eoghan,
Aindrias Mac Craith, Seán Clárach, Aodhgán,
A shower of poets.

Corkery embraced the purist doctrine expounded by the young Pearse with increasing fervour in his own later years. 'The English language, great as it is, can no more throw up an Irish literature than it can an Indian literature. Neither can the Irish nation have its say in both Irish and English.'[5] If Stalin and Zhdanov crippled Soviet artists in the 1930s with 'Girl Meets Tractor' prescriptions for socialist realism, Corkery came up with his own rigid formula, insisting that to qualify as Irish, literature must treat of three themes: religion, nation, and land. Joyce had fled those nets as tyrannies, yet by treating them in his books, he did at least concede their importance. He anticipated Ó Ríordáin in *A Portrait of the Artist as a Young Man*, where he pictures Irish youth caught between a native mindset and an English schooling, between a righteous Catholicism and a yearning for post-religious freedom.

In *A Portrait of the Artist as a Young Man* the mind of Stephen Daedalus remained saturated in the symbols of the religion it rejected: and so was Joyce's. Again and again he employed theological terms to describe artistic processes. The artist was like a priest at the consecration of the mass, 'transmuting the daily bread of experience into the radiant body of everliving life'.[6] Ó Ríordáin performed a similar set of manoeuvres, but he compared the artistic process to the sacrament of confession. In his aesthetic (somewhat Beckettian), the poem was analogous to a sin:

Do rugas don Eaglais
  Mo chnuasach nuapheacaí,
Do chuireas iad in eagar
  Don fhoilsitheoir a bhíonn
  Ag clódhearmad peacaí.[7]

I brought to the church
  My collection of new sins,
I edited them for
  The publisher who is
  Print-forgetting sins.

In 'Sos', another lyric from *Eireaball Spideoige*, the face that speaks from the mirror of the poet's verses is one 'a mhalartóidh liom faoistin' (which will exchange confessions with me).[8]

Whether in terms of confession or communion, both writers saw literature as a cleansing sacrament, and the artist as the priest of a post-Christian dispensation. Divested of Christian implication, religious vocabulary in their work becomes a technical terminology for the arts. Joyce's co-option of the word 'epiphany' is instructive: in theology it means the showing of the infant Jesus to the Magi, but to Joyce it was 'a sudden spiritual manifestation', possible in an evanescent moment when a character by a stray gesture indicated an essential aspect of personality.[9] So described, Joycean epiphany approximates to the 'beo-gheit' (start of recognition, quickening) conjured up by Ó Ríordáin in his Foreword to *Eireaball Spideoige*. According to his aesthetic, no poem is created without such a quickening, which casts all of creation under a new aspect, 'fé ghné eile'.[10] As with the epiphany, this is a poetic intensification of a quotidian image: a horse standing in the street; a man smoking tobacco; a cat soaking up the sun in the world of Ó Ríordáin. In that of Joyce, it might be a woman passing a coin to a man; men drinking in a pub; or boys on the lam from school. At such moments, the ordinary is invested with a symbolic quality and the matter-of-fact is tilted towards the miraculous.

Ó Ríordáin adopted as critical an attitude towards English literature as did Joyce towards Gaelic, but neither wished to make a final break with the 'opposing' culture. Joyce was forever haunted by images of the west and its people, and a similar set of tensions underlies Ó Ríordáin's poetry, which perpetually renews the choice between traditions. One voice urges him to purify the language of the tribe along the lines prescribed by Corkery, but another – stronger and subtler – advises him to follow Joyce's example and to tap the energies of English in the attempt to renovate the Irish language.

Corkery had cautioned repeatedly against such hybridity. Nineteenth-century Anglo-Irish writers had encased their themes in borrowed English forms, he complained:

> These moulds are not native to us for they were never fashioned at the bidding of the people of this land: in their making the intention was not to canalise some share of Irish consciousness so that consciousness would the better know itself. The intention was rather to discover some easy way in which the strange workings of that consciousness might entertainingly be exhibited to alien eyes.[11]

Corkery's strictures applied not just to comic novelists but, more poignantly, to serious poets from Thomas Davis to the younger Yeats, all of them bleak illustrations of a pitfall that Frantz Fanon found in the nationalist phase of a culture, when its elements are 'reinterpreted in the light of a borrowed aestheticism and of a conception of the world which was discovered under other skies'.[12] Against that depressing backdrop, Corkery's ringing claim that 'the tradition of the Irish people is to be understood and experienced with intimacy only in the Irish tongue'[13] may have had a seductive rigour, as well as a dangerous simplicity. This had been a theme-song of Revivalist writers like Fr Peter O'Leary, who contrasted pre-Famine Irish-speaking children with the post-Famine products of an anglicized schooling:

An páiste a múineadh Gaeilge mhaith dó, bhí sé go neamh-scáfar agus go seasmhach ina aigne, go súilaibí agus go hullamh chun freagra a thabhairt. Bhí sé dána gan a bheith droch-mhúinte . . . ach má thug sé roinnt ama i scoil ghallda, bhí sé ag smidireacht gáire in ionad freagra a thabhairt. Bhí sé droch-mhúinte gan a bheith dána . . .[14]

The child who had been taught good Irish was fearless and sturdy of mind, mature and alert with a ready answer. He was bold without being bad-mannered . . . but if he had spent some time at an English-speaking school, he was giggling rather than responsive. He was bad-mannered without being bold . . .

This essentialist account of an Irish nature deformed by English schooling seems to echo in Corkery's description of the conflicting signals given to a schoolchild in the early 1930s, when Ó Ríordáin was himself a pupil: 'No sooner does he begin to use his intellect than what he learns begins to undermine, to weaken and to harass his emotional nature. For practically all that he reads is English.'[15] Even in the 1930s, the intellectual material available to a young artist in Irish was limited: and so he or she was thrown back, willy-nilly, onto English publications for imaginative resources.

Ó Ríordáin had been caught between two cultures from the outset, born in Ballyvourney in 1916, at a time when the area was half Irish-speaking with the native language in sharp decline. Local schoolchildren spoke English and so did the poet's mother, with whom his relationship went very deep. All the same, this English was an impoverished, attenuated medium by contrast with the rich Irish of the storytellers and poets of the townland. In his

grandmother's house, the young boy listened spellbound to old tales
of Fionn:

> *Chonac saol mar scéal fiannaíochta*
> *Fadó, fadó, ar maidin . . .*[16]

> I saw life as a Fiannaíocht tale
> Long ago, long ago, in morning-time . . .

At the age of fifteen, he abandoned this half-Gaelic life and went to
school and later into a clerical post in the city of Cork. Which is to
say that he embarked on his secondary schooling, just one year after
Corkery had written of the contemporary schoolchild:

> For practically all that he reads is English – what he reads in
> Irish is not yet worth taking account of. It does not therefore
> focus the mind of his own people, teaching him the better to
> look about him, to understand both himself and his surround-
> ings. It focuses instead the life of another people. Instead of
> sharpening his gaze upon his own neighbourhood, his reading
> distracts it . . . His surroundings begin to seem unvital.[17]

Ó Ríordáin's contribution was to have given a clear account of this
crisis in art. Other poets, in English as well as Irish, often failed to
find a secure footing between the two cultures and to make their
diagnoses from an assured vantage point: they were often victims of
those tensions that ensued. Ó Ríordáin made of those tensions his
major theme and in the process he came up with a solution.

As a young artist in Cork, he soon realized that Irish was his fated
medium. It was less a case of an artist choosing a language than of a
language choosing an artist. On the streets of that city, however, he
met not the warriors of the Fianna but the hollow men of T.S. Eliot.
In Cork he found that he lacked the sustenance of a living poetic tradition and the support of a sympathetic, knowledgeable audience. He
sought his proper lineage in the Gaelic poets of earlier centuries:

> *A sheanfhilí, múinídh dom glao*
> *A mheallfadh corp dom shamhailtgharlach . . .*[18]

> Old poets, teach me a roar
> That will tease a body out of the child . . .

Seeking his own audience, he went to live in the Gaeltacht parish of

Dún Chaoin, regularly visiting Peig Sayers and Mícheál Ó Gaoithín, both authors of West Kerry autobiographies. In the poem called 'Na Blascaodaí' (The Blaskets), he equated the ancient lore with the traditional Gaelic culture, deliberately echoing the seventeenth-century poet Pádraigín Haicéad, as he addressed the Blasket fishermen:

> *Is fá thuairim ár seanaigne*
> *Déanam ólachán.*[19]

> And let us drink
> To our ancient mindset.

Yeats had, of course, written a lyric called 'The Fisherman', in which he explored the dilemma of a city poet unable to achieve an easy rapport with western people. He concluded in it that his ideal fisherman was probably

> *A man who does not exist,*
> *A man who is but a dream . . .* [20]

Although Ó Ríordáin would never go that far, the pathos of his lyric arises from a similar sense of himself as an interloper.

Many ideas that had no basis in Gaelic codes insinuated themselves into Ó Ríordáin's poetry, as did many forms without precedent in Irish. In a brave, complex lyric, he all but conceded that he was often thinking in English while using Irish words (the very reverse of those nineteenth-century peasants who found themselves thinking in Irish while using English words in the period of changeover). At a superficial level, of course, Ó Ríordáin was employing Irish words: but, deeper down, the ideas had about them a recognizably English structure of thought and feeling. The poems might indeed be printed in Irish, but they had the imprint of the English mind on every other line. Ó Ríordáin survived that cultural hybridization and reported it with compelling clarity:

> *A Ghaeilge im pheannsa*
> *Do shinsear ar chaillís?*
> *An teanga bhocht thabhartha*
> *Gan sloinne tú, a theanga?*

> *An leatsa na briathra*
> *Nuair a dheinimse peaca?*
> *Nuair is rúnmhar mo chroíse*
> *An tusa a thostann?*[21]

O Irish in my pen,
Have you lost your lineage?
Are you a poor fosterling
With no surname, o language?

When I pen my sin,
Do the words belong to you?
When my heart is secretive
Is it you who quieten?

Later in the lyric he concedes that even the ideas are often plagiarized
from a language he seeks only to escape:

Ag súrac atáirse
Ón striapach allúrach
Is sínim chugat smaointe
A ghoideas-sa uaithi.[22]

You are sucking from
The foreign harlot
And I proffer to you the thoughts
Which I have stolen from her.

The none-too-covert aggression in likening English to a soul for sale
cannot conceal the underlying conviction of the inadequacy of the
native codes, if left to themselves.

Máirtín Ó Direáin, another major poet of modern Irish, offered a
similar prose account of that process in his autobiography *Feamainn
Bhealtaine* (Maytime Seaweed): 'go ndí-bhéarlaíonn an file an
tábhar ina aigne agus go gcuireann sé de chomaoin ar an nGaeilge
é a chumadh inti ansin'[23] (so that the poet deanglicizes such material
in his imagination, before submitting it to the imprint of the Gaelic
mind). Ó Direáin in this book gives a poignant account of how, in
his youth, he was estranged from his Aran comrades on Inis Mór by
his intellectual tendencies, only to be estranged in middle age from
his Dublin contemporaries by his memories of the island. His major
literary exemplar is Chekhov, because of his injunction to forget the
group and hold to the individual. Ó Direáin castigates members of
the Irish-language movement for their introversion, their great
refusal of the complexities and uncertainties of modern living. Such
a life demands wide reading in biography, history, philosophy,
ethics, politics, psychology and humanism, all of it done in English,
so that it becomes hard to maintain the pretence that English is

really a foreign language. Nevertheless, for Ó Direáin, whose English was somewhat weak, Irish must remain the most natural medium, the mother tongue: and in Ó Ríordáin's exemplary de-anglicization of material he finds the only feasible solution. There are risks attendant on the method: the likelihood that many recent converts will produce a writing that is neither good Irish nor good poetry, but a weak echo of English ideas and forms. Those who have managed to create a modernist poetry in Irish have done so because theirs was already a versatile and muscular idiom before these challenges were confronted by it. Ó Ríordáin, because of his dedication and talent, was one of these exceptions.

None the less, the formal strains of the manoeuvre sometimes showed through. Many poems of his first collection are clearly written in familiar English metres of a kind to be found in schoolbooks of the 1920s and 1930s: and it may be no coincidence that some are now listed in school anthologies, such as 'Cúl an Tí' (Behind the House):

> *Tá Tír na nÓg ar chúl an tí,*
> *Tír álainn trína chéile,*
> *Lucht ceithre cos ag siúl na slí*
> *Gan bróga orthu ná léine,*
> *Gan Béarla acu ná Gaeilge.*[24]

> Tír na nÓg is behind the house,
> A beautiful land entirely,
> The four-footed folk walk that way
> Without shoes on them or shirt,
> Without English or Irish.

It is obvious from the metre that the poet himself is also trapped in a liminal area, another soul lacking a full command of either Irish or English codes. The problem is not that the form derives from English nursery rhymes, so much as that it does not fuse seamlessly with the sense: what is offered is an over-schematic pattern of sound extraneously imposed on the material.

Again in 'Oileán agus Oileán Eile' (An Island and Another Island), a too-measured metre becomes an obstacle to the reader's encounter with the words themselves. Rhythm and language do not fully harmonize and the stress may seem to fall on the inappropriate word. The final effect is of rhythms that betray, as often as bring out, the underlying sense. If the English tourist fishing on the lake troubles the writer, so (in a far deeper sense) the English

poetic tradition disturbs the poem. Even the title evokes the two
islands of Ireland and Britain, and the subtitle of the final section,
'An Sasannach agus Mé Féin'(The Englishman and Myself) brings
these concerns down to the fundamental question. Even the distortion wrought by the English-accented metre might be seen as an
illustration, whether intended or not, of the poem's central thesis:
but while the schematic metres may dramatize that problem, they
cannot solve it. Ó Ríordáin is an Anglo-Gaelic poet in that profound sense too.

In the case of 'Scagadh' (Separation), a lyric composed in 1951,
one critic has complained that here too rhythm is extraneous rather
than integral:

> Do scagas ceann is cos mo ghrá
> Is glún is cíoch is dul a cnámh[25]

Here the iambic becomes deadly, without redeeming variation or
surprise. Critics have repeatedly convicted the early Ó Ríordáin of
such transgressions, while arguing that after *Eireaball Spideoige* he
deanglicized his forms and achieved a closer rapprochement with
Gaelic modes. That is both true and untrue. It is true in as much as
Ó Ríordáin had a far greater command of Irish in his later writings: but it is untrue in so far as he continued to imitate English
structures. His second collection, *Brosna* (Kindling, 1964), was
dedicated to the people of Dún Chaoin, as if the author were
declaring a wish to return and immerse himself in the native element: but it is, in fact, here that he concedes for the first time that
he is borrowing material from English. Not only that, but many
phrases have been isolated by critics as examples of *Béarlachas*
(anglicized Gaelic idiom). Poetic licence might be cited in Ó
Ríordáin's defence: his rather abstract phrasing can sound foreign
in Irish precisely because much intellectual content disappeared
from the language in the seventeenth century. He saw himself as
restoring a gift for abstraction to an idiom that, by his own time,
was far too concrete.

When Ó Ríordáin wrote 'do thuirling aer na bhFlaitheas ar an
uaigh sin' (the air of Paradise alighted on that grave), he was in all
likelihood thinking of the line 'Brightness falls from the air': but
simply by writing it that way he sounded a new, necessary note in
Irish-language poetry. Equally, his use of compound words, while
owing much to Ó Rathaille and the *filí*, was also an application of
Hopkins's ideas of 'instress'. More pressing than either of these palpable influences was the example of Yeats, who loved to compose

phrases like 'mackerel-crowded seas' or 'swan-delighting river'. A hyphenated race indeed. Ó Ríordáin's use of compound words

> *Thit real na gealaí i scamallsparán*[26]

> *The sixpence of moon fell into a cloud-purse*

or

> *Is éistfead leis na scillingsmaointe*
> *A malairtítear*
> *Mar airgead . . .*[27]

> And I will listen to the shilling thoughts
> Which are exchanged
> Like money . . .

is, if anything, closer to Yeats than to the *filí*.

In his earlier work Ó Ríordáin used forms of nursery rhyme and ballad, but in later collections such as *Línte Liombó* (Lines of Limbo, 1979) he relied on more complex borrowings from sophisticated writers of English. A major source was Wordsworth's 'Ode on the Intimations of Immortality'. Lines like

> *Not in entire forgetfulness,*
> *And not in utter nakedness,*
> *But trailing clouds of glory do we come*
> *From God who is our home . . .*

or

> *The Rainbow comes and goes*
> *And lovely is the Rose . . .* [28]

are quoted in 'Cló' (Imprint):

> *Gach rud dá dtagann,*
> *Imíonn is ath-thagann*
> *Is filleann arís ár gcéad ghlóire;*
> *Is deineann fear aibidh*
> *Mar a dhein sé ina leanbh,*
> *Níl i ndán ach athnuachan na hóige.*[29]

> Everything that comes

Goes and comes again,
And our first glory returns:
And the grown man does
As he did when a child;
There is no fate but the renewal of youth.

'Imíonn is ath-thagann' is derived from 'The Rainbow comes and goes'. Wordsworth's child is presented for our approval in the first person plural: and 'ár gcéad ghlóire' is manifestly based on 'trailing clouds of glory do we come'. More telling still is the fact that the central lines of 'Cló', come from the epigraph to Wordsworth's ode:

The Child is father of the Man;
And I could wish my days to be
Bound each to each by natural piety.[30]

Is deineann fear abidh
Már a dhein sé ina leanbh;
Níl i ndán ach athnuachan na hóige.

Even the metrical scheme seems to follow Wordsworth's: two short lines and then a longer third, with the rhyming section aab, ccb: and in this case the metre is wonderfully attuned to the themes. In such a context, Corkery's denunciation of 'the want of native moulds' in Anglo-Irish literature seems misdirected. His recommendation of Irish as the only remedy for this lack seems equally simplistic. Ó Ríordáin had the courage to show that, no matter what language the poet finally mastered, the same formal challenges would arise. Corkery had been right in remarking of the aspiring writer that 'his education provides him with an alien medium through which he is henceforth to look at his native land', but his mistake had been to suppose that Irish could, by some mysterious privilege, remain immune to outside influence. Ó Ríordáin suffered from no such delusions. He had steeped himself in foreign philosophy and in English literature. From Eliot, for instance, he had learned that the test of a great poet is not whether he borrows so much as how the borrowings are used.

Although – perhaps because – much of Ó Ríordáin's work was written for the people of Dún Chaoin, it repeatedly stresses the fact that there can be no final 'farewell to English'. Again and again he urges himself to say that last goodbye:

bain ded mheabhair
Srathar shibhialtacht an Bhéarla,

Shelley, Keats, is Shakespeare:
Fill arís ar do chuid . . .
Dein d'fhaoistin is dein
Síocháin led ghiniúin féinig.[31]

           remove from your mind
The surfaces of English civilization,
Shelley, Keats, and Shakespeare:
Return again to your kind . . .
Make your confession and make
Peace with your own family tree.

– but it can never be more than a fanciful, impractical injunction. In a poem titled 'A Theanga Seo Leath-Liom' (O This Language Which Is Half-Mine), the writer explores the dilemma of one born in the semi-Gaeltacht, educated and employed in English-speaking areas, and anxious now to return to native ways:

Ní mór dúinn dul in aice leat
Go sloigfí sinn ionat;
Ní mheileann riamh leath-aigne,
Caithfeam dul ionat . . .[32]

We must align with you,
Until we are swallowed by you;
A half commitment will achieve nothing,
We must immerse ourselves in you . . .

If Ó Ríordáin's soul fretted in the shadow of an Irish he could never hope to know in all its intensity, this was similar to the scruples Joyce often felt about his knowledge of English. English was to him 'so familiar and so foreign',[33] a language only half his too. Joyce may have been one of the masters of English prose, but he faced the same tests in English as Ó Ríordáin did in Irish. Although Joyce gave up Pearse's Irish classes at an early stage, he knew enough to appreciate the Gaelic syntax and imagery embedded in Hiberno-English. When he has Stephen Daedalus assert in *A Portrait of the Artist as a Young Man* that Ireland is the sow that eats her own farrow, he is inverting two lines of Seathrún Céitinn:

Deor níor fágadh i gclár do bhrollaigh mhínghil
nár dheolsad ál gach cránach coigríche . . .[34]

A drop wasn't left in your bright gentle breast
That was not slurped down by the farrow of every
    foreign sow.

For Céitinn a sow devours the land, but for Joyce the land itself is the
sow. For Céitinn that sow is a foreign predator, but in Joyce's view
the oppression comes from within. It was a creative rewriting like
Joyce's which Flann O'Brien had in mind when he wrote, years later,
to Sean O'Casey:

> I agree absolutely with you when you say that the Irish lan-
> guage is essential, particularly for any sort of literary worker. It
> supplies that unknown quantity in us that enables us to trans-
> form the English language – and this seems to hold good for
> people who know little or no Irish, like Joyce. It seems to be an
> inbred thing.[35]

It might, however, also be claimed that Ó Ríordáin used English to
transform the Irish language, to renovate the consciousness of its
intellectuals, to shake it free of longstanding constrictions. In doing
this, he disproved some of the more chauvinistic theories of Daniel
Corkery but also the defeatist assumption (made by many) that Irish
was no longer fit to grapple with the problems of the modern world.
No poet in English has given as complete a rendition of the experience of living in two cultures simultaneously as did Seán Ó Ríordáin.
From that rendition one thing is clear: the choice of a language in
which to work is important but never final. Ó Ríordáin considered
that he had opted, early on, for Irish, but he continued at some level
to work also in English. Similarly, Synge, though he chose English as
medium, never ceased to interweave elements of Gaelic syntax into
his texts. Like all policemen of literature, Corkery was convinced
that language was the authentic repository of the national mind: but
Ó Ríordáin showed that what was going on in the deeper structures,
below the level of mere words, was what counted. In those deeper
zones, he found what other great imaginations encountered, the
experience of poetry as a struggle with the self, and between 'natural'
and 'cultural' forces which had become so intertwined that it was
only with difficulty that they could be distinguished. It is part of his
achievement – though he would have been reluctant to admit this –
that he made the very distinction almost impossible to sustain.

35

Irish Narrative: A Short History

The first recorded *file* was named Aimhirgin, who lived in the first century AD. He tabulated the laws and told immense lies. Confronted with his wild exaggerations, the sardonic men of Ulster felt obliged to make a plea for the reality-principle, but it was a plea well qualified by the claims of the imagination: 'What you say is frankly incredible, Aimhirgin, but we believe you, because you are a poet; and when a poet says a thing, it becomes true.'[1] Coded into that rich response is a clear implication: that in an oral culture a word is not just an act but itself also an action. The poet has such power that society may in time be refashioned to reflect the ideas or arrangements of a work of art. The future is, as Oscar Wilde said, what artists already are.

In other countries, readers and critics have found in art a zone of imaginative freedom, which at its purest cannot be contaminated by matters of politics and society. That is not an ignoble vision, for most persons in their moments of grace would like to enjoy the blessedness of dream in a state of wakefulness, to live in a world unconstrained by conditions. It is good that art should never be expected to reflect in a myopic way the constraints of actually existing society, for that would leave artists no better than tape-recorders, denying to them and their audiences the imaginative capacity by which everyone must live. However, it is quite another thing to suggest that the radical audacity of the creative mind has nothing of social value or wisdom to offer fellow-citizens. To see a work of art as solely a beautiful internal arrangement of words and images is to put oneself in the position of an ostrich who sticks his head in the sand for the pleasure of admiring the relationship between the grains.

This was not the view taken by the *filí*, nor by the English forces who extirpated them and their lords from the old Gaelic order. Both groups knew that the *filí* were seers, prophets and thus bearers in their texts of blueprints for possible worlds. English poets like Edmund Spenser were envious of the social power of the *filí*. More than two centuries later, when Shelley wrote his famous description of poets as unacknowledged legislators of the world, he went on at once to lament that such a power was seldom recognized by the poets themselves: there spoke a man who would have much preferred to have been cast in the role of Irish bard.[2]

In one sense, the criticism of Irish narrative begins with Spenser's attack on the Irish character as nomadic, disloyal, and devoid of a sense of chronology. This, in turn, elicited from the priest, poet and proseman Seathrún Céitinn not only a reasoned defence, but also a devastating critique of English narrative methods. At the centre of Céitinn's complaint is a view of Spenser as pure textualist rather than a man responding to felt experience. He further alleges, in the preface to *Foras Feasa ar Éirinn* (The Basis for a Knowledge of Ireland) that Spenser relied mainly on English documents rather than taking Gaelic texts also into his account. What is remarkable about that exchange is how monotonously it would be repeated within the discipline of Irish Studies over the centuries to come. In these changing contexts, much the same allegations would be made against two seemingly disparate groups: revisionist historians and aesthetic critics. It would be said that their narrowed eyes saw only what they had been trained to see by previous exponents of the approved textual mode; that they privileged the literary and textual over the spoken voices of the world; that even their textualism was myopic since it paid scant heed to Gaelic written sources; and that simple-minded theories of the native propensity to violence, licence and unreliability were allowed to override the actual experience of Ireland.

When the Gaelic order collapsed, the *filí* crumbled with it: yet as artists who carried the once and future wisdom of a culture with them, they were looked up to by many people as a group that might some day help to renovate the national consciousness. Strangely, this view of the *normative* social power of literature was reinforced, perhaps inadvertently, by the educators of the new colonial regime. An English play or book, when read in Ireland, provided more than just a good story: it was also an etiquette manual, which might teach a person how to walk across a room or how to greet a noble lord. The idea that a society might be no more than a set of inferences drawn from the classic texts served only to emphasize the central importance of literature in Irish society. This conferred on books a social influence out of all proportion to that which they had in England, where they were treated more as ornaments and sources of fancy.

It was left to the people of the Enlightenment to seek in culture a zone of grace, in which the strife between Gael and Gall might come to a happy truce. Charlotte Brooke's *Reliques of Irish Poetry* (1789) was perhaps the first attempt at a narrative that accorded 'parity of esteem' to both island traditions. Her project was to defend the Anglo-Irish aristocracy against the charge of being muscular, horse-riding dullards and to remind colonial administrators in Dublin and London of the dignity and beauty of the literature of the ancient Gael. It is a nice, Swiftian irony that such early involvements of the Anglo-Irish with what is known now as Irish Studies should have derived less from a Spenserian desire to combat native immorality than from an honest indignation against the ignorance of English administrators and English readers: 'As yet we are too little known to our noble neighbour of Britain; were we better acquainted, we should be better friends.'[3] That is a warning that the British must blend the Gaelic tradition with their own, if they wish to administer a peaceful and prosperous land. Charlotte Brooke did not share Spenser's belief that contact with the natives would lead to a decline in morale or to a dangerously hybrid condition. On the contrary, she saw her own easy commerce with the labourers on her father's Cavan estate as a model for Anglo-Irish relations in general.

Yet the confident sentiments of her preface cannot conceal her anxiety that, as so often in the past, the British just don't and won't understand:

The British Muse is not yet informed that she has an elder sister in this isle; let us then introduce them to each other. Together let them walk in cordial union between two countries that seem formed by nature to be joined by every bond of interest and of amity. Let them entreat of Britain to cultivate a nearer acquaintance with her neighbouring isle. Let them conciliate for us her esteem, and her affection will follow of course. Let them tell her, that the portion of her blood which flows in their veins is rather ennobled than disgraced by the mingling tides that descended from our heroic ancestors. Let them come – but will they listen to a voice like mine?[4]

They did not come. Instead, the bloody uprising of 1798, led by

Tone against an obtuse but manipulative administration, was answered with an even greater ferocity: and Charlotte Brooke's hopes of a cultural fusion were lost. The consequence was a more rigid master–servant relationship than the relatively happy commerce between classes that had characterized the pre-Union Ireland described by Maria Edgeworth in *Castle Rackrent*. A growing contempt for all things Gaelic seemed to dominate state discourse, and eventually to possess the minds of the peasantry too.

Brooke's call, for all its unsuccess, reverberated through the decades of the nineteenth century. It was taken up in the 'union of hearts' policy espoused by Matthew Arnold in the mid-1860s in lectures calling for the establishment of a chair of Celtic Studies at Oxford. If Brooke's summons had been issued in a land on the verge of insurrection, it was no coincidence that Matthew Arnold's preceded the Fenian rising of 1867. This shows that Irish Studies, for all its hopes of academic objectivity, remains a crisis-driven discipline. Some of its exponents in high-profile posts are routinely accused of being fellow travellers of the Irish Republican Army; others of being pro-British stooges – yet most write what they honestly believe to be as objective an account as possible in the given circumstances. As a matter of record, a chair of Celtic Studies was finally funded at Oxford, and is now accompanied by a chair of Irish History of much more recent vintage. These foundations indicate the desire of the official British mind to understand not only the Celtic temperament but also the byzantine complexities of Irish politics. It is one of the curiosities of cultural history that the study of Celtic languages was seen by some as a means of spreading the Protestant reformation among peoples who spoke Irish, Welsh or Scots Gaelic, and as a way of exploring the form of feudal society best suited to native temperaments. Hence the rediscovery of Gaelic saga in the 1870s by such landlords as Standish J. O'Grady – this was a last-ditch attempt to hold back 'the filthy modern tide' in the days of the Land War.

Neither Oxford nor Cambridge yet houses a chair of Irish Literature and students at both institutions may still feel able to treat Irish or Anglo-Irish writing as an exotic offshoot of English literature. This, of course, is how the subject until recent decades was also viewed in Irish colleges: and it is only fair to record how grateful were many poets, from Oliver Goldsmith to W.B. Yeats, to assimilate their work to a tradition as prestigious and global as that of English literature. Yet writers even as early as Swift could not help reading that literature against the grain of their rather different Irish experience. Hence the undertow felt in the direction of the native culture by a succession of Anglo-Irish artists from Swift, Goldsmith and Sheridan down to Edgeworth and Wilde. Hence also the radical reinterpretation by such authors of the classics of English literature. For Yeats, the clash in Shakespeare's history plays between Bolingbroke and Richard simply re-creates the victory of English administrative guile over doomed Celtic complexity in Ireland. For Joyce, the 'note of banishment' is what sounds in the plays from *The Two Gentlemen of Verona* until Prospero breaks his staff. Each man reread Shakespeare as a version of himself.[5]

These reinterpretations of the English canon were subversive, and it is difficult for us today to imagine the excitement with which they were first received. It is likely that Yeats's rewriting of *Richard II* in his own Cuchulain cycle, with its underlying notion that he who loses life shall save it, helped to shape the thinking of those rebels who rose at Easter 1916. English departments in an independent Ireland after 1921 did not, however, respond to the challenge of further developing these interpretative methods. Few tested English literature against their Irish experience, and many failed to consider the Irish expressive achievement in English at all. Two rare exceptions to this were Thomas MacDonagh and Daniel Corkery. It was the distinction of both men to have taken the study of Gaelic and Anglo-Irish literatures out of their self-imposed quarantine and to have treated them as part of a cultural continuum. MacDonagh was a lecturer in the English department of University College Dublin at the time of the Easter Rising. He was executed along with other rebel leaders shortly after, but some months later in 1916 his *Literature in Ireland: Studies Irish and Anglo-Irish* appeared. Although he did not share Brooke's ascendancy perspective, he did endorse her argument for the essential continuity of the two cultures.

MacDonagh argued that by the time of the Penal Laws, literature had become decadent, but for more than a century afterwards, English 'was not yet able to carry on the tradition or to syllable anew for itself here'. It was only after 1900 that a writer such as Synge had emerged who was 'at once sufficiently Gaelic to express the feeling of the central Irish tradition, and sufficiently master of English style to use it as one uses the air one breathes'.[6] Rejecting the contention that a national literature could only be created in Irish, he suggested that the native language suffered from the same defects that afflicted modern English – journalese, cliché, fatigued imprecision. The ideal solution had been found in the Hiberno-English of Synge, 'more vigorous, fresh and simple than either of the two languages between which it stands'. He believed that, once all the major works in Irish had been translated into English, that translated work could go forward as a central element in the culture of modern Ireland.[7]

Although he was overdismissive of the creative potentials in modern Irish, MacDonagh worked valuably for a rapprochement between Irish and English, something Patrick Pearse had also begun to favour in the closing years of his life. Sadly, it was the more strident doctrine of the teenaged Pearse that Daniel Corkery chose to reassert for the next generation of writers. In his pamphlet *What's This About the Gaelic League?* (1941), he said downrightly that 'the English language, great as it is, can no more throw up an Irish literature than it can an Indian literature. Neither can Irish nationality have its say in both English and Irish.'[8] The fact that his own grasp of Irish was uncertain and that his fame both as a professor and writer of English extended to Britain and North America did not seem to blunt Corkery's ardour in expounding this extreme theory. In his most influential critical work, *Synge and Anglo-Irish Literature* (1931), he had gone even further, arguing that no writer could truly claim to be Irish unless his work contained three specific notes – nationality, religion and the land. By these rigid criteria, Yeats and his colleagues were written off as mere interlopers. Unsurprisingly, Corkery's three notes were not far removed from those forces ('nationality, language, religion') that drove Joyce's Stephen Daedalus into exile.[9]

It is only just to add, however, that Corkery's influence was more often healthy than harmful. Like many dogmatists, he tended to flout his worst theories by his best practices. Though foolish enough in theory to deny the very existence of Anglo-Irish writing as a distinct body of literature, he wrote the best critical book of his generation on an Irish author: his patient, non-reductive, wholly engaged study of Synge. In his own critical practice, he simply ignored the classroom division all across the island between Irish and English. So he produced brilliant essays that contrasted the 'Nativity Ode' as practised by Aodh Mac Aingil and John Milton or he penned pages comparing the homely intensity of Eoghan Rua Ó Súilleabháin and Robbie Burns. He discovered an English source – Richard Savage's 'The Bastard' – for *Cúirt an Mheán-Oíche*; and in *The Hidden Ireland* (1924) he produced the first sustained literary criticism of eighteenth-century Gaelic poetry. In that book he called eloquently for the practice of Celtic Studies to embrace the work of imaginative interpretation, as well as the disciplines of grammar and linguistic scholarship. In effect, he founded the school of literary critics working on the Irish language, though it was not until the later 1960s that this work fully blossomed.

Corkery and MacDonagh were exceptional figures, quite unrepresentative of the English departments to which they belonged. They were teachers in an absolute sense, gurus who created an exciting debate, inspiring students. The same could hardly be said of most of their colleagues. Seán Ó Faoláin has left a rather savage account of the low level of teaching at University College Cork in the 1920s. Corkery's predecessor, a man named Stockley, he described as 'having a mind like a sewing basket after a kitten had been through it'.[10] After political independence, images of Irish possibility tended to freeze, especially among the intelligentsia. It was as if the energy expanded in dislodging the British had left all too little for a truly creative national debate (Salman Rushdie in *Midnight's Children* reports a very similar kind of failure from India after 1948). The essays produced in English departments were largely exercises in ventriloquism, done as if the scholar were writing in Liverpool and London. Even when the subject was Swift or Goldsmith, little enough was made of the Irish background: and no academic saw fit to invoke the republicanism of Milton, Blake, Shelley or Wilde as a challenge to that critical approach which confidently proclaimed English literature as predominantly royalist and Anglo-Catholic.

How does one explain this? For where, but in the literature departments of universities in a free state and young republic, would one have expected such a criticism to flourish? It would not have been entirely surprising to find that some exponents of an Anglo-Irish culture which felt itself under threat might choose to fight a rearguard action from one or another department. Some sort of exchange between Corkeryite nationalists and exponents of Anglo-Irish culture could have made for a very lively department, which had some interesting choices to put to its students. Authoritative voices were raised on behalf of Anglo-Ireland, but these were the voices of trenchant critics safely installed at foreign universities – T.R. Henn at Cambridge, A. Norman Jeffares at Leeds, Peter Allt in London. At home, however, the analysis initiated by MacDonagh and Corkery was all but postponed for over fifty years. Universities instead became centres of an aesthetic criticism, devoted to the study of genre and to the practical criticism of a narrowly defined canon of high literature.

These trends were typical of their time in other countries, other continents. After all, in leading American universities of the same period, there was little study of the classic texts of the American Renaissance and much devotion to Jane Austen, Arnold, Tennyson and the English canon. The mid-twentieth-century generation became obsessed with questions of taste and value, and with the making of 'nice' discriminations in defence of 'standards'. Professional academics were hugely distrustful of popular authors or low-brow culture. Their lectures were daily demonstrations of their right to hold their exalted positions. They gave to Henry James the status of most favoured novelist and to the poetry of John Donne the highest praise that practical criticism could bestow: but they were less at home with the vernacular energies and cheerful vulgarity of a Swift or a Joyce.

An amusing instance of this may be found in the reception of Vivian Mercier's *The Irish Comic Tradition* (1962). Mercier was a Protestant gentleman and Trinity graduate who took an equal pleasure in the learned and the obscene. His book was, in the spirit of Brooke and MacDonagh, a demonstration of how the Irish love of the macabre, grotesque and ribald had survived the transition from Irish to English. In his middle years, following a protracted exile in New York, Mercier had taught himself Old and Middle Irish during a sabbatical year in Dublin and had gone on in his book to fuse the methods of Kuno Meyer and Gerald Murphy, of Sigmund Freud and James Frazer. In effect, his volume relaunched the contemporary discipline that now goes by the name of Irish Studies. It was a great success with students and younger scholars, but came in for heavy attack from the territorial interests entrenched in particular English and Irish departments. Jibes were made about its author being a Jack of all trades and master of none.

In a lucid essay called 'Our Wits About Us', Conor Cruise O'Brien defended his friend's book (the men had been roommates during their student years at Trinity College Dublin). He endorsed its thesis that 'the ribald, the dangerously satirical, the grotesque and the obscene' were major elements of the national literary heritage, but wickedly observed that for a certain kind of purist Irishman, it was now a point of honour to have no sense of humour at all. For such tremulous souls, *The Irish Comic Tradition* 'is a veritable *danse macabre* of the skeletons in the family cupboard'. This national puritan he christened Paddy Solemn:

> Paddy Solemn shudders at the thought, and cringes at the sight or sound, of Brendan Behan; Paddy Solemn likes to use precise-sounding terminology in a vague way, and derives from this a bracing sense of intellectual rigour; Paddy Solemn likes to be thought of as a Thomist, and knows – for he is no fool, despite appearances – that this will do him no harm at all in an academic career bounded on all sides by bishops . . . Paddy Solemn has, however, a secret fear. It is that Ireland Will Let Him

Down. Of what avail his national respectability if he is dragged down by a national entity that refuses to be respectable?[11]

The Irish Comic Tradition was indeed a book of the 1960s, for it celebrated that combination of wit and vulgarity which linked both Joyce and Swift back to Gaelic lore: and it openly regretted the long-standing separation of those elements in Anglo-Saxon writing since the days of Shakespeare and Jonson. It savoured the laughter of underlings, as something that did not negate so much as complete seriousness. Mercier's Ireland was one which relished robust dialect, witty oaths, flytings and curses, for he found in their energies a real alternative to po-faced authority. He agreed with Stanislaus Joyce that his brother was a mocker and his work an elaborate joke at the expense of high culture. In its handling of ideas of the 'grotesque' and 'macabre', the book remarkably overlapped with the sketch made by Mikhail Bakhtin in *Rabelais and His World* (written at the height of the Stalinist terror in the 1930s, but published in Russian only in 1965 and in English in 1984). The English-language version delighted Mercier, for it helped to confirm not just the audacity but the rightness of his approach, especially in his celebration of the human body as an image of the restored community.

Conor Cruise O'Brien's essay was no pal's puff, however. Having defined and defended Mercier's argument for comedy, he went on to question his underlying assumption of an unbroken, unproblematic Irish tradition spanning the two languages. In O'Brien's view, such a tradition was notable only for its absence: what he found was a gapped and broken narrative. Opposing Mercier's model of an essentialist, all-Ireland identity, he proposed an alternative which might be labelled behaviourist: there was really no Irish mind as such, only a plurality of Irish minds, each caught up in an Irish predicament, 'which has produced common characteristics in a number of those who have been involved in it'.[12] Chief among these were wit and irony. Words were the only weapons available to a dis-armed people who had sought, over centuries, to expose the difference between official pretence and actual reality. These alter-native models of Irish identity would dominate cultural debate in the three decades to follow, as all the younger critics grappled with the arguments adumbrated in this energetic exchange (broadly speak-ing, the Field Day analysts, led by Seamus Deane, tended to follow the Mercier line, while the so-called revisionists, who followed Edna Longley, took a position closer to O'Brien's). It was Mercier and O'Brien, rather than the Paddy Solemns, who regenerated the debate made possible by MacDonagh and Corkery: yet for neither of these most productive and gifted of critics would there ever be a post in a literature department of an Irish university.

The situation through these decades was much the same in other college disciplines in Ireland. A black humorist might even consider the travelling scholarships initiated to enable the brightest graduates of the National University to study overseas as a tacit admission that there was little intellectual challenge to be found at home. 'Devoting time to Irish affairs', observed Joseph Lee in a devastating critique of his fellow academics, 'is often a waste of time for those Irish thinkers who can play in the first division internationally.' That would explain why the leading lawyers, geographers and mathematicians went international, but given the immensity of the Irish achievement in literature, it can hardly account for the long silences in criticism through the period. The best energies of understaffed departments were invested in teaching: but perhaps also the fact that Irish writing was still viewed as an offshoot of English literature (until the mid-1960s there was no separate 'Irish' category in most Dublin city bookshops) led to the belief that it was interpretable by the same essential rules. As Lee himself suggests: 'analytical tools were rarely refined and honed in response to the specific challenge of understanding the Irish situation. Imports substituted for the theoretical originality the situation required.'[13]

There are other explanations for the intellectual somnolence of English departments in the period. The courses taught in secondary schools remained virtually unreformed between 1921 and 1969, 'a monument to an essentially Edwardian sensibility'.[14] Under the influence of F.R. Leavis and the 1944 Education Acts, English schools modernized their syllabi: but in Ireland everything froze. The expressive works of the mature Yeats, O'Casey, O'Brien, Kavanagh or Beckett (and many more) were hardly represented in curricula, which stuck generally to nineteenth-century writing. A key factor in all this was the Irish language. The representation of Anglo-Irish writing in this attenuated fashion helped to confirm a pet nationalist theory that the Irish mind could express itself fully in the native language alone. One writer for the *Catholic Bulletin* in 1933 went so far as to suggest that *no* English literature should penetrate the secondary school curriculum: 'Its whole line of writers from Bacon to Macaulay, from Spenser to Wordsworth, Tennyson, Masefield, drips at every pore with intellectual and moral poison.'[15] At much the same time, a Trinity College professor was warning Protestant parents that sustained exposure to Irish-language texts might lead large numbers of their offspring to convert to Roman Catholicism.[16]

Such worries were unfounded. Religious practice had never waned in Ireland to anything like the extent it had in Britain or Continental Europe; and so its study, along with that of Irish, remained the central element of an official national pedagogy. In that context, English could never hope to assume the almost messianic role reserved for it by the followers of Matthew Arnold as the central humanist activity in a liberal education. Instead, it was viewed, like it was viewed in many another postcolonial state, as a subject necessary for passing those examinations that led to secure jobs in the professions and the civil service.

Matthew Arnold had contended that the task of English was to sustain a national ideal and to teach students to transcend self-interest for its sake. In Ireland, Patrick Pearse adapted those precepts wholesale, applying them to the study of Irish. A reading of heroic saga would produce 'manly' qualities in students: and, indeed, Irish was felt to have certain advantages over English, which was often accused of being a 'soft option'. The disciplined study of an ancient language filled with difficult declensions of the noun and many irregular verbs seemed as character-forming as that of Greek or Latin.

In European universities and schools, philosophy stood at the centre of a national curriculum, compelling all teachers and students to theorize their positions. In England, on the other hand, most of the values felt to be inherent in English Studies were seldom explicitly construed. It was seriously suggested that to construe them too obviously might actually imperil such values. Thus was produced a literary criticism which found it a mark of excellence in a writer that he or she had a mind so fine that no single idea could violate it. It was this form of criticism which was ventriloquized in most English departments in Ireland.

The great critic of Irish literature throughout this period was Richard Ellmann. He wrote definitive and brilliant books on Yeats, Joyce and Wilde, as well as a major essay on Beckett. In each of these he produced a narrative which argued that the writer made himself 'modern' to precisely the extent that he transcended his own Irishness. An American humanist liberal of Jewish background, Ellmann had been in the armies that helped to liberate Europe from the Nazis in 1944, and he had a personal stake in wishing to recruit Irish writers into the gaps left in European high modernism after the Holocaust. Needless to add, his project of 'Europeanizing' the interpretation of Irish art blended easily with that of the Irish elites from the 1950s onwards, as they sought entry to the European Economic Community. Yet the analyses of Ellmann also had the strange, surely unintended, effect of convincing a whole generation of readers that it was very possible that the

great Irish modernists were in no meaningful sense of the word
'Irish' at all. In his essay 'Yeats without Analogue', Ellmann pronounced himself willing to admit that Irish nationalism was
perhaps an absurdity: yet, he charitably added, Yeats himself did
not consider it so. Still, the critic insisted, it wasn't really very helpful to consider Yeats as one of a group of poets who simply
freshened up Celtic legends. 'When he wrote *A Vision*, he forgot he
was an Irishman. And while he calls the fairies by their Irish name
of Sidhe, I suspect that they are internationalists.'[17] So there it was:
even the little people (in Ellmann's scheme) were secret subscribers
to the Fourth International.

The central argument of this book has been a direct reversal of
Ellmann's: my contention is that, for writers as disparate as Ó Bruadair
and Yeats, to be Irish was to be modern anyway, whether one liked it
or not. That is what links the artists covered here: each has had to
cope, in his or her way, with the coercive onset of modernity. Each has
generated a narrative that seeks to salvage something of value from the
past, even as the forces of the new world are embraced. The Belfast
Agreement of April 1998 might be read as just the most recent version
of that paradigm: for coded into it are many of the same ideas which
animated people like Edgeworth and Carleton, Burke and
MacDonagh. One is the understanding that when the *nostra* of the
recent past seem no longer serviceable, the unsentimental and useful
thing to do is to dispose of them fast. Another is the suggestion that
there should be 'parity of esteem' for both languages and cultures. In
this document a native criticism finally comes of age, at least in the
sense that it 'catches up' with the insights afforded over many years by
Irish writers. The language of the Belfast Agreement is richly indebted
not just to postcolonial theory and to recent forms of Irish criticism,
but even more potently to the preface of Charlotte Brooke and the
postscript of Maria Edgeworth.

Central to the Belfast Agreement is the proposition that people in
Northern Ireland have a birthright 'to identify themselves and be
accepted as Irish or British, or both, as they may so choose'; accordingly the agreement confirms 'that their right to hold both British
and Irish citizenships is accepted by both Governments and would
not be affected by any future change in the status of Northern
Ireland'.[18] Oscar Wilde had likewise offered himself as a very English
kind of Irishman, one who believed that, just as every Irishman had
a sort of honorary Englishman occluded in himself, so every woman
had an element of the 'masculine' coded into her identity. And vice
versa, of course. His entire art was an attempt to dissolve the manic
Victorian urge to create an antithesis between England and Ireland,

male and female, good and evil, and so on. The truth in art was one whose opposite might also be true. The phrase 'Irish or British, *or both*' perfectly captures his cheerfully paradoxical approach. That phrase may, in due time, mean that Northern Irish people can carry two passports but also that they may vote in elections to four major assemblies – the European and Westminster parliaments, the Belfast Assembly and the Dáil in Dublin.

Perhaps the most interesting of all the institutions postulated in the agreement is the British–Irish Council (or, as it is sometimes called, the Council of the Isles). This is to work on an east–west trajectory, and this particular strand of the document contains a seemingly innocuous but radical possibility:

> Membership of the British–Irish Council will comprise representatives of the British and Irish Governments, devolved institutions in Northern Ireland, Scotland and Wales, when established, and if appropriate, elsewhere in the United Kingdom, together with representatives of the Isle of Man and the Channel islands.[19]

This may refer to proposed assemblies for the North of England, Devon and Cornwall, or wherever; but it seems also to recognize that England itself may have an unresolved national question, soluble only by a parliament of its own. The recent essays of Tom Nairn in *Faces of Nationalism* confirm the view that more and more left-liberals, and not just Tory Little Englanders, have come to the same conclusions reached by Wilde: that England itself might be the most deeply penetrated of all British colonies. That view, which has been sponsored over the intervening century by thinkers as diverse as H.G. Wells, George Orwell and Tony Benn, was first ventilated by Wilde with his suggestion that England might become a republic and that a republic was the form of government most favourable to art.

Of all the measures written into the Belfast Agreement, the most astonishing is that by which the citizens of the Republic are to remove the territorial claim on the six northern counties currently part of the United Kingdom. Every schoolchild in the Republic has been taught to see that claim as a force of nature, confirmed by the very shape of Ireland as an island. Yet over 94 per cent of the southern electorate voted in 1998 to rescind the claim, for the sake of peace and good relations with unionist fellow-islanders for whose welfare they care deeply. It is hard to do justice to the audacity or intrepidity of that gesture (or to the massive majority by which it was effected). Has any other nation-state in modern history so voted to reduce the extent of its territorial claims? The vote was, in fact, a recognition that any people's claims need no longer be mediated by means of the nation and that identity is rooted less in the relation between persons and territory than in the relations of persons to one another.

Much of the language of the Belfast Agreement is vague, even 'poetic'. That is because it offers a version of multiple identities, of a kind for which no legal language yet exists. The Wilde who suggested that the only way to intensify personality was to multiply it would have approved: but where is the lawyer who can offer a constitutional definition of identity as open rather than fixed, as a process rather than a conclusion? The Belfast Agreement effectively sounds the death-knell for old-style constitutions. A common bond now uniting the majority north and south who voted for it is fidelity to its thirty-five pages, a fidelity that will probably override their actual relation to their respective sovereign powers.

One weakness of the document is its treatment of cultural issues. For a paper that is remarkably hospitable to theories of hybridity and ideas of perpetual negotiation, it is somewhat reticent about the cultural implications. It offers 'parity of esteem' for both the Irish language and Ulster Scots dialect, but doesn't go much further. That reticence is understandable, given that the document was written by politicians and civil servants under pressure of a Good Friday deadline after four sleepless nights, but it may come back to haunt its architects. After all, Jean Monnet, a founder of the European Economic Community, once said that his greatest regret was that he had never evolved a coherent cultural policy for a united Europe, one that might have helped it get through its rougher moments of economic and political crisis. He believed in his later years that then-fashionable neo-Marxian ideas of economic determinism after World War Two had led people to discount the vital importance of culture as a creator of social forces. Whatever the case about other parts of western Europe, culture in Ireland has often caused major developments in politics. The 1916 Rising and the establishment of a separate state would have been inconceivable without the literary revival and language movements that preceded them.

Even if the Belfast Agreement lapses through a failure of unionists and nationalists to recognize one another's difficulties with their respective constituencies, it will none the less serve as a useful statement of the workings of 'tradition' in Ireland. In it a political nationalism that had existed for more than a century as a seemingly sacred value has been unceremoniously dumped by the vast majority of the electorate. In much the same way, and as a direct consequence of the scandals of recent decades, the teaching authority of the Catholic bishops has been rejected by many. In other words, the two main forces that filled the vacuum after the decline of the Irish language have now all but evaporated.

The Irish language itself underwent a similar fate after the Great Famine of the 1840s. It was the people themselves who resolved not to speak it any more, but set their children to master English as the language of modernity. The profound lack of sentimentality behind all these gestures suggests that, far from being worshippers of the past, what Irish people really worship is their own power over it, including the power to bury it at a time of their own choosing.

There is, as I have argued throughout this narrative, no real tradition in Ireland, other than the persistent and largely successful endeavour to oppose any attempt to impose a tradition as 'official'. That is what has given the place its modernist edge over the past four centuries, for by very definition modernism, in order to maintain itself, must never lapse into an official style. Rather, it must constantly renew and reformulate itself. The Irish language may have declined, but it was reborn in the Hiberno-English of Hyde, Synge and Augusta Gregory. Similarly, that Catholicism that is being shattered at an institutional level has been remoulded in books like *AnamChara* (Soul-Friend), a bestseller that links Celtic soul and Catholic devotionalism (of that kind whose subversive potential delighted Wilde) but strictly outside all institutional frameworks.

Even as political nationalism disappears, a truly comprehensive national culture may for the first time be born. After all, political nationalism was just another in the long line of attempts to cope with modernity – it was nothing more than a means by which to implement the Celtic values of a people which had never achieved a satisfactory embodiment under the British imperial scheme. By attaching itself to forms of the state inherited from British days and by leaving those forms unmodified, it doomed itself to frustration, to mistaking the means of liberation for the end in itself. The Belfast Agreement at least gives everyone the chance to start again. It may in time produce political and cultural models that could be of use to communities in other war-torn parts of the world, where the problem of 'blood and belonging' cries out for cultural rather than military solutions. Its central intuition – that an unprecedented knowledge is possible in zones where cultures collide – would not have fazed any of the major writers treated in this book. The seeds of the Belfast Agreement were sown in the works of Irish literature, a fact recognized by Patrick Mayhew, the Secretary of State for Northern Ireland who helped to initiate the peace process of the 1990s.

One day, as this process was beginning to take shape, Mayhew read the prison letters of Ernie O'Malley, an IRA veteran of the War of Independence. He found in them to his amazement an unambiguous celebration of the masterpieces of English literature. This confirmed – even if Mayhew might not have so phrased it himself – those postcolonial theories which held that nationalism was doomed to frustration by the myth of its own singularity: only by contact with the art of other peoples could anything approaching a national culture be born. O'Malley clearly revered English literature just as deeply as many of the great Anglo-Irish writers had admired Gaelic culture. What struck Patrick Mayhew most was an account of how the wounded IRA man, as he lay waiting for first aid during a long gun battle, took comfort from his pocket edition of the sonnets of Shakespeare. On the basis of that strange epiphany he concluded – rightly, as it turned out – that a meaningful peace process between ancient enemies might yet be possible. Irish, or British, or both.[20]

Notes

In citing works in the notes, short titles have generally been used. References to *FDA* are to the *Field Day Anthology of Irish Writing* (3 Vols), Derry 1991.

1 Gaelic Ireland: Apocalypse Now?

1   Eleanor Knott ed., *Ériu 8*, Dublin 1915, 192–5.
2   Marc Caball, *Poets and Politics: Reaction and Continuity in Irish Poetry 1558–1625*, Cork 1998, 118.
3   Robin Flower, *The Irish Tradition*, London 1947, 168, 166.
4   Nina Witoszek and Pat Sheeran, *Talking to the Dead: A Study of Irish Funerary Traditions*, Amsterdam 1998, 67.
5   Tomás Ó Fiaich, Réamhrá, *Imeacht na nIarlaí* (henceforth *II*), ed. Pádraig de Barra, Áth Cliath 1972, 50–4.
6   Seán Mac Airt, 'The Development of Early Modern Irish Prose', in *Seven Centuries of Irish Learning*, ed. Brian Ó Cuív, Cork 1971, 109.
7   *II*, 64.
8   *II*, 86.
9   *II*, 179.
10 Réamhrá, *II*, 34.
11 Osborn Bergin, *Irish Bardic Poetry* (henceforth *IBP*), ed. Fergus Kelly, Dublin 1970, 88.
12 *IBP*, 90.
13 Caball, 113, 97.
14 Vivian Mercier, *The Irish Comic Tradition*, Oxford 1962, 155.
15 N.J.A. Williams ed., *Pairlement Chloinne Tomáis* (henceforth *PCT*), Dublin 1981, 3. Both first and second versions are included in the Williams edition.
16 *PCT*, 40
17 Ibid.
18 Ibid.
19 *PCT*, 6.
20 *PCT*, 30.

21 *PCT*, 59.
22 *PCT*, 42.
23 *PCT*, 20.
24 Caball, 44.
25 Caball, passim.
26 Brian Ó Cuív ed., *Éigse*, Dublin 1973–4, 272–3.
27 Quoted in Brian Ó Cuív ed., *A View of the Irish Language*, Dublin 1969, 104.
28 The sources for these reports are Ó Cuív ed., *A View of the Irish Language*, 104, and Daniel Corkery, *The Fortunes of the Irish Language*, Cork 1968, 71.
29 Ó Cuív ed., *A View of the Irish Language*, 105.
30 David Greene, 'The Professional Poets', in Ó Cuív ed., *Seven Centuries of Irish Learning*, 42.
31 Ibid., 38.
32 See Joep Leerssen, *Mere Irish and Fíor-Ghael: Studies in the Idea of Irish Nationality, Its Development and Literary Expression Prior to the Nineteenth Century*, Cork 1996, 190,
33 Caball, 48, 52.

2 Bardic Poetry: The Loss of Aura

1   David Greene, in *Seven Centuries of Irish Learning*, ed. Brian Ó Cuív, Cork 1971, 48–9.
2   *Irish Bardic Poetry* (henceforth *IBP*), ed. Fergus Kelly, Dublin 1970, 145–6.
3   Quoted by Walter Benjamin, *Charles Baudelaire: A Lyric Poet in the Era of High Capitalism*, translated by Harry Zohn, London 1983, 34.
4   Ibid.
5   Osborn Bergin in *IBP*, 127.
6   *IBP*, 127–8.
7   *IBP*, 128.
8   *IBP*, 129.
9   *IBP*, 120.
10 *IBP*, 121: S. McKibben, 'Lamenting the Language', M.Phil, UCD 1997, 31.
11 Eleanor Knott, *Irish Classical Poetry*, Dublin 1960, 53.
12 *IBP*, 122.
13 Cited by Benjamin, *Charles Baudelaire*, 153.
14 Susan Buck-Morss, *The Dialectics of Seeing: Walter Benjamin and the Arcades Project*, Cambridge, Mass. 1990, 190.
15 Cited by Benjamin, *Charles Baudelaire*, 193.
16 Mark Caball, *Poets and Politics: Reaction and Continuity in Irish Poetry 1558–1625*, Cork 1998, 24.
17 Benjamin, *Charles Baudelaire*, 154.
18 I heard this said at a wake in Indreabhán, June 1972.
19 Ellsworth Mason and Richard Ellmann eds., *The Critical Writings of James Joyce*, New York 1959, 174.
20 Samuel Beckett, *Molloy: Malone Dies: The Unnamable*, London 1959, 302.

21 Woody Allen, *Without Feathers*, London 1978, 98.
22 Quoted by Catherine Stanley, 'On Death and Dying', *Minneapolis Star-Tribune*, 25 May 1997, 51.
23 Caball, 111.
24 Flaithrí Ó Maolchonaire, *Desiderius*, ed. T.F. O'Rahilly, Dublin 1955, 2.
25 Cited in Daniel Corkery, *The Fortunes of the Irish Language*, Cork 1968, 73–4.
26 Seathrún Céitinn, *Foras Feasa ar Éirinn 1*, ed. David Comyn, London 1902, 76. Spelling modernized.
27 Frank Kermode, *The Sense of an Ending*, Oxford 1967, 68.
28 For a contrapuntal artistic analysis of Gaelic and English poets of the period, see Frank McGuinness's play *Mutabilitie*, London 1997.
29 Kermode, 27, 82.
30 Kenneth Muir ed., *King Lear* (Arden Shakespeare), London 1952, 148.
31 Kermode, 82.

3 Saving Civilization: Céitinn and Ó Bruadair

1   Wallace Stevens, cited in Frank Kermode, *The Sense of an Ending*, Oxford 1967, 31.
2   Frank O'Connor, *The Backward Look*, London 1967, 111.
3   Patrick Kavanagh, *Collected Poems*, London 1972, 84.
4   O'Connor, *The Backward Look*, 105.
5   Pádraig de Brún, Breandán Ó Buachalla, Pádraig Ó Concheanainn eds., *Nua-Dhuanaire*, Áth Cliath 1971, 15–16.
6   For these debates see Aodh de Blácam, *Gaelic Literature Surveyed*, Dublin 1924, 259–60; his account offers a lively revivalist counterblast to the emerging narrow-gauge readings.
7   *Nua-Dhuanaire*, 18.
8   James Joyce, *A Portrait of the Artist as a Young Man*, ed. S. Deane, London 1992, 220.
9   De Blácam, *Gaelic Literature Surveyed*, 259.
10 O'Connor, *The Backward Look*, 107.
11 P.H. Pearse, 'About Literature', *An Claidheamh Soluis*, 26 Bealtaine (May) 1906, 6.
12 Douglas Hyde, *A Literary History of Ireland*, London 1899, 542.
13 Cainneach Ó Maonaigh, 'Scríbhneoirí Gaeilge an Seachtú hAois Déag', *Studia Hibernica*, No. 2, 1962, 182–208.
14 J.C. MacErlean SJ ed., *Duanaire Dháibhidh Uí Bhruadair*, Vol. 3, London 1917, 180. Spelling slightly modernized by me.
15 *Nua-Dhuanaire*, 49.
16 Quoted by Walter Benjamin in *Charles Baudelaire: A Lyric Poet in the Era of High Capitalism*, translated by Harry Zohn, London 1983, 153–4.
17 Quoted by Roger McHugh, 'Anglo-Irish Poetry 1700–1850', *Irish Poets in English*, ed. Seán Lucy, Cork 1972, 81.
18 For example, the critic Piaras Béaslaoí in *Éigse Nua Ghaedhige*, Áth Cliath, n.d.
19 Breandán Ó Buachalla, 'Canóin na Creille: An File ar Leaba a Bháis',

Nua-Léamha: Gnéithe de Chultúr, Stair agus Polaitíocht na hÉreann 1600–1900, ed. Máirín Ní Dhonnchadha, Áth Cliath 1996, 153ff.

4   Dying Acts: Ó Rathaille and Others

1   Samuel Beckett, *All That Fall*, London 1957, 31–2.

2   Jacques Derrida, 'Des Tours de Babel', in *Theories of Translation*, eds. R. Schutte and J. Biguenet, Chicago 1992, 219.

3   Samuel Beckett, *More Pricks than Kicks*, London 1934, 272.

4   *Irish Bardic Poetry* (henceforth *IBP*), ed. Fergus Kelly, Dublin 1970, 150.

5   *IBP*, 183.

6   *IBP*, 159–60.

7   Caoimhghín Ó Góilidhe ed., *Dánta Árdteastais*, Áth Cliath 1967, 28–30.

8   The strongest argument to this effect is Ó Buachalla's 'Canóin na Creille', but see also the meticulously researched dissertation by Sarah McKibben, 'Lamenting the Language: On the Metaphor of Dying Irish', M. Phil., University College Dublin 1997.

9   *Dánta Árdteastais*, 66.

10 Seán Ó Tuama, *Repossessions: Selected Essays on the Irish Literary Heritage*, Cork 1995, 116–17; also his *Filí faoi Sceimhle*, Áth Cliath 1978, 123. The essay on Synge makes the connection in *Repossessions*, 219–33.

11 J.M. Synge, *Collected Works: Prose*, ed. Alan Price, Oxford 1966, 75.

12 W.B. Yeats, *Collected Poems*, London 1950, 350.

13 W.B. Yeats, *Autobiographies*, London 1955, 189.

14 Arthur H. Scouten, 'Jonathan Swift's Progress from Prose to Poetry', in *Critical Essays on Jonathan Swift*, ed. Frank Palmeri, New York 1993, 46.

15 Jonathan Swift, *Complete Poems*, ed. Pat Rogers, Harmondsworth 1983, 498.

16 Edward W. Said, *The World, the Text and the Critic*, London 1984, 66.

17 Ó Tuama, *Filí faoi Sceimhle*, 106–19.

18 Seán Ó Tuama and Thomas Kinsella eds., *An Duanaire: An Irish Anthology 1600–1900 – Poems of the Dispossessed*, Philadelphia 1981, 160–2.

19 Bruce Redford ed., *The Letters of Samuel Johnson*, Vol. 1, Princeton 1992, 94–7.

20 Aogán Ó Rathaille, *Dánta*, ed. Dáibhí Mac Conmara, Limerick 1968, 35. Spelling slightly modernized.

21 Jane H. Jack, 'The Periodical Essayists', *The Pelican Guide to English Literature 4*, ed. B. Ford, Harmondsworth 1968, 217–29.

22 Pádraig Ó Fiannachta, 'An Barántas', *Léachtaí Cholm Cille*, Vol. 4, Má Nuad 1975, 132–50.

23 Cited by Pat Rogers, *The Augustan Vision*, London 1978, 154.

24 *An Duanaire*, 146–8. Spelling slightly altered.

25 Alexander Pope, *Collected Poems*, ed. Bonamy Dobrée, London 1956, 84.

26 Ibid., 87.

27 Ó Tuama, *Filí faoi Sceimhle*, 140.

28 Daniel Corkery, *The Hidden Ireland*, Dublin 1967, 101.

29 Breandán Ó Buachalla, 'Canóin na Creille', *Nua-Léamha: Gnéithe de*

Chultúr, Stair agus Polaitíocht na hÉireann 1600–1900, ed. Máirín Ní Dhonnchadha, Áth Cliath 1996, 155.

30 Thomas Kinsella, 'The Divided Mind', *Irish Poets in English*, ed. Seán Lucy, Cork 1972, 209.

5 Endings and Beginnings: Mac Cuarta and After

1   Louis Cullen, 'Hidden Ireland: Reassessment of a Concept', *Studia Hibernica*, No. 9, 1969, 7–47.

2   Seán Ó Tuama and Thomas Kinsella eds., *An Duanaire*, Philadelphia 1981, 130–2. Spelling slightly altered.

3   Pat Rogers, *The Augustan Vision*, London 1978, 171.

4   J.M. Synge, *Collected Works: Plays 1*, ed. A. Saddlemyer, Oxford 1968, 9–11.

5   Ibid., 9.

6   Mac Cuarta, *An Duanaire*, 128–30. Spelling slightly altered.

7   J. Bush, *Hibernia Curiosa*, Dublin 1764.

8   Seán Ó Neachtain, *Stair Éamuinn Uí Chléire*, ed. E. Ó Neachtain, Áth Cliath 1918, 32.

9   Seosamh Watson ed., *Mac na Míchomhairle*, Áth Cliath 1979.

10 R.A. Breatnach, 'The End of a Tradition', *Studia Hibernica*, No. 1, 1960, 142.

11 Cathal Ó Háinle, 'An tÚrscéal nár Tháinig', *Promhadh Pinn*, Áth Cliath 1978, 74–98.

12 Quoted by Aodh de Blácam, *Gaelic Literature Surveyed*, Dublin 1924, 308.

13 Jane H. Jack, 'The Periodical Essayists', in *The Pelican Guide to English Literature 4*, ed. B. Ford, Harmondsworth 1968, 221–7.

14 Diarmud Ó Muirithe, *An tAmhrán Macarónach*, Áth Cliath 1980, 11.

15 Sarah McKibben, 'Lamenting the Language', M. Phil. dissertation, University College Dublin 1997, 3ff.

16 Jonathan Swift, 'Thoughts on Religion', in Temple Scott ed., *Prose Works of Jonathan Swift*, London 1898, Vol. 3. 309.

17 On this see Seamus Deane, 'Remembering the Irish Future', *Ireland: Dependence and Independence*, Crane Bag Special Issue, Vol. 8, No. 1, Dublin 1984, 87.

18 McKibben, especially 79–111: also Edward Said, *Orientalism*, New York 1978, 240–3.

19 Caoimhín Ó Danachair, 'The Gaeltacht', in *A View of the Irish Language*, ed. Brian Ó Cuív, Dublin 1969, 119.

20 McKibben, 7.

21 W.B. Yeats, *Autobiographies*, London 1955, 189; also Stanislaus Joyce, *My Brother's Keeper*, ed. R. Ellmann, London 1958, 18.

22 James Joyce, *Ulysses: Student's Annotated Edition*, annotated by Declan Kiberd, London 1992, 139ff.

23 Quoted by Ruth Dudley Edwards, *Patrick Pearse: The Triumph of Failure*, London 1977, 236–7.

24   Cullen, 'Hidden Ireland: Reassessment', 7–47 passim.
25   Synge, *Plays 1*, 33: see Witozsek and Sheeran, passim.
26   Fiona Macintosh, *Dying Acts*, Cork 1994, 124.
27   Ernest Becker, *The Denial of Death*, New York 1973, passim.
28   Peter Kavanagh, *Patrick Kavanagh: Man and Poet*, Newbridge 1987, 129.
29   Peter Kavanagh, *Patrick Kavanagh: Sacred Keeper*, Newbridge 1979, 168–9.
30   On the persistence of the motif, see Seán Ó Súilleabháin, *Irish Wake Amusements*, Cork 1967, 154ff.
31   Peter Kavanagh, *Patrick Kavanagh: Sacred Keeper*, 170.
32   Cainneach Ó Maonaigh, 'Scríbhneoirí Gaeilge an Seachtú hAois Déag', *Studia Hibernica*, No. 2, 1962, 207.
33   Antoinette Quinn, *Patrick Kavanagh: Born-Again Romantic*, Dublin 1991, 101.
34   Patrick Kavanagh, *Collected Poems*, London 1972, 76–7.
35   Patrick Kavanagh, 'A Poet's Country', *Ireland of the Welcomes*, March 1953.

6   Jonathan Swift: A Colonial Outsider?

1   Deane Swift, *An Essay Upon the Life, Writing and Character of Dr Jonathan Swift*, London 1755, 26.
2   *The Correspondence of Jonathan Swift*, ed. Harold Williams, Oxford 1963–72, Vol. 3, 329.
3   All quotations in this paragraph from Roger McHugh, 'The Life of Jonathan Swift', in *Swift Revisited*, ed. D. Donoghue, Cork 1968, 9–10.
4   Swift, *Correspondence*, Vol. 1, 29: on this see also Louis A. Landa, *Swift and the Church of Ireland*, Oxford 1965, 21–3.
5   *The Prose Works of Jonathan Swift*, ed. Herbert Davis *et al.*, Oxford 1939–68, Vol. 4, 281.
6   Swift, *Prose Works*, Vol. 9, 200.
7   Cited by McHugh, 14.
8   Swift, *Correspondence*, Vol. 4, 229.
9   The most recent scholarly edition is Joseph McMinn ed., *Swift's Irish Pamphlets*, Gerards Cross 1991, 23: it has a brilliant introduction and commentary on which I greatly rely here.
10   Oliver W. Ferguson, *Jonathan Swift and Ireland*, Urbana 1962, 49.
11   Joseph McMinn, 'A Weary Patriot: Swift and Anglo-Irish Identity', *Eighteenth Century Ireland*, Dublin 1987, Vol. 2, 104.
12   W.E.H. Lecky, *A History of Ireland in the Eighteenth Century*, London 1892, Vol. 1, 146.
13   Andrew Carpenter, 'Double Vision in Anglo-Irish Literature', in *Place, Personality and the Irish Writer*, ed. A. Carpenter, Gerrards Cross 1977, 182–3. See also Edith Mary Johnston, *Ireland in the Eighteenth Century*, Dublin 1974, 1 and 17–52.
14   Carpenter, 182.
15   Swift, *Prose Works*, Vol. 12, 53.
16   Louis A. Landa, 'Jonathan Swift and Charity', *Essays in Eighteenth*

Century English Literature, Princeton 1980, 56ff.

17   McMinn, *Swift's Irish Pamphlets*, 54.
18   Landa, 'Swift's Economic Views', *Essays in Eighteenth Century English Literature*, 22.
19   Quoted by Ferguson, 49: 3 February 1718 to William Nicholson.
20   Swift, *Prose Works*, Vol. 12, 18.
21   Ibid., 19.
22   Carole Fabricant, *Swift's Landscape*, Baltimore 1982, passim.
23   Swift, *Correspondence*, Vol. 4, 33–5.
24   Pat Rogers, *The Augustan Vision*, London 1978, 57.
25   Ferguson, 51.
26   Douglas Hyde, 'The Necessity for Deanglicising Ireland', *The Revival of Irish Literature*, London 1894, 120ff.
27   Swift, *Prose Works*, Vol. 12, 80.
28   Jonathan Swift, *Complete Poems*, ed. Pat Rogers, Harmondsworth 1983, 453.
29   Cited by Landa, *Essays in Eighteenth Century English Literature*, 32: from *The Querist*, Part 1, No. 150.
30   Swift, *Complete Poems*, 449–50.
31   Art Mac Cumhaigh, *Dánta*, ed. Tomás Ó Fiaich, Áth Cliath 1973, 102.
32   Marc Caball, *Poets and Politics: Reaction and Continuity in Irish Poetry 1558–1625*, Cork 1998, 45ff.
33   Swift, *Complete Poems*, 554.
34   Joseph McMinn, 'Jonathan's Travels: Swift's Sense of Ireland', *Swift Studies 7*, 1992, 45.
35   Andrew Carpenter and Alan Harrison, 'Swift's "O'Rourke's Feast" and Sheridan's "Letter": Early Transcripts by Anthony Raymond', *Proceedings of the First Munster Symposium on Jonathan Swift*, eds. H. Read and H. Vienken, Munich 1985, 27–46.
36   Robert Hogan ed. *The Poems of Thomas Sheridan*, Newark 1994, 133, lines 27–30.
37   John Flood of Trinity College Dublin has cast some doubt on the likelihood that 'Cill Cais' existed in Swift's day, but McMinn thinks that it did.
38   Daniel Corkery, *The Hidden Ireland*, Dublin 1967, 160.
39   Swift, *Prose Works*, Vol. 10, 129.
40   Mackie L. Jarrell, 'Jack and the Dane": Swift Traditions in Ireland', in A.N. Jeffares ed., *Fair Liberty Was All His Cry: Swift – A Tercentenary Tribute*, London 1967, 329.
41   Swift, *Correspondence*, Vol. 4, 328.
42   Swift, *Correspondence*, Vol. 3, 359–60.
43   J.C. Beckett, *The Anglo-Irish Tradition*, London 1976, 143–7.
44   Irwin Ehrenpreis, *The Man, His Works and the Age: Dean Swift*, London 1983, 5.
45   Swift, *Correspondence*, Vol. 4, 537.
46   See Ehrenpeis, 730,
47   Homi Bhabha, 'Of Mimicry and Man', *October 28*, Spring 1984, 126ff.
48   Ibid.
49   Swift, *Complete Poems*, 253.
50   Ehrenpreis, 67.

51 Bhabha, 126.
52 Ibid., 131.
53 Swift, *Prose Works*, Vol. 9, 17.
54 On this see Denis Donoghue, *Jonathan Swift: A Critical Introduction*, Cambridge 1969, 148.
55 Cited in Ferguson, 119.
56 Mark Kinkead-Weekes, 'The Dean and the Drapier', in Donoghue ed., 46.
57 Ferguson, 98.
58 Ibid., 118.
59 Cited in Ehrenpreis, 255.
60 Cited in Robert Mahony, *The Irish Swift*, New Haven 1995, 105.
61 Swift, *Correspondence*, Vol. 4, 266.
62 Cited by Mahony, 62.
63 D.F. MacCarthy, *The Poets and Dramatists of Ireland*, Dublin 1846, Vol. 1, 130–1.
64 *The Nation*, 2 August 1845, 698.

7 Home and Away: *Gulliver's Travels*

1 Edward Young, *Conjectures on Original Composition*, London 1759, 64.
2 Reported by George Faulkner, 'To the Reader', *The Works of Jonathan Swift*, 1762.
3 C.J. Rawson, *Order From Confusion Sprung: Studies in Eighteenth Century Literature from Swift to Cowper*, New Jersey 1985, 113–20.
4 Jonathan Swift, *Gulliver's Travels* (henceforth *GT*), in *The Portable Swift*, ed. Carl Van Doren, London 1948, 342.
5 Quoted in Irwin Ehrenpreis, *The Man, His Works and the Age: Dean Swift*, London 1983, 67.
6 Thomas Sheridan, *Life of Rev. Dr. Jonathan Swift*, London 1787, 236.
7 Rawson, 82–3; also Herbert Davis, commentary to *The Prose of Jonathan Swift*, Vols 9 and 10, Oxford 1939–68.
8 Cited by Nicholas Mansergh, *The Irish Question 1840–1921*, London 1965, 89.
9 *The Correspondence of Jonathan Swift*, ed. Harold Williams, Oxford 1963–72, Vol. 3, 158.
10 Vivian Mercier, 'Swift and the Gaelic Tradition', in A.N. Jeffares ed., *Fair Liberty Was All His Cry*, London 1967, 284. This may not be a case of direct influence so much as one of a number of correspondences or analogies between Swift's world and a Gaelic Ireland not so different from it as many critics have suggested.
11 Jonathan Swift, *Drapier's Letters*, ed. H. Davis, Oxford 1965, 128.
12 *GT*, 230.
13 *GT*, 239.
14 *GT*, 251.
15 *GT*, 256.
16 *GT*, 258.
17 *GT*, 266.

18   Louis A. Landa, *Swift and the Church of Ireland*, Oxford 1965, 17.

19   *GT*, 526.

20   Albert Memmi, *The Coloniser and the Colonised*, translated by Howard Greenfeld, Boston 1967.

21   *GT*, 350.

22   *GT*, 312.

23   See J.K. Walton, 'The Unity of the *Travels*', *Hermathena*, CIV, 1967, 5–50: and Warren Montag, *The Unthinkable Swift: The Spontaneous Philosophy of a Church of England Man*, London 1994, 156ff.

24   *GT*, 295.

25   *GT*, 312.

26   *GT*, 346.

27   *GT*, 391.

28   Arthur E. Case, 'Personal and Political Satire in *Gulliver's Travels*', in D. Donoghue ed., *Jonathan Swift: Penguin Critical Anthologies*, Harmondsworth 1971, 330.

29   See Seamus Deane, 'Swift: Virtue, Travel and the Enlightenment', in *Walking Naboth's Vineyard*, eds. Brenda Toohey and Christopher Fox, Indiana 1995, 17–39.

30   *GT*, 386.

31   Walton's article (see note 23) is the fullest treatment of this aspect known to me. The Lindalino episode, Chapter Three of Book Three, was only published as late as 1899 in Volume 8 of the Temple Scott edition, so the world had to wait 173 years for the 'Irish' section.

32   *GT*, 394.

33   This is a durable tradition in Irish writing. Early parts of *Ulysses* were intercepted in the mail during World War One by officers who suspected that they might be part of a secret enemy code.

34   *GT*, 421.

35   *GT*, 518.

36   For instance in 1758 one visitor saw a connection between Yahoos and the Irish peasantry: see Robert Mahony, *The Irish Swift*, New Haven 1995, 59.

37   Swift, *Prose Works*, Vol. 9, 66.

38   Swift, *Correspondence*, Vol. 4, 312.

39   *GT*, 435.

40   *GT*, 440.

41   T.S.Eliot, '*Ulysses*, Order and Myth', *The Dial*, Vol. 75, November 1923: in *The Modern Tradition*, eds R. Ellmann and C. Feidelson, Oxford 1965, 680

42   Peadar Ó Doirnín, *Amhráin*, ed. Breandán Ó Buachalla, Áth Cliath 1969, 34–6.

43   *GT*, 456.

44   Cited by Ferguson, 173. In *A Modest Proposal* Swift offered an even more devastating confusion of the human and animal.

45   *GT*, 458.

46   *GT*, 495.

47   On this see Joseph McMinn, *Jonathan's Travels: Swift and Ireland*, Belfast 1994, passim.

48   For an interesting, earlier reading of the Yahoos as mere Irish and the

Houyhnhnms as slave-owners see Anne Kline Kelly, *PMLA*, XLI, 1976, 845–55.

49   *GT*, 469–70.
50   George Orwell, 'Politics v. Literature: An Examination of *Gulliver's Travels*', in Donoghue ed., 354.
51   *GT*, 482; previous quotation from 475–6.
52   *GT*, 526.
53   Ibid.
54   *GT*, 472.
55   See Kathleen Williams, *Jonathan Swift and the Age of Compromise*, London 1959.
56   Robert Martin Adams, 'Swift and Kafka', in Donoghue ed., 240.
57   Jonathan Swift, *A Tale of a Tub and Other Satires*, ed. Kathleen Williams, London 1975, 114.
58   Cited by Williams, *Jonathan Swift and the Age of Compromise*, 96.
59   Edmund Leach, *Lévi-Strauss*, London 1970, 18; and see *World on the Wane*, London 1961, 392 (the English version of Lévi-Strauss's *Tristes Tropiques*).
60   Edward W. Said, 'Swift's Tory Anarchy', in his *The World, the Text and the Critic*, London 1984, 65.
61   *GT*, 523.
62   Swift, *Prose Works*, Vol. 12, 82.
63   Said, *The World*, 67.
64   Ibid., 69. On Swift and historians see also Alan Harrison, *Ag Cruinniú Meala*, Áth Cliath 1988 and Carole Fabricant, 'Swift as an Irish Historian', in Toohey and Fox eds., *Walking Naboth's Vineyard*, 40–72.
65   On this see C.J. Rawson, *Gulliver and the Gentle Reader*, New Jersey 1993, 82ff.
66   Ehrenpreis, Vol. 3, 6.
67   Ibid., 133.

8   Nostalgia as Protest: Goldsmith's 'Deserted Village'

1   Seamus Deane, *Field Day Anthology of Irish Writing*, Derry 1991, Vol. 1 (hereafter *FDA 1*), 659.
2   W.B. Yeats, *Uncollected Prose*, Vol. 2, eds. John P. Frayne and Colton Johnson, London 1975, 328.
3   Peter Dixon, *Oliver Goldsmith Revisited*, Boston 1991, 4: the quotation is on 8.
4   A. Lytton Sells, *Oliver Goldsmith: His Life and Works*, London 1974, 29.
5   Arthur Friedman ed., *Collected Works of Oliver Goldsmith*, Vol. 1, Oxford 1966, 336.
6   Sells, 33.
7   Katharine Worth, *Sheridan and Goldsmith*, London 1992, 18.
8   Terry Eagleton, *Crazy John and the Bishop*, Cork 1998, 112.
9   Sells, 37.
10   James Prior, *The Life of Oliver Goldsmith*, Vol. 2, London 1837, 359.
11   Katherine Balderstone ed., *Collected Letters of Oliver Goldsmith*, Cambridge 1928, 17 and 18.

12   Sells, 45.
13   *Collected Works*, Vol. 2, 60–2; and Vol. 4, 251.
14   *Collected Letters*, 28–30.
15   Ibid., 5.
16   R.S. Crane ed., *New Essays by Oliver Goldsmith*, Chicago 1927, 14.
17   Stephen Gwynn, *Memorials of an Eighteenth Century Painter*, London 1898, 96.
18   G.K. Chesterton, *The Autobiography of G.K. Chesterton*, New York 1936, 139.
19   *Collected Letters*, 13.
20   Ibid., 87.
21   Ibid., 58. The second quotation is from Dixon, 10.
22   James Boswell, *Life of Johnson*, London 1893, Vol. 3, 240.
23   Ricardo Quintana, *Oliver Goldsmith*, London 1967, 16.
24   Cited by Boris Ford, 'Oliver Goldsmith', *The Pelican Guide to English Literature 4*, ed. B. Ford, Harmondsworth 1968, 373–4.
25   *Collected Works*, Vol. 1, 154.
26   Ibid., 91–2.
27   Quoted by Ford, *Pelican Guide 4*, 380.
28   *FDA 1*, 665.
29   Ibid., 665.
30   Raymond Williams, *The Country and the City*, London 1985, 76.
31   Quoted by Andrew Swarbrick, in A. Swarbrick ed., *The Art of Oliver Goldsmith*, London 1978, 15–16.
32   *FDA 1*, 450.
33   Quoted by John Montague, *The Figure in the Cave and Other Essays*, Syracuse 1989, 62.
34   *FDA 1*, 448.
35   Ibid., 449.
36   *Collected Letters*, 162.
37   *FDA 1*, 450.
38   Ibid., 449.
39   Ibid., 451.
40   Ibid.
41   Ford, *Pelican Guide 4*, 384.
42   *FDA 1*, 451.
43   Ibid.
44   See John Lucas, *England and Englishness*, London 1991, 55–70.
45   *FDA 1*, 452.
46   Ibid.
47   See W.J. McCormack, 'Goldsmith, Biography and the Phenomenology of Anglo-Irish Literature', in A. Swarbrick ed., *The Art of Oliver Goldsmith*, 168–94.
48   *FDA 1*, 452.
49   Quoted by Lucas, *England and Englishness*, 60.
50   *Collected Works*, Vol. 4, 266.
51   Cited in Brian Ó Cuív ed., *A View of the Irish Language*, Dublin 1969, 105.
52   *FDA 1*, 453.
53   Ibid.

54 This anonymous poem is included in Brendan Kennelly ed., *The Penguin Book of Irish Verse*, London 1970, 76.
55 Williams, *The Country and the City*, 79.
56 Lucas, 60, 60.
57 Quoted by Montague, 62.
58 *Collected Works*, Vol. 4, 298.
59 Williams, 78.
60 *FDA 1*, 448.
61 Quoted by R. Ellmann, *Yeats: The Man and the Masks*, London 1949, 116.
62 Quoted by Peter Costello, *The Heart Grown Brutal*, Dublin 1975, 28–9.
63 *FDA 1*, 452.
64 Goldsmith, *New Essays*, 116–24.
65 Karl Marx and Friedrich Engels, *The Communist Manifesto*; cited by Marshall Berman, *All That Is Solid Melts into Air*, London 1983, 21.

9 Radical Pastoral: Goldsmith's *She Stoops to Conquer*

1   K. Balderstone ed., *Collected Letters of Oliver Goldsmith*, Cambridge 1928, 166–8.
2   Aodh de Blácam, *Gaelic Literature Surveyed*, Dublin 1924, 238–9.
3   *FDA 1*, 573.
4   Ibid., 574.
5   Seán Lucy ed., *Irish Poets in English*, Cork 1972, 81.
6   Louis MacNeice, *The Poetry of W.B. Yeats*, London 1941.
7   *FDA 1*, 575.
8   Ibid., 590.
9   Ibid., 575.
10 A. Lytton Sells, *Oliver Goldsmith: His Life and Works*, London 1974, 343.
11 Richard Quintana, *Oliver Goldsmith*, London 1967, 151.
12 Ibid., 158.
13 *FDA 1*, 577.
14 Ibid.
15 Quoted by Katharine Worth, *Sheridan and Goldsmith*, London 1992, 82.
16 *FDA 1*, 578.
17 Ibid., 579.
18 Ibid., 581.
19 Ibid., 583.
20 Richard Sennett, *The Fall of Public Man: On the Social Psychology of Capitalism*, New York 1978, 66–7.
21 *FDA 1*, 583.
22 Philip Zimbardo, *Shyness*, London 1981, 33.
23 Ibid., 70–1.
24 Ibid., 74.
25 *FDA 1*, 589.
26 Ibid., 591.
27 Ibid.
28 Ibid., 594.
29 Ibid.

30 Ibid., 588.
31 Quoted by Quintana, 31.
32 *FDA 1*, 600.
33 Ibid., 601.
34 Ibid.
35 Ibid.
36 Oliver Goldsmith, 'Retaliation', in Friedman ed., *Collected Works of Oliver Goldsmith*, Oxford 1966, Vol. 4, 351–9.
37 Peter Dixon, *Oliver Goldsmith Revisited*, Boston 1991, 134 offers telling examples of this.
38 Cited by Quintana, 151.

10 Sheridan and Subversion

1   Fintan O'Toole, *A Traitor's Kiss: The Life of Richard Brinsley Sheridan*, London 1997, 87.
2   Katharine Worth, *Sheridan and Goldsmith*, London 1992, 22.
3   O'Toole, 63.
4   Ibid., 75.
5   Ibid., 84.
6   Ibid., 71.
7   See F.N. Lees, 'John Dryden', in *The Pelican Guide to English Literature 4*, ed. B. Ford, Harmondsworth 1968, 97–113.
8   O'Toole, 134.
9   Richard Brinsley Sheridan, *The School for Scandal and Other Plays* (henceforth *SSOP*), ed. Eric Rump, London 1988, 199.
10 Ibid., 49.
11 Ibid., 50.
12 Ibid., 68.
13 *FDA 1*, 450.
14 *SSOP*, 51.
15 Quoted by Benedict Kiely, 'Dialect and Literature', *The English Language in Ireland*, ed. D. Ó Muirithe, Dublin 1977, 99.
16 *SSOP*, 52.
17 Ibid., 78.
18 Peter Davison ed., *Sheridan's Comedies: A Casebook*, London 1986, 85.
19 Quoted by Worth, 63.
20 *SSOP*, 96.
21 Quoted by G. Duggan, *The Stage Irishman*, Dublin and Cork 1937, 291.
22 *SSOP*, 87.
23 Ibid.
24 Ibid., 102.
25 Ibid., 89.
26 Ibid., 90.
27 Ibid., 53.
28 Ibid., 34.
29 Cecil Price ed., *Dramatic Works of Richard Brinsley Sheridan*, Oxford 1973, 47 and 43.

30   O'Toole, 93.
31   *SSOP*, 34.
32   Ibid., 56.
33   Ibid., 82.
34   Ibid., 71.
35   Ibid., 98.
36   Ibid., 109.
37   Ibid.
38   Ibid., 98.
39   Ibid., 55.
40   A.N. Kaul, 'A Note on Sheridan', in Davison ed., 106.
41   Ibid., 101.
42   *SSOP*, 47.
43   Kaul, 103.
44   *SSOP*, 211.
45   Review in the *Morning Chronicle*, 24 May 1777; Davison ed., 134.
46   T.S. Eliot, '*Ulysses*, Order and Myth', in *The Modern Tradition*, eds. R. Ellmann and C. Feidelson, Oxford 1965, 681.
47   *SSOP*, 195.
48   Ibid., 202.
49   Ibid., 193.
50   Ibid., 203.
51   Ibid., 236.
52   Ibid., 219.
53   Ibid., 227.
54   Ibid., 215.
55   Ibid., 266.
56   Ibid., 267.
57   George Bernard Shaw, cited in Davison ed., 149.
58   O'Toole, 120.
59   Worth, 39–59.
60   Louis Kronenberger, 'The Polished Surface', in Davison ed., 179.
61   William Hazlitt, 'The New English Drama', in Davison ed., 89.
62   O'Toole, 204.
63   *SSOP*, 97.
64   Quoted by Worth, *Sheridan and Goldsmith*, 34–5.
65   Quoted by Worth, 35.
66   Sheridan, cited in Davison ed., 28.
67   Sheridan, quoted by Worth, 33.
68   Pitt's dismissals are quoted in Davison ed., 15.
69   O'Toole, 340.
70   Davison ed., 31.
71   O'Toole, 443.

11 Eibhlín Dhubh Ní Chonaill: The Lament for Art Ó Laoghaire

1   Seán Ó Tuama, *Repossessions: Selected Essays on the Irish Literary Heritage*, Cork 1995, 84.

2   Louis Cullen, 'The Contemporary and Later Politics of *Caoineadh Airt Uí Laoghaire*', *Eighteenth Century Ireland*, Vol. 8, 1993, 17.
3   Ibid., 21.
4   Ó Tuama, *Repossessions*, 85.
5   Peter Levi, *The Lamentation of the Dead*, London 1984, 18.
6   Walter J. Ong, *Orality and Literary: The Technologizing of the Word*, London 1982, 22.
7   Ong, 22; and Breandán Ó Buachalla, *An Caoine agus an Chaointeoireacht*, Áth Cliath 1998, 38.
8   Rachel Bromwich, 'The Keen for Art O'Leary', *Éigse 5*, 1948, 242.
9   Mr and Mrs Samuel Hill: cited in Ó Tuama, *Repossessions*, 81.
10   Eavan Boland, 'Daughters of Colony: A Personal Interpretation of the Place of Gender Issues in the Postcolonial Interpretation of Irish Literature', *Éire-Ireland*, Vol. XXXII, Nos. 2 and 3, Summer–Fall 1997, 15.
11   Eleanor Hull, 'The Story of Deirdre', *Folk-Lore*, XV, 1904, 25.
12   Tomás Ó Raithbheartaigh, *Máistrí san Fhilíocht*, Áth Cliath 1939, 233.
13   Richard Poirier, *The Performing Self: Compositions and Decompositions in the Languages of Contemporary Life*, New York 1971, 12.
14   Angela Bourke, 'Performing, Not Writing: The Reception of an Irish Woman's Lament', in *Dwelling in Possibility: Women Poets and Critics on Poetry*, eds. Yopie Prins and Maeera Shreiber, Ithaca 1997, 145.
15   Cullen, 22.
16   T. Crofton Croker, *The Keen of the South of Ireland*, London 1844, xxxiv.
17   Cullen, 20.
18   Bourke, 134.
19   Seán Ó Tuama ed., *Caoineadh Airt Uí Laoghaire*, Áth Cliath 1961, 33.
20   Ibid., 43.
21   James Carney, *The Irish Bardic Poet*, Dublin 1967, 38.
22   June Singer, *Androgyny: Towards a New Theory of Sexuality*, London 1977, 314–15.
23   Ó Tuama, *Caoineadh*, 35.
24   Cited by Ó Tuama, *Repossessions*, 22.
25   Ó Tuama, *Caoineadh*, 36.
26   Ibid., 37.
27   Ibid., 43.
28   Ibid., 39.
29   Ibid.
30   Ibid., 43.
31   Ibid.
32   Ibid., 44.
33   Cullen, 25.
34   Ó Tuama, *Réamhrá, Caoineadh*, 20.
35   Ó Tuama, *Caoineadh*, 45.
36   Ibid.
37   Sylvia Plath, 'Daddy', *The Penguin Book of Contemporary American Verse*, ed. Geoffrey Moore, Harmondsworth 1977, 577.
38   J.M. Synge, *Collected Works: Prose*, ed. Alan Price, Oxford 1966, 75.
39   Ibid., 349.

40 Seán Ó Súilleabháin, *Irish Wake Amusements*, 113; Cullen, 19; and Bourke, 'Performing', passim.
41 Ó Tuama, *Repossessions*, 87.
42 Bourke, 133.
43 T.S. Eliot, 'Tradition and the Individual Talent', in *English Critical Texts*, eds. D.J. Enright and Ernst de Chickera, Oxford 1962, 294.
44 Bourke, 133.
45 Ibid., 140.
46 Eliot, 294.
47 Ó Buachalla, 24.
48 Bourke, 142.
49 Julia Kristeva, 'Women's Time', *The Kristeva Reader*, ed. Toril Moi, Oxford 1986, 189.
50 Ibid., 194–5.
51 Bourke, 142–3.
52 Fiona Macintosh, *Dying Acts*, Cork 1994, 21.

12   Brian Merriman's *Midnight Court*

1   Harold Bloom, *The Anxiety of Influence: A Theory of Poetry*, Oxford 1973, 152.
2   Seán Ó Tuama, 'Brian Merriman and His Court', *Repossessions*, Cork 1995, 63.
3   Gearóid Ó Crualaoich, 'The Vision of Liberation in *Cúirt an Mheán-Oíche*', *Folia Gadelica: Essays Presented to R.A. Breatnach*, Cork 1983, 102.
4   Seán Ó Tuama and Thomas Kinsella eds., *An Duanaire: An Irish Anthology 1600–1900 – Poems of the Dispossessed*, Philadelphia 1981, 158.
5   Ó Crualaoich, 98.
6   Gearóid Ó Tuathaigh, 'The Role of Women in Ireland under the New English Order', *Women in Irish Society: The Historical Dimension*, eds. Margaret Mac Curtain and Donncha Ó Corráin, Dublin 1978, 34.
7   Cecile O'Rahilly ed., 'An Síogaí Rómhánach', *Five Seventeenth Century Political Poems*, Dublin 1952, 17–18.
8   Liam P. Ó Murchú, *Cúirt an Mheon-Oíche*, Áth Cliath 1982, 19.
9   Alexander Pope, *Collected Poems*, ed. Bonamy Dobrée, London 1956, 25.
10 Ó Murchú, 19.
11 Quoted by Alan Titley, 'An Breithiúnas ar *Cúirt an Mheán-Oíche*', *Studia Hibernica*, No. 25, Dublin 1989–90, 127.
12 Angela Bourke, 'The Virtual Reality of Irish Fairy Legend', *Éire-Ireland*, Spring–Summer 1996, Vol. XXXI, Nos. 1 and 2, 9–10. Bourke first drew my attention to the Bakhtinian parody of *aisling* conventions in the Cúirt.
13 Ó Murchú, 20.
14 Cited by Colbert Kearney, *The Writings of Brendan Behan*, Dublin 1977.
15 Ó Murchú, 26–7.
16 Ibid., 33.
17 Ibid., 35.
18 Quoted by Daniel Corkery, *The Hidden Ireland*, Dublin 1967, 231.

19 Ó Murchú, 36.
20 Ibid., 37.
21 Ibid., 38.
22 Ibid., 40.
23 Ibid., 46.
24 Frank O'Connor, *The Backward Look*, London 1967, 130.
25 Piaras Béaslaí, *Éigse Nua-Ghaedhilge 2*, Áth Cliath, no date cited, 204ff.
26 Corkery, *The Hidden Ireland*, 237.
27 Ó Tuama, *Repossessions*, 63: Ó Murchú, Réamhrá, 12–13.
28 Mikhail Bakhtin, *Rabelais and His World*, translated by Helene Iwolsky, Bloomington 1984, 123.
29 Karl Marx, *Collected Works*, Vol. 1, 418.
30 Bakhtin, *Rabelais*, London 1971, 91.
31 Ó Tuama, *Repossessions*, 63–77.
32 Seán Ó Tuama, 'Cúirt an Mheán-Oíche', *Studia Hibernica*, 1964, 7–27.
33 W.B. Yeats, cited in Vivian Mercier, *The Irish Comic Tradition*, Oxford 1962, 193ff.
34 Anraí Mac Giolla Chomhaill ed., *Díolaim Próis 1450–1850*, Áth Cliath 1971, 131. See the original text in Brian Ó Cuív ed., *Párliament na mBan*, Dublin 1977, 11.
35 August Knock, quoted in Donncha Ó Corráin, 'Women in Early Irish Society', *Women in Irish Society: The Historical Dimension*, 5.
36 Donncha Ó Corráin, in ibid., 9.
37 Ibid., 10.
38 Ibid., 11.
39 For the foregoing references and further commentary, see Pat Rogers, *The Augustan Vision*, London 1978, 87–98.
40 *Díolaim Próis*, 131.
41 Jane Austen, cited by Pat Rogers, *The Augustan Vision*, 97.
42 Piaras Béaslaí, quoted by Corkery, *The Hidden Ireland*, 236.
43 James Joyce, cited in a lecture by Richard Ellmann, Gulbenkian Theatre, Oxford University, 2 April 1974.
44 Frank O'Connor, preface, *The Midnight Court*, London 1945, 10.
45 Seamus Heaney, *The Redress of Poetry: Oxford Lectures*, London 1995, 61.
46 Ó Murchú, 46.
47 Corkery, *The Hidden Ireland*, 230.
48 Ó Murchú, 23.
49 Richard Sennett, *The Fall of Public Man*, New York 1978, 185–90.
50 Heaney, *The Redress of Poetry*, 56.
51 Ó Crualaoich, 98.
52 Ibid., 101–2.
53 Tim Pat Coogan, *De Valera: Long Fellow, Long Shadow*, London 1993, 126.

13 Burke, Ireland and Revolution

1 Conor Cruise O'Brien, *The Great Melody: A Thematic Biography of Edmund Burke*, London 1992, 20.

2   Ibid., 23.
3   Edmund Burke, *Irish Affairs* (henceforth *IA*), London 1988, 47.
4   Quoted by Cruise O'Brien, *Great Melody*, 70.
5   Quoted in ibid., 75, 82.
6   Ibid., 85.
7   Edmund Burke, *Correspondence*, eds. A. Cobban and R.A. Smith, Chicago 1967, Vol. 6, 10.
8   Quoted in John C. Weston Jr., 'Edmund Burke's View of History', *Review of Politics*, No. 23, 1961, 223–4.
9   Burke, *Correspondence*, Vol. 4, 48.
10 Conor Cruise O'Brien, Introduction, in Edmund Burke, *Reflections on the Revolution in France*, Harmondsworth 1969, 34.
11 Burke, *IA* 349.
12 J.C. Beckett, *The Anglo-Irish Tradition*, London 1976, 65.
13 Burke, *Correspondence*, Vol. 1, 147–8.
14 J.C. MacErlean sj ed., *Duanaire Dháibhidh Uí Bhruadair*, Vol. 1, London 1910, 18.
15 Ibid., Vol. 2, London 1913, 34.
16 Edmund Burke, *Works*, Boston 1869, Vol. 10, 217: Speech on the Impeachment of Warren Hastings, 21 April 1789; and *Works*, Vol. 2, 222: Speech on Mr Fox's East India Bill.
17 Burke, *Correspondence*, Vol. 5, 255: 19 January 1786.
18 Burke, *Works*, Vol. 2, 195.
19 Burke, *Works*, Vol. 12, London 1887, 23–4, 7 June 1794.
20 Burke, *Works*, Vol. 2, 320.
21 For a somewhat different analysis of the paradoxical Burke, see Michael Freeman, *Edmund Burke and the Critique of Political Radicalism*, Oxford 1980; and Isaac Kramnick, *The Rage of Edmund Burke: Portrait of an Ambivalent Conservative*, New York 1977, passim.
22 Burke, quoted in Freeman, 121.
23 Burke, cited by Weston, 225; and *Correspondence*, Vol. 7, 218.
24 Burke, *Correspondence*, Vol. 8, 147–8.
25 Edmund Burke, *A Philosophical Enquiry into the Origin of Our Ideas on the Sublime and the Beautiful*, ed. J.T. Boulton, London 1958, 51.
26 On Arnold and Burke, see Conor Cruise O'Brien, Introduction, *IA*, vii–xxxvi.
27 *IA*, 71.
28 Ibid., 128.
29 Karl Mannheim, *Ideology and Utopia*, translated by Louis Wirth and Edward Shils, New York 1936, passim.
30 *IA*, 6–7.
31 Ibid., 9–11. Burke is in some self-contradiction here. In an ideal world he sought to balance the masculine sublime with the feminine beautiful, but in this essay he seems to privilege the masculine. For a somewhat similar confusion on addressing these themes, see remarks by Wolfe Tone in this volume, 234–6.
32 *IA*, 13.
33 Burke, *Works*, Vol. 5, 'Letters on a Regicide Peace', 210–11.
34 *IA*, 47.

35 Ibid., 271.
36 See David Simpson, *Romanticism, Nationalism and the Revolt against Theory*, Chicago 1993.
37 *IA*, 417.
38 Ibid., 64.
39 Ibid., 170.
40 Ibid.
41 Burke, *Works*, Vol. 5, 225.
42 *IA*, 74.
43 Burke, *Works*, Vol. 2, 31–2: and quoted by Bertram Srasan, 'Burke's Two Notes on America', *Burke Newsletter*, 6, No. 1, Autumn 1964, 127.
44 *IA*, 141, 210.
45 Ibid., 243.
46 Ibid., 315.
47 Ibid., 350.
48 Ibid., 424–5.
49 On this see Alfred Cobban, *Edmund Burke and the Revolt Against the Eighteenth Century*, London 1960.
50 For more on this inner conflict see Kramnick, especially 100–210: and Ronald Paulson, *Representations of Revolution 1789–1820*, New Haven 1983, 70ff.
51 Burke, *Works*, Vol. 5, 148: 'A Letter to a Noble Lord'.
52 Burke, *Correspondence*, Vol. 8, 592.
53 James Boswell, *Life of Johnson*, London 1893, Vol. 3, 390

14 Republican Self-Fashioning: The Journal of Wolfe Tone

1 W.B. Yeats, *Autobiographies*, London 1955, 69.
2 Ibid., 84.
3 Stephen Spender, 'Confessions and Autobiography', in James Olney ed., *Autobiography: Essays Theoretical and Critical*, Princeton 1980, 120.
4 *Letters of John Keats*, ed. Frederick Page, London 1968, 53.
5 Quoted by Lionel Trilling, *Sincerity and Authenticity*, Oxford 1972, 25.
6 Jacques Barzun, *Classic, Romantic and Modern*, London 1962, 63.
7 Marianne Elliott, *Wolfe Tone: Prophet of Irish Independence*, London 1989, 27.
8 Thomas Bartlett ed., *Life of T.W. Tone*, Dublin 1998, 19. This volume contains both the autobiographical memoirs and the journals which are the main subject of this chapter.
9 Tone, in ibid., 19.
10 Ibid., 20.
11 Elliott, 30. Martha Worthington was either 15 or 16 when they eloped. Tone preferred to call her Matilda.
12 On this see Trilling, 75ff.
13 Bartlett, 26.
14 Ibid., 33.
15 Ibid., 30.
16 Ibid., 125.
17 Cited in ibid., 438.

18 Ibid., 439.
19 Ibid., 135.
20 Ibid., 136.
21 Ibid., 120. Tone's youthful support for empire was not inconsistent with his anti-Englishness: he simply wanted an independent Ireland to be in a position to found an empire of its own. He voiced (at various times) sympathy for Louis XVI and George III. As a republican, he did not *have* to be anti-monarchical, at least until the 1790s, when republicanism became strongly separatist.
22 Ibid., 122.
23 Ibid., 124.
24 Richard Sennett, *The Fall of Public Man*, New York 1978, 64–6.
25 Bartlett, 131.
26 Ibid., 138.
27 Ibid., 288.
28 Ibid., 281. This may be a boost for Paine at the expense of Burke, who was accused by Paine of noticing only the plumage of society and missing the dead bird beneath.
29 Ibid., 39.
30 Ibid., 151.
31 Ibid., 475.
32 Ibid., 562.
33 Ibid., 734.
34 Edmund Burke, *Reflections on the Revolution in France*, Harmondsworth 1969, 85–6, 92.
35 Bartlett, 573. Matilda Tone was very tolerant in including this passage in the first edition of 1826.
36 Ronald Paulson, *Representations of Revolution 1789–1820*, New Haven 1983, 70.
37 Mary Wollstonecraft, quoted in ibid., 71.
38 Bartlett, 477.
39 Ibid., 504–5.
40 Ibid., 567, 576.
41 Ibid., 404.
42 Ibid., 464.
43 Ibid., 465.
44 Rousseau, quoted by Trilling, *Sincerity and Authenticity*, 65.
45 Rousseau, quoted by Jean Starobinski, *Jean-Jacques Rousseau: Transparency and Obstruction*, translated by Arthur Goldhammer, Chicago 1988, 93.
46 Bartlett, 495.
47 Ibid., 154.
48 Ibid., 198.
49 Starobinski, 125–6.
50 Bartlett, 591, 853.
51 Ibid., 791.
52 Ibid., 628.
53 Ibid., 664.
54 Rainer Maria Rilke, *Von der Landschaft, Ausgewählte Werke*, 1938, II,

218: cited by J.H. Van den Berg, 'The Subject and his Landscape', in *Romanticism and Consciousness: Essays in Criticism*, ed. Harold Bloom, New York 1970, 61.

55 John Mitchel, introduction, *James Clarence Mangan: Poems*, ed. Mitchel, New York 1859, 32.
56 Authoritative examples are Elliott's ground-breaking biography; Tom Dunne's *Theobald Wolfe Tone: Colonial Outsider* (Cork 1982); and Frank MacDermot, *Theobald Wolfe Tone* (Dublin 1926).
57 Bartlett, 23.
58 Ibid., xxxviii.
59 Kevin Whelan, *The Tree of Liberty*, Cork 1996, 168.
60 Bartlett, 40.

15   Native Informants: Maria Edgeworth and *Castle Rackrent*

1 W.B. Yeats, *Explorations*, New York 1962, 345.
2 John Cronin, *The Anglo-Irish Novel*, Vol. 1, Belfast 1990, 25.
3 Oliver MacDonagh, *States of Mind: A Study of Anglo-Irish Conflict 1780–1980*, London 1983, 44–5.
4 Maria Edgeworth ed., *Memoirs of Richard Lovell Edgeworth*, Vol. 2, Boston 1821, 133–42.
5 Stanislaus Joyce, *My Brother's Keeper*, New York 1958, 124.
6 Maria Edgeworth, *Castle Rackrent* (henceforth *CR*), London 1992, 61.
7 Ibid., 61.
8 Julian Moynahan, *Anglo-Irish: The Literary Imagination in a Hyphenated Culture*, Princeton 1995, 39.
9 Homi Bhabha, 'Of Mimicry and Man: The Ambivalence of Colonial Discourse', *October 28*, Spring 1984, 129.
10 Seamus Deane, *A Short History of Irish Literature*, London 1986, 97.
11 Ibid., 97.
12 *CR*, 63.
13 William Wilde, preface, *Irish Popular Superstitions*, Dublin and London 1852.
14 F.V. Berry ed., *Maria Edgeworth: Chosen Letters*, Boston 1931, 243–4.
15 Moynahan, 22.
16 Oscar Wilde, *The Artist as Critic*, ed. R. Ellmann, London 1970, 137.
17 Marilyn Butler, quoted by Cronin, *The Anglo-Irish Novel*, Vol. 1, 38.
18 *CR*, 63.
19 Brendan Barrington, 'The Eighteenth Century Maria Edgeworth: History, Colony and Ideology in *Castle Rackrent*', MA dissertation, University College Dublin 1996, 92.
20 Oliver MacDonagh, *Ireland: The Union and Its Aftermath*, London 1977, 33–4.
21 Terry Eagleton, *Heathcliff and the Great Hunger: Studies in Irish Culture*, London 1995, 176.
22 *CR*, 63.
23 Ibid., 65.
24 Ibid., 66.

25 Ibid., 69.
26 Ibid., 70.
27 Ibid., 71.
28 Ibid., 137.
29 Ibid., 129.
30 Ibid.
31 Ibid., 81.
32 Ibid., 73.
33 Vera Kreilkamp, *The Anglo-Irish Novel and the Big House*, Syracuse 1998, 53ff.
34 Kevin Whelan, *The Tree of Liberty*, Cork 1996, passim.
35 CR, 74.
36 Ibid., 76.
37 Ibid., 77.
38 Ibid., 83.
39 Ibid., 96.
40 Ibid., 97.
41 Ibid., 100. For further links between the narrative and the period 1792–1800 see W.J. McCormack, *Ascendancy and Tradition*, Oxford 1985, 108ff.
42 CR, 105.
43 Cronin, *The Anglo-Irish Novel*, Vol. 1, 36.
44 Bhabha, 129–32.
45 CR, 108.
46 Ibid., 109.
47 Ibid.
48 Ibid., 112.
49 Theodor Adorno, *Minima Moralia: Reflections from a Damaged Life*, translated by E.F.N. Jephcott, London 1974, 120.
50 CR, 119.
51 Ibid., 121.
52 Ibid., 122.
53 Ibid.
54 Ibid.
55 Seamus Deane, *Strange Country*, Oxford 1997: 'it is not merely a nostalgic lament for the traditional pieties and values they produce. It is a lament for the idea of the traditional in which nostalgia is a constitutive element . . . lostness is central to its meaning.'
56 Maria Edgeworth ed., *Memoirs of Richard Lovell Edgeworth*, 251.
57 Eagleton, *Heathcliff and the Great Hunger*, 168.
58 Moynahan, 39.
59 The fear that a distinctively Irish way of life is about to die recurs. By 1907 James Joyce was voicing it, and by 1916 Desmond FitzGerald. Brian Friel's plays of the 1980s and 1990s explore it consistently.
60 Marilyn Butler sees Edgeworth as 'bipartisan' in her sympathies through the 1790s (*Jane Austen and the War of Ideas*, Oxford 1987, 124): but David Lloyd argues that her novel cannot but be partisan, with the people therein represented becoming its 'antagonists as well as its objects' (*Anomalous States*, Dublin 1993, 141).

61   Clíona Ó Gallchóir, 'Maria Edgeworth and the Rise of National Literature', PhD thesis, Cambridge University 1998, 104.

62   Maria and Richard Lovell Edgeworth, *Essay Upon Irish Bulls*, London 1802, 97.

63   McCormack, 80.

64   *Irish Bulls*, 97.

65   Ibid., 211.

66   For more, see the brilliant analysis in Ó Gallchóir, 105ff.

67   *Irish Bulls*, 59–60.

68   Edmund Burke, *Irish Affairs*, London 1988, 64.

69   Book Notes in *Monthly Review*, May 1800, 90–1.

70   Richard Lovell Edgeworth, 26 April 1800 to David Beaufort: National Library of Ireland, MS 13176 (4).

71   Hobart, quoted by McCormack, 69.

72   Quoted by Oliver MacDonagh, *States of Mind*, 134: the speaker was Lord Lieutenant Westmoreland.

73   Ibid., 135.

74   See Michael Hurst, *Maria Edgeworth and the Social Scene: Intellect, Fine Feeling and Landlordism in the Age of Reform*, London 1969, passim.

75   Berry ed., 384.

16   Confronting Famine: Carleton's Peasantry

1   *The Autobiography of William Carleton*, London 1968, 77.

2   Ibid., 114.

3   Ibid., 73.

4   Ibid., 51.

5   William Carleton, *Tales of Ireland*, Dublin 1836.

6   *Autobiography*, 92.

7   Ibid., 18 and 61.

8   Ibid., 59.

9   Ibid., 169.

10   Ibid., 170.

11   Ibid.

12   John Montague, 'William Carleton: The Fiery Gift', *The Figure in the Cave and Other Essays*, Dublin 1989, 81.

13   Eoghan Rua Ó Súilleabháin in Seán Ó Tuama and Thomas Kinsella eds., *An Duanaire: An Irish Anthology 1600–1900 – Poems of the Dispossessed*, Philadelphia 1981, 196.

14   William Carleton, *Traits and Stories of the Irish Peasantry* (henceforth *TSIP*), Vol. 2, Gerrards Cross 1990, 115.

15   Ibid., 159.

16   Ibid., 113.

17   Ibid., 195.

18   Ibid., 203.

19   Ibid., 244.

20   Carleton, *Traits and Stories of the Irish Peasantry*, Dublin 1833 edition, 448.

21   On this see R.F. Foster, *Paddy and Mr Punch*, London 1993, 281–305.
22   Julian Moynahan, *Anglo-Irish: The Literary Imagination in a Hyphenated Culture*, Princeton 1995, 75.
23   Carleton, *TSIP* 1990, Vol. 2, 238.
24   Ibid., 256.
25   See *TSIP*, Vols 1 and 3 in particular.
26   *Autobiography*, 129.
27   Frank O'Connor, *The Lonely Voice*, London 1963, 13–45.
28   Christopher Morash, *Writing the Irish Famine*, Oxford 1995, 75.
29   *TSIP*, Vol. 1, v.
30   Quoted by Benedict Kiely, *Poor Scholar*, Dublin 1974, 107.
31   On the question of Carleton's authorial intrusiveness, see Neasa Coen, MA dissertation, University College Dublin 1998, 'The Narrator and the Reader: Aspects of Narrative Perspective in William Carleton's *Traits and Stories*'.
32   Norman Vance, *Irish Literature: A Social History*, Oxford 1990, 137.
33   Thomas Davis, *Memoir, Essays and Poems*, Dublin 1945, 112.
34   Thomas Davis, *Literary and Historical Essays*, Dublin 1846, 209.
35   *TSIP*, i. Vol. 1.
36   Karl Marx and Friedrich Engels, *On Literature*, London 1971, 403.
37   *TSIP*, i–ii. Vol. 1.
38   Ibid., ii.
39   Ibid., iii.
40   Ibid., v.
41   Ibid., xviii.
42   Ibid., xix.
43   Ibid.
44   Kiely, *Poor Scholar*, 122.
45   Seán de Fréine, *The Great Silence*, Dublin 1966, 69–71.
46   Carleton, quoted in Kiely, 123.
47   Peadar Ó Laoghaire, *Mo Scéal Féin*, Áth Cliath 1964, 48–9.
48   Raymond Crotty, *Ireland in Crisis: A Study in Capitalist Colonial Underdevelopment*, Dingle 1986.
49   See Harold Bloom, *The Anxiety of Influence*, New York 1973, and S. Deane, *Strange Country*, Oxford 1997, 52.
50   Antain Mac Lochlainn, 'The Famine in Gaelic Tradition', *The Irish Review*, Nos. 17–18, Winter 1995, 90–108.
51   Morash, 113–14.
52   Mrs Asenath Nicholson, *Lights and Shades of Ireland*, London 1850, 9. The same point would be made by Primo Levi in *If This is a Man*, London 1987, 129, in a discussion of the Nazi death camps.
53   Quoted by Kevin Whelan, *The Great Irish Famine*, Dublin 1995, 32.
54   Maria Edgeworth, quoted by Peter Quinn, 'An Interpretation of Silences', *Éire-Ireland*, XXXII, No. 1, Spring 1997, 10.
55   Charles Maturin, *Women: or Pour et Contre*, Vol. 3, London 1818, 295.
56   Seamus Deane, *A Short History of Irish Literature*, London 1986, 110.
57   Declan Kiberd, 'Storytelling: The Gaelic Tradition', in *The Irish Short Story*, eds. P. Rafroidi and T. Brown, Lille 1979, 19ff.

58 *TSIP*, Vol. 1, x.
59 W.B. Yeats, 'Irish National Literature 1: From Carleton to Callanan', *Uncollected Prose*, Vol. 1, ed. John P. Frayne, London 1970, 361.
60 J.M. Synge, *Collected Works: Prose*, ed. Alan Price, Oxford 1966, 149.
61 *TSIP*, Vol. 1, xv.
62 Kiely, 15.
63 Ibid.
64 Douglas Hyde, *A Literary History of Ireland*, Dublin 1899, 631ff, for a fascinating discussion.
65 William Curran, *The Life of John Philpott Curran*, ed. R. Shelton Mackenzie, Chicago 1882, 523.
66 Matthew Arnold, quoted by Frank O'Connor, *The Backward Look*, London 1967, 154.
67 Mac Lochlainn, 90–8.
68 See Isaac Butt, *The Irish People and Irish Land*, Dublin 1867, 267–8, for a full account, two decades later, of Butt's ideas.
69 William Carleton, preface to *Valentine M'Clutchy*, Dublin 1847, vi.
70 *TSIP*, Vol. 1, xi.
71 Quoted by Máirín Wall, 'The Decline of the Irish Language', in *A View of the Irish Language*, ed. Brian Ó Cuív, Dublin 1969, 87.
72 Quoted by Frank O'Connor, *The Backward Look*, 110.
73 Cited by Hyde, 631.
74 Cited in ibid., 636.
75 Synge, *Prose*, 341.
76 De Fréine, 242.
77 Ibid., 159.
78 See Morash (148–9) on how A.M. Sullivan saw the famine as transforming a feckless peasantry into bourgeois subjects; and on how Justin McCarthy saw 'much good in it'.
79 Morash, 160: and John Cronin, *The Anglo-Irish Novel*, Vol. 1, Belfast 1990, 88–97.

17 Feudalism Falling: *A Drama in Muslin*

1   George Moore, *A Drama in Muslin* (henceforth *DM*), Gerrards Cross 1986, 88–9.
2   Ibid., 90.
3   Ibid., 92.
4   Ibid., 38.
5   Ibid., 193.
6   Ibid., 32.
7   Ibid., 100.
8   Ibid., 149.
9   Ibid., 156.
10 On this see Mark Bence-Jones, *Twilight of the Ascendancy*, London 1987, 43–53.
11 *DM*, 171.
12 Ibid.

13   Ibid., 159.
14   Joseph Hone, *The Life of George Moore*, London 1936, 100–11.
15   *DM*, 160.
16   Ibid., 172.
17   These details are from Bence-Jones, 43–52.
18   Ibid., 47.
19   Ibid., 29.
20   Ibid., 16.
21   *DM*, 218.
22   Ibid., 203–4.
23   George Moore, *Hail and Farewell*, London 1911–14, passim.
24   *DM*, 151.
25   Ibid., 1.
26   On this see Julian Moynahan, *Anglo-Irish: The Literary Imagination in a Hyphenated Culture*, Princeton 1995, 158.
27   *DM*, 69.
28   Ibid., 70.
29   Ibid., 71.
30   Moynahan, *Anglo-Irish*, 157.
31   For a different reading, see John Cronin, *The Anglo-Irish Novel*, Vol. 1, Belfast 1990, 115–34.
32   *DM*, 39.
33   Ibid., 86.
34   George Moore, *Parnell and His Ireland*, London 1887, 7–8.
35   George Moore, *Confessions of a Young Man*, London 1888, 104.
36   *DM*, 159.
37   Ibid., 191.
38   These quotations are from Tony Gray, *A Peculiar Man: A Life of George Moore*, London 1996, 87–9.
39   Patrick Kavanagh, *Collected Pruse*, London 1973, 282.
40   James Joyce, *Ulysses: Student's Annotated Edition*, annotated by Declan Kiberd, London 1992, 246.
41   See Declan Kiberd, 'George Moore's Gaelic Lawn-Party', in *The Way Back, George Moore's The Untilled Field and The Lake*, ed. R. Welch, Dublin 1982, 13–28.
42   *DM*, 38.
43   George Eliot, *Middlemarch*, Harmondsworth 1965, 119.
44   Ibid., 25, 51; and *DM*, 98.
45   *DM*, 137.
46   Quotations in Gray, 323.

18   The *Love Songs of Connacht*

1   Royal Irish Academy, MS 4B43, Athair Peadar Ó Laoire go Seosamh Laoide, 7 Deire Fómhair 1895.
2   'Gan focal ar bith do chur i gclódh sa Ghaedhilg, nach beidheach l'án-oireamhnach ar a chur i gclódh sa Bhéarla', ibid.
3   *Freeman's Journal*, Wednesay 30 January 1907, 7.

4   Quoted by Tomás Ó Fiaich, 'The Great Controversy', in *The Gaelic League Idea*, ed. Seán Ó Tuama, Cork 1972, 67.

5   Ibid., 67–8.

6   Charlotte Brooke, *Reliques of Irish Poetry*, Dublin 1789, iii.

7   Ibid., viii.

8   Michael Cronin, *Translating Ireland*, Cork 1996, 100ff.

9   Brooke, viii.

10   Cronin, 108.

11   James Hardiman, *Irish Minstrelsy: or Bardic Remains of Ireland with English Poetical Translations*, London 1831, xxxvii.

12   Samuel Ferguson, 'Irish Minstrelsy No 2', *Dublin University Magazine*, Vol. 4, No. 22 (1834), 154.

13   Cronin, 112–13.

14   Mary Colum, *Life and the Dream*, London 1947, 107–8.

15   Ibid., 113.

16   Ibid., 114.

17   On dowry, see Richard Breen, 'Dowry Payments and the Irish Case', *Comparative Studies in Society and History*, Vol. 26, No. 2, April 1984, 280–96.

18   Colum, *Life*, 114.

19   Douglas Hyde, *Love Songs of Connacht*, Shannon 1968, 43. On the popularity of 'Ringleted Youth of My Love', see Janet Egleson Dunleavy and Gareth W. Dunleavy, *Douglas Hyde: A Maker of Modern Ireland*, Berkeley 1991, 173.

20   Homi K. Bhabha, foreword to Frantz Fanon, *Black Skin, White Masks*, London 1986, xxiii.

21   Tom Garvin, *The Evolution of Irish Nationalist Politics*, Dublin 1981, 101.

22   *Love Songs of Connacht*, 40–3.

23   Ibid., 43.

24   W.B. Yeats, *Explorations*, London 1962, 193.

25   Augusta Gregory, *Poets and Dreamers*, Gerrards Cross 1974, 251.

26   W.B. Yeats, letter to the editor, *The Leader*, September 1900.

27   Michael Cronin, 135–6.

28   Ibid., 136.

29   W.B. Yeats, 'Notes', *Samhain*, October 1902.

30   Dominic Daly, *The Young Douglas Hyde*, Dublin 1974, 133.

31   Douglas Hyde, 'The Necessity for Deanglicising Ireland', *The Revival of Irish Literature*, London 1894, 159ff.

32   George Moore, *Vale*, London 1914, 250. On these questions see also Declan Kiberd, *Idir Dhá Chultúr*, Áth Cliath 1993, passim and Thomas MacDonagh, *Literature in Ireland*, Nenagh 1996, 112ff.

33   *Love Songs of Connacht*, 41.

34   MacDonagh, *Literature in Ireland*, 71. He also believed that Arthur O'Shaughnessy's versions in English exceeded the original poems of Sully Prudhomme, a now-forgotten Nobellist, in French: see *Literature in Ireland*, 86.

35   Ibid., 73.

36   Ibid., 72.

37   See Declan Kiberd, *Synge and the Irish Language*, London 1993, 30.
38   J. M. Synge, *Collected Works: Plays 2*, Oxford 1968, ed. Ann Saddlemyer, 125.
39   *Love Songs of Connacht*, 91.
40   Synge, *Plays 2*, 163.
41   Synge, *Plays 1*, ed. Ann Saddlemyer, Oxford 1968, 55.
42   See W.B. Yeats, *Memoirs*, ed. D. Donoghue, London 1972, 177; and MacDonagh, *Literature in Ireland*, 47–8.
43   W.B. Yeats, preface to *Love Songs of Connacht*, Dun Emer Edition, Dublin 1904.
44   W.B. Yeats, 'Notes and Opinions', *Samhain*, November 1905; also October 1902, 3–7.
45   Tomás Ó Flannghaile, *For the Tongue of the Gael*, Dublin 1896, 156–7.
46   Ibid., 153.
47   J. M. Synge, *Collected Works: Prose*, ed. Alan Price, Oxford 1966, 112.
48   Ibid., 149.
49   Ibid., 133.
50   *Love Songs of Connacht*, 23, 7, 19, 33.
51   Cited by Walter Benjamin, *Illuminations*, translated by Harry Zohn, London 1973, 81.
52   Gilles Deleuze and Felix Guattari, *Kafka: Toward a Minor Literature*, translated by Dana Pelan, Minnesota 1986, 14.
53   Synge, *Prose*, 371.
54   Ibid.
55   W.B. Yeats, *Uncollected Prose*, Vol. 1, ed. John P. Frayne, London 1970, 361.
56   Samuel Ferguson, 'Hardiman's Irish Minstrelsy', *Dublin University Magazine*, October 1834, 453n.
57   Ibid., 529.
58   Synge, *Prose*, 372.
59   James Joyce, *Ulysses: Student's Annotated Edition*, annotated by Declan Kiberd, London 1992, 60.
60   Ibid., 168.
61   Ibid., 238. David Lloyd, *Anomalous States*, Dublin 1993, was first to suggest a vampire connection for this lyric, 103–5.
62   Joyce, *Ulysses: Student's Annotated Edition*.
63   *Love Songs of Connacht*, 28–31.
64   Yeats, *Uncollected Prose*, Vol. 1, 295ff.
65   Yeats, *Explorations*, 337.
66   For example, in Gonne's play *Dawn*.
67   Synge, *Prose*, 382.
68   Synge Manuscripts, Trinity College Dublin, MS 4347, fi–fii.
69   Ibid., MS 4392, f3r.
70   Quoted by Gregory, *Poets and Dreamers*, 76.
71   Synge, *Prose*, 367.
72   Archbishop John MacHale was an exception, and there were a few others.
73   J.J. Lee, 'Women and the Church Since the Famine', *Women in Irish Society: The Historical Dimension*, Dublin 1978, 40.
74   Friedrich Schleiermacher, 'On the Different Methods of Translating', in

Theories of Translation, eds. R. Schutte and J. Biguenet, Chicago 1992, 46–7.

19   Anarchist Attitudes: Oscar Wilde

1   Oscar Wilde, 'The Critic as Artist', in *The Artist as Critic*, (a collection of Wilde's prose writings) ed. R. Ellmann, London 1970, 348.

2   Regenia Gagnier, *Idylls of the Marketplace: Oscar Wilde and the Victorian Public*, Stanford 1986, 4.

3   Marina Warner, *From the Beast to the Blonde: On Fairy Tales and their Tellers*, London 1994, 20.

4   Even the Census of Ireland in 1901 found that 21 per cent of persons could neither read nor write.

5   Owen Dudley Edwards, introduction to Prose section, *Collected Works of Oscar Wilde*, Glasgow 1994, 14–15.

6   *Selected Letters of Oscar Wilde*, ed. Rupert Hart-Davis, London 1962, 208.

7   James Joyce, *A Portrait of the Artist as a Young Man*, ed. S. Deane, London 1991, 186.

8   Cyril Connolly, *The Unquiet Grave*: quoted by Edouard Roditi, *Oscar Wilde*, New York 1947, 157.

9   Gagnier, 82.

10   John Harrison, *The Reactionaries*, London 1966, 36.

11   Dominic Manganiello, *Joyce's Politics*, London 1980.

12   David H. Greene and Edward M. Stephens, *J.M. Synge 1871–1909*, New York 1961, 66.

13   Wilde, 'The Soul of Man under Socialism', in *The Artist as Critic*, 282.

14   E.H. Mikhail ed., *Oscar Wilde: Interviews and Recollections*, Vol. 1, London 1979, 232.

15   Cited by Gagnier, 31.

16   George Woodcock, 'The Social Rebel', in *Oscar Wilde: A Collection of Critical Essays*, ed. R. Ellmann, New Jersey 1965, 155.

17   Cited by Roditi, *Oscar Wilde*, 158.

18   Guy Debord, *Society of the Spectacle*, Detroit 1983.

19   Wilde, 'A Chinese Sage', in *The Artist as Critic*, 221–8.

20   Wilde, *Selected Letters*, 208.

21   William Morris, *Collected Works*, London 1918, 111 and 173.

22   Oscar Wilde, in *Field Day Anthology of Irish Writing*, Vol. 2, Derry 1991, 398.

23   Oscar Wilde, *Collected Letters*, London 1962, 488.

24   Yeats collected many of these later in the 1890s.

25   James Joyce, 'Oscar Wilde: The Poet of Salomé', in Ellmann ed., *Oscar Wilde: A Collection of Critical Essays*, 58.

26   H. Montgomery Hyde, *Oscar Wilde*, London 1976, 38ff.

27   Wilde, *Collected Letters*, 43.

28   Ibid., 478.

29   Ronald Schuchard, 'Wilde's Dark Angel and the Spell of Dissident Catholicism', in *Rediscovering Oscar Wilde*, ed. C. George Sandulescu, Gerrards Cross 1994, 371–96.

30 This is the subject of a doctoral thesis being completed by Jarlath Killeen at University College Dublin.

31 Cited by Hesketh Pearson, *Oscar Wilde: His Life and Art*, New York 1946, 58.

32 David Alderson, *Mansex Fine: Religion, Manliness and Imperialism in Nineteenth Century British Culture*, Manchester 1998, 79.

33 Ibid., 80–91.

34 James Joyce, 'Oscar Wilde', 59–60.

35 Wilde, *Collected Letters*, 878.

36 Wilde, *Selected Letters*, 205.

37 Ibid., 213.

38 Ibid., 184.

39 James Joyce, 'Oscar Wilde', 59.

40 Mary McCarthy, 'The Unimportance of Being Oscar', in Ellmann ed., *Oscar Wilde: A Collection of Critical Essays*, 107.

41 Wilde, *Selected Letters*, 164.

42 Wilde, quoted by John Albert OSO, 'The Christ of Oscar Wilde', *Critical Essays on Oscar Wilde*, ed. Regenia Gagnier, New York 1991, 249.

43 Gagnier, *Idylls*, 185.

44 Wilde, *Selected Letters*, 193.

45 Ibid., 216.

46 Richard Ellmann, *Oscar Wilde*, London 1987, 186.

47 Wilde, *Selected Letters*, 339.

48 Ibid., 339.

49 Wilde, *Complete Works*, London 1966, 845, 848–9, 857.

50 Wilde, 'The Soul of Man under Socialism', in *The Artist as Critic*, 266.

51 Ellmann, *Oscar Wilde*, 495–6; Montgomery Hyde, 324.

52 Wilde, quoted by Ellmann, *Oscar Wilde*, 548.

53 Davis Coakley, *Oscar Wilde: The Importance of Being Irish*, Dublin 1994, 215.

20 George Bernard Shaw: *Arms and the Man*

1   Shaw to Denis Johnston: quoted by Michael Holroyd, 'GBS and Ireland', *Sewanee Review*, Winter 1976, LXXXIV, No. 1, 39.

2   Stanley Weintraub ed., *Shaw: An Autobiography 1856–98*, London 1969, 184.

3   Holroyd, 54.

4   Weintraub ed., 86.

5   Ibid., 86.

6   Ibid., 58.

7   Eric Bentley, *Bernard Shaw*, New York 1985, 84.

8   Weintraub ed., 25.

9   Ibid., 36.

10 R.J. Kaufmann, Introduction, *G.B. Shaw: A Collection of Critical Essays*, New Jersey 1965, 10.

11 Holroyd, 51.

12 Weintraub ed., 3.

13 Bentley, 70.
14 Quoted in Bentley, 59.
15 Ibid., 63.
16 G.B. Shaw, *Christian Socialist*, April 1885; cited by Alick West, *A Good Man Fallen Among Fabians: A Study of George Bernard Shaw*, London 1950, 40.
17 West, 76.
18 Holroyd, 51.
19 Sir James Frazer, cited by R. Ellmann and C. Feidelson, *The Modern Tradition*, Oxford 1965, 531.
20 Lévi-Strauss, quoted by Edmund Leach, *Lévi-Strauss*, London 1970, 18.
21 Weintraub ed., 285.
22 Ibid., 286.
23 Ibid., 288.
24 G.B. Shaw, *The Complete Plays*, London 1937, 103 (*Arms and the Man*, henceforth *AM*).
25 *AM*, 100.
26 Ibid., 102.
27 Weintraub ed., 288.
28 Ibid.
29 Ibid., 290.
30 *AM*, 95.
31 Ibid., 97.
32 Ibid., 116.
33 Ibid., 122.
34 Quoted by Rodelle Weintraub, introduction, *Fabian Feminist: Bernard Shaw and Women*, Pennsylvania 1979, 1–13.
35 *AM*, 104.
36 Ibid.
37 Ibid., 105.
38 Mary Ellmann, *Thinking About Women*, London 1979, 127.
39 *AM*, 106.
40 *AM*, 113.
41 *AM*, 115.
42 Ibid.
43 Christopher Lasch, *The Revolt of the Elites and the Betrayal of Democracy*, New York 1995, 27.
44 R.H. Tawney, *Equality*, New York 1931: cited by Lasch, 41.
45 See Bentley, 28–9; also Gareth Griffith, *Socialism and Superior Brains*, London 1993, passim.
46 *AM*, 116.
47 *AM*, 117.
48 *AM*, 118.
49 Ibid.
50 *AM*, 120.
51 *AM*, 119.
52 *AM*, 122.
53 Bentley, 90.
54 Weintraub ed., 284.

55 Ibid., 12.
56 Ibid., 53.
57 W.B. Yeats, *Autobiographies*, London 1955, 283.
58 Shaw, quoted in Michael Holroyd, *Bernard Shaw: The Quest for Love*, London 1988, 298 and 303.

21 Somerville and Ross: *The Silver Fox*

1   Quoted by Declan Kiberd, 'The Perils of Nostalgia', in *Literature and the Changing Ireland*, ed. Peter Connolly, Gerrards Cross 1982, 19.
2   Edith Somerville and Martin Ross, *The Silver Fox* (henceforth *SF*), London 1897, 76.
3   Edith Somerville and Martin Ross, *Irish Memories*, London 1917, 91.
4   Ibid., 322 and 27.
5   Ibid., 125.
6   Somerville, quoted by Gifford Lewis, *Somerville and Ross: The World of the Irish RM*, Harmondsworth 1987, 134.
7   Quoted in ibid., 217.
8   Conor Cruise O'Brien, *Writers and Politics*, London 1965, 107.
9   Somerville, quoted by Lewis, 212.
10 Edith Somerville and Martin Ross, *Wheel-Tracks*, London 1923, 67: and *Irish Memories*, 195.
11 See Otto Rauchbauer, *The Edith Oenone Somerville Archive in Drishane*, Dublin 1995, 236ff.
12 Elizabeth Bowen, *Bowen's Court*, London 1964, 398.
13 Gifford Lewis ed., *The Selected Letters of Somerville and Ross*, London 1989, 256, 253, 253.
14 Ibid., 256, 252.
15 *SF*, 7, 7–8.
16 *SF*, 12.
17 *SF*, 23.
18 *SF*, 36.
19 *Irish Memories*, 103.
20 *SF*, 40.
21 *SF*, 51.
22 *SF*, 52, 53–4.
23 *SF*, 65.
24 *SF*, 73.
25 *SF*, 74, 76, 82.
26 *SF*, 83.
27 *SF*, 87, 106–7.
28 *SF*, 111.
29 *SF*, 116.
30 *SF*, 119.
31 *SF*, 125.
32 *SF*, 144.
33 *SF*, 147–8.
34 *SF*, 122.

35   *SF*, 68.
36   *SF*, 163.
37   *SF*, 164.
38   *SF*, 178.
39   *SF*, 199.
40   *SF*, 206.
41   Ezra Pound, 'A Retrospect', in *Modern Poets on Modern Poetry*, ed. James Scully, London 1966, 31.
42   *SF*, 213.
43   *SF*, 219.
44   On this phenomenon among Anglo-Irish writers, see R.F. Foster, 'Protestant Magic', in *Paddy and Mr Punch*, London 1993, 212–32.
45   *SF*, 242, 241.
46   P. Ó Canainn and Seán Ó Deaghdha, eds., *Filíocht na nGael*, Áth Cliath 1958, 39.
47   Julian Moynahan, *Anglo-Irish: The Literary Imagination in a Hyphenated Culture*, Princeton 1995, 191ff.
48   Ibid., 191.
49   *SF*, 243.
50   *SF*, 251.
51   *SF*, 249.
52   *SF*, 254.
53   Cruise O'Brien, *Writers and Politics*, 107.
54   Otto Rauchenbauer, 229: and MS LB 315 a.e., Drishane.
55   Cruise O'Brien, *Writers and Politics*, 107.
56   *SF*, 267.
57   *SF*, 274, 275.
58   Somerville, quoted in Lewis, 160.
59   Somerville, quoted in Lewis, 215.
60   Somerville, quoted in Lewis, 162.

22   Undead in the Nineties: Bram Stoker and *Dracula*

1   Letter to Bram Stoker 1875: cited in *Dracula* (henceforth *D*), London 1993 (Penguin Classics), 499.
2   See Peter Haining and Peter Tremayne, *The Un-Dead: The Legend of Bram Stoker and Dracula*, London 1997, 44.
3   Bram Stoker, College Historical Society: Address in Dining Hall of Trinity College, First Meeting of 128th session on 13 November 1872, Dublin 1872, 32.
4   Synge Manuscripts, Trinity College Dublin, MS 4373, f. 22.
5   Donald Harman Akenson, *The Church of Ireland: Ecclesiastical Reform and Revolution 1800–1885*, New Haven 1971, 308.
6   On this see Vivian Mercier, 'Evangelical Revival in the Church of Ireland', *Modern Irish Literature: Sources and Founders*, Oxford 1994, 64.
7   These phrases are taken from Julian Moynahan, *Anglo-Irish: The Literary Imagination in a Hyphenated Culture*, Princeton 1995, 127ff.

8   R. F. Foster, *Paddy and Mr Punch*, London 1993, 220.
9   Luke Gibbons, '"Some Hysterical Hatred": History, Hysteria and the Literary Revival', *Irish University Review*, 27, Spring–Summer 1997, 18.
10 Foster, 230.
11 Franco Moretti, *Signs Taken for Wonders*, London 1988, translated by S. Fischer, D. Torgacs and D. Miller, 105.
12 Some strong readings of the 'Irish' Dracula include Michael Valdez Moses, 'The Irish Vampire: *Dracula*, Parnell and the Troubled Dreams of Nationhood', *Journal X*, Vol. 2, No. 1, Autumn 1997, 66–111. On Irving, see Maurice Hindle, Introduction, *Dracula*, London 1993 (Penguin Classics), vii–xxiii.
13 *D*, 59.
14 *D*, 42.
15 See the extract quoted in Clive Leatherdale, *The Origins of Dracula: The Background to Bram Stoker's Gothic Masterpiece*, London 1997, 99–107; also George Stoker, *With 'The Unspeakables': or Two Years' Campaigning in European and Asiatic Turkey*, London 1878, 10.
16 See Seamus Deane, *Strange Country*, Oxford 1997, 89–94: and Terry Eagleton, *Heathcliff and the Great Hunger*, London 1995, 215–16.
17 *D*, 41.
18 *D*, 40.
19 *D*, 55.
20 *D*, 81.
21 *D*, 68.
22 *D*, 132.
23 *D*, 121.
24 *D*, 194.
25 *D*, 225.
26 See Ann Douglas, *The Feminization of American Culture*, New York 1978.
27 Henry James, *The Bostonians*, Harmondsworth 1966, 290.
28 *D*, 289.
29 On this see Nina Auerbach, *Our Vampires, Ourselves*, Chicago 1995, 66ff.
30 Mary E.F. FitzGerald, 'The Unveiling of Power: Nineteenth Century Gothic Fiction in Ireland, England and America', *Literary Inter-Relations: Ireland, England and the World*, Tübingen 1987, 15–25.
31 *D*, 411.
32 *D*, 389.
33 *D*, 218.
34 *D*, 257.
35 *D*, 277.
36 *D*, 270.
37 R.F. Foster, *Modern Ireland 1600–1972*, London 1988, 375.
38 Karl Marx, *Capital 1*, Harmondsworth 1976, 324. I take this reference from Maud Ellmann. On Connolly, see Owen Dudley Edwards, *The Mind of an Activist*, Dublin 1968, passim.
39 *D*, 306.
40 *D*, 302.
41 *D*, 397.

42 George Mills Harper, *Yeats's Golden Dawn*, Northamptonshire 1987.
43 Quoted in Haining and Tremayne, 46.
44 FitzGerald, 25.
45 Benedict Anderson, 'Exodus', *Critical Inquiry*, Vol. 20, No. 2, Winter 1994, 316.
46 See David Glover, *Vampires, Mummies and Liberals: Bram Stoker and the Politics of Popular Fiction*, Durham, North Carolina 1996, especially 44ff, for a fine analysis of this element.
47 George Sigerson, *Bards of the Gael and Gall*, London 1907, 395.
48 J.M. Synge, Collected Works: *Plays 1*, ed. Ann Saddlemyer, Oxford 1968, 48.
49 W.B. Yeats, *Collected Plays*, London 1952, 86; and Augusta Gregory, *Selected Writings*, eds. Lucy McDiarmid and Maureen Waters, London 1995, 309.
50 Quoted by Ruth Dudley Edwards, *Patrick Pearse: The Triumph of Failure*, London 1977, 236–7.

23 Augusta Gregory's Cuchulain: The Rebirth of the Hero

1 Lady Gregory, *Seventy Years 1852–1922*, ed. Colin Smythe, Gerrards Cross 1974, 394.
2 Lady Gregory, *Cuchulain of Muirthemne* (henceforth CM), Gerrards Cross 1970, 5.
3 Robert Welch, 'A Language for Healing', in *Lady Gregory: Fifty Years After*, eds. A. Saddlemyer and C. Smythe, Gerrards Cross 1987, 268ff.
4 Quoted by Augusta Gregory, *Gods and Fighting Men*, Gerrards Cross 1970, 355.
5 On this narrowing, see Gerry Smyth, *Decolonisation and Criticism*, London 1998, 123–32.
6 Lady Gregory, *Seventy Years*, 402.
7 Tomás Ó Cathasaigh, 'Between God and Man: The Hero of Irish Tradition', *Crane Bag*, Vol. 2, Nos. 1 and 2, 1978, 72–9.
8 G.M. Murphy, *Saga and Myth in Ancient Ireland*, Dublin 1955.
9 Patricia Kelly, 'The *Táin* as Literature', in *Aspects of the Táin*, ed. J.P. Mallory, Belfast 1992, 87.
10 Muireann Ní Bhrolcháin, 'Women in Early Irish Myths and Sagas', *Crane Bag*, Vol. 2, Nos. 1 and 2, 1978, 13; also Tomás Ó Máille, 'Medb Cruachna', *Zeitschrifte für Keltische Philologie*, 17, 129–46.
11 John V. Kelleher, 'The *Táin* and Its Annals', *Ériu* 22, 107–27.
12 Kelly, 72.
13 Claude Lévi-Strauss, 'Les mythes se pensent dans les hommes, et a leur insu', *Mythologies 1 : Le Cru et le Cuit*, Paris 1964, 20.
14 Standish J. O'Grady, *Toryism and Tory Democracy*, London 1886, 240 and 285–90.
15 Standish J. O'Grady, *Selected Essays and Passages*, ed. E.A. Boyd, Dublin 1918, 265.
16 Standish J. O'Grady, in *Samhain*, October 1902, No. 2, 5.
17 George Russell (AE), *Some Irish Essays*, Dublin 1928, 26 and 7.
18 Cited by Paul Zweig, *The Heresy of Self-love*, Princeton 1968, 196.
19 Ibid., 196.

20   W.B. Yeats, *Autobiographies*, London 1955, 220.
21   W.B. Yeats, *Plays and Controversies*, London 1923, 161 and 158.
22   Oscar Wilde, *The Artist as Critic*, ed. R. Ellmann, London 1970, 261.
23   Ibid., 271 and 271.
24   Ibid., 273.
25   Ibid., 131.
26   Angela Bourke, 'The Baby and the Bathwater: Cultural Loss in Nineteenth Century Ireland', in *Ideology and Ireland in the Nineteenth Century*, eds. Tadhg Foley and Sean Ryder, Dublin 1998, 84; and see also her 'The Virtual Reality of Irish Fairy Legend', *Éire-Ireland*, Spring–Summer 1996, Vol. XXXI, 1 and 2, 7–25.
27   Wilde, *The Artist as Critic*, 273.
28   W.B. Yeats, *Letters to the New Island*, ed. Horace Reynolds, Cambridge, Massachusetts 1934, 159.
29   Wilde, *The Artist as Critic*, 279.
30   W.B. Yeats, *Letters*, ed. Allan Wade, London 1954, 475.
31   Wilde, *The Artist as Critic*, 296.
32   Ibid., 285.
33   Lady Gregory, *Seventy Years*, 393.
34   Quoted by A. Saddlemyer ed., *Synge: Plays 2*, Oxford 1968, Introduction, xxvii.
35   Mary Colum, *Life and the Dream*, London 1947, 124.
36   Ruth Dudley Edwards, *Patrick Pearse: The Triumph of Failure*, London 1977, 20.
37   Quoted by P.S. O'Hegarty, *History of Ireland after the Union 1801–1922*, London 1952, 406.
38   P.H. Pearse, *Three Lectures*, Dublin 1898, 49.
39   Proinsias Mac Cana, 'Notes on the Early Irish Concept of Unity', *Crane Bag*, Vol. 2, Nos. 1 and 2, Dublin 1978, 60.
40   Stanley Weintraub ed., *Shaw: An Autobiography 1856–98*, London 1969, 24.
41   Otto Rank, *The Myth of the Birth of the Hero and Other Writings*, ed. Philip Freund, New York 1959, 84.
42   Patricia Kelly, 74; Gregory, *CM*, 25–34.
43   *CM*, 38.
44   Standish J. O'Grady, *The Coming of Cuculain*, London 1894, 52.
45   *CM*, 33.
46   Patricia Kelly, 89.
47   Walter Ong SJ, *Orality and Literacy: The Technologizing of the Word*, London 1982, 35–43.
48   Ibid., 45.
49   Ibid., 144.
50   *CM*, 16.
51   *CM*, 252. This scene became famous only in *later* versions.
52   *CM*, 204.
53   W.B. Yeats, *Uncollected Prose*, Vol. 1, ed. John P. Frayne, London 1970, 190.
54   *CM*, 256.
55   *CM*, 263.
56   Lady Gregory, *Seventy Years*, 400.

57 Powell, cited in ibid., 401.

58 George Moore, *Hail and Farewell*, ed. R. Cave, Gerrards Cross 1976, 549–52.

59 Lady Gregory, *Seventy Years*, 403.

60 J. M. Synge, *Collected Works: Prose*, ed. Alan Price, Oxford 1966, 366–70.

61 CM, 61.

62 Synge, *Prose*, 367.

63 Lady Gregory, *Seventy Years*, 403.

64 Quoted by A. Saddlemyer, 'Synge to McKenna: The Mature Years', in *Irish Renaissance*, eds. Robin Skelton and David Clark, Dublin 1965, 67.

65 Mary Lou Kohfelt, *Lady Gregory: The Woman Behind the Irish Renaissance*, London 1985, 139.

66 John Rees Moore, *Masks of Love and Death: Yeats as Dramatist*, Ithaca 1971, 37.

67 Declan Kiberd, *Synge and the Irish Language*, London 1979, 109–21.

68 Synge, *Plays 2*, 167.

69 Kiberd, *Synge and the Irish Language*, 176–95.

70 Synge, quoted by Saddlemyer, 'Synge to McKenna', 18.

71 Synge, *Plays 2*, 229.

72 Ibid., 215.

73 P.H. Pearse, 'Some Aspects of Irish Literature', *Collected Works: Songs of the Irish Rebels*, Dublin 1924, 157.

74 Cited by Ruth Dudley Edwards, *Patrick Pearse*, 120.

75 P.H. Pearse, *An Macaomh*, June 1909: cited in Ruth Dudley Edwards, *Patrick Pearse*, 123.

76 Cited by Ruth Dudley Edwards, *Patrick Pearse*, 117.

77 Desmond Ryan, *Remembering Sion*, Dublin 1934.

78 Cited by Ruth Dudley Edwards, *Patrick Pearse*, 119.

79 P.H. Pearse, *Collected Works: Plays, Stories and Poems*, Dublin 1924, 44.

80 Synge, *Prose*, 13.

81 P.H. Pearse, *Political Writings and Speeches*, Dublin 1924, 25.

82 Jonathan Rutherford, *Forever England: Reflections on Masculinity and Empire*, London 1997, 7.

83 Gauri Viswanathan, *Masks of Conquest*, London 1990 and 'The Voice Within', *Voice Literary Supplement*, New York, January–February 1989, 22; and Daniel Corkery, *Synge and Anglo-Irish Literature*, Cork 1931, Chapter 1.

84 Dean Stanley, *Life of Dr Arnold*, London 1844, 69.

85 See Ruth Dudley Edwards, *Patrick Pearse*, 90; and Seamus Deane, *Celtic Revivals*, London 1985, 65ff.

86 Standish J. O'Grady, cited by Yeats, *Autobiographies*, 424.

87 Augustine Birrell, *Things Past Redress*, London 1937, 214.

24 Synge's Tristes Tropiques: *The Aran Islands*

1 J.M. Synge, *Collected Works: Prose*, ed. Alan Price, Oxford 1966, 395.

2 David H. Greene and Edward M. Stephens, *J.M. Synge 1871–1909*, New York 1961, 83–4.

3   Synge, *Prose*, 163.
4   Ibid., 164.
5   Edward W. Said, *Orientalism*, New York 1978, passim.
6   Susan Sontag, *On Photography*, London 1979, 57.
7   Synge, *Prose*, 70.
8   J.M. Synge, *Collected Works: Plays 1*, ed. A. Saddlemyer, Oxford 1968, 169.
9   Quoted by Sontag, *On Photography*, 69.
10 Synge, *Prose*, 122.
11 Sontag, *On Photography*, 167.
12 John Berger, *About Looking*, London 1980, 58.
13 Synge, *Prose*, 106.
14 *Some Letters of J.M. Synge to Lady Gregory and W.B. Yeats*, selected by Ann Saddlemyer, Dublin 1971, 2: and Maurice Bourgeois, *John Millington Synge and the Irish Theatre*, London 1913, 82.
15 Synge, *Prose*, 141.
16 Ibid., 58.
17 Said, *Orientalism*, 160–85.
18 Ibid., 177.
19 Arthur Symons, 'The Isles of Aran' (henceforth *IA*), *The Savoy*, No. 8, London 1896, 75.
20 Synge, *Prose*, 49.
21 *IA*, 75.
22 Synge, *Prose*, 53.
23 Ibid.
24 *IA*, 85.
25 *IA*, 77.
26 *IA*, 81. For a fuller comparison see Declan Kiberd, 'Synge, Symons and the Isles of Aran', *Notes on Modern Irish Literature*, Vol. 1, 1989, Fenelton, Pennsylvania, 32–9.
27 Synge, *Prose*, 88.
28 Ibid., 89. Mary C. King in *The Drama of J.M. Synge*, London 1985, was the first critic to offer a full account of the traumatic effect on Synge of the export and eviction scenes, 18–47.
29 Synge, *Prose*, 95.
30 Oscar Wilde, *The Artist as Critic*, London 1970, 267. Synge was reading the essays of Wilde as he began writing *The Aran Islands* in 1898–9: MS 4378 TCD contains extracts from 'The Artist as Critic' (and from Frazer's *The Golden Bough*).
31 Wilde, *The Artist as Critic*, 261.
32 Synge, *Prose*, 116.
33 Ibid., 57.
34 Ibid., 74.
35 Ibid., 94.
36 Ibid., 100.
37 Ibid., 130.
38 Ibid., 132–3.
39 Synge, *Plays 1*, 9.
40 Synge, *Prose*, 149–50.

41 Ibid., 73.
42 Ibid., 56.
43 Ibid., 128.
44 Ibid., 114.
45 Ibid., 180.
46 Ibid., 66.
47 Ibid., 6.
48 Ibid., 78.
49 Ibid., 137
50 Ibid., 138.
51 Ibid.
52 Ibid., 114.
53 Synge Manuscripts TCD, Notebook 17: *Prose*, 143.
54 Alistair Horne, *The Fall of Paris: The Siege and the Commune 1870–71*, Harmondsworth 1981, 360ff.
55 Quoted by Greene and Stephens, 153.
56 Synge, *Prose*, 144.
57 Ibid., 75.
58 Ibid., 161.
59 Ibid., 162.
60 Ibid., 140.
61 Ibid., 80.
62 Synge, *Plays 1*, 41.
63 J.G. Frazer, *The Golden Bough*, London 1922, 49.
64 David Richards, *Masks of Difference: Cultural Representations in Literature, Anthropology and Art*, Cambridge 1994, 169.
65 Weldon Thornton, *J.M. Synge and the Western Mind*, Gerrards Cross 1979, 98ff.
66 Synge, *Prose*, 74.
67 Ibid., 347.
68 Ibid., 100.
69 Richards, 173.
70 Ibid., 193.
71 Synge Manuscripts TCD, Notebook 19: *Prose*, 103.
72 Susan Sontag, *Against Interpretation*, New York 1964, 70.
73 Synge, *Prose*, 114.
74 Ibid.
75 Ibid.
76 Richards, 233. Synge's most intense work on Petrarch was probably done after 1907.
77 Richards argues that T.S. Eliot had exactly the same view of this, 208.
78 T.S. Eliot, *Notes Toward a Definition of Culture*, London 1962, 41.
79 Claude Lévi-Strauss, *Tristes Tropiques*: cited by Sontag in *Against Interpretation*, 69.
80 Quoted by Sontag, ibid., 75.

25   W.B. Yeats: Building Amid Ruins

1   W.B. Yeats, *Autobiographies*, London 1955, 541.
2   For an extended discussion of this, see Louis MacNeice, *The Poetry of W.B. Yeats*, London 1967, 102–39.
3   *Autobiographies*, 27.
4   Ibid., 130.
5   W.B. Yeats, *Collected Poems* (henceforth *CP*), London 1950, 271.
6   Ibid., 105.
7   *Autobiographies*, 463.
8   *CP*, 142.
9   Peter Allt and Russell K. Alspach eds., *Variorum Edition of the Poems of W.B. Yeats*, London 1989, 778.
10   *CP*, 109.
11   J.M. Synge, *Letters to Molly: John M. Synge to Maire O'Neill*, ed. Ann Saddlemyer, Cambridge, Mass. 1971, passim.
12   Vivian Mercier, *Beckett/Beckett*, London 1977, 46.
13   Samuel Beckett, *Waiting for Godot*, London 1965, 12.
14   *CP*, 7–8.
15   Ibid., 392.
16   W.B. Yeats, *Uncollected Prose*, vol. 1, ed. John P. Frayne, London 1970, 361.
17   *CP*, 240.
18   *CP*, 237.
19   *CP*, 62.
20   *CP*, 141–2.
21   Quoted and discussed by John McCole, *Walter Benjamin and the Antinomies Tradition*, Ithaca, New York 1993, 284: from *Schriften 5*, 59.
22   *CP*, 211.
23   Synge, *Prose*, 348.
24   Cited by Benjamin, *Schriften 5*, 583.
25   *Field Day Anthology 2* (henceforth *FDA 2*), 471.
26   The anecdote was told by Ulick O'Connor, Trinity College Dublin, 3 May 1972; the interpretation of the stoppage is discussed by Susan Buck-Morss, *The Dialectics of Seeing: Walter Benjamin and the Arcades Project*, Cambridge, Mass. 1990, 92.
27   W.B. Yeats, *Ideals in Ireland*, ed. Augusta Gregory, London 1901, 106.
28   On this see McCole, 292–5.
29   W.B. Yeats, *Essays and Introductions*, London 1961, 155.
30   *CP*, 140.
31   *CP*, 149.
32   Walter Benjamin, *Schriften* 1, 875: and 4, 107.
33   W.B. Yeats, 'The Tables of the Law', *The Savoy*, No. 7, November 1896, 84.
34   Yeats, *Essays and Introductions*, 372.
35   Ibid., 318.
36   Quoted by Frank Tuohy, *Yeats*, Dublin 1975, 175.
37   W.B. Yeats, 'The Death of Oenone', *The Bookman*, 11 December 1892, 84.

38   *CP*, 140.
39   Yeats, *Essays and Introductions*, 310.
40   *Letters of W.B. Yeats*, 108.
41   Ursula Bridge ed., *W.B. Yeats and T. Sturge Moore: Their Correspondence 1901–1937*, London 1953, 154.
42   Richard Wolin, *Walter Benjamin: The Aesthetic of Redemption*, New York 1982, 53ff.
43   Theodor Adorno, *Minima Moralia: Reflections from a Damaged Life*, translated by E.F.N. Jephcott, London 1974, 120.
44   *CP*, 220.
45   *CP*, 222.
46   *Letters of W.B. Yeats*, 790.
47   Cited by McCole, 265: from *Schriften* 2, 321.
48   *CP*, 225.
49   *CP*, 230.
50   Ibid.
51   *CP*, 235.
52   *CP*, 235.
53   *CP*, 128.
54   *CP*, 113.
55   *CP*, 350.
56   *CP*, 351.
57   Ibid.
58   *Autobiographies*, 277.
59   *CP*, 398.
60   See Robert Langbaum, *The Mysteries of Identity: A Theme in Modern Literature*, Chicago 1982, 3–24.
61   W.B. Yeats, *On the Boiler*, Dublin 1939, 22.
62   *CP*, 381.
63   Ibid.
64   *CP*, 382.

26   *Ulysses*, Newspapers and Modernism

1   Richard Ellmann, *James Joyce*, London 1959, 640.
2   Mary Casteleyn, *A History of Literacy and Libraries in Ireland*, Aldershot 1984, 140–50.
3   Douglas Hyde, 'The Necessity for Deanglicising Ireland', *The Revival of Irish Literature*, London 1894, 159ff.
4   J.M. Synge, *Collected Works: Prose*, ed. Alan Price, Oxford 1966, 350.
5   See W.B. Yeats, *Uncollected Prose*, Vol. 1 ed. John P. Frayne, Vol. 2 ed. John P. Frayne and Colton Johnson, London 1970 and 1975.
6   Friedrich Nietzsche, *Thus Spoke Zarathustra*, translated by R.J. Hollingdale, Harmondsworth 1961, 77.
7   Ibid., 67.
8   Quoted by Richard Wolin, *Walter Benjamin: An Aesthetic of Redemption*, New York 1982, 119.
9   Peter Fritzsche, *Reading Berlin 1900*, Cambridge, Mass. 1996, 178. I am

much indebted to this marvellous book for many thoughts in this chapter and, as always, to the criticism of Walter Benjamin.

10 James Joyce, *Ulysses: Student's Annotated Edition* (henceforth *U*), annotated by Declan Kiberd, London 1992, 114.

11 *U*, 294.

12 James Joyce, *Exiles*, Harmondsworth 1973, 51.

13 *U*, 148.

14 *U*, 154.

15 Fritzsche, *Reading Berlin 1900*, passim.

16 *U*, 139.

17 *U*, 571.

18 See Hugh Kenner, *The Stoic Comedians: Flaubert, Joyce and Beckett*, Berkeley 1974 and *The Counterfeiters: An Historical Comedy*, Baltimore 1985, for Joyce and machines: and Dominic Manganiello, *Joyce's Politics*, on anarchism.

19 Walter Benjamin, cited by Susan Buck-Morss, *The Dialectics of Seeing: Walter Benjamin and the Arcades Project*, Cambridge, Mass. 1990, 144.

20 *U*, 586.

21 Fritzsche, 178.

22 Jack White, RTÉ Television, 15 August 1975.

23 Ellmann, *James Joyce*, 470.

24 Walter Benjamin, cited by Wolin, 221.

25 See chapters 28 and 32.

26 Frank Budgen, *James Joyce and the Making of Ulysses*, Oxford 1972, 94.

27 Irving Howe, *Literary Modernism*, New York 1968, 12.

28 *U*, 341.

29 *U*, 45.

30 Declan Kiberd, 'Joyce's Ellmann, Ellmann's Joyce', in *Classic Joyce*, Rome 1999, 53–68.

31 Cited by Buck-Morss, 101.

32 Ibid., 101.

33 Ellmann, *James Joyce*, 410.

34 *U*, 758–9.

35 *U*, 759.

36 Walter Benjamin, quoted by Wolin, 98.

37 Edna O'Brien, lecture, 2 September 1999, Newman House, Dublin.

38 Theodor Adorno, *Minima Moralia: Reflections from a Damaged Life*, translated by E.F.N. Jephcott, London 1974, 38–9, 120.

39 See Declan Kiberd, *Inventing Ireland: The Literature of the Modern Nation*, London 1995, 38.

40 *U*, 146.

41 Karl Marx, *The Eighteenth Brumaire of Louis Bonaparte*: cited in Marx and Engels, *Werke*, Berlin 1960, 115.

42 Richard Ellmann, *Eminent Domain*, Oxford 1967, 37.

43 *U*, 263.

44 W.B. Yeats, *Collected Poems*, London 1950, 240.

45 See Marilyn French, *The Book as World: James Joyce's Ulysses*, New York 1993, passim.

46   *U*, 34.
47   *U*, 98.
48   *U*, 98–9.
49   *U*, 131.
50   *U*, 75.
51   *U*, 782.
52   Karen Lawrence, *The Odyssey of Style in Ulysses*, Princeton 1981, 197.
53   Ellmann, *James Joyce*, 99.

27   After the Revolution: O'Casey and O'Flaherty

1   This statement is usually attributed to Denis Johnston.
2   Kevin O'Higgins, quoted by Declan Kiberd, *Inventing Ireland: The Literature of the Modern Nation*, London 1995, 163.
3   Augustine Birrell, *Royal Commission on the Rebellion in Ireland*, HM Stationery Office, Doc 8311, London 1916.
4   Sean O'Casey, *Juno and the Paycock* (henceforth *JP*) in *Three Plays*, London 1957, 24.
5   Cited by Michael Laffan, *The Resurrection of Ireland*, Cambridge 1999, 355.
6   *JP*, 18.
7   Raymond Williams, *Drama from Ibsen to Brecht*, Harmondsworth 1973, 161–9.
8   *JP*, 71.
9   *JP*, 71.
10   W.B. Yeats, *Collected Poems*, London 1950, 204.
11   *JP*, 27.
12   *JP*, 9.
13   *JP*, 67.
14   *JP*, 9.
15   *JP*, 21.
16   *JP*, 23.
17   *JP*, 70.
18   Cited by Richard Ellmann, *James Joyce*, London 1959, 61; Samuel Beckett, *Endgame*, New York 1958, 49; and W.B. Yeats, *Autobiographies*, London 1955, 106.
19   This reading revises the more critical assessment in *Inventing Ireland*, 218–38: but it derives from a sense of the emerging Protestant consciousness in the literature of the 1920s, a trend treated in that book in respect of authors other than O'Casey: 413–68. The possibility of explaining much in O'Casey by the application of a religious reading struck me only after the completion of *Inventing Ireland*.
20   Arthur Power, *Conversations with James Joyce*, Dublin 1974, 65.
21   Liam O'Flaherty, *The Life of Tim Healy*, London 1927, 35.
22   Patrick F. Sheeran, *The Novels of Liam O'Flaherty: A Study in Romantic Realism*, Dublin 1976, 35.
23   A.A. Kelly, ed., *Letters of Liam O'Flaherty*, Dublin 1996, 74.
24   Sean O'Casey, *Inishfallen, Fare Thee Well*, London 1972, 181.

25 Kelly, *Letters of Liam O'Flaherty*, 137.
26 Liam O'Flaherty, *Irish Statesman*, Vol. 5, 20 February 1926, 740.
27 Liam O'Flaherty, *Irish Statesman*, Vol. 3, 18 October 1924, 171.
28 Liam O'Flaherty, *Shame the Devil*, Dublin 1981, 190.
29 Ibid.
30 *Letters of Liam O'Flaherty*, 101–2.
31 Liam O'Flaherty, *The Informer* (henceforth *I*), London 1971, 22.
32 *I*, 24.
33 Austin Clarke, *A Penny in the Clouds*, London 1968, 99.
34 *I*, 32.
35 *I*, 43.
36 O'Flaherty, *Shame the Devil*, 100.
37 Liam O'Flaherty, 'My Life of Adventure', *TP's Weekly*, 20, October 1928, 256.
38 Vivian Mercier, 'Man against Nature: The Novels of Liam O'Flaherty', *Wascona Review*, No. 2, 1966, 45.
39 *I*, 84.
40 *I*, 107.
41 *I*, 111.
42 *I*, 138.
43 *I*, 172.
44 Quoted by James Cahalan, *Liam O'Flaherty: A Study of the Short Fiction*, Boston 1991, 35.
45 Liam O'Flaherty, *Two Years*, London 1930, 312.
46 *I*, 175.
47 Cited by A. Norman Jeffares, *W.B. Yeats: Man and Poet*, London 1949, 241 (Yeats to Olivia Shakespeare).
48 W.B. Yeats, Preface to *The King of the Great Clock Tower*, Dublin 1934.
49 'YO', 'Literature and Life: Heredity in Literature', *Irish Statesman*, Vol. 8, 4 June 1927, 304.
50 Seán Ó Faoláin, *The Bell*, June 1941, 29.
51 Liam O'Flaherty, *A Tourist's Guide to Ireland*, Dublin 1998, 43.
52 Cahalan, 31.

28   Gaelic Absurdism: *At Swim-Two-Birds*

1 George Russell, quoted by Francis MacManus, 'The Literature of the Period', *The Years of the Great Test 1926–39*, ed. F. MacManus, Cork 1967, 119.
2 Breandán Ó hEithir, *The Begrudger's Guide to Irish Politics*, Dublin 1986, 2.
3 John Butler Yeats, quoted by A. Norman Jeffares, *The Circus Animals*, London 1970, 139.
4 Ó Nualláin, 'A Sheaf of Letters', *Journal of Irish Literature*, Vol. 3, No. 1, January 1974, 69.
5 Flann O'Brien, *At Swim-Two-Birds* (henceforth *ASTB*), Harmondsworth 1967, 9.
6 Kevin O'Nolan, 'The First Furlongs', in *Myles: Portraits of Brian O'Nolan*, ed. Timothy O'Keeffe, London 1973, 29.

7 Niall Sheridan, 'Brian, Flann and Myles', in ibid., 36.
8 *ASTB*, 101.
9 *ASTB*, 77.
10 *ASTB*, 63.
11 *ASTB*, 29.
12 *ASTB*, 10.
13 *ASTB*, 73, 76.
14 *ASTB*, 80.
15 *ASTB*, 26.
16 *ASTB*, 156.
17 John Ryan, *Remembering How We Stood: Bohemian Dublin at the Mid-century*, Dublin 1975, 155.
18 Anthony Cronin, *No Laughing Matter: The Life and Times of Flann O'Brien*, London 1989, 9.
19 Brian O'Nolan, *The Best of Myles*, London 1974, 282–3.
20 *ASTB*, 15.
21 *ASTB*, 9.
22 Cathal Ó Háinle, 'Fionn and Suibhne at *At Swim-Two-Birds*', in *Conjuring Complexities: Essays on Flann O'Brien*, eds. A. Clune and T. Hurson, Belfast 1997, 21.
23 *ASTB*, 19.
24 *ASTB*, 31.
25 *ASTB*, 34.
26 Ó Háinle, 14.
27 J.C.C. Mays, 'Literalist of the Imagination', in O'Keeffe ed. *Myles: Portraits of Brian O'Nolan*, 84.
28 *ASTB*, 160. Stephen in Joyce's *A Portrait of the Artist as a Young Man* has a similar problem.
29 *ASTB*, 92.
30 *ASTB*, 32.
31 See Anne Clissmann, *Flann O'Brien: A Critical Introduction*, Dublin 1975, passim.
32 James Joyce, *Dubliners*, Harmondsworth 1956, 174.
33 *ASTB*, 19.
34 *ASTB*, 25, 25.
35 Niall Sheridan, in O'Keeffe ed. *Myles: Portraits of Brian O'Nolan*, 40.
36 *ASTB*, 99.
37 *ASTB*, 25.
38 Roland Barthes, 'The Death of the Author', in *Modern Literary Theory*, eds. A. Rice and P. Waugh, London 1989, 17.
39 *ASTB*, 68.
40 John Banville has solved some of these technical problems in *Doctor Copernicus*, London 1976.
41 Anon., *Times Literary Supplement*, 18 March 1939, on 'a schoolboy brand of mild vulgarity'.
42 Richard Poirier, *The Performing Self*, 45.
43 Richard Ellmann: reported conversation, 12 October 1982.
44 Cronin, *No Laughing Matter*, 142.
45 Fintan O'Toole, *A Mass for Jesse James*, Dublin 1988, passim.

46	Ellmann, conversation with the author, 12 October 1982.
47	*ASTB*, 85.
48	Matthew Arnold, *On the Study of Celtic Literature*, London 1891, 104.
49	*ASTB*, 53, 56.
50	*ASTB*, 59.
51	*ASTB*, 45, 48, 24, 34.
52	*ASTB*, 134.
53	Seosamh Mac Grianna, *Mo Bhealach Féin*, Áth Cliath 1940, 165.
54	Ryan, *Remembering How We Stood*, 161.
55	Anthony Cronin, *Dead as Doornails*, Oxford 1986, 112.
56	See Declan Kiberd, *Inventing Ireland: The Literature of the Modern Nation*, 497–512.
57	Brian O'Nolan, 'A Bash in the Tunnel', *Envoy*, V, 17, May 1951, 11.
58	*ASTB*, 153.
59	Ibid.
60	Cover of the Penguin Classics edition of *At Swim-Two-Birds*.
61	*ASTB*, 72.
62	*ASTB*, 77.
63	*ASTB*, 169.
64	Ibid.
65	*ASTB*, 175.
66	*ASTB*, 85.
67	O'Casey, quoted in Cronin, *No Laughing Matter*, 129.
68	Seamus Deane, *Strange Country*, Oxford 1997, 157–9.
69	*ASTB*, 98.

29   The Blasket Autobiographies

1	For a fuller account, see Muiris Mac Conghail, *The Blaskets: People and Literature*, Dublin 1987, 127–47.
2	Máire Mhac an tSaoi, 'An tOileánach', *The Pleasures of Gaelic Literature*, ed. John Jordan, Cork 1977, 25.
3	Seoirse Mac Thomáis, *An Blascaod Mar a Bhí*, Má Nuad 1977, 9; see also J.V. Luce, 'Homeric Qualities in the Life and Literature of the Great Blasket Island', *Greece and Rome*, Vol. XVI, 1969, 151–68.
4	Tomás Ó Criomhthain, *An tOileánach* (henceforth O), Áth Cliath 1929, 22.
5	On this see Cathal Ó Háinle, 'Tomás Ó Criomhthain agus *Caisleán Uí Néill*', *Irisleabhar Mhá Nuad*, 1985.
6	O, 163–4.
7	For more on this, see Declan Kiberd, *Men and Feminism in Modern Literature*, 123–4.
8	J.M. Synge, *Collected Works: Plays 1*, ed. Ann Saddlemyer, Oxford 1968.
9	Cathal Ó Háinle, 'Tóir an Chíosa', in *Promhadh Pinn*, Má Nuad 1978, 222–31.
10	O, 64.
11	O, 197.

12 *O*, 99.

13 *O*, 100.

14 Lecture by Máire Mhac an tSaoi, Department of Irish, Trinity College Dublin, 12 February 1972.

15 Tomas O'Crohan, *The Islandman*, translated from the Irish by Robin Flower, Oxford 1951, viii.

16 Ibid., viii. For Flower's own life, see Mícheál de Mórdha, *Bláithín: Flower*, An Daingean 1998; and for the connections with Ó Criomhthain, see Máire Ní Chéilleachair, *Tomás Ó Criomhthain 1855–1937*, An Daingean 1998.

17 J.M. Synge, *Collected Works: Prose*, ed. Alan Price, Oxford 1966, 132–3.

18 *O*, 51.

19 Pádraig Ó hÉalaithe, 'Na hOileánaigh agus a dTréithe', *Irisleabhar Mhuighe Nuadhat*, 1966, 7–18.

20 *O*, 126.

21 *O*, 265.

22 Synge, *Prose*, 73.

23 *O*, 138.

24 John McGahern, 'An tOileánach/The Islandman', *Irish Review*, Vol. 5, No. 1, 1991, 56.

25 Ibid., 57.

26 *O*, 47.

27 *O*, 265.

28 *O*, 265.

29 Seathrún Céitinn, *Foras Feasa ar Éirinn 1*, ed. David Comyn, London 1902, 76. The English-language version is by J.M. Synge.

30 *O*, 123.

31 Flower ed., *The Islandman*, viii–ix.

32 Mac Conghail, *The Blaskets*, 151ff.

33 Maurice O'Sullivan, *Twenty Years a-Growing*, translated by Mona Llewelyn Davies and George Thomson, Oxford 1953, v.

34 James Delargy, *The Gaelic Storyteller, Proceedings of the British Academy*, Vol. XXXI, London 1945, 8–33.

35 Ian Watt, *The Rise of the Novel: Studies in Defoe, Richardson and Fielding*, Berkeley 1957, 60–92.

36 Muiris Ó Súilleabháin, *Fiche Blian ag Fás* (henceforth *FBF*), Má Nuad 1976, 111.

37 Synge, *Prose*, 73.

38 *FBF*, 41.

39 Mac Thomáis, *An Blascaod Mar a Bhi*, 11.

40 Quoted by Máirtín Ó Cadhain, *Páipéir Bhána agus Páipéir Bhreaca*, Áth Cliath 1970, 38.

41 *FBF*, 196.

42 Bertrand Russell, *Autobiography*, London 1975, 52.

43 Thomson, quoted by Mac Conghail, 154.

44 Peig Sayers, *Peig* (henceforth *P*), Áth Cliath 1970, 97.

45 Stanislaus Joyce, *My Brother's Keeper*, New York 1958, 158–9.

46 *P*, 100.

47 *P*, 121.

48   *P*, 130.
49   *P*, 148.
50   *P*, 152.
51   *P*, 196.
52   *P*, 199.

30   Incorrigibly Plural: Louis MacNeice

1   Terence Brown, Lecture, Association of Teachers of English, University College Dublin, 30 June 1979.
2   Louis MacNeice, *Collected Poems* (henceforth *CP*), ed. E.R. Dodds, London 1966, 167.
3   Ibid., 168.
4   Ibid., 69.
5   Jon Stallworthy, *Louis MacNeice*, London 1995, 25.
6   Quoted by Peter MacDonald, *Louis MacNeice: The Poet in his Contexts*, Oxford 1991, 203.
7   Louis MacNeice, *The Strings Are False*, London 1982, 217.
8   *CP*, 225.
9   *CP*, 53.
10   Stallworthy, 274.
11   Ibid., 275.
12   Derek Mahon, *Journalism*, ed. T. Brown, Oldcastle 1996, 21–9.
13   *CP*, 183.
14   Stallworthy, 37.
15   Terence Brown, *Louis MacNeice: Sceptical Vision*, Dublin 1974, 7ff.
16   Louis MacNeice, *The Poetry of W.B. Yeats*, 50.
17   Stallworthy, 90.
18   Ibid., 107–8.
19   *CP*, 30.
20   Quoted by Terence Brown, *Louis MacNeice: Sceptical Vision*, 22.
21   Ibid., 23ff.
22   Ibid., 15.
23   MacNeice, quoted in ibid., 16.
24   *Letters of John Keats*, ed. Frederick Page, London 1954, 355.
25   MacNeice, *The Strings Are False*, 161.
26   Louis MacNeice, 'Impure Poetry', 1938: reproduced in Ronald Carter ed., *Thirties Poets: The Auden Group – A Casebook*, London 1984, 34–5.
27   Victor Hugo, quoted by Edward W. Said, *Orientalism*, New York 1978, 259.
28   Samuel Beckett, *Proust*, New York 1957, 8.
29   MacDonald, *Louis MacNeice*, 206.
30   *CP*, 132.
31   James Joyce, *A Portrait of the Artist as a Young Man*, ed. S. Deane, London 1992, 274.
32   Terence Brown, *Louis MacNeice: Sceptical Vision*, 10.
33   Quoted by Edna Longley, *Louis MacNeice: A Study*, London 1988, 21.

34   CP, 41.
35   Francis Scarfe, *Auden and After: The Liberation of Poetry 1930–1941*, London 1941, 62.
36   CP, 133.
37   CP, 132.
38   CP, 133.
39   Ibid.
40   CP, 125.
41   CP, 150.
42   For a moving and authoritative survey of these conjunctures and debates, see Samuel Hynes, 'Yeats and the Poets of the Thirties', *Modern Irish Literature: Essays in Honour of William York Tindall*, eds. Raymond Porter and James Brophy, New York 1972, 1–22.
43   MacNeice, quoted by Stallworthy, 232.
44   G.S. Fraser, 'Evasive Honesty: The Poetry of Louis MacNeice', in Carter ed., 128–35.
45   Letter from MacNeice to W.H. Auden, cited in Carter ed. 58.
46   CP, 203.
47   CP, 164.
48   Letter from MacNeice to E.R. Dodds: quoted in Edna Longley and Gerald Dawe eds., *Across a Roaring Hill*, Belfast 1985, 99.
49   Quoted by Anthony Cronin, *Heritage Now*, Dublin 1982, 202.
50   CP, 226.
51   CP, 145.
52   Stallworthy, 129.
53   Ibid., 310.

31   Kate O'Brien: *The Ante-Room*

1   Quoted by John Cronin, *The Anglo-Irish Novel*, Vol. 2 (the twentieth century), Belfast 1990, 138.
2   Eibhear Walshe ed., *Ordinary People Dancing*, Cork 1993, 11.
3   Ibid.
4   Lorna Reynolds, *Kate O'Brien: A Literary Portrait*, Gerrards Cross 1987, 38.
5   Adele Dalsimer, *Kate O'Brien: A Critical Study*, Dublin 1990, xiv.
6   Kate O'Brien, *The Ante-Room* (henceforth *AR*), London 1996, 125–6.
7   Eavan Boland, 'Daughter of the Middle Classes', *Irish Times*, 27 February 1987, 12.
8   Danny Mulqueen feared opinions or informations 'since they required a reaction' (*AR*, 28).
9   *AR*, 187.
10   Vivian Mercier, 'Kate O'Brien', *Irish Writing 1*, 1946, 98.
11   Kate O'Brien, 'George Eliot: A Moralising Fabulist', in *Essays by Divers Hands,* ed. G.R. Hamilton, *Transactions of the Royal Society of Literature*, No. 27, London 1955, 45.
12   Ibid., 42.
13   Vivian Mercier, 'The Land of Spices', *Spectator*, 14 February 1941, 184.

14   *AR*, 3.
15   *AR*, 20.
16   *AR*, 21, 21.
17   George Eliot, *Middlemarch*, ed. W.J. Harvey, Harmondsworth 1969, 25.
18   *AR*, 10.
19   Ibid. The following point I take from Michel Foucault, *The History of Sexuality*, Vol. 1, London 1979, 72.
20   *AR*, 5, 5.
21   *AR*, 9.
22   *AR*, 6.
23   *AR*, 32.
24   *AR*, 67.
25   *AR*, 66–7.
26   *AR*, 72. A more cynical sort of connoisseur would be Gilbert Osmond in Henry James's *The Portrait of a Lady*.
27   *AR*, 71.
28   *AR*, 95.
29   *AR*, 84.
30   *AR*, 99.
31   *AR*, 102.
32   *AR*, 105.
33   *AR*, 156.
34   *AR*, 161.
35   Patricia Coughlan, 'Kate O'Brien: Feminine Beauty, Feminist Writing and Sexual Role', in Walshe ed., 59–84.
36   *AR*, 152.
37   Coughlan, 61.
38   *AR*, 67.
39   James Joyce, *Ulysses: Student's Annotated Edition*, annotated by Declan Kiberd, London 1992, 915.
40   John Berger, *Ways of Seeing*, Harmondsworth 1972, 46.
41   Beatrice Faust, *Women, Sex and Pornography*, Harmondsworth 1982, 49.
42   *AR*, 67ff.
43   Anne Fogarty, 'The Business of Attachment: Romance and Desire in the Novels of Kate O'Brien', in Walshe ed., 115ff.
44   *AR*, 127.
45   *AR*, 134.
46   *AR*, 213.
47   Kate O'Brien, *The Last of Summer*, Dublin 1982, 48.
48   On this, see Gerardine Meaney, 'History, Nationality and Sexuality in Kate O'Brien', *Irish Journal of Feminist Studies*, 2:2, Winter 1997, 77–92.
49   *AR*, 213.
50   *AR*, 236.
51   *Letters of John Keats*, ed. Frederick Page, London 1968, 115.
52   *AR*, 127.
53   *Letters of John Keats*, 115–16.
54   *AR*, 245.
55   *AR*, 259.
56   *AR*, 255.

57   *AR*, 151.
58   *AR*, 306.
59   *AR*, 301.
60   *AR*, 173. The phrase about lying passion is cited by Cronin, *The Anglo-Irish Novel*, Vol. 2, 146.
61   *AR*, 267.
62   Dalsimer, xv: see also A. Fogarty and J. Madden, afterword to *AR*, 307–14.
63   Anthony Roche, 'The Ante-Room as Drama', in Walshe ed., 95.
64   John McGahern, lecture, University College Dublin, 17 February 1999.

32   All the Dead Voices: *Cré na Cille*

1   Máirtín Ó Cadhain, *Cré na Cille* (henceforth CC), Áth Cliath 1949, 49.
2   *CC*, 17.
3   Ibid.
4   Samuel Beckett, *Molloy: Malone Dies: The Unnamable* (henceforth *MMU*) London 1959, 240.
5   A. Alvarez, *Beckett*, London 1973, 61.
6   This may resemble the existential 'situation' as defined by Jean-Paul Sartre.
7   *MMU*, 242.
8   *CC*, 235.
9   *CC*, 247.
10 *CC*, 83.
11 *CC*, 99.
12 *CC*, 255.
13 *CC*, 51.
14 *CC*, 29.
15 *MMU*, 87.
16 Máirtín Ó Cadhain, *Páipéir Bhána agus Páipéir Bhreaca* (henceforth *PB*), Áth Cliath 1970, 24.
17 *MMU*, 135.
18 *CC*, 74.
19 *MMU*, 237.
20 *CC*, 89.
21 *MMU*, 310, 374, 302.
22 *MMU*, 302.
23 *PB*, 19.
24 *CC*, 208.
25 *PB*, 40.
26 *CC*, 176.
27 *CC*, 111.
28 *CC*, 77.
29 *CC*, 187.
30 Domhnall Ó Corcora, 'Cré na Cille', *Feasta*, Bealtaine 1950, 14–15. See also Breandán Ó Doibhlín, 'Athléamh ar *Chré na Cille*', *Léachtaí Cholm Cille*, Má Nuad 1974, v, 40–53.
31 *CC*, 41.
32 *PB*, 41.

33 Samuel Beckett, *Three Dialogues* (with Georges Duthuit), in M. Esslin ed., *Beckett: A Collection of Critical Essays*, New Jersey 1965, 17.
34 CC, 30–1.
35 CC, 32.
36 Cited on the jacket of the 1949 edition of *Cré na Cille*.
37 MMU, 28.
38 MMU, 26.
39 Breandán Ó hEithir quotes this from *Ar Aghaidh*, in 'Cré na Cille: Máirtín Ó Cadhain', *The Pleasures of Gaelic Literature*, 73.
40 Cited by Alan Titley, *Máirtín Ó Cadhain: Clár Saothair*, Áth Cliath 1975, 18.
41 James Joyce, *Stephen Hero*, London 1944, 221.
42 See Michael D. Higgins, 'The Gombeen Man in Irish Fact and Fiction', *Études Irlandaises*, December 1985, No. 10, 31–52 for a developed version of this critique.
43 Ó Cadhain, cited by Titley, 18.
44 P.H. Pearse, *An Claidheamh Soluis*, 13 and 26 Bealtaine 1906, 6.
45 Ó Cadhain, cited by Titley, 19.
46 P.H. Pearse, *An Claidheamh Soluis*, 14 Márta 1903, 3 and 26 Bealtaine 1906, 6.
47 Ó Cadhain, cited by Titley, 19.
48 Samuel Beckett, *Waiting for Godot*, New York 1954, 40a.

33   Underdeveloped Comedy: Patrick Kavanagh

1 Gilles Deleuze and Felix Guattari, *Kafka: Toward a Minor Literature*, Minneapolis 1986, 26.
2 Samuel Beckett, *Malloy, Molone Dies, The Unnamable* (henceforth *MMU*) London 1959, 223.
3 Samuel Beckett, *Waiting for Godot*, New York 1954, 44a.
4 Israel Shenker, interview, in *Samuel Beckett: The Critical Heritage*, eds. L. Graver and R. Federman, London 1979, 146–9.
5 Patrick Kavanagh, *Collected Poems* (henceforth *CP*), London 1972, 173.
6 Ibid., 144.
7 Ibid., 121.
8 Patrick Kavanagh, *Collected Pruse*, London 1973, 266–7.
9 Samuel Beckett, *Disjecta*, New York 1984, 70ff.
10 Kavanagh, *CP*, xiv.
11 CP, 34.
12 CP, 52.
13 CP, 53.
14 CP, 42.
15 *Collected Pruse*, 19.
16 James Joyce, *A Portrait of the Artist as a Young Man*, ed. S. Deane, London 1992, 198.
17 *Collected Pruse*, 19; also 28.
18 Ibid., 19.
19 Samuel Beckett, *Watt*, London 1963, 254.

20   *Collected Pruse*, 22.
21   *CP*, 150.
22   Darcy O'Brien, *Patrick Kavanagh*, New Jersey 1975, 62–3.
23   *CP*, 147.
24   *CP*, 153.
25   *Collected Pruse*, 26.
26   Samuel Beckett, *MMU*, 170.
27   *CP*, 70.
28   Brendan Kennelly, 'Patrick Kavanagh', *Irish Poets in English*, ed. Seán Lucy, Cork 1972, 181.
29   Patrick Kavanagh, quoted by Darcy O'Brien, 64.
30   Peter Kavanagh ed., *Patrick Kavanagh: Sacred Keeper*, Newbridge 1979, 162–3.
31   Ibid., 165.
32   *Collected Pruse*, 13.
33   *CP*, xiii.
34   Peter Kavanagh, *November Haggard*, New York 1971, 34.
35   Peter Kavanagh ed., *Patrick Kavanagh: Man and Poet*, Newbridge 1987, 258.
36   Peter Kavanagh, *November Haggard*, 120.

34   Anglo-Gaelic Literature: Seán Ó Ríordáin

1   Quoted by Ruth Dudley Edwards, *Patrick Pearse: The Triumph of Failure*, London 1977, 30–1.
2   See Declan Kiberd, *Inventing Ireland: The Literature of the Modern Nation*, London 1995, 162.
3   Declan Kiberd, *Synge and the Irish Language*, London 1979, 219–20.
4   Seán Ó Ríordáin, *Scáthán Véarsaí* (henceforth *SV*), Áth Cliath 1980, 30.
5   Daniel Corkery, *What's This about the Gaelic League?*, pamphlet, Áth Cliath 1941.
6   James Joyce, *A Portrait of the Artist as a Young Man*, ed. S. Deane, London 1992, 240.
7   *SV*, 20.
8   *SV*, 25.
9   James Joyce, *Stephen Hero*, London 1944, 188. See also Peter Garrett, introduction to *Dubliners: Twentieth Century Interpretations*, New Jersey 1968, 11.
10   Seán Ó Ríordáin, réamhrá do *Eireaball Spideoige*, Áth Cliath 1952.
11   Daniel Corkery, *Synge and Anglo-Irish Literature*, Cork 1966, 6.
12   Frantz Fanon, *The Wretched of the Earth*, translated by Constance Farrington, Harmondsworth 1967, 178–80.
13   Daniel Corkery, *The Fortunes of the Irish Language*, Cork 1968, 13.
14   Peadar Ó Laoghaire, *Mo Scéal Féin*, Áth Cliath 1964, 48–9.
15   Corkery, *Synge*, 14.
16   *SV*, 22.
17   Ibid.
18   *SV*, 17.

19 *SV*, 51.
20 W.B. Yeats, *Collected Poems*, London 1950, 167.
21 *SV*, 69.
22 *SV*, 70.
23 Máirtín Ó Direáin, *Feamainn Bhealtaine*, Áth Cliath 1961, 87–88ff.
24 *SV*, 37.
25 *SV*, 63.
26 *SV*, 20.
27 *SV*, 56.
28 William Wordsworth, 'Ode on the Intimations of Immortality in Early Childhood', *The Norton Anthology of English Literature*, Vol. 2, eds S. Greenblatt, L. Lipking *et al.*, New York 2000, 287.
29 Seán Ó Ríordáin, *Línte Liombó*, Áth Cliath 1971, 31.
30 Wordsworth, 'Ode on the Intimations', *Norton 2*, 287.
31 *SV*, 96.
32 *SV*, 85.
33 James Joyce, *Portrait*, 205.
34 'A drop wasn't left in your bright gentle breast, that was not slurped down by the farrow of every foreign sow.'
35 Quoted by Anne Clissmann, *Flann O'Brien: A Critical Introduction*, Dublin 1975, 79.

35   Irish Narrative: A Short History

1   For further comment, see Declan Kiberd, 'Irish Literature and Irish History', *Oxford Illustrated History of Ireland*, Oxford 1989, passim.
2   P.B. Shelley, 'A Defence of Poetry', *English Critical Texts*, eds. D.J. Enright and Ernst de Chickera, London 1962, 225–55.
3   Charlotte Brooke, preface to *Reliques of Irish Poetry*, Dublin 1789, v–viii: also in *FDA1*, 980.
4   Ibid., 980.
5   See Declan Kiberd, *Inventing Ireland*, London 1995, 268–79.
6   Thomas MacDonagh, *Literature In Ireland*, Nenagh 1996, 17.
7   Ibid., 73.
8   Daniel Corkery, *What's This About the Gaelic League?*, Áth Cliath 1941.
9   Daniel Corkery, *Synge and Anglo-Irish Literature*, Cork 1931, Chapter 1.
10 Seán Ó Faoláin, *Vive Moi: An Autobiography*, London 1965, 129ff.
11 Conor Cruise O'Brien, *Writers and Politics*, London 1965, 102.
12 Ibid., 104.
13 J.J. Lee, *Ireland 1912–1985: Politics and Society*, Cambridge 1989, 622 and 628.
14 John Devitt, 'English for the Irish', *Crane Bag*, Vol. 6, No. 1, 1982, 106.
15 Cited by Devitt, ibid.
16 A.A. Luce, professor of philosophy and the most distinguished Berkeley scholar of his age.
17 Richard Ellmann, 'Yeats without Analogue', *Along the Riverrun*, New York 1990, 25.

18 Agreement Reached in the Multi-Party Negotiations, Dublin, Belfast, London 1998, 2.
19 Ibid., 16.
20 For an interesting study of this background, see Richard English, *Ernie O'Malley: IRA Intellectual*, Oxford 1998, 200–13.

Index